BLACKSTONE'S GUIDE TO

The Proceeds of Crime Act 2002

Second Edition

BLACKSTONE'S GUIDE TO

The Proceeds of Crime Act 2002

Second Edition
by
Edward Rees QC and Richard Fisher

OXFORD
UNIVERSITY PRESS

OXFORD
UNIVERSITY PRESS

Great Clarendon Street, Oxford OX2 6DP

Oxford University Press is a department of the University of Oxford.
It furthers the University's objective of excellence in research, scholarship,
and education by publishing worldwide in

Oxford New York

Auckland Cape Town Dar es Salaam Hong Kong Karachi
Kuala Lumpur Madrid Melbourne Mexico City Nairobi
New Delhi Shanghai Taipei Toronto

With offices in
Argentina Austria Brazil Chile Czech Republic France Greece
Guatemala Hungary Italy Japan South Korea Poland Portugal
Singapore Switzerland Thailand Turkey Ukraine Vietnam

Oxford is a registered trade mark of Oxford University Press
in the UK and in certain other countries

Published in the United States
by Oxford University Press Inc., New York

British Library Cataloguing in Publication Data

Data available

Library of Congress Cataloging-in-Publication Data

Rees, Edward.
Blackstone's guide to the Proceeds of Crime Act 2002 / by Edward Rees
and Richard Fisher. — 2nd ed.
p. cm
ISBN 0–19–927765–6 (alk. paper)
1. Great Britain. Proceeds of Crime Act 2002. 2. Forfeiture—England.
3. Money laundering—England. I. Title: Guide to the Proceeds of Crime
Act 2002. II. Fisher, Richard, 1971– III. Great Britain. Proceeds of
Crime Act 2002. IV. Title.
KD8460.A3122R44 2005
345.42′0268—dc22   2004026516

1 3 5 7 9 10 8 6 4 2

Typeset by Hope Services (Abingdon) Ltd
Printed in Great Britain
on acid-free paper by
Biddles Ltd., King's Lynn

Contents—Summary

Visit the Blackstone's Guide Series website: www.oup.com/uk/law/practitioner/bgseries

Contents

Contents

Contents

Preface to the Second Edition

Since the publication of the first edition of the Guide by Edward Rees and Andrew Hall, Andrew has been appointed Chairman of the Remuneration Committee of the General Council of the Bar—a post in which he continues to represent the barristers of England and Wales in difficult and time-consuming negotiations with the newly formed Department of Constitutional Affairs. We wish him well.

The preface to the first edition was written at the end of January 2003. At that point, very few provisions of the Act had actually been brought into effect. Now we are starting to see and feel the implications as the provisions come on stream. Examples of practical developments since the first edition include:

- Enthusiastic and proactive direction of law enforcement agencies by the Assets Recovery Agency;
- Wide judicial interpretation of the compliance duties of the regulated financial sector (now including most solicitors) in suspected money laundering situations;
- The use of the Crown Court as a one-stop asset recovery 'shop';
- The pronouncement by the Court of Appeal (in *R v Silcock*, 29 January 2004) that Parliament had intended to make 'express provision for the rules of evidence . . . to be different from those in criminal trials' and, in particular, for inadmissible evidence to be acceptable in criminal confiscation cases;
- The frequent use of the cash seizure and forfeiture provisions throughout the United Kingdom;
- The first successful applications for Civil Recovery orders in the High Court.

New Crown Court rules and Codes of Practice are in force. These, along with other relevant texts, are printed in full and referred to at appropriate points in the body of the Guide.

The second edition is intended for legal practitioners and those in the regulated sector who will inevitably confront the Proceeds of Crime Act head on in their daily professional lives. It is hoped that the Guide will provide a clear and practical routemap through the changed legal landscape.

E.P.R.
R.F.
31 August 2004

Table of Cases

Tables of European and International Cases

Table of Primary Legislation

Tables of Secondary Legislation

Table of Conventions

List of Abbreviations

ARA   Assets Recovery Agency
CICFA   Concerted Inter-Agency Criminal Finances Action Group
CJA   Criminal Justice Act
CLS   Community Legal Service
DTA   Drug Trafficking Act
DTOA   Drug Trafficking Offences Act
FI   Financial Investigators
HRA   Human Rights Act
LSC   Legal Services Commission
MLRO   Money Laundering Reporting Officer
NCIS   National Criminal Intelligence Service
PACE   Police and Criminal Evidence Act
POCA   Proceeds of Crime Act
RAIF   Recovered Assets Incentivisation Fund
RART   Regional Asset Recovery Team
TA   Terrorism Act

1
INTRODUCTION

A. PURPOSE OF THE LEGISLATION

1. The Statutory Agenda

The Proceeds of Crime Act 2002 (POCA) is the embodiment of a consensus   **1.01** among the international law enforcement community that the epic scale of money laundering and the profitability of organized crime in general can be dismantled by the co-ordinated and aggressive pursuit of 'asset recovery'.[1] Rightly or wrongly, the consensus holds that modern necessity requires robust 'modern' law-making and, as a consequence, the displacement of outmoded and inappropriate norms of criminal procedure and investigation. Happily, this coincides with the present Government's avowedly illiberal and authoritarian instincts.

The immediate impetus for new legislation came in June 2000 with the report   **1.02** of the government's Performance and Innovation Unit, 'Recovering the Proceeds of Crime'.[2] The Unit argued that the potential for the recovery of the proceeds of crime was 'seriously under-utilized'. It identified particular shortcomings:

---

[1] See, for example, the United Nations Convention against Illicit Traffic in Narcotic Drugs and Psychotropic Substances (1988), Council of Europe Convention on Laundering, Search, Seizure and Confiscation of the Proceeds from Crime (Strasbourg, 1990) and earlier statutes including the Criminal Justice (International Co-operation) Act 1990, the Northern Ireland (Emergency Provisions) Act 1991, the Criminal Justice Act 1993, the Drug Trafficking Act 1994, and the Proceeds of Crime Act 1995 (amending the provisions the Criminal Justice Act 1988).

[2] Available at www.cabinet-office.gov.uk/seu/1988/trhome.htm.

(a) Less than 20 per cent of drug trafficking convictions, and an even smaller proportion of other cases, resulted in confiscation orders.

(b) The value of cash seizures at the border represented a tiny proportion of the known proceeds of drug trafficking in the United Kingdom.

(c) There was considerable variation in the use and standards of financial investigation between different police forces.

(d) The enforcement of confiscation orders was poor with less than 50 per cent being successfully achieved annually.

(e) The number of money laundering prosecutions was disproportionately small when compared with the true extent of the problem.

1.03 The proposed solution was a significant shift in emphasis: 'the Asset Recovery Strategy'. Henceforth, the pursuit of criminal property should be elevated to a principal imperative of crime reduction policy which would be centrally driven by a new and proactive 'Assets Recovery Agency'. The engine of the new strategy would be strong and radical law which would consolidate and extend the patchy framework of existing legislation.

1.04 Criminal property is to be identified, frozen and confiscated in whatever form and wherever it is found. Confiscation rules are not to be mitigated by judicial discretion. Civil procedures and standards of proof shape new forms of proceedings which are otherwise criminal in nature. Criminal 'benefit' is to be assumed unless the contrary is proved. It is sufficient to observe at this stage that the Act represents a conscious avoidance of the normal criminal process. Thus, the House of Lords, the Privy Council, and the European Court itself have all held that similar confiscation provisions in earlier statutes do not even engage the presumption of innocence in Article 6(2) of the European Convention because they do not involve the 'determination of a criminal charge'.

1.05 Significantly, the Home Secretary, David Blunkett, launching the White Paper, 'One Step Ahead: A 21st Century Strategy to Defeat Organised Criminals' in March 2004 felt able to state: 'Modern crime bosses are sophisticated, organised and determined. No group of defendants is more adept at exploiting our legal safeguards for their own ends.'

1.06 The intended message for both the public and the criminal community is that the notion that 'crime does not pay' is no longer to be perceived as empty and ironic. Criminal organizations are to be disrupted and frustrated by intervention and confiscation; public confidence in the administration of justice is to be restored. In the words of the Prime Minister, the political mission statement is to:

... turn the tide against criminals ... we will deter people from crime by ensuring that criminals do not hang on to their unlawful gains. We will enhance confidence in the law by demonstrating that nobody is beyond its reach. We will make it easier for courts to recover the proceeds of crime from convicted criminals. And we will return to society the assets that have been unlawfully taken.

More prosaically, the message for financial institutions and lawyers is that they **1.07** must expect the new laws to become part of their daily practice. In an enormously significant shift, the 'regulated' financial sector (now defined to include most solicitors firms) is thrust into the front line of money laundering detection and intelligence gathering. A significant penal burden is placed squarely upon the sector to report suspicious client activity and to monitor its own compliance.

Complex issues will arise for solicitors who hold client funds and conduct **1.08** commercial and property transactions on their behalf. They are now exposed to criminal sanctions for poor compliance with statutory disclosure requirements. In addition, the tension between permissible, privileged legal advice given to clients under investigation and the offence of 'prejudicing an investigation' will pose serious professional dilemmas. We have endeavoured to highlight these areas where they arise and to give cautious practical advice as to how they might be approached. It is clear that the solicitors' profession, in particular, will need to develop training systems, and protocols within firms, which will provide warning signals for advisers and employees when these issues arise in client contact.

As the POCA 2002 comes on stream, all criminal lawyers must additionally **1.09** prepare themselves for a culture in which the automatic confiscation of criminal assets, real and 'assumed' under the Act, is a routine part of the processing of convicted defendants. The intended use of the Crown Court as 'a one-stop shop' purveying the complete asset recovery sequence of restraint order, the appointment of receivers, conviction and confiscation will be commonplace. At appropriate points in the text we deal with these aspects where they arise.

B. THE NEW LAW

1. The Assets Recovery Agency

The powers of the Agency are fully covered in Chapter 2.[3] In short, the Agency is **1.10** responsible for implementing and directing the Asset Recovery Strategy. It advises and supports other law enforcement agencies and may conduct criminal confiscation and civil recovery proceedings itself. It may also take over the taxation powers of the Inland Revenue in particular cases.

It came into being as a corporate body on 13 January 2003. Since then it has **1.11** issued two enthusiastic, if not evangelical, annual reports under the stewardship of its first director, Jane Earl. It publishes a 'Proceeds of Crime Update' fortnightly and 'Money Laundering News' monthly.[4] There has even been a special issue of a 'canine' newsletter lauding the successes of cash sniffing dogs!

Between February 2003 and May 2004, the Agency has received 142 referrals **1.12** from other agencies (twenty-three for confiscation and 119 for civil recovery or

---

[3] enquiries@ara.gsi.gov.uk; www.assetsrecovery.gov.uk.
[4] Contact Julie.Davis@ara.gsi.gov.uk.

taxation). According to the 2003–4 report it had 62 cases under investigation thereby exceeding its first year target by 24 per cent; by 31 March 2004, it had obtained £14.8 million in freezing orders, interim receiving orders, and tax assessments—as against £10 million required by its Business Plan.

1.13 Implementation of the Asset Recovery Strategy is intended to be self-financing. A multi-agency 'Enforcement Taskforce' is determinedly pursuing enforcement of existing confiscation orders through the magistrates' courts and has swelled the Consolidated Fund with the collection of over £30 million since it began work in December 2002. In turn, finance specifically diverted from the Fund under the Asset Recovery Strategy has generated numerous purposeful initiatives (and acronyms!). On 2 October 2003, the Home Secretary established the 'Recovered Assets Incentivisation (sic) Fund' (RAIF) for projects which 'boost front line agencies' ability to recover'. Proposals for funding are assessed by the 'Concerted Inter-Agency Criminal Finances Action Group' (CICFA). The Fund is spending over £12 million in its first three years on the creation of five 'Regional Asset Recovery Teams' (RARTs) covering the West Midlands, the North West, the North East, London, and Wales. The teams are made up of police, Customs, Assets Recovery Agency, Inland Revenue, National Criminal Intelligence Service, and Crown Prosecution Service staff, each working under a detective chief inspector.

2. Money Laundering

1.14 The POCA removes the previous statutory distinction between laundering the proceeds of drug trafficking activities and the proceeds of other acquisitive crime. For offences of failing to report knowledge or suspicion of money laundering, a subjective test is substituted for the objective approach of the Drug Trafficking Act 1994 (DTA) and the Criminal Justice Act 1988 (CJA). However, for those in the regulated business sector, the objective test is retained—'has reason for knowing or suspecting'. It will be sufficient to show that a person within the regulated sector should have known or suspected on the basis of information available to them and in keeping with any relevant guidance. The Performance and Innovation Unit Report, concluded that a subjective test placed 'unacceptable obstacles' in the way of prosecutions and that the introduction of a 'negligence test' was necessary as a deterrent against those who failed to act competently and responsibly. The provisions are dealt with in detail in Chapter 6.

3. 'One-Stop Shopping'

1.15 The jurisdiction to make anticipatory restraint orders and to appoint and direct receivers is transferred from the High Court to the Crown Court. As a consequence, the Crown Court is now declared to be a 'One-Stop Shop' in which the prosecution can now 'purchase' pre-trial restraint of assets, criminal conviction, sentence and, ultimately, confiscation of the restrained assets.

4. Criminal Confiscation

It is fair to say that both the DTA 1994 and the CJA 1988 (as heavily amended by   1.16
the POCA 1995) provide limited templates for the post-conviction confiscation
provisions in the POCA 2002. To that extent, concepts such as the 'assumption'
that any property received by a defendant in the previous six years is criminal
benefit are not new. The DTA 1994 provided for mandatory assumptions in drugs
cases, whereas the CJA 1988 allowed for judicial discretion in all other cases. The
new Act consolidates and extends the two previous regimes. It is full of features
such as reverse burdens of proof, the now universal assumption that a defendant
has benefited from crime, the concept of a 'criminal lifestyle', compulsory self-
incrimination under production, and disclosure orders. The provisions are dealt
with in greater detail in Chapter 3.

5. Civil Recovery, Cash Seizure, and Taxation

An entirely new High Court jurisdiction has been created for the making of a   1.17
'recovery order' enabling the Director of the Agency to recover property which is,
or which represents, 'property obtained through unlawful conduct' regardless of
whether any crime has actually been proved against any given individual. Thus far,
the fledgling jurisdiction has also survived challenges to its compatibility with the
Human Rights Act. Civil recovery is covered in Chapter 7.

Existing powers to seize drug trafficking cash at UK borders have been   1.18
extended to all cash wherever found in the United Kingdom which is believed to
be associated with all forms of criminal conduct, past or future. Magistrates may
then order the forfeiture of the cash. Cash seizure and forfeiture are dealt with in
Chapter 8.

Lastly, the Director has power to take over specific and general tax collection   1.19
functions of the Inland Revenue where it is believed that a person's income or gain
or company profit arise as a result of that person's or another's criminal conduct.

C. SCHEME OF THE COMMENTARY

The complete text of the Act is contained within this edition[5] (except those parts   1.20
relating exclusively to Scotland or Northern Ireland); it runs to twelve Parts, 462
sections, and twelve schedules. The statutory language is another triumph for the
Parliamentary draftspersons in their subversive pursuit of unnecessary obscurity
and convolution.

Accordingly, the authors of this Guide have endeavoured to summarize the   1.21
main provisions of the new legislation in a form which is digestible, to highlight

---

[5] See Appendix 1.

issues of novelty or complexity, and to address points of uncertainty. The text is designed primarily for the practitioner. In dealing with the new criminal confiscation provisions, for example, it does so by means of a step-by-step analysis of the procedure and the applicable principles. Practical advice is similarly provided to practitioners in relation to the money laundering provisions and the traps which exist for the unwary lawyer.

1.22 The meaning of many features of the Act can be deduced from judicial consideration of earlier legislation and, therefore, much earlier case law remains relevant. However, in places we have had to attempt to predict likely interpretations. Lacking the confidence that our predictions are necessarily accurate, we recommend that there is no substitute for a detailed examination of the actual provisions themselves.

1.23 The law is applicable to England and Wales, although the scheme of the Act for the most part makes identical provision for Northern Ireland. Part 4 is a separate confiscation regime which we do not cover. The Agency will cover Northern Ireland, but its distinctive historical needs will be addressed through the appointment of an assistant to the Director, who will have specific responsibility for carrying out his functions there, and the Director will need to set out in his annual plan the local strategies which are to be pursued. Part 3 of the Act, applying a similar assets recovery and money laundering regime to Scotland is also omitted.

1.24 The law contained in the Guide is as we believe it to be as of 18 August 2004.

2

THE ASSETS RECOVERY AGENCY

A. OVERVIEW

1. Structure of the Agency

The creation of the free standing Assets Recovery Agency (ARA) heralds **2.01** significant changes in the detection, investigation and prosecution of crime and the confiscation of property derived from crime. Consistent with the Government's intention to promote joined up inter-agency co-operation, the ARA is now part of the 'Organized Crime Task Force', made up with the Police Service of Northern Ireland, HM Customs and Excise, the Inland Revenue, the National Criminal Intelligence Service (NCIS), the Home Office, and the Northern Ireland Office. This is so even though the ARA will primarily concentrate upon the investigation and recovery of criminal assets as opposed to the investigation and prosecution of crimes.

Part 1 of the POCA 2002 creates the ARA and makes provision for the appoint- **2.02** ment and powers of the Director by the Secretary of State, s 1(2). The Director is defined as a 'corporation sole' under s 1(3) and he may authorize any ARA member of staff or other 'person providing services under arrangements' to exercise the full powers of the Director themself by virtue of s 1(6). It seems therefore that other agencies will deploy manpower to the ARA (and perhaps vice versa) in the pursuit of the aim of co-operation, sharing of techniques and information and overall crime reduction. This is likely to include the police (including NCIS, etc), HM Customs and Excise, and the Inland Revenue. These organizations as 'persons who have functions relating to the investigation or prosecution of offences' are required under s 4 to co-operate with the Director and the Director is required to co-operate with them in the exercise of functions they have under the Act.

2.03   The exercise of the functions of the Director by any person so authorized will not in fact be fully extended in every respect. Police officers, for example, may not discharge the Director's civil recovery powers (s 313).

2. Functions of the Agency

2.04   The ARA has three distinct operational functions: criminal confiscation, civil recovery, and the taxation of income related to crime. Whilst these operational functions are directed towards the overall goal of the reduction of crime as so stated in s 2(1), only one of them has its foundations firmly in the criminal justice system. The ARA will be able to initiate confiscation proceedings under s 6(3)(a) and can act as the enforcement authority in respect of Crown Court confiscation orders under s 34 (via associated powers in ss 6, 19, 20, 27, 28, 31, and 33). In addition to the powers under the criminal regime, controversially the ARA can pursue those individuals in the civil courts who are perceived to be in possession of 'property obtained through unlawful conduct' as per s 304(1) without necessarily being able to identify any particular index criminal offence.

3. Director's Guidance

2.05   Section 2(5) and (6) of the POCA states that 'the Director must have regard to any guidance given to him by the Secretary of State' and that this 'guidance must indicate that the reduction of crime is in general best secured by means of criminal investigations and criminal proceedings'. For the purposes of contributing to the reduction of crime, the Director should:

(a)   not normally act without a referral from the law enforcement or prosecution authorities;

(b)   consult the relevant law enforcement or prosecution authority before exercising any of his operational functions, in order to enquire whether doing so would prejudice a criminal investigation or criminal proceedings and give due weight to any advice so received;

(c)   keep under review the extent to which taking, continuing, or refraining from any course of action has a potential to prejudice a criminal investigation or criminal proceedings and avoid such prejudice where possible;

(d) ensure where possible that information relevant to a criminal investigation or criminal proceedings is disclosed to the relevant law enforcement or prosecution authority at the earliest practical opportunity.[1]

Where there is evidence of a particular crime having been committed by a particular person, it would be envisaged that the ARA would turn over the individual case it was investigating to one of the available prosecuting authorities whilst retaining the potential for input at a later stage such as with the making of a confiscation order or, if criminal proceedings fail, by civil recovery. **2.06**

We will have to wait to see what significance there may be as to the interpretation of the phrase 'in general' in s 2(6) as to the perceived effectiveness of criminal investigations and criminal proceedings in contributing to crime reduction. Does this leave open the potential for the guidance from the Secretary of State to change if the reduction of crime is subsequently considered to be best achieved outside of the Criminal Justice System? Might there be particular categories of crime where the reduction of it is not 'in general best secured by means of criminal investigations and criminal proceedings'? Would this open up the greater proliferation of allegations of unlawful conduct being heard by the civil courts? **2.07**

One view might be to suggest that vigorously pursued civil recovery could in fact overlook and even prejudice the reduction of crime aim. It may be that those individuals said to have obtained property through unlawful conduct would far prefer to be subjected to a financial penalty under civil recovery rather than face the potential for the dual and significant penalties of the loss of liberty and asset confiscation under the criminal justice system. Such a perception may not in fact deter the sophisticated criminals at whom the creation of the ARA was aimed, but instead merely encourage them to view any such civil recovery as a form of business cost allowing them to continue their unlawful activity. **2.08**

For a detailed exposition of the relevant procedures involved in civil recovery see Chapter 7 below. As an accompaniment to that chapter practitioners are directed to Appendix 12 concerned with the Legal Services Commission publication of 'Guidance to Solicitors and Applicants Seeking Community Legal Services Funding for Proceedings under the Proceeds of Crime Act 2002 Involving the Assets Recovery Agency'. **2.09**

4. Revenue Functions

Part 6 of the POCA provides for the ARA to exercise taxation functions under powers delegated by the Inland Revenue. These apply in circumstances where income, gains or profits are believed to arise from criminal conduct and in any event are unlikely to have been declared. General matters are considered here and Chapter 9 below further explores the extent of the provisions. **2.10**

---

[1] Source: Guidance by the Secretary of State to the Director of the Assets Recovery Agency.

2. The Assets Recovery Agency

2.11 The Director will only become involved where there are reasonable grounds for suspecting that any income, gains or profits derive from the proceeds of crime. If such a suspicion ceases to exist then the matter will be referred back to the Revenue for them to handle in the normal way and the Director will cease to take responsibility.

2.12 In addition to responsibility for income tax, capital gains tax, and corporation tax, the Director will also have jurisdiction in respect of inheritance tax, and functions relating to the payment of PAYE and National Insurance contributions in respect of employer suspects. These additional functions enable a comprehensive investigation of the tax affairs of suspect companies and their directors. In each case, the ARA will not simply act as investigator, passing information back to the Revenue for action, but rather will be responsible for all stages of the process of taxing a person in respect of the relevant period, including the recovery of unpaid tax, interest and financial penalties.

2.13 This comprehensive approach is intended to have two important effects. First, important information will be gathered by the ARA which will enable it to determine whether there has been a benefit from criminal proceeds or conduct, and to what extent. Secondly, the ARA will be able to raise a revenue demand without the need to identify the source of income, thus placing the onus on the taxpayer to displace the assessment on appeal and to prove that the income derived from a non-taxable (and non-criminal) source.

2.14 In order to carry out tax functions the ARA requires to have access to Inland Revenue information. The mechanisms are provided in Pt 6 by vesting in the Director the statutory functions of the Board of the Inland Revenue and, in addition, by permitting the Inland Revenue to disclose information to the Director under ss 436 and 437, subject to the provisions of the Data Protection Act 1998 and Pt 1 of the Regulation of Investigatory Powers Act 2000. However, it is of significance that, once received, the information can be used in connection with the exercise of any of the Director's functions and is not confined to the transferred taxation function. In other words, Inland Revenue documentation obtained additionally may be used in confiscation and civil recovery proceedings by the ARA by virtue of s 435, and may be disclosed under s 437 to other agencies or persons for limited purposes and with the consent of the Commissioners of Inland Revenue. General provisions relating to the disclosure of information for the following purposes:

(a) criminal investigations and proceedings, both here and abroad;

(b) confiscation proceedings by a prosecutor in any part of the United Kingdom;

(c) summary recovery proceedings initiated by police or customs officers;

(d) safeguarding national security,

are specifically *excluded* in relation to Inland Revenue information by s 438(2).

5. Aims and Objectives of the Asset Recovery Strategy

The strategy is, in part, a response to the publication in June 2000 of the study   2.15
conducted by the Performance and Innovation Unit on Recovering the Proceeds
of Crime. This study expressed the clear view that financial investigation and asset
recovery were seriously under utilized. It emphasized the importance of the
pursuit and recovery of the proceeds of crime as a crime fighting measure and as
a means to instil public confidence in the rule of law. The report identified the
weaknesses in the present system, particularly the failings in the investigation,
making and enforcement of confiscation orders.

The four aims of the strategy are: 2.16

(i)   To make greater use of the investigation of criminal assets in the fight against
      crime.
(ii) To recover money that has been made from crime or which is intended for use
      in crime.
(iii) To prevent criminals and their associates from laundering the proceeds of
      criminal conduct, and to detect and penalize such laundering where it occurs.
(iv) To use the proceeds recovered for the benefit of the community.

B. THE DIRECTOR'S ROLE AND FUNCTIONS

1. Appointment and Terms

Schedule 1 to the Act contains the Director's terms of appointment in office, the   2.17
staffing of the ARA and the funding of the ARA. Under Sch 1, the Director is
required to prepare an Annual Plan before the beginning of each financial year
which is subject to the approval of the Secretary of State. Additionally the
Director is required to produce an Annual Report at the end of each financial year
to be published and laid before Parliament.

2. Training and Accreditation of Financial Investigators

Under s 3 of the Act the Director is required to establish a system for the accredi-   2.18
tation of financial investigators (FIs). It is claimed that the Assets Recovery
Agency's Financial Investigation Centre of Excellence trained 1,417 financial
investigators, primarily police and customs officers between September 2002 and
March 2003.[2] However the ARA Annual Report states that in response to the
target of delivering high quality training to financial investigators '431 FIs had
been trained as at 31 March 2004. The report also states that 205 FIs received

---

[2] *Proceeds of Crime Update*, issue No.8, 31 July 2003.

enhanced training in confiscation.'[3] The vast differences in the two sets of figures produced by the ARA themselves cannot be explained.

3. Investigative Tools

2.19 In considering the extent of the authority of the Director and the available tools at the disposal of Agency staff it is interesting to note the miscellaneous provisions provided for under Pt 12 of the Act. Under s 449 any member of staff of the Agency if authorized 'to do anything by the Director for the purposes of this act', and 'it is necessary or expedient for the purposes of doing the thing', may for that purpose identify himself by means of a pseudonym.[4] Quite how 'doing the thing' will be interpreted in practice will only be seen as ARA cases flow through the courts. The authorization of the use of pseudonyms is not a new feature to criminal investigations concerned with serious crime (undercover police officers for instance), but of course the ARA is not primarily concerned with these. Under s 449(4) a member of staff to whom the section has been applied 'must not be asked (and if he is asked is not required to answer) any question which is likely to reveal his true identity'. This section illustrates the dual role that the ARA will play in the fight against crime and the recovery of the proceeds of crime.

4. Confiscation Orders and Enforcement

2.20 Chapter 3 considers in detail the Act's revolutionary revision of the process of confiscation orders in a criminal context. However it is relevant to consider confiscation at this stage because the Act now provides that the Director must be made responsible for the enforcement of confiscation orders where the Director asked the court to proceed under s 6 of the Act or where the Director was appointed as the enforcement authority upon an application by the Director prior to the making of the confiscation order under s 34. The Director can also be appointed in cases where a defendant has absconded[5] or an appeal is instigated from the Crown Court's order.[6] In all other cases it appears that s 34 does not authorize the court to appoint the Director as the enforcement authority, for example where the court has made a confiscation order as a result of the application of the prosecutor and the order has been made without any application by the Director to be appointed as the enforcement authority. In such cases the old regime will apply and the confiscation order will be treated as akin to a Crown Court fine having been imposed on the defendant. In those circumstances the order will be enforced by the Magistrates Court under s 35. In such a case the provisions of the Powers of Criminal Courts (Sentencing) Act 2000 will apply,[7]

---

[3] ARA, *Annual Report 2003–4*, 32.　　[4] See s 449(2).　　[5] See ss 27–30.
[6] See ss 31–33.　　[7] Referred to in s 35 as 'the Sentencing Act'.

the Crown Court having set a period of imprisonment in default of the satisfaction of the confiscation order.[8]

Where the Director is properly appointed to enforce a confiscation order under **2.21**
the Act and the defendant has failed to satisfy the confiscation order there are two
main regimes provided for by the Act under ss 37 and 52. Firstly under s 37 the
Director may apply *ex parte* to the Crown Court for the issuing of a summons
against a defendant for his committal to prison or detention for default in payment. If it appears to the Crown Court that the conditions have been satisfied (the
conditions include establishing that 'because of the defendant's wilful refusal or
culpable neglect the order is not satisfied') then a summons may be issued requiring the defendant's attendance at court. If a defendant fails to attend in answer to
the summons the court may issue a warrant for his arrest under s 37(4). It appears
that the Director cannot apply for a warrant for the defendant's arrest at the first
stage, only if they fail to appear in answer to the summons issued under s 37(3).
When a defendant appears and the court is satisfied that the conditions set out in
s 37(2) are satisfied it may issue a warrant committing the defendant to prison or
detention.[9] The Act further provides under s 39 for the reduction of the original
default term of imprisonment in circumstances where the confiscation order is
met in part or varied and the Act additionally provides for the increase of the
default term of imprisonment subject to the variation of the original order, for
example on appeal.[10]

The second main mechanism under the Act for enforcement by the Director of **2.22**
the ARA is contained in ss 52, 53, and 56. This provides for the appointment of
'Director's Receivers' which must follow in any case where the Director is
appointed as the enforcement authority (in cases where the Director is not
appointed the Crown Court may appoint a receiver, see s 50(2) 'Enforcement
Receivers). In this context the Director's Receiver appointed to enforce the
confiscation order may be a member of staff of the ARA or a specialist who provides services to the ARA. In the exercise of those powers the Director appointed
receiver is to have regard to s 69 of the Act so as to make available the value of realizable property in order to satisfy the outstanding confiscation order. Those sums
retrieved by the Director or the Director's Receiver appointed under s 52 are to be
distributed having regard to the provisions of ss 56 and 57 of the Act. It is worthy
of note that there are differing sections to apply to the distinct methods of enforcing a confiscation order. For example if the Director is not appointed to enforce
an order but an Enforcement Receiver is appointed under s 50, the receiver must
apply s 54 of the Act as to the distribution of the sums held. Depending upon the
section of the Act under which the order is to be enforced there are corresponding
distribution of sums provisions.

---

[8] See Powers of Criminal Courts Act 2000, ss 139 and 140.
[9] See s 37(2)(a) to (e).   [10] See ss 21, 22, 23, 29, 32, and 33.

C. PROGRESS OF THE ARA SINCE IMPLEMENTATION

1. Asset Recovery Updates

2.23 Since the implementation of the ARA and the appointment of the Director, the ARA has published regular newsletters in two separate publications.[11] Published up to three times a month these updates laud the value of those assets that have been recovered and highlight the political and legal developments as pertain to the 'assets recovery community' such as the growth of the inter-agency co-operation.

2.24 Although not directly relevant to this chapter but of particular interest in assessing more broadly the effect of the increased powers under the POCA are the reports as to cash seizures. In June 2003 the ARA newsletter claimed that the Metropolitan Police had made cash and asset seizures of £4.7 million and that HM Customs and Excise had been seizing £1 million each week within the first four weeks of the new powers available under the Act.[12]

2.25 The money laundering updates have also usefully recorded the manner in which the POCA has been received particularly by the financial services industry, with examples of the new systems deployed by banking institutions to detect and report suspicious activity.[13] Such updates can be of significant assistance in assessing how investigations into criminal proceeds and the money laundering provisions of the POCA are being practically applied.

2. ARA Annual Report

2.26 The ARA has now been operating for just over a year and has recently published its Annual Report for the financial year 2003–4.[14] On the whole the report claims that the ARA has had a successful year in a number of respects including exceeding the target of training 400 financial investigators (432 trained), exceeding the target number of fifty 'cases under investigation' (sixty-two cases) and exceeding the target of £10 million of 'orders and tax assessments' (£14.8 million in freezing orders, interim receiving orders, and tax assessments).[15]

2.27 In terms of the ARA's involvement in criminal confiscation it is still early days in assessing the impact. Many of the POCA offences came into force in February and March 2003 and any alleged unlawful activity after that date could potentially attract charges under the POCA and upon conviction, POCA confiscation with ARA input. However any alleged unlawful acquisitive activity before that date would be covered by offences and confiscation regimes provided by the Drug Trafficking Act 1994 and/or the Criminal Justice Act 1988. Therefore even over a

---

[11] *Proceeds of Crime Update* and *Proceeds of Crime Update—Money Laundering News.*
[12] *Proceeds of Crime Update*, Issue No.4, 5 June 2003.
[13] The updates are available at the ARA Website www.assetsrecovery.gov.uk.   [14] ibid.
[15] ARA, Annual Report 2003–4, 2.

year after the coming into force of the Act the ARA is only able to claim a single case of adopting a confiscation investigation outright.[16]

It is therefore still quite difficult to objectively assess the claimed success of the   **2.28** ARA in pursuing its strategies and targets. However the creation of the ARA and the scope for its multi-faceted powers remain one of the most significant developments in the fight against crime in recent memory.

3. ARA Business Plan 2004–5

Published together with the Annual Report for 2003–4, the Business Plan for the   **2.29** current year emphasizes the Director's commitment to working together with the ARA's law enforcement partners in order to deliver 'the maximum possible contribution we can make to ensuring that crime really does not pay.' The specified objectives include 'disrupting organised criminal organisations,' to 'deliver high quality training to Financial Investigators,' and to 'become effectively self financing no later than 2005–6 and to increase the ratio of receipts to operating cost by at least 5% a year thereafter.'

The 'activity' identified to achieve the targets includes continuing to assist in the   **2.30** investigation of the existing nineteen adopted criminal confiscation cases and adopting a further fifteen cases. In addition the ARA is to continue to investigate the existing forty-five adopted civil recovery/tax cases and adopt a further twenty-five. In financial terms the ARA is aiming to disrupt criminal enterprises by early restraint of assets in all cases to the value of £12 million, obtain confiscation orders to the value of £5 million, recovery orders and tax assessments to the value of at least £10 million, and realize receipts in civil recovery/taxation cases to the value of at least £7.5 million. The progress of this activity in achieving the targets set out in the business plan can no doubt be monitored in the regular ARA publications already identified.

---

[16] ibid 7.

3
CRIMINAL CONFISCATION

A. OVERVIEW

1. Previous Legislation

Part 2 of the Proceeds of Crime Act 2002 (POCA) creates a single model **3.01** for confiscation following conviction in criminal cases.[1] It came into force on 24 March 2003.[2]

The scheme of the Act is meant to be severe and unforgiving. Anyone with legal **3.02** training coming fresh to confiscation law may feel disoriented. Part 2 appears to occupy some parallel legal universe which has no apparent relationship with the normal rules of criminal process. Speaking of an earlier template, Tucker J once said: 'evidential burdens are cast upon (the defendant) which are, to say the least, unusual in the area of the criminal law'.[3] An examination of the Act shows this to be a masterly understatement.

Accordingly, defendants are penalized for conduct which is unproven; civil **3.03** standards and methods of proof apply to most issues; assumptions and reverse burdens of proof punctuate the various stages; hardship is never a consideration. It cannot be fathomed without an appreciation that it is public policy, not procedural fairness, which drives its workings.

However, those with a knowledge of existing confiscation law will recognize **3.04** many of the features of previous legislation. The basic framework of the POCA is a merger and extension of the two similar but separate schemes contained in the Drug Trafficking Act 1994 (DTA) for drug offences and in the Criminal Justice Act 1988 (CJA) (as heavily amended by the Proceeds of Crime Act 1995) for other

---

[1] Other than for certain terrorist offences which have separate legislation.
[2] See further para 3.24 below.   [3] *Comiskey* (1991) 93 Cr App R 227.

offences. For that reason, many of the earlier cases remain useful guides to the application of the new Act.

2. Principal Changes

3.05 The Act changes the previous law in five important ways:

(i) the Crown Court is now the 'one-stop shop' for confiscation and ancillary orders;

(ii) the Act creates a single, unified system for confiscation following a criminal conviction;

(iii) an enquiry is mandatory if the prosecution applies for a hearing;

(iv) the Act introduces the notion of a 'criminal lifestyle' which triggers an unlimited review of the proceeds of the defendant's 'general criminal conduct';

(v) it gives the prosecution a straightforward right of appeal.[4]

3. The Human Rights Act

3.06 The Home Secretary, David Blunkett, has attached a statement of compatibility under s 19 of the Human Rights Act 1998 (HRA). However, this in itself is probably meaningless. In *A (No 2)*,[5] Lord Hope remarked that such statements 'may serve a useful purpose in Parliament . . . But they are no more than expressions of opinion by the minister. They are not binding on the court, nor do they have any persuasive authority.'

3.07 Unfortunately for defendants, the higher courts have tended to agree with the Minister when testing similar constructs in the CJA 1988 and in the DTA 1994. Thus far, all arguments that these provisions breach the European Convention on Human Rights ('the Convention') have been rejected. We consider some of these in turn.

(a) *Reverse burdens of proof and the presumption of innocence*

3.08 The basic argument is that a defendant in confiscation proceedings, as a person 'charged with a criminal offence', is entitled to the express presumption of innocence in Article 6(2). The mandatory assumption in confiscation proceedings (see below) that the defendant has benefited from criminal conduct unless he can show the assumption to be 'incorrect' is an unfair reversal of the burden of proof. This argument has been roundly rejected root and branch.[6]

---

[4] But see *Flowers (A-G's References (Nos 114–116 of 2002)* (CA, 26 November 2003) where the judge erred in law as to his power to proceed under the CJA 1988.

[5] [2002] 1 AC 45.

[6] Note, however, that it has also been held that a confiscation hearing is, nevertheless, the determination of a 'criminal charge' and, therefore, attracts the general fair trial guarantees of Art 6(1). See, for example, *Lloyd v Bow Street Magistrates' Court* [2003] EWHC 2294 (Admin); *Re S* [2004] EWHC 1011 (Admin).

The most crushing domestic decision is that of the House of Lords in 2002 in   **3.09**
Benjafield and Rezvi.[7] However, the point had already been effectively resolved a
year earlier by the Privy Council (albeit in relation to similar Scottish legislation)
in *McIntosh v Lord Advocate*.[8] They unanimously held that the defendant is not
'charged with a criminal offence'. The confiscation order was categorized as 'a
financial penalty (with a custodial penalty in default of payment) but it is a
penalty imposed for the offence of which he has been convicted and involves no
accusation of any other offence'.

Given that 'criminal conduct' includes other criminal offences and that the   **3.10**
assumptions can operate to require the court to find that the defendant has
benefited from 'criminal conduct' beyond the index offence, this is a little difficult
to follow. Nevertheless, the court in *Rezvi* regarded the Privy Council's character-
ization as 'an accurate description' of the process. Moreover, the European Court
of Human Rights itself appears to agree. Between the decisions in *McIntosh* and
Rezvi, the European Court visited a similar point under the DTA 1994 in *Phillips
v UK*:[9]

. . . the right to be presumed innocent under article 6(2) arises only in connection with the
particular offence 'charged'. Once an accused has properly been proved guilty of that
offence, article 6(2) can have no application in relation to allegations made about the
accused's character and conduct as part of the sentencing process, unless such accusations
are of such a nature and degree as to amount to the bringing of a new 'charge' within the
autonomous Convention meaning.

The court considers that . . . [the presumption of innocence] . . . is not . . . absolute, since
presumptions of fact or of law operate in every criminal law system and are not prohibited
in principle by the Convention, as long as states remain within certain limits, taking into
account the importance of what is at stake and maintaining the rights of the defence.

(b) *Proportionality*

The House of Lords in *Benjafield and Rezvi* purported to weigh the interests of   **3.11**
defendants against the wider needs of society as a whole. In the two linked appeals
the House was considering both the mandatory assumptions of the DTA 1994
and the discretionary rules of the CJA 1988 respectively. In both they again followed the reasoning in *Phillips v UK* which concerned the 1994 Act. Referring to
Phillips, Lord Steyn stated in his speech in *Rezvi*:

Overall . . . the application . . . of the 1994 Act 'was confined within reasonable limits given
the importance of what was at stake and that the rights of the defence were fully respected'.

It is a notorious fact that professional and habitual criminals frequently take steps to
conceal their profits from crime. Effective but fair powers of confiscating the proceeds of
crime are therefore essential. The provisions . . . are aimed at depriving such offenders of
the proceeds of their criminal conduct. Its purposes are to punish convicted offenders, to
deter the commission of further offences and to reduce the profits available to fund further
criminal enterprises. These objectives reflect not only national but also international policy.

---

[7] [2002] 1 AC 45.   [8] [2001] 3 WLR 107.   [9] 11 BHRC 280.

The United Kingdom has undertaken, by signing and ratifying treaties agreed under the auspices of the United Nations and the Council of Europe, to take measures necessary to ensure that the profits of those engaged in drug trafficking or other crimes are confiscated ... It is clear that the [legislation] was passed in furtherance of a legitimate aim and that the measures are rationally connected with that aim ... The only question is whether the statutory means adopted are wider than is necessary to accomplish the objective ...

3.12 Lord Steyn went on to quote from the judgment of the Court of Appeal[10]:

Parliament has clearly made efforts to balance the interest of the defendant against that of the public in the following respects:

(a) It is only after the necessary convictions that any question of confiscation arises. This is of significance, because the trial which results in the conviction or convictions will be one where the usual burden and standard of proof rests upon the prosecution. In addition, a defendant who is convicted of the necessary offence or offences can be taken to be aware that if he committed the offences of which he has been convicted, he would not only be liable to imprisonment or another sentence, but he would also be liable to confiscation proceedings.

(b) The prosecution has the responsibility for initiating the confiscation proceedings unless the court regards them as inappropriate ...

(c) There is also the responsibility placed upon the court not to make a confiscation order when there is a serious risk of injustice. As already indicated, this will involve the court, before it makes a confiscation order, standing back and deciding whether there is a risk of injustice. If the court decides there is, then the confiscation order will not be made.

(d) There is the role of this court on appeal to ensure there is no unfairness.

3.13 Lord Steyn placed great reliance on the existence of this discretion in the making of assumptions in the CJA 1988. He spoke of 'the role of the court in standing back and deciding whether there is or might be a risk of serious or real injustice and, if there is, or might be, in emphasising that a confiscation order ought not be made.'

3.14 That may be right in so far as the discretion in the 1988 Act may temper the assumptions, but those of the DTA 1994 and of the POCA 2002 are mandatory. Nevertheless, in the *Benjafield* appeal, Lord Steyn again drew upon the judge's power to prevent injustice:

The critical point is that under the 1994 Act, as under the 1988 Act, the judge must be astute to avoid injustice. If there is or might be a serious or real risk of injustice, he must not make a confiscation order. In these circumstances a challenge to the compatibility of the legislation must fail.

3.15 This has been seized upon by some commentators as a future basis for a positive, proactive judicial approach to the making of orders even under these mandatory provisions—in other words, no unjust order may be made. However, there is

---

[10] [2001] 3 WLR 75.

actually little scope for this in the statutory language and it may be over-optimistic because the Court of Appeal has made it plain in cases such as *Dore* (1997)[11] that, as a matter of construction, the injustice must arise from the operation of the assumptions and not from the severe consequences of a confiscation order. Hardship arising from the making of a confiscation order is not considered injustice in this sense.[12] What is contemplated is some internal contradiction in the process of assumption or between the assumption and the factual basis for sentence which leads to an unjust calculation of the proceeds.

B. THE PROCESS—A SUMMARY

1. Summary

The expression 'confiscation order' has been accurately described as a misnomer as the order itself does not confiscate any property but, instead, requires the defendant to pay over a sum of money.   3.16

In the language of the Act, this sum is termed the 'recoverable amount'. This will be either (a) the full amount of what the court has found to be his 'benefit' from his 'criminal conduct' or (b) the value of all of the defendant's remaining assets, called the 'available amount', if that can be proved to be less.   3.17

An order may be made in the Crown Court against anyone convicted of an indictable offence or committed by the magistrates. Procedure is governed by the Crown Court (Confiscation, Restraint and Receivership) Rules 2003.[13] The outcome of the hearing may be agreed and last only a few minutes or it may be hard fought, run into days and involve vast international wealth. In all cases, the process is inexorable and must proceed to its conclusion once judge or prosecution sets it in motion.   3.18

The Act has its own form of pleadings. The prosecution must provide a 'Statement of Information'. In turn, the court can order the defendant to respond to the prosecution's Statement or to divulge information.   3.19

Normally, the confiscation order must be made before sentence. However, the court can sentence the defendant or order compensation (although not impose monetary penalties) and postpone the confiscation hearing for up to two years from the date of conviction. In 'exceptional circumstances' longer postponements are possible.   3.20

There are extensive provisions allowing the prosecution or the Director to re-open the issues where, for example, new material comes to light. The defendant   3.21

---

[11] [1997] 2 Cr App R (S) 152.

[12] For example, in *Danison v UK* (1998) (Application No 45042/98) the Commission held that 'the extent of the relevance' of a spouse's interest in the matrimonial home is 'within the appreciation' of the domestic court.

[13] SI 2003/421.

may return to court for a reduction in the order if it subsequently turns out that his assets prove to be inadequate to meet the order in full.

2. The Order of Events

3.22 A strict chronology must be followed (see the chart at the end of this chapter):

(a) The process starts when the prosecution asks for an enquiry or when 'the court (itself) believes it is appropriate for it to do so'.

(b) The judge must then decide whether the defendant has a 'criminal lifestyle'. This depends solely upon the nature of the offence or offences of which the defendant has been convicted in the current or earlier proceedings. For example, anyone convicted of a drug trafficking or money laundering offence is automatically deemed to have a criminal lifestyle.

(c) The judge must then determine whether the defendant 'has benefited from . . . criminal conduct'. There are two alternatives:

(i) If the defendant has been found to have a criminal lifestyle, the court must determine whether the defendant has benefited from 'his *general* criminal conduct'.

(ii) If, on the other hand, the defendant does not have a criminal lifestyle, the court must determine whether he has benefited from 'his *particular'* criminal conduct'—that is, from the particular offence(s) of which he has been convicted or has taken into consideration.

(d) Next, the judge must determine the gross market value of the proceeds/benefit—'the recoverable amount'. In calculating benefit from 'general criminal conduct', the judge must apply the relevant assumptions as to income and expenditure in the previous six years and as to property 'held' by the defendant on conviction (unless the defendant can show an assumption to be incorrect or that 'there would be a serious risk of injustice if an assumption were made').

(e) Lastly, the judge must make a confiscation order in that sum *unless* the defendant can prove that the value of all his existing assets, known as 'the available amount' (including artificial or 'tainted' gifts to others), is less than the value of the benefit. If so, the 'available amount' becomes the 'recoverable amount' and, therefore, is the amount of the confiscation order.

C. WHEN DOES THE ACT APPLY?

1. The Crown Court

3.23 Anyone facing sentence in the Crown Court can find himself the subject of a POCA enquiry. The 'first condition' for an enquiry is that the defendant has been:

(a) convicted of an offence in the Crown Court;

(b) committed to the Crown Court for sentence; or

(c) committed to the Crown Court under s 70 of the POCA itself for specific consideration of a confiscation order (s 6(2)).

It is important to note that the Act does not apply if any of the offences upon which the defendant was convicted or committed took place before 24 March 2003. Where an offence occurs over a period, it is taken to have occurred on the earliest day in the period.[14]   **3.24**

2. Magistrates' Courts

Magistrates no longer have power to make a confiscation order. However, if the prosecution asks them to do so, they must commit a convicted defendant 'with a view to a confiscation order being considered' (s 70). It would appear that this even includes summary only offences. The Magistrates' Court must state whether it would have also committed the defendant for sentence.   **3.25**

D. MANDATORY ENQUIRY

1. Prosecution Application

The 'second condition' is fulfilled and the process becomes mandatory when either: **3.26**

(a) the prosecutor asks the court to proceed, or

(b) the court itself considers that it is appropriate to do so (s 6(3)).

So, if the prosecution wants a determination, the Crown Court '*must* proceed towards the making of a confiscation order'.

2. Abuse of Process

It is conceivably arguable that an unmerited prosecution application should be refused on the basis that a hearing would amount to an abuse of process—for example, in a case where there is nothing to suggest any significant discrepancy between the defendant's property and expenditure and his known sources of income. Lord Bingham has said that 'unless the accounting details reveal such a discrepancy the prosecutor will not in practice apply for an order' (*McIntosh v Lord Advocate* (2001).[15] This seems to imply that it might be an abuse to apply in some circumstances.   **3.27**

---

[14] POCA 2002 (Transitional Provisions, Savings and Amendment) Order (SI 2003/333).
[15] [2001] 3 WLR 107.

3.28 Admittedly, the language of the Act does not limit the prosecution's right to make an application. Even so, prosecutors are ministers of justice whose independent discretion should be exercised judicially and who ought not to embark on opportunistic 'fishing expeditions'. The decision to apply for a hearing ought to be based upon some rational ground for believing that it will produce a result.

3.29 One might have thought that it would be an abuse if a prosecutor leaves charges on the file in return for guilty pleas but then nevertheless goes on to invite the judge to make the assumption that monies received in the period covered by those charges is the benefit of criminal conduct. However, the House of Lords has held that it cannot be an abuse simply to apply primary legislation as intended and, in particular, to apply the assumptions which the Act demands (*Benjafield and Rezvi* (2002)).[16]

E. EVIDENCE AND PROOF

1. The Burden and Standard of Proof

3.30 In strict terms the burden of proving both the fact that the defendant has benefited from crime and the amount of his benefit is borne by the prosecution. Accordingly, it is for the prosecution to prove, for example, that the defendant received a particular payment before any assumption can be made that it represents the proceeds of crime. Pausing there, this could be established in a variety of ways: for example, by producing the defendant's bank statements or calculations in the defendant's 'working notes' or frequently by inference from all the circumstances.[17]

3.31 The standard of proof is that of 'the balance of probabilities' (s 6(7)). This, it should be noted, is a quite deliberate departure from the DTA 1994 and the CJA 1988 which both use the expression, '. . . that applicable to civil proceedings'. Without doubt, this is intended to evade the flexibility of the civil standard and the principle that civil proceedings involving criminal allegations require a higher degree of proof.

3.32 Some prosecutors may choose to limit themselves to evidence of the defendant's finances within a definite period when there is clear evidence of benefit from criminal conduct—for example, where a marked change in the defendant's bankings can be shown. However, in large-scale drug and fraud cases, it may be considered that a complete review of the defendant's activities is justified on the basis that a principal player must have worked his way up the criminal hierarchy and benefited accordingly over the years.

---

[16] [2002] 2 WLR 235.
[17] See *Dickens* [1999] 2 QB 102; Enwezor (1991) 93 Cr App R 233; Redbourne (1993) 96 Cr App R 201; Khan (CA, 26 February 1996).

Negotiation and compromise will not necessarily limit the scope of the enquiry. **3.33** Because the required assumptions are mandatory, the judge may have to determine the proceeds to be greater than the parties have agreed (see, for example, Atkinson (1993).[18]

2. Sources of Proof

In *Dickens* (above), Lord Lane, considering the determination of benefit, stated **3.34** 'The evidence upon which that judgement is based will come in part from the trial, if there has been one, in part from the statements tendered by the parties . . . and in part from evidence adduced before the court'.

3. Trial Evidence

Where the POCA investigation has been preceded by a contested trial, the judge is **3.35** entitled to rely on the trial evidence without having it all repeated in the POCA hearing. He is not bound to adopt the view which is most favourable to the defence (*Threapleton* (2002)[19]). However, the defendant must be allowed to give evidence at this stage, whether or not he gave evidence in the trial (*Jenkins* (1990)[20]).

Where more than one view of the facts is consistent with the verdict, the judge **3.36** may form his own view in light of the evidence.[21] It is not clear how the judge must approach split verdicts—in other words, where the defendant has been convicted of some offences but acquitted of others—either on the verdict of the jury or because the prosecution has offered no evidence. Admittedly, the standard of proof is lower in a POCA enquiry. It is, nevertheless, submitted that the correct approach is to treat an acquittal as having decided the relevant issues for all purposes. For example, if the trial issue was whether the defendant had, in fact, received certain monies, the judge ought not to go behind the verdict in the POCA determination to find differently; if the trial issue was whether the monies were received as a result of crime, it would be unjust for the judge to assume the monies to be benefit from criminal conduct.

4. Prosecution Statements of Information

The procedure has its own form of pleadings governed by the new Crown Court **3.37** Rules. First, the prosecution (or Director) must set out its stall in a 'Statement of Information' outlining the matters which it believes are relevant to the various stages of the POCA enquiry (s 16). The judge sets a time table.

---

[18] (1993) 14 Cr App R (S) 182.   [19] [2002] Crim LR 229.
[20] (1990–91) 12 Cr App R (S) 582.
[21] See *Boyer* (1981) 3 Cr App R (S) 35; *Solomon and Triumph* (1984) 6 Cr App R (S) 120; *McGlade* (1990–91) 12 Cr App R (S) 105.

3.38   The statement must set out the underlying material for any of the required assumptions; equally, however, 'if the prosecutor or Director believes there would be a serious risk of injustice' (see below) in making an assumption, the statement must include information to that effect. There is no obligation for the prosecution to estimate or detail the defendant's available property—that is something for the defendant himself to establish.

3.39   Frequently, the statement will be compiled by the officer in the case and it will catalogue the defendant's assets, apparent income and expenditure. Its thoroughness will often depend on the seriousness of the conduct involved and obviously whether the Director has the conduct of the case. For example, there may be comparisons between the defendant's bankings or the cost of his lifestyle and his declared sources of income. The value of property will be estimated. The value of drugs may be fixed according to national and local databases of prices. Strong reliance will be placed on inference. The statement may include hearsay but is not evidence in itself, however, and facts such as the value or ownership of property require proof.

3.40   Much may turn on the accuracy of property valuations. The defendant is perfectly entitled to call expert evidence. Forensic accountants may be able to reconcile the defendant's apparent income with his legitimate activities. Expert reports must be served 'as soon as practicable' under the new Crown Court Rules.

5. Defence Responses

3.41   In return, the defendant can be ordered to 'indicate . . . in a manner ordered by the court' the extent to which he accepts the allegations in the statement and, if he does not accept any allegation, 'to give particulars of any matters he proposes to rely on' (s 17).

3.42   If the defendant disputes any of the primary factual aspects of the statement, the prosecution must then adduce evidence proving the fact. On the other hand, the court is entitled to treat acceptance of an allegation as conclusive on the point. Moreover, if the defendant fails 'in any respect' to comply with an order to respond to the prosecution statement, he can be treated as having accepted 'every allegation' in the statement apart from (a) those to which he has responded and (b) the basic allegation that he has benefited from criminal conduct (see *Crutchley and Tonks* (1994)[22]).

3.43   Note that the defendant's acceptance that he has benefited is not admissible evidence in proceedings for an offence (s 17(6)).

6. Provision of Information by Defendant

3.44   In addition, the court has a freestanding ability at any time to order the defendant to provide it with information 'to help it in carrying out its functions' (s 18). Thus,

---

[22] (1994) 15 Cr App R (S) 627.

it may order information to be provided at any point (including the pre-enquiry stage when the court may be considering whether to proceed of its own motion under s 6(3)(b)). Under the Crown Court Rules, the information must be given in writing. Failure to comply without reasonable excuse entitles the court to draw an adverse inference against the defendant.

The judge cannot order a third party such as a solicitor to provide information **3.45** (*R (on the application of Dechert Solicitors) v Southwark Crown Court* (2002).[23]

7. Evidence in the POCA Hearing

In an extraordinary construction of the Criminal Justice Act 1988 (as amended) **3.46** the Court of Appeal has recently decided for the first time that 'the ordinary rules of criminal evidence (do) not apply and that the confiscation hearing . . . is an extension of the sentencing hearing' (*Silcock* (2004)[24]).

Accordingly, it was for the judge simply to decide the weight to be attached to **3.47** material, inadmissible or not—in that case, the contents of a co-defendant's interviews and contested witness statements appended to the prosecutor's statement which had not been relied upon at trial.

The Court in *Silcock* accepted that its decision cut across earlier cases under the **3.48** Drug Trafficking Offences Act 1986 which plainly held that matters in dispute in a confiscation hearing must be proved by admissible evidence.[25] However, it noted that these cases all predated amendments of the DTOA (and of the CJA 1988) which introduced (a) the civil standard of proof and (b) the power to postpone a confiscation hearing for the purpose of obtaining further 'information'. These two modifications amounted to a significant 'change in the procedural landscape' which revealed Parliament's intent to make 'express provision for the rules of evidence . . . to be different from those in criminal trials'.

The overall rationale for abandoning notions of admissibility was as follows: **3.49**

First, the burden (sic) of proof is now the civil burden. Second, the court may make far-reaching assumptions. Third, the court may require the defendant to provide information and may draw inferences from his failure to do so. Fourth, the court may rely both on evidence at trial and on any relevant information, properly obtained both before trial and thereafter, in order to determine a defendant's benefit and the amount to be recovered.

These are, and are intended to be, far-reaching provisions with the aim of separating criminals from the proceeds of their crimes. The determining judge must, of course, examine both the evidence and the information obtained judicially and with great care as to its weight.

The reasoning appears to apply equally to the provisions of the POCA 2002. It **3.50** is remarkable that the Court refused to certify a point of public importance to

---

[23] [2001] EWHC Admin 477 (QBD).   [24] 29 January 2004.
[25] See *Dickens* (1990) 12 Cr App R (S) 191; *Chrastny (No 2)* [1991] 1 WLR 1385; *Rose* (1993) 97 Cr App R 253.

enable an appeal to the House of Lords. Presumably the defendant can also attempt to rely upon inadmissible material. In our opinion, there is a danger that, as a result of this decision, confiscation hearings may now turn into an evidential 'free for all'.

8. The Role of the Assumptions

3.51 As will be explained below, a finding that the defendant has a 'criminal lifestyle' leads inexorably to an examination of 'his general criminal conduct' and to the compulsory assumptions imposed by s 10. It is this mechanism that overlays the entire procedure for determining the fact and amount of benefit in the previous six years. The court *must* apply the assumptions unless satisfied that they are incorrect or unjust.

F. STAGE ONE OF THE PROCESS: DETERMINING 'CRIMINAL LIFESTYLE'

1. The Meaning of 'Criminal Lifestyle'

3.52 In the first step in a POCA enquiry the court must decide whether the defendant has a 'criminal lifestyle' (s 6(4)(a)). This is the gateway into the general confiscation scheme because it triggers an unlimited historical enquiry into the defendant's 'general criminal conduct'. By way of example, anyone convicted in the proceedings of possession of a controlled drug with intent is automatically deemed to have a criminal lifestyle and is subject to the rigour of an enquiry which must assume that all his income over the previous six years represents the proceeds of crime.

3.53 Thus, in April 2004 at Derby Crown Court, a defendant who pleaded guilty to four offences of stealing petrol to a value of £219.58 was ordered to pay a confiscation order of £1.5 million. The local Financial Investigations Unit had discovered that millions of pounds had gone through UK and Swiss bank accounts even though he had been claiming state benefits since 1966. If he fails to pay within twelve months he will face a further six years imprisonment with no remission.

3.54 Determination of a criminal lifestyle is a purely formulaic exercise in which the defendant qualifies if one of the offences of which he has been convicted falls within the statutory catalogue (s 75).[26] There are three sub-divisions:

(a) **Offences specified in Sch 2**. The Schedule includes aiding and abetting, etc, and attempts, conspiracy and incitement to commit any of the offences listed. The reader is asked to refer to the Act for the full list, but it may be summarized as follows:

---

[26] See also POCA 2002 (Commencement No 5) (Amendment of Transitional Provisions) Order (SI 2003/531).

(i) *A drug trafficking offence.* This takes in the principal drug offences under the Misuse of Drugs Act 1971, the Customs and Excise Management Act 1979, and the Criminal Justice (International Co-operation) Act 1990. A notable exception is 'simple' possession. Nor has cultivation been listed but this is of limited significance as it is a means of production which is a listed offence (*Taylor v Chief Constable of Kent* (1981)[27]);

(ii) *A money laundering offence.* In other words, an offence under ss 327 or 328 of the POCA itself.

(iii) *Directing terrorism;*

(iv) *Assisting illegal entry;*

(v) *Arms trafficking;*

(vi) *Counterfeiting;*

(vii) *Pimping and brothelkeeping;*

(viii) *Blackmail.*

(b) **An offence which 'constitutes conduct forming part of a course of criminal activity'.** To qualify, either the defendant must have been convicted:

(i) of three or more other offences in the current proceedings, each of which was committed on or after 24 March 2003 and which constitutes conduct from which he has benefited (accordingly, at least four offences in all), or

(ii) of such an offence on at least two separate occasions in the six years before the current proceedings were started (notwithstanding that any of the offences was committed before March 2003).

Note (1) that, in order to qualify, the defendant's benefit from the offences or TICs must be at least £5,000. (The ARA advises prosecutors that they should meet defence arguments that this means £5,000 on each offence by referring to Lord Falconer's explanatory remarks to the contrary (Hansard, 22 July 2002).

Note (2) that proceedings are started when a summons or warrant is issued, when the defendant is charged following arrest without warrant, or when a Voluntary Bill of Indictment is preferred (s 85).

(c) **An offence committed over a period of at least six months.** In most cases this will be determined by the particulars of the charge. However, cautious prosecutors often draft particulars more widely than necessary. There may well be instances where, on the evidence, the true period covered by the offence is shorter. It is submitted that this ought to be a question of fact to be decided by the judge.

Note again that the defendant's benefit must be at least £5,000.

---

[27] (1981) 72 Cr App R 318.

G. STAGE TWO: HAS THE DEFENDANT BENEFITED FROM CRIMINAL CONDUCT?

1. The Meaning of Criminal Conduct

3.55 Unsurprisingly, 'criminal conduct' means crime. It is conduct which either constitutes an offence in England and Wales or which would constitute an offence if it occurred here (s 76(1)).

3.56 There are two types of criminal conduct: 'particular' and 'general'. If the defendant does not qualify as having a criminal lifestyle, then the court must consider whether he has nevertheless benefited from 'his *particular* criminal conduct' (s 6(4)(a)). If, on the other hand, he does qualify, it must consider whether he has benefited from 'his general criminal conduct' (s 6(4)(b)).

2. Particular Criminal Conduct

3.57 The crucial distinction is that an enquiry into particular criminal conduct is restricted to the offences which are proved or admitted in the current proceedings, including offences taken into consideration (s 76(3)). The prosecution cannot embark on a trawl through the past and the judge cannot apply the assumptions. The benefit resulting from the offences must be proved on the balance of probabilities by evidence and necessary inference from the circumstances.

3.58 Plainly advisers need to weigh up the advantages of offences being taken into consideration if this only serves to increase the amount of benefit and, therefore, the size of the confiscation order.

3. General Criminal Conduct

3.59 In determining the benefit from general criminal conduct the court *must* apply the required assumptions to the previous six years. However, in theory, the enquiry is not confined to the six years. General criminal conduct is quite simply *all* the defendant's criminal conduct regardless of when it occurred (s 76(2)) up to the time when the court makes its decision (s 8(2)). The court is entitled to calculate the benefit of earlier crime, but the criminal conduct and the benefit must be proved to the civil standard without reliance on the assumptions.

4. The Meaning of Benefit

3.60 At its simplest, a person benefits from criminal conduct 'if he obtains property as a result of or in connection with the conduct' (s 76(4)). 'His benefit *is the value of the property obtained*' (s 76(7)) (see below).

3.61 Property is 'obtained' by a person 'if he obtains an interest in it' (s 84(2)(b)). An interest in land includes 'any legal estate or equitable interest or power' (s 84(2)(f));

an interest in property other than land means a right including a right to possession (s 84(2)(h)).

Pausing there, in 'criminal lifestyle' cases the operation of the assumptions requires the court to find that any property transferred to the defendant in the previous six years or held by him after conviction was 'obtained' as a result of his general criminal conduct. Property held or obtained abroad is nevertheless benefit notwithstanding that no offence has been committed in that jurisdiction (*McKinnon* (2004)[28]). **3.62**

However, in most cases the property which is the subject-matter of the offence(s) of which the defendant has been convicted will itself form the core 'benefit'. **3.63**

As long as the defendant does actually obtain the property, he need only do so momentarily. In *Patel*[29] the defendant was a dishonest postmaster who had taken cash from the till and given half of it to an accomplice as part of a benefit book racket. It was held that the fact that he paid over a share was irrelevant and that he had obtained all the property. A courier of cash obtains the whole amount that he has carried; it is not necessary for the property to pass to the defendant (*Simpson* (1998).[30] The burglar caught in the act obtains what he has momentarily taken: 'Success or otherwise is irrelevant' (*Wilkes* (2003)[31]). **3.64**

Even so, the prosecution must nevertheless prove that the defendant has, in fact, 'obtained' property or a pecuniary advantage himself and not simply that it has been received or obtained by others. There have been differences of approach in first instance decisions but the position has been clarified recently by the Court of Appeal under the identical provisions of the CJA 1988 (as amended). In *Olubitan* (2003)[32] it ruled: **3.65**

We reject . . . (the) extreme submission that . . . where there is a conspiracy, anyone who joins the conspiracy as a matter of law becomes liable for his proportion of the total amount by which the conspirators as a whole may have benefited. (The Act requires) findings of fact . . . The court may often be entitled to make robust inferences if convicted defendants remain unhelpful as to which of them obtained what benefit as defined by the Act. In many cases, an equal division of the benefit which the conspirators as a whole obtained between the defendants before the court may constitute a fair and reasonable inference. But, in our judgement, the section is not to be construed so that a person may be held to have obtained property or derived a pecuniary advantage when a proper view of the evidence demonstrates that he has not in fact done so.

This is in keeping with the approach of Buxton J in *Gokal* (1999)[33] in which there had been fraudulent loans of £548 million from BCCI to a conglomerate of companies in which the defendant had interests known as the Gulf Group. The **3.66**

---

[28] CA, 19 January 2004.   [29] [2000] 2 Cr App R (S) 10.
[30] [1998] 2 Cr App R (S) 111; See also *Alagobola* (CA, 21 January 2004).
[31] CA, 3 March 2003.   [32] 7 November 2003; [2003] EWCA Crim 2940.
[33] 11 March 1999 (See also *Martens* (Langley J, 20 April 1999).

benefit finding was limited to the funds actually obtained by the defendant and family and not funds that he caused to be received by others.

3.67   There appears to be an anomalous single exception to this approach where the defendant has been convicted of obtaining by deception or of conspiracy to obtain by deception contrary to s 15 of the Theft Act 1968. In that case, his benefit is deemed to be the whole of the property obtained. This is said to follow from the definition of 'obtains by deception' in s 15(2) of that Act: 'obtaining for another or enabling another to obtain or to retain' (see *Rees* (Auld J (1990)[34]). In *Gokal* (above) Buxton J held that *Rees* should be confined to its own facts.

3.68   But even a conspiracy to obtain property by deception must still result in some property having been obtained *by someone*. In *Davy* (2003)[35] the defendant had conspired to obtain and sell on fake ecstasy tablets. The tablets were seized in transit and, accordingly, he had neither obtained any property nor derived any pecuniary advantage.

5. The Meaning of Property

3.69   'Property' has the same meaning throughout the Act. It is fairly safe for the reader to work on the basis that it includes anything of value, anywhere in the world, in which the defendant has or had some interest.

3.70   Property is all property wherever situated and includes:

(a) money;

(b) all forms of real or personal property;

(c) things in action and other intangible or incorporeal property.

6. Obtaining a Pecuniary Advantage

3.71   Of course, in many types of fraud and importation of goods cases, the defendant does not obtain any property as such but, instead, avoids payment of duties or monies due—the evasion of tax or import duty being classic examples. Accordingly, where the defendant's benefit is a pecuniary advantage, he is taken to have obtained a sum of money equal to the value of the advantage (s 76(5)).

3.72   Giving the expression 'pecuniary advantage' its ordinary and natural meaning (see *US v Montgomery* (1999)[36]) the deferment of a debt is sufficient. So that, where a fraudulent scheme to cheat the Revenue results in the evasion of income tax, the amount of unpaid tax is a pecuniary advantage notwithstanding that the defendant still owes the tax and remains liable for payment (*Dimsey and Allen* (2000)[37]).

---

[34] 19 July 1990.   [35] CA, 5 March 2003; [2003] EWCA Crim 781.
[36] [1999] 1 All ER 84.   [37] [2000] 1 Cr App R (S) 497.

Further, in *Smith (David)* (2002)[38] the House of Lords decided that it makes no **3.73** difference if, after he obtains the pecuniary advantage, the property is destroyed or damaged or forfeited by customs officers. In that case, the defendant was held to have obtained an advantage when he sailed a boat with contraband cigarettes past Customs points (at which duty should have been paid) only to find the goods seized on landing.

Even so, the benefit should not be held to be greater than the amount of the **3.74** advantage. A distinction can be drawn between cases of evading tax on profit from lawful sales and unlawful profit from unlawful sales. Accordingly, in *Attorney-General's Reference (No 25 of 2001) (Moran)*[39]), a market trader who had been evading tax by underdeclaring his income for years was liable only for the unpaid tax plus interest and not for the whole of his undeclared profit.

However, if the defendant unlawfully sells goods upon which he has evaded **3.75** payment of duty, his benefit consists not only of the amount of unpaid duty but also the amount which he received unlawfully for the goods. His proceeds of sale separately and additionally qualify as property obtained as a result of or in connection with criminal conduct. So, if he acquires and sells goods without paying VAT, he is liable for the amount of unpaid VAT *and* for the value of his sales.

Much depends on the particular circumstances and whether the defendant has **3.76** obtained an overall pecuniary advantage from his activities. Where, for example, he has cheated the Revenue by diverting company income into a secret account for his own use, he may be liable for the whole amount and not just the amount of the evaded tax (*Foggon* (2003)[40]).

7. 'Obtained as a Result of or in Connection with Criminal Conduct'

In almost all situations there will be some core evidence proving an income result- **3.77** ing from crime. Moreover, in lifestyle cases, the mandatory assumptions operate to make the link between property and criminal conduct; the assumption in either case being that the property was obtained 'as a result of' criminal conduct.

However, the complete definition of benefit is much wider. It catches property **3.78** which is proved merely to have been obtained 'in connection with' the defendant's criminal conduct (s 76(4)).

Accordingly, the benefit can include payment of incidental expenses, whether **3.79** by way of reward or not. In *Osei* (1988),[41] 'payment' under the DTA included an airline ticket given to a courier and even money which she was given to show to immigration officers to enable her to obtain a visa. In *Finch* (1993),[42] money which the defendant claimed to have obtained by 'ripping-off' a drugs dealer was held to be the proceeds of trafficking.

Nor does the obtaining of the property need to be exclusively connected with **3.80** the criminal conduct as long as it has some connection with it (s 76(6)). In *Randle*

---

[38] [2002] 1 WLR 54.   [39] CA, 27 July 2001.   [40] CA, 14 February 2003.
[41] [1988] Crim LR 775.   [42] (1993) 14 Cr App R (S) 226.

and Pottle (1991),[43] the two journalists who published an account of the escape of George Blake, the spy, obtained financial benefits both directly from lawful sales of their book and indirectly from unlawfully assisting in his escape which provided the subject-matter of the book.

3.81 The present definition of benefit follows the scheme of the CJA 1988. However, the DTA 1994 defined benefit as the receipt of 'any payment or other reward' in connection with drug trafficking. Applying the narrower DTA definition of benefit, the Court of Appeal had held that the drugs themselves should not be regarded as a payment in the absence of clear evidence (*Agenkin* (1995)[44]).

3.82 However, there may be problems of definition now that the wider meaning of benefit is extended to drugs cases. Should drugs which are or have been in the defendant's possession be regarded as property 'obtained as a result of or in connection with' criminal conduct and, therefore, be treated as benefit (to be given their gross/street market value)? On the face of it, they fall squarely within this wider definition whether or not they represent payment or reward.

3.83 The answer may be found in the approach of the Court of Appeal in *Dore* (1997).[45] It held that controlled drugs have no 'market value' as they cannot be sold or realised lawfully. It, therefore, seems somewhat pointless to include the drugs as part of the benefit if their value is nil. Presumably, this principle applies equally to any property in the defendant's possession which cannot be converted lawfully.

3.84 In our view it is preferable to treat the possession of and value of drugs as evidence of wholesale expenditure. Property in the defendant's possession which has no lawful value should not be counted as benefit.

H. THE ASSUMPTIONS

3.85 The simplest way to approach the first three assumptions is to work on the basis that they respectively deal with the calculation of the defendant's benefit represented by (a) what he has received, (b) what he has retained, and (c) what he has spent. The fourth assumption credits him with a full interest in any property assumed or proved to have been obtained from criminal conduct.

1. The First Assumption—Transferred Property

3.86 The first assumption is that any property transferred to the defendant within the six-year period that preceded the start of the proceedings for the index offence(s) was obtained by him (a) as a result of his general criminal conduct, and (b) at the earliest time he appears to have held it (s 10(2)).

---

[43] [1991] COD 369.   [44] [1995] 16 Cr App R 499.   [45] [1997] 2 Cr App R (S) 152.

Proceedings start when a summons or warrant is issued or when the defendant **3.87**
is charged following arrest without warrant or when a Voluntary Bill is preferred.
Property is transferred if 'an interest' in it is transferred or granted by another
(s 84(2)(c)). In other words, the judge must assume that anything of value that has
been transferred to date since the beginning of that six-year period and the POCA
enquiry is the proceeds of crime.

2. The Second Assumption—Property Held by the Defendant after Conviction

The second assumption is that any property held by the defendant at any time **3.88**
after the date of conviction was obtained as a result of his general criminal conduct (at the earliest time he appears to have held it) (s 10(3)). Where there is more
than one conviction in the proceedings, the date is the latest of those convictions.

More starkly put, all of the property which he holds at that point is assumed to **3.89**
be the proceeds of crime unless he can prove otherwise. It is irrelevant when he
acquired the property—in other words, it does not need to be shown that he
obtained his interest in the previous six years as with the first and third assumptions (*Chrastny* (*No 2*) (1991)[46]).

Section 84 states that 'property is held by a person if he holds an interest in it'. **3.90**
It also catches bankruptcy or liquidation as devices to deflect the operation of the
Act so that the defendant still holds the property even where it is vested in a trustee
in bankruptcy or liquidator.

An interest in land includes 'any legal estate or equitable interest or power'. **3.91**
References to an interest in property other than land include 'references to a right
(including a right to possession)'.

This is an area with considerable risk of double-counting. For example, the **3.92**
defendant may own a house bought out of criminal money. Potentially, the
assumptions could work so that the money is treated as benefit because it was
originally property transferred to the defendant (the first assumption) while the
house is simultaneously treated as benefit as property held by him (the second
assumption). However, to apply both would be logically unfair as the house
represents the converted money. In this situation the court should disapply one of
the assumptions as to do otherwise would work injustice (see below).

This does not mean that in the above example the defendant can profit from an **3.93**
increase in the value of the house. If, as is generally the case, the court chooses the
approach which treats the house as representing the benefit, the value of the
benefit will be its market value at the time of the determination, if higher, and not
the amount that he used to buy it (unless, for some reason, that is higher) (see
below).

---

[46] [1991] 1 WLR 1385.

3. The Third Assumption—Expenditure

3.94 The third assumption is that any expenditure incurred by the defendant at any time after the start of the six-year period was met from property obtained by him as a result of his general criminal conduct (s 10(4)).

3.95 The primary fact of expenditure cannot itself be assumed; it must be proved. But once the prosecution proves that the defendant has made some expenditure, the court must then assume that he has funded it from the proceeds of earlier crime unless he can prove otherwise.

3.96 Drugs cases classically lend themselves to the inference that there has been expenditure in the acquisition of the drugs. The apparent simplicity of the expenditure approach is shown by cases such as *Dellaway* (2001).[47] Counsel argued that the drugs may have been provided on credit and that it was not proved that there had been any expenditure in acquiring them. The Court of Appeal thought otherwise:

> This is a perfectly proper inference to make, as a matter of common sense . . . In relation to a large quantity of drugs of this sort, approaching the matter on the balance of probabilities where there is no alternative credible explanation, the inference is obvious: money would be required to pay for the drugs. Those who traffic in the drugs trade do not normally extend credit or trust to others involved.

3.97 That must be right where there is evidence of repeated transactions, but the position may not be so clear if there is a single consignment. There will be situations in which it will be impossible to infer from his possession of drugs that the defendant has paid for them and there is no scope for the assumption that they represent expenditure—for example, where he has been entrusted with possession of the drugs (*J* (2001)[48]), or where it is accepted that the offence represents his first venture into drugs supply (*Butler* (1993)[49]) or where the judge had found as a fact that he was a minder with no beneficial interest (*Johannes* (2002).[50]

3.98 It is important to remember (a) that the amount of the expenditure itself is not to be assumed, and (b) it is the actual amount which the defendant paid out—in drugs cases, normally the wholesale price and not the gross street value. Nevertheless, it is equally important to grasp that the benefit is not necessarily limited to that amount. Strictly speaking, it is the amount of the (assumed) earlier payment out of which it was funded. The required assumption is simply the fact that the expenditure was met from property obtained as a result of earlier criminal conduct. The benefit is the value of *that* property.

3.99 However, this is not an approach to be encouraged. An enthusiastic court can make sweeping and expensive findings which have no tangible foundation in the evidence. It must, therefore, be stressed that findings as to the value of that property must have some evidential basis.

---

[47] [2001] 1 Cr App R (S) 77. [48] [2001] 1 Cr App R (S) 273.
[49] (1993) 14 Cr App R (S) 537. [50] [2002] Crim LR 147.

The limits of the exercise were illustrated in *Williams (Errol)* (2001).[51] The judge properly calculated drugs expenditure of £500,000. However, he then purported to work out the gross amount of the payment out of which the expenditure was met. He said it was well known that the profit on drugs was very high, but it was difficult to state the mark up precisely. He nevertheless decided to use a mark up of one quarter and, accordingly, multiplied the expenditure by four, making nearly £2 million, which he then added to the net benefit, making a total of nearly £2.5 million. The Court of Appeal quashed the order, observing: **3.100**

> The mistake of the judge in the present case was to take the figure produced by the application of the proper approach, (£½ million), and then to subject it to a series of further hypotheses for which there was no evidential basis, namely:
>
> (i) that it was the product of a particular form of drug trafficking i.e. wholesale supply,
>
> (ii) that it represented net profits of such activity and
>
> (iii) that a hypothetical quantity and value of drugs must have been required to be purchased during the preceding 6 years to enable such a profit to be calculated.
>
> The judge was wrong to employ the 'expenditure' assumption . . . for this purpose and his device of calculating a figure for the working capital required to produce a profit equal to the proceeds figure . . . was incorrect. There was simply no evidence as to the defendant's possession of such drugs, or that they were funded from previous dealing . . . the problem seems to us to have stemmed from the fact that the sentencing judge . . . sought to redefine (the proceeds) and treat them as 'profits', and to base his further calculations on that redefinition. That approach does not seem to us to be one permitted by the Act. It is also one likely to lead to arbitrary and unjust results.

4. The Fourth Assumption—Property Free of Other Interests

The starting point for the valuation of property proven or assumed to have been obtained by the defendant is the further assumption that he is or was the only person with any interest in the property (s 10(5)) (see below for cases on joint benefit in property obtained). **3.101**

5. Defeating the Assumptions

(a) *Incorrect assumptions*
The judge cannot make a particular assumption if it is 'shown to be incorrect' (s 10(6)(a)). So, for example, if the defendant can prove on the balance of probabilities that a particular source of income is legitimate, the court must not treat it as benefit of criminal conduct. This may be something that can be agreed with the prosecutor but frequently it is the principal battleground in contested cases. Once the prosecutor proves, for example, the existence of a particular credit in a bank **3.102**

---

[51] [2001] 2 Cr App R (S) 44.

statement, the full force of the assumptions is felt. The defendant may then have to make the decision whether to give evidence and expose himself to unlimited cross-examination on his bankings.

3.103   If the court finds an assumption to be incorrect, it must give reasons for its conclusion (s 10(7)). Presumably, this is intended to allow review of the decision should the prosecution exercise its newly-provided right of appeal.

(b) *Serious risk of injustice*

3.104   The only other circumstance in which a mandatory assumption can be avoided is when 'there would be a serious risk of injustice if the assumption were made' (s 10(6)(b)). Note that the language of the two sub-sections is different in that there is no express burden placed on the defendant to prove injustice. This aspect was emphasized by Lord Steyn in *Benjafield and Rezvi* (2002):[52]

> ... the judge had misdescribed his function by saying 'it has not been shown on the balance of probabilities that there was any risk of injustice'... that is putting it too high. The judge must avoid any real risk of injustice.

3.105   As pointed out in the introduction to this chapter, this may be a deceptively narrow safety net because the Court of Appeal has made it plain that, as a matter of construction, the perceived risk of injustice must arise from the operation of the assumptions not from hardship. What is contemplated is some internal contradiction either in the process of assumption which leads to an unjust calculation of the proceeds—for example, if money was to be double counted as both income and expenditure—or a contradiction between an assumption and the factual basis for sentence.

3.106   Thus, in *Lunnon* (2004),[53] the appellant was one of a number of defendants convicted of drug importation. He pleaded guilty to involvement only as a driver. It was accepted by the Crown that he had no previous involvement in drug trafficking and he was sentenced on that basis. The trial judge nevertheless assumed that the purchase cost of the drugs was expenditure and, therefore, benefit to be apportioned between all the defendants. The Court of Appeal rejected the Crown's argument that the court could compartmentalize the sentencing and confiscation aspects in this way:

> What is plainly unacceptable is for the concession to be made for part of the sentencing process, without qualification, but for reliance to be placed, tacitly, on the assumptions when it comes to the confiscation hearing... It is clear from ... *Benjafield* ... that the obligation ... to 'stand back' and make its own independent assessment is of fundamental importance, since this is what makes the reverse burden of proof compatible with the requirements of Article 6 ... Once the the Crown has made a concession, such as in this case, unless and until it is withdrawn, there would be an apparent injustice in the court's ignoring it for the purposes of a confiscation hearing.

---

[52] [2002] 2 WLR 235 at [13].   [53] CA, 5 May 2004; [2004] EWCA Crim 1125.

Final resistance to the full force of the assumptions could be based on the deci- **3.107** sion in *Deprince* (2004[54]) in which it was held that, even if the assumptions are not proved to be incorrect, if the court is satisfied of the serious risk of injustice, it may 'in an appropriate case' make a percentage discount in order to guard against a remote possibility that a small part of the property held or transferred, or the expenditure incurred, had a legitimate source.

What if the property is liable to be forfeited under some other provision; can the **3.108** property or its value still be counted as part of the benefit? It has been argued unsuccessfully that forfeiture of drugs under s 27 of the Misuse of Drugs Act should take their value out of the benefit calculation altogether—otherwise the defendant is penalized twice over. First, he loses the value of the drugs and, secondly, the value as expenditure is additionally counted as part of the benefit (*Dore* (1997)[55]). The court held there was no double penalty. The drugs themselves have no lawful value; the cost of the drugs was counted once only as expenditure.

In the case of cash, there should be no double-counting if the Act is properly **3.109** applied. The court must make the confiscation order before making any forfeiture order and once the confiscation order is made there is no cash left to forfeit (*Barker* 1996).[56]

Note that the prosecutor's statement of information must itself include any **3.110** relevant information that the prosecutor 'believes is relevant . . . for the purpose of enabling the court to decide if the circumstances are such that it must not make . . . an assumption' (s 16(4)(b)).

Again, if the court declines to make an assumption because of injustice, it must **3.111** state its reasons for so doing.

I. STAGE THREE: DETERMINING THE RECOVERABLE AMOUNT

1. General

Having determined that the defendant has benefited (from either general or par- **3.112** ticular criminal conduct), the court must (a) decide the recoverable amount, and (b) make an order (a confiscation order) requiring him to pay that amount (s 6(5)). For these purposes, 'the recoverable amount . . . is an amount equal to the defendant's benefit from the conduct concerned' (s 7(1)).

Pausing there, as will be seen below, the defendant can reduce the amount of the **3.113** order if he can prove that the value of his actual assets ('the available amount') is less than the benefit figure—in which case the lesser amount becomes the 'recoverable amount'.

---

[54] CA, 9 March 2004.   [55] [1997] 2 Cr App R (S) 152.   [56] CA, 15 December 1996.

3.114   However, we have not yet reached that point in the exercise and (except where a victim is bringing civil proceedings, see para 3.133) the court is bound to determine the amount of the benefit at this stage.

2. Taking Account of All of the Criminal Conduct

3.115   In fixing the recoverable amount, the court must 'take account' of (a) conduct up to the time it makes its decision, and (b) property obtained up to that time (s 8(2)). This has profound implications for anyone deemed to have a 'criminal lifestyle'. Section 76(2) defines the defendant's general criminal conduct as 'all his criminal conduct' and appears to mean just that—regardless of whether the conduct occurred or the benefit was obtained before the passing of the Act.

3.116   Putting all the provisions in the Act together, the defendant's benefit in lifestyle cases is the amount of all the property which he is proved to have obtained from criminal conduct whenever and wherever it occurred—not forgetting that, broadly speaking, if he obtained the property in the previous six years, it will be assumed that it was obtained from criminal conduct.

3. The Value of the Benefit

(a)   *Valuation of property obtained*

3.117   The court applies two fundamental rules. The first principle, expressed at its simplest, is that the amount of the defendant's benefit is literally 'the value of the property obtained' (s 76(7)).

3.118   It follows that benefit does not mean profit. In other words, all of the property obtained is to be accounted and not merely the profit element; confiscation is concerned with gross turnover even where the profit is small. The principle was plainly spelt out in the context of the Drug Trafficking Offences Act 1986 by Lord Lane CJ in *Smith* (1989):[57]

> The words 'any payments' are on the face of them quite clear. They must mean, indeed it is clear from the wording, any payment in money or kind. It does not mean . . . net profit derived from the payment after the deduction of expenses, whether those expenses are of purchase, travelling, entertainment or otherwise valued. It seems to us that the section is deliberately worded so as to avoid the necessity . . . of having to carry out an accountancy exercise . . . It may be that the wording is draconian and that it produces a draconian result. But it seems to us that if that is the case, it was the result intended by those who framed the Act.

3.119   It does not matter if the defendant holds the property momentarily and does not retain it. This is well illustrated by some of the decided cases. In *Simons* (1994)[58]

---

[57] (1989) 89 Cr App R 135; See also *Smith* (1989) 11 Cr App R (S) 55; *Simons* (1994) 15 Cr App R (S) 126; *Banks* [1997] 2 Cr App R (S) 110; *Simpson* [1998] 2 Cr App R (S) 111.

[58] (1994) 98 Cr App R 100; See also *Banks* [1997] 2 Cr App R (S) 110.

there was a chain of contracts of sale of drugs—from a Hong Kong supplier to the appellant in the United Kingdom and from him to South Africa. The Hong Kong dealer had received £166,000 from the appellant who had received that sum plus a further £40,000 from South Africa. His profit was the £40,000 but his benefit was held to be the whole amount. In *Simpson* (1998)[59] the defendant had carried large sums of cash back and forth to Ireland as a courier in a drugs money laundering exercise. His benefit was adjudged to be the total amount that he had carried and not merely the amount that he had been paid for so doing. He argued that it cannot have been Parliament's intention to permit multiple recovery from a succession of bailees. But it was held that it was not necessary that property should pass to a defendant for him to obtain it. In *Currey* (1995)[60] the defendant was liable for the full value of obscene material which he had imported notwithstanding that he made little personal profit.

Still more controversially, it appears that the defendant who has obtained property as a result of crime (for example, a house purchased partly with criminal proceeds and partly with a mortgage) is liable for the full value of the property even where he has contributed some of his own funds towards its acquisition. **3.120**

Under the CJA 1988, a number of well-known but unreported cases have upheld the 'full value approach' to the calculation of benefit (*In Re K* (1990);[61] *Layode* (1993);[62] *Rees* (1990)[63]). 'The answer to the simple question required by [the CJA] "what property did he obtain?' must be "the house" '—*per* McCullough LJ in *In Re K*, above. **3.121**

It should be noted that a different approach has been held to prevail under the regime of the DTA 1994 (see *Walls (Andrew)* (2002)[64] and *Johnson* (1991)[65]). Nevertheless, the language of the POCA 2002 is closer to that of the CJA 1988. **3.122**

It is important to grasp that, while at this stage of the determination (the calculation of the benefit amount) the existence of a charge on the property is irrelevant—the charge will nevertheless be deducted at the later stage of determining the 'available amount' (see below). **3.123**

Where the property obtained has no value then, plainly, the benefit is nil—for example, a worthless cheque (*Johnson* (1990).[66] Controlled drugs are not lawfully saleable and, therefore, have no value as property in themselves (*Dore* (1997)[67]) (but see the value of drugs as evidence of expenditure). **3.124**

(b) *Market value*
The second principle is expressly referred to as 'the basic rule' and applies to the valuation of property throughout the Act, namely that the value of property is its market value at the material time (s 79(2)). **3.125**

---

[59] [1998] 2 Cr App R (S) 111.   [60] (1995) 16 Cr App R (S) 42.
[61] CA, 6 July 1990.   [62] CA, 12 March 1993.
[63] Plymouth Crown Court 19 July 1990, Auld J.
[64] [2003] 1 WLR 731 (leave has been granted to appeal to the House of Lords).
[65] [1991] 2 QB 249.   [66] (1990) 91 Cr App R 332.
[67] [1997] 2 Cr App R (S) 152.

3.126   Under s 80(1) the material time for valuing the property comprising the defendant's benefit from particular or general criminal conduct 'is the time the court makes its decision'. Under s 80(2) its value at that time is the *greater* of the following:

(a) its (market) value at the time it was obtained by the defendant (adjusted for subsequent inflation); or

(b) if he still holds the property, its current market value or, if he no longer holds the property, the market value of any property which 'directly or indirectly represents' it, or a combination of both if he has converted only part of the property which he originally obtained.

3.127   In other words: tails, the defendant loses; heads, the prosecution wins. As may not be uncommon, if he has nothing left to show for his efforts because he has dissipated everything, the benefit would still be the market value of the property at the time he obtained it. (Bear in mind also that there is no requirement that the defendant should have retained the property at all; all that is necessary is that he obtained it.)

3.128   Equally, if the market value of the property has declined since the defendant obtained it, then his benefit is its original market value adjusted upwards for inflation. In *Foxley* (1995)[68] the Judge correctly applied the retail price index to the purchase price of property notwithstanding evidence from chartered surveyors that the value had, in fact, fallen.

3.129   There may be an argument that the relevant market value will vary according to whether goods have been obtained wholesale, for example by theft from containers in transit, or from a retail outlet (see *Ascroft* (2003)[69]—albeit a case decided under the different language of the CJA 1988).

4. Joint Benefit

3.130   An order cannot be made jointly and severally against defendants. As a basic rule the court should attempt to apportion the value of the proceeds according to the degree of involvement and a separate confiscation order should be made against each individual. The Act requires findings of fact to be made and, in general, a defendant's benefit should not include property or pecuniary advantage which he himself has not obtained (See further the meaning of 'obtains': para 3.60 *et seq*).

3.131   In the absence of any explanation from the defendant and of evidence to the contrary, it may be taken that the proceeds were equally shared (*Porter* (1990–91);[70] *Gibbons* (2003).[71] This may be 'acceptable and fair' where the principal participants are together before the court. When they are not all present, a different approach may be permissible if the defendant who is present has sufficient

---

[68] (1995) 16 Cr App R (S) 879.
[70] (1990–91) 12 Cr App R (S) 377.

[69] [2003] EWCA Crim 2365.
[71] [2003] EWCA Crim 3161.

control over jointly held existing property to realize it. Depending on the circumstances, jointly held property can be treated as 'property held by the (remaining) defendant . . . after the date of conviction' and, therefore, *that* defendant's benefit.

The leading case is *Chrastny (No 2)* (1991)[72] in which the defendant had been convicted of conspiracy to supply drugs with her husband; the husband had escaped. The Court of Appeal held there was no unfairness in treating their joint property as her benefit and in not apportioning the benefit between them: 'where only one defendant has been convicted and had sufficient control to realise the property, we see no reason why an order in the total sum should not be made'. If she satisfied the order, no further order could be made against the husband on his apprehension as the property would no longer be in his possession or control. **3.132**

5. Proceedings by a Victim

A court need not calculate the recoverable amount and make an order 'if it believes that any victim of the conduct has at any time started or intends to start proceedings against the defendant in respect of loss, injury or damage sustained in connection with the conduct' (s 6(6)). **3.133**

If the court does choose to determine the recoverable amount in that situation, it is 'such amount as the court believes just' (as long as it does not exceed the value of 'the available amount'). **3.134**

6. Recovery, Forfeiture, and Previous Confiscation Orders

In calculating benefit the court must ignore any property over which there is a recovery or forfeiture order in force (s 7(4)). A recovery order is a High Court order in civil recovery proceedings vesting property in a civil recovery trustee (s 266) (see Chapter 7); a forfeiture order is a magistrates' court order forfeiting cash (s 298). In the case of general criminal conduct, the court must deduct any previous confiscation orders (s 8(3)). **3.135**

J. STAGE FOUR: DETERMINING THE AVAILABLE AMOUNT

1. General

This is literally 'the bottom line' and often the most meaningful point of the contest between the defendant and the prosecution. Its manifest importance to the defendant is that the court cannot confiscate more than he is worth—'the available amount'. **3.136**

So, if the defendant can manage to prove on the balance of probabilities that he is worth less than the amount of his benefit, then he can only be ordered to pay the **3.137**

---

[72] [1991] 1 WLR 1385.

lesser amount. In the scheme of the Act, the 'available amount' then becomes the 'recoverable amount' (s 7(2)(a)). If the available amount is nil, then the recoverable amount is a nominal amount (s 7(2)(b).

3.138   The 'available amount' is the aggregate of:

(a) the total value at the time of the order of 'all the free property then held by the defendant' (minus the total amount of any priority obligations), and

(b) the total value of all 'tainted gifts' (s 9(1)).

3.139   As noted elsewhere, following the universal definitions in s 84, property is 'held' by a person 'if he holds an interest in it' and an interest (a) in land includes 'any legal estate or equitable interest or power' or (b) in other property includes 'references to a right (including a right to possession)'. Property is still held by a person even where it is vested in a trustee in bankruptcy or liquidator.

3.140   Property is 'free' unless there is already a forfeiture or deprivation order in force (s 82).

3.141   We deal with the meaning of expressions such as 'priority obligations' and 'tainted gifts' below. In essence, however, the process of calculating the total available amount is as follows:

(a) identify the free property in which the defendant has interests at the time of the order;

(b) calculate the total current market value of his beneficial interests in that property;

(c) deduct the amount of his priority obligations (ie fines, etc and preferential debts);

(d) lastly, add the total value of any 'tainted gifts'.

3.142   If the court determines the available amount, the confiscation order must include 'a statement of its findings as to the matters relevant for deciding that amount' (s 7(5)).

2. Assets not Proceeds

3.143   In earlier legislation the term 'the realizable amount' was used instead of 'available amount'. The meaning is probably identical. Two misconceptions were prevalent.

3.144   First, it was sometimes believed that the calculation could only take into account property which was itself the proceeds of crime. This is emphatically not the case. The assessments, first of the amount of benefit, and then of the available amount, are entirely separate exercises. The calculation of the available amount is simply a computation of the defendant's realizable assets regardless of their origins.

3.145   For example, he may find himself having to sell the matrimonial home notwithstanding that the purchase price came from a legitimate source.

The Appellant's real complaint is that the houses which he owns, and which were not the product of drug trafficking, should be realised to pay the confiscation order. But that is the result for which the Act provides and the court has . . . no discretion to mitigate the intentionally harsh consequences of a confiscation order. Even if this result were to be regarded as an injustice, it is not an injustice which results from making the assumption . . . (*Dore* (1997).[73]

The elasticity of the definition can be judged from *Walbrook and Glasgow* (1994).[74] There it was held that a contingent interest under the will of the appellant's late grandmother which set up a trust fund that would vest absolutely in the appellant if he survived her by five years was realizable property.   **3.146**

3. Burden of Proof

The second misconception was that, in calculating the value of the available amount, the court can only take into account property which the prosecution can prove to exist. This misunderstands the burden of proving that the available amount is less than the amount of benefit. Section 7(2) squarely places the burden upon the defendant.   **3.147**

The case of *Ilsemann* (1990–91)[75] is a cautionary tale which illustrates the strict operation of the Act. The prosecution had itself tendered a schedule of the defendant's realizable assets as far as they were known to the prosecution. The defence accepted the figure. Nevertheless, the Court of Appeal upheld a confiscation order for the full and greater value of the benefit: **3.148**

. . . in the present case one starts with (the benefit figure) . . . The Crown might, had the defence put forward a statement as to what was capable of being realised, either have accepted it or not. Nor was any evidence called on behalf of the appellant . . . [The appellant's counsel] put it on this basis, that if the Crown put that figure forward and the defence agree it, then why should the court not accept it?

In our judgement that is a misconception. The Crown were not putting this figure forward for agreement as the amount realisable; all they were doing was putting it forward as the amount that they were able actually to prove without conceding that it was all that was realisable. If the appellant wished to say that that was all that was realisable, then it was for him to satisfy the court to that effect. He did not do so, either by seeking to call evidence or by putting in any statement which the Crown might or might not have agreed. Accordingly, the court was left without anything to put against the [benefit figure].

There are further endorsements in *Comiskey* (1991):[76]   **3.149**

There can be no doubt that the Defendant is in an incomparably better position to . . . [satisfy the court that the amount that might be realised is less than the recoverable amount] since he alone knows what has become of the proceeds. In our judgement, the object of the

---

[73] [1997] 2 Cr App R (S) 152.   [74] (1994) 15 Cr App R (S) 783.
[75] (1990–91) 12 Cr App R (S) 398.
[76] (1991) 93 Cr App R 227 (and see *Carroll* (1992) 13 Cr App R (S) 99).

Act is to oblige a Defendant to reveal this information so as to enable the court to make an effective order.

3.150   Even so, the court in *Comiskey* acknowledged that, as a matter of common sense, the amount that might be realized must be less than the value of the proceeds by reason of the expenses that must necessarily have been involved in the operation:

> There can be no question of carrying out an accountancy exercise, but it does seem to us that some acknowledgement ought to be made of the realities of the situation.

3.151   As in all other aspects of the criminal process, findings of fact are regularly made on the basis of inference. Even when there are no identifiable assets, judges have been known to reject claims of impoverishment when the circumstances suggest otherwise. Thus, a judge may properly determine the amount to be realized by finding that the defendant must have invested cash proceeds to keep pace with inflation if the circumstances support that conclusion; in *Barwick* (2001)[77] there was a finding that a conman like the defendant was 'inherently unlikely' to have kept his money as cash.

3.152   In *Cukovic* (1996),[78] the defendant's case was that, while he had assets in Yugoslavia, none of those assets were realizable. However, the Court of Appeal endorsed the approach of the judge who 'did not accept that a person in such a position, responsible for such a huge importation of cocaine, had no realisable assets outside Yugoslavia'.

3.153   Cash in a defendant's possession which has been lent for a specific purpose is nevertheless 'held by a defendant' and, therefore, part of his 'realisable property' (*McQueen* (2002)[79]). It is not an 'obligation having priority'.

3.154   It is sometimes overlooked that in Customs and Excise cases, seizure of the instruments of crime, such as motor vehicles used for smuggling, results in their immediate forfeiture under the Customs and Excise Management Act 1979 so that they no longer belong to the defendant and cannot, therefore, form part of the available amount (see *Thacker* (1995)).[80]

4. Priority Obligations

(a) *Fines or Other Orders*

3.155   The available amount must be reduced by the amount of any outstanding fine or other order made following a conviction at any time before the confiscation order is made (s 9(2)(a)).

---

[77] [2001] 1 Cr App R (S) 129.   [78] [1996] 1 Cr App R (S) 131.
[79] [2002] 2 Cr App R (S) 9.   [80] [1995] 16 Cr App R (S) 461.

(b) *Preferential Debts*

A further discount must be given for any sum 'which would be included among the   **3.156**
preferential debts' if the defendant's bankruptcy had commenced or his winding-
up been ordered on the date of the confiscation order (s 9(2)(b)).

'Preferential debt' has the same meaning as in s 386 of the Insolvency Act 1986   **3.157**
and includes tax owed to the Inland Revenue, VAT, car tax, betting and gaming
duties, remuneration of employees, and social security and pension scheme
contributions.

5. Tainted Gifts

As noted above, the total value of 'all tainted gifts' must be added to the value of   **3.158**
the property still held by the defendant (s 9(1)(b)). It is the value of the gift that is
accounted and, accordingly, any difficulty that the defendant may have in retriev-
ing the actual gift itself is immaterial: *Tighe*.[81] (For the valuation of gifts, see paras
3.163 *et seq*)

6. The Meaning of 'Tainted Gift'

The defendant makes a gift if he transfers property to another for 'significantly   **3.159**
less' consideration than its value at the time he obtained it (s 78(1)). The process of
then identifying whether a gift is 'tainted' varies according to whether or not the
defendant has a criminal lifestyle (s 77). Once again, a finding that he does have a
criminal lifestyle triggers deeming provisions which are similar to those which
apply the required assumptions earlier in the Act—only in this context gifts take
on tainted characteristics if made within the previous six years.

(a) *Criminal lifestyle (or no decision)*

Where it has been decided that the defendant has a criminal lifestyle or where 'no   **3.160**
court has made a decision', a gift is tainted if it was made since the start of the six-
year period preceding the commencement of the proceedings (s 77(2)).

Alternatively, a gift is tainted, regardless of when it was made, if it is proved to   **3.161**
consist of property obtained by the defendant 'as a result of or in connection with
his general criminal conduct' or of property in his hands which represented such
property 'in whole or part . . . directly or indirectly' (s 77(3)). Thus, there is an
apparent parallel with the required assumptions: if the six-year period applies,
then the gift is deemed to be tainted; but there is no time limit if the property can
actually be proved to have been obtained from crime.

---

[81] [1996] 1 Cr App R (S) 314.

(b) *No criminal lifestyle*

3.162 If, on the other hand, it is decided that the defendant does not have a criminal lifestyle, any gift is tainted if made after he committed the earliest index offence or offence taken into consideration in the proceedings (s 77(5)). A continuing offence is deemed to be committed 'on the first occasion when it is committed'.

7. The Value of a Tainted Gift

3.163 If the defendant literally gives the property away, the entire gift is added to the available amount. However, in many cases, there may have been an attempt to disguise the transaction as a transfer for value. In those circumstances, the gift element in the transfer has to be determined according to a statutory formula. The Act uses the phrase, 'the property given'. Effectively, this means the share which the defendant has given away expressed as a proportionate fraction of the whole (s 78(2)). Applying the formula, if the property was worth £100 when he transferred it, and he transferred it for £20, 'the property given' is 80 per cent of the whole.

3.164 The 'basic rule' now again applies and the value of the 'property given' is its market value. Moving on in the process, its market value is the greater of the following:

(a) its value at the time it was given (adjusted for subsequent inflation); or

(b) its value at the time of the confiscation order—but calculated to take account of whether the recipient of the gift has himself converted the property (s 81).

3.165 Accordingly, if the recipient still holds the property, the value of the tainted gift is the current value of the property given; on the other hand, if the recipient has retained none or only part of the property, its value is that of 'any property which directly or indirectly represents it in his hands' or a combination of the value of what he has retained and such property.

8. The Value of the Available Amount

3.166 Applying 'the basic rule' of valuation of property held and of tainted gifts at their market values can be a speculative and controversial exercise. Prosecution valuations of the defendant's property are often incorrect; historically, they have often relied upon the best efforts of the officer in the case. The Court of Appeal has stressed the necessity for up to date valuations of houses (*Lemmon* (1992)).[82] It has also conceded that the market value of property means its net market value after the costs of sale have been deducted (*Cramer* (1992)).[83]

---

[82] (1992) 13 Cr App R (S) 66.   [83] (1992) 13 Cr App R (S) 390.

Needless to say, the market value of property such as a house may vary according to whether it has to be a 'quick sale' or whether it can remain on the market for longer. Accordingly, the court is often provided with differing valuations which range from an immediate forced sale to one following several months' exposure in an open market. In these circumstances, the court may choose to allow the defendant a lengthy period in which to satisfy the order (see below) and value the house on the basis that he can take advantage of that period to achieve a higher price and, therefore, a larger available amount. **3.167**

9. Third Party Interests

The defendant is deemed to hold any and all property in which he has an interest. He 'holds' property notwithstanding that others may have legitimate and even greater interests in the same property. However, the scheme of the Act is to factor in and deduct a third party's interest such as a mortgage from the available amount at the point of valuing the property. Accordingly, where there is a third party, the value of the property held by the defendant (and, therefore, the figure to be included in the available amount) is the market value of his interest at the time of the order (s 79(3)). **3.168**

The genuineness of an encumbrance, such as a mortgage loan, will be a question of fact to be determined on the evidence (*Harvey*[84]). The balance of a negative equity cannot be set off against the recoverable amount (*Ghadami* (1998)[85]). There are frequent disputes: the defendant may claim simply that he has no beneficial interest in the particular property; conversely the prosecution may argue that, not only does he have an interest, but that his true interest includes the other party's share which, in reality, ought to be included in the available amount. **3.169**

The court should first determine whether the defendant himself has any beneficial interest. This may run to a detailed investigation of the actual circumstances and a necessary finding that it was the parties' common intention to provide the defendant with a beneficial interest.[86] The fact that he is living in the premises and paying the owner's mortgage in lieu of rent is not necessarily conclusive of the owner's intention to provide the defendant with a beneficial interest (*Robson* (1991)[87]). **3.170**

Once it is found that the defendant does have an interest, the judge should then go on to consider whether the other party's share is genuinely beneficial or whether it is a tainted gift and caught by the Act (*Buckman* (1997)[88]). In either of these aspects the evidence may show that the legal reality of the defendant's interest or, as the case may be, the interest of the other party, is a beneficial interest under a resulting or constructive trust. **3.171**

---

[84] [1999] 1 Cr App R (S) 354. [85] [1998] 1 Cr App R (S) 42.
[86] See *Eves v Eves* [1975] 1 WLR 1338; *Grant v Edwards* [1986] 3 WLR 114.
[87] (1991) 12 Cr App R (S) 387; but see also *Cowcher v Cowcher* [1972] 1 WLR 425.
[88] [1997] 1 Cr App R (S) 325.

3.172   The court will find a resulting trust where there is a common intention, express or inferred, that the person is to hold a beneficial interest proportionate to his direct or indirect financial contributions to the capital acquisition cost of the asset; there is a constructive trust where there is a common intention that the person is to have a specific interest (for example, one half) or an interest to be ascertained by taking into account his contribution over the years to the cost of acquiring or improving the asset so that he is induced to act to his detriment in the reasonable belief that he is acquiring an agreed beneficial interest.

10. The Matrimonial Home

3.173   In theory, a similar process should be applied to the matrimonial home—first, the determination of the respective interests of husband and wife (or couples living as such) followed by a determination of whether the interest of the partner who is not a defendant is tainted. In practice, the attitude of the prosecution will vary according to the circumstances and will frequently occupy a principal ground of negotiation between prosecution and defence.

3.174   By way of example, if, in the aftermath of a criminal enterprise, the defendant provided all of the purchase price of a house which was purchased in joint names, the prosecution is likely to treat the partner's share as tainted. On the other hand, the prosecution may be inclined to accept the integrity of joint ownership in the context of a lengthy relationship to which the partner has genuinely contributed in other ways.

3.175   In any event, the defendant's own interest in the matrimonial home frequently amounts to at least half of its market value and it is sometimes necessary to sell the home so that he can realize his share and satisfy the compensation order. This can mean that an innocent partner (and children) are forced to leave the home. However, the court has no discretion—hardship arising from the enforced loss of the matrimonial home is not a consideration. In *Danison v UK* (1998)[89] the Commission held that 'the extent of the relevance' of a spouse's interest in the matrimonial home is 'within the appreciation' of the domestic court.

3.176   Nevertheless, where there are concurrent matrimonial proceedings it may be possible to regularize the interests in shared property so as to avoid hardship for the innocent partner. In *Customs and Excise Commissioners v MCA* (2002),[90] the prosecution sought to enforce a DTA order by realizing the home (and two endowment policies). The wife, who had filed for divorce before the offences occurred, sought their transfer to her as ancillary relief under the Matrimonial Causes Act 1973. It was held that it would be disproportionate to any legitimate public interest to force a sale of the home and that the appropriate course in these circumstances is to order the transfer of the defendant's entire beneficial and legal interests to the wife. However, this should not be regarded as 'open season to

---

[89] Application No 45042/98.   [90] The Times, 25 July 2002.

collusive agreements between dishonest former spouses'. Such an order could be set aside subsequently on the ground that the court had not been given full disclosure or had not been told that the assets represented the proceeds of crime. (See further: *CPS v Grimes; Grimes v Grimes* (2003)[91] for the considerations which the court should apply).

11. Third Party Representations

Traditional advice for third parties wishing to protect property in their possession was to await enforcement proceedings. Of course, during the determination hearing itself, the defendant himself might call the third party as a witness in order to prove an interest which reduced the amount of the defendant's available property. But, there has never been any procedure allowing for third parties to make their own free-standing representations at that stage. They have no control of the proceedings and no right of appeal.

3.177

However, at the enforcement stage (and in relation to the management of property under a restraint order), the Act does permit third parties to protect their interests. First, where a receiver has been appointed (either as a management receiver following a restraint order, as an enforcement receiver, or as a Director's receiver—see below), the court cannot confer powers to manage or realize property 'unless it gives persons holding interests in the property a reasonable opportunity to make representations' (ss 51 and 53).

3.178

Further, persons who are or may be affected by the receiver's actions may apply for the Crown Court to 'make such order as it believes is appropriate' (s 62) or for the order to be discharged or varied (s 63).

3.179

Under previous legislation, confiscation orders were enforced by the High Court under a discrete civil jurisdiction. In *Norris* (2001)[92] the House of Lords held that a third party could not be prevented from a re-hearing at that stage notwithstanding that her evidence had already been rejected by the Crown Court. Admittedly, notwithstanding that this jurisdiction is now retained by the Crown Court, it still remains separate from the determination of benefit so that the third party will still be able to make her own representations and to call evidence at the enforcement stage rather than have to rely on the presentation of her interests as part of the defendant's case. However, it seems highly likely that judges who have already heard the third party give evidence on the defendant's behalf and have made adverse findings of fact, particularly on credibility, will decline to hear the same evidence all over again. This is a strong argument for adhering to the traditional advice to keep their powder dry until enforcement in any but the clearest cases.

3.180

---

[91] [2003] FLR 510.   [92] [2001] 1 WLR 1388.

K. CONFISCATION ORDERS AND SENTENCE

1. General Relationship with Sentence

3.181 The judge has a choice whether to make a confiscation order before sentence or whether to postpone the determination (s 14(1)). The implication is that, unless there is a postponement, the making of the confiscation order must always precede sentence (see further below).

3.182 One of the obvious problems of this sequence for a defendant is that, by the time the judge comes to sentence, the defendant's 'lifestyle' may reveal greater criminality than that comprised in the index offences.

3.183 Nevertheless, the most basic principle of sentencing must still prevail—that a person cannot be sentenced for offences of which he has not been convicted or which he has not asked to be taken into consideration, unless he accepts that the offences are specimen examples of a wider course of conduct.[93] Even so, the sentencer may '. . . pay some regard to the evidence placed before him . . . in the same way as he might pay regard to general evidence placed before him' to find, for example, that this was not the first occasion on which the defendant had offended.

> The correct way of approaching the matter was this: the judge must sentence only on the counts that have been proved . . . : he could, of course, mitigate that sentence from what would have been appropriate on the facts, because of good character or because the offence was shown to be an isolated incident, or he could take the view, if there was evidence that it was not an isolated incident, that he should not mitigate what would otherwise be the appropriate sentence (*Harper* (1989)[94]).

3.184 It has also been said that an enquiry is 'akin to a Newton hearing' and (if findings are made to the criminal standard of proof) 'material could be used to inform the court of the seriousness of the offence . . . and (the defendant's) degree of involvement in it' (*Thompson and Smith* (1997)[95]). The proper approach was outlined in *Saunders* (1990–91):[96]

> . . . we consider it would be absurd to say that, if in the course of the . . . investigation the defendant, for example, admitted extensive drug trafficking, the sentencing judge should entirely disregard that in determining the appropriate sentence. He could and should take it into account . . . Equally clearly, however, he should be careful not to take into account factual matters of which he has not been satisfied beyond reasonable doubt. Above all, he should not allow the unusual and . . . very adverse [statutory] assumptions to lead him to make findings adverse to the defendant in the realm of sentencing which he would not have made applying the ordinary burden of proof.

---

[93] See *Bragason* (1988) 10 Cr App R (S) 258; *Ayensu* (1982) 4 Cr App R (S) 248.
[94] (1989) 11 Cr App R (S) 240.   [95] [1997] 1 Cr App R (S) 289.
[96] (1990–91) 12 Cr App R (S) 344.

It is, therefore, wrong to deny a defendant sentencing credit for having no pre- **3.185** vious convictions notwithstanding that the application of the assumptions resulted in a finding that he had been previously involved in drug trafficking (*Callan* (1994)[97]). Where the outcome of a confiscation enquiry results in a conflict with other features of the case, the judge is entitled to then hold a *Newton* hearing. In *McNulty* (1994),[98] the agreed basis for a guilty plea was that the defendant had supplied cannabis on a 'social basis'. The DTA enquiry, on the other hand, led to a finding that cash in his possession was profit. The judge *then* held a *Newton* hearing to determine to the criminal standard whether the defendant was, in fact, a commercial supplier for the purposes of sentence.

2. Relationship with Other Orders

The interaction between confiscation orders and other sentencing powers is reg- **3.186** ulated by s 13. The effect of the confiscation order varies according to the type of sentencing order. A distinction is made between the principal financial orders (but not including compensation) and other orders.

The judge cannot make certain financial orders (fines, deprivation orders or **3.187** forfeiture orders under the Misuse of Drugs Act 1971 or the Terrorism Act 2000) without taking account of the confiscation order and reducing the defendant's available means accordingly (s 13(2) and (3)). The court has no power to make a deprivation order in respect of property which it would otherwise have confiscated—for example, cash in the defendant's possession (*Stuart and Bonnet* (1989)[99]).

Generally, however, the judge must 'leave the confiscation order out of account **3.188** in deciding the appropriate sentence' (s 13(4)), for example, in deciding whether to impose a custodial sentence.[100]

3. Relationship with Compensation Orders

The Act has particular rules to ensure the primacy of compensation for victims **3.189** and losers over confiscation. The route of the Act must still be followed—in other words, the court must still go through the process of making the confiscation order, then fixing the amount of compensation without regard to the existence of the confiscation order. It then looks at the situation in the round. If 'the court believes . . . [the defendant] . . . will not have sufficient means to satisfy both the orders in full', it must order the shortfall in compensation to be paid out of the confiscated sum (s 13(5) and (6)).[101] On the other hand, if the defendant does have

---

[97] (1994) 15 Cr App R (S) 574.   [98] (1994) 15 Cr App R (S) 606.
[99] (1989) 11 Cr App R (S) 89.
[100] See *Rogers* [2002] 1 Cr App R (S) 337 and *Andrews* [1997] 1 Cr App R (S) 279.
[101] See *Mitchell* [2001] 2 Cr App R (S) 141; *Williams* [2001] 1 Cr App R 500.

the means, he can be ordered to pay the money twice over both as confiscation and compensation (see *Brazil* (1995)[102]); *Williams* above; *Mitchell* above).

4. Costs

3.190   An order for costs ought not to be made where the judge has assessed the available amount to be less than the benefit figure. The implication of such an assessment is that no further funds are available.[103]

L. POSTPONEMENT

1. Postponement and Sentence

3.191   Either side may apply for a postponement or the court may order a postponement of its own motion (s 14(7)). Otherwise the court should make the confiscation order before the defendant is sentenced. Prosecutors should always make their position clear.

3.192   Under previous law it has been held that, if the prosecutor had not asked for a determination (nor the judge deemed it appropriate) before sentence, the jurisdiction to hold a determination 'falls away': *Phillips* (2002).[104]

3.193   However, late amendments to the Bill appear to have been intended to ensure that a reversal of the sequence will no longer sustain an appeal by itself. They included (a) the removal of an express provision that the order of events is mandatory and (b) the addition of a rule that orders are not to be quashed only on the ground that 'the procedure connected with the application for or the granting of a postponement' was defective (s 14(11)).

3.194   There may still be arguments that a decision to sentence is not part of the procedure of postponement. Nevertheless, the Act clearly contemplates otherwise because it expressly withholds the procedural immunity from cases where the court has fined or made other financial orders before sentence (s 14(12)). This appears to imply that the immunity does otherwise cover all other forms of sentence.

3.195   If the determination is postponed, the judge may sentence in the meantime so long as he does not impose a fine or make a compensation, forfeiture or deprivation order (s 15(2)) (they can be imposed after a postponed DTA determination but only in the twenty-eight days immediately following).

3.196   A court which postpones the determination and proceeds to sentence should not make an order for costs before making the confiscation order (*Threapleton*

---

[102] CA, 12 January 1995.
[103] *Ahmed and Choudhury* [1997] 2 Cr App R (S) 8; *Szrajber* (1994) 15 Cr App R (S) 821.
[104] [2002] Crim LR 232. See also *Ross* [2001] 2 Cr App R (S) 109.

$(2002)^{105}$). Under the new Crown Court Rules, the court may grant a postponement without a hearing—presumably only where the parties agree.

2. Powers of Postponement

Postponements are frequent—for example, where one side or the other requires further time to obtain information, or, increasingly, where it is necessary to await the outcome of co-defendants' trials likely to last many months. **3.197**

The judge has now an unfettered discretion to postpone for specified periods up to a maximum of two years from the date of conviction (or longer in exceptional circumstances) (s 14). This quadruples the six-month period previously allowed by the CJA and DTA (and then only when further information was required). The new period undoubtedly reflects the fact that previous judicial efforts to sustain longer postponements led to 'almost unparalleled muddle and confusion'. **3.198**

In our view, this lengthening of the basic period of postponement is likely to add to the existing prosecution culture of delay. Historically, the POCA enquiry has often been a post-trial afterthought and a dilatory prosecutor's statement was commonly expected. Of course, for different reasons, elasticity may also suit a defendant on occasions. **3.199**

As noted above, procedural defects in the postponement will not alone invalidate a confiscation order (s 14(11)). However, the following principles have emerged from cases decided under the CJA and DTA and remain relevant. **3.200**

The leading case on postponement is *Steele and Shevki* $(2001)^{106}$, in which the Court of Appeal reviewed the authorities. The main point in *Steele and Shevki* holds good for the POCA—the discretion to postpone is to be exercised judicially and carefully. **3.201**

Confiscation orders should normally form part of the ordinary sentencing process [but] . . . this will often be impractical . . . These decisions involve the court's discretion, judicially exercised when the statutory conditions are present, taking full account of the preferred statutory sequence as well as the express direction in the statute that save in exceptional circumstances, confiscation determinations should not be postponed for more than [the permitted period] . . . after conviction.

It does not follow from the fact that an order has not been made, when it might have been, that the order must have been postponed, or be deemed to have been postponed. Mere temporising, delay or inaction did not amount to a postponement of a determination. In short, following an application by one side or the other, or as a result of the court acting on its own initiative, . . . a judicial decision was needed . . . and, unless made within the permitted period (whether for a postponement or for an extension in exceptional circumstances), the jurisdiction to make the order for postponement lapses.

[105] [2002] Crim LR 229; *Smart* [2003] 2 Cr App R (S) 384.
[106] [2001] 2 Cr App R (S) 178; see also *Kelly* [2000] 2 Cr App R (S) 129; *Khan* [2000] 2 Cr App R (S) 76; *Tuegel* [2000] 2 Cr App R 361; *Miranda* [2000] 2 Cr App R (S) 347; *Woodhead* [2002] Crim LR 323.

3.202 To avoid problems, the judge should set a time-table on conviction dealing with service of the prosecutor's statement and the defendant's response when ordering a postponement.

3.203 While a decision to postpone need not be expressed in any particular form of words, the judge must make it clear in advance of passing sentence that he has exercised his discretion to postpone. It will suffice if, at that stage, he sets out a time table for reciprocal service of information and sets a hearing date or even a band of possible hearing dates. It is preferable for a precise date to be set, but not fatal to the subsequent order if it is not (see *Ruddick* (2003)[107]).

3. Exceptional Circumstances

3.204 The two-year period may be exceeded in 'exceptional circumstances'. The Court of Appeal has not hitherto given a great deal of guidance. In *Gadsby* (2001)[108] it was held that the judge was entitled to find that there were exceptional circumstances where the defence solicitor had wrongly refused service of the prosecutor's statement leaving no time available in which to complete a hearing within the permitted period.

3.205 However, no particular principle has emerged and the court simply recognized that in general two judges might legitimately differ in their approaches with the question on appeal being whether the judge was entitled to find the circumstances 'exceptional'.

3.206 The failure to refer expressly to 'exceptional circumstances' will not invalidate a postponement if it can be inferred that the court had the appropriate test in mind and if the order can be justified (*Chuni* (2002)[109]). But there must be some appraisal of the circumstances and a finding that there are exceptional circumstances (*Soneji and Bullen* (2003)[110]).

3.207 There currently appear to be two schools of thought as to whether 'ordinary' listing difficulties entitle the Court and, in particular, listing officers to extend hearing dates beyond the permitted period. In *Groombridge* (2004),[111] a case in which the list office had varied the date because of the defendant's illness, the Court of Appeal considered that:

> circumstances which arise within the ordinary ambit of the duties of the list officer . . . are not to be regarded as matters taking place within the ambit of . . . (the legislation) . . . and they are not susceptible of challenge on the basis that a judicial decision should be made . . . as opposed to an administrative decision by a listing officer in the ordinary course of business.

---

[107] [2003] EWCA Crim 1061; *Haisman* [2004] 1 Cr App R (S) 383; *Sekhon* (CA, 16 December 2002) (at time of writing, leave to appeal to the House of Lords granted), preferring *Copeland* [2002] EWCA Crim 736 to *Davis* [2001] EWCA Crim 2790; *Pisciotto* [2002] Crim LR 678; *Palmer* [2002] EWCA Crim 2202; and *Ross* [2001] EWCA Crim 560).

[108] [2001] Crim LR 828.

[109] [2002] 2 Cr App R (S) 82.

[110] CA, 20 June 2003.

[111] [2004] 1 Cr App R (S) 84.

On the other hand, in *Young* (2003)[112] it was thought that a stricter approach **3.208** was unavoidable:

... a bald proposition that, whatever the circumstances, listing difficulties are incapable of being exceptional circumstances would be wrong. (However)The mere convenience of counsel, witnesses or the court would certainly not justify a postponement or adjournment of any significance on the grounds that the circumstances were exceptional. The plain policy of the legislation must be faithfully adhered to ... It may well be necessary for counsels' other commitments to be interfered with, for witnesses to be inconvenienced, and for the court to promote confiscation hearings at the expense of other business ... But there may be a small minority of cases in which in all the circumstances difficulties with dates cannot justly be accommodated without a small overrun. These rare cases will be capable of constituting exceptional circumstances ... there has to be a proper and sufficient judicial enquiry ... the say-so of the listing officer is insufficient.

An order for an exceptional postponement is only valid if made before the **3.209** expiry of the original specified period(s).

4. Common Law Adjournments

In order to uphold overlong postponements in some of the earlier cases where the **3.210** statutory rules had been ignored or misunderstood, the Court of Appeal was driven to fall back on the Crown Court's inherent common law power to adjourn its own proceedings.[113] The existence of the power is undeniable but again there is a danger of abuse if it is resorted to when there is no possibility of an extension under the Act itself. The court in *Steele and Shevki* explained that the approach should be restrictive:

So far as practicable, adjournments which would have the effect of postponing the determination beyond [the permitted period] ..., or in exceptional cases, beyond the period envisaged when the decision to postpone was made, should be avoided. Nevertheless, when the circumstances in an individual case compel an adjournment which would have this effect, then ... it may be ordered, for example, to take account of illness on one side or the other, or the unavailability of the judge, without depriving a subsequent order of its validity.

In principle, the confiscation order must be made within the period permitted **3.211** by the statute and there is some authority that an adjournment beyond that period also requires exceptional circumstances (*Soneji and Bullen* (2003)[114]). The power to sentence before a confiscation hearing can only be exercised where the court uses the statutory power of postponement (s 14(1)). It, therefore, seems that a confiscation order made after sentence and following a common law adjournment

---

[112] [2003] EWCA Crim 3481.

[113] See *Lingham* [2001] 1 Cr App R (S) 46; *Zelzele* [2001] Crim LR 830; *Fairhead* [1975] 2 All ER 737; *Teugal* [2000] 2 All ER 872; *Menocal* [1980] AC 598; *Annesley* (1976) 62 Cr App R 113; *Ingle* (1974) 59 Cr App R 306.

[114] CA, 20 June 2003; see also *Young* (CA, 4 February 2003); cf *October* (CA, 27 February 2003).

is invalid. Whether that amounts to a sufficient ground of appeal is debatable in the light of the procedural saving in s 14(11) (see paras 3.191 *et seq*). As the POCA now contains a general power to postpone which could be used in those examples, it is submitted that retrospective reliance on the common law could rarely be justified.

5. Postponement on Appeal

3.212   The court may also postpone the determination while the defendant appeals against conviction—presumably for a determined period which starts to run on disposal of the appeal (s 14(6)). If the appeal takes more than two years, the Act permits postponement for up to three months after the appeal.

M. THE MAKING OF THE ORDER

1. Fixed Amount

3.213   The court must fix the recoverable amount. By way of example, an order referring to the defendant's assets as the equity of a particular property 'valued at not less than £26,000' has been held to be defective (*Jubb* (2002)[115]).

2. Time for Payment

3.214   The ordinary principle is that the order must be satisfied immediately (s 11(1)). However, if the defendant shows that he needs time to pay, he can be allowed a specified period of up to six months to meet the order. If he applies before the end of that period, it can be extended in exceptional circumstances to a maximum of twelve months from the date of the order.

3.215   As mentioned above, the court may be prepared to allow him longer to realize assets such as houses if a better price can be obtained as a result.

N. ENFORCEMENT

1. The Enforcement Authority

3.216   In most cases the order is effectively treated as a fine to be collected and enforced by a specified magistrates' court or, if none is specified, by the committing magistrates' court (s 35(2)).

3.217   However, the Director must be appointed as 'the enforcement authority for the order' in any case in which the Director applied for the determination or has applied to be the enforcement authority (s 34).

---

[115] [2002] 2 Cr App R (S) 8.

2. Default in Payment

If the amount of the order is not paid in time, interest accrues on the unpaid amount for the period for which it remains unpaid (s 12). **3.218**

The mechanism for imposing terms of imprisonment or detention for default is almost identical to that used in the enforcement of fines and many of the provisions of the Powers of Criminal Courts (Sentencing) Act 2000 are expressly incorporated in the POCA. **3.219**

Thus, the Crown Court must fix a default term in accordance with the scale set out in s 139(4) of the Powers of Criminal Courts (Sentencing) Act. (Failure to do so, however, will not invalidate the order (*Ellis* (1996)[116]). The scale ranges from seven days for an amount not exceeding £200 up to ten years for anything over £1 million. These are maximum terms and it follows that the Crown Court may fix lesser terms within the bands (*Szrajber* (1994)[117]). **3.220**

The Crown Court may itself go on to commit the defendant to serve the default period immediately but only where: **3.221**

(a) he appears to have the means to pay forthwith;

(b) he is unlikely to remain in the jurisdiction long enough for payment to be enforced by another method; or

(c) he is serving or is sentenced to imprisonment or detention.

Where the defendant is also sentenced to imprisonment, the default period is served consecutively. Default imprisonment is remitted if payment is made. However, anyone hoping to avoid payment by serving the term in default may face disappointment because 'his serving that term does not prevent the confiscation order from continuing to have effect so far as any other method of enforcement is concerned' (s 38(5)). In other words, the court could still appoint an enforcement receiver to take over and realize the defendant's property (see below). **3.222**

If the defendant does default, the magistrates must summons and then commit him to serve the default period. What they may not do is allow further time or payment by instalments or hold a further means enquiry (s 35(3)). **3.223**

The Administrative Court has held that proceedings to enforce a confiscation order by commitment to prison are part of the entire criminal proceedings and, therefore, part of the determination of a criminal charge within Article 6(1) of the Convention. Accordingly, the defendant is entitled to have the proceedings determined 'within a reasonable time'. Regard should be had to any efforts made to extract the money by other means and to the conduct of the defendant. A delay of two years ten months (including ten months for which the defendant may have been responsible) was unreasonable where no material had been advanced to explain the delay and the proceedings were stayed: *Lloyd v Bow Street* **3.224**

---

[116] [1996] 2 Cr App R (S) 403.   [117] (1994) 15 Cr App R (S) 821.

Magistrates' Court (2003).[118] Note, however, that the court was careful to limit the decision to the enforcement of a confiscation order by the issue of a warrant of commitment to prison.

3.225   Where the Director is the enforcement authority and the order has not been satisfied because of the defendant's 'wilful refusal or culpable neglect', he may apply for a summons requiring the defendant to appear before the court (s 37). The court may commit him to prison in default of payment. He must be released on payment.

3.226   In December 2002 the 'Enforcement Taskforce' was set up consisting of staff from Customs and Excise, police, and CPS working alongside magistrates' courts to ensure full payment of orders made before the 2002 Act. By mid 2004 it had obtained £30 million. Presumably, the Taskforce or some similar unit will also pursue the enforcement of orders made under the Act.

3. Enforcement Receivers

3.227   If the order is not satisfied (and not appealed) the prosecution may ask the Crown Court to appoint an enforcement receiver (s 50). The court may then confer powers on the receiver to:

(a) take possession of realizable property;

(b) manage 'or otherwise deal with' the property;

(c) realize the property 'in such manner as the court may specify';

(d) bring or defend legal proceedings (s 51(2)).

It may also authorize the receiver to exercise various more specific management functions.

3.228   Third parties holding interests in realizable property may be ordered to pay the receiver 'in respect of a beneficial interest held by the defendant or the recipient of a tainted gift' (s 51(6)). (As noted above, third parties have a right to make representations at that stage.)

4. Director's Receivers

3.229   If the Director is the enforcement authority, the court 'must make an order for the appointment of a receiver' (s 52(3)). The Director then has power to nominate a receiver who may be a member of the ARA staff. The court may be grant powers similar to those of an enforcement receiver.

---

[118] 8 October 2003; [2003] EWHC 2294 (Admin).

5. Sums Realized by Receivers

These must be applied in strict order: first, in payment of the expenses of insol- **3.230** vency practitioners; secondly, 'in making any payments directed by the Crown Court'; thirdly, to satisfy the confiscation order by payment to the Justices' Chief Executive or to the Director as the case may be (ss 54 and 56).

If there is any money remaining, the receiver must distribute it to those who **3.231** hold/held interests in the property in such proportions as the court directs. They have a right to make representations.

6. Seized Money

Where a restraint order has effect but the confiscation order has not been satisfied, **3.232** justices may order banks and building societies to pay over money towards a confiscation order where:

(a) the money is held by a person in such an account;

(b) the money which has been seized by the police or Customs and Excise under their general power of seizure (Police and Criminal Evidence Act 1984, s 19) and is held by them in such an account (s 67).

7. Enforcement Abroad

Where the prosecutor or Director believes that realizable property is situated out- **3.233** side the United Kingdom they may send a Request for Assistance to the Home Secretary who may, in turn, forward the request to the relevant government (s 74). A Request for Assistance asks the receiving country to apply the various co-operation treaties and, in particular, to prohibit anyone from dealing in the property and to ensure that the proceeds 'are applied in accordance with the law of the receiving country'. If property is realized abroad, the amount which the defendant has been ordered to pay under the order is reduced accordingly.

O. RECONSIDERATION

1. General

Confiscation orders can be varied within twenty-eight days under the general **3.234** 'slip-rule', particularly where further information comes to light (Powers of Criminal Courts (Sentencing) Act 2000, s 155).[119]

However, the Act itself anticipates that the full extent of the defendant's assets **3.235** may not emerge for some considerable time or, alternatively, that his assets

---

[119] And see *Miller* (1990-91) 12 Cr App R (S) 519.

actually amount to less than originally thought. Accordingly, the court retains powers to vary findings (a) as to the existence or amount of benefit for up to six years from conviction or (b) indefinitely as to the available amount. Recalculations of benefit or of the available amount must take account of any change in the value of money.

3.236   Under the new Crown Court Rules 1982 (as amended), applications for reconsideration under previous legislation have to specify the grounds and the evidence supporting of the application.

2. Prosecution Application

3.237   First, the prosecution or the Director have six years from the date of conviction in which to ask the court to consider evidence of benefit which was 'not available' to them at the time of conviction or when the court decided not to proceed with a determination. The court has some latitude in fixing the recoverable amount which can be such amount that 'the court believes is just'. Moreover, the court cannot apply the s 10 assumptions to property obtained or expenditure made after that date.

3.238   The court must proceed with a further enquiry if, having considered the evidence, it believes that it is 'appropriate' to do so in the following situations:

(a) where no order was previously made because:
   (i) there has been no POCA enquiry (s 19), or
   (ii) the court previously decided that the defendant has not benefited from criminal conduct (s 20); or

(b) where the court has made a confiscation order, and 'the prosecutor or Director believes' that the amount of benefit would exceed the earlier finding (s 21).

3.239   Secondly, the prosecutor or Director (or a receiver) may apply at any point for reconsideration of the available amount (s 22). The section even catches property which has accrued to the defendant after the date of the confiscation order and regardless of whether the prosecution can prove that it is the result of crime (*Tivnan* (1999)[120]).

3.240   Note that, while it has been held that 'a defendant enjoys full benefit of all the rights conferred by Article 6(1) in all aspects of confiscation proceedings', it has been held simultaneously that the entitlement to 'a hearing within a reasonable time' does not apply to reconsideration of the available amount—precisely because Parliament stipulated no time limit (*Re S* (2004)[121]).

---

[120] [1999] 1 Cr App R (S) 92.   [121] [2004] EWHC 1011 (Admin).

3. Inadequacy of Available Amount

The defendant (or an appointed receiver) may apply to the Crown Court for the amount of the order to be reduced if the available amount is inadequate for payment in full (s 23). Again, the court can substitute 'such smaller amount as the court believes is just'. It can disregard any shortfall attributable to anything done by the defendant to frustrate the realization of tainted gifts.   **3.241**

This is an example of the Crown Court acting as a 'one-stop shop'. Prior to the Act, a convoluted process had to be gone through in which the defendant or the receiver had to apply to the High Court for a 'Certificate of Inadequacy' which then entitled the defendant to go back to the Crown Court to apply for a reduction. There are certain oddities. There is no time limit on applications and it appears that an application does not require fresh evidence. No doubt, in practice applications will not be entertained without some change in the circumstances.   **3.242**

An application for a certificate does not provide an opportunity to try and make good deficiencies in the case presented at the time of the confiscation order. It is not enough for the defendant to come to court and say that his assets are inadequate to meet the order unless at the same time he condescends to demonstrate what has happened since the making of the order to the realisable property found by the trial judge when the order was made (*Gokal v Serious Fraud Office* (2001)[122]).   **3.243**

It has been held that certificates under the DTA 1994 should only be issued where there has been a reduction in the value of the realizable assets since the making of the order; the fact that the defendant might have difficulties in realising the assets is irrelevant (*Re R* (2002)[123]).   **3.244**

4. Discharge of Small or Inadequate Amounts

Where less than £1,000 of the order remains to be paid, the justices' chief executive can apply to the Crown Court for the order to be discharged. The court can then discharge the order if satisfied that the current available amount is inadequate and that the inadequacy is due to a fluctuation in currency rates or to 'any reason specified by the Secretary of State by order' (s 24). At the time of writing, no such order has been made.   **3.245**

Where the unpaid part of an order is £50 or less, the justices' chief executive can simply apply to the Crown Court for the order to be discharged (s 25).   **3.246**

---

[122] [2001] EWCA Civ 368; see also *R v C* (CA, 18 November 1997); *R v W* (CA, 29 January 1998).

[123] Silber J (QB, 29 July 2002); see also *R v Liverpool Magistrates' Court, ex p Ansen* [1998] 1 All ER 692.

P. ABSCONDING DEFENDANTS

1. Convicted Defendants

3.247   Once a convicted defendant absconds it seems that the prosecution cannot proceed in the normal way (s 6(8)). They may, instead, apply to proceed under s 27 but the court has a discretion rather than a duty to do so and the price is a more limited form of enquiry. The court may proceed if (a) the prosecutor or Director applies for it to proceed, *and* (b) 'the court believes it is appropriate for it to do so' (s 27(3)). The court then proceeds as if the defendant were present but with certain important 'modifications' (s 27(5)). These include:

(a) 'any person the court believes is likely to be affected by an order' is entitled to appear and to make representations;

(b) no order can be made unless the prosecutor or Director has taken reasonable steps to contact the defendant;

(c) the required assumptions and the provisions requiring defence disclosure must be ignored.

3.248   If an order is made in these circumstances and then he re-appears, the defendant himself can do little other than to apply for a variation on the basis that the available amount is inadequate to meet the order (s 23).

3.249   If, on the other hand, the prosecution applied to proceed under s 27 in his absence but 'no court has proceeded' under that section, the prosecution may take a second bite at the cherry if it has fresh evidence. Thus, if it has evidence which was 'not available' when the court earlier made the decision not to proceed with an enquiry in the defendant's absence or, if no such decision was made, on the date of conviction, it may apply within six years of conviction for the court to consider the evidence (s 19).

3.250   If, after considering the evidence, the court believes it is appropriate to proceed, it must do so. Again, there are restrictions on application of the assumptions. The recoverable amount is 'such amount as the court believes is just'.

2. Unconvicted Defendants

3.251   There is a similar discretion to proceed where the defendant absconds before the proceedings for the index offence(s) have been concluded (s 28). Once two years have elapsed from the day that 'the court believes he absconded', a similarly modified form of enquiry can take place—notwithstanding that he remains unconvicted.

3.252   If he then re-appears before the proceedings for the offence(s) are concluded, the court may discharge the order if it finds either that there has been 'undue delay' in continuing the prosecution or that the prosecutor does not intend to continue with the prosecution (s 30(4)).

However, if on his re-appearance, the defendant is 'tried and acquitted', a 3.253
confiscation order made earlier in his absence must be discharged (s 30(2)). This
includes a verdict of not guilty formally entered after the prosecution offers no
evidence. Criminal Law Act 1967, s 17 provides that such a verdict 'shall have the
same effect as if the defendant had been tried and acquitted on the verdict of a
jury'.

Q. APPEALS

1. Court of Appeal—by the Defendant

A confiscation order or variation (apart from variations based upon inadequacy 3.254
of the available amount) constitutes a sentence for the purposes of appeal
(Criminal Appeal Act 1968, s 50(1) as amended by the POCA 2002, Sch 8).
Accordingly, the defendant may appeal against the making or the amount of an
order with the leave of the Court of Appeal. Even an order for postponement has
been regarded as a sentence in the much criticized decision in *Davis* (2002).[124]
There the order being appealed was the judge's refusal to rule that on a previous
occasion he had improperly postponed the determination.

The court may confirm, quash or vary the order (s 86). An order remains sub- 3.255
ject to appeal 'until there is no possibility of an appeal on which the order could
be varied or quashed' (s 87(2)). It follows that the right of appeal exists while there
remains a possibility of variation or reconsideration. Presumably the normal
twenty-eight day time limit applies once the decision to vary has been made
(Criminal Appeal Act 1968, s 18).

The new Crown Court Rules[125] bring the procedural aspects broadly in line 3.256
with the Criminal Appeal Act and Rules.

2. Court of Appeal—by the Prosecution or Director

As noted above, a confiscation order constitutes a sentence. Prior to the Act, an 3.257
Attorney-General's reference to the Court of Appeal was possible in respect of
sentences for indictable only offences and for certain specified offences, including
the importation of controlled drugs (Criminal Appeal Act 1988, s 35).[126]

For the first time in the evolution of confiscation law, the prosecutor or Director 3.258
now has a general right of appeal 'in respect of' the making of an order and
against a decision not to make an order. This also requires leave. They may not

---

[124] [2002] Crim LR 224.
[125] The Proceeds of Crime Act 2002 (Appeals under Part 2) Order 2003 (SI 2003 /82) and the
Criminal Appeal (Confiscation, Restraint and Receivership) Rules 2003 (SI 2003/428).
[126] See *Flowers (A-G's References (Nos 114–116 of 2002)* (CA, 26 November 2003) where the judge
erred in law as to his power to proceed under the CJA 1988.

appeal against refusals to reconsider whether to proceed, to reconsider the amount of benefit or to hold an enquiry for an absconder (s 31).

3.259　Where the Court of Appeal believes the decision not to proceed was wrong, it may conduct its own enquiry or direct the Crown Court to proceed afresh (s 32).

3. House of Lords

3.260　The parties may appeal further to the House of Lords whose powers are similar to those of the Court of Appeal (s 33). Appeals lie with the leave of either court on a certified point of law of general public importance.

R. COMPENSATION

3.261　Perhaps as some acknowledgement of the potential for unfairness in the processes of restraint and confiscation, the Act itself contains detailed provisions under which the court may order such compensation it 'believes is just' where there has been a 'serious default' by the authorities (s 72). This applies to the police, Crown Prosecution Service, Serious Fraud Office, Customs and Excise and Inland Revenue.

3.262　In order to qualify, the person has to meet three conditions:

(a) a criminal investigation has been started but has not resulted in conviction (or the conviction is quashed on appeal);

(b) there has been a serious default without which the investigation would not have continued; and

(c) a person who held realizable property suffered loss in consequence of an order under this part of the Act.

The court may also order compensation to a person who has suffered loss from an order which is subsequently varied.

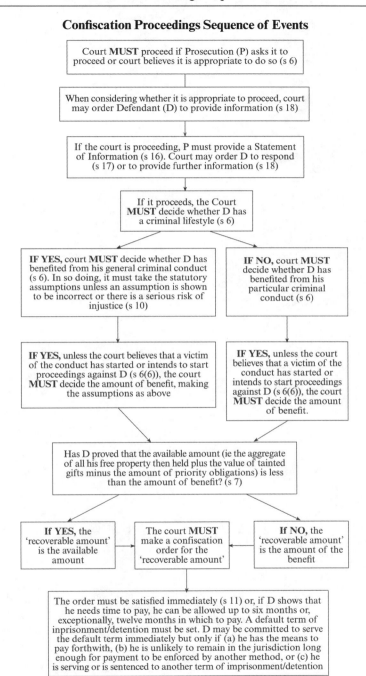

Confiscation Proceedings Sequence of Events 3.263

Court **MUST** proceed if Prosecution (P) asks it to proceed or court believes it is appropriate to do so (s 6)

When considering whether it is appropriate to proceed, court may order Defendant (D) to provide information (s 18)

If the court is proceeding, P must provide a Statement of Information (s 16). Court may order D to respond (s 17) or to provide further information (s 18)

If it proceeds, the Court **MUST** decide whether D has a criminal lifestyle (s 6)

IF YES, court **MUST** decide whether D has benefited from his general criminal conduct (s 6). In so doing, it must take the statutory assumptions unless an assumption is shown to be incorrect or there is a serious risk of injustice (s 10)

IF NO, court **MUST** decide whether D has benefited from his particular criminal conduct (s 6)

IF YES, unless the court believes that a victim of the conduct has started or intends to start proceedings against D (s 6(6)), the court **MUST** decide the amount of benefit, making the assumptions as above

IF YES, unless the court believes that a victim of the conduct has started or intends to start proceedings against D (s 6(6)), the court **MUST** decide the amount of benefit.

Has D proved that the available amount (ie the aggregate of all his free property then held plus the value of tainted gifts minus the amount of priority obligations) is less than the amount of benefit? (s 7)

If YES, the 'recoverable amount' is the available amount

The court **MUST** make a confiscation order for the 'recoverable amount'

If NO, the 'recoverable amount' is the amount of the benefit

The order must be satisfied immediately (s 11) or, if D shows that he needs time to pay, he can be allowed up to six months or, exceptionally, twelve months in which to pay. A default term of inprisonment/detention must be set. D may be committed to serve the default term immediately but only if (a) he has the means to pay forthwith, (b) he is unlikely to remain in the jurisdiction long enough for payment to be enforced by another method, or (c) he is serving or is sentenced to another term of imprisonment/detention

FIG. 3.1: Confiscation Proceedings—Sequence of Events

4

INVESTIGATIONS INTO CRIMINAL PROCEEDS

A. OVERVIEW

1. Ambit of the Powers

4.01 The powers conferred by Pt 8 of the POCA 2002 are similar to, and will exist in tandem with, those powers already in existence under other statutory regimes such as the Police and Criminal Evidence Act 1984 (PACE), the Drug Trafficking Act 1994 (DTA) and the Terrorism Act 2000 (TA). Where they differ is that their primary focus is not solely in the realms of criminal investigations. In that sense the creation of the Assets Recovery Agency (ARA) and its wide ranging functions will draw upon the provisions contained in ss 341 to 379 as applicable to England and Wales. Although the primary focus of the investigatory powers contained in this part of the Act may not be the investigation of crime, it is envisaged that there will clearly be overlap with criminal investigations and this is discussed in greater detail below.

4.02 Part 8 controls three types of investigation as defined under s 341:

(i) confiscation investigation;

(ii) civil recovery investigation; and

(iii) money laundering investigation.

4.03 A confiscation investigation is defined under s 341(1)(a) and (b) as an investigation into whether a person has benefited from his criminal conduct or the extent or whereabouts of his benefit from his criminal conduct. A civil recovery investigation is defined as an investigation into whether property is recoverable property or associated property, who holds the property or what is its extent or its whereabouts.[1] In defining a civil recovery investigation, the POCA excludes under s 341(3), investigations conducted in connection with recovery order proceedings, interim receiving or administration orders or the detention of property (cash) under s 295. A money laundering investigation is defined for the purposes of this part to be an investigation into whether a person has committed a money laundering offence. Under s 343 applications directed at either a confiscation investigation or a money laundering investigation must be made to a judge who 'is

[1] See ss 304 to 310 of the POCA 2002 for the appropriate definitions of recoverable property.

entitled to exercise the jurisdiction of the Crown Court'.[2] We expect that this phrase will be construed to include High Court judges, circuit judges and recorders. Any application pursued in respect of a civil recovery investigation must be made to a High Court judge.[3]

2. The Investigatory Powers

Under the POCA there are now five tools available in investigating whether **4.04** persons have benefited from criminal conduct, where these proceeds are and what their extent is/are. The powers are:

  (i)   production orders;

  (ii) search and seizure warrants;

  (iii) disclosure orders;

  (iv) customer information orders; and

  (v) account monitoring orders.

These specific powers are considerable and provide the investigator with **4.05** additional options in tracing the whereabouts of criminal property to financial institutions, bank accounts, or other supposed more secure locations. In the case of production orders and orders to grant entry, the powers are enforceable under the threat of a contempt of court under s 351(7), as it stipulates that they 'have effect as if they were orders of the court' and therefore if such an order is not complied with such an individual could face contempt proceedings and a fine and/or imprisonment. Furthermore a new and specific offence is created under s 342 of the Act, this offence of 'prejudicing an investigation' may be committed by an individual in several ways and is punishable summarily with a fine and/or imprisonment for up to six months. Following trial on indictment an individual convicted under s 342 faces imprisonment for up to five years. The exercise of these new powers must be considered in association with the Code of Practice issued under s 377 of the Act. The Code is considered in section G below as a general topic but it is advisable to consider the specific section of the Code as it pertains to the individual investigative tool. The Code of Practice is printed in full in Appendix 3.

3. Legal Professional Privilege

The POCA powers will have clear practical implications for the practitioner and **4.06** their clients particularly where they are faced with either an order in the terms of (i), (ii) or (iii) above. In respect of a production order, by virtue of s 348(1) a person does not have to produce, or give access to, privileged material. This is defined

---

     [2] See s. 343(2).   [3] See s. 343(3).

under s 348(2) as any material which the person would be entitled to refuse to produce on grounds of legal professional privilege in proceedings in the High Court. There are similar provisions in relation to search and seizure warrants under s 354 and disclosure orders under s 361 of the Act.

4.07   Section 10 of the PACE 1984 defines 'items subject to legal privilege' as follows:

10.—(1) Subject to subsection (2) below, in this Act 'items subject to legal privilege' means–

(a) communications between a professional legal adviser and his client or any person representing his client made in connection with the giving of legal advice to the client;

(b) communications between a professional legal adviser and his client or any person representing his client or between such an adviser or his client or any such representative and other person made in connection with or in contemplation of legal proceedings and for the purposes of such proceedings; and

(c) items enclosed with or referred to in such communications and made—

(i) in connection with the giving of legal advice; or

(ii) in connection with or in contemplation of legal proceedings and for the purposes of such proceedings,

when they are in the possession of a person who is entitled to possession of them.

(2) Items held with the intention of furthering a criminal purpose are not items subject to legal privilege.

4.08   The existing case authorities on these topics continue to be of relevance. Communications made by a client to his solicitor with the intention of furthering a criminal enterprise are not protected by legal professional privilege (*R v Cox and Railton*[4] and *R v Central Criminal Court, ex p Francis and Francis (a firm)*[5]). Items which may otherwise come within the definition of 'items subject to legal privilege' will be excluded if they were held with the intention of either the holder or any other person of furthering a criminal purpose, whether the purpose be that of the client, the solicitor or any other person.

4.09   Conveyance documents, and records showing how the transaction was financed, do not of themselves amount to the giving of advice, nor do attendance notes or diary entries recording the details of the client and his visits to the solicitor in connection with the transfer (*R v Inner London Crown Court, ex p Baines & Baines (a firm)*[6]). However correspondence between a solicitor and his client relating to such matters may be privileged or alternatively, the materials might fall under the rubric of 'excluded materials' due to their confidential nature (*R v Guildhall Magistrates' Court, ex p Primlaks Holdings Co (Panama) Inc*[7]). It seems that pre-existing documents placed in the hands of a solicitor, rather than created

---

[4] (1884) 14 QBD 153a.   [5] [1989] AC 346, HL.   [6] [1988] QB 579, DC.
[7] [1990] 1 QB 261.

or transferred for the purposes of providing or receiving advice, are not of themselves privileged. Certainly, if the documents are forged by the solicitor, they are neither privileged nor held under any duty of confidence, 'there being no confidence in iniquity' (*R v Leeds Magistrates' Court, ex p Dumbleton*[8]).

It may not always be clear whether particular material identified under a **4.10** production order, search and seizure warrant or disclosure order is subject to 'legal privilege'. In the case of *R v Southampton Crown Court, ex p J and P*[9] the court gave guidance where applications are made to a judge. In each case it will be necessary to balance the competing interests of the investigation of crime and the confidentiality of communications between solicitor and client. The police (or other authorized applicant under the POCA) should draw to the judge's attention that material that may be subject to legal privilege and provide him with sufficient information to enable him to make a decision whether or not the material is privileged. Where there is doubt legal advice should be obtained for the judge's assistance. The material should be capable of distinction where possible otherwise it may not be possible to satisfy a judge that every document in a file, or every file in a category is not legally privileged.

4. Other Exclusions and Provisions

A production order does not require a person to produce, or give access to, **4.11** 'excluded material' as defined under s 11 of the PACE 1984 such as personal records created in the course of an occupation and held in confidence, human tissue or fluid taken for the purposes of diagnosis or medical treatment and held in confidence, and journalistic documents or records held in confidence.[10] In addition s 348 states that an order will cover material in spite of any 'restriction on the disclosure of information' which is likely to include claims under contractual terms, data protection legislation or general duties of confidentiality. Such material is not therefore excluded by the section and would therefore have to be produced as might 'special procedure material' of which the section is silent.[11]

It is possible that the exercise of the powers of search under the POCA might, **4.12** in certain circumstances, be frustrated by an arrested suspect making arrangements through third parties to remove, conceal or destroy property which is the subject of the investigation or represents his proceeds of crime. Schedule 11 to the POCA amends ss. 56, 58 and 116 of PACE 1984[12] and Sch 8 to the Terrorism Act 2000[13] so as to authorize the delay of the right to have someone informed when arrested and authorize the delay of access to legal advice. The basis for this delay requires reasonable grounds for believing that the person detained for the serious arrestable offence has benefited from his criminal conduct and that the recovery of the value of the property constituting the benefit will be hindered by telling the

---

[8] [1993] Crim LR 866, DC.
[10] See PACE 1984 ss 11, 12, 13, and 14.
[12] See para. 14 of Schedule 11 POCA 2002.

[9] [1993] Crim LR 962, DC.
[11] See PACE 1984 s 14.
[13] See ibid para 39.

named person of the arrest or by exercising the right to access to legal advice whichever is appropriate to the circumstances.

B. PRODUCTION ORDERS

1. Introduction

4.13 The purpose of a production order is to obtain material already in existence relating to a known person, for example bank statements and correspondence and may be served on any person or institution. The POCA provisions are based upon the provisions contained in s 93H of the CJA 1988, s 55 of the DTA 1994, and art 50 of the Proceeds of Crime (Northern Ireland) Order 1996.

4.14 A production order may be sought in respect of all three forms of 'investigation', confiscation, civil recovery, and money laundering. Only an 'appropriate officer' may apply. The definition of 'appropriate officer' will vary according to the nature of the order sought. For example if the investigation is a 'confiscation investigation' as defined, the appropriate officer(s) may be the Director (of the ARA), an accredited financial investigator, a constable, or a customs officer.[14] If however the application pertains to a 'money laundering investigation' as defined, the appropriate officer does *not* include the Director as such an investigation is more rooted in criminal investigations.[15]

4.15 A production order requires the person in possession or control of material to produce it to the appropriate officer for removal or for inspection within the maximum time specified in the order.[16] The maximum period is defined as a period of seven days beginning with the day on which the order is made unless the judge who makes the order considers the particular circumstances are such that a longer or shorter period is necessary.[17]

2. Applying for the Order

4.16 The application must state that the specified person or property is subject to a confiscation, money laundering or civil recovery investigation.[18] Note that for the purposes of s 341(3) a civil recovery investigation is defined so as to exclude 'investigations' that include civil recovery proceedings that have already begun or where an interim receiving or administration order applies to the property in question, or it is 'seized cash'[19] and has already been detained under s 295.

4.17 The application must be made by an appropriate officer and must be made to a judge. Provision is made in s 351 to permit applications to be made *ex parte* to a judge in chambers. The application must state three matters about the order, first that it is sought for the purposes of the investigation, secondly that it is sought in

---

[14] See s 378(1).   [15] See s 378(4).   [16] See s 345(4).   [17] See s 345(5).
[18] See s 345(2).   [19] See s 294.

relation to material, or material of a description specified in the order, and thirdly that a person as specified in the application appears to be in possession or control of the material.[20]

There are four 'requirements' that must be satisfied under s 346 for the making of a production order. Under s 346 (2) the first requirement is that there must be 'reasonable grounds for suspecting' either that the specified person has benefited from his criminal conduct (confiscation investigation), that the specified property is recoverable or associated property (civil recovery investigation) or that the subject of the investigation has committed a money laundering offence (money laundering investigation). **4.18**

Secondly, there must be reasonable grounds for believing that the specified person is, in fact, in possession or control of the material (s 346(3)). Thirdly, there must be reasonable grounds for believing that such material is likely to be of substantial value to the investigation. Lastly, there must be reasonable grounds for believing that it is in the public interest for the material to be produced, or access provided to it, having regard to the benefit likely to accrue to the investigation and the circumstances in which the possessor of the material holds it. Note that, while all the conditions for the making of an order are objective, the first requires reasonable suspicion whereas the remainder require the higher state of reasonable belief. **4.19**

The original Bill did not contain any 'public interest' component. The addition is presumably intended to cater for the requirement of Article 8 of the European Convention that any interference with the right to a private life must be necessary in a democratic society. **4.20**

3. Breaching an Order

Under s 351 production orders and entry orders 'have effect as if they were orders of the court' except in relation to a civil recovery investigation. Contempt proceedings would therefore be available in the Crown Court. In addition, a person may face the prospect of being charged with the offence of 'prejudicing an investigation' contrary to s 342 of the POCA. If an individual, knows or suspects that an appropriate officer is acting (or proposing to act) in connection with one of the three types of relevant investigation,[21] and in order to frustrate it, removed or destroyed the relevant material (sought under a production order) that would be a commission of the offence. **4.21**

4. Entry to Premises and Access to Materials

A judge can make an order under s 347 requiring a person to permit access to materials on any premises, or permit an appropriate officer to gain entry to **4.22**

---

[20] See s 345(3).   [21] Confiscation, civil recovery, or money laundering.

premises in order to obtain access to such materials. In the case of materials that are held on computer, s 349 is similar to other statutory provisions.[22] If any of the material specified in an application for a production order consists of material contained in a computer one of two alternatives applies. First if the order is one which requires the person to produce material for an officer to take away, it requires the material to be produced in a form in which it can be taken away by him and in which it is visible and legible. In the alternative, if the order requires a person to give an appropriate officer access to the material it is to be in a form which is visible and legible. A production order does not allow for the situation where information is held on a computer that the officers do not know about, the existence of the material must be known and the identification of the material must be possible before an application for a production order can be made. An application for a search and seizure warrant[23] may be more appropriate in circumstances where the content of the material held on a computer has not been identified and cannot therefore be specified.

4.23   An appropriate officer may take copies of any material which is produced, or to which access is given under s 348(5). Material produced in compliance with a production order may be retained for 'so long as is necessary to retain it' (as opposed to copies of it) in connection with the relevant investigation. In addition if an appropriate officer has reasonable grounds for believing that the material may need to be produced for the purposes of any legal proceedings and it might otherwise be unavailable if not held, it can be held until the proceedings are concluded.[24] If information required for an investigation is held by a government department s 350 of the Act can be applied. The information may be obtained by serving a production order upon any officer of the department (whether named in the order or not) to comply with it. The order is to be served as if the proceedings were civil proceedings against the department. If such an order is served the person on whom it is served must take all reasonable steps to bring it to the attention of the 'officer concerned', this is likely to be the relevant officer in the department. Failure to do so may require the person on whom the order was served to appear before a Crown Court or High Court judge under s 350(5).

C. SEARCH AND SEIZURE WARRANTS

1. Introduction

4.24   A search and seizure warrant under s 352 is a warrant authorizing an 'appropriate person' to enter and search the premises specified in the application for the warrant and to thereafter seize and retain any material found there which is likely to be of substantial value (whether or not by itself) to the investigation for the pur-

---

[22] See PACE 1984, s 20, CJA 1988, s 93H and DTA 1994, s 55.
[23] See POCA 2002, ss 352 and 353.   [24] See s 348(7).

poses of which the application is made.[25] The search and seizure warrant applies to premises[26] and does not empower any appropriate officer to effect a stop, arrest or to search a person. The warrant can only be applied for by an appropriate officer, defined as a constable or customs officer if the warrant is sought for the purposes of a confiscation investigation or a money laundering investigation. If the warrant is sought for the purposes of a civil recovery investigation then the appropriate person is a named member of staff of the ARA.

These provisions in ss 352 to 356 are derived from the existing powers contained within the DTA 1994 and CJA 1988.[27] They are limited in their scope to those investigative purposes set out in the POCA in contrast with 'search warrants' which may be granted under separate provisions in the context of a general criminal investigation. The first purpose of the provisions is to permit the recovery of identifiable materials in circumstances where a production order has not been complied with, such as where it is not possible to locate or communicate with the possessor of the materials. This may be because that person is out of the jurisdiction and in those circumstances clearly a production order would have no effect. Secondly, the provisions aim to meet the need to obtain access to specified premises where it may not be possible to describe the material satisfactorily for the purposes of a production order application, and obtaining access to premises without a warrant is likely to prove impossible; for example, because the premises are where the particular suspect resides. **4.25**

2. Applying for the Warrant

A judge may issue a search and seizure warrant on application by an appropriate officer where one of the specified statutory alternatives are satisfied. The first is if a production order under s 345 has not been complied with and there are reasonable grounds for believing that the material specified in the warrant (or previously on the production order) is on the premises specified.[28] In the alternative under s 353 a series of complicated provisions distinguish between what must be established in each type of investigation. This depends upon the reasons why a production order is not available, and the sort of material, identifiable or otherwise, which it is believed might be recovered. The practicalities of communicating with the possessor of the material, or obtaining access without a warrant, including the risk of serious prejudice to any investigation in the absence of immediate access, are provided for by s 353(4) and (9). **4.26**

Under s 352(2) and (3) an application must state that a person specified in the application is subject to a confiscation investigation, a money laundering investigation or property specified in the application is subject to a civil recovery investigation. In addition the application must state the following: that the warrant is **4.27**

---

[25] Subject to qualifications in s 354.
[26] See PACE 1984 s 23 as to definition of 'premises'.
[27] See CJA 1988, s 93I and DTA 1994, s 56.
[28] See s 352(6)(a).

sought for the purposes of the investigation, that the warrant is sought in relation to premises specified and that the material is specified in the application, or there is material falling within s 353(6), (7), or (8) on the premises.

4.28   The requirement for the issue of a warrant contained in s 352(6)(a) is straightforward but the provisions of s 353 are likely to test the mind of the person drafting and making the application and may test the patience of the judge hearing the application. The section is satisfied if sub-section (2) applies and either of the first or second 'set of conditions' is complied with. Sub-section (2) applies if there are reasonable grounds for suspecting that certain circumstances exist—depending upon the particular type of investigation, for example, in a money laundering investigation, that the person specified in the application for the warrant has committed a money laundering offence.

4.29   The applicant must then satisfy one of two sets of 'conditions'. The 'first set of conditions'[29] is that there are reasonable grounds for believing that any material on the premises specified is likely to be of substantial value to the investigation, that it is in the public interest for the material to be obtained and it would not be appropriate to make a production order for any one or more of the 'reasons' in s 353(4). There are three 'reasons', that it is not practicable to communicate with any person against whom a production order could be made, secondly that it is not practicable to communicate with any person who would be required to comply with an order to grant entry to the premises and/or thirdly that the investigation might be seriously prejudiced unless an appropriate person is able to secure immediate access to the material.

4.30   The 'second set of conditions' are set out under sub-section (5). There are three 'conditions', first that there are reasonable grounds for believing that there is material on the premises specified and the material falls within sub-section (6), (7), or (8). Secondly that there are reasonable grounds for believing that it is in the public interest for the material to be obtained, and thirdly that any of the 'requirements' in sub-section (9) are met. Having regard to sub-sections (6), (7), or (8) the material is defined distinctly in terms of the type of investigation. In the case of a confiscation investigation[30] this includes material which cannot be identified at the time of the application, but it relates to the person specified in the application, relates to the issue of whether he has benefited from his criminal conduct or to the extent or whereabouts of his benefit and finally that it is likely to be of substantial value to the investigation for the purposes of which the warrant is sought. The third of the 'second set of conditions' as prescribed by sub-section (9) defines the 'requirements' in the following way: that it is not practicable to communicate with any person entitled to grant entry to the premises, that entry to the premises will not be granted unless a warrant is produced and that the investigations might be seriously prejudiced unless an appropriate person arriving at the premises is able to secure immediate entry to them.

---

[29] See s 353(3).   [30] See s 353(6).

The overall scheme of the provisions is best illustrated in Figure 4.1 at the end **4.31** of this chapter.

3. Additional Provisions and Execution of the Warrant—Confiscation and Money Laundering investigations

There are important provisions contained in ss 355 and 356. In confiscation and **4.32** money laundering investigations in relation to applications for and execution of search warrants the Secretary of State has the power to make modifications to the general rules that apply under PACE 1984, ss 15 (search warrants—safeguards), 16 (execution of warrants), 21 (access and copying) and 22 (retention). The applicable PACE 1984 provisions at ss 15 and 16 do 'have effect in relation to the issue to constables under any enactment, including an enactment contained in an Act passed after this Act'.[31]

Modifications have been made and the relevant Statutory Instrument[32] con- **4.33** tains in its Schedules the modified PACE 1984 sections as listed above. These modifications include the removal of the word 'constables' and the insertion of the phrase 'appropriate officer'. Thereafter the sections are modified so that they are distinctly POCA worded and relevant so as to pertain to 'a search and seizure warrant under section 352 of the Proceeds of Crime Act 2002 for the purposes of a confiscation investigation or a money laundering investigation'. Furthermore the modified s 15 specifically states that 'an entry on or search of premises under such a warrant is unlawful unless it complies with this section and is executed in accordance with section 16' (of the PACE 1984). The effect of those provisions and the safeguards continued within them remains the same as in the PACE and therefore any search and seizure warrant shall authorize an entry on one occasion only, entry and search under the warrant must be within one month from the date of its issue and must be at a reasonable hour unless it appears to the appropriate person executing it that the purpose of a search may be frustrated on an entry at a reasonable hour. Where the occupier, or another person, is present the appropriate person shall identify himself, the warrant should be produced and a copy provided as per s 16(5). Searches may only be conducted 'to the extent required for the purpose for which the warrant was issued' under s 16(8) and any items seized should be noted on the warrant which may subsequently be inspected by the occupier of the premises as per s 16(9) and (12). A record of seized items should also be provided, if requested, within a reasonable time under s 21(2), and supervised access provided to the materials themselves on application to the officer in charge of the investigation. In addition, photocopies ought to be provided unless the effect of this would be to prejudice the investigation (s 21(4) and (8)). A refusal may be challenged by way of judicial review of the Chief Constable's refusal to

---

[31] See PACE 1984, s 15(1).
[32] See Proceeds of Crime Act 2002 (Application of Police and Criminal Evidence Act 1984 and Police and Criminal Evidence (Northern Ireland) Order 1989) Order 2003 (S.I. 2003 No.174).

comply (see *Allen v Chief Constable of Cheshire Constabulary*[33]). Items seized may be retained 'for as long as is necessary in all the circumstances' (s 22(1)), although this does not apply to original documents or materials where a photocopy would suffice (s 22(4)).

4.34   In common with seizure of cash, existing search and production powers have been rationalized in the POCA for use in respect of the proceeds of all criminal conduct, whether drugs related or otherwise. Accordingly, the current powers contained within ss 55 and 56 of the DTA 1994 and ss 93H and 93I of the CJA 1988 are replaced. In addition, the power to apply for warrants to a circuit judge may now be exercised by the Director of the ARA and also any 'accredited financial investigator' as well as police and customs officers.

4.35   The modified s 22 extends the purposes for which anything seized under a confiscation or money laundering investigation may be retained. In its original form under PACE 1984, s 22 permitted retention of anything seized for use as 'evidence at a trial for an offence' and for 'forensic examination or for investigation in connection with an offence.' In its modified form there are two further uses, first 'as evidence in proceedings relating to the making of a confiscation order under the Drug Trafficking Offences Act 1986, Part VI of the Criminal Justice Act 1988, Part I of the Drug Trafficking Act 1994 or Part 2 of the Proceeds of Crime Act 2002' and secondly 'for forensic examination or for investigation in connection with a confiscation investigation or money laundering investigation.' As to the use of documents and materials for purposes other than the purpose of the investigation or resulting criminal proceedings, see *Preston BC v McGrath*.[34]

4. Additional Provisions and Execution of the Warrant – Civil Recovery Investigations

4.36   The modification of ss 15, 16, 21, and 22 of the PACE 1984 under SI 2003/174 relate only to a search and seizure warrant under section 352 of the POCA for the purposes of a confiscation investigation or a money laundering investigation. In relation to a search and seizure warrant sought in a civil recovery investigation separate provisions are provided for in s 356 of the Act. It is clear that warrants may be issued subject to conditions imposed by the High Court judge. This power is particularly important for two reasons: first, that the application may be made *ex parte* to a judge in chambers under s 356(2) and secondly, that the protections and safeguards contained in s 356 are not as extensive, nor as explicit, as those contained within the PACE 1984. There are, for example, no corresponding provisions to match the 'reasonable hour' provision of s 16(4), or other protective safeguards of the PACE 1984, s 16. Similarly, there are no specific provisions relating to facilities to be provided for access to or copying of documents seized under a confiscation or money laundering investigation warrant obtained by the

---

[33] *The Times*, 16 July 1988, CA.   [34] *The Times*, 19 May 2000, CA.

Director. It should be remembered that a search and seizure warrant does not merely encompass 'recoverable property' and 'associated property' identified in any production order, but also any materials relating to an investigation of its possession or location. The only limitation is that the material is likely to be of substantial value to the investigation and that it is in the public interest to recover it. Such material might well include documentation such as bank accounts, accounting documents and records, share certificates and registers, correspondence, company and personal files and many other forms of 'materials'. The absence of detailed safeguards is an unhelpful lacuna in the Act and likely to lead to considerable difficulty. These powers are available only where civil recovery proceedings have not yet begun and before the High Court is seized of the substantive case. The remedy may lie in an application to the issuing court which will have an inherent jurisdiction to control its own procedures. Alternatively, a civil action would have to be brought to recover the documents which might then be compromised by an undertaking to provide the necessary copies.

The warrant issued must be executed within a month from issue according to **4.37** s 356(4). Where the relevant materials are contained on a computer in the premises the warrant will provide authority for the information required to be produced in a form which is visible and legible and can be taken away (s 356(5)). Other materials seized may be copied (s 356(8)), although it is unclear whether this provision is designed to make such copies available to the investigator or the possessor of the documents. The originals of materials, as opposed to copies, may only be retained for so long as they are required for the purposes of the investigation for which the warrant was issued (s 356(9)), although this may include retaining them for the purposes of 'any legal proceedings' where the Director has reasonable grounds for believing that they might otherwise not be available as per s 356(10) and they may be retained until the proceedings are concluded.

5. Execution of the Warrant—Extent and Consequences

Under s 354 a search and seizure warrant does not confer the right to seize 'privi- **4.38** leged' material, defined in High Court terms. Furthermore a search and seizure warrant does not confer the right to seize 'excluded' material (for discussion in relation to production orders see para 4.13 above). The provisions will therefore seem to permit the seizure of 'special material' as they are silent as to any exclusion of the sort stated in s 354 in relation to material covered by privilege or defined as excluded.[35] In common with the exercise of other functions under the Act, s 449 provides protection for ARA staff when executing a search and seizure warrant. Under this section they are permitted, with the specific and personal authorization of the Director, to use pseudonyms in order to disguise their identities.

---

[35] See PACE 1984, s 14 for definitions of 'special material'.

D. DISCLOSURE ORDERS

1. Introduction

4.39 A disclosure order empowers the Director of the ARA to send a written notice to compel an individual to answer questions, provide information or produce documents. It can be sent to anyone 'the Director considers' has information that is relevant to the investigation. The power is available only to the Director and only in respect of confiscation and civil recovery investigations. No such order may be in relation to money laundering investigations.

2. Applying for the Order

4.40 In order to obtain a disclosure order the Director must apply to a judge. Under s 357(3) the application must state either that a person specified in the application is subject to a confiscation investigation carried out by the Director and the order is sought for the purposes of the investigation, or it must state that the property specified in the application is subject to a civil recovery investigation. The judge may make an order if the three 'requirements' in s 358 are met and these are first, that there must be reasonable grounds for suspecting that in the case of a confiscation investigation, the person specified in the application has benefited from his criminal conduct[36] or in the case of a civil recovery investigation, the property specified in the application for the order is recoverable property or associated property.[37] Secondly there must be reasonable grounds for believing that the information which may be provided under the order is likely to be of substantial value (whether or not by itself) to the investigation for the purposes of which the order is sought. The third requirement is that there must be reasonable grounds for believing that it is in the public interest for the information to be provided, having regard to the benefit likely to accrue to the investigation if the information is obtained.

4.41 In considering any application for a disclosure order it is thought that a judge should have regard to whether any other applications have been made, for example for a production order, and whether those applications were granted and if so whether they were effective. In addition consideration may have to be given as to whether alternative investigative tools such as a production order, would in the circumstances be inadequate. Applications may have to have regard to these factors as the proportionality test (the public interest) has been specifically included in s 358(4).

---

[36] See ss 413 and 416.   [37] See ss 304–310, 316, 414, and 416.

3. Effect of the Order

The notice may require the recipient to respond in any or all of three ways, first to **4.42** answer questions, either at a time specified or at once, at a place so specified, secondly to provide information specified in the notice, by a time and in a manner so specified and/or thirdly to produce documents or documents of a description specified in the notice, either at or by a time so specified or at once, and in a manner so specified.[38] The section defines 'relevant information' as information (whether or not contained in a document) which the Director considers to be relevant to the investigation. That is a convenient and circular assertion akin to saying 'it is relevant because I say so' but one which is expected will have to pass the discretion of the judge who considers the application and evaluates the 'substantial value' and 'public interest' requirements in s 358. A person may not in any event by virtue of s 361, be required to answer any privileged question, provide any privileged information or produce any privileged document, except that a lawyer may be required to provide the name and address of a client of his. In addition by virtue of s 361(5) a person may not be required to produce excluded material. The definitions of privilege and excluded material are consistent with those parts of the Act as discussed previously. Similarly this part of the Act is silent on 'special material' and there is no other express statement in relation to any other type of material. It would appear therefore that the Act seeks to overrule any apparent restriction on the disclosure of information which may arise by virtue of contract or otherwise.

A disclosure order has the benefit for the Director of giving continuing **4.43** powers for the duration of the investigation rather than having to make separate applications for a production order. Furthermore a disclosure order will allow for relevant individuals to be identified and interviewed in order to further the investigation, particularly where there may be complex material to consider.

The Code of Practice issued under s 377 of the POCA is discussed later in this **4.44** chapter but it is worthy of note that in respect of disclosure orders, the Code is very detailed in respect of all stages of the order's life. The Code contains sections dedicated to the application stage, execution, interview, legal and financial advice, persons who may be present at interviews (appropriate adults), the role of persons who may be present at interviews, the conduct of interviews, the interviewer's obligations, tape recording and the recording of any action taken under a disclosure order. In any case the Code should be considered at each stage to ensure that the appropriate safeguards are followed.

4. Use of a Disclosure Order

There is potential for concern as to how these orders might be used. The Director **4.45** is not permitted to apply for them as a tool in a general criminal investigation,

---

[38] See s 357(4).

because the Director can only apply for them in a criminal confiscation investigation. However what of the situation where in a confiscation investigation the Director successfully applies for a disclosure order and under it information is disclosed to the Director that suggests the commission of a separate offence unconnected to the matter upon which the confiscation investigation is based? Alternatively what of the position where a respondent complies with compelled disclosure and then a separate criminal investigation is mounted which seeks to use that information provided under the disclosure order?

4.46 In the light of *Saunders v UK*[39] the Government no doubt included s 360 of the Act so as to protect a person who makes a statement in response to a disclosure order, the section states that any such statement 'may not be used in evidence against him in criminal proceedings'. In sub-section (2) there are four qualifications to that bar contained in s 360(1), first in relation to confiscation proceedings, secondly in relation to a prosecution for having failed without reasonable excuse to comply with the disclosure order,[40] and thirdly in respect of an offence under s 5 of the Perjury Act 1911.[41] It is the fourth qualification of the bar to using a compelled statement that is of greater concern. Under sub-section (2)(d) the bar does not apply 'on a prosecution for some other offence where, in giving evidence, the person makes a statement inconsistent with the statement mentioned in subsection (1)'. The ability to make use of the statement is qualified itself by sub-section (3) which states that a statement may not be used by virtue of sub-section (2)(d) against a person unless evidence relating to it is adduced or a question relating to it is asked 'by him or on his behalf in proceedings arising out of the prosecution.'

4.47 Quite how the provisions of this section will be interpreted in practice will be particularly interesting to follow. There is no indication given in the Act that leave of the judge is required before such an inconsistent statement can be used against an individual. It would seem to be fundamental that leave would need to be granted in such circumstances otherwise a defendant's right to a fair trial under Article 6 might be infringed (as might his Article 8(2) rights have been in the first place through the application of a disclosure order and the criminal offence contained in s 359(1)). Furthermore the Act does not indicate which party in a case may use such rebuttal evidence and therefore it may be open for use by the Crown and/or co-defendants.

5. Penalties for Failure to Comply

4.48 Failure to comply, without reasonable excuse, with a disclosure order is an offence punishable summarily with imprisonment up to six months or a fine not exceeding level 5, or both under s 359(2). False or misleading statements in response to

---

[39] 23 EHRR 313.
[40] See s 359.
[41] Or art. 10 of the Perjury (Northern Ireland) Order 1979 (SI 1979/1714).

an order, whether deliberate or reckless, also amount to an offence punishable on summary conviction with six months' imprisonment and/or a fine. On indictment that sentence may be up to a maximum of two years, as per s 359(4).

E. CUSTOMER INFORMATION ORDERS

1. Introduction

A customer information order requires banks or other financial institutions to **4.49** provide details of any accounts held by the person under investigation. The order may require all such institutions, or a selection of them, or named institutions, to comply with the order. The scheme applies to each type of proceeds of crime investigation but, in this context, the definition of 'money laundering offence' is extended from the main offences under ss 327–329 to cover offences under s 18 of the Terrorism Act 2000, and conduct abroad which would constitute any such offence if carried out in the United Kingdom.

Such potentially disruptive orders should not be made speculatively and under **4.50** ss 369(7) and 378(2) applications are required to be made or authorized by the Director of the ARA or a police superintendent or senior investigator of similar rank. The precise requirements relating to the applicant depend on the nature of the investigation and are set out in detail in s 378. An application for a customer information order may be made *ex parte* to a judge in chambers.[42]

The definition of 'customer information' under s 364 is modelled on that con- **4.51** tained in Sch 6 to the Terrorism Act 2000 and requires detailed information to be produced, in accordance with the lists in s 364(2) and (3), depending upon whether the person named is an individual or a corporate entity. This includes information in relation to a person who holds, or has held, an account or accounts at the financial institution. Under sub-sections (2) and (3) the information includes account number(s), the person's full name, date of birth, most recent address and any previous addresses, the date of opening and closing the account, the identification evidence as obtained by the financial institution under or for the purposes of any legislation relating to money laundering, any joint account details and any details of accounts of which he is a signatory. By virtue of s 364(4) the Secretary of State may by order add to or subtract from these categories of information.

As with the disclosure order, there are penalties to secure compliance, although, **4.52** since the subjects of the orders are institutions rather than individuals, these are purely financial. Fines for knowingly or recklessly making false or misleading statements are unlimited. Once again, since this is a power to compel disclosure of information with sanctions, there are provisions to prevent the use of information in criminal proceedings against any institution, save in limited and defined circumstances. These are discussed further at para 4.56 below.

---

[42] See s 368.

2. Applying for the Order

4.53 Applications may be made *ex parte* to a judge in chambers under s 369(1) and the rules of court will govern both applications for orders in the Crown Court in confiscation and money laundering cases, and for their variation and discharge s 369(2)–(6). Proceedings in the High Court in relation to civil recovery will be the subject of separate rules. An accredited financial adviser, a constable, or a customs officer may not make an application, or apply to vary or discharge an application, unless he is a 'senior appropriate officer' as defined in s 378. In relation to a civil recovery investigation only the Director of the ARA falls within this category for these purposes.[43]

4.54 Under s 363(2) the application must state that the person specified is subject to a confiscation or money laundering investigation, or alternatively, that the property specified is subject to a civil recovery investigation and that the person specified in the application appears to hold the property. The application must also state that the order is sought for the purposes of the investigation and must identify the financial institution or financial institutions, either individually or by class or description.[44] The statutory requirements depend upon the nature of the investigation, whether it be a confiscation, a civil recovery or a money laundering investigation.

4.55 Under s 365 there are three requirements and for these purposes they are considered in the context of a money laundering investigation only.[45] First there must be reasonable grounds for suspecting that the person specified in the application for the order has committed a money laundering offence, secondly there must be reasonable grounds for believing that customer information which may be provided is likely to be of substantial value (whether or not by itself) to the investigation and lastly that there are reasonable grounds for believing that it is in the public interest for the customer information to be provided, having regard to the benefit likely to accrue to the investigation if the information is obtained. As commented upon before, the distinction between reasonable 'suspicion' and reasonable 'belief' is worthy of note as the latter requires a greater degree of objective proof.

3. Non-compliance Offences

4.56 The statute requires a customer information order to have effect in spite of any restriction on the disclosure of information however imposed. It therefore could not be resisted for example upon the basis of contract, confidentiality or data protection legislation. Under s 366 a financial institution may commit two potential offences. The summary only offence under s 366(1) is committed if without reasonable excuse the financial institution fails to comply with a requirement

---

[43] See s 378(3).　　[44] See s 363(3) and (4).　　[45] See s 364.

imposed on it under a customer information order. This offence is punishable by a fine not exceeding level 5 on the standard scale. The triable either way offence under s 366(3) is committed if a financial institution in 'purported compliance' makes a statement which it knows to be false or misleading in a material particular or recklessly makes a statement which is false or misleading in a material particular. This offence is punishable on summary conviction with a fine not exceeding the statutory maximum and on conviction on indictment, to a fine.

The provisions of s 367 are similar to those in s 360 relating to disclosure orders **4.57** and the use or otherwise of statements made under compulsion. Under s 367 statements made by financial institutions in response to customer information orders may not be used in evidence against that financial institution in criminal proceedings. However that bar does not apply if the statement is to be used in proceedings relating to 'confiscation'[46] or for the prosecution of an offence under s 366(1) or (3) or in a prosecution of 'some other offence' where in giving evidence the financial institution makes a statement inconsistent with the statement made under the customer information order. In this instance the statement may not be used unless evidence relating to it is adduced or a question relating to it is asked by or on behalf of the financial institution in the proceedings arising out of the prosecution. See para 4.45 above for a consideration of the ambit of using the respondent's previously compelled statement.

F. ACCOUNT MONITORING ORDERS

1. Introduction

An account monitoring order requires a financial institution to provide to an **4.58** appropriate officer details of all transactions on a specified suspect account or accounts for the specified period stated in the order. The order is limited to ninety days beginning with the day on which the order is made. An application for an account monitoring order may be made *ex parte* to a judge in chambers.[47] Under s 374 an account monitoring order 'has effect in spite of any restriction on the disclosure of information however imposed'. As would also appear to be the case with customer information orders, an account monitoring order could not be resisted for example upon the basis of contract, confidentiality or data protection legislation.

As with disclosure and customer information orders, the institution is being **4.59** compelled to provide information, and accordingly the section spells out the limitations on the use of this evidence in any criminal prosecution of the provider so as to avoid a breach of the rule against self-incrimination. However, unlike these other new powers, no separate offence is created to sanction non-compliance with this provision, and so it is simply policed by the ordinary powers arising in

---

[46] Parts 2 or 4 of the Act.   [47] See s 373.

contempt proceedings. Account monitoring orders have effect as if they were orders of the Crown Court and are enforceable as such.

2. Applying for the Order

4.60 Under s 370(2) and (3)(a) the application must state that a person or property specified in the application is the subject of a proceeds of crime investigation, and confirm that the order is sought for the purposes of the investigation. The 'account information' sought must be specified in the application and must relate to an account or accounts held at the institution by the person specified, whether solely or jointly with another as per s 370(4). Applying s 370(5) the application may cover all accounts so held by the person specified, or a particular description of accounts, or a particular account or accounts and requires the institution to provide to an appropriate officer the information specified in the order in the manner and at the time and frequency indicated. The length of the order, up to a maximum of ninety days, will also be included in the application and set out in any order.

4.61 The requirements that must be met under s 371 are identical to those pertaining to production orders under s 353, and customer information orders under s 365, in that an association between the identified person or property and the particular investigation must be established. In the case of a money laundering investigation, the relationship is a direct one arising from the suspicion (on reasonable grounds) that *he* has committed a money laundering offence. Similarly, in confiscation cases, the person specified must be suspected (on reasonable grounds) of having 'benefited' from *his* criminal conduct. In civil recovery cases, the relationship with culpable conduct is indirect. There must be reasonable grounds for believing that the property specified is recoverable or associated property, and accordingly linked to criminal conduct. However, the conduct of the holder of the property is not in question. The mere fact that there are reasonable grounds to suspect that he holds all or some of the property, innocently or otherwise, is sufficient to trigger the power to apply for an order.

4.62 Similarly as before, tests of 'substantial value to the investigation' and ' public interest' must be considered by the judge hearing the application[48] and in that sense consideration may need to be given to alternative, less intrusive orders which may be more proportionate. Clearly each application must be considered upon its own facts but there may be cases where other orders might be deemed more appropriate in the circumstances.

4.63 As before with disclosure orders and customer information orders there is a bar (in this case under s 372) to the use of a statement made by a financial institution in response to an account monitoring order, against it in criminal proceedings.

---

[48] See s 371(5) and (6).

The caveats in s 372(2) to that general bar are identical to those as discussed before in the case of customer information orders.

G. CODE OF PRACTICE GOVERNING THE INVESTIGATION POWERS

The Code of Practice issued under s 377 applies to functions undertaken under **4.64** Chap 2 of Pt 8 of the Act. It places obligations on all those who apply for or execute any of the five powers listed above (at para 4.04) and stipulates how applications should be made and how the execution of the various powers should be conducted.

It should be noted that if an investigator is seeking to perform a duty prescribed **4.65** under this part of the Act then the Code applies to the exclusion of any other code of practice, for example as issued pursuant to the PACE 1984. In conducting investigations into the commission of drug trafficking *offences* under the DTA 1994, investigators will still have recourse to those production order and search warrant provisions under the DTA which are still in force and this code does not apply to them. However in respect of investigations into the *benefit* derived from such offences, the provisions of the POCA now apply and therefore if the appropriate POCA provisions are adopted during the course of an investigation into such benefit[49] this Code will apply.

Importantly the Code seeks to emphasize the need for European Convention **4.66** rights to be afforded proper consideration before an application is made and to consider whether there may be less intrusive means which could achieve the necessary objectives. The most obvious example is that contained in Article 8 and the right to privacy, clearly an order or warrant has the potential to infringe an individual's convention right. The Code affirms the need for such an infringement to be 'proportionate to the benefit to be gained from making an order or warrant.' This affirmation contained in the Code will not by itself automatically legitimise any application which may be subsequently challenged. It is at least indicative of the care that is suggested is taken in applying for orders and warrants. The Code is evidence itself therefore that the officers must apply that test themselves in the application stage.[50]

The Code emphasizes that the officer making the application should have close **4.67** regard to the statutory requirements that must be met in order to obtain an order or warrant before making the application, including the importance of the objective test involved in considering whether there are reasonable grounds for suspecting that a person has benefited from his criminal conduct or has committed a money laundering offence. An application stating that the officer has reasonable

---

[49] Such as in relation to a production order or search and seizure warrant.
[50] See paras 10 to 12 of the Code of Practice.

grounds clearly must still pass the statutory tests as applied by the individual judge who of course may not be so satisfied. The Code clearly states the need for the basis for any application on terms of the reasonable grounds for believing that the material or information is likely to be of substantial value to the investigation and that it is in the public interest to obtain it. The Code advises that any officer carefully balance the public interest against the disadvantages to the person against whom the order is being made. This is necessary and practical advice as the basis for such an application (successful or otherwise) may be a matter for subsequent challenge in a number of possible ways, such as a complaint that Article 8 rights have been infringed.

4.68 The Code advises the officer serving any order, warrant or notice as to the information that should be provided to the recipient and the warnings that ought to be given as to non-compliance. In addition the Code advises that an application may be made, and the service of an order or warrant may be effected by, an officer identifying themselves with a pseudonym subject to the appropriate authority of the Director. This extreme permission does not extend to appropriate officers working outside the ARA such as police officers or accredited financial investigators.

4.69 It is stated under s 377(6) that a failure to comply with any provision of the Code of Practice does not *of itself* render the individual liable to criminal or civil proceedings. However by virtue of s 377(7) the Code of Practice is admissible in evidence in criminal or civil proceedings and 'a court' may take account of any failure to comply with its provisions 'in determining any question in the proceedings' (guilt or liability). The Code of Practice will clearly be vital in monitoring the stages involved in applying for the different types of specified warrants and orders and the subsequent service and execution of them.

H. OVERSEAS EVIDENCE

1. Principles and Application

4.70 Obtaining evidence from overseas in confiscation proceedings is governed by s 376 of the Act. In order to seek the assistance of the overseas authorities in this regard a letter of request must be issued. Under s 376 there are two ways in which a letter of request may be issued, first on an application to a judge under s 376(2), or secondly by the Director himself under the provisions of s 376(3). The considerations in respect of both routes for obtaining overseas evidence are the same. The issuing of a letter of request is triggered if either thinks that there is 'evidence' in a country or territory outside the United Kingdom either that a person subject to the investigation has benefited from his criminal conduct or of the extent or whereabouts of that person's benefit from his criminal conduct. In an application to a judge to issue a letter of request either the Director or 'a person subject to the investigation' may apply. It seems unlikely that such a person would initiate such a procedure as in order to do so they would be submitting to the judge that they had benefited from their own criminal conduct.

On a literal reading of the provision, the evidence must be probative of the fact   **4.71** that he *has* benefited and, if so, where his benefit is to be found. There appears to be no provision for letters of request to issue to trace material showing the opposite to be the case. What if there may be evidence overseas that a person subject to a confiscation investigation might not have benefited to the extent submitted against him? If the Director's assertions in the confiscation proceedings were based on evidence of 'foreign' funds coming to the person's benefit in this jurisdiction, the individual concerned may wish to seek for themselves the evidence that establishes that these funds relate to an entirely unconnected and innocent matter. It may be in the circumstances that the evidence required to rebut any assertion would not be available to them through the procedure in s 376. Whether this will be interpreted, in accordance with the HRA 1998, so as to provide 'equality of arms' is clearly open for debate.

2. Process after Grant

Once a letter of request is issued in either of the two ways, it must be sent to the   **4.72** Secretary of State. Thereafter under s 376(6) if the Secretary of State 'believes it is appropriate to do so' he may forward it to a relevant court, tribunal, or other authority in the jurisdiction identified. In cases of urgency the letters may be sent directly to the court or tribunal without intervention by the Home Office under s 376(6) and (7). Generally in its fight against crime the Government has sought to broaden the means for international mutual assistance and the POCA provisions are consistent with that. As of 26 April 2004 Pt 1 of the Crime (International Co-operation) Act 2003 came into force and published at the same time was 'Mutual Legal Assistance Guidelines: Obtaining Assistance in the UK and Overseas.'[51]

I. PREJUDICING AN INVESTIGATION

1. Elements of the Offence

Under s 342 an offence is committed if a person knows or suspects that an 'inves-   **4.73** tigation'[52] is being or is about to be conducted and makes a disclosure which is likely to prejudice it or 'falsifies, conceals, destroys or otherwise disposes of relevant documents or causes or permits another to do so.'[53] The person concerned must know or suspect that the documents are relevant to the investigation or he

---

[51] Available at www.homeoffice.gov.uk.
[52] In this context 'investigation' is a confiscation, a civil recovery, or a money laundering investigation.
[53] s 342(2)(a) and (b).

intends to conceal any fact disclosed by the documents from the 'appropriate officer.'[54] If the opposite is the case, in either case, under s 342(6) no offence would be committed without the requisite knowledge or suspicion of relevance or intention to conceal.

2. Avoiding Liability

4.74 The section provides for several exemptions where either the existence of particular facts will mean that no offence is committed or, in the alternative, the absence of particular facts will have the same effect. Those contained in s 342(6) are identified above. In addition no offence will be committed if a person does not know or suspect that the disclosure is likely to prejudice an investigation, or if the disclosure is made in the exercise of a function under the POCA or other 'enactment relating to criminal conduct'[55] or importantly in the context of the legal profession, if the person is a professional legal adviser and the disclosure was made to a client, or representative of a client, in connection with the giving of legal advice or to any person in connection with legal proceedings or contemplated legal proceedings.

3. Legal Profession

4.75 Legal advisers must ensure that they work within the Act and apply the guidance issued by the relevant professional bodies. In Chapter 6 'Money Laundering' the duties and obligations of solicitors and barristers are considered in detail having regard to the judgment of Dame Elizabeth Butler-Sloss, P in the case of *P v P*[56] and the coming into force of the Money Laundering Regulations 2003. The *P v P* case was principally concerned with the potential effect of ancillary relief in matrimonial proceedings for liability under the money laundering offences and the impact upon the ambit of legal professional privilege and what information may be provided to a client and/or other person in the giving of legal advice.

4.76 The reader is recommended to consider those appropriate paragraphs not least because there are clear parallels between the 'prejudicing an investigation' offence and the 'tipping off' offence under s 333, and the potential for solicitors and barristers to be placed in demanding situations by virtue of the POCA provisions is clear.

4.77 A solicitor may be consulted by his client who believes that investigations are being made into his financial affairs. The client makes it clear that if this is the case he will destroy his accounting records. The solicitor suspects, with good cause, that an investigation has begun or is imminent. If he tells the client this, and the

---

[54] As defined in s 378.
[55] To include investigators and law enforcement officials who make disclosures during the course of an investigation.
[56] [2003] EWHC 2260 (Fam).

reasons for his suspicion, he may plainly prejudice the investigation. The client is undoubtedly about to embark upon a criminal offence. Obviously, if the solicitor assists him in destroying materials, or in forging accounts or documents, the position would seem to be clear enough. Incriminating documents in the possession of the solicitor are more difficult. Here retention alone may amount to concealment from the investigation. In addition, does the solicitor possess the 'intention' to further this criminal purpose by making a mere disclosure which he knows will have inevitable and criminal consequences? If so, the legal privilege exemption would appear to have very limited effect.

We suspect that the prudent solicitor would avoid a situation in which such an argument had to be relied upon. In any event, the confirmation of the client's suspicions from information known to the solicitor might well be considered to fall outside 'the giving of legal advice' or 'in connection with legal proceedings or contemplated legal proceedings' under s 342(4). These difficulties strongly underline the increased need for caution on the part of legal advisers, and that specialist professional advice should be sought at the earliest moment should such a dilemma arise.   **4.78**

4. Penalties

An offence under this section is triable either way and is punishable summarily with a fine and/or imprisonment for up to six months and on indictment to a maximum of five years (s 342(7)).   **4.79**

4.80

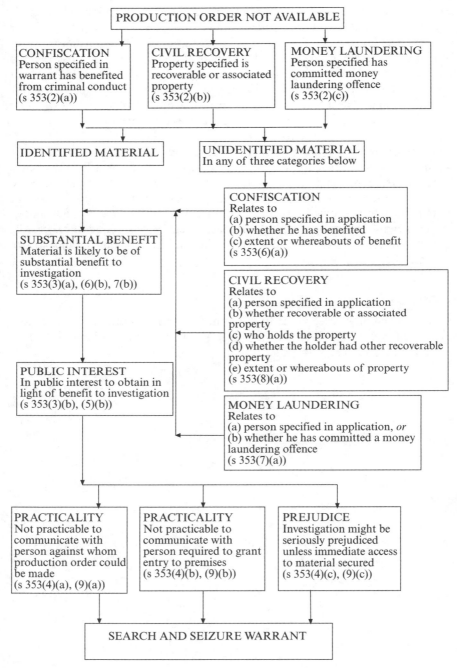

PRODUCTION ORDER NOT AVAILABLE

CONFISCATION
Person specified in
warrant has benefited
from criminal conduct
(s 353(2)(a))

CIVIL RECOVERY
Property specified is
recoverable or associated
property
(s 353(2)(b))

MONEY LAUNDERING
Person specified has
committed money
laundering offence
(s 353(2)(c))

IDENTIFIED MATERIAL

UNIDENTIFIED MATERIAL
In any of three categories below

CONFISCATION
Relates to
(a) person specified in application
(b) whether he has benefited
(c) extent or whereabouts of benefit
(s 353(6)(a))

SUBSTANTIAL BENEFIT
Material is likely to be of
substantial benefit to
investigation
(s 353(3)(a), (6)(b), 7(b))

CIVIL RECOVERY
Relates to
(a) person specified in application
(b) whether recoverable or associated
property
(c) who holds the property
(d) whether the holder had other recoverable
property
(e) extent or whereabouts of property
(s 353(8)(a))

PUBLIC INTEREST
In public interest to obtain in
light of benefit to investigation
(s 353(3)(b), (5)(b))

MONEY LAUNDERING
Relates to
(a) person specified in application, *or*
(b) whether he has committed a money
laundering offence
(s 353(7)(a))

PRACTICALITY
Not practicable to
communicate with
person against whom
production order could
be made
(s 353(4)(a), (9)(a))

PRACTICALITY
Not practicable to
communicate with
person required to grant
entry to premises
(s 353(4)(b), (9)(b))

PREJUDICE
Investigation might be
seriously prejudiced
unless immediate access
to material secured
(s 353(4)(c), (9)(c))

SEARCH AND SEIZURE WARRANT

Fig. 4.1

4.81

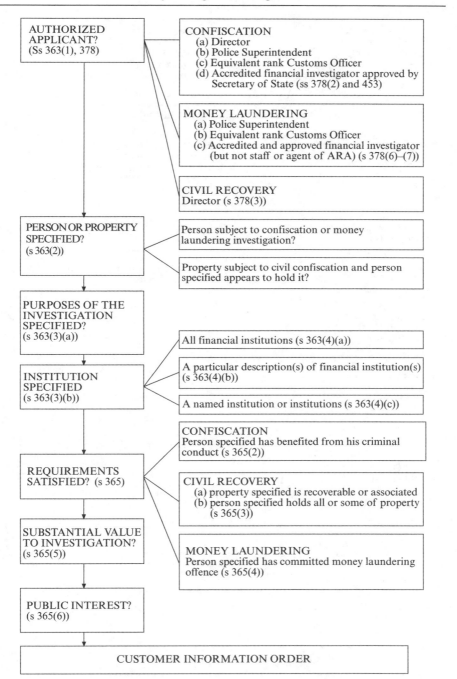

FIG. 4.2

4.82

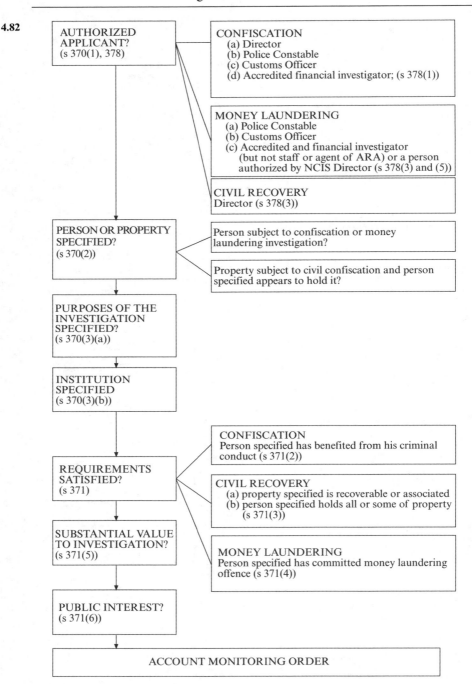

CONFISCATION
(a) Director
(b) Police Constable
(c) Customs Officer
(d) Accredited financial investigator; (s 378(1))

MONEY LAUNDERING
(a) Police Constable
(b) Customs Officer
(c) Accredited and financial investigator
(but not staff or agent of ARA) or a person
authorized by NCIS Director (s 378(3) and (5))

CIVIL RECOVERY
Director (s 378(3))

AUTHORIZED
APPLICANT?
(s 370(1), 378)

PERSON OR PROPERTY
SPECIFIED?
(s 370(2))

Person subject to confiscation or money
laundering investigation?

Property subject to civil confiscation and person
specified appears to hold it?

PURPOSES OF THE
INVESTIGATION
SPECIFIED?
(s 370(3)(a))

INSTITUTION
SPECIFIED
(s 370(3)(b))

REQUIREMENTS
SATISFIED?
(s 371)

CONFISCATION
Person specified has benefited from his criminal
conduct (s 371(2))

CIVIL RECOVERY
(a) property specified is recoverable or associated
(b) person specified holds all or some of property
(s 371(3))

MONEY LAUNDERING
Person specified has committed money laundering
offence (s 371(4))

SUBSTANTIAL VALUE
TO INVESTIGATION?
(s 371(5))

PUBLIC INTEREST?
(s 371(6))

ACCOUNT MONITORING ORDER

Fig. 4.3

5

RESTRAINT PROCEEDINGS

A. OVERVIEW

1. Introduction

The relevant provisions are contained in Pt 2 of the Proceeds of Crime Act **5.01** (POCA) 2002. A restraint order has the effect of freezing property in order to preserve those assets that may subsequently be the subject of a confiscation order. It prohibits the person specified in the order from dealing with any 'realizable property held by him' whether or not he is the suspected offender (or the defendant if criminal proceedings have commenced).

5.02   Under earlier legislation, either a restraint or charging order could be made in the High Court only where:

(a) proceedings had been started;

(b) an investigation was under way and charges were anticipated, or

(c) an application had been, or was about to be, made for further confiscation (for example, on reconsideration of the amount of a defendant's benefit).

5.03   The POCA 2002 makes a number of important changes to the previous regime. First, charging orders are abolished. Secondly, the jurisdiction in respect of restraint orders is transferred to the Crown Court. Thirdly, the law is amended to permit a power to apply for a restraint order at a point in advance of the apprehension of any criminal charges. Accordingly, changes in legal aid provision ensure that funding from the Legal Services Commission is available pre-charge for restraint proceedings under the Access to Justice Act 1999. Previously, the High Court exercised a discretion to release restrained funds for the purposes of reasonable living and legal expenses. This discretion is maintained in the Crown Court, although it is in an extremely restricted form. By virtue of s 41(4), the court is prevented from releasing funds, either to the defendant or the recipient of a tainted gift, for legal expenses in relation to 'offences in respect of which the restraint order is made'. Instead, such a person has access to public funds provided by the Legal Services Commission for any proceedings in the Crown Court. Once again, this appears to be a deliberate strategy on the part of the Government to avoid the dissipation of restrained assets, and has the likely effect of forcing a respondent to instruct a lawyer who is prepared to act on a public funded basis.

5.04   The relevant ss 40 to 47 provide the Crown Court with the power to make a variety of orders for the purpose of ensuring that relevant property is properly restrained and preserved, including the power to require a person to disclose his assets. In fact s 41(7) states very clearly that 'the court may make such order as it believes is appropriate for the purpose of ensuring that the restraint order is effective'. The powers are similar to those previously available under residuary High Court powers. Failure to comply with such an order, or with any order restraining property, will be punished as a contempt of court. Under the High Court jurisdiction, in order to comply with the common law rule against self-incrimination, a principle developed that orders for a statement of assets to be provided ought to be conditional upon the information not being used in a prosecution for any offence of the maker (*Re O (Disclosure Order: Disclosure of Assets)*.[1]

---

[1] [1991] 2 WLR 475.

It is submitted that orders drawn under the new procedures in the Crown Court should contain a clear and specific statement to this effect. That may not, of course, restrict the use of such statements following conviction for the purposes of making a confiscation order.

5.05 There are no less than seven situations in which a restraint order can be imposed under s 40. They are termed 'conditions' and a restraint order can be made if any of them are satisfied. The first five conditions are triggered by the court having reasonable cause to believe that an alleged offender (or defendant) has benefited from 'his criminal conduct' but that a final confiscation order has not yet been achieved. The remaining two are concerned with preserving property held by a convicted defendant which may form the subject of a final confiscation order, adjusted to take account of new evidence as to calculation of the defendant's benefit or the available amount to be confiscated. It is important to remember that the court retains a discretion as to whether or not to make a restraint order even where the statutory conditions are satisfied. The underlying principle of the legislation is to protect against the dissipation of assets. In the words of Glidewell LJ, a restraint order should only be made:

if there is a reasonable apprehension that, without it, realisable property may be dissipated ... if there is no such risk or the risk is merely fanciful, the order ought not to be made since, ex hypothesi, it would not be necessary for the achievement of its only proper purpose (Re AJ and DJ[2]).

5.06 The detailed provisions relating to applications, discharge, variation and appeals against restraint orders are summarized below, and the principles to be applied by the courts and receivers in the exercise of their powers are set out in detail below.

B. CONDITIONS FOR EXERCISE OF POWERS

1. Crown Court Rules

5.07 Practitioners must consult the Crown Court (Confiscation, Restraint and Receivership) Rules 2003 (SI 2003/421)(hereafter referred to as the Crown Court Rules 2003). These Rules came into force on 24 March 2003 and make provision for the procedure to be followed in proceedings in the Crown Court under Pt 2 of the POCA relating to confiscation orders, restraint orders and the appointment of receivers. They are included in full in Appendix 7.

5.08 Under r 16 the application for a restraint order may be made without notice, it must be made in writing and it must be supported by a witness statement which must contain certain specified features. These features are as follows:

(a) the grounds for the application;

---

[2] CA, 9 December 1992.

(b) the details of the realizable property in respect of which the applicant is seeking the order and specify the person holding that property;

(c) the grounds for, and full details of, any application for an ancillary order under s 41(7) of the Act for the purposes of ensuring that the restraint order is effective; and

(d) where the application is made by an accredited financial investigator, a statement that he has been authorized to make the application under s 68 of the Act.

2. Application Before Charge

5.09 The earliest time an application can arise is where a criminal investigation has been initiated in England or Wales.[3] It is unnecessary for the prosecution to await the formulation of charges or even anticipate a charge arising. There may be insufficient evidence to charge with any offence, or even generate the necessary suspicion to arrest a suspect for an offence, and yet enough to form the view that a person 'has benefited from his criminal conduct'. The very broad definitions contained in s 76 of 'benefit' and 'criminal conduct' apply to this provision and, accordingly, it is irrelevant where or when any such criminal behaviour took place. In these circumstances the investigation team is entitled to commence restraint proceedings, notwithstanding that no criminal charge may ever be brought. The team will do so by persuading the court, to the civil standard, of its reasonable suspicions, and by indicating that an investigation into an unspecified offence is under way. Hearsay evidence is admissible, in whatever degree, to establish 'reasonable cause to believe' by virtue of s 46(1).

5.10 The provision highlights an uncomfortable fit between restraint as a mechanism for preserving property for confiscation following conviction, and the wider purposes of the Act, which are to recover the proceeds of criminal conduct irrespective of whether a conviction is achieved. The former has a focus upon criminal charges and the commencement of proceedings which may conclude with the making of a confiscation order on conviction. Previous arrangements, which required a charge to be 'anticipated', reflected that focus. The wider focus of the POCA 2002 requires the time frame to be shifted back and uncoupled from the decision to charge with an offence. This is necessary because confiscation is no longer confined to an offender's particular criminal conduct but may, if he has a 'criminal lifestyle', also attach to benefits from his general criminal conduct. The results of this shift are an extended power with reduced protection against precipitate use, and the need to build in provisions to compensate those who may have been adversely effected.

5.11 The practical difficulties and potential adverse effects should not be underestimated. On the face of it, an individual's assets may be frozen for a protracted

---

[3] See s 40(2)(a).

period whether or not he is accused, or may be accused, of a drugs trafficking or acquisitive offence. There need be no nexus between an offence being investigated and the criminal conduct which has led to benefit in the past. The initial application is likely to be made ex parte to a judge in chambers as is permitted under s 42(1)(b). Evidence, including hearsay evidence, is admissible and is likely to be based in large part upon intelligence materials. Public interest immunity principles may deny access to these on the part of the suspect or his lawyers. No time limit is placed on any subsequent investigation save that the order may be discharged on application by the respondent if 'within a reasonable time proceedings for the offence are not started' (s 42(7)).

An ill-judged action for restraint, coupled with a protracted investigation, may **5.12** spell commercial disaster or financial ruin for an individual. It seems unlikely that the power of a circuit judge to order compensation to be paid in cases 'of serious default' is an adequate remedy in such circumstances. Whether, as a result, the regime is compliant with Convention rights to peaceful enjoyment of property is a matter of some interest.

3. Application Following Charge

After a suspect has been charged, an order for restraint may be made against any **5.13** criminal defendant prior to the conclusion of his trial where 'there is reasonable cause to believe that [he] has benefited from his criminal conduct' (s 40(3)). Under s 42(6) the order will be discharged automatically at the conclusion of the proceedings. At that stage either the defendant will be acquitted or upon conviction the court will exercise its powers to make a confiscation order in respect of the preserved property. Where no confiscation order is ultimately made, but the defendant is convicted of the offence for which proceedings were started, no compensation under s 72 is available for any loss arising as a result of restraint.

4. Application Following Conviction

There are a number of circumstances following conviction in which considera- **5.14** tion, or reconsideration, of a confiscation order against a defendant may require property to be preserved. These include applications for reconsideration under ss 19, 20, 21, or 22, and applications to proceed with confiscation proceedings against an absconding defendant under ss 27 or 28. Where such applications are pending, or have been made but not yet concluded, s 40(4)–(6) provides power to apply to the court for restraint. The court must consider the prospects of the relevant application succeeding, but will make the order where there is 'reasonable cause to believe' that it will succeed, unless the court accepts that 'there has been undue delay in continuing the application' or it is satisfied that the prosecutor does not 'intend to proceed' (s 40(8)). 'Undue delay' is not defined or expanded upon in the Act. Where an initial application for confiscation has failed—for example, because of a failure to establish 'benefit'—or is considered by the prosecution to be unsatisfactory in relation to the 'available amount' confiscated under the order, there will be a strong temptation to preserve the asset position, pending continuing enquiries, in the hope of new evidence coming to light. Such investigations may be extensive. The Act does not appear to recognize the potential for loss suffered by the subject of any application for a variation of an order in providing for compensation under s 72. Since the defendant fails to satisfy the first condition of being acquitted, he is not eligible even where serious default is shown.

C. EFFECTS OF A RESTRAINT ORDER

5.15 The effect of an order is to prohibit 'any specified person' from dealing with any realizable property held by him, including transferring the property abroad. In addition, as already identified s 41(7) allows the court to may 'make such order as it believes is appropriate for the purpose of ensuring that the restraint order is effective'.

5.16 Under existing arrangements, a High Court restraint order, in addition to prohibiting the disposal of specified assets, may require information to be provided by the defendant as to the extent and whereabouts of his assets. In the interim, he may be prohibited from removing any of his assets out of the jurisdiction or otherwise dealing with his funds save in accordance with any exceptions or permissions set out in the order. The text of the order will normally set out the consequences of breaching the order, provide undertakings as to service and a specified duration for the order, and include provisions as to variation and discharge.

5.17 No limit is placed by the Act on the discretion to make such order as appropriate, although plainly issues of proportionality will arise. In theory it might include depositing with the court or prosecution bank books, Land Registry title deeds, share certificates and similar items to prevent access to or transfer of property. The physical seizure of property, and the use of reasonable force to do this, are not excluded from the directions which may be applied, although such directions would be highly unusual. On the other hand, s 45 specifically provides a power to enable a constable or a customs officer to seize any realizable property subject to a restraint order to prevent it being removed from England or Wales. Thereafter the court may make such further order in relation to that property as it thinks appropriate. Arguably, the existence of this specific power suggests that the seizure of property ought to be confined to cases in which there is a clear risk of it being moved outside the jurisdictional reach of the court.

5.18 It is important for the practitioner to consider the terms of the order with care. Those representing clients whose assets have been restrained should carefully note what the client is prohibited from doing, in relation to which particular assets, and the nature of the information he is required to provide within the time limits available. It may be possible to obtain a variation of the order by consent to overcome any aspect of immediate difficulty in relation, for example, to the continued running of a business or trade, or the need to have access to additional funds for living expenses. As a general rule the defendant is entitled to enjoy the standard of life he previously experienced and is entitled to meet continuing expenses as they arise, although this may not extend to keeping up an excessively 'Rolls Royce lifestyle' (*In re Peters* (1988);[4] *Re D* (1992)[5]).

In order to give further effect to restraint of property, s 48 specifically empow- **5.19** ers the court to appoint a receiver to receive and manage the property pending future consideration of a confiscation order. The powers and duties of such a management receiver are considered further below.

The person specified in the order may be the suspected offender (or defendant) **5.20** or any other person who holds the property. The order will prevent any dealing with specified property but may be phrased so as to attach to 'all realisable property held by the specified person whether or not . . . described in the order' and all realizable property transferred to the specified person after the date of the order (s 41(2)).

Under s 41(3) the judge may exempt property which is required for legitimate **5.21** purposes and 'in particular' the order may make provision:

(a) for 'reasonable living expenses' and reasonable legal expenses;

(b) to enable a person to carry on any trade, profession or occupation;

(c) other exemptions subject to any conditions imposed.

Specifically excluded by virtue of s 41(4) from the legal expenses exemption is the power to release funds to pay for legal help for the defendant/suspect or recipient of a 'tainted gift' in relation to the suspected or charged offence which triggered the restraint proceedings. Such a person would be entitled to apply for reasonable legal expenses in relation to other matters which are not so excluded.

D. DEFINITIONS

1. Realizable Property

The scope of the order will depend on the identity of the holder, and his relation- **5.22** ship with the suspect/offender, as well as the type and nature of the property thought to represent the latter's benefit from criminal conduct. The provision is drafted with sufficient breadth to cover every conceivable variety of circumstances. 'Property' has the familiar broad definition contained in s 84 and 'realizable property' means that it is any such property which is not subject to an existing order for forfeiture or deprivation under this or similar legislation, or to a receiving or recovery order under the POCA 2002. Cash seized under the provisions of s 295 is similarly excluded, perhaps for obvious reasons.[6]

---

[4] [1988] 1 QB 871.   [5] QB, 28 October 1992.   [6] See also ss 82 and 83.

2. Holding and Interests in Property

5.23 Section 84(2) contains a number of additional general provisions which relate to the holding of property. Property is 'held' by a person if he holds an interest in it and, in relation to land in the jurisdiction, this includes any legal estate or beneficial interest or power by virtue of s 84(2). References to an 'interest' in property other than land include a right to possession. Property vested in a trustee in bankruptcy or a liquidator will also be caught by the provision. In relation to assets held by a company which is not a defendant, it would appear that these are not realizable property, even if the defendant himself holds all of the shares. His realizable property is the shareholding rather than the assets of the company, and the latter may not be the subject of restraint unless it can be established that the company is a mere sham or device to avoid the defendant's obligations or disguise his true interests in the property (*Trustor v Smallbone*[7]). In exceptional circumstances, where the relevant companies, for example, have been used for fraud, the court may permit the 'corporate veil' to be lifted (*Re H*[8]).

E. APPLICATION, VARIATION, AND DISCHARGE

1. Scope of Applicants

5.24 The power to apply for a restraint order has been extended to the Director of the ARA and to 'accredited financial investigators', as defined in the Act (s 42(2)). However, in order to make an application, or seek to vary or discharge an order, or initiate any appeal, the accredited financial investigator must either be one of the following, or authorized to act by one of the following (s 68):

(a) a police officer of superintendent rank or higher;

(b) an equivalent rank customs officer;

(c) an accredited financial investigator falling within a description specified by the Secretary of State under s 453.

The court will have a power to discharge an order on application by the original applicant or 'any person affected by the order' (s 42(3)). The requirement to discharge an order is mandatory when either the relevant proceedings or application have concluded, or if 'within a reasonable time' the proceedings or application anticipated are not initiated.

2. Appeal

5.25 Where an application to discharge or vary the terms of an order is made, both the original applicant or any person affected by the order has a right of appeal to the

---

[7] [2001] 1 WLR 1177.   [8] [1996] 2 All ER 391.

Court of Appeal, and thereafter to the House of Lords, under ss 43 and 44. There is no right of appeal in connection with the making of the original order which will normally have been obtained on an ex parte basis. An aggrieved person must first apply to the Crown Court for variation or discharge and, if appropriate, appeal a refusal subsequently. The appellate court may confirm or discharge any order, or make 'such order as it believes is appropriate'.

3. Evidence

Restraint proceedings are essentially civil in nature, notwithstanding that juris- **5.26** diction now resides in the Crown Court and that the aim is to facilitate the making of a confiscation order following a criminal trial. It follows that the burden of proof in such proceedings is upon the balance of probability.

Civil rules of evidence are imported by s 46(2) which applies to the proceedings **5.27** (ss 2–4 of the Civil Evidence Act 1995). Section 2(1) of the Civil Evidence Act 1995 ordinarily requires a party intending to adduce hearsay evidence to provide notice to the other party or parties of that fact but by virtue of r 39 of the Crown Court Rules 2003 that provision does *not* apply to evidence in 'restraint proceed- ings'[9] and 'receivership proceedings'.[10]

The proper approach to what 'weight' ought to be attached to hearsay evidence **5.28** is set out in s 4. The court is required to have regard 'to any circumstances from which any inference can be drawn as to the reliability or otherwise of the evidence'. In particular, the court must take into account whether:

(a) it would have been reasonable and practicable to call the maker of the state- ment as a witness;

(b) the statement was made contemporaneously with the described event of existence of the matters stated;

(c) the evidence involves multiple hearsay;

(d) any person involved had a motive to conceal or misrepresent matters;

(e) the original statement was edited, or made in collaboration with another or for a particular purpose;

(f) the circumstances of adducing the hearsay evidence suggest an attempt to prevent a proper evaluation of its weight.

For the avoidance of any doubt, s 46(1) permits the use of hearsay evidence 'of **5.29** whatever degree' in the proceedings, and defines 'hearsay' as evidence given other- wise than orally by a witness which is 'tendered as evidence of the matters stated'. Section 46(5) confirms that evidence which would otherwise be admissible is not affected by these hearsay provisions.

---

[9] Defined as proceedings under ss 42 and 58(2) and (3) of the POCA 2002.
[10] Defined as proceedings under ss 48 to 53 and 54(4), 56(4), 59(2) and (3), 60(2) and (3), 62, and 63 of the POCA 2002.

5.30   The general effect of these provisions is that hearsay evidence, even second or third hand, may not be excluded by judges hearing restraint applications. Breach of the notice and information rules may have an effect upon the weight to be attached to the material, but only in so far as the defect has an effect upon reliability. Moreover, the prosecution need not call the witness for the purposes of cross-examination. In these circumstances the other party may apply to call the witness itself for cross-examination, in effect using the witness's statement as evidence in chief (Civil Evidence Act 1995, s 3). Where the witness is out of the jurisdiction and unwilling to co-operate this may prove to be impossible.

5.31   The overall 'fairness' of the proceedings is, of course, a matter to which the court must have constant regard in considering the way in which such proceedings are litigated. However, European human rights jurisprudence has displayed a marked unwillingness to interfere with domestic evidential rules or the exercise of judicial discretion in relation to admissibility. Once again, the provisions are extremely wide and generously drawn so far as the applicant for restraint is concerned, and quite deliberately so.

4. Variation and Discharge

5.32   Applications to vary and/or discharge may be made by a person affected by the order and/or by the person who applied for the order. The Crown Court Rules 2003 specify that such applications to vary or discharge, if made by the person affected by the order, must be made in writing and made on notice. The application itself must be served upon the person who applied for the restraint order and any other person affected by the order at least two days before the fixed date of the hearing unless the crown court specifies a shorter period. By virtue of r 19(2) if the party who applied for the original restraint order wishes to apply to vary it they may do so on an *ex parte* basis if the application is urgent or there are reasonable grounds for believing that giving notice would cause dissipation of realizable property which is the subject of the application. Under r 20 if the person who applied for the order wishes to discharge it the application may be made *ex parte* and must be in writing.

F. APPOINTMENT OF MANAGEMENT RECEIVERS

1. Scope

5.33   The Act makes provision for the appointment of receivers in connection with restraint proceedings and any confiscation orders which may follow. The Crown Court Rules make further provision as to the relevant applications, remuneration, and provision of accounts.

5.34   The appointment of 'management receivers' in connection with restraint is, as the title suggests, for the purpose of receiving and managing any restrained property pending the outcome of proceedings. Once an order for confiscation is made, there is provision for the appointment of 'enforcement receivers' under s 50 where the order is not satisfied and it is necessary to take possession of, manage and dispose of realizable property so as to give effect to it. As we have seen, the enforcement receiver will often be the ARA. It is important to note that a court appointed receiver is not an agent of either party but, in effect, an officer of the court (*Re Andrews*[11]). He must accordingly act in accordance with general principles of justice and honest dealing. However, since he may recover his expenses and costs from property which is realized, any restrained assets may rapidly be expended on this alone. There appears to be no protection in the legislation for a defendant to recover the receiver's management costs in the event that the balance of property is released from restraint and no forfeiture order is made. This is because the receiver's remuneration is considered to be an expense of the receivership and not of the proceedings themselves. The power to award compensation under the new Act is confined to defaults in the investigation or prosecution of offences and not to provide for such management expenses. The court in *Andrews* recognized that, on the face of it, this was plainly unfair to a defendant who might later be acquitted, but that the matter might be reviewed on further consideration of the Human Rights Act 1998. The implications for an innocent defendant subjected to this process can be severe and might amount to the complete dissipation of his property. In a subsequent case, arguments based upon Article 6 were specifically argued, but without success (*Hughes & Others v HM Customs and Excise; R & Another v Crown Prosecution Service; Anderson v HM Customs & Excise* (2002)[12]). The court concluded that the decision in *Andrews* was correct and such costs were irrecoverable by the defendant. However, it went on to say that this is a matter which must plainly be weighed in the balance by any court considering an application for the appointment of a receiver.

2. Appointment and Powers

Section 48 provides for management receivers to be appointed when a restraint order is made, or at any time after it is in force, on the request of the original applicant (s 48(1)). The order will take effect in respect of any realizable property to which the restraint order applies (s 48(2)). The order may also empower the receiver to exercise a number of powers identical to those of the enforcement receiver, although it does not permit him to realize any of the property save for the purposes of meeting his own remuneration and expenses (s 49(2)). The difference between this provision and s 51(2), in relation to enforcement receivers, is that the latter are intended to realize the property in order to meet the confiscation order, whereas the former are intended to preserve it in case such an order may be made.

5.35

---

[11] [1991] 3 WLR 1236 at 1242, *per* Ward LJ.
[12] [2003] 1 WLR 1777, CA, Simon Brown, Laws and Arden LJJ, 20 May 2002.

5.36　In order to give effect to these powers, the receiver may be required to:

(a)　search for or inspect things authorized by the court;

(b)　make or obtain copies or photographs or records of material;

(c)　remove and take possession of items.

5.37　Section 49(3) enables the court to include such powers, with any appropriate limitations, on the order of appointment and s 49(5) permits the court to order that any person in possession of realizable property should give possession of it to the receiver. In addition, the receiver may be authorized to engage in a number of general management functions in relation to the property, including entering into contracts, employing agents, and executing powers of attorney, deeds and other instruments. Essentially, the court can authorize any appropriate steps considered necessary for the proper exercise of the receiver's functions (s 49(4)) and for his management of, and dealing with, the property. In order to satisfy the need to preserve the property for confiscation purposes, the receiver may have to carry on an existing business, or make arrangements for another to do so. He may also have to incur capital expenditure in respect of certain property and realize other elements in order to do so. All of these various contingencies are provided for by s 49(9).

5.38　In cases of urgency, where it is feared that alerting the defendant to an application for restraint and appointment of a receiver will result in the dissipation of the property, the application to appoint a receiver may be made at the same time as an *ex parte* restraint application. The orders made must, however, be on the narrowest terms consistent with the need to act effectively, and ought not to include a general power of sale. In such circumstances, should it become necessary for the receiver to dispose of property, he should return to court on notice for further directions (*Re P* (2000)[13]).

3.　Third Parties

5.39　Third parties holding realizable property, including an equitable interest in it or right to possession, may obviously be adversely affected by the making of a restraint order and the activities of a management receiver. The receiver may decide to take possession of the property, or manage it in a way which defeats or diminishes the rights of the innocent third party. The property may be sold to realize either the receiver's expenses and remuneration, or to provide funds for his management functions. In order to do so the receiver may be entitled, for example, to initiate possession proceedings to evict the third party who has a right or licence to occupy premises under s 49(2)(b), (d) and (10). A court order may require someone holding an interest in realizable property to make payment to the receiver of a sum equivalent to the defendant's (or suspected person's) beneficial interest in the property, or that of the recipient of a tainted gift (s 49(6)).

---

[13]　[2000] 1 WLR 473.

In any of these circumstances, the court must not authorize the power in s 49(2)(a) or (b), or make the order in s 49(6) without providing persons holding such interests with a reasonable opportunity to make representations to it s 49(8)). The principles to be applied in exercise of the court's powers are considered further below. Furthermore, under s 49(9), the court may make any order subject to such conditions and exceptions as it thinks appropriate, taking into account the legitimate interests of third parties. For example, an order permitting a receiver to take possession of real property owned by the defendant or suspected person, or to obtain possession by legal proceedings, might exclude the house in which he or any spouse or children live, or include a term permitting possession only to be sought against parties other than the defendant and his dependants. **5.40**

Where any person has been, or may be, affected by an action by a receiver, he may apply to the Crown Court under s 62(3) for directions as to the exercise of the receiver's powers. The court may make any order it thinks appropriate in these circumstances. Similarly, any person affected by an order may apply for it to be discharged or varied under s 63(1) and (2). **5.41**

The Act also anticipates the actions of third parties who are not currently in possession of realizable property exercising lawful rights in order to obtain possession. The effect of this would be to defeat the court's attempts to preserve the property. A defendant or suspect might attempt to frustrate a possible confiscation order by incurring debt which might lead to his assets being the subject of distress, or non-payment of rent which might cause him to lose a tenancy. Section 58 accordingly provides that no distress may be levied against any realizable property, nor may forfeiture by re-entry on breach of a tenancy agreement be exercised save with the leave of the Crown Court and subject to any conditions it thinks appropriate. Where court proceedings have commenced in relation to any property, that court has power to stay the proceedings where it knows that a restraint order has been made or applied for in the Crown Court by virtue of s 58(5). It should not act, either to stay or permit the proceedings to continue— either with or without conditions—without giving the applicant for the restraint order and any receiver appointed an opportunity to be heard (s 58(6)). **5.42**

Situations will arise in which a receiver takes action in respect of property which is not realizable property and loss or damage results from his actions, including loss or damage to third parties. Where the receiver would have been entitled to take such action if the property had been 'realizable property', and he believed on reasonable grounds that he was entitled to take that action, then the receiver will be protected from an action for damages unless he behaved negligently (s 61). **5.43**

4. Discharge of Management Receivers

A management receiver will be discharged by the court upon the appointment either of an enforcement receiver under s 50 or a Director's receiver under s 52 (s 64(1)). The court will then order the management receiver to transfer all of the property. The transfer will take effect once the further appointment vests the **5.44** replacement with his powers and applies to all property save any realised to pay the management receiver's expenses and fees (s 64(4)). Once the transfer is made, the management receiver is released from his appointment and from any obligation arising under the Act.

G. RESTRAINT PROCEEDINGS AND SEIZED MONEY

1. Scope and Extent

5.45 Section 67 makes provision to enable confiscation to take effect in relation to cash sums which are in the possession of banks and building societies, rather than in the possession of a management receiver. Here the funds must have been subject to a restraint order (s 67(4)(a)). Since any such order expires on the making of a confiscation order, and the cash remains in the hands of third party institutions rather than an enforcement or Director's receiver, then there must be a power to compel payment to be made in satisfaction of the order. The power extends to banks and building societies into which funds have been deposited by the enforcement agencies following cash seizures under the general powers contained in s 19 of the PACE 1984. Once any time allowed for satisfaction of the confiscation order has expired, a magistrates' court may order the bank or building society to transfer the funds (s 67(4) and (5)). Failure to do so will result in a penalty of up to £5,000 (s 67(6)).

H. PRINCIPLES TO BE FOLLOWED IN EXERCISE OF POWERS

1. Purpose

5.46 The exercise of powers of restraint by the Crown Court, including the powers to appoint receivers, and the powers of receivers themselves, are designed to serve the purposes of the Act in preserving property for possible confiscation. However, they undoubtedly amount to a serious infringement of the right to quiet enjoyment of property and, potentially, to the right to family life. They affect not merely defendants or suspected persons against whom confiscation orders may eventually be made, but also innocent third parties. The court and the receiver must exercise those wide powers with the first aims in mind, but also responsibly and in accordance with the principles set out in s 69 of the Act.

2. Specific Principles

5.47 The powers which are available must be exercised:

(a) with a view to securing the availability of the property to satisfy any confiscation order;

(b) in a case where no order has yet been made, with a view to ensuring that the property does not decrease in value;

(c) without taking account of any conflicting obligation of the defendant or a recipient of a tainted gift.

However, those three objectives are subject to the rules that: **5.48**

(i) a person other than the defendant or recipient of a tainted gift should be allowed to retain or recover the value of any interest held by him;

(ii) in respect of realizable property held by the recipient of a tainted gift, the powers should be exercised with a view to realizing no more than the value for the time being of that gift;

(iii) where no confiscation order has yet been made, and the defendant or the recipient of a tainted gift makes application, the court should not order the sale of property which it is satisfied cannot be replaced

6

MONEY LAUNDERING

A. OVERVIEW

1. Introduction

6.01 The term 'money laundering' applies to the process by which funds derived from illicit activity are given apparent legitimacy. Although the term is said to have derived in origin from the use of 'Laundromats' by organized crime syndicates in the United States to process the proceeds of their illegitimate 'businesses' through legitimate business, in a colloquial sense the term conveniently lends itself to describe the process of 'cleaning' the criminal proceeds.

6.02 The process of money laundering is international in its extent and as a major financial centre Britain has seen a significant volume of activity in recent years both as a source from where criminal proceeds begin their movement, as a temporary location or as the final destination for conversion. Those proceeds of crime may be UK generated or generated from criminal activity elsewhere, the process of laundering can be done in a number of alternative ways. It can range from the unsophisticated physical transportation of cash in a suitcase across borders and then seeking to integrate it at its destination, to the placement of the criminal proceeds in bank accounts which are then moved about the system of international banking from the United Kingdom to elsewhere taking advantage of a myriad of separate accounts in several different countries. There is clearly scope for the proceeds of crime generated from illicit activities abroad to be placed into the UK economy in order to provide apparent legitimacy to them. Wherever the predicate crime occurred or by whatever the means the proceeds are laundered, those concerned with the process will aim to move funds and/or convert them in such a way as to place as many stages/layers between the initial criminal activity and the funds/property concerned.

6.03 The National Criminal Intelligence Service (NCIS) has previously identified that the proceeds from crime in the United Kingdom are anywhere between £19 billion and £48 billion each year and that the amount actually laundered is realistically £25 billion per year.[1]

2. Perceived Aims of the POCA

6.04 Part 7 of the POCA, ss 327–340 builds upon the Government's commitment to the fight against crime particularly that termed as 'organised' although it will be noted that the definition of 'criminal property' is sufficiently wide to include the merest of transgressions. In order to perpetuate its illegal activities organized crime must at some stage seek to launder its proceeds so that they can be accessed without detection or at least without arousing suspicion. Unless the criminal proceeds are successfully laundered the beneficiaries may not be able to enjoy the profits and

---

[1] Source: NCIS Annual Threat Assessment 2003.

without apparent legitimacy the transparency of new found wealth may be their undoing.

The POCA focuses upon seeking to disrupt the ease with which it is possible to **6.05** clean tainted funds in three main ways. First, the Act penalizes those who attempt to assist, agree to assist, or do in fact assist in laundering criminal property. Secondly. the Act enforces disclosure by those in the 'regulated sector' who come across suspicious transactions in the course of their business or professional activities. Thirdly, the Act eases the means by which an investigation may be instigated and continued by the threat of penalizing those who warn the money launders of any interest in their activities.

3. Relationship with Earlier Legislation

The POCA significantly shifts the focus and extent of those provisions previously **6.06** contained in the Drug Trafficking Act 1994 (DTA) and the Criminal Justice Act 1988 (CJA). The POCA consolidates the money laundering offences in an attempt to simplify the framework by creating three principal offences of 'concealing criminal property' under s 327, 'facilitating the retention or control of criminal property' under s 328, and 'possessing criminal property' under s 329, punishable by fourteen years imprisonment. In addition two ancillary offences are created of 'failure to disclose: regulated sector' under s.330 and 'tipping off' under s 333 both punishable by five years imprisonment on conviction on indictment. The offences are triable either way and due to their broad ambit there is clearly scope for a great number of prosecutions in the magistrates' court.

The POCA provisions remove any distinction between offences concerning the **6.07** proceeds generated by general criminal conduct and drug trafficking activity as had previously been the case under the former prevailing offences contained in the DTA and CJA legislation. This clearly simplifies the position as was previously the case where the Crown could prove that property was the proceeds of illicit activity but could not prove whether they were the proceeds of drug trafficking or some other criminal activity.

4. Definition of Terms

The POCA money laundering provisions are directed towards detecting criminal **6.08** proceeds through three types of individuals. First, those who 'benefit' from 'property' which is derived from 'criminal conduct', secondly those who 'use' and thirdly those who come into possession of 'property' which is derived from 'criminal conduct'. These terms are defined elsewhere in the Act in similar terms, particularly in the context of criminal confiscation.[2]

---

[2] See Chap 3.

6.09 'Money laundering'—This is defined in s 340(11) of the POCA as an act which constitutes an offence under ss 327, 328, or 329, or an attempt, conspiracy, or incitement to commit any of those offences, or aiding, abetting, counselling, or procuring their commission. Under s 340(11)(d) the crime need not have been committed in the United Kingdom nor must it be a criminal offence in the jurisdiction in which it took place, provided that it would be an offence in the United Kingdom if it had been committed in the United Kingdom that satisfies the definition.

6.10 'Property'—This includes all forms of property wherever situated and in whatever form, including money, real or personal property, things in action, and other tangible or incorporeal property. An individual will have 'obtained' property if they acquire an interest in it, including an equitable interest or power in relation to land in England and Wales, or a right (including a right to possession) in relation to property other than land. [3]

6.11 'Possession'—The possession of property is widely defined as including doing any act in relation to it.

6.12 'Criminal Property'—This is defined widely under s 340(3). 'Property is criminal property if it constitutes a person's benefit from criminal conduct or it represents such a benefit, and the alleged offender knows or suspects that it constitutes or represents such a benefit.' The benefit therefore can be direct or indirect or in whole or in part. The definition establishes a critical necessary element, that of knowledge or suspicion, which must be established in order to found the basis of an allegation under the offences contained in ss 327, 328, and 329. This element protects the unwitting who may be engaged in 'converting' property for example that is in fact the proceeds of criminal conduct but about which they neither knew or suspected say in the case of exchanging currency. This required proof of the state of mind is vital as it is the knowledge or suspicion of the illegitimacy of the property which would trigger the offence as opposed to knowledge or suspicion of the criminal activities of a person with whom the potential defendant was dealing. It is immaterial who carried out the original criminal conduct or who benefited and the fact that the criminal conduct occurred prior to the act is irrelevant.

6.13 'Criminal Conduct'—This is defined under s 340(2) in wide terms so as to include any activity which constitutes an offence in any part of the United Kingdom or would constitute an offence in any part of the United Kingdom if it occurred there, thereby including 'criminal conduct' that occurred abroad but the proceeds of which come into the United Kingdom. Under s 340(5) a person is deemed to have benefited from 'conduct' (and thereby 'criminal' conduct) 'if he obtains property as a result of or in connection with the conduct' and this is broad enough to include payments and rewards for criminal conduct as well as property which is derived from or connected to its commission (which might be 'criminal property' in any event).

---

[3] See s 340(9) and (10).

B. CONCEALING THE PROCEEDS OF CRIMINAL CONDUCT (s 327)

1. Basic Elements of the Offence

The offence under s 327 of the Act can be committed in five separately listed ways **6.14** although it must be recognized that there may be overlap between them, particularly with regard to (i) and (ii). Under the section a person commits an offence if he:

(i)   conceals; or

(ii)   disguises; or

(iii)   converts; or

(iv)   transfers; or

(v)   removes criminal property from England and Wales or from Scotland or from Northern Ireland.

Concealing and disguising criminal property are defined further at s 327(3) as **6.15** including 'concealing or disguising its nature, source, location, disposition, movement or ownership or any rights with respect to it'. In sub-section (1)(e), represented by (v) above it is clear that the offence will be committed if the criminal property is moved from any of the three legal jurisdictions within the United Kingdom. Therefore an individual who takes criminal property (including therefore the requisite *mens rea* contained in s 340) in the form of cash from Glasgow to Cardiff would commit an offence under s 327. It is still important to note the additional provisions of s 340 identified at para 6.12 above, as to the fact that it is immaterial who committed the particular criminal act or when they did it.

2. Avoiding Liability

Liability may be avoided through disclosure before acting or where a reasonable **6.16** excuse exists for not having done so. These availing provisions are included within s 327 itself and additionally by reference to s 338 of the Act.[4] Under s 327(2) where the individual who would otherwise have committed an offence under s 327, makes an 'authorized disclosure' under s 338 of the Act and obtains the appropriate consent 'he does not commit such an offence'.

Subsections 2(b) and (c) of s 327 provide further protection if the person **6.17** intended to make such a disclosure[5] but had a reasonable excuse for not doing so, and if the act is done in carrying out a function the person has in relation to the enforcement of any provision of the POCA or 'any other enactment relating to criminal conduct or benefit from criminal conduct'. This would clearly protect

---

[4] See section E, paras 6.47 *et seq.*   [5] Under s 338.

any investigating officers who seize 'criminal property' in the form of cash or bank credits which are transferred into accounts held by the authorities.

3. Revision of Previous Provisions

6.18 There are important developments to note in the POCA offences compared to the equivalent provisions contained in the DTA 1994 and the CJA 1988. Previously under s 93C(2) of the CJA 1988 'concealing or transferring proceeds of criminal conduct' the commission of the offence required that the act of concealment or transfer of the proceeds of criminal conduct was for the purposes of avoiding prosecution for an offence (under that part of the Act) or the making or enforcement of a confiscation order. No such condition appears in the POCA and thus it is much simpler to establish.

6.19 In pursuit of simplifying the law the POCA has removed the distinction contained in the previous provisions[6] between laundering the proceeds of crime of another and laundering one's own proceeds. The s 327 offence is therefore now simpler and broader than its predecessors and many of the concepts that formerly applied under previous legislation have, for the moment, been consigned to legal history.

6.20 The Crown will succeed in a prosecution under this section if they can satisfy the tribunal of fact (lay magistrates or district judge in the magistrates court or the jury in the Crown Court) that the accused conducted the relevant act[7] in relation to the relevant property in the knowledge or suspicion that it derived from criminal conduct.

6.21 In a case where the person who is said to have conducted the relevant act is also said to have been the original perpetrator of the originating criminal conduct the Crown may face less difficulty in securing a conviction. In such an example it is submitted that the Court will have to be satisfied of his responsibility for that originating criminal conduct. In such circumstances thought would have to be given to whether a separate offence should be charged on the same indictment and this would be dependent upon the circumstances of the particular case. There may be prevailing tactical, evidential, or legal reasons why a particular course is adopted over another by the Crown and there may be defence applications such as severance, in response.

6.22 In a case where the accused is not said to have been the original perpetrator of the original crime the position will be more difficult for the prosecution particularly having regard to the relationship between the instant defendant and the original offender. Even so the POCA is indiscriminate and will potentially catch those who are several stages removed from the original crime and the original offender. The requisite knowledge or suspicion on their part coupled with any

---

[6] See s 93C of the CJA 1988 and s 49 of the DTA 1994.
[7] That amounts to 'conceals, disguises, converts, transfers or removes'.

relevant act will lead to potential criminal sanctions whoever they are and in whatever circumstances it originally came into their possession.

4. The Legal Profession

The POCA money laundering provisions and their potential application must become part of the everyday working knowledge of the legal profession, solicitors and barristers alike. All must have a working knowledge and understanding of the legislation, case law, and their respective professional guidelines. Both must be aware of the extent of their own business and how their respective functions in providing professional services to their clients are to be regarded in the eyes of the Act. Only through a careful assessment of the provisions will legal advisers be able to protect their clients and themselves particularly having regard to those provisions requiring reports to be made to NCIS and/or potential liability for failing to make the required disclosure under s 330.   **6.23**

The legal profession must adopt relevant compliance procedures and staff training[8] so that the Act and the associated Money Laundering Regulations[9] are complied with. The care that must be taken in applying the POCA provisions was emphasised in the case of *P v P,* heard before Dame Elizabeth Butler-Sloss, President of the Family Division,[10] where in the context of ancillary relief proceedings the provisions under this part of the Act were in focus, particularly s 328. These matters are considered in further detail at the relevant points in the remainder of this chapter.   **6.24**

C. ASSISTING ANOTHER TO RETAIN THE BENEFITS OF CRIMINAL CONDUCT (s 328)

1. Basic Elements of the Offence

The POCA offence under s 328 is derived from s 50 of the DTA 1994 and s 93A of the CJA 1988. An offence will be committed where a person enters into or becomes concerned in an arrangement which he knows or suspects facilitates (by whatever means) the acquisition, retention, use or control of criminal property by or on behalf of another person. As with s 327 discussed above, no offence is committed if a disclosure pursuant to s 338 has been made in respect of the criminal property and he has the appropriate consent, or if the person intended to make such a disclosure but had a reasonable excuse for not doing so or if the act is done in carrying out a function he has relating to the enforcement of the Act.   **6.25**

---

[8] Not all barristers will meet the definition of having 'employees' but understanding of such definitions and appropriate training will be essential where appropriate.

[9] Money Laundering Regulations 2003 (SI 2003/3075) came into force 1 March 2004.

[10] Judgment of 8 October 2003, [2003] EWHC Fam 2260.

6.26 The first part of the section is widely drawn and embraces the actions of, for example, any professional adviser, bank employee, administrator, or other person who might deal with the property in the course of his business and who suspects the provenance of the property or funds. The 'assistance' must be known or suspected to facilitate retention or control of the criminal property by or on behalf of A (whether by concealment, removal from the jurisdiction, transfer to nominees, or otherwise) or to enable A to have access to his criminal property or be used for his benefit to acquire other property by way of investment. The definition of 'proceeds of criminal conduct' is as before, including property which in whole or in part, directly or indirectly, represents 'benefit from criminal conduct'. Again it is of significance that under the POCA the criminal property need not be the product of criminal conduct by A but could be that arising from the criminal activities of a third party. The replaced provision, CJA 1988, s 93A, had a different focus and associated culpability with knowledge or suspicion of A's criminal activities in addition to knowledge or suspicion that the property represented his proceeds of crime, see s 93A(2) and the statutory defences provided by s 93A(4). This position, and the changing burden of proof it gave rise to, seemed 'designed to create the maximum of confusion for judges and juries'.[11]

6.27 Unlike the provisions in s 93A(4) of the CJA 1988, s 328 of the POCA does not place any onus upon the defendant to establish a statutory defence of lack of guilty knowledge or disclosure to the authorities. The reverse burden is removed by the new Act and, accordingly, it is submitted that no offence will be committed by the defendant unless the prosecution can prove that:

(i) he knew or suspected that the arrangement related to any person's proceeds of criminal conduct; and

(ii) he knew or suspected that by the arrangement he was facilitating retention or control by A or, as appropriate, access to or use by or for the benefit of A; and

(iii) he failed to make an 'authorized disclosure' to the relevant authority about the arrangement and has no reasonable excuse for failing to do so on his own and timely initiative.

6.28 In respect of each element, the burden of proof will lie on the prosecution and knowledge or suspicion under this section are to be evaluated subjectively. Evidence tending to show that a defendant ought to have known or suspected is likely to have weight in establishing that he did, in fact, possess the relevant state of mind. The position is to be contrasted with the offence of failing to disclose knowledge or suspicion of money laundering by those in the regulated sector under s 330 where a combination of a subjective and objective test is applied by the statute.

---

[11] See commentary by Professor JC Smith, *R v Butt* [1999] Crim LR 414.

Where 'failing to disclose' assists another to retain criminal proceeds, or to **6.29** conceal them, there will be a temptation to prefer charges under s 330 (failing to disclose) in addition to ss 327 or 328. If the court concludes that the subjective test in ss 327 or 328 is not satisfied then it may convict of the lesser offence[12] for which an objective test of knowledge or suspicion may suffice. The burden of proving each element lies with the prosecution to the ordinary standard avoiding the reversed burden of proof difficulty of *R v DPP, ex p Kebeline*.[13]

2. Avoiding Liability

As with s 327 discussed above, s 328 contains within it availing provisions relating **6.30** to authorized disclosures under s 338 or if the person intended to make such a disclosure but had a reasonable excuse for not doing so or if the act is done in carrying out a function he has relating to the enforcement of the Act or 'any other enactment relating to criminal conduct or benefit from criminal conduct'.

3. Revision of Previous Provisions

As discussed above at paras 6.26 to 6.28, the POCA moves the focus away from the **6.31** criminal persona to criminal property and removes the burden for establishing the statutory defence.

4. The Legal Profession

It is imperative that the profession understands the workings of the Act. Of **6.32** particular importance to the legal profession are the circumstances in which the provision of legal services may involve an 'arrangement' which facilitates the acquisition, retention, use or control of criminal property (and the appropriate knowledge or suspicion exists).

In light of the case of *P v P*[14] solicitors and barristers must exercise great care in **6.33** considering whether the particular circumstances of a case and the particular stage of the case will engage the POCA provisions. Time will tell how far the interpretation of the POCA provisions in that case will have general application beyond its clear relevance to family proceedings. In her judgment the President of the Family Division, Dame Elizabeth Butler-Sloss deliberately set the context as that of family proceedings. However, it was clearly considered sufficiently important for the NCIS, the Inland Revenue, the Law Society and the Bar Council to be represented at the hearing.

In *P v P* the solicitor acting for the wife made an 'authorized disclosure' under **6.34** s 338 to NCIS and sought the 'appropriate consent' under s 335. The wife's legal

---

[12] See s 334 for penalties under this part of the Act.   [13] [1999] 4 All ER 801, HL.
[14] See n 10 above.

team were concerned that they might commit an offence under s 328 of the Act. This conclusion was based upon the disclosure in the proceedings of Accountant's Forensic Reports which indicated tax evasion by the husband. Having considered this information and the advice from their own forensic accountant, the wife and her legal team became suspicious that part of the matrimonial assets might be 'criminal property' as defined in the Act. Therefore in continuing to act for the wife in any litigation and/or settlement they might become 'concerned in an arrangement' which might 'facilitate the acquisition, retention, use or control of criminal property' by the wife. In addition the wife's legal team were concerned as to the 'tipping off' provisions under s 333.

6.35   Following a protracted and unsuccessful series of communications (including non responses from the NCIS) between the wife's solicitors and the NCIS, directions were sought from the court, initially *ex parte* and then at a full hearing. Butler-Sloss, P determined that there were two main issues 'in the context of family proceedings':

(a) whether and in what circumstances it is permitted to act in relation to an arrangement; and

(b) whether and in what circumstances a legal adviser, having made an authorized disclosure, is permitted to tell others of the fact he or she has done so.

6.36   As to the issue at (a), the s 328 offence would not be committed only on the point of execution of the arrangement. Butler-Sloss, P accepted the unchallenged submission that the act of negotiating an arrangement would equally amount to being 'concerned in an arrangement'. We wonder whether, in circumstances where no 'arrangement' actually comes into being (but there is negotiation and the requisite criminal property), a prosecution *under this section* would be mounted as opposed to conspiracy or an attempt. Butler-Sloss, P deemed there was nothing in s 328 to prevent a solicitor or barrister from taking instructions from a client. If having taken instructions, the solicitor or barrister knows or suspects that the client will become involved in an arrangement that might involve the acquisition, retention, use, or control of criminal property, then the solicitor or barrister may commit an offence under s 328 unless he brings himself within s 328(2) and makes an authorized disclosure under s 338 in advance of the otherwise prohibited act followed by receiving the appropriate consent to the act under s 335. Alternatively the solicitor or barrister would not commit the offence where they intended to make such a disclosure and has a good reason for not having made it.

6.37   Applying the provisions of ss 335 and 338 and the 'good practice' recommended by Butler-Sloss, if a disclosure is made to the NCIS seeking consent to continue taking steps in relation to an arrangement no further steps in relation to the matter may be taken until one of three alternative scenarios exist. First, either NCIS consent is received within seven working days from the next working day after the disclosure is made, or secondly seven working days expire without a response from NCIS in which case the person is regarded as having deemed consent to resume acting in relation to the arrangement. Thirdly where notice of refusal of consent is received within the notice period, the person must not act in relation to the arrangement for the duration of the moratorium period of thirty-one days. In practice the longest period a person could be prevented from taking steps in relation to an arrangement after sending notice to NCIS would be seven working days plus thirty-one days. This is calculated on the basis that having made disclosure and sought the appropriate consent the individual must wait for at least seven working days. If on the seventh day NCIS refuse the individual will have to allow the thirty-one day moratorium period to elapse.

As to (b) above (at para 6.35) where a solicitor or barrister makes an authorized **6.38** disclosure, if they inform another of that fact they will be protected from liability for 'tipping off' under s 333 and/or 'prejudicing an investigation' under s 342 provided they come within the protection given by s 333(3) and/or 342(4). These provisions permit a disclosure to a client or client's representative 'in connection with the giving of legal advice' or to any person 'in connection with legal proceedings or contemplated legal proceedings'. A disclosure will not fall within those permitted circumstances when it is 'made with the intention of furthering a criminal purpose' and the requisite improper intention related to that of the solicitor. At para [66] of the judgment Butler-Sloss, P stated that:

unless the requisite improper intention is there the solicitor should feel free to communicate such information to his/her client or opponent as is necessary and appropriate in connection with the giving of legal advice or acting in connection with actual or contemplated proceedings.

Full and frank disclosure is required in family proceedings and therefore **6.39** Butler-Sloss, P's assessment of the parameters of a legal adviser's duty to their client, their opponent and to the court is consistent with that. That is not to say that in the context of other proceedings a legal adviser should adopt a different approach, but the specific circumstances of each case and the application of the Act must be carefully applied. Subsequently both the Law Society and the Bar Council have published amended guidance reflecting the judgment in the *P v P* case. All practitioners should consider the judgment and the guidance issued in response and family practitioners particularly must adapt their working understanding of the Act in the light of this case.

D. ACQUISITION, USE, AND POSSESSION OF THE PROCEEDS OF CRIME (s 329)

1. Basic Elements of the Offence

Section 329 replaces both DTA 1994, s 51 and CJA 1988, s 93B with a unified pro- **6.40** vision dealing with those who acquire, use, or come into possession of property representing the proceeds of crime. As before, the sanction only applies to those who have the requisite subjective knowledge or suspicion as to the provenance of the property concerned. A person who is in possession of property without the requisite knowledge is not guilty if the property they are in possession of is in fact the proceeds of crime. In that sense the argument could be posited in this way, the property is not 'criminal property' as defined under the Act because the accused did not know or suspect that it constituted the benefit of criminal conduct.

6.41 As is common with the provisions under ss 327 and 328 a person does not commit an offence if he makes an authorized disclosure under s 338, or he intended to do so but had a reasonable excuse for not doing so. An exemption is provided to the police and other enforcement agencies who take possession of the proceeds of crime in the course of their official duties.

6.42 Under s 329(2)(c) a person does not commit an offence if they acquired, used or had possession of the property for 'adequate consideration'. This provision seeks to protect those such as retailers who may be paid for ordinary consumer goods with funds they are suspicious of, the provision only bites where the person acquired or used or had possession of the property for less than 'adequate consideration'. The adequacy or otherwise of the 'consideration' at issue is to be evaluated by reference to the criteria in sub-section (3) such as (3)(a) 'a person acquires property for inadequate consideration if the value of the consideration is significantly less than the value of the property'. Under CJA 1988, s 93B, adequate consideration was expressed as a defence and accordingly the burden of proving the issue to the civil standard fell on the defendant. The position, illustrated by cases such as *R v Gibson*,[15] is now corrected by the new Act in the light of *R v DPP, ex p Kebeline*.[16]

6.43 Goods or services provided in exchange, which are known or suspected to help another to carry out criminal conduct, will not count as 'consideration'. Thus, a supplier of a getaway car to be used in a robbery, who is paid from the proceeds of an earlier robbery, will not be availed by an argument that the vehicle was sold at, or possibly above, the market rate. In any event he may face alternative allegations such as being a co-conspirator in the armed robbery itself.

2. Avoiding Liability

6.44 Similar protection is provided for under s 329 where the person concerned makes, or intends to make, an authorized disclosure to a constable, or to an employer where the person is employed and procedures have been established by his employer for the reporting of suspicions or knowledge of criminal proceeds. The provisions are in identical terms as those contained in the earlier sections.[17]

3. The Legal Profession

6.45 The provisions of s 329 could clearly have direct application to the payment of fees for the provision of legal services where a legal adviser forms the requisite know-

---

[15] [2000] Crim LR 479.   [16] See n 13 above.   [17] See ss 329, 335, and 338.

ledge or belief as to the provenance of the funds. A solicitor who acts on the basis of private funding either to be paid by the client or a third party must carefully consider their position. If the solicitor forms the appropriate suspicion then they must consider whether they are then obliged to make an authorized disclosure. However as the solicitor would submit that they had received such funds for the payment of their fees, for work reasonably and properly done, they may seek to rely upon the 'adequate consideration' provision in s 329. In the particular circumstances of each case legal advisers would do well to consider all of their options and if appropriate take advice from the relevant professional body.

The position of barristers must also be considered in this light. Most privately **6.46** funded work is not in the field of criminal defence where the potential for concern is perhaps greater than in other areas. In any case does a barrister avoid potential liability simply because his fees are the responsibility of, and paid directly by, the solicitor? If the solicitor receives funding on account is the barrister entitled to work upon the basis that the solicitor has undertaken all the necessary checks, considered the relevant guidance, and performed the necessary compliance? Should the barrister obtain confirmation as to the individual solicitor's compliance? These are interesting and testing issues which must be considered in the appropriate cases. As is discussed later in this chapter the position of legal advisers has developed significantly in the light of the Money Laundering Regulations 2003. Those regulations and the appropriate guidance issued by the Law Society and Bar Council must be considered so that legal advisers adopt the practices required and do not fall foul of the Act. These are discussed further in sections F and I below and can be obtained from the respective websites.[18]

E. REPORTING UNDER s 338

1. The Reporting Procedure

Section 338 of the POCA is important. This provision is broadly the same as in **6.47** previous money laundering legislation, encouraging the making of a disclosure so that a transaction or transfer may still be completed notwithstanding the belief that an offence under ss 327 to 329 would be committed. A disclosure is 'authorized' under the section if it is made to the relevant persons (constable,[19] customs officer or a nominated officer[20]) and in the form and manner (if any) prescribed. It is worthy of note at this point that in the context of 'employment',[21] subject to

---

[18] www.lawsociety.org.uk and www.barcouncil.org.uk.

[19] Defined under s 340(13) of the POCA 2002—as a person authorized by the Director General of the National Criminal Intelligence Service (NCIS).

[20] Includes a Money Laundering Reporting Officer (MLRO), see further regarding the Money Laundering Regulations 2003, above.

[21] Defined under s 340(12)—to include any function, paid or unpaid, carried out for any body, association or organization including voluntary organizations.

the appropriate compliance procedures having been installed, disclosure by an employee to the company's 'nominated officer' will afford that individual the statutory protection under s 338(5).

6.48 The disclosure itself requires fundamentally an admission that the 'property is criminal property'. The authorization (and the protection) may be obtained prior to the offender undertaking the prohibited act and obtaining consent to proceed. Alternatively the disclosure is classed as 'authorized' if it is made after the offender undertakes the prohibited act provided 'there is good reason for his failure to make the disclosure before he did the act' and the disclosure was made 'on his own initiative' and as soon as it is practicable for him to make it. A record may need to be kept detailing the information that was within the individual's contemplation at the time they formed the relevant suspicion and the reasons for not making the disclosure then. The absence of a record could potentially lead to an inference being drawn that is adverse to the individual concerned.

6.49 The consideration of the term 'appropriate consent' and its application to the matters under ss 327 to 329 and s 338 is to be found at s 335 of the Act. The term is defined as the consent of a nominated officer, constable, or customs officer (whichever is appropriate) to do a prohibited act if an authorized disclosure is made. If the authorized disclosure is made to a constable or a customs officer and the statutory notice period of seven working days[22] passes without the consent having been refused, then the person may undertake the 'prohibited act'. In addition if the authorized disclosure is made to a constable or a customs officer and the person receives notice that consent *is* refused, thereafter if the statutory 'moratorium' period of thirty-one days[23] passes the individual may proceed to undertake the prohibited act.

2. Protected and Authorized Disclosures

6.50 Section 337 of the Act must be considered at this point due to the interrelationship with the provisions of s 338. A 'protected disclosure' does not breach any restriction on the disclosure of information (however imposed): a disclosure will be 'protected' if three conditions are satisfied, first that the information disclosed came to the discloser during the course of his trade, profession, business, or employment. Secondly, the information causes the discloser to know or suspect or provides reasonable grounds for so suspecting, that another is engaged in money laundering. Thirdly the disclosure is made to a constable, a customs officer, or a nominated officer as soon as is practicable after the information comes to the discloser. The effect of this section is to provide immunity from any action based, for example, on a breach of contract or confidentiality and is not limited to those within the 'regulated sector' who are required to make disclosure.

---

[22] Starting on the first working day *after* the person makes the disclosure.
[23] Starting with the day on which the person receives notice that consent to doing the act is refused.

In May 2004 the NCIS published 'Guidance Notes for the NCIS Regulated   **6.51**
Sector Disclosure Report'.[24] It is directly relevant to the completion of protected
disclosures and authorized disclosures under ss 337 and 338. The form has not
been prescribed by the Secretary of State under s 339 of the Act and therefore it is
not mandatory to use it in making reports to the NCIS. Those concerned should
consider their respective industry guidance and apply that to the NCIS forms.

Anyone coming within the definition of the regulated sector as conducting   **6.52**
'relevant business' will potentially face criminal sanctions for not reporting. This
is closely linked, but also separate to, the application of 'authorized disclosure'
under s 338.

F. FAILURE TO DISCLOSE KNOWLEDGE OR SUSPICION OF MONEY LAUNDERING (s 330)

1. Introduction

The regime creating the obligation to report 'drug' money laundering suspicions   **6.53**
to a law enforcement 'constable' was established by the DTA 1986. The application of this obligation has evolved thereafter with subsequent legislation to its
POCA 2002 form. The removal of any distinction between proceeds of general
criminal activity and that generated by 'drug trafficking' has been discussed
already[25] and the current regime for reporting money laundering activity mirrors
that although in a particular case, the basis for the report may involve providing
information that in fact reveals a distinction. Where there is a distinction in terms
of reporting, is that between money laundering connected to general crime and
money laundering connected to terrorism. 'Terrorist' reports suspecting money
laundering activity are prioritised for obvious reasons.

2. The Regulated Sector

Particular duties under ss 330, 331 and 332 originally fell upon persons employed   **6.54**
in the regulated sector of business as originally defined in Sch 9 to the Act. Such
persons were expected to exercise a greater degree of diligence in handling transactions than those employed in other businesses and, accordingly, an objective
test of knowledge or belief of money laundering was applied to them.

The definitions of 'regulated sector' and 'relevant business' closely follow the   **6.55**
provisions in the Money Laundering Regulations 1993 (SI 1993/1933) and 2001
(SI 2001/3641), the latter adding certain money service businesses, including
bureaux de change, to the meaning of 'relevant financial business'. These have
now been revoked and replaced by the Money Laundering Regulations 2003 (SI

---

[24] Available at www.ncis.co.uk.
[25] In the context of the definition of 'criminal property'.

2003/3075) which reflect the European Parliament's 'Second European Money Laundering Directive 2001/97/EC'. The implementation of the Directive is important as it covers a sufficiently broad range of activities that almost all solicitors and many barristers will fall within the definition of 'regulated sector' and potentially liable therefore to the sanctions of s 330 of the Act.

6.56   Aside from potential criminal liability under the POCA for offences under ss 327 to 331, professional advisers must be aware that it is a criminal offence not to comply with the 2003 Money Laundering Regulations.

3. The Regulated Sector—The Position of Legal Advisers

6.57   Under paragraph 2(2)(l) of the 2003 Regulations 'relevant business' is defined to include:

the provision by way of business of legal services by a body corporate or unincorporate or, in the case of a sole practitioner, by an individual and which involves participation in a financial or real property transaction (whether by assisting in the planning or execution of any such transaction or otherwise by acting for, or on behalf of, a client in any such transaction

6.58   The effect of this will be to impose upon those engaged in any aspect of this work the full requirements of the regulated sector. Part II of the 2003 Regulations details the relevant obligations on persons who carry on relevant business and this includes the requirement of implementing systems and training, identification procedures, record-keeping, internal reporting procedures, and the following of relevant guidance issued by a 'supervisory authority' or any other 'appropriate body'. Under reg 3(3) such guidance is to be approved by the Treasury and published in a manner approved by the Treasury as appropriate in their opinion to bring the guidance to the attention of persons likely to be affected by it.

6.59   In this respect 'supervisory authority' includes under reg 2(7) the Bank of England, the Council of Lloyd's, and the Office of Fair Trading. We think that 'or other appropriate body' under reg 3(3) will clearly include the Law Society and the Bar Council. At this point both the Law Society and the Bar Council have published guidance but as the procedure for Treasury approval is not in place it is not Treasury approved as per the regulations. Even so it is recommended that the relevant guidance is carefully considered as in the unfortunate event of a prosecution, in its present form it may be considered in evaluating the conduct of the accused solicitor or barrister.[26]

6.60   It remains a concern that the regulatory burden may:

have a disproportionate impact on smaller firms that are currently unregulated, and do not have well-developed compliance mechanisms. These firms may find it more difficult to absorb new regulatory costs: and some unqualified practitioners may not already have the

---

[26] Available at the relevant websites: www.lawsociety.org.uk and www.barcouncil.org.uk.

same expertise and training as qualified professionals in detecting suspicious activity. However, it can be argued that the obligations will be proportionate to the risk that such firms would otherwise be targeted by money launderers, as it became more difficult for them to use the services of qualified practitioners.[27]

4. Other Professions

Other professions have to consider the effect of the POCA and the most recent Money Laundering Regulations. A Home Office Informal Consultation titled 'The Proceeds of Crime Act 2002 & The Money Laundering Regulations 2003: Obligations of Accountants to Report Money Laundering' was published on 4 August 2004. It considers in the main, whether auditors, external accountants, and tax advisers 'providing directly comparable services' as lawyers, ought to be provided with the same privilege exemption from reporting money laundering. The European Second Money Laundering Directive suggests that such a provision should equally apply and failing to extend it to accountants may be the subject of challenge. This informal consultation seeks to consider the relevant submissions. It is indicated that the Government's proposal is to amend s 330 of the POCA so as to include the term 'relevant professional adviser' in s 330(6)(b) and (10). This would have the effect of extending the protection of non-disclosure where the information or other matter came to the adviser in privileged circumstances. It is suggested that a 'relevant professional adviser' would include an accountant, auditor or tax adviser 'who is a member of a professional body which is established for accountants, auditors or tax advisers.' **6.61**

5. The s 330 Offence of Failing to Disclose

It is clear that once brought within the regulated sector those concerned must comply with the additional statutory burden within s 330. It replaces DTA 1994, s 52 and creates a new obligation upon the regulated sector to report to the appropriate authorities suspicions of the laundering of criminal proceeds. As is the case with the provisions discussed before, 'criminal conduct' has the wide definition contained within s 340(2) and can include offences committed abroad. The scope of s 330 is also extended to inchoate offences such as conspiracy by reason of the definition of 'money laundering' contained in s 415(2). An offence under s 330 will be committed where three 'conditions' are satisfied: **6.62**

   (a) First that he/she:

       (i)   knows or suspects, or

       (ii) has reasonable grounds for knowing or suspecting,

     that another person is engaged in money laundering.

---

[27] HM Treasury Consultation Document—Option 2.

(b) Secondly that the information or other matter

    (i)   on which his/her knowledge or suspicion is based, or

    (ii) which gives reasonable grounds for such knowledge or suspicion,

came to him/her in the course of a business in the regulated sector.

(c) Thirdly that he/she does not make the required disclosure as soon as is practicable after the information or other matter came to him/her.

6.63   The impact of the test for knowledge or suspicion is significant as it can be met in three alternative ways, as follows:

(a) the accused knows that another person is engaged in money laundering; or

(b) the accused suspects that another person is engaged in money laundering; or

(c) the accused has reasonable grounds for knowing or suspecting that another person is engaged in money laundering.

6.64   Therefore the accused may be found to have formed the appropriate *mens rea* in a subjective or objective manner. The individual may 'know or suspect' which could be established by admission (unlikely) or from evidence from which it could be inferred or there may be evidence as to the facts available to the accused at the relevant time that no disclosure was made which establish reasonable grounds for knowing or suspecting. It may be that the Crown in most prosecutions are more likely to concentrate upon (c) above as more straightforward of proof.

6.65   It is likely to be of concern that the test can be met in such a broad and alternative manner but at least there is some protection provided against complete negligent culpability by s 330(6)(c) and (7). Where a person does not in fact know of or suspect money laundering and they have not been provided by their employer with such training as the Secretary of State has specified by order, then they will not be guilty of an offence. 'Employers' in the regulated sector are required by virtue of the Money Laundering Regulations 2003 to provide such training or face prosecution for not complying with the regulations. If that training is provided to the requisite standard then that protection would not be available.

6.66   The 'money laundering' that the individual accused of the s 330 offence 'knew or suspected' includes any offence under ss 327 to 329 or an attempt to commit, or conspiracy to commit.[28]

6.67   There are additional exceptions under s 330(6) and if they apply no offence will be committed where:

(a) the person has a reasonable excuse for not disclosing the matter; or

(b) a professional legal adviser fails to disclose any information or matter which came to him in privileged circumstances.

---

[28] See s 340(11) for full definitions.

The ambit of this protection is tightly defined by s 330(10) and specifically excludes disclosures made with a view to furthering a criminal purpose. What the protection will cover are circumstances where the information or matter was given either:

(a) by a client or by a representative of a client in connection with the legal adviser giving legal advice to the client;

(b) by a person or by a representative of a person seeking legal advice from a legal adviser;

(c) by a person or by a representative of a person in connection with legal proceedings or contemplated legal proceedings.

In the absence of any exception, such a person must make disclosure of the information as soon as reasonably practicable after it comes to his attention. This must be to a nominated officer or a person authorized by the Director General of the NCIS and in the form and manner prescribed by order made by the Secretary of State under s 339. **6.68**

The Act adds further reinforcement to these provisions in the regulated sector by creating offences committed by 'nominated officers' who fail to pass on to the authorities the information about money laundering received from employees under the provisions of s 330. Under s 331, required disclosure must be made as soon as practicable to an authorized person[29] in the manner prescribed unless there is a reasonable excuse for failing to do so. In deciding whether an offence has been committed, under s 331(7) the court must consider whether the nominated officer followed any Treasury approved guidance, issued by any supervisory or other appropriate body designated under Sch 9, and published in a manner to bring it to the attention of relevant persons. Similarly in a prosecution for an offence under s 330, the court must make the same assessment as to whether the individual followed any relevant guidance. The issue of 'guidance' and 'Treasury approval' has been discussed in the context of the legal profession at paragraph 6.59 above. **6.69**

Section 332 provides similar measures to deal with other nominated officers in the non-regulated sector who receive information as a result of disclosures made by employees under ss 337 and 338. Where such information gives rise to a knowledge or suspicion that another person is engaged in money laundering, the officer must make the required disclosure to an authorized person in the form prescribed as soon as practicable. In the absence of a reasonable excuse for failing to do so, an offence will be committed. The test for knowledge or suspicion, unlike that applying in the regulated sector, is a subjective one. This illustrates in a straightforward way the increased focus the Act places on those in the regulated sector. **6.70**

---

[29] See s 331(5).

G. TIPPING OFF

1. Introduction

6.71 The offences of 'tipping off' contrary to s 333 and 'prejudicing an investigation' under s 342 share common features but are aimed at distinctly different offending actions. The 'tipping off' provisions are directed towards the individual who knows or suspects a disclosure has been made[30] as opposed to knowledge of the existence of an investigation, the disclosure of which may be 'prejudiced' which s 342 envisages.

2. Basic Elements of the Offence

6.72 Section 333 replaces DTA 1994, ss 53 and 58 and CJA 1988, s 93D(1). As in s 330, this provision extends to inchoate offences such as conspiracy. Under this section, a person will be guilty of an offence where:

    (a) he knows or suspects that protected or authorized disclosure has been made to a constable or employer of the kind in s 337 or s 338; and

    (b) he makes a disclosure which is likely to prejudice any investigation that might be conducted as a result.

6.73 Under s 333(2) no offence will be committed where the relevant person did not know or suspect that the disclosure was likely to be prejudicial in the way mentioned above or where the disclosure is made in carrying out any function he has in relation to the enforcement of money laundering legislation.

6.74 The tipping off provisions relate to any person, including professional advisers. However, nothing in s 333 will make it an offence for a professional legal adviser to disclose any information:

    (a) to his client or a representative of his client in connection with the giving of legal advice to the client; or

    (b) to any person in contemplation of, or in connection with, legal proceedings and for the purpose of those proceedings (s 333(3)),

unless the disclosure was made with a view to furthering a criminal purpose s 333(4).

3. Practical Dilemmas for the Legal Profession

6.75 In regard to the above, the judgment in the case of *P v P*[31] provides some practical assistance and the reader should consider those paragraphs at 6.32 to 6.39 above

---

[30] Pursuant to s 337 or 338.   [31] [2003] EWHC Fam 2260.

in this chapter. The advice proffered by the Law Society in the guidance published in February 2004 should be consulted. Solicitors may face very real practical dilemmas when faced with circumstances where they are aware a person has been named in a report and/or that the authorities are carrying out, or are intending to carry out, a money laundering investigation. At para 2.58 of Chapter 2 the following advice is given:

Solicitors will often want to make preliminary enquiries of their client, or third party to obtain further information to help the solicitor to decide whether they have a suspicion. Solicitors might also need to raise questions during a transaction to clarify such issues. There is nothing in the law to prevent a firm from making normal enquiries about the client's instructions, and the proposed transaction in order to remove, if possible, any concerns and enable the firm to decide whether to take on, or continue, the retainer. These enquiries will not amount to tipping off, unless you know or suspect that a report (internal or external) has already been made or that an investigation is current or pending and make enquiries in a way which discloses those facts. It is also not tipping off to include a paragraph about your obligations under the money laundering legislation in your firm's standard client care letter.[32]

The replaced s 93D of the CJA 1988 gave rise to a number of difficulties that the courts had to resolve by balancing the competing interests of the investigating authorities, subjects of investigation and third parties caught up in the process of investigation. The POCA powers and duties will require similar concepts to be examined and two case authorities are worthy of consideration.   **6.76**

In *Governor and Company of the Bank of Scotland v A Ltd* (2001),[33] the bank made enquiries in respect of a number of accounts opened by A Ltd into which substantial sums of money were transferred. Police advised them that money laundering investigations were being carried out into the activities of the company and asked the bank not to reveal the information to A Ltd. The bank was fearful that it would risk being sued by the company if it failed to pay out money held in the accounts, or by third parties as constructive trustees if it did. The Court of Appeal indicated that the proper approach in such a case was for the bank to seek an interim declaration under CPR 25.1(1)(b), naming the Serious Fraud Office as the defendant. In determining such an application, the court would pay careful attention to the defendant's submissions as to what might frustrate its enquiries, but that the life of the declaration would be likely to be short since the need to conceal the investigation would, in most cases, be for a fairly limited period. In these circumstances the bank would clearly be protected against criminal liability for 'tipping off'. If proceedings were subsequently taken by the customer against the bank then it would have to take a commercial decision as to whether to contest those proceedings since the relief would not automatically protect the bank from actions taken by either the customer or third parties. However, *per curiam*, it seemed unlikely in those circumstances that the bank would be held liable for any liability under the accessory principle.   **6.77**

---

[32] Available at www.lawsociety.org.uk.   [33] [2001] 1 WLR 751, CA.

6.78   An earlier case, *C v S* (1999),[34] led to the publication of a Practice Note dealing with the situation arising where the subject of a money laundering investigation sought disclosure in an action of documents which might have revealed the existence of ongoing enquiries by the NCIS. The purpose of the application was an attempt by the company, C, to trace sums of money that it alleged had been misappropriated by others. A bank had earlier made a disclosure to the NCIS of suspicious transactions and was fearful that disclosure of the documents might breach the tipping off provisions of s 93D. It was in an invidious position. On the one hand, it faced criminal liability if it complied with a first instance order for disclosure; on the other hand, it was liable in contempt if it failed to do so. An *ex parte* application was made to the High Court *in camera* in an attempt to resolve the dilemma and the original disclosure order was revoked. The company subsequently applied to another judge who re-ordered disclosure. A third judge was then approached, *inter partes* but *in camera*, and he reversed the previous decision on undertakings from the bank to take all necessary steps to resolve the issue and to give an immediate notification to the parties once the risk of prosecution had passed.

6.79   In attempting to resolve this procedural and jurisdictional morass, the Court of Appeal was critical of the approach of the NCIS which appeared unconcerned as to the difficulties that its investigations and the prohibition against tipping off had created for the bank.

> It was submitted that the NCIS is entitled, having warned those involved of its interests, to await developments and then leave it to those responsible for determining whether there should be a prosecution to decide whether to prosecute or not. The civil courts should not involve the NCIS as to do so resulted in its limited resources being diverted from the purpose for which they should be used. Whilst recognizing the importance of not causing the NCIS unnecessary expense, this approach is neither sensible nor appropriate. First of all it will deter financial institutions [from] . . . doing their duty to make reports if their co-operation does not result in a sympathetic and helpful response in relation to their difficulties being adopted by the authorities in return . . . In addition, if a financial institution has made a disclosure in compliance with an order of the court, after placing all of the relevant facts of which it is aware before the court, as happened in this case, it would be, absent exceptional circumstances which are difficult to envisage, an abuse of process to prosecute the institution for making that disclosure. The fact that the statutory provisions make it an offence to tip off in the specified circumstances provides considerable, but not unqualified, protections of investigations into money laundering from the adverse consequences of orders of the court which could interfere with the investigation. The court will not make an order which it would otherwise make if it would result in a person being required to commit a criminal offence . . . However, courts are required to protect the interests of litigants who find themselves in a similar position to that which exists here. They are therefore entitled to satisfy themselves that an offence will be likely to be committed if disclosure were to be made before refusing an order for disclosure. In addition, they will want to explore the possibility of reconciling the position of the party to the litigation seeking the assistance of

---

[34] [1999] 1 WLR 1551.

the court and the investigating authority by making a more restricted order for disclosure than would otherwise be made (*per* Lord Woolf MR at 1533–4).

The guidance provided by the Court of Appeal is worthy of detailed summary **6.80** as follows:

(a) As soon as a financial institution (or other regulated body) is aware of an application for discovery by an investigated subject then the NCIS should be informed and the material identified.

(b) Where the NCIS is not concerned with the subject being aware of the investigation it may simply require an undertaking to be provided that the disclosed material should be kept confidential.

(c) Where partial disclosure is possible without disclosing the existence of an investigation then this should be made. If this does not satisfy the applicant then he should be advised that application will have to be made to the court. Whether any explanation for partial disclosure is provided will be conditioned by advice from the NCIS.

(d) Where the application is to be pursued before the court, then the way in which the proceedings are dealt with will be determined by the particular circumstances and may be on an application to set aside an *ex parte* order or for directions. In any event, the court should be warned in advance of the difficulties by way of a sealed letter to the judge in charge of the court and/or by provision of a skeleton argument.

(e) The degree to which the subject of the investigation can be involved, and whether or not proceedings can be conducted in open court, will also depend on the particular circumstances of the case. However, the general approach should be that ordinary principles will apply to the extent that this is possible. A transcript of any such hearing should be made available to the subject as soon as possible once the need for secrecy has ended.

(f) The court will decide what evidence it requires, if any, from the investigating agency and may require its attendance, if necessary by making the NCIS or the relevant agency a party to the proceedings.

(g) The onus will be on the investigating agency to persuade the court that, were disclosure to be made, there would be a real likelihood of prejudice to the investigation. If co-operation from the agency was not received, or the court was not so persuaded, then the disclosure order would be made and the institution would not be at any risk of prosecution.

(h) The court must recognize its responsibility to protect the interests of absent applicants and must have material upon which to act if an applicant is to be deprived of his normal rights. The court may consider in many cases that a partial order is better than no order at all.

H. PENALTIES

6.81 The penalties for the principal offences in ss 327, 328 and 329 are, on summary conviction, six months' imprisonment and/or a fine not exceeding the statutory maximum and, on indictment, fourteen years' imprisonment or a fine or both. For offences under the failure to disclose and tipping off provisions, ss 330 to 333, the sentences on summary conviction are the same although the maximum sentence of imprisonment on indictment is five years. Sentences for money laundering can be severe (see *Simpson* (1998);[35] *Sabharwal* (2001)[36]). In an exceptional case, the sentence may be the maximum prescribed (*Reader* (1988)[37]). The argument that sentences should be limited to the maximum sentence for the offence giving rise to the tainted funds has not found favour in cases in which a conspiracy to launder money has existed over a long period of time and may not relate to any particular individual offence (*R v Everson* (2002);[38] *R v Singh Basra* (2002)[39]). However, the gravity of the connected offence may have the effect of aggravating any laundering of proceeds—see *O'Meally and Morgan* (1994)[40] in which Gage J indicated the court's approval of the remark of the sentencing judge that 'Those who launder money from drugs are nearly as bad as those who actually deal in them. It is merely one step along the line.'

---

[35] [1998] 2 Cr App R (S) 111.   [36] [2001] 2 Cr App R (S) 81.
[37] (1988) 10 Cr App R (S) 210.   [38] [2002] 1 Cr App R (S) 131.
[39] [2002] 2 Cr App R (S) 99.   [40] (1994) 15 Cr App R (S) 831.

7

CIVIL RECOVERY OF THE PROCEEDS OF UNLAWFUL CONDUCT

A. INTRODUCTION

1. General

7.01   Chapters 1 and 2 of Pt 5 of the POCA 2002 came into force on 24 February 2003. They create an entirely new High Court jurisdiction for the making of a 'recovery order'. The order enables the Director of the Assets Recovery Agency ('the enforcement authority'), to recover property which is, or which represents, 'property obtained through unlawful conduct' (s 240). This is termed 'recoverable property'. The Home Secretary has by order set a minimum threshold of £5,000.

7.02   Proceedings may not be taken in respect of cash alone (s 282(2)). The preferred procedure for the seizure of cash alone is set out in Ch 3 of Pt 5 of the Act (see Chapter 8 below).

7.03   If the Director proves the existence of recoverable property (or property which represents it) the court must make an order vesting the property in a trustee for civil recovery who will then realize it for the benefit of the Director.

7.04   According to the Agency's 2004 Report, it applies the following criteria for proceeding:

(a)   The case must normally be referred by a Law Enforcement Agency or prosecuting authority;

(b)   Criminal prosecution must have been considered and either failed or proved impossible to complete;

(c)   Recoverable property must have been identified and have an estimated value of at least £10,000;

(d)   The recoverable property must include property other than cash or negotiable instruments;

(e)   There must be evidence of criminal conduct supported to the criminal standard.

7.05   By May 2004, the Agency had received 119 referrals for civil recovery or taxation; fifty-nine had been adopted for civil recovery investigations involving £50 million of associated recoverable assets; a further twenty-seven cases were being assessed. It had commenced litigation in twenty-four cases, obtaining nine freezing orders, three 'Mareva' injunctions, and twelve interim receiving orders. Full orders have been obtained in Northern Ireland (and Scotland). On 14 May 2004 the Agency obtained its first recovery order in England and Wales against one Billy Liversedge for £16,049. According to the 2004 Report, the Agency will apply a 'realistic settlement policy'.

2. Representation

Community Legal Service (CLS) funding is available for respondents and for third parties who claim to be the innocent owners of property. Representation is 'licensed work'. Solicitors with either civil or criminal franchises may apply. They may 'self-grant' emergency work, otherwise all applications are referred to the Legal Services Commission's Special Investigations Unit. The statutory charge applies which means that any property that is recovered or maintained for a funded client must be used to repay the cost of the case to the CLS fund.   7.06

Schedule 2 to the Access to Justice Act 1999 purports to exclude from public funding certain types of proceedings, notably 'matters arising out of the carrying on of a business'. However, negotiations with the Department of Constitutional Affairs have resulted in a Direction by the Home Secretary that funding may be authorized for proceedings under the POCA which are 'in the scope of the scheme'. Guidance issued by the LSC confidently states that 'in reality, none of the proceedings listed . . . (in the 1999 Act) . . . are likely to arise in the proceedings brought by the ARA'.[1]   7.07

3. Relationship with Criminal Proceedings

Proceedings may be brought whether or not there has been a connected criminal case. Moreover, even an acquittal in criminal proceedings is no bar to the bringing of recovery proceedings in respect of the very same conduct. According to the Explanatory Notes to the POCA 2002 (para 290) civil claims 'may include cases where a defendant has been acquitted, or where a conviction did not result in a confiscation order'.   7.08

The Agency's first successful order (above) was such a case. Mr Billy Liversedge had defeated criminal confiscation under the Drug Trafficking Act by asserting that his premium bonds and cash were the proceeds of other non-drug related crime namely, the sale of smuggled cigarettes and tobacco. In a significant example of inter-agency co-operation, his case was then referred to the Agency by the West Mercia Economic Crime Unit. No doubt, there was some broad justice in his own assertions being turned against him in the civil proceedings.[2]   7.09

It has been argued with some force that the procedure has potential for use as an uneasy and unsatisfactory substitute for the criminal process. Criminal allegations are made and acted upon without the protections of criminal procedure: a clear indictment, the criminal standard of proof, determination by a jury and so   7.10

---

[1] See further: 'Guidance to Solicitors and Applicants' available at www.legalservices.gov.uk.
[2] 'The Liversedge defence' is not uncommon in DTA hearings and it may be that in such cases in future legal advice should include the possibility of an irresistible civil recovery order.

on. There is no collateral relationship with criminal proceedings at all and presently there is nothing to prevent the Director opting for civil recovery as by far the easier option.

7.11   Of considerable concern is the suggestion in the Agency's 2004 Report that a civil claim may be a proper alternative to criminal proceedings where there is 'a sensitive disclosure issue'. This is not an attractive prospect if, for example, it means that the civil process will be used to conceal Customs and Excise conduct in respect of informants of the sort that, notoriously and repeatedly, has been held to amount to abuse of the criminal process (see, for example, *Early* (2003)[3]).

4. The Human Rights Act

7.12   The safeguards of fairness that are said to underpin the criminal confiscation process do not obviously apply to civil recovery. Part of the reasoning of the House of Lords in the leading case of *Benjafield and Rezvi* (2002)[4] was that the Crown Court confiscation process is not unfair because it is triggered only when there has first been a conviction under criminal rules. No such consideration applies to civil recovery. On the contrary, as has been stated, even an acquittal may be irrelevant. Admittedly, the Act provides that, even if the property is found to be recoverable, the order may not contain any provision which is incompatible with the Human Rights Act 1998 (s 266(3)(b)). It is inevitable that the actual process of proving that the property is recoverable (and other features such as mandatory self-incrimination in response to a disclosure or production order) will face challenges under the Human Rights Act. There is appreciable irony in the predictable counter-argument that the proceedings cannot amount to the determination of a criminal charge under Article 6 precisely because there is no indictment, conviction, etc. Nor, it is said, does the process qualify for criminal safeguards as it imposes no penalty or punishment for criminal conduct. The respondent to the proceedings is not necessarily the perpetrator of the conduct but rather the holder of the property. Accordingly, the focus is on the recovery of property rather than penalizing the conduct. This has been unselfconsciously spelt out in the United States:

> The forfeiture of such proceeds, like the confiscation of money stolen from a bank, does not 'punish' respondents because it exacts no price in liberty or lawfully deprived property from them (*US v Usery* (1996)[5]).

7.13   Already, similar reasoning has defeated an Article 6 challenge in the Belfast High Court to the Northern Ireland civil recovery provisons of the POCA 2002:

> . . . the essential focus of the statutory scheme is recovery of property and not the conviction and punishment of individuals for breaches of the criminal law. The purpose of the legislation is essentially preventative in that it seeks to reduce crime by removing from

---

[3] [2003] 1 Cr App R 19.   [4] [2002] 2 WLR 235.
[5] 135 L Ed 2D 549 (1996) *per* Justice Stevens.

circulation property which can be shown to have been obtained by unlawful conduct thereby diminishing the productive efficiency of such conduct and rendering less attractive the 'untouchable' image of those who have resorted to it for the purpose of accumulating wealth and status.[6]

While there are no directly comparable procedures in other countries, civil recovery or forfeiture regimes have existed for some time in countries such as the United States, Ireland, Denmark, France, Canada, Australia, New Zealand and Italy. The equivalent in the Irish Republic, the Proceeds of Crime Act 1996 has also survived constitutional challenge (see *Gilligan v Criminal Assets Bureau* (1998)[7]).   **7.14**

Part 5 of the Act is a statement of law enforcement at its most pragmatic. Lord Steyn has recently remarked 'Perhaps it is an illusion that all problems can be solved; sometimes one may have to settle for containment and the least bad choice'.[8] The judgment of whether this path forward is 'the least bad choice' may depend upon the readiness of the Agency to utilize this process in any but the clearest cases. In the meantime, the Act simply permits the authority to bring proceedings against 'any person who the authority thinks holds recoverable property' (s 243(1)).   **7.15**

B. DEFINITIONS

1. Recoverable Property

'Property obtained through unlawful conduct is recoverable property' (s 304(1)). Property which *represents* 'the original property' is also deemed to be 'recoverable property' (s 305(1)) (see para 7.28 below).   **7.16**

2. Property and Value

Property bears the meaning that it has elsewhere in the Act, namely: **7.17**

  (a) money;

  (b) all forms of property, real or personal, heritable or movable;

  (c) things in action and other intangible or incorporeal property (s 316(4)).

References to a person's property include references to any interest which he holds in the property. The 'value' of property means its market value (s 316(1)).

---

[6] *Per* Coughlin J: 'In the matter of the Director of the Assets Recovery Agency and in the matter of Cecil Stephen Walsh and in the matter of the Proceeds of Crime Act 2002', Belfast High Court, 1 April 2004.

[7] [1998] 3 IR 185; See also *Murphy v GM PB PC Ltd and GH* (HC, 4 June 1999); *Murphy v Mitchell; Gilligan v Criminal Assets Bureau* (SC, 18 October 2001).

[8] Robin Cooke Lecture, 18 September 2002.

3. Unlawful Conduct

7.18 In broad terms, unlawful conduct means crime wherever it is committed—more precisely, if it is unlawful under UK criminal law or, if it occurs in another country, is contrary to the criminal law of that country and would be unlawful if it occurred here (s 241).

4. Property Obtained through Unlawful Conduct

7.19 A person obtains property through unlawful conduct if he obtains it 'by or in return for the conduct' (s 242(1)). The unlawful conduct need not be his own.

7.20 It is immaterial whether any money, goods or services 'were provided in order to put the person in question in a position to carry out the conduct' (s 242(2)(a)). The purpose of this provision, according to the Explanatory Notes, is:

> to ensure that property counts as having been obtained through unlawful conduct regardless of any investment in that conduct. So if a person buys illicit drugs with honestly come by money, and sells them at a profit, the whole of the proceeds of sale will count as having been obtained through unlawful conduct (para 295).

7.21 Nor does the Director have to prove that the conduct was a particular kind of crime 'if it is shown that the property was obtained through conduct of one of a number of kinds, each of which would have been unlawful conduct' (s 242(2)(b)). Again according to the Explanatory Notes, this means that:

> . . . it will not matter, for example, that it cannot be established whether certain funds are attributable to drug dealing, money laundering, brothel-keeping or other unlawful activities, provided it can be shown that they are attributable to one or other of these in the alternative, or perhaps some alternative (para 296).

5. Exceptions

7.22 Property ceases to be recoverable in the following situations (s 308):

(a) where a person obtains the property in good faith, for value and without notice that it was a recoverable acquisition (see below);

(b) where a person obtains the property following a civil judgment based upon unlawful conduct;

(c) where payment is made under a compensation or various forms of restitution order;

(d) while a restraint order applies to the property;

(e) where the property has been taken into account in making a criminal confiscation order.

Recoverable property does not include property which has been disposed of under the forfeiture provisions of the statutes listed in the POCA 2002 (Exemption from Civil Recovery) Order.[9]   **7.23**

6. Associated Property

Associated property essentially means innocently held property which has some physical or legal connection with the recoverable property. The court may make orders dramatically affecting rights in the associated property including seizure and realization of the property. However, there must then be repayment for value or severance of the interest.   **7.24**

More specifically, associated property means any of the following descriptions *which is not itself the recoverable property*:   **7.25**

(a) any interest in the recoverable property;

(b) any other interest in the property in which the recoverable property subsists;

(c) if the recoverable property is a tenancy in common, the other tenancy;

(d) if the recoverable property is an inseparable part of a larger property, the remainder of that property (s 245).

C. ACQUISITION IN GOOD FAITH

As mentioned above, property ceases to be recoverable if obtained for value by a bona fide purchaser without notice that it is recoverable (s 308).   **7.26**

In addition, where the property is not acquired for value, the court has a discretion not to include recoverable property in an order if it would not be just and equitable to do so and if each of the following conditions is met (s 266(3)(a)):   **7.27**

(a) the respondent obtained the property in good faith;

(b) he took steps after obtaining it which he would not otherwise have taken or he took steps before obtaining it which he would not have taken had he not believed he was going to obtain it;

(c) when he did so, he had no notice that the property was recoverable; and

(d) because of the steps he took, a recovery order would be detrimental.

In determining whether the requirements of justice and equity are met in the particular case, the court must have regard both to the degree of detriment and to the authority's interest in receiving the realized proceeds of the property (s 266(6)).

---

[9] SI 2003/336.

D. TRACING PROPERTY

1. Disposal of Original Property

7.28 The claim follows the property so that recovery cannot be thwarted by simply converting the recoverable property into something else or by granting an interest in it. Where there has been a disposal of the original property, a 'pick and mix' approach is available. The Director may choose to trace the original property itself through various hands or he may prefer to recover property which now represents the original property. 'Disposal' includes disposal of part of the property or granting an interest in the property including under a will or intestacy or by operation of law or simply by making a payment (s 314).

7.29 He can, therefore, follow the property 'into the hands' of anyone obtaining it up to the point of its innocent acquisition for value by a person acting in good faith—for example, where a stolen painting is passed from thief to handler and, if necessary, on through a chain of recipients, the painting remains recoverable (s 304(3)).

7.30 Alternatively, if the actual property itself is no longer accessible, either because it no longer exists or because it now belongs to a bona fide purchaser for value, the Act also permits the recovery of property which represents the original property (s 305(1)).

7.31 So that, in the above example, if the thief swaps the painting for a motor car, the car is 'recoverable property' because it represents the original property. If the thief then sells the car for cash or other property, the cash or other property is recoverable (s 305(2)). Finally, as a further alternative, the car in the example may itself be followed into the hands of the person who obtains it (s 305(3)).

2. Mixing Property

7.32 Frequently, of course, a person's recoverable property will be mixed up with other non-recoverable property (his own or that of another). The Act itself gives examples such as increasing funds in a bank account, part payment for the acquisition of an asset, the restoration or improvement of land and the acquisition of a freehold by a leaseholder. In those sorts of situation, the portion which is attributable to the recoverable property is deemed to represent the recoverable property (s 306(2)). However, profits which have accrued out of the recoverable property are themselves recoverable (s 307).

E. PROCEDURE

1. Procedure Generally

The procedure for the making of claims and applications is governed by the 'Practice Direction—Proceeds of Crime Act 2002 Parts 5 and 8: Civil Recovery' (2004) which largely adopts the existing Civil Procedure Rules.

7.33

It appears that such aspects as pleadings, default judgments, discovery, exchange of witness statements, and the conduct of hearings are governed by the normal rules of procedure and evidence. Compulsory discovery in the shape of disclosure and production orders (see Chapter 4 above and para 7.42 below) is already available to the Director elsewhere in the Act. Third parties, against whom no cause of action lies, such as financial institutions, are likely to be ordered to supply information. Confidentiality is not a bar in the face of public interest (see *C v S* (1999);[10] *Norwich Pharmacal v Customs and Excise Commissioners* (1974)[11]).

7.34

Under the Civil Evidence Act 1995 criminal convictions prove their own facts. Undoubtedly, they will be admissible to prove the criminal conduct itself or to support an inference that the probable source of property is criminal.

7.35

2. Commencing Proceedings

In practice, an application for an interim receiving order freezing the assets before proceedings are issued is likely to prove the most common method of launching the recovery process (see para 7.47 below).

7.36

A claim or application must commence in the Administrative Court which 'will thereupon consider whether to transfer (it) to another Division or Court of the High Court'.[12] The claim itself must originate with a claim form, governed by Pt 8 of the Civil Procedure Rules, to be served on the respondent 'wherever domiciled, resident or present'. If, in addition, the Director wishes to obtain an order in respect of associated property, he must also serve the form on anyone that he 'thinks holds any associated property' unless the court dispenses with service (s 243). If the property is not specified, it must at least be described in general terms in the claim form or in the particulars of claim (s 243(3)). The form must state whether it is recoverable or associated property.

7.37

3. Limitation

The Director may not bring proceedings (either by issuing a claim form or by applying for an interim order) after the expiration of twelve years from the date on which the original criminal property was obtained (s 288).

7.38

---

[10] [1999] 1 WLR 1551.   [11] [1974] AC 133.   [12] Practice Direction, para 2.2.

4. Burden of Proof

7.39   The burden of proving that property was obtained by criminal conduct lies on the Director. However, this does not mean proving that the respondent or anyone further up the line has committed any particular crime, but merely proving that the property is probably criminal in origin. In practice, this burden will often be discharged by inference from the circumstances, leaving the respondent with the task of providing an alternative explanation. One can anticipate claims based upon an analysis of the respondent's means in which, for example, bankings or assets are compared with known sources of income. Inevitably, reconciliation will be a matter for the respondent.

5. Standard of Proof

7.40   The standard required to prove whether any matters alleged to constitute unlawful conduct have occurred or that any person intended to use cash in unlawful conduct is 'the balance of probabilities' (s 241).

7.41   As in Pt 2 of the Act (criminal confiscation—see Chapter 3 above), this represents a departure from the language of earlier legislation which stipulated the standard 'applicable in civil proceedings'. As a matter of statutory construction, the change can only be interpreted as intentional and purposive. The purpose may be to anticipate any reliance on the principle that a claim of criminal conduct requires a high probative standard even in civil proceedings—fraud being the classic example.[13]

7.42   However, one notes that the Agency's own criteria for bringing proceedings include the existence of 'evidence of criminal conduct supported to the *criminal standard*'.

6. Production and Disclosure Orders, Search and Seizure Warrants

7.43   These orders are covered in Chapter 4 above. They may be granted on an *ex parte* application. A production order requires any person who is in possession or control of material to produce it or give access to it to 'an appropriate officer' (ie a constable or customs officer or member of the Agency staff) (s 345).

7.44   The court must be satisfied that there are reasonable grounds:

  (a) for suspecting that the specified property is recoverable or associated property;

  (b) for believing that the person is in possession or control of it;

  (c) for believing that the material is likely to be of 'substantial value to the investigation'; and

---

[13]   See *Bater v Bater* [1951] P 35; *Hornal v Neuberger Products Ltd* [1957] 1 QB 247; *R v Secretary of State for the Home Department, ex p Khawaja* [1984] AC 74.

(d) that the order is in the public interest, having regard to the benefit to the investigation and the circumstances in which the person holds the material.

There are similar powers exercisable on similar conditions to grant extensive 7.45 search and seizure warrants (s 352) and to make disclosure orders requiring 'any person the Director considers has relevant information' to answer questions, provide specified information or produce documents (s 357). It is an offence to fail to comply with the order or to make a deliberate or reckless statement. Relevant information is 'information which the Director considers to be relevant'!

There is a likelihood that hearsay information from undisclosed informants will 7.46 have a role in the establishment of reasonable grounds for granting orders or warrants (see *Smith (Joe)* (2001)[14]).

Statements made by someone in response to an order are not admissible in 7.47 criminal proceedings against him (s 360). This protection does not apply in confiscation proceedings, breaches of the order, perjury proceedings or generally as a previous inconsistent statement. No disclosure order can be made in relation to a money laundering investigation.

F. INTERIM RECEIVING ORDERS

1. General

The Director can apply for an interim order before or after starting the proceed- 7.48 ings (s 246(1)). This can be done secretly 'if the circumstances are such that notice . . . would prejudice any right of the enforcement authority' to obtain an order. Plainly, this is aimed at preventing the frustration of recovery proceedings by advance destruction or concealment of the property.

The court may only make an order if satisfied that there is a 'good arguable case' 7.49 that the property is or includes recoverable property or is associated property. The court may order compensation if it eventually decides that the property is neither recoverable nor associated property (s 283).

As a matter of basic principle, there must be a duty of frankness which includes 7.50 a duty to draw to the court's attention any matters in the respondent's favour which might cause the court to refuse the application. In addition, where the property includes associated property and the identity of 'the person who holds it' has not been established, the court must be satisfied that all reasonable steps have been taken to do so.

---

[14] [2001] 1 WLR 1034; *Fox, Campbell and Hartley v UK* (1990) 13 EHRR 157; and cf *Lamothe v Commissioner of Police for the Metropolis* (CA, 25 October 1999).

2. The Effect of an Order

7.51 An order has four effects:

(a) it permits 'the detention, custody or preservation of property' (s 246(2)(a));

(b) it appoints an interim receiver (s 246(2)(b));

(c) any 'civil recovery investigation' by the Director must cease (s 341(3)(b)) (see chapter 4);

(d) subject to express exclusions, it prevents 'any person to whose property the order applies' from dealing with it (s 252).

7.52 Two examples of discretionary 'exclusions' from the bar on dealing with the property are (i) reasonable living expenses and (ii) the carrying on of any trade, business, profession or occupation. However, (and sadly for some) an order may not make provision for expenditure of private finances on legal expenses for the purpose of resisting the civil recovery claim itself. As mentioned above, legal aid will normally be available.

7.53 The power to exclude property from the order must be exercised with a view to ensuring that the Director's rights are not prejudiced.

7.54 The order may include a requirement that a respondent must produce or preserve the property or relevant documents (s 250). 'Document' means anything in which information of any description is recorded.

3. Receivers

7.55 The application must nominate a qualified receiver who, in this situation, may not be a member of the ARA staff. The court can give the receiver such powers as it thinks 'appropriate' for the statutory purposes (summarized below).

7.56 The receiver, any party to the proceedings or anyone affected by the actions or proposed actions of the receiver may apply to the court for directions regulating the receiver's functions. However, the reality of the situation may be that, once the authority discharges the burden of establishing a 'good arguable case', it is the interim receiver rather than the court who effectively determines whether the property is, in fact, recoverable. Indeed, the order 'must' require the interim receiver to take necessary steps to establish whether the property in the order is recoverable or associated property and also whether any other property is recoverable and, if so, who holds it (s 247(2)). Thus, there may be an inevitability about the process if it is already established at the outset that the property is the proceeds of crime.

7.57 Express powers are set out in Sch 6 and include the following:

(a) Power to seize the property.

(b) Power to obtain information or to require 'a person to answer any question'. As with disclosure orders, there are limitations on the subsequent use of compulsory statements in criminal prosecutions. The order itself must 'make provision in respect of legal professional privilege'. This wording is unhelpfully vague: for example, should the court expressly exempt matters that are or matters that merely may be privileged?

(c) Power to enter and search premises, to copy or remove relevant material. Again, 'provision' must be made in the order for legal privilege.

(d) Power to manage property. This includes selling or disposing of property that is perishable or has diminishing value, continuing trade or business, or incurring capital expenditure.

(e) Power to require any person to return property or documents to the jurisdiction (s 250).

7.58 The order must require the receiver to report as soon as reasonably practicable if he thinks that the property is neither recoverable nor associated property. But, equally, he must report if he considers that any property outside the order is recoverable or associated property or if the property turns out to be held by someone different from the person claimed in the application or if there has been a change in circumstances (s 255). Copies of the report must be served on anyone who holds property to which the order applies or 'who may otherwise be affected by the report' (s 255(2)). An interim receiver is not liable for non-negligent loss or damage to property.

4. Collateral Proceedings

7.59 During the currency of an interim order, the court can stay 'any action, execution or other legal process' in respect of the property; and no distress can be levied against the property without the court's permission (s 253). In addition, any court in which there are pending proceedings over the property can stay or control the continuance of the proceedings if satisfied that an interim order has been applied for or made. No landlord may exercise any right of forfeiture by re-entry for breaches of the tenancy without the court's permission.

G. THE MAKING OF A RECOVERY ORDER

1. General

7.60 Once satisfied that the property is recoverable, the court must make a recovery order vesting the property in a 'trustee for civil recovery' (s 266). This is called a 'Part 5 Transfer'. The trustee is 'a suitably qualified person' nominated by the Director (s 267).

7.61 An order pre-empts any provision 'of whatever nature' which otherwise restricts the vesting of the property (s 269). The court may also order severance of any property or impose conditions as to the manner in which the trustee may deal with the property for the purpose of realising it (s 266(8)). Schedule 10, Pt 2 contains detailed taxation rules following Part 5 transfers.

2. Exceptions

7.62 Even if the property is found to be recoverable, the order may not contain any provision affecting the property if it is incompatible with the Human Rights Act 1998 (s 266(3)(b)).

7.63 The court also has discretion not to include recoverable property in an order if it would not be just and equitable so to do *and* if various conditions regarding acquisition in good faith are satisfied (s 266(6)) (see para 7.27 above).

3. Victims of Theft

7.64 The procedure permits someone who has been deprived of property 'by unlawful conduct' to apply to the court for a declaration to that effect with the result that the property cannot be treated as recoverable (s 281).

4. Holders of Associated Property and Joint Tenants

(a) *Agreed payments*

7.65 As an alternative to the vesting of the property in the trustee, the Act allows agreed payments in limited situations. For example, where the property includes associated property and the owner has been served with the claim form or service dispensed with, the person holding the property can agree with the Director to make a payment equivalent to the value of the recoverable property instead of having it taken away and vested in the trustee (ss 270 and 271). A similar disposal is potentially available if the recoverable property belongs to joint tenants and one of them obtained it in circumstances in which it would not be recoverable against him. This allows for payment of the value of the recoverable property less that tenant's share.

7.66 If, in either of these situations, the authority agrees that the person has suffered loss as a result of an interim receiving order, the payment may be reduced by agreement 'having regard to that loss and to any other relevant circumstances' (s 271(4)).

(b) *Payments by the trustee for civil recovery*

7.67 Where there is no agreement in these situations, the recovery order may vest the property in the trustee but simultaneously provide for recompense if 'the court thinks it just and equitable to do so'. The mechanism is for the recovery order to provide for the trustee to pay an amount to the person holding the associated property or the joint tenant and/or provide for the creation of interests in the vested property (s 272). Again where there has been loss as a result of an interim order reasonable compensation can be ordered.

5. Pension Rights

Where the recoverable property includes rights under a pension scheme, the order   **7.68** requires the pension trustees or managers to pay the value of the rights (as determined by them) to the trustee for civil recovery (s 273). There are detailed provisions defining the term 'pension scheme' and the methods of calculation (ss 274 and 275).

6. Insolvency

Special rules apply in situations such as those where the property is an asset of a   **7.69** company that is being voluntarily wound up, or part of the estate of a person adjudged bankrupt. Recovery proceedings may not be taken or continued unless the relevant court grants leave (s 311).

7. Consent Orders

As with most civil actions, the court may stay the proceedings and adopt 'terms   **7.70** agreed by the parties for the disposal of the proceedings' in the form of a consent order (s 276).

H. THE TRUSTEE FOR CIVIL RECOVERY

1. Functions

In general terms the role of the trustee is to realize the value of the recovered prop-   **7.71** erty and pay it over to the Director. In effect, he is the agent of the Director. He acts on behalf of the Director and must comply with the Director's directions (s 267(4)). He must perform any function conferred by the Act (s 267(3)) and, in particular, must act:

  (a) to secure the detention, custody or preservation of property vested in him;

  (b) to realise the value of such property (apart from money) 'for the benefit' of the authority. This is also expressed as a duty to realise the value, 'so far as practicable, in the manner best calculated to maximise the amount payable' to the Director (s 267(5)).

Extensive enabling powers are granted by Sch 7 as follows: **7.72**

  (a) to sell all or any part of the property;

  (b) to incur expenditure in acquiring any part of or interest in the property not vested in him, or to discharge liabilities or extinguish rights;

  (c) to manage the property;

  (d) to commence, continue or defend legal proceedings;

(e) to compromise any claim;

(f) to 'do any other act which is necessary or expedient'.

8

CASH SEIZURE

A. INTRODUCTION

The historical origins of the power to seize criminal cash are to be found in the **8.01** Criminal Justice (International Cooperation) Act 1990. This resulted from complaints made by American and British law enforcement agencies to the Home Affairs Select Committee that international suppression of money laundering, together with the absence of UK exchange control, had led to large-scale movements of 'dirty money' into this country.[1] The powers in the 1990 Act were replaced by Pt II of the Drug Trafficking Act 1994 which permitted the seizure, detention, and forfeiture of cash 'which is being imported into or exported from the United Kingdom' and which represented proceeds of drug trafficking.

---

[1] See 7th Report 1989, Vol 1, para 87.

155

8.02 Chapter 3 of Pt 5 of the POCA 2002 extends the powers in the 1994 Act in two highly significant ways: (a) to include cash which is related to all forms of unlawful conduct; and (b) to provide for the seizure of such cash 'found at any place in the United Kingdom', regardless of its geographical provenance or destination.

8.03 Cash seized may only be held for a period of forty-eight hours although this may be extended by a magistrate for a further initial period of three months, and thereafter by further order(s) up to two years.

8.04 The magistrates' court may order the forfeiture of the cash. The powers of seizure and forfeiture respectively are both founded upon the the same conditions: namely, that the cash is either 'recoverable property' or was 'intended for use by any person in unlawful conduct'.

8.05 This measure was the first part of the POCA 2002 to come into force on 30 December 2002 and has been used enthusiastically since then. Compared to civil proceedings for other 'recoverable property' (for which the Agency estimates a two-year turnaround), summary seizure and forfeiture of cash provide fast and effective tools for the disruption of criminal activity and benefits. Inter-agency co-operation has proved particularly fruitful. By way of a vivid illustration of the new 'joined up' approach under the Act, in March 2004 a high street bank submitted a consent request to the NCIS, regarding a request to withdraw £30,000 from an account. Avon and Somerset Financial Investigations Unit established that the account holder was the unemployed mother of an alleged local heroin dealer. Having withdrawn the money at a pre-arranged time, the woman was stopped outside the bank, the cash seized, and a money laundering prosecution is to follow.

B. DEFINITIONS

1. 'Cash'

8.06 Cash is defined as:

(a) notes and coins in any currency;

(b) postal orders;

(c) cheques of any kind, including travellers' cheques;

(d) bankers' drafts;

(e) bearer bonds and bearer shares; and

(f) any kind of monetary instrument specified by the Home Secretary.[2]

---

[2] See s 289(6) and (7).

2. 'Recoverable Property'

Part 5 of the Act, which also includes civil recovery, adopts universal definitions. **8.07** Thus, 'recoverable property' is simply expressed as property 'obtained through unlawful conduct' (s 304(1)). If such property has been disposed of, property which *represents* 'the original property' is also deemed to be 'recoverable property' (s 305(1)). Thus, if stolen goods are sold for cash, the cash itself is recoverable property (see further para 7.28).

3. 'Unlawful Conduct'

In broad terms, 'unlawful conduct' means crime wherever it is committed—more **8.08** precisely, if it is unlawful under UK criminal law or, if it occurs in another country, is contrary to the criminal law of that country and would be unlawful if it occurred here (s 241).

4. 'Property Obtained through Unlawful Conduct'

A person obtains property through unlawful conduct if he obtains it 'by or in **8.09** return for the conduct' (s 242(1)). The unlawful conduct need not be his own (see further para 7.19).

C. SEARCH AND SEIZURE

1. Search Powers

A customs officer or constable may search any premises or person for cash 'which **8.10** is recoverable property or is intended by any person for use in unlawful conduct' (s 289(1)) (see below). Where premises are to be searched, the officer must be on the premises lawfully, ie in a public place, on private premises by invitation of the owner, or in the exercise of an existing power of entry under the Police and Criminal Evidence Act 1984 or the Customs and Excise Management Act 1979. The powers are exercisable 'only so far as reasonably required for the purpose of finding cash'.

The powers may only be exercised where the officer has reasonable grounds for **8.11** suspecting (a) that such cash is on the premises or is being carried by the person, and (b) that the amount of cash is not less than £5,000.[3]

---

[3] The original minimum of £10,000 has been revised downwards with effect from 16th March 2004 (The Proceeds of Crime 2002 (Recovery of Cash in Summary Proceedings: Minimum Amount) Order 2004 (SI 2004/420). The Code of Practice (see below) continues to refer to the higher amount but is overridden by the statutory instrument.

8.12   In the case of customs officers, searches are only permitted if the officer has reasonable grounds for suspecting that the unlawful conduct relates to an 'assigned matter' as defined by the Customs and Excise Management Act 1979— essentially any matter in relation to which the Commissioners are 'for the time being required in pursuance of any enactment to perform any duties'.

8.13   Involuntary 'intimate' or 'strip searches' are not permitted within the meaning of s 164 of the Customs and Excise Management Act 1979 (s 289(8)). An 'intimate search' is one involving a physical rather than merely visual examination of a person's body orifices. A 'strip search' is any search which involves the removal of any article of clothing worn wholly or partly on the trunk and either next to the skin or next to an article of underwear. Only an outer coat, jacket or gloves may be required to be removed and the search of inner clothing must be confined to superficial examination of outer garments. This does not prevent an officer from putting his hands inside pockets or feeling around the inside of collars, socks, shoes, and the like. Reasonable force may be used for the purposes of the search and, by virtue of s 289(4), the officer may detain the suspected person for so long as is necessary to exercise these powers.

8.14   It should be noted that both Customs and Excise and regional police forces are using and training dogs to detect concealed cash. The ARA has even released a special 'canine newsletter' trumpeting successful discoveries.

2. Prior Approval

8.15   Searches need prior approval from a magistrate, police inspector or above or the Customs and Excise equivalent unless 'in the circumstances it is not practicable to obtain that approval' beforehand (s 290). The hearings are likely to be *ex parte* and without notice, but with a written application. However, if a search is conducted without the authority of a magistrate, and no cash is recovered or any cash is released within forty-eight hours, a written report must be completed specifying the reasons for the search and why prior approval was not practicable (s 290(6)). The intention is that such reports should be submitted to an independent person (the 'appointed person') appointed by the Secretary of State to review such matters and to provide reports to him and to Parliament. This may be of little comfort to an aggrieved individual but will provide evidence of an unlawful search, which might in turn give rise to a civil action for assault and/or trespass.

3. Code of Practice

8.16   A statutory Code of Practice came into operation on 30 December 2002.[4] It closely follows PACE 1984 Code A (Stop and Search) and Code B (Searching of Premises and Seizure of Property) and anticipates that the standard recording requirements will be followed. Officers are reminded that:

---

[4] Proceeds of Crime (Cash Searches: Code of Practice) Order 2002 (SI 2002 /3115).

the right to respect for private life and home—and the right to peaceful enjoyment of possessions—are both safeguarded by the Human Rights Act 1998. Powers of search may involve significant interference with the privacy of those whose premises and persons are searched and therefore need to be fully and clearly justified before they are used. In particular, officers should consider at every stage whether the necessary objectives can be achieved by less intrusive means (Draft Code, para 5).

8.17 Perhaps more in hope than expectation, the Code addresses the proper meaning of 'reasonable suspicion':

reasonable suspicion can never be supported on the basis of personal factors alone without reliable supporting intelligence or information or some specific behaviour by the person concerned. For example, a person's race, age, appearance, or the fact that a person is known to have a previous conviction, cannot be used alone or in combination with each other as the reason for searching that person. Reasonable suspicion cannot be based on generalisations or stereotypical images of certain groups or categories of people being more likely to be involved in criminal activity.

4. Seizure

8.18 Constables or customs officers may seize cash on a similar basis: namely, if they have reasonable grounds for suspecting that it is recoverable property or intended by any person for use in unlawful conduct (s 294(1)). The whole of a cash amount may be seized if it is not reasonably practicable to sever it from a suspected amount.

D. DETENTION OF CASH

8.19 Once seized, the cash may be retained for so long as the reasonable suspicion is maintained. In the first instance there is also an upper limit of forty-eight hours (s 295). This may be extended by a magistrates' court for a period of three months, and thereafter by order(s) for a maximum of two years 'beginning with the date of the first order' (s 295(2)). There are two conditions: first that the initial operating condition still applies in respect of the cash—namely, thought to be recoverable proceeds or for use in unlawful conduct—and, secondly, that either:

(a) its derivation is still being investigated ; or

(b) consideration is being given to bringing 'in the United Kingdom or elsewhere' proceedings against 'any person' for an offence with which the cash is 'connected'; or

(c) such proceedings have commenced but have not concluded.

8.20 Where cash is detained in excess of forty-eight hours, it must be paid into an interest-bearing account and the accrued interest added to the sum eventually forfeited or released. The provisions are widely drawn and will result in cash being detained where, for example, a foreign police force continues its investigations against third parties who may have some link with the cash.

E. FORFEITURE

1. Powers

8.21 An application for forfeiture may be made to the magistrates' court by a constable or by the Commissioner of Customs and Excise who must demonstrate to the civil standard that all or part of the cash is either recoverable property or was intended for use by any person in criminal conduct (s 298).

8.22   The evidence in support of an application is likely to be that which first gave rise to suspicion and justified exercise of search and seizure powers, together with the fruits of any subsequent investigation. The cash may have been hidden and untruthful or inconsistent explanation(s) offered for its possession. The background circumstances may be relevant; for example, that the suspected person was travelling to a well-known centre for the supply of drugs. The cash itself may be contaminated with traces of drugs which are not explicable in terms of normal contamination of notes in circulation (see *Pruijsen v Customs and Excise Commissioners* (1999)[5]). Moreover, there may be specific evidence to associate the carrier of cash with illegal activity on a previous occasion. This, it is submitted, should be more than the mere fact of a previous record. In certain circumstances, the applicant may even rely upon a previous acquittal. *Customs and Excise Commissioners v Thorpe* (1996)[6] was such a case. The defendant was stopped en route to Spain in possession at the airport of £12,500 in cash which was seized under the DTA powers. On a previous occasion, four and a half years earlier, the same man had been seen to go to a helicopter that had just landed, and to take a holdall that contained cannabis and amphetamines to a waiting car. Proceedings against him for drugs offences were later withdrawn and his acquittal was directed. In applying for forfeiture of the cash, the Customs were not precluded from relying on the facts of the earlier incident, it being held by the Divisional Court that his argument as to issue estoppel had no application.

8.23   Where the property belongs to joint tenants, one of whom is an excepted joint owner, such share 'as the court thinks is attributable to the excepted joint owner's share' will not be forfeit (s 298(3)). This might, for example, include a joint account holder who has deposited legitimate funds into an account used by another to hold the proceeds of drugs trafficking. Where the other account holder removes the whole, and it is subsequently seized, then the innocent party's share may be returned.

8.24   Appeals against forfeiture lie to the Crown Court (s 299). The cash must be retained pending any appeal against the forfeiture order. The application must be

---

[5] QB, 18 October 1999.   [6] 18 November 1996.

made within thirty days of the forfeiture order. Notice must be given to certain persons with an interest in the proceedings who may not have been joined as parties in the magistrates' courts.[7]

2. Representation

Community Legal Service funding is available to resist an application for forfei- **8.25**
ture[8] for respondents and for third parties who claim to be the innocent owners of property. They are treated as civil proceedings and, therefore, subject to the required means and merits tests. Representation is 'licensed work'. Solicitors with either civil or criminal franchises may apply. They may 'self-grant' emergency work, otherwise all applications are referred to the Legal Services Commission's Special Investigations Unit.

F. RELEASE OF DETAINED CASH

An order for the return of cash will require proof that the conditions contained in **8.26**
s 295 for the detention of the cash are no longer met in respect of the cash or any part of it. The provisions envisage two situations in which seized cash will be returned, namely:

(a) return by the investigating authorities on the basis that detention can no longer be justified;

(b) on application to the magistrates' court by the person from whom the cash was seized (s 297).

G. VICTIMS AND OTHER OWNERS

Any person who claims that the detained cash belongs to him can apply to the **8.27**
magistrates' court for its release in the course of detention or forfeiture proceedings 'or at any other time'. This provision essentially allows the 'true owner' of property to apply to the court for its release in circumstances where:

(a) some or all of the cash belongs to the applicant, or represents his property, and it was taken from him by unlawful conduct; and

(b) it was not, immediately before that time, 'recoverable property'.

The provision protects the interests of third parties in respect of property which could not otherwise be recovered from them by civil recovery proceedings.

---

[7] Crown Court (Amendment) (No 2) Rules 2002 (SI 2002/2997).
[8] See para 3, Sch 2 to the Access to Justice Act 1999 as amended by Sch 11 to the POCA 2002.

H. COMPENSATION

8.28 Section 302 provides that, where no forfeiture order is made, the person from whom the cash was seized or the person to whom it belongs, may apply to the magistrates' court for compensation. This will normally be no more than the interest accruing to the interest-bearing account into which the money has been deposited. If, however, the court is satisfied that the person has suffered loss as a result of the detention and 'the circumstances are exceptional', it may order reasonable additional compensation.

9

REVENUE FUNCTIONS

A. GENERAL

Prior to the POCA 2002, Customs and Excise and the Inland Revenue regularly pooled intelligence. Since 1996 (when self-assessment was introduced) random investigations into tax returns have occurred in a small number of cases. The Anti-Terrorism, Crime and Security Act 2001 created an 'information gateway' which allowed the Revenue to disclose information to law enforcement agencies.   **9.01**

However, Pt 6 of the POCA goes a great deal further and gives the Director of the Assets Recovery Agency a novel power to take over the specific and general tax collection functions of the Inland Revenue. It came into force on 24 February 2003. It is arguably a second or even third best option where the state cannot directly attack proceeds of crime through post-conviction confiscation or by civil recovery. Everyone is familiar with the famous example of Al Capone.   **9.02**

It has been held that the 'principle of fiscal neutrality' allows for no generalized differentiation between lawful and unlawful transactions (except where certain products have special characteristics, such as counterfeit money or dangerous drugs[1]). Accordingly, income tax is chargeable on income whether the source is legitimate or not; capital gains tax applies to capital assets and has never depended on the source, and stamp duty is a tax on documents, not on transactions.   **9.03**

---

[1] See *Customs and Excise Commissioners v Polok* [2002] STC 361; *Staatssecrataris van Financien v Coffeeshop 'Siberie' vof* [1999] STC 742.

9.04   As of 31 March 2004, the ARA had received 119 referrals from other agencies for either civil recovery proceedings or taxation. By that date, the Agency had adopted seven cases for taxation. In four of those cases tax assessments have been raised totalling £730,000. The Agency has what it describes as a 'realistic settlement policy'.

9.05   By way of practical example under Irish legislation, in July 1998 the Irish High Court entered judgment against one George Mitchell for £103,350 for VAT and interest while he was serving a sentence of imprisonment in Holland. Between October 1996 and December 2001 the Irish Criminal Assets Bureau demanded 56 million euros and collected 36 million euros in taxes and interest under the Irish Proceeds of Crime Act 1996.

9.06   The general Revenue functions that may be vested in the Director are as follows (s 323):

- income tax;
- capital gains tax;
- corporation tax;
- national insurance contributions;
- statutory sick pay;
- statutory maternity pay;
- statutory paternity pay;
- statutory adoption pay;
- student loans.

B. REASONABLE GROUNDS FOR SUSPICION

9.07   In the most general terms, the Director must first have reasonable grounds to suspect that taxable income, gains, or profits are the proceeds of crime. Accordingly, the standard of proof is not whether criminal conduct can be proved but whether reasonable grounds exist for the Director's suspicion. Note also that in order to exercise his powers, the Director need not necessarily believe that the property is criminal but merely suspect it to be such. It is immaterial whether the tax liability arose before or after the Act.

9.08   The whole raison d'être of these powers is that they provide a method of taxing income with no apparent legitimate origin. Accordingly, it is immaterial that the Director cannot identify any source for the income (s 319(1)).

C. NOTICE TO THE COMMISSIONERS

1. Vesting of Functions

The takeover occurs when the Director serves notice on the Inland Revenue   9.09
Commissioners ('the Board') vesting in himself the Revenue functions specified in
the notice. The notice does not, however, operate to divest the Board of the same
functions. Notices may be served in respect of three areas of taxation:

(a) personal income, gain and company profits;

(b) inheritance tax;

(c) settlements.

2. Personal Income, Gain, and Company Profits

The Director may serve a notice when he reasonably suspects that a person's   9.10
income or gain is chargeable to tax or that company profits are chargeable to corporation tax and that the income, gain or profits in a chargeable period arise or
accrue 'as a result of the person's or another's criminal conduct' (wholly or partly,
directly or indirectly) (s 317).

'Criminal conduct' means conduct whenever it occurred which amounts to an   9.11
offence in the United Kingdom or would do so if it occurred here (s 326(1) and
(2)).

The Director is not required to take over functions which relate to a company in   9.12
its capacity as an employer or to self-employed Class 2 contributions and which
relate to a year of assessment that does not fall within the chargeable period
(s 318).

3. Inheritance Tax

The Director may serve a notice when he reasonably suspects that (a) there has   9.13
been a transfer of value within the meaning of the Inheritance Tax Act 1984; and
(b) the value transferred is 'attributable (in whole or in part) to criminal property'
(s 321).

Property is 'criminal' if it constitutes or represents (wholly or partly, directly or   9.14
indirectly) 'a person's benefit from criminal conduct' (s 326(4)). It does not matter
who carried out the conduct nor who benefited from it. Criminal conduct is
defined above. The definitions of terms such as 'benefit', 'property', and 'obtaining' mirror those found in Pt 2 of the Act and the reader is referred to Chapter 3
above for more detail. As before, 'criminal conduct' means conduct whenever it
occurred which amounts to an offence in the United Kingdom or would do so if it
occurred here (s 326).

4. Settlements

9.15 Here notice depends upon reasonable suspicion that:

(a) all or part of the property comprised in a settlement is 'relevant property' for the purposes of the Inheritance Tax Act 1984 (ie a settlement without interest in possession); and

(b) the relevant property is (in whole or part) criminal property (as defined above) (s 322).

D. APPEALS

9.16 An appeal 'in respect of the exercise by the Director of general Revenue functions' lies as of right to the Special Commissioners who may nominate one or more specialist assessors from a panel appointed by the Lord Chancellor (s 320).

APPENDIX 1

Proceeds of Crime Act 2002

CHAPTER 29

CONTENTS

PART 1
ASSETS RECOVERY AGENCY

PART 2
CONFISCATION: ENGLAND AND WALES

PART 3

PART 4

PART 5
CIVIL RECOVERY OF THE PROCEEDS ETC. OF UNLAWFUL CONDUCT

CHAPTER 1
INTRODUCTORY

CHAPTER 3
RECOVERY OF CASH IN SUMMARY PROCEEDINGS

CHAPTER 2
ENGLAND AND WALES AND NORTHERN IRELAND

PROCEEDS OF CRIME ACT 2002

CHAPTER 29

An Act to establish the Assets Recovery Agency and make provision about the appointment of its Director and his functions (including Revenue functions), to provide for confiscation orders in relation to persons who benefit from criminal conduct and for restraint orders to prohibit dealing with property, to allow the recovery of property which is or represents property obtained through unlawful conduct or which is intended to be used in unlawful conduct, to make provision about money laundering, to make provision about investigations relating to benefit from criminal conduct or to property which is or represents property obtained through unlawful conduct or to money laundering, to make provision to give effect to overseas requests and orders made where property is found or believed to be obtained through criminal conduct, and for connected purposes.

[24th July 2002]

BE IT ENACTED by the Queen's most Excellent Majesty, by and with the advice and consent of the Lords Spiritual and Temporal, and Commons, in this present Parliament assembled, and by the authority of the same, as follows:—

PART 1
ASSETS RECOVERY AGENCY

1. The Agency and its Director

(1) There shall be an Assets Recovery Agency (referred to in this Act as the Agency).
(2) The Secretary of State must appoint a Director of the Agency (referred to in this Act as the Director).
(3) The Director is a corporation sole.
(4) The Director may—
   (a) appoint such persons as members of staff of the Agency, and
   (b) make such arrangements for the provision of services, as he considers appropriate for or in connection with the exercise of his functions.
(5) But the Director must obtain the approval of the Minister for the Civil Service as to the number of staff appointed under subsection (4)(a).
(6) Anything which the Director is authorised or required to do may be done by—
   (a) a member of staff of the Agency, or
   (b) a person providing services under arrangements made by the Director, if authorised by the Director (generally or specifically) for that purpose.
(7) Schedule 1 contains further provisions about the Agency and the Director.

2. Director's functions: general

(1) The Director must exercise his functions in the way which he considers is best calculated to contribute to the reduction of crime.
(2) In exercising his functions as required by subsection (1) the Director must—
   (a) act efficiently and effectively;

(b) have regard to his current annual plan (as approved by the Secretary of State in accordance with Schedule 1).

(3) The Director may do anything (including the carrying out of investigations) which he considers is—

(a) appropriate for facilitating, or

(b) incidental or conducive to,

the exercise of his functions.

(4) But subsection (3) does not allow the Director to borrow money.

(5) In considering under subsection (1) the way which is best calculated to contribute to the reduction of crime the Director must have regard to any guidance given to him by the Secretary of State.

(6) The guidance must indicate that the reduction of crime is in general best secured by means of criminal investigations and criminal proceedings.

3. Accreditation and training

(1) The Director must establish a system for the accreditation of financial investigators.

(2) The system of accreditation must include provision for—

(a) the monitoring of the performance of accredited financial investigators, and

(b) the withdrawal of accreditation from any person who contravenes or fails to comply with any condition subject to which he was accredited.

(3) A person may be accredited—

(a) in relation to this Act;

(b) in relation to particular provisions of this Act.

(4) But the accreditation may be limited to specified purposes.

(5) A reference in this Act to an accredited financial investigator is to be construed accordingly.

(6) The Director may charge a person—

(a) for being accredited as a financial investigator, and

(b) for the monitoring of his performance as an accredited financial investigator.

(7) The Director must make provision for the training of persons in—

(a) financial investigation, and

(b) the operation of this Act.

(8) The Director may charge the persons who receive the training.

4. Co-operation

(1) Persons who have functions relating to the investigation or prosecution of offences must co-operate with the Director in the exercise of his functions.

(2) The Director must co-operate with those persons in the exercise of functions they have under this Act.

5. Advice and assistance

The Director must give the Secretary of State advice and assistance which he reasonably requires and which—

(a) relate to matters connected with the operation of this Act, and

(b) are designed to help the Secretary of State to exercise his functions so as to reduce crime.

PART 2
CONFISCATION: ENGLAND AND WALES

Confiscation orders

6. Making of order

(1) The Crown Court must proceed under this section if the following two conditions are satisfied.

(2) The first condition is that a defendant falls within any of the following paragraphs—

(a) he is convicted of an offence or offences in proceedings before the Crown Court;

(b) he is committed to the Crown Court for sentence in respect of an offence or offences under section 3, 4 or 6 of the Sentencing Act;

(c) he is committed to the Crown Court in respect of an offence or offences under section 70 below (committal with a view to a confiscation order being considered).

(3) The second condition is that—

(a) the prosecutor or the Director asks the court to proceed under this section, or

(b) the court believes it is appropriate for it to do so.

(4) The court must proceed as follows—

(a) it must decide whether the defendant has a criminal lifestyle;

(b) if it decides that he has a criminal lifestyle it must decide whether he has benefited from his general criminal conduct;

(c) if it decides that he does not have a criminal lifestyle it must decide whether he has benefited from his particular criminal conduct.

(5) If the court decides under subsection (4)(b) or (c) that the defendant has benefited from the conduct referred to it must—

(a) decide the recoverable amount, and

(b) make an order (a confiscation order) requiring him to pay that amount.

(6) But the court must treat the duty in subsection (5) as a power if it believes that any victim of the conduct has at any time started or intends to start proceedings against the defendant in respect of loss, injury or damage sustained in connection with the conduct.

(7) The court must decide any question arising under subsection (4) or (5) on a balance of probabilities.

(8) The first condition is not satisfied if the defendant absconds (but section 27 may apply).

(9) References in this Part to the offence (or offences) concerned are to the offence (or offences) mentioned in subsection (2).

7. Recoverable amount

(1) The recoverable amount for the purposes of section 6 is an amount equal to the defendant's benefit from the conduct concerned.

(2) But if the defendant shows that the available amount is less than that benefit the recoverable amount is—

(a) the available amount, or

(b) a nominal amount, if the available amount is nil.

(3) But if section 6(6) applies the recoverable amount is such amount as—

    (a) the court believes is just, but

    (b) does not exceed the amount found under subsection (1) or (2) (as the case may be).

(4) In calculating the defendant's benefit from the conduct concerned for the purposes of subsection (1), any property in respect of which—

    (a) a recovery order is in force under section 266, or

    (b) a forfeiture order is in force under section 298(2),

    must be ignored.

(5) If the court decides the available amount, it must include in the confiscation order a statement of its findings as to the matters relevant for deciding that amount.

8. Defendant's benefit

(1) If the court is proceeding under section 6 this section applies for the purpose of—

    (a) deciding whether the defendant has benefited from conduct, and

    (b) deciding his benefit from the conduct.

(2) The court must—

    (a) take account of conduct occurring up to the time it makes its decision;

    (b) take account of property obtained up to that time.

(3) Subsection (4) applies if—

    (a) the conduct concerned is general criminal conduct,

    (b) a confiscation order mentioned in subsection (5) has at an earlier time been made against the defendant, and

    (c) his benefit for the purposes of that order was benefit from his general criminal conduct.

(4) His benefit found at the time the last confiscation order mentioned in subsection (3)(c) was made against him must be taken for the purposes of this section to be his benefit from his general criminal conduct at that time.

(5) If the conduct concerned is general criminal conduct the court must deduct the aggregate of the following amounts—

    (a) the amount ordered to be paid under each confiscation order previously made against the defendant;

    (b) the amount ordered to be paid under each confiscation order previously made against him under any of the provisions listed in subsection (7).

(6) But subsection (5) does not apply to an amount which has been taken into account for the purposes of a deduction under that subsection on any earlier occasion.

(7) These are the provisions—

    (a) the Drug Trafficking Offences Act 1986 (c. 32);

    (b) Part 1 of the Criminal Justice (Scotland) Act 1987 (c. 41);

    (c) Part 6 of the Criminal Justice Act 1988 (c. 33);

    (d) the Criminal Justice (Confiscation) (Northern Ireland) Order 1990 (S.I. 1990/2588 (N.I. 17));

    (e) Part 1 of the Drug Trafficking Act 1994 (c. 37);

    (f) Part 1 of the Proceeds of Crime (Scotland) Act 1995 (c. 43);

    (g) the Proceeds of Crime (Northern Ireland) Order 1996 (S.I. 1996/1299 (N.I. 9));

    (h) Part 3 or 4 of this Act.

(8) The reference to general criminal conduct in the case of a confiscation order made under any of the provisions listed in subsection (7) is a reference to conduct in

respect of which a court is required or entitled to make one or more assumptions for the purpose of assessing a person's benefit from the conduct.

9. Available amount

(1) For the purposes of deciding the recoverable amount, the available amount is the aggregate of—
  (a) the total of the values (at the time the confiscation order is made) of all the free property then held by the defendant minus the total amount payable in pursuance of obligations which then have priority, and
  (b) the total of the values (at that time) of all tainted gifts.
(2) An obligation has priority if it is an obligation of the defendant—
  (a) to pay an amount due in respect of a fine or other order of a court which was imposed or made on conviction of an offence and at any time before the time the confiscation order is made, or
  (b) to pay a sum which would be included among the preferential debts if the defendant's bankruptcy had commenced on the date of the confiscation order or his winding up had been ordered on that date.
(3) 'Preferential debts' has the meaning given by section 386 of the Insolvency Act 1986 (c. 45).

10. Assumptions to be made in case of criminal lifestyle

(1) If the court decides under section 6 that the defendant has a criminal lifestyle it must make the following four assumptions for the purpose of—
  (a) deciding whether he has benefited from his general criminal conduct, and
  (b) deciding his benefit from the conduct.
(2) The first assumption is that any property transferred to the defendant at any time after the relevant day was obtained by him—
  (a) as a result of his general criminal conduct, and
  (b) at the earliest time he appears to have held it.
(3) The second assumption is that any property held by the defendant at any time after the date of conviction was obtained by him—
  (a) as a result of his general criminal conduct, and
  (b) at the earliest time he appears to have held it.
(4) The third assumption is that any expenditure incurred by the defendant at any time after the relevant day was met from property obtained by him as a result of his general criminal conduct.
(5) The fourth assumption is that, for the purpose of valuing any property obtained (or assumed to have been obtained) by the defendant, he obtained it free of any other interests in it.
(6) But the court must not make a required assumption in relation to particular property or expenditure if—
  (a) the assumption is shown to be incorrect, or
  (b) there would be a serious risk of injustice if the assumption were made.
(7) If the court does not make one or more of the required assumptions it must state its reasons.
(8) The relevant day is the first day of the period of six years ending with—

(a) the day when proceedings for the offence concerned were started against the defendant, or

(b) if there are two or more offences and proceedings for them were started on different days, the earliest of those days.

(9) But if a confiscation order mentioned in section 8(3)(c) has been made against the defendant at any time during the period mentioned in subsection (8)—

(a) the relevant day is the day when the defendant's benefit was calculated for the purposes of the last such confiscation order;

(b) the second assumption does not apply to any property which was held by him on or before the relevant day.

(10) The date of conviction is—

(a) the date on which the defendant was convicted of the offence concerned, or

(b) if there are two or more offences and the convictions were on different dates, the date of the latest.

11. Time for payment

(1) The amount ordered to be paid under a confiscation order must be paid on the making of the order; but this is subject to the following provisions of this section.

(2) If the defendant shows that he needs time to pay the amount ordered to be paid, the court making the confiscation order may make an order allowing payment to be made in a specified period.

(3) The specified period—

(a) must start with the day on which the confiscation order is made, and

(b) must not exceed six months.

(4) If within the specified period the defendant applies to the Crown Court for the period to be extended and the court believes there are exceptional circumstances, it may make an order extending the period.

(5) The extended period—

(a) must start with the day on which the confiscation order is made, and

(b) must not exceed 12 months.

(6) An order under subsection (4)—

(a) may be made after the end of the specified period, but

(b) must not be made after the end of the period of 12 months starting with the day on which the confiscation order is made.

(7) The court must not make an order under subsection (2) or (4) unless it gives—

(a) the prosecutor, or

(b) if the Director was appointed as the enforcement authority for the order under section 34, the Director,

an opportunity to make representations.

12. Interest on unpaid sums

(1) If the amount required to be paid by a person under a confiscation order is not paid when it is required to be paid, he must pay interest on the amount for the period for which it remains unpaid.

(2) The rate of interest is the same rate as that for the time being specified in section 17 of the Judgments Act 1838 (c. 110) (interest on civil judgment debts).

(3) For the purposes of this section no amount is required to be paid under a confiscation order if—
- (a) an application has been made under section 11(4),
- (b) the application has not been determined by the court, and
- (c) the period of 12 months starting with the day on which the confiscation order was made has not ended.

(4) In applying this Part the amount of the interest must be treated as part of the amount to be paid under the confiscation order.

13. Effect of order on court's other powers

(1) If the court makes a confiscation order it must proceed as mentioned in subsections (2) and (4) in respect of the offence or offences concerned.

(2) The court must take account of the confiscation order before—
- (a) it imposes a fine on the defendant, or
- (b) it makes an order falling within subsection (3).

(3) These orders fall within this subsection—
- (a) an order involving payment by the defendant, other than an order under section 130 of the Sentencing Act (compensation orders);
- (b) an order under section 27 of the Misuse of Drugs Act 1971 (c. 38) (forfeiture orders);
- (c) an order under section 143 of the Sentencing Act (deprivation orders);
- (d) an order under section 23 of the Terrorism Act 2000 (c. 11) (forfeiture orders).

(4) Subject to subsection (2), the court must leave the confiscation order out of account in deciding the appropriate sentence for the defendant.

(5) Subsection (6) applies if—
- (a) the Crown Court makes both a confiscation order and an order for the payment of compensation under section 130 of the Sentencing Act against the same person in the same proceedings, and
- (b) the court believes he will not have sufficient means to satisfy both the orders in full.

(6) In such a case the court must direct that so much of the compensation as it specifies is to be paid out of any sums recovered under the confiscation order; and the amount it specifies must be the amount it believes will not be recoverable because of the insufficiency of the person's means.

Procedural matters

14. Postponement

(1) The court may—
- (a) proceed under section 6 before it sentences the defendant for the offence (or any of the offences) concerned, or
- (b) postpone proceedings under section 6 for a specified period.

(2) A period of postponement may be extended.

(3) A period of postponement (including one as extended) must not end after the permitted period ends.

(4) But subsection (3) does not apply if there are exceptional circumstances.

(5) The permitted period is the period of two years starting with the date of conviction.

(6) But if—

(a) the defendant appeals against his conviction for the offence (or any of the offences) concerned, and

(b) the period of three months (starting with the day when the appeal is determined or otherwise disposed of) ends after the period found under subsection (5), the permitted period is that period of three months.

(7) A postponement or extension may be made—

(a) on application by the defendant;

(b) on application by the prosecutor or the Director (as the case may be);

(c) by the court of its own motion.

(8) If—

(a) proceedings are postponed for a period, and

(b) an application to extend the period is made before it ends, the application may be granted even after the period ends.

(9) The date of conviction is—

(a) the date on which the defendant was convicted of the offence concerned, or

(b) if there are two or more offences and the convictions were on different dates, the date of the latest.

(10) References to appealing include references to applying under section 111 of the Magistrates' Courts Act 1980 (c. 43) (statement of case).

(11) A confiscation order must not be quashed only on the ground that there was a defect or omission in the procedure connected with the application for or the granting of a postponement.

(12) But subsection (11) does not apply if before it made the confiscation order the court—

(a) imposed a fine on the defendant;

(b) made an order falling within section 13(3);

(c) made an order under section 130 of the Sentencing Act (compensation orders).

15. Effect of postponement

(1) If the court postpones proceedings under section 6 it may proceed to sentence the defendant for the offence (or any of the offences) concerned.

(2) In sentencing the defendant for the offence (or any of the offences) concerned in the postponement period the court must not—

(a) impose a fine on him,

(b) make an order falling within section 13(3), or

(c) make an order for the payment of compensation under section 130 of the Sentencing Act.

(3) If the court sentences the defendant for the offence (or any of the offences) concerned in the postponement period, after that period ends it may vary the sentence by—

(a) imposing a fine on him,

(b) making an order falling within section 13(3), or

(c) making an order for the payment of compensation under section 130 of the Sentencing Act.

(4) But the court may proceed under subsection (3) only within the period of 28 days which starts with the last day of the postponement period.

(5) For the purposes of—

    (a) section 18(2) of the Criminal Appeal Act 1968 (c. 19) (time limit for notice of appeal or of application for leave to appeal), and

    (b) paragraph 1 of Schedule 3 to the Criminal Justice Act 1988 (c. 33) (time limit for notice of application for leave to refer a case under section 36 of that Act),

the sentence must be regarded as imposed or made on the day on which it is varied under subsection (3).

(6) If the court proceeds to sentence the defendant under subsection (1), section 6 has effect as if the defendant's particular criminal conduct included conduct which constitutes offences which the court has taken into consideration in deciding his sentence for the offence or offences concerned.

(7) The postponement period is the period for which proceedings under section 6 are postponed.

16. Statement of information

(1) If the court is proceeding under section 6 in a case where section 6(3)(a) applies, the prosecutor or the Director (as the case may be) must give the court a statement of information within the period the court orders.

(2) If the court is proceeding under section 6 in a case where section 6(3)(b) applies and it orders the prosecutor to give it a statement of information, the prosecutor must give it such a statement within the period the court orders.

(3) If the prosecutor or the Director (as the case may be) believes the defendant has a criminal lifestyle the statement of information is a statement of matters the prosecutor or the Director believes are relevant in connection with deciding these issues—

    (a) whether the defendant has a criminal lifestyle;

    (b) whether he has benefited from his general criminal conduct;

    (c) his benefit from the conduct.

(4) A statement under subsection (3) must include information the prosecutor or Director believes is relevant—

    (a) in connection with the making by the court of a required assumption under section 10;

    (b) for the purpose of enabling the court to decide if the circumstances are such that it must not make such an assumption.

(5) If the prosecutor or the Director (as the case may be) does not believe the defendant has a criminal lifestyle the statement of information is a statement of matters the prosecutor or the Director believes are relevant in connection with deciding these issues—

    (a) whether the defendant has benefited from his particular criminal conduct;

    (b) his benefit from the conduct.

(6) If the prosecutor or the Director gives the court a statement of information—

    (a) he may at any time give the court a further statement of information;

    (b) he must give the court a further statement of information if it orders him to do so, and he must give it within the period the court orders.

(7) If the court makes an order under this section it may at any time vary it by making another one.

17. Defendant's response to statement of information

(1) If the prosecutor or the Director gives the court a statement of information and a copy is served on the defendant, the court may order the defendant—

  (a) to indicate (within the period it orders) the extent to which he accepts each allegation in the statement, and

  (b) so far as he does not accept such an allegation, to give particulars of any matters he proposes to rely on.

(2) If the defendant accepts to any extent an allegation in a statement of information the court may treat his acceptance as conclusive of the matters to which it relates for the purpose of deciding the issues referred to in section 16(3) or (5) (as the case may be).

(3) If the defendant fails in any respect to comply with an order under subsection (1) he may be treated for the purposes of subsection (2) as accepting every allegation in the statement of information apart from—

  (a) any allegation in respect of which he has complied with the requirement;

  (b) any allegation that he has benefited from his general or particular criminal conduct.

(4) For the purposes of this section an allegation may be accepted or particulars may be given in a manner ordered by the court.

(5) If the court makes an order under this section it may at any time vary it by making another one.

(6) No acceptance under this section that the defendant has benefited from conduct is admissible in evidence in proceedings for an offence.

18. Provision of information by defendant

(1) This section applies if—

  (a) the court is proceeding under section 6 in a case where section 6(3)(a) applies, or

  (b) it is proceeding under section 6 in a case where section 6(3)(b) applies or it is considering whether to proceed.

(2) For the purpose of obtaining information to help it in carrying out its functions the court may at any time order the defendant to give it information specified in the order.

(3) An order under this section may require all or a specified part of the information to be given in a specified manner and before a specified date.

(4) If the defendant fails without reasonable excuse to comply with an order under this section the court may draw such inference as it believes is appropriate.

(5) Subsection (4) does not affect any power of the court to deal with the defendant in respect of a failure to comply with an order under this section.

(6) If the prosecutor or the Director (as the case may be) accepts to any extent an allegation made by the defendant—

  (a) in giving information required by an order under this section, or

  (b) in any other statement given to the court in relation to any matter relevant to deciding the available amount under section 9,

the court may treat the acceptance as conclusive of the matters to which it relates.

(7) For the purposes of this section an allegation may be accepted in a manner ordered by the court.

(8) If the court makes an order under this section it may at any time vary it by making another one.

(9) No information given under this section which amounts to an admission by the defendant that he has benefited from criminal conduct is admissible in evidence in proceedings for an offence.

Reconsideration

19. No order made: reconsideration of case

(1) This section applies if—
- (a) the first condition in section 6 is satisfied but no court has proceeded under that section,
- (b) there is evidence which was not available to the prosecutor on the relevant date,
- (c) before the end of the period of six years starting with the date of conviction the prosecutor or the Director applies to the Crown Court to consider the evidence, and
- (d) after considering the evidence the court believes it is appropriate for it to proceed under section 6.

(2) If this section applies the court must proceed under section 6, and when it does so subsections (3) to (8) below apply.

(3) If the court has already sentenced the defendant for the offence (or any of the offences) concerned, section 6 has effect as if his particular criminal conduct included conduct which constitutes offences which the court has taken into consideration in deciding his sentence for the offence or offences concerned.

(4) Section 8(2) does not apply, and the rules applying instead are that the court must—
- (a) take account of conduct occurring before the relevant date;
- (b) take account of property obtained before that date;
- (c) take account of property obtained on or after that date if it was obtained as a result of or in connection with conduct occurring before that date.

(5) In section 10—
- (a) the first and second assumptions do not apply with regard to property first held by the defendant on or after the relevant date;
- (b) the third assumption does not apply with regard to expenditure incurred by him on or after that date;
- (c) the fourth assumption does not apply with regard to property obtained (or assumed to have been obtained) by him on or after that date.

(6) The recoverable amount for the purposes of section 6 is such amount as—
- (a) the court believes is just, but
- (b) does not exceed the amount found under section 7.

(7) In arriving at the just amount the court must have regard in particular to—
- (a) the amount found under section 7;
- (b) any fine imposed on the defendant in respect of the offence (or any of the offences) concerned;
- (c) any order which falls within section 13(3) and has been made against him in respect of the offence (or any of the offences) concerned and has not already been taken into account by the court in deciding what is the free property held by him for the purposes of section 9;

(d) any order which has been made against him in respect of the offence (or any of the offences) concerned under section 130 of the Sentencing Act (compensation orders).

(8) If an order for the payment of compensation under section 130 of the Sentencing Act has been made against the defendant in respect of the offence or offences concerned, section 13(5) and (6) above do not apply.

(9) The relevant date is—
  (a) if the court made a decision not to proceed under section 6, the date of the decision;
  (b) if the court did not make such a decision, the date of conviction.

(10) The date of conviction is—
  (a) the date on which the defendant was convicted of the offence concerned, or
  (b) if there are two or more offences and the convictions were on different dates, the date of the latest.

20. No order made: reconsideration of benefit

(1) This section applies if the following two conditions are satisfied.

(2) The first condition is that in proceeding under section 6 the court has decided that—
  (a) the defendant has a criminal lifestyle but has not benefited from his general criminal conduct, or
  (b) the defendant does not have a criminal lifestyle and has not benefited from his particular criminal conduct.

(3) If the court proceeded under section 6 because the Director asked it to, the second condition is that—
  (a) the Director has evidence which was not available to him when the court decided that the defendant had not benefited from his general or particular criminal conduct,
  (b) before the end of the period of six years starting with the date of conviction the Director applies to the Crown Court to consider the evidence, and
  (c) after considering the evidence the court concludes that it would have decided that the defendant had benefited from his general or particular criminal conduct (as the case may be) if the evidence had been available to it.

(4) If the court proceeded under section 6 because the prosecutor asked it to or because it believed it was appropriate for it to do so, the second condition is that—
  (a) there is evidence which was not available to the prosecutor when the court decided that the defendant had not benefited from his general or particular criminal conduct,
  (b) before the end of the period of six years starting with the date of conviction the prosecutor or the Director applies to the Crown Court to consider the evidence, and
  (c) after considering the evidence the court concludes that it would have decided that the defendant had benefited from his general or particular criminal conduct (as the case may be) if the evidence had been available to it.

(5) If this section applies the court—
  (a) must make a fresh decision under section 6(4)(b) or (c) whether the defendant has benefited from his general or particular criminal conduct (as the case may be);

     (b) may make a confiscation order under that section.

(6) Subsections (7) to (12) below apply if the court proceeds under section 6 in pursuance of this section.

(7) If the court has already sentenced the defendant for the offence (or any of the offences) concerned, section 6 has effect as if his particular criminal conduct included conduct which constitutes offences which the court has taken into consideration in deciding his sentence for the offence or offences concerned.

(8) Section 8(2) does not apply, and the rules applying instead are that the court must—

     (a) take account of conduct occurring before the date of the original decision that the defendant had not benefited from his general or particular criminal conduct;

     (b) take account of property obtained before that date;

     (c) take account of property obtained on or after that date if it was obtained as a result of or in connection with conduct occurring before that date.

(9) In section 10—

     (a) the first and second assumptions do not apply with regard to property first held by the defendant on or after the date of the original decision that the defendant had not benefited from his general or particular criminal conduct;

     (b) the third assumption does not apply with regard to expenditure incurred by him on or after that date;

     (c) the fourth assumption does not apply with regard to property obtained (or assumed to have been obtained) by him on or after that date.

(10) The recoverable amount for the purposes of section 6 is such amount as—

     (a) the court believes is just, but

     (b) does not exceed the amount found under section 7.

(11) In arriving at the just amount the court must have regard in particular to—

     (a) the amount found under section 7;

     (b) any fine imposed on the defendant in respect of the offence (or any of the offences) concerned;

     (c) any order which falls within section 13(3) and has been made against him in respect of the offence (or any of the offences) concerned and has not already been taken into account by the court in deciding what is the free property held by him for the purposes of section 9;

     (d) any order which has been made against him in respect of the offence (or any of the offences) concerned under section 130 of the Sentencing Act (compensation orders).

(12) If an order for the payment of compensation under section 130 of the Sentencing Act has been made against the defendant in respect of the offence or offences concerned, section 13(5) and (6) above do not apply.

(13) The date of conviction is the date found by applying section 19(10).

21. Order made: reconsideration of benefit

(1) This section applies if—

     (a) a court has made a confiscation order,

     (b) there is evidence which was not available to the prosecutor or the Director at the relevant time,

(c) the prosecutor or the Director believes that if the court were to find the amount of the defendant's benefit in pursuance of this section it would exceed the relevant amount,

(d) before the end of the period of six years starting with the date of conviction the prosecutor or the Director applies to the Crown Court to consider the evidence, and

(e) after considering the evidence the court believes it is appropriate for it to proceed under this section.

(2) The court must make a new calculation of the defendant's benefit from the conduct concerned, and when it does so subsections (3) to (6) below apply.

(3) If a court has already sentenced the defendant for the offence (or any of the offences) concerned section 6 has effect as if his particular criminal conduct included conduct which constitutes offences which the court has taken into consideration in deciding his sentence for the offence or offences concerned.

(4) Section 8(2) does not apply, and the rules applying instead are that the court must—

(a) take account of conduct occurring up to the time it decided the defendant's benefit for the purposes of the confiscation order;

(b) take account of property obtained up to that time;

(c) take account of property obtained after that time if it was obtained as a result of or in connection with conduct occurring before that time.

(5) In applying section 8(5) the confiscation order must be ignored.

(6) In section 10—

(a) the first and second assumptions do not apply with regard to property first held by the defendant after the time the court decided his benefit for the purposes of the confiscation order;

(b) the third assumption does not apply with regard to expenditure incurred by him after that time;

(c) the fourth assumption does not apply with regard to property obtained (or assumed to have been obtained) by him after that time.

(7) If the amount found under the new calculation of the defendant's benefit exceeds the relevant amount the court—

(a) must make a new calculation of the recoverable amount for the purposes of section 6, and

(b) if it exceeds the amount required to be paid under the confiscation order, may vary the order by substituting for the amount required to be paid such amount as it believes is just.

(8) In applying subsection (7)(a) the court must—

(a) take the new calculation of the defendant's benefit;

(b) apply section 9 as if references to the time the confiscation order is made were to the time of the new calculation of the recoverable amount and as if references to the date of the confiscation order were to the date of that new calculation.

(9) In applying subsection (7)(b) the court must have regard in particular to—

(a) any fine imposed on the defendant for the offence (or any of the offences) concerned;

(b) any order which falls within section 13(3) and has been made against him in respect of the offence (or any of the offences) concerned and has not already been taken into account by the court in deciding what is the free property held by him for the purposes of section 9;

(c) any order which has been made against him in respect of the offence (or any of the offences) concerned under section 130 of the Sentencing Act (compensation orders).

(10) But in applying subsection (7)(b) the court must not have regard to an order falling within subsection (9)(c) if a court has made a direction under section 13(6).

(11) In deciding under this section whether one amount exceeds another the court must take account of any change in the value of money.

(12) The relevant time is—

(a) when the court calculated the defendant's benefit for the purposes of the confiscation order, if this section has not applied previously;

(b) when the court last calculated the defendant's benefit in pursuance of this section, if this section has applied previously.

(13) The relevant amount is—

(a) the amount found as the defendant's benefit for the purposes of the confiscation order, if this section has not applied previously;

(b) the amount last found as the defendant's benefit in pursuance of this section, if this section has applied previously.

(14) The date of conviction is the date found by applying section 19(10).

22. Order made: reconsideration of available amount

(1) This section applies if—

(a) a court has made a confiscation order,

(b) the amount required to be paid was the amount found under section 7(2), and

(c) an applicant falling within subsection (2) applies to the Crown Court to make a new calculation of the available amount.

(2) These applicants fall within this subsection—

(a) the prosecutor;

(b) the Director;

(c) a receiver appointed under section 50 or 52.

(3) In a case where this section applies the court must make the new calculation, and in doing so it must apply section 9 as if references to the time the confiscation order is made were to the time of the new calculation and as if references to the date of the confiscation order were to the date of the new calculation.

(4) If the amount found under the new calculation exceeds the relevant amount the court may vary the order by substituting for the amount required to be paid such amount as—

(a) it believes is just, but

(b) does not exceed the amount found as the defendant's benefit from the conduct concerned.

(5) In deciding what is just the court must have regard in particular to—

(a) any fine imposed on the defendant for the offence (or any of the offences) concerned;

(b) any order which falls within section 13(3) and has been made against him in respect of the offence (or any of the offences) concerned and has not already been taken into account by the court in deciding what is the free property held by him for the purposes of section 9;

(c) any order which has been made against him in respect of the offence (or any of the offences) concerned under section 130 of the Sentencing Act (compensation orders).

(6) But in deciding what is just the court must not have regard to an order falling within subsection (5)(c) if a court has made a direction under section 13(6).

(7) In deciding under this section whether one amount exceeds another the court must take account of any change in the value of money.

(8) The relevant amount is—
   (a) the amount found as the available amount for the purposes of the confiscation order, if this section has not applied previously;
   (b) the amount last found as the available amount in pursuance of this section, if this section has applied previously.

(9) The amount found as the defendant's benefit from the conduct concerned is—
   (a) the amount so found when the confiscation order was made, or
   (b) if one or more new calculations of the defendant's benefit have been made under section 21 the amount found on the occasion of the last such calculation.

23. Inadequacy of available amount: variation of order

(1) This section applies if—
   (a) a court has made a confiscation order, and
   (b) the defendant, or a receiver appointed under section 50 or 52, applies to the Crown Court to vary the order under this section.

(2) In such a case the court must calculate the available amount, and in doing so it must apply section 9 as if references to the time the confiscation order is made were to the time of the calculation and as if references to the date of the confiscation order were to the date of the calculation.

(3) If the court finds that the available amount (as so calculated) is inadequate for the payment of any amount remaining to be paid under the confiscation order it may vary the order by substituting for the amount required to be paid such smaller amount as the court believes is just.

(4) If a person has been adjudged bankrupt or his estate has been sequestrated, or if an order for the winding up of a company has been made, the court must take into account the extent to which realisable property held by that person or that company may be distributed among creditors.

(5) The court may disregard any inadequacy which it believes is attributable (wholly or partly) to anything done by the defendant for the purpose of preserving property held by the recipient of a tainted gift from any risk of realisation under this Part.

(6) In subsection (4) 'company' means any company which may be wound up under the Insolvency Act 1986 (c. 45) or the Insolvency (Northern Ireland) Order 1989 (S.I. 1989/2405 (N.I. 19)).

24. Inadequacy of available amount: discharge of order

(1) This section applies if—
   (a) a court has made a confiscation order,
   (b) a justices' chief executive applies to the Crown Court for the discharge of the order, and

    (c) the amount remaining to be paid under the order is less than £1,000.

(2) In such a case the court must calculate the available amount, and in doing so it must apply section 9 as if references to the time the confiscation order is made were to the time of the calculation and as if references to the date of the confiscation order were to the date of the calculation.

(3) If the court—

    (a) finds that the available amount (as so calculated) is inadequate to meet the amount remaining to be paid, and

    (b) is satisfied that the inadequacy is due wholly to a specified reason or a combination of specified reasons,

it may discharge the confiscation order.

(4) The specified reasons are—

    (a) in a case where any of the realisable property consists of money in a currency other than sterling, that fluctuations in currency exchange rates have occurred;

    (b) any reason specified by the Secretary of State by order.

(5) The Secretary of State may by order vary the amount for the time being specified in subsection (1)(c).

25. Small amount outstanding: discharge of order

(1) This section applies if—

    (a) a court has made a confiscation order,

    (b) a justices' chief executive applies to the Crown Court for the discharge of the order, and

    (c) the amount remaining to be paid under the order is £50 or less.

(2) In such a case the court may discharge the order.

(3) The Secretary of State may by order vary the amount for the time being specified in subsection (1)(c).

26. Information

(1) This section applies if—

    (a) the court proceeds under section 6 in pursuance of section 19 or 20, or

    (b) the prosecutor or the Director applies under section 21.

(2) In such a case—

    (a) the prosecutor or the Director (as the case may be) must give the court a statement of information within the period the court orders;

    (b) section 16 applies accordingly (with appropriate modifications where the prosecutor or the Director applies under section 21);

    (c) section 17 applies accordingly;

    (d) section 18 applies as it applies in the circumstances mentioned in section 18(1).

Defendant absconds

27.   Defendant convicted or committed

(1) This section applies if the following two conditions are satisfied.

(2) The first condition is that a defendant absconds after—

     (a) he is convicted of an offence or offences in proceedings before the Crown Court,

     (b) he is committed to the Crown Court for sentence in respect of an offence or offences under section 3, 4 or 6 of the Sentencing Act, or

     (c) he is committed to the Crown Court in respect of an offence or offences under section 70 below (committal with a view to a confiscation order being considered).

(3) The second condition is that—

     (a) the prosecutor or the Director applies to the Crown Court to proceed under this section, and

     (b) the court believes it is appropriate for it to do so.

(4) If this section applies the court must proceed under section 6 in the same way as it must proceed if the two conditions there mentioned are satisfied; but this is subject to subsection (5).

(5) If the court proceeds under section 6 as applied by this section, this Part has effect with these modifications—

     (a) any person the court believes is likely to be affected by an order under section 6 is entitled to appear before the court and make representations;

     (b) the court must not make an order under section 6 unless the prosecutor or the Director (as the case may be) has taken reasonable steps to contact the defendant;

     (c) section 6(9) applies as if the reference to subsection (2) were to subsection (2) of this section;

     (d) sections 10, 16(4), 17 and 18 must be ignored;

     (e) sections 19, 20 and 21 must be ignored while the defendant is still an absconder.

(6) Once the defendant ceases to be an absconder section 19 has effect as if subsection (1)(a) read—

     '(a) at a time when the first condition in section 27 was satisfied the court did not proceed under section 6,'.

(7) If the court does not believe it is appropriate for it to proceed under this section, once the defendant ceases to be an absconder section 19 has effect as if subsection (1)(b) read—

     '(b) there is evidence which was not available to the prosecutor or the Director on the relevant date,'.

28. Defendant neither convicted nor acquitted

(1) This section applies if the following two conditions are satisfied.

(2) The first condition is that—

     (a) proceedings for an offence or offences are started against a defendant but are not concluded,

     (b) he absconds, and

     (c) the period of two years (starting with the day the court believes he absconded) has ended.

(3) The second condition is that—

     (a) the prosecutor or the Director applies to the Crown Court to proceed under this section, and

     (b) the court believes it is appropriate for it to do so.

(4) If this section applies the court must proceed under section 6 in the same way as it must proceed if the two conditions there mentioned are satisfied; but this is subject to subsection (5).

(5) If the court proceeds under section 6 as applied by this section, this Part has effect with these modifications—

    (a) any person the court believes is likely to be affected by an order under section 6 is entitled to appear before the court and make representations;

    (b) the court must not make an order under section 6 unless the prosecutor or the Director (as the case may be) has taken reasonable steps to contact the defendant;

    (c) section 6(9) applies as if the reference to subsection (2) were to subsection (2) of this section;

    (d) sections 10, 16(4) and 17 to 20 must be ignored;

    (e) section 21 must be ignored while the defendant is still an absconder.

(6) Once the defendant has ceased to be an absconder section 21 has effect as if references to the date of conviction were to—

    (a) the day when proceedings for the offence concerned were started against the defendant, or

    (b) if there are two or more offences and proceedings for them were started on different days, the earliest of those days.

(7) If—

    (a) the court makes an order under section 6 as applied by this section, and

    (b) the defendant is later convicted in proceedings before the Crown Court of the offence (or any of the offences) concerned,

section 6 does not apply so far as that conviction is concerned.

29. Variation of order

(1) This section applies if—

    (a) the court makes a confiscation order under section 6 as applied by section 28,

    (b) the defendant ceases to be an absconder,

    (c) he is convicted of an offence (or any of the offences) mentioned in section 28(2)(a),

    (d) he believes that the amount required to be paid was too large (taking the circumstances prevailing when the amount was found for the purposes of the order), and

    (e) before the end of the relevant period he applies to the Crown Court to consider the evidence on which his belief is based.

(2) If (after considering the evidence) the court concludes that the defendant's belief is well founded—

    (a) it must find the amount which should have been the amount required to be paid (taking the circumstances prevailing when the amount was found for the purposes of the order), and

    (b) it may vary the order by substituting for the amount required to be paid such amount as it believes is just.

(3) The relevant period is the period of 28 days starting with—

    (a) the date on which the defendant was convicted of the offence mentioned in section 28(2)(a), or

    (b) if there are two or more offences and the convictions were on different dates, the date of the latest.

 (4) But in a case where section 28(2)(a) applies to more than one offence the court must not make an order under this section unless it is satisfied that there is no possibility of any further proceedings being taken or continued in relation to any such offence in respect of which the defendant has not been convicted.

30. Discharge of order

 (1) Subsection (2) applies if—

    (a) the court makes a confiscation order under section 6 as applied by section 28,

    (b) the defendant is later tried for the offence or offences concerned and acquitted on all counts, and

    (c) he applies to the Crown Court to discharge the order.

 (2) In such a case the court must discharge the order.

 (3) Subsection (4) applies if—

    (a) the court makes a confiscation order under section 6 as applied by section 28,

    (b) the defendant ceases to be an absconder,

    (c) subsection (1)(b) does not apply, and

    (d) he applies to the Crown Court to discharge the order.

 (4) In such a case the court may discharge the order if it finds that—

    (a) there has been undue delay in continuing the proceedings mentioned in section 28(2), or

    (b) the prosecutor does not intend to proceed with the prosecution.

 (5) If the court discharges a confiscation order under this section it may make such a consequential or incidental order as it believes is appropriate.

Appeals

31. Appeal by prosecutor or Director

 (1) If the Crown Court makes a confiscation order the prosecutor or the Director may appeal to the Court of Appeal in respect of the order.

 (2) If the Crown Court decides not to make a confiscation order the prosecutor or the Director may appeal to the Court of Appeal against the decision.

 (3) Subsections (1) and (2) do not apply to an order or decision made by virtue of section 19, 20, 27 or 28.

32. Court's powers on appeal

 (1) On an appeal under section 31(1) the Court of Appeal may confirm, quash or vary the confiscation order.

 (2) On an appeal under section 31(2) the Court of Appeal may confirm the decision, or if it believes the decision was wrong it may—

    (a) itself proceed under section 6 (ignoring subsections (1) to (3)), or

    (b) direct the Crown Court to proceed afresh under section 6.

 (3) In proceeding afresh in pursuance of this section the Crown Court must comply with any directions the Court of Appeal may make.

 (4) If a court makes or varies a confiscation order under this section or in pursuance of a direction under this section it must—

(a) have regard to any fine imposed on the defendant in respect of the offence (or any of the offences) concerned;

(b) have regard to any order which falls within section 13(3) and has been made against him in respect of the offence (or any of the offences) concerned, unless the order has already been taken into account by a court in deciding what is the free property held by the defendant for the purposes of section 9.

(5) If the Court of Appeal proceeds under section 6 or the Crown Court proceeds afresh under that section in pursuance of a direction under this section subsections (6) to (10) apply.

(6) If a court has already sentenced the defendant for the offence (or any of the offences) concerned, section 6 has effect as if his particular criminal conduct included conduct which constitutes offences which the court has taken into consideration in deciding his sentence for the offence or offences concerned.

(7) If an order has been made against the defendant in respect of the offence (or any of the offences) concerned under section 130 of the Sentencing Act (compensation orders)—

(a) the court must have regard to it, and

(b) section 13(5) and (6) above do not apply.

(8) Section 8(2) does not apply, and the rules applying instead are that the court must—

(a) take account of conduct occurring before the relevant date;

(b) take account of property obtained before that date;

(c) take account of property obtained on or after that date if it was obtained as a result of or in connection with conduct occurring before that date.

(9) In section 10—

(a) the first and second assumptions do not apply with regard to property first held by the defendant on or after the relevant date;

(b) the third assumption does not apply with regard to expenditure incurred by him on or after that date;

(c) the fourth assumption does not apply with regard to property obtained (or assumed to have been obtained) by him on or after that date.

(10) Section 26 applies as it applies in the circumstances mentioned in subsection (1) of that section.

(11) The relevant date is the date on which the Crown Court decided not to make a confiscation order.

33. Appeal to House of Lords

(1) An appeal lies to the House of Lords from a decision of the Court of Appeal on an appeal under section 31.

(2) An appeal under this section lies at the instance of—

(a) the defendant or the prosecutor (if the prosecutor appealed under section 31);

(b) the defendant or the Director (if the Director appealed under section 31).

(3) On an appeal from a decision of the Court of Appeal to confirm, vary or make a confiscation order the House of Lords may confirm, quash or vary the order.

(4) On an appeal from a decision of the Court of Appeal to confirm the decision of the Crown Court not to make a confiscation order or from a decision of the Court of Appeal to quash a confiscation order the House of Lords may—

(a) confirm the decision, or

(b) direct the Crown Court to proceed afresh under section 6 if it believes the decision was wrong.

(5) In proceeding afresh in pursuance of this section the Crown Court must comply with any directions the House of Lords may make.

(6) If a court varies a confiscation order under this section or makes a confiscation order in pursuance of a direction under this section it must—

(a) have regard to any fine imposed on the defendant in respect of the offence (or any of the offences) concerned;

(b) have regard to any order which falls within section 13(3) and has been made against him in respect of the offence (or any of the offences) concerned, unless the order has already been taken into account by a court in deciding what is the free property held by the defendant for the purposes of section 9.

(7) If the Crown Court proceeds afresh under section 6 in pursuance of a direction under this section subsections (8) to (12) apply.

(8) If a court has already sentenced the defendant for the offence (or any of the offences) concerned, section 6 has effect as if his particular criminal conduct included conduct which constitutes offences which the court has taken into consideration in deciding his sentence for the offence or offences concerned.

(9) If an order has been made against the defendant in respect of the offence (or any of the offences) concerned under section 130 of the Sentencing Act (compensation orders)—

(a) the Crown Court must have regard to it, and

(b) section 13(5) and (6) above do not apply.

(10) Section 8(2) does not apply, and the rules applying instead are that the Crown Court must—

(a) take account of conduct occurring before the relevant date;

(b) take account of property obtained before that date;

(c) take account of property obtained on or after that date if it was obtained as a result of or in connection with conduct occurring before that date.

(11) In section 10—

(a) the first and second assumptions do not apply with regard to property first held by the defendant on or after the relevant date;

(b) the third assumption does not apply with regard to expenditure incurred by him on or after that date;

(c) the fourth assumption does not apply with regard to property obtained (or assumed to have been obtained) by him on or after that date.

(12) Section 26 applies as it applies in the circumstances mentioned in subsection (1) of that section.

(13) The relevant date is—

(a) in a case where the Crown Court made a confiscation order which was quashed by the Court of Appeal, the date on which the Crown Court made the order;

(b) in any other case, the date on which the Crown Court decided not to make a confiscation order.

Enforcement authority

34. Enforcement authority

(1) Subsection (2) applies if a court makes a confiscation order and any of the following paragraphs applies—

    (a) the court proceeded under section 6 after being asked to do so by the Director;

    (b) the court proceeded under section 6 by virtue of an application by the Director under section 19, 20, 27 or 28;

    (c) the court proceeded under section 6 as a result of an appeal by the Director under section 31(2) or 33;

    (d) before the court made the order the Director applied to the court to appoint him as the enforcement authority for the order.

(2) In any such case the court must appoint the Director as the enforcement authority for the order.

Enforcement as fines etc

35. Director not appointed as enforcement authority

(1) This section applies if a court—

    (a) makes a confiscation order, and

    (b) does not appoint the Director as the enforcement authority for the order.

(2) Sections 139(2) to (4) and (9) and 140(1) to (4) of the Sentencing Act (functions of court as to fines and enforcing fines) apply as if the amount ordered to be paid were a fine imposed on the defendant by the court making the confiscation order.

(3) In the application of Part 3 of the Magistrates' Courts Act 1980 (c. 43) to an amount payable under a confiscation order—

    (a) ignore section 75 of that Act (power to dispense with immediate payment);

    (b) such an amount is not a sum adjudged to be paid by a conviction for the purposes of section 81 (enforcement of fines imposed on young offenders) or a fine for the purposes of section 85 (remission of fines) of that Act;

    (c) in section 87 of that Act ignore subsection (3) (inquiry into means).

36. Director appointed as enforcement authority

(1) This section applies if a court—

    (a) makes a confiscation order, and

    (b) appoints the Director as the enforcement authority for the order.

(2) Section 139(2) to (4) and (9) of the Sentencing Act (functions of court as to fines) applies as if the amount ordered to be paid were a fine imposed on the defendant by the court making the confiscation order.

37. Director's application for enforcement

(1) If the Director believes that the conditions set out in subsection (2) are satisfied he may make an ex parte application to the Crown Court for the issue of a summons against the defendant.

(2) The conditions are that—

    (a) a confiscation order has been made;

(b) the Director has been appointed as the enforcement authority for the order;

(c) because of the defendant's wilful refusal or culpable neglect the order is not satisfied;

(d) the order is not subject to appeal;

(e) the Director has done all that is practicable (apart from this section) to enforce the order.

(3) If it appears to the Crown Court that the conditions are satisfied it may issue a summons ordering the defendant to appear before the court at the time and place specified in the summons.

(4) If the defendant fails to appear before the Crown Court in pursuance of the summons the court may issue a warrant for his arrest.

(5) If—

(a) the defendant appears before the Crown Court in pursuance of the summons or of a warrant issued under subsection (4), and

(b) the court is satisfied that the conditions set out in subsection (2) are satisfied, it may issue a warrant committing the defendant to prison or detention for default in payment of the amount ordered to be paid by the confiscation order.

(6) Subsection (7) applies if the amount remaining to be paid under the confiscation order when the warrant under subsection (5) is issued is less than the amount ordered to be paid.

(7) In such a case the court must substitute for the term of imprisonment or detention fixed in respect of the order under section 139(2) of the Sentencing Act such term as bears to the original term the same proportion as the amount remaining to be paid bears to the amount ordered to be paid.

(8) Subsections (9) and (10) apply if—

(a) the defendant has been committed to prison or detention in pursuance of a warrant issued under subsection (5), and

(b) a payment is made in respect of some or all of the amount remaining to be paid under the confiscation order.

(9) If the payment is for the whole amount remaining to be paid the defendant must be released unless he is in custody for another reason.

(10) If the payment is for less than that amount, the period of commitment is reduced so that it bears to the term fixed under section 139(2) of the Sentencing Act the same proportion as the amount remaining to be paid bears to the amount ordered to be paid.

38. Provisions about imprisonment or detention

(1) Subsection (2) applies if—

(a) a warrant committing the defendant to prison or detention is issued for a default in payment of an amount ordered to be paid under a confiscation order in respect of an offence or offences, and

(b) at the time the warrant is issued the defendant is liable to serve a term of custody in respect of the offence (or any of the offences).

(2) In such a case the term of imprisonment or of detention under section 108 of the Sentencing Act (detention of persons aged 18 to 20 for default) to be served in default of payment of the amount does not begin to run until after the term mentioned in subsection (1)(b) above.

(3) The reference in subsection (1)(b) to the term of custody the defendant is liable to serve in respect of the offence (or any of the offences) is a reference to the term of imprisonment, or detention in a young offender institution, which he is liable to serve in respect of the offence (or any of the offences).

(4) For the purposes of subsection (3) consecutive terms and terms which are wholly or partly concurrent must be treated as a single term and the following must be ignored—

(a) any sentence suspended under section 118(1) of the Sentencing Act which has not taken effect at the time the warrant is issued;

(b) in the case of a sentence of imprisonment passed with an order under section 47(1) of the Criminal Law Act 1977 (c. 45) (sentences of imprisonment partly served and partly suspended) any part of the sentence which the defendant has not at that time been required to serve in prison;

(c) any term of imprisonment or detention fixed under section 139(2) of the Sentencing Act (term to be served in default of payment of fine etc) for which a warrant committing the defendant to prison or detention has not been issued at that time.

(5) If the defendant serves a term of imprisonment or detention in default of paying any amount due under a confiscation order, his serving that term does not prevent the confiscation order from continuing to have effect so far as any other method of enforcement is concerned.

39. Reconsideration etc: variation of prison term

(1) Subsection (2) applies if—

(a) a court varies a confiscation order under section 21, 22, 23, 29, 32 or 33,

(b) the effect of the variation is to vary the maximum period applicable in relation to the order under section 139(4) of the Sentencing Act, and

(c) the result is that that maximum period is less than the term of imprisonment or detention fixed in respect of the order under section 139(2) of the Sentencing Act.

(2) In such a case the court must fix a reduced term of imprisonment or detention in respect of the confiscation order under section 139(2) of the Sentencing Act in place of the term previously fixed.

(3) Subsection (4) applies if paragraphs (a) and (b) of subsection (1) apply but paragraph (c) does not.

(4) In such a case the court may amend the term of imprisonment or detention fixed in respect of the confiscation order under section 139(2) of the Sentencing Act.

(5) If the effect of section 12 is to increase the maximum period applicable in relation to a confiscation order under section 139(4) of the Sentencing Act, on the application of the appropriate person the Crown Court may amend the term of imprisonment or detention fixed in respect of the order under section 139(2) of that Act.

(6) The appropriate person is—

(a) the Director, if he was appointed as the enforcement authority for the order under section 34;

(b) the prosecutor, in any other case.

Restraint orders

40. Conditions for exercise of powers

(1) The Crown Court may exercise the powers conferred by section 41 if any of the following conditions is satisfied.

(2) The first condition is that—
   (a) a criminal investigation has been started in England and Wales with regard to an offence, and
   (b) there is reasonable cause to believe that the alleged offender has benefited from his criminal conduct.

(3) The second condition is that—
   (a) proceedings for an offence have been started in England and Wales and not concluded, and
   (b) there is reasonable cause to believe that the defendant has benefited from his criminal conduct.

(4) The third condition is that—
   (a) an application by the prosecutor or the Director has been made under section 19, 20, 27 or 28 and not concluded, or the court believes that such an application is to be made, and
   (b) there is reasonable cause to believe that the defendant has benefited from his criminal conduct.

(5) The fourth condition is that—
   (a) an application by the prosecutor or the Director has been made under section 21 and not concluded, or the court believes that such an application is to be made, and
   (b) there is reasonable cause to believe that the court will decide under that section that the amount found under the new calculation of the defendant's benefit exceeds the relevant amount (as defined in that section).

(6) The fifth condition is that—
   (a) an application by the prosecutor or the Director has been made under section 22 and not concluded, or the court believes that such an application is to be made, and
   (b) there is reasonable cause to believe that the court will decide under that section that the amount found under the new calculation of the available amount exceeds the relevant amount (as defined in that section).

(7) The second condition is not satisfied if the court believes that—
   (a) there has been undue delay in continuing the proceedings, or
   (b) the prosecutor does not intend to proceed.

(8) If an application mentioned in the third, fourth or fifth condition has been made the condition is not satisfied if the court believes that—
   (a) there has been undue delay in continuing the application, or
   (b) the prosecutor or the Director (as the case may be) does not intend to proceed.

(9) If the first condition is satisfied—
   (a) references in this Part to the defendant are to the alleged offender;
   (b) references in this Part to the prosecutor are to the person the court believes is to have conduct of any proceedings for the offence;

(c) section 77(9) has effect as if proceedings for the offence had been started against the defendant when the investigation was started.

41. Restraint orders

(1) If any condition set out in section 40 is satisfied the Crown Court may make an order (a restraint order) prohibiting any specified person from dealing with any realisable property held by him.

(2) A restraint order may provide that it applies—
  (a) to all realisable property held by the specified person whether or not the property is described in the order;
  (b) to realisable property transferred to the specified person after the order is made.

(3) A restraint order may be made subject to exceptions, and an exception may in particular—
  (a) make provision for reasonable living expenses and reasonable legal expenses;
  (b) make provision for the purpose of enabling any person to carry on any trade, business, profession or occupation;
  (c) be made subject to conditions.

(4) But an exception to a restraint order must not make provision for any legal expenses which—
  (a) relate to an offence which falls within subsection (5), and
  (b) are incurred by the defendant or by a recipient of a tainted gift.

(5) These offences fall within this subsection—
  (a) the offence mentioned in section 40(2) or (3), if the first or second condition (as the case may be) is satisfied;
  (b) the offence (or any of the offences) concerned, if the third, fourth or fifth condition is satisfied.

(6) Subsection (7) applies if—
  (a) a court makes a restraint order, and
  (b) the applicant for the order applies to the court to proceed under subsection (7) (whether as part of the application for the restraint order or at any time afterwards).

(7) The court may make such order as it believes is appropriate for the purpose of ensuring that the restraint order is effective.

(8) A restraint order does not affect property for the time being subject to a charge under any of these provisions—
  (a) section 9 of the Drug Trafficking Offences Act 1986 (c. 32);
  (b) section 78 of the Criminal Justice Act 1988 (c. 33);
  (c) Article 14 of the Criminal Justice (Confiscation) (Northern Ireland) Order 1990 (S.I. 1990/2588 (N.I. 17));
  (d) section 27 of the Drug Trafficking Act 1994 (c. 37);
  (e) Article 32 of the Proceeds of Crime (Northern Ireland) Order 1996 (S.I. 1996/1299 (N.I. 9)).

(9) Dealing with property includes removing it from England and Wales.

42. Application, discharge and variation

(1) A restraint order—
  (a) may be made only on an application by an applicant falling within subsection (2);

(b) may be made on an ex parte application to a judge in chambers.

(2) These applicants fall within this subsection—
   (a) the prosecutor;
   (b) the Director;
   (c) an accredited financial investigator.

(3) An application to discharge or vary a restraint order or an order under section 41(7) may be made to the Crown Court by—
   (a) the person who applied for the order;
   (b) any person affected by the order.

(4) Subsections (5) to (7) apply to an application under subsection (3).

(5) The court—
   (a) may discharge the order;
   (b) may vary the order.

(6) If the condition in section 40 which was satisfied was that proceedings were started or an application was made, the court must discharge the order on the conclusion of the proceedings or of the application (as the case may be).

(7) If the condition in section 40 which was satisfied was that an investigation was started or an application was to be made, the court must discharge the order if within a reasonable time proceedings for the offence are not started or the application is not made (as the case may be).

43. Appeal to Court of Appeal

(1) If on an application for a restraint order the court decides not to make one, the person who applied for the order may appeal to the Court of Appeal against the decision.

(2) If an application is made under section 42(3) in relation to a restraint order or an order under section 41(7) the following persons may appeal to the Court of Appeal in respect of the Crown Court's decision on the application—
   (a) the person who applied for the order;
   (b) any person affected by the order.

(3) On an appeal under subsection (1) or (2) the Court of Appeal may—
   (a) confirm the decision, or
   (b) make such order as it believes is appropriate.

44. Appeal to House of Lords

(1) An appeal lies to the House of Lords from a decision of the Court of Appeal on an appeal under section 43.

(2) An appeal under this section lies at the instance of any person who was a party to the proceedings before the Court of Appeal.

(3) On an appeal under this section the House of Lords may—
   (a) confirm the decision of the Court of Appeal, or
   (b) make such order as it believes is appropriate.

45. Seizure

(1) If a restraint order is in force a constable or a customs officer may seize any realisable property to which it applies to prevent its removal from England and Wales.

(2) Property seized under subsection (1) must be dealt with in accordance with the directions of the court which made the order.

46. Hearsay evidence

(1) Evidence must not be excluded in restraint proceedings on the ground that it is hearsay (of whatever degree).

(2) Sections 2 to 4 of the Civil Evidence Act 1995 (c. 38) apply in relation to restraint proceedings as those sections apply in relation to civil proceedings.

(3) Restraint proceedings are proceedings—
   (a) for a restraint order;
   (b) for the discharge or variation of a restraint order;
   (c) on an appeal under section 43 or 44.

(4) Hearsay is a statement which is made otherwise than by a person while giving oral evidence in the proceedings and which is tendered as evidence of the matters stated.

(5) Nothing in this section affects the admissibility of evidence which is admissible apart from this section.

47. Supplementary

(1) The registration Acts—
   (a) apply in relation to restraint orders as they apply in relation to orders which affect land and are made by the court for the purpose of enforcing judgments or recognisances;
   (b) apply in relation to applications for restraint orders as they apply in relation to other pending land actions.

(2) The registration Acts are—
   (a) the Land Registration Act 1925 (c. 21);
   (b) the Land Charges Act 1972 (c. 61);
   (c) the Land Registration Act 2002 (c. 9).

(3) But no notice may be entered in the register of title under the Land Registration Act 2002 in respect of a restraint order.

(4) The person applying for a restraint order must be treated for the purposes of section 57 of the Land Registration Act 1925 (inhibitions) as a person interested in relation to any registered land to which—
   (a) the application relates, or
   (b) a restraint order made in pursuance of the application relates.

Management receivers

48. Appointment

(1) Subsection (2) applies if—
   (a) the Crown Court makes a restraint order, and
   (b) the applicant for the restraint order applies to the court to proceed under subsection (2) (whether as part of the application for the restraint order or at any time afterwards).

(2) The Crown Court may by order appoint a receiver in respect of any realisable property to which the restraint order applies.

49. Powers

(1) If the court appoints a receiver under section 48 it may act under this section on the application of the person who applied for the restraint order.

(2) The court may by order confer on the receiver the following powers in relation to any realisable property to which the restraint order applies—

    (a) power to take possession of the property;

    (b) power to manage or otherwise deal with the property;

    (c) power to start, carry on or defend any legal proceedings in respect of the property;

    (d) power to realise so much of the property as is necessary to meet the receiver's remuneration and expenses.

(3) The court may by order confer on the receiver power to enter any premises in England and Wales and to do any of the following—

    (a) search for or inspect anything authorised by the court;

    (b) make or obtain a copy, photograph or other record of anything so authorised;

    (c) remove anything which the receiver is required or authorised to take possession of in pursuance of an order of the court.

(4) The court may by order authorise the receiver to do any of the following for the purpose of the exercise of his functions—

    (a) hold property;

    (b) enter into contracts;

    (c) sue and be sued;

    (d) employ agents;

    (e) execute powers of attorney, deeds or other instruments;

    (f) take any other steps the court thinks appropriate.

(5) The court may order any person who has possession of realisable property to which the restraint order applies to give possession of it to the receiver.

(6) The court—

    (a) may order a person holding an interest in realisable property to which the restraint order applies to make to the receiver such payment as the court specifies in respect of a beneficial interest held by the defendant or the recipient of a tainted gift;

    (b) may (on the payment being made) by order transfer, grant or extinguish any interest in the property.

(7) Subsections (2), (5) and (6) do not apply to property for the time being subject to a charge under any of these provisions—

    (a) section 9 of the Drug Trafficking Offences Act 1986 (c. 32);

    (b) section 78 of the Criminal Justice Act 1988 (c. 33);

    (c) Article 14 of the Criminal Justice (Confiscation) (Northern Ireland) Order 1990 (S.I. 1990/2588 (N.I. 17));

    (d) section 27 of the Drug Trafficking Act 1994 (c. 37);

    (e) Article 32 of the Proceeds of Crime (Northern Ireland) Order 1996 (S.I. 1996/1299 (N.I. 9)).

(8) The court must not—

    (a) confer the power mentioned in subsection (2)(b) or (d) in respect of property, or

    (b) exercise the power conferred on it by subsection (6) in respect of property,

unless it gives persons holding interests in the property a reasonable opportunity to make representations to it.

(9) The court may order that a power conferred by an order under this section is subject to such conditions and exceptions as it specifies.

(10) Managing or otherwise dealing with property includes—

    (a) selling the property or any part of it or interest in it;

    (b) carrying on or arranging for another person to carry on any trade or business the assets of which are or are part of the property;

    (c) incurring capital expenditure in respect of the property.

Enforcement receivers

50. Appointment

(1) This section applies if—

    (a) a confiscation order is made,

    (b) it is not satisfied, and

    (c) it is not subject to appeal.

(2) On the application of the prosecutor the Crown Court may by order appoint a receiver in respect of realisable property.

51. Powers

(1) If the court appoints a receiver under section 50 it may act under this section on the application of the prosecutor.

(2) The court may by order confer on the receiver the following powers in relation to the realisable property—

    (a) power to take possession of the property;

    (b) power to manage or otherwise deal with the property;

    (c) power to realise the property, in such manner as the court may specify;

    (d) power to start, carry on or defend any legal proceedings in respect of the property.

(3) The court may by order confer on the receiver power to enter any premises in England and Wales and to do any of the following—

    (a) search for or inspect anything authorised by the court;

    (b) make or obtain a copy, photograph or other record of anything so authorised;

    (c) remove anything which the receiver is required or authorised to take possession of in pursuance of an order of the court.

(4) The court may by order authorise the receiver to do any of the following for the purpose of the exercise of his functions—

    (a) hold property;

    (b) enter into contracts;

    (c) sue and be sued;

    (d) employ agents;

    (e) execute powers of attorney, deeds or other instruments;

    (f) take any other steps the court thinks appropriate.

(5) The court may order any person who has possession of realisable property to give possession of it to the receiver.

(6) The court—

    (a) may order a person holding an interest in realisable property to make to the receiver such payment as the court specifies in respect of a beneficial interest held by the defendant or the recipient of a tainted gift;

(b) may (on the payment being made) by order transfer, grant or extinguish any interest in the property.
(7) Subsections (2), (5) and (6) do not apply to property for the time being subject to a charge under any of these provisions—
   (a) section 9 of the Drug Trafficking Offences Act 1986 (c. 32);
   (b) section 78 of the Criminal Justice Act 1988 (c. 33);
   (c) Article 14 of the Criminal Justice (Confiscation) (Northern Ireland) Order 1990 (S.I. 1990/2588 (N.I. 17));
   (d) section 27 of the Drug Trafficking Act 1994 (c. 37);
   (e) Article 32 of the Proceeds of Crime (Northern Ireland) Order 1996 (S.I. 1996/1299 (N.I. 9)).
(8) The court must not—
   (a) confer the power mentioned in subsection (2)(b) or (c) in respect of property, or
   (b) exercise the power conferred on it by subsection (6) in respect of property,
   Unless it gives persons holding interests in the property a reasonable opportunity to make representations to it.
(9) The court may order that a power conferred by an order under this section is subject to such conditions and exceptions as it specifies.
(10) Managing or otherwise dealing with property includes—
   (a) selling the property or any part of it or interest in it;
   (b) carrying on or arranging for another person to carry on any trade or business the assets of which are or are part of the property;
   (c) incurring capital expenditure in respect of the property.

Director's receivers

52. Appointment

(1) This section applies if—
   (a) a confiscation order is made, and
   (b) the Director is appointed as the enforcement authority for the order under section 34.
(2) But this section does not apply if—
   (a) the confiscation order was made by the Court of Appeal, and
   (b) when the Crown Court comes to proceed under this section the confiscation order has been satisfied.
(3) If this section applies the Crown Court must make an order for the appointment of a receiver in respect of realisable property.
(4) An order under subsection (3)—
   (a) must confer power on the Director to nominate the person who is to be the receiver, and
   (b) takes effect when the Director nominates that person.
(5) The Director must not nominate a person under subsection (4) unless at the time he does so the confiscation order—
   (a) is not satisfied, and
   (b) is not subject to appeal.
(6) A person nominated to be the receiver under subsection (4) may be—
   (a) a member of the staff of the Agency;

    (b) a person providing services under arrangements made by the Director.

(7) If this section applies section 50 does not apply.

53. Powers

(1) If the court makes an order for the appointment of a receiver under section 52 it may act under this section on the application of the Director.

(2) The court may by order confer on the receiver the following powers in relation to the realisable property—

    (a) power to take possession of the property;

    (b) power to manage or otherwise deal with the property;

    (c) power to realise the property, in such manner as the court may specify;

    (d) power to start, carry on or defend any legal proceedings in respect of the property.

(3) The court may by order confer on the receiver power to enter any premises in England and Wales and to do any of the following—

    (a) search for or inspect anything authorised by the court;

    (b) make or obtain a copy, photograph or other record of anything so authorised;

    (c) remove anything which the receiver is required or authorised to take possession of in pursuance of an order of the court.

(4) The court may by order authorise the receiver to do any of the following for the purpose of the exercise of his functions—

    (a) hold property;

    (b) enter into contracts;

    (c) sue and be sued;

    (d) employ agents;

    (e) execute powers of attorney, deeds or other instruments;

    (f) take any other steps the court thinks appropriate.

(5) The court may order any person who has possession of realisable property to give possession of it to the receiver.

(6) The court—

    (a) may order a person holding an interest in realisable property to make to the receiver such payment as the court specifies in respect of a beneficial interest held by the defendant or the recipient of a tainted gift;

    (b) may (on the payment being made) by order transfer, grant or extinguish any interest in the property.

(7) Subsections (2), (5) and (6) do not apply to property for the time being subject to a charge under any of these provisions—

    (a) section 9 of the Drug Trafficking Offences Act 1986 (c. 32);

    (b) section 78 of the Criminal Justice Act 1988 (c. 33);

    (c) Article 14 of the Criminal Justice (Confiscation) (Northern Ireland) Order 1990 (S.I. 1990/2588 (N.I. 17));

    (d) section 27 of the Drug Trafficking Act 1994 (c. 37);

    (e) Article 32 of the Proceeds of Crime (Northern Ireland) Order 1996 (S.I. 1996/1299 (N.I. 9)).

(8) The court must not—

    (a) confer the power mentioned in subsection (2)(b) or (c) in respect of property, or

    (b) exercise the power conferred on it by subsection (6) in respect of property, unless it gives persons holding interests in the property a reasonable opportunity to make representations to it.

(9) The court may order that a power conferred by an order under this section is subject to such conditions and exceptions as it specifies.

(10) Managing or otherwise dealing with property includes—

(a) selling the property or any part of it or interest in it;

(b) carrying on or arranging for another person to carry on any trade or business the assets of which are or are part of the property;

(c) incurring capital expenditure in respect of the property.

Application of sums

54. Enforcement receivers

(1) This section applies to sums which are in the hands of a receiver appointed under section 50 if they are—

(a) the proceeds of the realisation of property under section 51;

(b) sums (other than those mentioned in paragraph (a)) in which the defendant holds an interest.

(2) The sums must be applied as follows—

(a) first, they must be applied in payment of such expenses incurred by a person acting as an insolvency practitioner as are payable under this subsection by virtue of section 432;

(b) second, they must be applied in making any payments directed by the Crown Court;

(c) third, they must be applied on the defendant's behalf towards satisfaction of the confiscation order.

(3) If the amount payable under the confiscation order has been fully paid and any sums remain in the receiver's hands he must distribute them—

(a) among such persons who held (or hold) interests in the property concerned as the Crown Court directs, and

(b) in such proportions as it directs.

(4) Before making a direction under subsection (3) the court must give persons who held (or hold) interests in the property concerned a reasonable opportunity to make representations to it.

(5) For the purposes of subsections (3) and (4) the property concerned is—

(a) the property represented by the proceeds mentioned in subsection (1)(a);

(b) the sums mentioned in subsection (1)(b).

(6) The receiver applies sums as mentioned in subsection (2)(c) by paying them to the appropriate justices' chief executive on account of the amount payable under the order.

(7) The appropriate justices' chief executive is the one for the magistrates' court responsible for enforcing the confiscation order as if the amount ordered to be paid were a fine.

55. Sums received by justices' chief executive

(1) This section applies if a justices' chief executive receives sums on account of the amount payable under a confiscation order (whether the sums are received under section 54 or otherwise).

(2) The chief executive's receipt of the sums reduces the amount payable under the order, but he must apply the sums received as follows.

(3) First he must apply them in payment of such expenses incurred by a person acting as an insolvency practitioner as—

(a) are payable under this subsection by virtue of section 432, but

(b) are not already paid under section 54(2)(a).

(4) If the justices' chief executive received the sums under section 54 he must next apply them—

(a) first, in payment of the remuneration and expenses of a receiver appointed under section 48, to the extent that they have not been met by virtue of the exercise by that receiver of a power conferred under section 49(2)(d);

(b) second, in payment of the remuneration and expenses of the receiver appointed under section 50.

(5) If a direction was made under section 13(6) for an amount of compensation to be paid out of sums recovered under the confiscation order, the justices' chief executive must next apply the sums in payment of that amount.

(6) If any amount remains after the justices' chief executive makes any payments required by the preceding provisions of this section, the amount must be treated for the purposes of section 60 of the Justices of the Peace Act 1997 (c. 25) (application of fines etc) as if it were a fine imposed by a magistrates' court.

(7) Subsection (4) does not apply if the receiver is a member of the staff of the Crown Prosecution Service or of the Commissioners of Customs and Excise; and it is immaterial whether he is a permanent or temporary member or he is on secondment from elsewhere.

56. Director's receivers

(1) This section applies to sums which are in the hands of a receiver appointed under section 52 if they are—

(a) the proceeds of the realisation of property under section 53;

(b) sums (other than those mentioned in paragraph (a)) in which the defendant holds an interest.

(2) The sums must be applied as follows—

(a) first, they must be applied in payment of such expenses incurred by a person acting as an insolvency practitioner as are payable under this subsection by virtue of section 432;

(b) second, they must be applied in making any payments directed by the Crown Court;

(c) third, they must be applied on the defendant's behalf towards satisfaction of the confiscation order by being paid to the Director on account of the amount payable under it.

(3) If the amount payable under the confiscation order has been fully paid and any sums remain in the receiver's hands he must distribute them—

(a) among such persons who held (or hold) interests in the property concerned as the Crown Court directs, and

(b) in such proportions as it directs.

(4) Before making a direction under subsection (3) the court must give persons who held (or hold) interests in the property concerned a reasonable opportunity to make representations to it.

(5) For the purposes of subsections (3) and (4) the property concerned is—
    (a) the property represented by the proceeds mentioned in subsection (1)(a);
    (b) the sums mentioned in subsection (1)(b).

57. Sums received by Director

(1) This section applies if the Director receives sums on account of the amount payable under a confiscation order (whether the sums are received under section 56 or otherwise).

(2) The Director's receipt of the sums reduces the amount payable under the order, but he must apply the sums received as follows.

(3) First he must apply them in payment of such expenses incurred by a person acting as an insolvency practitioner as—
    (a) are payable under this subsection by virtue of section 432, but
    (b) are not already paid under section 56(2)(a).

(4) If the Director received the sums under section 56 he must next apply them—
    (a) first, in payment of the remuneration and expenses of a receiver appointed under section 48, to the extent that they have not been met by virtue of the exercise by that receiver of a power conferred under section 49(2)(d);
    (b) second, in payment of the remuneration and expenses of the receiver appointed under section 52.

(5) If a direction was made under section 13(6) for an amount of compensation to be paid out of sums recovered under the confiscation order, the Director must next apply the sums in payment of that amount.

(6) Subsection (4) does not apply if the receiver is a member of the staff of the Agency or a person providing services under arrangements made by the Director.

Restrictions

58. Restraint orders

(1) Subsections (2) to (4) apply if a court makes a restraint order.

(2) No distress may be levied against any realisable property to which the order applies except with the leave of the Crown Court and subject to any terms the Crown Court may impose.

(3) If the order applies to a tenancy of any premises, no landlord or other person to whom rent is payable may exercise a right within subsection (4) except with the leave of the Crown Court and subject to any terms the Crown Court may impose.

(4) A right is within this subsection if it is a right of forfeiture by peaceable re-entry in relation to the premises in respect of any failure by the tenant to comply with any term or condition of the tenancy.

(5) If a court in which proceedings are pending in respect of any property is satisfied that a restraint order has been applied for or made in respect of the property, the court may either stay the proceedings or allow them to continue on any terms it thinks fit.

(6) Before exercising any power conferred by subsection (5), the court must give an opportunity to be heard to—
    (a) the applicant for the restraint order, and
    (b) any receiver appointed in respect of the property under section 48, 50 or 52.

59. Enforcement receivers

(1) Subsections (2) to (4) apply if a court makes an order under section 50 appointing a receiver in respect of any realisable property.

(2) No distress may be levied against the property except with the leave of the Crown Court and subject to any terms the Crown Court may impose.

(3) If the receiver is appointed in respect of a tenancy of any premises, no landlord or other person to whom rent is payable may exercise a right within subsection (4) except with the leave of the Crown Court and subject to any terms the Crown Court may impose.

(4) A right is within this subsection if it is a right of forfeiture by peaceable re-entry in relation to the premises in respect of any failure by the tenant to comply with any term or condition of the tenancy.

(5) If a court in which proceedings are pending in respect of any property is satisfied that an order under section 50 appointing a receiver in respect of the property has been applied for or made, the court may either stay the proceedings or allow them to continue on any terms it thinks fit.

(6) Before exercising any power conferred by subsection (5), the court must give an opportunity to be heard to—

   (a) the prosecutor, and
   (b) the receiver (if the order under section 50 has been made).

60. Director's receivers

(1) Subsections (2) to (4) apply if—

   (a) the Crown Court has made an order under section 52 for the appointment of a receiver in respect of any realisable property, and
   (b) the order has taken effect.

(2) No distress may be levied against the property except with the leave of the Crown Court and subject to any terms the Crown Court may impose.

(3) If the order is for the appointment of a receiver in respect of a tenancy of any premises, no landlord or other person to whom rent is payable may exercise a right within subsection (4) except with the leave of the Crown Court and subject to any terms the Crown Court may impose.

(4) A right is within this subsection if it is a right of forfeiture by peaceable re-entry in relation to the premises in respect of any failure by the tenant to comply with any term or condition of the tenancy.

(5) If a court (whether the Crown Court or any other court) in which proceedings are pending in respect of any property is satisfied that an order under section 52 for the appointment of a receiver in respect of the property has taken effect, the court may either stay the proceedings or allow them to continue on any terms it thinks fit.

(6) Before exercising any power conferred by subsection (5), the court must give an opportunity to be heard to—

   (a) the Director, and
   (b) the receiver.

Receivers: further provisions

61. Protection

If a receiver appointed under section 48, 50 or 52—
    (a) takes action in relation to property which is not realisable property,
    (b) would be entitled to take the action if it were realisable property, and
    (c) believes on reasonable grounds that he is entitled to take the action,
he is not liable to any person in respect of any loss or damage resulting from the action, except so far as the loss or damage is caused by his negligence.

62. Further applications

(1) This section applies to a receiver appointed under section 48, 50 or 52.
(2) The receiver may apply to the Crown Court for an order giving directions as to the exercise of his powers.
(3) The following persons may apply to the Crown Court—
    (a) any person affected by action taken by the receiver;
    (b) any person who may be affected by action the receiver proposes to take.
(4) On an application under this section the court may make such order as it believes is appropriate.

63. Discharge and variation

(1) The following persons may apply to the Crown Court to vary or discharge an order made under any of sections 48 to 53—
    (a) the receiver;
    (b) the person who applied for the order or (if the order was made under section 52 or 53) the Director;
    (c) any person affected by the order.
(2) On an application under this section the court—
    (a) may discharge the order;
    (b) may vary the order.
(3) But in the case of an order under section 48 or 49—
    (a) if the condition in section 40 which was satisfied was that proceedings were started or an application was made, the court must discharge the order on the conclusion of the proceedings or of the application (as the case may be);
    (b) if the condition which was satisfied was that an investigation was started or an application was to be made, the court must discharge the order if within a reasonable time proceedings for the offence are not started or the application is not made (as the case may be).

64. Management receivers: discharge

(1) This section applies if—
    (a) a receiver stands appointed under section 48 in respect of realisable property (the management receiver), and
    (b) the court appoints a receiver under section 50 or makes an order for the appointment of a receiver under section 52.
(2) The court must order the management receiver to transfer to the other receiver

all property held by the management receiver by virtue of the powers conferred on him by section 49.

(3) But in a case where the court makes an order under section 52 its order under subsection (2) above does not take effect until the order under section 52 takes effect.

(4) Subsection (2) does not apply to property which the management receiver holds by virtue of the exercise by him of his power under section 49(2)(d).

(5) If the management receiver complies with an order under subsection (2) he is discharged—
  (a) from his appointment under section 48;
  (b) from any obligation under this Act arising from his appointment.

(6) If this section applies the court may make such a consequential or incidental order as it believes is appropriate.

65. Appeal to Court of Appeal

(1) If on an application for an order under any of sections 48 to 51 or section 53 the court decides not to make one, the person who applied for the order may appeal to the Court of Appeal against the decision.

(2) If the court makes an order under any of sections 48 to 51 or section 53, the following persons may appeal to the Court of Appeal in respect of the court's decision—
  (a) the person who applied for the order;
  (b) any person affected by the order.

(3) If on an application for an order under section 62 the court decides not to make one, the person who applied for the order may appeal to the Court of Appeal against the decision.

(4) If the court makes an order under section 62, the following persons may appeal to the Court of Appeal in respect of the court's decision—
  (a) the person who applied for the order;
  (b) any person affected by the order;
  (c) the receiver.

(5) The following persons may appeal to the Court of Appeal against a decision of the court on an application under section 63—
  (a) the person who applied for the order in respect of which the application was made or (if the order was made under section 52 or 53) the Director;
  (b) any person affected by the court's decision;
  (c) the receiver.

(6) On an appeal under this section the Court of Appeal may—
  (a) confirm the decision, or
  (b) make such order as it believes is appropriate.

66. Appeal to House of Lords

(1) An appeal lies to the House of Lords from a decision of the Court of Appeal on an appeal under section 65.

(2) An appeal under this section lies at the instance of any person who was a party to the proceedings before the Court of Appeal.

(3) On an appeal under this section the House of Lords may—
  (a) confirm the decision of the Court of Appeal, or
  (b) make such order as it believes is appropriate.

Seized money

67. Seized money

(1) This section applies to money which—
   (a) is held by a person, and
   (b) is held in an account maintained by him with a bank or a building society.

(2) This section also applies to money which is held by a person and which—
   (a) has been seized by a constable under section 19 of the Police and Criminal Evidence Act 1984 (c. 60) (general power of seizure etc), and
   (b) is held in an account maintained by a police force with a bank or a building society.

(3) This section also applies to money which is held by a person and which—
   (a) has been seized by a customs officer under section 19 of the 1984 Act as applied by order made under section 114(2) of that Act, and
   (b) is held in an account maintained by the Commissioners of Customs and Excise with a bank or a building society.

(4) This section applies if the following conditions are satisfied—
   (a) a restraint order has effect in relation to money to which this section applies;
   (b) a confiscation order is made against the person by whom the money is held;
   (c) the Director has not been appointed as the enforcement authority for the confiscation order;
   (d) a receiver has not been appointed under section 50 in relation to the money;
   (e) any period allowed under section 11 for payment of the amount ordered to be paid under the confiscation order has ended.

(5) In such a case a magistrates' court may order the bank or building society to pay the money to the justices' chief executive for the court on account of the amount payable under the confiscation order.

(6) If a bank or building society fails to comply with an order under subsection (5)—
   (a) the magistrates' court may order it to pay an amount not exceeding £5,000, and
   (b) for the purposes of the Magistrates' Courts Act 1980 (c. 43) the sum is to be treated as adjudged to be paid by a conviction of the court.

(7) In order to take account of changes in the value of money the Secretary of State may by order substitute another sum for the sum for the time being specified in subsection (6)(a).

(8) For the purposes of this section—
   (a) a bank is a deposit-taking business within the meaning of the Banking Act 1987 (c. 22);
   (b) 'building society' has the same meaning as in the Building Societies Act 1986 (c. 53).

Financial investigators

68. Applications and appeals

(1) Subsections (2) and (3) apply to—
   (a) an application under section 41, 42, 48, 49 or 63;
   (b) an appeal under section 43, 44, 65 or 66.

(2) An accredited financial investigator must not make such an application or bring such an appeal unless he falls within subsection (3).

(3) An accredited financial investigator falls within this subsection if he is one of the following or is authorised for the purposes of this section by one of the following—
    (a) a police officer who is not below the rank of superintendent,
    (b) a customs officer who is not below such grade as is designated by the Commissioners of Customs and Excise as equivalent to that rank,
    (c) an accredited financial investigator who falls within a description specified in an order made for the purposes of this paragraph by the Secretary of State under section 453.

(4) If such an application is made or appeal brought by an accredited financial investigator any subsequent step in the application or appeal or any further application or appeal relating to the same matter may be taken, made or brought by a different accredited financial investigator who falls within subsection (3).

(5) If—
    (a) an application for a restraint order is made by an accredited financial investigator, and
    (b) a court is required under section 58(6) to give the applicant for the order an opportunity to be heard,

the court may give the opportunity to a different accredited financial investigator who falls within subsection (3).

Exercise of powers

69. Powers of court and receiver

(1) This section applies to—
    (a) the powers conferred on a court by sections 41 to 60 and sections 62 to 67;
    (b) the powers of a receiver appointed under section 48, 50 or 52.

(2) The powers—
    (a) must be exercised with a view to the value for the time being of realisable property being made available (by the property's realisation) for satisfying any confiscation order that has been or may be made against the defendant;
    (b) must be exercised, in a case where a confiscation order has not been made, with a view to securing that there is no diminution in the value of realisable property;
    (c) must be exercised without taking account of any obligation of the defendant or a recipient of a tainted gift if the obligation conflicts with the object of satisfying any confiscation order that has been or may be made against the defendant;
    (d) may be exercised in respect of a debt owed by the Crown.

(3) Subsection (2) has effect subject to the following rules—
    (a) the powers must be exercised with a view to allowing a person other than the defendant or a recipient of a tainted gift to retain or recover the value of any interest held by him;
    (b) in the case of realisable property held by a recipient of a tainted gift, the powers must be exercised with a view to realising no more than the value for the time being of the gift;
    (c) in a case where a confiscation order has not been made against the defendant, property must not be sold if the court so orders under subsection (4).

(4) If on an application by the defendant, or by the recipient of a tainted gift, the court decides that property cannot be replaced it may order that it must not be sold.

(5) An order under subsection (4) may be revoked or varied.

Committal

70. Committal by magistrates' court

(1) This section applies if—
   (a) a defendant is convicted of an offence by a magistrates' court, and
   (b) the prosecutor asks the court to commit the defendant to the Crown Court with a view to a confiscation order being considered under section 6.

(2) In such a case the magistrates' court—
   (a) must commit the defendant to the Crown Court in respect of the offence, and
   (b) may commit him to the Crown Court in respect of any other offence falling within subsection (3).

(3) An offence falls within this subsection if—
   (a) the defendant has been convicted of it by the magistrates' court or any other court, and
   (b) the magistrates' court has power to deal with him in respect of it.

(4) If a committal is made under this section in respect of an offence or offences—
   (a) section 6 applies accordingly, and
   (b) the committal operates as a committal of the defendant to be dealt with by the Crown Court in accordance with section 71.

(5) If a committal is made under this section in respect of an offence for which (apart from this section) the magistrates' court could have committed the defendant for sentence under section 3(2) of the Sentencing Act (offences triable either way) the court must state whether it would have done so.

(6) A committal under this section may be in custody or on bail.

71. Sentencing by Crown Court

(1) If a defendant is committed to the Crown Court under section 70 in respect of an offence or offences, this section applies (whether or not the court proceeds under section 6).

(2) In the case of an offence in respect of which the magistrates' court has stated under section 70(5) that it would have committed the defendant for sentence, the Crown Court—
   (a) must inquire into the circumstances of the case, and
   (b) may deal with the defendant in any way in which it could deal with him if he had just been convicted of the offence on indictment before it.

(3) In the case of any other offence the Crown Court—
   (a) must inquire into the circumstances of the case, and
   (b) may deal with the defendant in any way in which the magistrates' court could deal with him if it had just convicted him of the offence.

Compensation

72. Serious default

(1) If the following three conditions are satisfied the Crown Court may order the payment of such compensation as it believes is just.

(2) The first condition is satisfied if a criminal investigation has been started with regard to an offence and proceedings are not started for the offence.

(3) The first condition is also satisfied if proceedings for an offence are started against a person and—
    (a) they do not result in his conviction for the offence, or
    (b) he is convicted of the offence but the conviction is quashed or he is pardoned in respect of it.

(4) If subsection (2) applies the second condition is that—
    (a) in the criminal investigation there has been a serious default by a person mentioned in subsection (9), and
    (b) the investigation would not have continued if the default had not occurred.

(5) If subsection (3) applies the second condition is that—
    (a) in the criminal investigation with regard to the offence or in its prosecution there has been a serious default by a person who is mentioned in subsection (9), and
    (b) the proceedings would not have been started or continued if the default had not occurred.

(6) The third condition is that an application is made under this section by a person who held realisable property and has suffered loss in consequence of anything done in relation to it by or in pursuance of an order under this Part.

(7) The offence referred to in subsection (2) may be one of a number of offences with regard to which the investigation is started.

(8) The offence referred to in subsection (3) may be one of a number of offences for which the proceedings are started.

(9) Compensation under this section is payable to the applicant and—
    (a) if the person in default was or was acting as a member of a police force, the compensation is payable out of the police fund from which the expenses of that force are met;
    (b) if the person in default was a member of the Crown Prosecution Service or was acting on its behalf, the compensation is payable by the Director of Public Prosecutions;
    (c) if the person in default was a member of the Serious Fraud Office, the compensation is payable by the Director of that Office;
    (d) if the person in default was a customs officer, the compensation is payable by the Commissioners of Customs and Excise;
    (e) if the person in default was an officer of the Commissioners of Inland Revenue, the compensation is payable by those Commissioners.

73. Order varied or discharged

(1) This section applies if—
    (a) the court varies a confiscation order under section 29 or discharges one under section 30, and
    (b) an application is made to the Crown Court by a person who held realisable property and has suffered loss as a result of the making of the order.

(2) The court may order the payment of such compensation as it believes is just.

(3) Compensation under this section is payable—
    (a) to the applicant;
    (b) by the Lord Chancellor.

Enforcement abroad

74. Enforcement abroad

(1) This section applies if—

    (a) any of the conditions in section 40 is satisfied,

    (b) the prosecutor or the Director believes that realisable property is situated in a country or territory outside the United Kingdom (the receiving country), and

    (c) the prosecutor or the Director (as the case may be) sends a request for assistance to the Secretary of State with a view to it being forwarded under this section.

(2) In a case where no confiscation order has been made, a request for assistance is a request to the government of the receiving country to secure that any person is prohibited from dealing with realisable property.

(3) In a case where a confiscation order has been made and has not been satisfied, discharged or quashed, a request for assistance is a request to the government of the receiving country to secure that—

    (a) any person is prohibited from dealing with realisable property;

    (b) realisable property is realised and the proceeds are applied in accordance with the law of the receiving country.

(4) No request for assistance may be made for the purposes of this section in a case where a confiscation order has been made and has been satisfied, discharged or quashed.

(5) If the Secretary of State believes it is appropriate to do so he may forward the request for assistance to the government of the receiving country.

(6) If property is realised in pursuance of a request under subsection (3) the amount ordered to be paid under the confiscation order must be taken to be reduced by an amount equal to the proceeds of realisation.

(7) A certificate purporting to be issued by or on behalf of the requested government is admissible as evidence of the facts it states if it states—

    (a) that property has been realised in pursuance of a request under subsection (3),

    (b) the date of realisation, and

    (c) the proceeds of realisation.

(8) If the proceeds of realisation made in pursuance of a request under subsection (3) are expressed in a currency other than sterling, they must be taken to be the sterling equivalent calculated in accordance with the rate of exchange prevailing at the end of the day of realisation.

Interpretation

75. Criminal lifestyle

(1) A defendant has a criminal lifestyle if (and only if) the following condition is satisfied.

(2) The condition is that the offence (or any of the offences) concerned satisfies any of these tests—

    (a) it is specified in Schedule 2;

    (b) it constitutes conduct forming part of a course of criminal activity;

    (c) it is an offence committed over a period of at least six months and the defendant has benefited from the conduct which constitutes the offence.

(3) Conduct forms part of a course of criminal activity if the defendant has benefited from the conduct and—

    (a) in the proceedings in which he was convicted he was convicted of three or more other offences, each of three or more of them constituting conduct from which he has benefited, or

    (b) in the period of six years ending with the day when those proceedings were started (or, if there is more than one such day, the earliest day) he was convicted on at least two separate occasions of an offence constituting conduct from which he has benefited.

(4) But an offence does not satisfy the test in subsection (2)(b) or (c) unless the defendant obtains relevant benefit of not less than £5000.

(5) Relevant benefit for the purposes of subsection (2)(b) is—

    (a) benefit from conduct which constitutes the offence;

    (b) benefit from any other conduct which forms part of the course of criminal activity and which constitutes an offence of which the defendant has been convicted;

    (c) benefit from conduct which constitutes an offence which has been or will be taken into consideration by the court in sentencing the defendant for an offence mentioned in paragraph (a) or (b).

(6) Relevant benefit for the purposes of subsection (2)(c) is—

    (a) benefit from conduct which constitutes the offence;

    (b) benefit from conduct which constitutes an offence which has been or will be taken into consideration by the court in sentencing the defendant for the offence mentioned in paragraph (a).

(7) The Secretary of State may by order amend Schedule 2.

(8) The Secretary of State may by order vary the amount for the time being specified in subsection (4).

76. Conduct and benefit

(1) Criminal conduct is conduct which—

    (a) constitutes an offence in England and Wales, or

    (b) would constitute such an offence if it occurred in England and Wales.

(2) General criminal conduct of the defendant is all his criminal conduct, and it is immaterial—

    (a) whether conduct occurred before or after the passing of this Act;

    (b) whether property constituting a benefit from conduct was obtained before or after the passing of this Act.

(3) Particular criminal conduct of the defendant is all his criminal conduct which falls within the following paragraphs—

    (a) conduct which constitutes the offence or offences concerned;

    (b) conduct which constitutes offences of which he was convicted in the same proceedings as those in which he was convicted of the offence or offences concerned;

    (c) conduct which constitutes offences which the court will be taking into consideration in deciding his sentence for the offence or offences concerned.

(4) A person benefits from conduct if he obtains property as a result of or in connection with the conduct.

(5) If a person obtains a pecuniary advantage as a result of or in connection with conduct, he is to be taken to obtain as a result of or in connection with the conduct a sum of money equal to the value of the pecuniary advantage.

(6) References to property or a pecuniary advantage obtained in connection with conduct include references to property or a pecuniary advantage obtained both in that connection and some other.

(7) If a person benefits from conduct his benefit is the value of the property obtained.

77. Tainted gifts

(1) Subsections (2) and (3) apply if—
  (a) no court has made a decision as to whether the defendant has a criminal lifestyle, or
  (b) a court has decided that the defendant has a criminal lifestyle.

(2) A gift is tainted if it was made by the defendant at any time after the relevant day.

(3) A gift is also tainted if it was made by the defendant at any time and was of property—
  (a) which was obtained by the defendant as a result of or in connection with his general criminal conduct, or
  (b) which (in whole or part and whether directly or indirectly) represented in the defendant's hands property obtained by him as a result of or in connection with his general criminal conduct.

(4) Subsection (5) applies if a court has decided that the defendant does not have a criminal lifestyle.

(5) A gift is tainted if it was made by the defendant at any time after—
  (a) the date on which the offence concerned was committed, or
  (b) if his particular criminal conduct consists of two or more offences and they were committed on different dates, the date of the earliest.

(6) For the purposes of subsection (5) an offence which is a continuing offence is committed on the first occasion when it is committed.

(7) For the purposes of subsection (5) the defendant's particular criminal conduct includes any conduct which constitutes offences which the court has taken into consideration in deciding his sentence for the offence or offences concerned.

(8) A gift may be a tainted gift whether it was made before or after the passing of this Act.

(9) The relevant day is the first day of the period of six years ending with—
  (a) the day when proceedings for the offence concerned were started against the defendant, or
  (b) if there are two or more offences and proceedings for them were started on different days, the earliest of those days.

78. Gifts and their recipients

(1) If the defendant transfers property to another person for a consideration whose value is significantly less than the value of the property at the time of the transfer, he is to be treated as making a gift.

(2) If subsection (1) applies the property given is to be treated as such share in the property transferred as is represented by the fraction—
  (a) whose numerator is the difference between the two values mentioned in subsection (1), and

(b) whose denominator is the value of the property at the time of the transfer.

(3) References to a recipient of a tainted gift are to a person to whom the defendant has made the gift.

79. Value: the basic rule

(1) This section applies for the purpose of deciding the value at any time of property then held by a person.

(2) Its value is the market value of the property at that time.

(3) But if at that time another person holds an interest in the property its value, in relation to the person mentioned in subsection (1), is the market value of his interest at that time, ignoring any charging order under a provision listed in subsection (4).

(4) The provisions are—

(a) section 9 of the Drug Trafficking Offences Act 1986 (c. 32);

(b) section 78 of the Criminal Justice Act 1988 (c. 33);

(c) Article 14 of the Criminal Justice (Confiscation) (Northern Ireland) Order 1990 (S.I. 1990/2588 (N.I. 17));

(d) section 27 of the Drug Trafficking Act 1994 (c. 37);

(e) Article 32 of the Proceeds of Crime (Northern Ireland) Order 1996 (S.I. 1996/1299 (N.I. 9)).

(5) This section has effect subject to sections 80 and 81.

80. Value of property obtained from conduct

(1) This section applies for the purpose of deciding the value of property obtained by a person as a result of or in connection with his criminal conduct; and the material time is the time the court makes its decision.

(2) The value of the property at the material time is the greater of the following—

(a) the value of the property (at the time the person obtained it) adjusted to take account of later changes in the value of money;

(b) the value (at the material time) of the property found under subsection (3).

(3) The property found under this subsection is as follows—

(a) if the person holds the property obtained, the property found under this subsection is that property;

(b) if he holds no part of the property obtained, the property found under this subsection is any property which directly or indirectly represents it in his hands;

(c) if he holds part of the property obtained, the property found under this subsection is that part and any property which directly or indirectly represents the other part in his hands.

(4) The references in subsection (2)(a) and (b) to the value are to the value found in accordance with section 79.

81. Value of tainted gifts

(1) The value at any time (the material time) of a tainted gift is the greater of the following—

(a) the value (at the time of the gift) of the property given, adjusted to take account of later changes in the value of money;

(b) the value (at the material time) of the property found under subsection (2).

(2) The property found under this subsection is as follows—

(a) if the recipient holds the property given, the property found under this subsection is that property;

(b) if the recipient holds no part of the property given, the property found under this subsection is any property which directly or indirectly represents it in his hands;

(c) if the recipient holds part of the property given, the property found under this subsection is that part and any property which directly or indirectly represents the other part in his hands.

(3) The references in subsection (1)(a) and (b) to the value are to the value found in accordance with section 79.

82. Free property

Property is free unless an order is in force in respect of it under any of these provisions—

(a) section 27 of the Misuse of Drugs Act 1971 (c. 38) (forfeiture orders);

(b) Article 11 of the Criminal Justice (Northern Ireland) Order 1994 (S.I. 1994/2795 (N.I. 15)) (deprivation orders);

(c) Part 2 of the Proceeds of Crime (Scotland) Act 1995 (c. 43) (forfeiture of property used in crime);

(d) section 143 of the Sentencing Act (deprivation orders);

(e) section 23 or 111 of the Terrorism Act 2000 (c. 11) (forfeiture orders);

(f) section 246, 266, 295(2) or 298(2) of this Act.

83. Realisable property

Realisable property is—

(a) any free property held by the defendant;

(b) any free property held by the recipient of a tainted gift.

84. Property: general provisions

(1) Property is all property wherever situated and includes—

(a) money;

(b) all forms of real or personal property;

(c) things in action and other intangible or incorporeal property.

(2) The following rules apply in relation to property—

(a) property is held by a person if he holds an interest in it;

(b) property is obtained by a person if he obtains an interest in it;

(c) property is transferred by one person to another if the first one transfers or grants an interest in it to the second;

(d) references to property held by a person include references to property vested in his trustee in bankruptcy, permanent or interim trustee (within the meaning of the Bankruptcy (Scotland) Act 1985 (c. 66)) or liquidator;

(e) references to an interest held by a person beneficially in property include references to an interest which would be held by him beneficially if the property were not so vested;

(f) references to an interest, in relation to land in England and Wales or Northern Ireland, are to any legal estate or equitable interest or power;

(g) references to an interest, in relation to land in Scotland, are to any estate, interest, servitude or other heritable right in or over land, including a heritable security;

(h) references to an interest, in relation to property other than land, include references to a right (including a right to possession).

85. Proceedings

(1) Proceedings for an offence are started—

    (a) when a justice of the peace issues a summons or warrant under section 1 of the Magistrates' Courts Act 1980 (c. 43) in respect of the offence;

    (b) when a person is charged with the offence after being taken into custody without a warrant;

    (c) when a bill of indictment is preferred under section 2 of the Administration of Justice (Miscellaneous Provisions) Act 1933 (c. 36) in a case falling within subsection (2)(b) of that section (preferment by Court of Appeal or High Court judge).

(2) If more than one time is found under subsection (1) in relation to proceedings they are started at the earliest of them.

(3) If the defendant is acquitted on all counts in proceedings for an offence, the proceedings are concluded when he is acquitted.

(4) If the defendant is convicted in proceedings for an offence and the conviction is quashed or the defendant is pardoned before a confiscation order is made, the proceedings are concluded when the conviction is quashed or the defendant is pardoned.

(5) If a confiscation order is made against the defendant in proceedings for an offence (whether the order is made by the Crown Court or the Court of Appeal) the proceedings are concluded—

    (a) when the order is satisfied or discharged, or

    (b) when the order is quashed and there is no further possibility of an appeal against the decision to quash the order.

(6) If the defendant is convicted in proceedings for an offence but the Crown Court decides not to make a confiscation order against him, the following rules apply—

    (a) if an application for leave to appeal under section 31(2) is refused, the proceedings are concluded when the decision to refuse is made;

    (b) if the time for applying for leave to appeal under section 31(2) expires without an application being made, the proceedings are concluded when the time expires;

    (c) if on appeal under section 31(2) the Court of Appeal confirms the Crown Court's decision, and an application for leave to appeal under section 33 is refused, the proceedings are concluded when the decision to refuse is made;

    (d) if on appeal under section 31(2) the Court of Appeal confirms the Crown Court's decision, and the time for applying for leave to appeal under section 33 expires without an application being made, the proceedings are concluded when the time expires;

    (e) if on appeal under section 31(2) the Court of Appeal confirms the Crown Court's decision, and on appeal under section 33 the House of Lords confirms the Court of Appeal's decision, the proceedings are concluded when the House of Lords confirms the decision;

    (f) if on appeal under section 31(2) the Court of Appeal directs the Crown Court to reconsider the case, and on reconsideration the Crown Court decides not to make a confiscation order against the defendant, the proceedings are concluded when the Crown Court makes that decision;

    (g) if on appeal under section 33 the House of Lords directs the Crown Court to reconsider the case, and on reconsideration the Crown Court decides not to make a confiscation order against the defendant, the proceedings are concluded when the Crown Court makes that decision.

(7) In applying subsection (6) any power to extend the time for making an application for leave to appeal must be ignored.

(8) In applying subsection (6) the fact that a court may decide on a later occasion to make a confiscation order against the defendant must be ignored.

86. Applications

(1) An application under section 19, 20, 27 or 28 is concluded—

    (a) in a case where the court decides not to make a confiscation order against the defendant, when it makes the decision;

    (b) in a case where a confiscation order is made against him as a result of the application, when the order is satisfied or discharged, or when the order is quashed and there is no further possibility of an appeal against the decision to quash the order;

    (c) in a case where the application is withdrawn, when the person who made the application notifies the withdrawal to the court to which the application was made.

(2) An application under section 21 or 22 is concluded—

    (a) in a case where the court decides not to vary the confiscation order concerned, when it makes the decision;

    (b) in a case where the court varies the confiscation order as a result of the application, when the order is satisfied or discharged, or when the order is quashed and there is no further possibility of an appeal against the decision to quash the order;

    (c) in a case where the application is withdrawn, when the person who made the application notifies the withdrawal to the court to which the application was made.

87. Confiscation orders

(1) A confiscation order is satisfied when no amount is due under it.

(2) A confiscation order is subject to appeal until there is no further possibility of an appeal on which the order could be varied or quashed; and for this purpose any power to grant leave to appeal out of time must be ignored.

88. Other interpretative provisions

(1) A reference to the offence (or offences) concerned must be construed in accordance with section 6(9).

(2) A criminal investigation is an investigation which police officers or other persons have a duty to conduct with a view to it being ascertained whether a person should be charged with an offence.

(3) A defendant is a person against whom proceedings for an offence have been started (whether or not he has been convicted).

(4) A reference to sentencing the defendant for an offence includes a reference to dealing with him otherwise in respect of the offence.

(5) The Sentencing Act is the Powers of Criminal Courts (Sentencing) Act 2000 (c. 6).

(6) The following paragraphs apply to references to orders—

(a) a confiscation order is an order under section 6;

(b) a restraint order is an order under section 41.

(7) Sections 75 to 87 and this section apply for the purposes of this Part.

General

89. Procedure on appeal to the Court of Appeal

(1) An appeal to the Court of Appeal under this Part lies only with the leave of that Court.

(2) Subject to rules of court made under section 53(1) of the Supreme Court Act 1981 (c. 54) (distribution of business between civil and criminal divisions) the criminal division of the Court of Appeal is the division—

(a) to which an appeal to that Court under this Part is to lie, and

(b) which is to exercise that Court's jurisdiction under this Part.

(3) In relation to appeals to the Court of Appeal under this Part, the Secretary of State may make an order containing provision corresponding to any provision in the Criminal Appeal Act 1968 (c. 19) (subject to any specified modifications).

90. Procedure on appeal to the House of Lords

(1) Section 33(3) of the Criminal Appeal Act 1968 (limitation on appeal from criminal division of the Court of Appeal) does not prevent an appeal to the House of Lords under this Part.

(2) In relation to appeals to the House of Lords under this Part, the Secretary of State may make an order containing provision corresponding to any provision in the Criminal Appeal Act 1968 (subject to any specified modifications).

91. Crown Court Rules

In relation to—

(a) proceedings under this Part, or

(b) receivers appointed under this Part,

Crown Court Rules may make provision corresponding to provision in Civil Procedure Rules.

PART 3

. . .

PART 4

. . .

PART 5
CIVIL RECOVERY OF THE PROCEEDS ETC.
OF UNLAWFUL CONDUCT

CHAPTER 1
INTRODUCTORY

240. General purpose of this Part

(1) This Part has effect for the purposes of—

    (a) enabling the enforcement authority to recover, in civil proceedings before the High Court or Court of Session, property which is, or represents, property obtained through unlawful conduct,

    (b) enabling cash which is, or represents, property obtained through unlawful conduct, or which is intended to be used in unlawful conduct, to be forfeited in civil proceedings before a magistrates' court or (in Scotland) the sheriff.

(2) The powers conferred by this Part are exercisable in relation to any property (including cash) whether or not any proceedings have been brought for an offence in connection with the property.

241. 'Unlawful conduct'

(1) Conduct occurring in any part of the United Kingdom is unlawful conduct if it is unlawful under the criminal law of that part.

(2) Conduct which—

    (a) occurs in a country outside the United Kingdom and is unlawful under the criminal law of that country, and

    (b) if it occurred in a part of the United Kingdom, would be unlawful under the criminal law of that part,

is also unlawful conduct.

(3) The court or sheriff must decide on a balance of probabilities whether it is proved—

    (a) that any matters alleged to constitute unlawful conduct have occurred, or

    (b) that any person intended to use any cash in unlawful conduct.

242. 'Property obtained through unlawful conduct'

(1) A person obtains property through unlawful conduct (whether his own conduct or another's) if he obtains property by or in return for the conduct.

(2) In deciding whether any property was obtained through unlawful conduct—

    (a) it is immaterial whether or not any money, goods or services were provided in order to put the person in question in a position to carry out the conduct,

    (b) it is not necessary to show that the conduct was of a particular kind if it is shown that the property was obtained through conduct of one of a number of kinds, each of which would have been unlawful conduct.

231

CHAPTER 2
CIVIL RECOVERY IN THE HIGH COURT OR COURT OF SESSION

Proceedings for recovery orders

243. Proceedings for recovery orders in England and Wales or Northern Ireland

(1) Proceedings for a recovery order may be taken by the enforcement authority in the High Court against any person who the authority thinks holds recoverable property.

(2) The enforcement authority must serve the claim form—
   (a) on the respondent, and
   (b) unless the court dispenses with service, on any other person who the authority thinks holds any associated property which the authority wishes to be subject to a recovery order, wherever domiciled, resident or present.

(3) If any property which the enforcement authority wishes to be subject to a recovery order is not specified in the claim form it must be described in the form in general terms; and the form must state whether it is alleged to be recoverable property or associated property.

(4) The references above to the claim form include the particulars of claim, where they are served subsequently.

244. Proceedings for recovery orders in Scotland

(1) Proceedings for a recovery order may be taken by the enforcement authority in the Court of Session against any person who the authority thinks holds recoverable property.

(2) The enforcement authority must serve the application—
   (a) on the respondent, and
   (b) unless the court dispenses with service, on any other person who the authority thinks holds any associated property which the authority wishes to be subject to a recovery order, wherever domiciled, resident or present.

(3) If any property which the enforcement authority wishes to be subject to a recovery order is not specified in the application it must be described in the application in general terms; and the application must state whether it is alleged to be recoverable property or associated property.

245. 'Associated property'

(1) 'Associated property' means property of any of the following descriptions (including property held by the respondent) which is not itself the recoverable property—
   (a) any interest in the recoverable property,
   (b) any other interest in the property in which the recoverable property subsists,
   (c) if the recoverable property is a tenancy in common, the tenancy of the other tenant,
   (d) if (in Scotland) the recoverable property is owned in common, the interest of the other owner,
   (e) if the recoverable property is part of a larger property, but not a separate part, the remainder of that property.

(2) References to property being associated with recoverable property are to be read accordingly.

(3) No property is to be treated as associated with recoverable property consisting of rights under a pension scheme (within the meaning of sections 273 to 275).

Interim receiving orders (England and Wales and Northern Ireland)

246. Application for interim receiving order

(1) Where the enforcement authority may take proceedings for a recovery order in the High Court, the authority may apply to the court for an interim receiving order (whether before or after starting the proceedings).

(2) An interim receiving order is an order for—

(a) the detention, custody or preservation of property, and

(b) the appointment of an interim receiver.

(3) An application for an interim receiving order may be made without notice if the circumstances are such that notice of the application would prejudice any right of the enforcement authority to obtain a recovery order in respect of any property.

(4) The court may make an interim receiving order on the application if it is satisfied that the conditions in subsections (5) and, where applicable, (6) are met.

(5) The first condition is that there is a good arguable case—

(a) that the property to which the application for the order relates is or includes recoverable property, and

(b) that, if any of it is not recoverable property, it is associated property.

(6) The second condition is that, if—

(a) the property to which the application for the order relates includes property alleged to be associated property, and

(b) the enforcement authority has not established the identity of the person who holds it, the authority has taken all reasonable steps to do so.

(7) In its application for an interim receiving order, the enforcement authority must nominate a suitably qualified person for appointment as interim receiver, but the nominee may not be a member of the staff of the Agency.

(8) The extent of the power to make an interim receiving order is not limited by sections 247 to 255.

247. Functions of interim receiver

(1) An interim receiving order may authorise or require the interim receiver—

(a) to exercise any of the powers mentioned in Schedule 6,

(b) to take any other steps the court thinks appropriate, for the purpose of securing the detention, custody or preservation of the property to which the order applies or of taking any steps under subsection (2).

(2) An interim receiving order must require the interim receiver to take any steps which the court thinks necessary to establish—

(a) whether or not the property to which the order applies is recoverable property or associated property,

(b) whether or not any other property is recoverable property (in relation to the same unlawful conduct) and, if it is, who holds it.

(3) If—
   (a) the interim receiver deals with any property which is not property to which the order applies, and
   (b) at the time he deals with the property he believes on reasonable grounds that he is entitled to do so in pursuance of the order, the interim receiver is not liable to any person in respect of any loss or damage resulting from his dealing with the property except so far as the loss or damage is caused by his negligence.

248. Registration

(1) The registration Acts—
   (a) apply in relation to interim receiving orders as they apply in relation to orders which affect land and are made by the court for the purpose of enforcing judgements or recognisances,
   (b) apply in relation to applications for interim receiving orders as they apply in relation to other pending land actions.
(2) The registration Acts are—
   (a) the Land Registration Act 1925 (c. 21),
   (b) the Land Charges Act 1972 (c. 61), and
   (c) the Land Registration Act 2002 (c. 9).
(3) But no notice may be entered in the register of title under the Land Registration Act 2002 in respect of an interim receiving order.
(4) A person applying for an interim receiving order must be treated for the purposes of section 57 of the Land Registration Act 1925 (inhibitions) as a person interested in relation to any registered land to which—
   (a) the application relates, or
   (b) an interim receiving order made in pursuance of the application relates.

249. Registration (Northern Ireland)

(1) A person applying for an interim receiving order must be treated for the purposes of section 66 of the Land Registration Act (Northern Ireland) 1970 (c. 18 (N.I.)) (cautions) as a person interested in relation to any registered land to which—
   (a) the application relates, or
   (b) an interim receiving order made in pursuance of the application relates.
(2) Upon being served with a copy of an interim receiving order, the Registrar must, in respect of any registered land to which an interim receiving order or an application for an interim receiving order relates, make an entry inhibiting any dealing with the land without the consent of the High Court.
(3) Subsections (2) and (4) of section 67 of the Land Registration Act (Northern Ireland) 1970 (inhibitions) apply to an entry made under subsection (2) as they apply to an entry made on the application of any person interested in the registered land under subsection (1) of that section.
(4) Where an interim receiving order has been protected by an entry registered under the Land Registration Act (Northern Ireland) 1970 or the Registration of Deeds Acts, an order setting aside the interim receiving order may require that entry to be vacated.
(5) In this section—

'Registrar' and 'entry' have the same meanings as in the Land Registration Act (Northern Ireland) 1970, and

'Registration of Deeds Acts' has the meaning given by section 46(2) of the Interpretation Act (Northern Ireland) 1954 (c. 33 (N.I.)).

250. Duties of respondent etc.

(1) An interim receiving order may require any person to whose property the order applies—
   (a) to bring the property to a place (in England and Wales or, as the case may be, Northern Ireland) specified by the interim receiver or place it in the custody of the interim receiver (if, in either case, he is able to do so),
   (b) to do anything he is reasonably required to do by the interim receiver for the preservation of the property.

(2) An interim receiving order may require any person to whose property the order applies to bring any documents relating to the property which are in his possession or control to a place (in England and Wales or, as the case may be, Northern Ireland) specified by the interim receiver or to place them in the custody of the interim receiver.

'Document' means anything in which information of any description is recorded.

251. Supervision of interim receiver and variation of order

(1) The interim receiver, any party to the proceedings and any person affected by any action taken by the interim receiver, or who may be affected by any action proposed to be taken by him, may at any time apply to the court for directions as to the exercise of the interim receiver's functions.

(2) Before giving any directions under subsection (1), the court must (as well as giving the parties to the proceedings an opportunity to be heard) give such an opportunity to the interim receiver and to any person who may be interested in the application.

(3) The court may at any time vary or set aside an interim receiving order.

(4) Before exercising any power under this Chapter to vary or set aside an interim receiving order, the court must (as well as giving the parties to the proceedings an opportunity to be heard) give such an opportunity to the interim receiver and to any person who may be affected by the court's decision.

252. Restrictions on dealing etc. with property

(1) An interim receiving order must, subject to any exclusions made in accordance with this section, prohibit any person to whose property the order applies from dealing with the property.

(2) Exclusions may be made when the interim receiving order is made or on an application to vary the order.

(3) An exclusion may, in particular, make provision for the purpose of enabling any person—
   (a) to meet his reasonable living expenses, or
   (b) to carry on any trade, business, profession or occupation,
and may be made subject to conditions.

(4) But an exclusion may not be made for the purpose of enabling any person to meet any legal expenses in respect of proceedings under this Part.

(5) If the excluded property is not specified in the order it must be described in the order in general terms.

(6) The power to make exclusions must be exercised with a view to ensuring, so far as practicable, that the satisfaction of any right of the enforcement authority to recover the property obtained through unlawful conduct is not unduly prejudiced.

253. Restriction on proceedings and remedies

(1) While an interim receiving order has effect—
    (a) the court may stay any action, execution or other legal process in respect of the property to which the order applies,
    (b) no distress may be levied against the property to which the order applies except with the leave of the court and subject to any terms the court may impose.

(2) If a court (whether the High Court or any other court) in which proceedings are pending in respect of any property is satisfied that an interim receiving order has been applied for or made in respect of the property, the court may either stay the proceedings or allow them to continue on any terms it thinks fit.

(3) If the interim receiving order applies to a tenancy of any premises, no landlord or other person to whom rent is payable may exercise any right of forfeiture by peaceable re-entry in relation to the premises in respect of any failure by the tenant to comply with any term or condition of the tenancy, except with the leave of the court and subject to any terms the court may impose.

(4) Before exercising any power conferred by this section, the court must (as well as giving the parties to any of the proceedings in question an opportunity to be heard) give such an opportunity to the interim receiver (if appointed) and any person who may be affected by the court's decision.

254. Exclusion of property which is not recoverable etc.

(1) If the court decides that any property to which an interim receiving order applies is neither recoverable property nor associated property, it must vary the order so as to exclude it.

(2) The court may vary an interim receiving order so as to exclude from the property to which the order applies any property which is alleged to be associated property if the court thinks that the satisfaction of any right of the enforcement authority to recover the property obtained through unlawful conduct will not be prejudiced.

(3) The court may exclude any property within subsection (2) on any terms or conditions, applying while the interim receiving order has effect, which the court thinks necessary or expedient.

255. Reporting

(1) An interim receiving order must require the interim receiver to inform the enforcement authority and the court as soon as reasonably practicable if he thinks that—
    (a) any property to which the order applies by virtue of a claim that it is recoverable property is not recoverable property,
    (b) any property to which the order applies by virtue of a claim that it is associated property is not associated property,
    (c) any property to which the order does not apply is recoverable property (in relation to the same unlawful conduct) or associated property, or

(d) any property to which the order applies is held by a person who is different from the person it is claimed holds it,

or if he thinks that there has been any other material change of circumstances.

(2) An interim receiving order must require the interim receiver—

    (a) to report his findings to the court,

    (b) to serve copies of his report on the enforcement authority and on any person who holds any property to which the order applies or who may otherwise be affected by the report.

Interim administration orders (Scotland)

256. Application for interim administration order

(1) Where the enforcement authority may take proceedings for a recovery order in the Court of Session, the authority may apply to the court for an interim administration order (whether before or after starting the proceedings).

(2) An interim administration order is an order for—

    (a) the detention, custody or preservation of property, and

    (b) the appointment of an interim administrator.

(3) An application for an interim administration order may be made without notice if the circumstances are such that notice of the application would prejudice any right of the enforcement authority to obtain a recovery order in respect of any property.

(4) The court may make an interim administration order on the application if it is satisfied that the conditions in subsections (5) and, where applicable, (6) are met.

(5) The first condition is that there is a probabilis causa litigandi—

    (a) that the property to which the application for the order relates is or includes recoverable property, and

    (b) that, if any of it is not recoverable property, it is associated property.

(6) The second condition is that, if—

    (a) the property to which the application for the order relates includes property alleged to be associated property, and

    (b) the enforcement authority has not established the identity of the person who holds it, the authority has taken all reasonable steps to do so.

(7) In its application for an interim administration order, the enforcement authority must nominate a suitably qualified person for appointment as interim administrator, but the nominee may not be a member of the staff of the Scottish Administration.

(8) The extent of the power to make an interim administration order is not limited by sections 257 to 264.

257. Functions of interim administrator

(1) An interim administration order may authorise or require the interim administrator—

    (a) to exercise any of the powers mentioned in Schedule 6,

    (b) to take any other steps the court thinks appropriate,

for the purpose of securing the detention, custody or preservation of the property to which the order applies or of taking any steps under subsection (2).

(2) An interim administration order must require the interim administrator to take any steps which the court thinks necessary to establish—

    (a) or not any other property is recoverable property (in relation to the same unlawful conduct) and, if it is, who holds it.

(3) If—

    (a) the interim administrator deals with any property which is not property to which the order applies, and

    (b) at the time he deals with the property he believes on reasonable grounds that he is entitled to do so in pursuance of the order,

the interim administrator is not liable to any person in respect of any loss or damage resulting from his dealing with the property except so far as the loss or damage is caused by his negligence.

258. Inhibition of property affected by order

(1) On the application of the enforcement authority, the Court of Session may, in relation to the property mentioned in subsection (2), grant warrant for inhibition against any person specified in an interim administration order.

(2) That property is heritable property situated in Scotland to which the interim administration order applies (whether generally or such of it as is specified in the application).

(3) The warrant for inhibition—

    (a) has effect as if granted on the dependence of an action for debt by the enforcement authority against the person and may be executed, recalled, loosed or restricted accordingly, and

    (b) has the effect of letters of inhibition and must forthwith be registered by the enforcement authority in the register of inhibitions and adjudications.

(4) Section 155 of the Titles to Land Consolidation (Scotland) Act 1868 (c. 101) (effective date of inhibition) applies in relation to an inhibition for which warrant is granted under subsection (1) as it applies to an inhibition by separate letters or contained in a summons.

(5) The execution of an inhibition under this section in respect of property does not prejudice the exercise of an interim administrator's powers under or for the purposes of this Part in respect of that property.

(6) An inhibition executed under this section ceases to have effect when, or in so far as, the interim administration order ceases to apply in respect of the property in relation to which the warrant for inhibition was granted.

(7) If an inhibition ceases to have effect to any extent by virtue of subsection (6) the enforcement authority must—

    (a) apply for the recall or, as the case may be, the restriction of the inhibition, and

    (b) ensure that the recall or restriction is reflected in the register of inhibitions and adjudications.

259. Duties of respondent etc.

(1) An interim administration order may require any person to whose property the order applies—

    (a) to bring the property to a place (in Scotland) specified by the interim administrator or place it in the custody of the interim administrator (if, in either case, he is able to do so),

    (b) to do anything he is reasonably required to do by the interim administrator for the preservation of the property.

(2) An interim administration order may require any person to whose property the order applies to bring any documents relating to the property which are in his possession or control to a place (in Scotland) specified by the interim administrator or to place them in the custody of the interim administrator.

'Document' means anything in which information of any description is recorded.

260. Supervision of interim administrator and variation of order

(1) The interim administrator, any party to the proceedings and any person affected by any action taken by the interim administrator, or who may be affected by any action proposed to be taken by him, may at any time apply to the court for directions as to the exercise of the interim administrator's functions.

(2) Before giving any directions under subsection (1), the court must (as well as giving the parties to the proceedings an opportunity to be heard) give such an opportunity to the interim administrator and to any person who may be interested in the application.

(3) The court may at any time vary or recall an interim administration order.

(4) Before exercising any power under this Chapter to vary or set aside an interim administration order, the court must (as well as giving the parties to the proceedings an opportunity to be heard) give such an opportunity to the interim administrator and to any person who may be affected by the court's decision.

261. Restrictions on dealing etc. with property

(1) An interim administration order must, subject to any exclusions made in accordance with this section, prohibit any person to whose property the order applies from dealing with the property.

(2) Exclusions may be made when the interim administration order is made or on an application to vary the order.

(3) An exclusion may, in particular, make provision for the purpose of enabling any person—

   (a) to meet his reasonable living expenses, or

   (b) to carry on any trade, business, profession or occupation,

and may be made subject to conditions.

(4) But an exclusion may not be made for the purpose of enabling any person to meet any legal expenses in respect of proceedings under this Part.

(5) If the excluded property is not specified in the order it must be described in the order in general terms.

(6) The power to make exclusions must be exercised with a view to ensuring, so far as practicable, that the satisfaction of any right of the enforcement authority to recover the property obtained through unlawful conduct is not unduly prejudiced.

262. Restriction on proceedings and remedies

(1) While an interim administration order has effect, the court may sist any action, execution or other legal process in respect of the property to which the order applies.

(2) If a court (whether the Court of Session or any other court) in which proceedings are pending in respect of any property is satisfied that an interim administration order has been applied for or made in respect of the property, the court may either sist the proceedings or allow them to continue on any terms it thinks fit.

(3) Before exercising any power conferred by this section, the court must (as well as giving the parties to any of the proceedings in question an opportunity to be heard) give such an opportunity to the interim administrator (if appointed) and any person who may be affected by the court's decision.

263. Exclusion of property which is not recoverable etc.

(1) If the court decides that any property to which an interim administration order applies is neither recoverable property nor associated property, it must vary the order so as to exclude it.

(2) The court may vary an interim administration order so as to exclude from the property to which the order applies any property which is alleged to be associated property if the court thinks that the satisfaction of any right of the enforcement authority to recover the property obtained through unlawful conduct will not be prejudiced.

(3) The court may exclude any property within subsection (2) on any terms or conditions, applying while the interim administration order has effect, which the court thinks necessary or expedient.

264. Reporting

(1) An interim administration order must require the interim administrator to inform the enforcement authority and the court as soon as reasonably practicable if he thinks that—
 (a) any property to which the order applies by virtue of a claim that it is recoverable property is not recoverable property,
 (b) any property to which the order applies by virtue of a claim that it is associated property is not associated property,
 (c) any property to which the order does not apply is recoverable property (in relation to the same unlawful conduct) or associated property, or
 (d) any property to which the order applies is held by a person who is different from the person it is claimed holds it,
or if he thinks that there has been any other material change of circumstances.

(2) An interim administration order must require the interim administrator—
 (a) to report his findings to the court,
 (b) to serve copies of his report on the enforcement authority and on any person who holds any property to which the order applies or who may otherwise be affected by the report.

265. Arrestment of property affected by interim administration order

(1) On the application of the enforcement authority or the interim administrator the Court of Session may, in relation to moveable recoverable property to which an interim administration order applies (whether generally or such of it as is specified in the application), grant warrant for arrestment.

(2) An application by the enforcement authority under subsection (1) may be made at the same time as the application for the interim administration order or at any time thereafter.

(3) Such a warrant for arrestment may be granted only if the property would be arrestable if the person entitled to it were a debtor.

(4) A warrant under subsection (1) has effect as if granted on the dependence of an action for debt at the instance of the enforcement authority or, as the case may be, the interim administrator against the person and may be executed, recalled, loosed or restricted accordingly.

(5) The execution of an arrestment under this section in respect of property does not prejudice the exercise of an interim administrator's powers under or for the purposes of this Part in respect of that property.

(6) An arrestment executed under this section ceases to have effect when, or in so far as, the interim administration order ceases to apply in respect of the property in relation to which the warrant for arrestment was granted.

(7) If an arrestment ceases to have effect to any extent by virtue of subsection (6) the enforcement authority or, as the case may be, the interim administrator must apply to the Court of Session for an order recalling or, as the case may be, restricting the arrestment.

Vesting and realisation of recoverable property

266. Recovery orders

(1) If in proceedings under this Chapter the court is satisfied that any property is recoverable, the court must make a recovery order.

(2) The recovery order must vest the recoverable property in the trustee for civil recovery.

(3) But the court may not make in a recovery order—
   (a) any provision in respect of any recoverable property if each of the conditions in subsection (4) or (as the case may be) (5) is met and it would not be just and equitable to do so, or
   (b) any provision which is incompatible with any of the Convention rights (within the meaning of the Human Rights Act 1998 (c. 42)).

(4) In relation to a court in England and Wales or Northern Ireland, the conditions referred to in subsection (3)(a) are that—
   (a) the respondent obtained the recoverable property in good faith,
   (b) he took steps after obtaining the property which he would not have taken if he had not obtained it or he took steps before obtaining the property which he would not have taken if he had not believed he was going to obtain it,
   (c) when he took the steps, he had no notice that the property was recoverable,
   (d) if a recovery order were made in respect of the property, it would, by reason of the steps, be detrimental to him.

(5) In relation to a court in Scotland, the conditions referred to in subsection (3)(a) are that—
   (a) the respondent obtained the recoverable property in good faith,
   (b) he took steps after obtaining the property which he would not have taken if he had not obtained it or he took steps before obtaining the property which he would not have taken if he had not believed he was going to obtain it,
   (c) when he took the steps, he had no reasonable grounds for believing that the property was recoverable,
   (d) if a recovery order were made in respect of the property, it would, by reason of the steps, be detrimental to him.

(6) In deciding whether it would be just and equitable to make the provision in the recovery order where the conditions in subsection (4) or (as the case may be) (5) are met, the court must have regard to—

    (a) the degree of detriment that would be suffered by the respondent if the provision were made,

    (b) the enforcement authority's interest in receiving the realised proceeds of the recoverable property.

(7) A recovery order may sever any property.

(8) A recovery order may impose conditions as to the manner in which the trustee for civil recovery may deal with any property vested by the order for the purpose of realising it.

(9) This section is subject to sections 270 to 278.

267. Functions of the trustee for civil recovery

(1) The trustee for civil recovery is a person appointed by the court to give effect to a recovery order.

(2) The enforcement authority must nominate a suitably qualified person for appointment as the trustee.

(3) The functions of the trustee are—

    (a) to secure the detention, custody or preservation of any property vested in him by the recovery order,

    (b) in the case of property other than money, to realise the value of the property for the benefit of the enforcement authority, and

    (c) to perform any other functions conferred on him by virtue of this Chapter.

(4) In performing his functions, the trustee acts on behalf of the enforcement authority and must comply with any directions given by the authority.

(5) The trustee is to realise the value of property vested in him by the recovery order, so far as practicable, in the manner best calculated to maximise the amount payable to the enforcement authority.

(6) The trustee has the powers mentioned in Schedule 7.

(7) References in this section to a recovery order include an order under section 276 and references to property vested in the trustee by a recovery order include property vested in him in pursuance of an order under section 276.

268. Recording of recovery order (Scotland)

(1) The clerk of the court must immediately after the making of a recovery order which relates to heritable property situated in Scotland send a certified copy of it to the keeper of the register of inhibitions and adjudications for recording in that register.

(2) Recording under subsection (1) is to have the effect, as from the date of the recovery order, of an inhibition at the instance of the trustee for civil recovery against the person in whom the heritable property was vest prior to that date.

269. Rights of pre-emption, etc.

(1) A recovery order is to have effect in relation to any property despite any provision (of whatever nature) which would otherwise prevent, penalise or restrict the vesting of the property.

(2) A right of pre-emption, right of irritancy, right of return or other similar right does not operate or become exercisable as a result of the vesting of any property under a recovery order.

A right of return means any right under a provision for the return or reversion of property in specified circumstances.

(3) Where property is vested under a recovery order, any such right is to have effect as if the person in whom the property is vested were the same person in law as the person who held the property and as if no transfer of the property had taken place.

(4) References to rights in subsections (2) and (3) do not include any rights in respect of which the recovery order was made.

(5) This section applies in relation to the creation of interests, or the doing of anything else, by a recovery order as it applies in relation to the vesting of property.

270. Associated and joint property

(1) Sections 271 and 272 apply if the court makes a recovery order in respect of any recoverable property in a case within subsection (2) or (3).

(2) A case is within this subsection if—
   (a) the property to which the proceedings relate includes property which is associated with the recoverable property and is specified or described in the claim form or (in Scotland) application, and
   (b) if the associated property is not the respondent's property, the claim form or application has been served on the person whose property it is or the court has dispensed with service.

(3) A case is within this subsection if—
   (a) the recoverable property belongs to joint tenants, and
   (b) one of the tenants is an excepted joint owner.

(4) An excepted joint owner is a person who obtained the property in circumstances in which it would not be recoverable as against him; and references to the excepted joint owner's share of the recoverable property are to so much of the recoverable property as would have been his if the joint tenancy had been severed.

(5) Subsections (3) and (4) do not extend to Scotland.

271. Agreements about associated and joint property

(1) Where—
   (a) this section applies, and
   (b) the enforcement authority (on the one hand) and the person who holds the associated property or who is the excepted joint owner (on the other) agree,

the recovery order may, instead of vesting the recoverable property in the trustee for civil recovery, require the person who holds the associated property or who is the excepted joint owner to make a payment to the trustee.

(2) A recovery order which makes any requirement under subsection (1) may, so far as required for giving effect to the agreement, include provision for vesting, creating or extinguishing any interest in property.

(3) The amount of the payment is to be the amount which the enforcement authority and that person agree represents—
   (a) in a case within section 270(2), the value of the recoverable property,

    (b) in a case within section 270(3), the value of the recoverable property less the value of the excepted joint owner's share.

(4) But if—

    (a) an interim receiving order or interim administration order applied at any time to the associated property or joint tenancy, and

    (b) the enforcement authority agrees that the person has suffered loss as a result of the interim receiving order or interim administration order, the amount of the payment may be reduced by any amount the enforcement authority and that person agree is reasonable, having regard to that loss and to any other relevant circumstances.

(5) If there is more than one such item of associated property or excepted joint owner, the total amount to be paid to the trustee, and the part of that amount which is to be provided by each person who holds any such associated property or who is an excepted joint owner, is to be agreed between both (or all) of them and the enforcement authority.

(6) A recovery order which makes any requirement under subsection (1) must make provision for any recoverable property to cease to be recoverable.

272. Associated and joint property: default of agreement

(1) Where this section applies, the court may make the following provision if—

    (a) there is no agreement under section 271, and

    (b) the court thinks it just and equitable to do so.

(2) The recovery order may provide—

    (a) for the associated property to vest in the trustee for civil recovery or (as the case may be) for the excepted joint owner's interest to be extinguished, or

    (b) in the case of an excepted joint owner, for the severance of his interest.

(3) A recovery order making any provision by virtue of subsection (2)(a) may provide—

    (a) for the trustee to pay an amount to the person who holds the associated property or who is an excepted joint owner, or

    (b) for the creation of interests in favour of that person, or the imposition of liabilities or conditions, in relation to the property vested in the trustee,

or for both.

(4) In making any provision in a recovery order by virtue of subsection (2) or (3), the court must have regard to—

    (a) the rights of any person who holds the associated property or who is an excepted joint owner and the value to him of that property or, as the case may be, of his share (including any value which cannot be assessed in terms of money),

    (b) the enforcement authority's interest in receiving the realised proceeds of the recoverable property.

(5) If—

    (a) an interim receiving order or interim administration order applied at any time to the associated property or joint tenancy, and

    (b) the court is satisfied that the person who holds the associated property or who is an excepted joint owner has suffered loss as a result of the interim receiving order or interim administration order, a recovery order making any provision by virtue of subsection (2) or (3) may require the enforcement authority to pay compensation to that person.

(6) The amount of compensation to be paid under subsection (5) is the amount the court thinks reasonable, having regard to the person's loss and to any other relevant circumstances.

273. Payments in respect of rights under pension schemes

(1) This section applies to recoverable property consisting of rights under a pension scheme.

(2) A recovery order in respect of the property must, instead of vesting the property in the trustee for civil recovery, require the trustees or managers of the pension scheme—

    (a) to pay to the trustee for civil recovery within a prescribed period the amount determined by the trustees or managers to be equal to the value of the rights, and

    (b) to give effect to any other provision made by virtue of this section and the two following sections in respect of the scheme.

This subsection is subject to sections 276 to 278.

(3) A recovery order made by virtue of subsection (2) overrides the provisions of the pension scheme to the extent that they conflict with the provisions of the order.

(4) A recovery order made by virtue of subsection (2) may provide for the recovery by the trustees or managers of the scheme (whether by deduction from any amount which they are required to pay to the trustee for civil recovery or otherwise) of costs incurred by them in—

    (a) complying with the recovery order, or

    (b) providing information, before the order was made, to the enforcement authority, interim receiver or interim administrator.

(5) None of the following provisions applies to a court making a recovery order by virtue of subsection (2)—

    (a) any provision of section 159 of the Pension Schemes Act 1993 (c. 48), section 155 of the Pension Schemes (Northern Ireland) Act 1993 (c. 49), section 91 of the Pensions Act 1995 (c. 26) or Article 89 of the Pensions (Northern Ireland) Order 1995 (S.I. 1995/3213 (N.I. 22)) (which prevent assignment and the making of orders that restrain a person from receiving anything which he is prevented from assigning),

    (b) any provision of any enactment (whenever passed or made) corresponding to any of the provisions mentioned in paragraph (a),

    (c) any provision of the pension scheme in question corresponding to any of those provisions.

274. Consequential adjustment of liabilities under pension schemes

(1) A recovery order made by virtue of section 273(2) must require the trustees or managers of the pension scheme to make such reduction in the liabilities of the scheme as they think necessary in consequence of the payment made in pursuance of that subsection.

(2) Accordingly, the order must require the trustees or managers to provide for the

liabilities of the pension scheme in respect of the respondent's recoverable property to which section 273 applies to cease.

(3) So far as the trustees or managers are required by the recovery order to provide for the liabilities of the pension scheme in respect of the respondent's recoverable property to which section 273 applies to cease, their powers include (in particular) power to reduce the amount of—

    (a) any benefit or future benefit to which the respondent is or may be entitled under the scheme,

    (b) any future benefit to which any other person may be entitled under the scheme in respect of that property.

275. Pension schemes: supplementary

(1) Regulations may make provision as to the exercise by trustees or managers of their powers under sections 273 and 274, including provision about the calculation and verification of the value at any time of rights or liabilities.

(2) The power conferred by subsection (1) includes power to provide for any values to be calculated or verified—

    (a) in a manner which, in the particular case, is approved by a prescribed person, or

    (b) in accordance with guidance from time to time prepared by a prescribed person.

(3) Regulations means regulations made by the Secretary of State after consultation with the Scottish Ministers; and prescribed means prescribed by regulations.

(4) A pension scheme means an occupational pension scheme or a personal pension scheme; and those expressions have the same meaning as in the Pension Schemes Act 1993 (c. 48) or, in relation to Northern Ireland, the Pension Schemes (Northern Ireland) Act 1993 (c. 49).

(5) In relation to an occupational pension scheme or a personal pension scheme, the trustees or managers means—

    (a) in the case of a scheme established under a trust, the trustees,

    (b) in any other case, the managers.

(6) References to a pension scheme include—

    (a) a retirement annuity contract (within the meaning of Part 3 of the Welfare Reform and Pensions Act 1999 (c. 30) or, in relation to Northern Ireland, Part 4 of the Welfare Reform and Pensions (Northern Ireland) Order 1999),

    (b) an annuity or insurance policy purchased, or transferred, for the purpose of giving effect to rights under an occupational pension scheme or a personal pension scheme,

    (c) an annuity purchased, or entered into, for the purpose of discharging any liability in respect of a pension credit under section 29(1)(b) of the Welfare Reform and Pensions Act 1999 (c. 30) or, in relation to Northern Ireland, Article 26(1)(b) of the Welfare Reform and Pensions (Northern Ireland) Order 1999.

(7) References to the trustees or managers—

    (a) in relation to a retirement annuity contract or other annuity, are to the provider of the annuity,

    (b) in relation to an insurance policy, are to the insurer.

(8) Subsections (3) to (7) have effect for the purposes of this group of sections (that is, sections 273 and 274 and this section).

276 Consent orders

(1) The court may make an order staying (in Scotland, sisting) any proceedings for a recovery order on terms agreed by the parties for the disposal of the proceedings if each person to whose property the proceedings, or the agreement, relates is a party both to the proceedings and the agreement.

(2) An order under subsection (1) may, as well as staying (or sisting) the proceedings on terms—

(a) make provision for any property which may be recoverable property to cease to be recoverable,

(b) make any further provision which the court thinks appropriate.

(3) Section 280 applies to property vested in the trustee for civil recovery, or money paid to him, in pursuance of the agreement as it applies to property vested in him by a recovery order or money paid under section 271.

277. Consent orders: pensions

(1) This section applies where recoverable property to which proceedings under this Chapter relate includes rights under a pension scheme.

(2) An order made under section 276—

(a) may not stay (in Scotland, sist) the proceedings on terms that the rights are vested in any other person, but

(b) may include provision imposing the following requirement, if the trustees or managers of the scheme are parties to the agreement by virtue of which the order is made.

(3) The requirement is that the trustees or managers of the pension scheme—

(a) make a payment in accordance with the agreement, and

(b) give effect to any other provision made by virtue of this section in respect of the scheme.

(4) The trustees or managers of the pension scheme have power to enter into an agreement in respect of the proceedings on any terms on which an order made under section 276 may stay (in Scotland, sist) the proceedings.

(5) The following provisions apply in respect of an order under section 276, so far as it includes the requirement mentioned in subsection (3).

(6) The order overrides the provisions of the pension scheme to the extent that they conflict with the requirement.

(7) The order may provide for the recovery by the trustees or managers of the scheme (whether by deduction from any amount which they are required to pay in pursuance of the agreement or otherwise) of costs incurred by them in—

(a) complying with the order, or

(b) providing information, before the order was made, to the enforcement authority, interim receiver or interim administrator.

(8) Sections 273(5) and 274 (read with section 275) apply as if the requirement were included in an order made by virtue of section 273(2).

(9) Section 275(4) to (7) has effect for the purposes of this section.

278. Limit on recovery

(1) This section applies if the enforcement authority seeks a recovery order—

(a) in respect of both property which is or represents property obtained through unlawful conduct and related property, or

   (b) in respect of property which is or represents property obtained through unlawful conduct where such an order, or an order under section 276, has previously been made in respect of related property.

(2) For the purposes of this section—
   (a) the original property means the property obtained through unlawful conduct,
   (b) the original property, and any items of property which represent the original property, are to be treated as related to each other.

(3) The court is not to make a recovery order if it thinks that the enforcement authority's right to recover the original property has been satisfied by a previous recovery order or order under section 276.

(4) Subject to subsection (3), the court may act under subsection (5) if it thinks that—
   (a) a recovery order may be made in respect of two or more related items of recoverable property, but
   (b) the making of a recovery order in respect of both or all of them is not required in order to satisfy the enforcement authority's right to recover the original property.

(5) The court may in order to satisfy that right to the extent required make a recovery order in respect of—
   (a) only some of the related items of property, or
   (b) only a part of any of the related items of property, or both.

(6) Where the court may make a recovery order in respect of any property, this section does not prevent the recovery of any profits which have accrued in respect of the property.

(7) If—
   (a) an order is made under section 298 for the forfeiture of recoverable property, and
   (b) the enforcement authority subsequently seeks a recovery order in respect of related property, the order under section 298 is to be treated for the purposes of this section as if it were a recovery order obtained by the enforcement authority in respect of the forfeited property.

(8) If—
   (a) in pursuance of a judgment in civil proceedings (whether in the United Kingdom or elsewhere), the claimant has obtained property from the defendant ('the judgment property'),
   (b) the claim was based on the defendant's having obtained the judgment property or related property through unlawful conduct, and
   (c) the enforcement authority subsequently seeks a recovery order in respect of property which is related to the judgment property,
the judgment is to be treated for the purposes of this section as if it were a recovery order obtained by the enforcement authority in respect of the judgment property.

In relation to Scotland, 'claimant' and 'defendant' are to be read as 'pursuer' and 'defender'.

(9) If—
   (a) property has been taken into account in deciding the amount of a person's benefit from criminal conduct for the purpose of making a confiscation order, and
   (b) the enforcement authority subsequently seeks a recovery order in respect of related property,

the confiscation order is to be treated for the purposes of this section as if it were a recovery order obtained by the enforcement authority in respect of the property referred to in paragraph (a).

(10)   In subsection (9), a confiscation order means—

(a) an order under section 6, 92 or 156, or

(b) an order under a corresponding provision of an enactment mentioned in section 8(7)(a) to (g),

and, in relation to an order mentioned in paragraph (b), the reference to the amount of a person's benefit from criminal conduct is to be read as a reference to the corresponding amount under the enactment in question.

279. Section 278: supplementary

(1) Subsections (2) and (3) give examples of the satisfaction of the enforcement authority's right to recover the original property.

(2) If—

(a) there is a disposal, other than a part disposal, of the original property, and

(b) other property (the representative property) is obtained in its place,

the enforcement authority's right to recover the original property is satisfied by the making of a recovery order in respect of either the original property or the representative property.

(3) If—

(a) there is a part disposal of the original property, and

(b) other property (the representative property) is obtained in place of the property disposed of,

the enforcement authority's right to recover the original property is satisfied by the making of a recovery order in respect of the remainder of the original property together with either the representative property or the property disposed of.

(4) In this section—

(a) a part disposal means a disposal to which section 314(1) applies,

(b) the original property has the same meaning as in section 278.

280. Applying realised proceeds

(1) This section applies to—

(a) sums which represent the realised proceeds of property which was vested in the trustee for civil recovery by a recovery order or which he obtained in pursuance of a recovery order,

(b) sums vested in the trustee by a recovery order or obtained by him in pursuance of a recovery order.

(2) The trustee is to make out of the sums—

(a) first, any payment required to be made by him by virtue of section 272,

(b) second, any payment of expenses incurred by a person acting as an insolvency practitioner which are payable under this subsection by virtue of section 432(10),

and any sum which remains is to be paid to the enforcement authority.

Exemptions etc.

281. Victims of theft, etc.

(1) In proceedings for a recovery order, a person who claims that any property alleged to be recoverable property, or any part of the property, belongs to him may apply for a declaration under this section.

(2) If the applicant appears to the court to meet the following condition, the court may make a declaration to that effect.

(3) The condition is that—

    (a) the person was deprived of the property he claims, or of property which it represents, by unlawful conduct,

    (b) the property he was deprived of was not recoverable property immediately before he was deprived of it, and

    (c) the property he claims belongs to him.

(4) Property to which a declaration under this section applies is not recoverable property.

282. Other exemptions

(1) Proceedings for a recovery order may not be taken against any person in circumstances of a prescribed description; and the circumstances may relate to the person himself or to the property or to any other matter.

In this subsection, prescribed means prescribed by an order made by the Secretary of State after consultation with the Scottish Ministers.

(2) Proceedings for a recovery order may not be taken in respect of cash found at any place in the United Kingdom unless the proceedings are also taken in respect of property other than cash which is property of the same person.

(3) Proceedings for a recovery order may not be taken against the Financial Services Authority in respect of any recoverable property held by the authority.

(4) Proceedings for a recovery order may not be taken in respect of any property which is subject to any of the following charges—

    (a) a collateral security charge, within the meaning of the Financial Markets and Insolvency (Settlement Finality) Regulations 1999 (S.I. 1999/2979),

    (b) a market charge, within the meaning of Part 7 of the Companies Act 1989 (c. 40),

    (c) a money market charge, within the meaning of the Financial Markets and Insolvency (Money Market) Regulations 1995 (S.I. 1995/2049),

    (d) a system charge, within the meaning of the Financial Markets and Insolvency Regulations 1996 (S.I. 1996/1469) or the Financial Markets and Insolvency Regulations (Northern Ireland) 1996 (S.R. 1996/252).

(5) Proceedings for a recovery order may not be taken against any person in respect of any recoverable property which he holds by reason of his acting, or having acted, as an insolvency practitioner.

Acting as an insolvency practitioner has the same meaning as in section 433.

Miscellaneous

283. Compensation

(1) If, in the case of any property to which an interim receiving order or interim administration order has at any time applied, the court does not in the course of the proceedings decide that the property is recoverable property or associated property, the person whose property it is may make an application to the court for compensation.

(2) Subsection (1) does not apply if the court—
   (a) has made a declaration in respect of the property by virtue of section 281, or
   (b) makes an order under section 276.

(3) If the court has made a decision by reason of which no recovery order could be made in respect of the property, the application for compensation must be made within the period of three months beginning—
   (a) in relation to a decision of the High Court in England and Wales, with the date of the decision or, if any application is made for leave to appeal, with the date on which the application is withdrawn or refused or (if the application is granted) on which any proceedings on appeal are finally concluded,
   (b) in relation to a decision of the Court of Session or of the High Court in Northern Ireland, with the date of the decision or, if there is an appeal against the decision, with the date on which any proceedings on appeal are finally concluded.

(4) If, in England and Wales or Northern Ireland, the proceedings in respect of the property have been discontinued, the application for compensation must be made within the period of three months beginning with the discontinuance.

(5) If the court is satisfied that the applicant has suffered loss as a result of the interim receiving order or interim administration order, it may require the enforcement authority to pay compensation to him.

(6) If, but for section 269(2), any right mentioned there would have operated in favour of, or become exercisable by, any person, he may make an application to the court for compensation.

(7) The application for compensation under subsection (6) must be made within the period of three months beginning with the vesting referred to in section 269(2).

(8) If the court is satisfied that, in consequence of the operation of section 269, the right in question cannot subsequently operate in favour of the applicant or (as the case may be) become exercisable by him, it may require the enforcement authority to pay compensation to him.

(9) The amount of compensation to be paid under this section is the amount the court thinks reasonable, having regard to the loss suffered and any other relevant circumstances.

284. Payment of interim administrator or trustee (Scotland)

Any fees or expenses incurred by an interim administrator, or a trustee for civil recovery appointed by the Court of Session, in the exercise of his functions are to be reimbursed by the Scottish Ministers as soon as is practicable after they have been incurred.

285. Effect on diligence of recovery order (Scotland)

(1) An arrestment or poinding of any recoverable property executed on or after the appointment of the trustee for civil recovery is ineffectual in a question with the trustee.

(2) Any recoverable property so arrested or poinded, or (if the property has been sold) the proceeds of sale, must be handed over to the trustee for civil recovery.

(3) A poinding of the ground in respect of recoverable property on or after such an appointment is ineffectual in a question with the trustee for civil recovery except for the interest mentioned in subsection (4).

(4) That interest is—
   (a) interest on the debt of a secured creditor for the current half yearly term, and
   (b) arrears of interest on that debt for one year immediately before the commencement of that term.

(5) On and after such appointment no other person may raise or insist in an adjudication against recoverable property or be confirmed as an executor-creditor on that property.

(6) An inhibition on recoverable property shall cease to have effect in relation to any heritable property comprised in the recoverable property on such appointment.

(7) The provisions of this section apply in relation to—
   (a) an action of maills and duties, and
   (b) an action for sequestration of rent,

as they apply in relation to an arrestment or poinding.

286. Scope of powers (Scotland)

(1) Orders under this Chapter may be made by the Court of Session in respect of a person wherever domiciled, resident or present.

(2) Such an order may be made by the Court of Session in respect of moveable property wherever situated.

(3) But such an order in respect of a person's moveable property may not be made by the Court of Session where—
   (a) the person is not domiciled, resident or present in Scotland, and
   (b) the property is not situated in Scotland,

unless the unlawful conduct took place in Scotland.

287. Financial threshold

(1) At any time when an order specifying an amount for the purposes of this section has effect, the enforcement authority may not start proceedings for a recovery order unless the authority reasonably believes that the aggregate value of the recoverable property which the authority wishes to be subject to a recovery order is not less than the specified amount.

(2) The power to make an order under subsection (1) is exercisable by the Secretary of State after consultation with the Scottish Ministers.

(3) If the authority applies for an interim receiving order or interim administration order before starting the proceedings, subsection (1) applies to the application instead of to the start of the proceedings.

(4) This section does not affect the continuation of proceedings for a recovery order which have been properly started or the making or continuing effect of an

interim receiving order or interim administration order which has been properly applied for.

288. Limitation

(1) After section 27 of the Limitation Act 1980 (c. 58) there is inserted—

'27A. Actions for recovery of property obtained through unlawful conduct etc.

(1) None of the time limits given in the preceding provisions of this Act applies to any proceedings under Chapter 2 of Part 5 of the Proceeds of Crime Act 2002 (civil recovery of proceeds of unlawful conduct).

(2) Proceedings under that Chapter for a recovery order in respect of any recoverable property shall not be brought after the expiration of the period of twelve years from the date on which the Director's cause of action accrued.

(3) Proceedings under that Chapter are brought when—

    (a) a claim form is issued, or

    (b) an application is made for an interim receiving order,

whichever is the earlier.

(4) The Director's cause of action accrues in respect of any recoverable property—

    (a) in the case of proceedings for a recovery order in respect of property obtained through unlawful conduct, when the property is so obtained,

    (b) in the case of proceedings for a recovery order in respect of any other recoverable property, when the property obtained through unlawful conduct which it represents is so obtained.

(5) If—

    (a) a person would (but for the preceding provisions of this Act) have a cause of action in respect of the conversion of a chattel, and

    (b) proceedings are started under that Chapter for a recovery order in respect of the chattel,

section 3(2) of this Act does not prevent his asserting on an application under section 281 of that Act that the property belongs to him, or the court making a declaration in his favour under that section.

(6) If the court makes such a declaration, his title to the chattel is to be treated as not having been extinguished by section 3(2) of this Act.

(7) Expressions used in this section and Part 5 of that Act have the same meaning in this section as in that Part.'

(2) After section 19A of the Prescription and Limitation (Scotland) Act 1973 (c. 52) there is inserted—

'19B. Actions for recovery of property obtained through unlawful conduct etc.

(1) None of the time limits given in the preceding provisions of this Act applies to any proceedings under Chapter 2 of Part 5 of the Proceeds of Crime Act 2002 (civil recovery of proceeds of unlawful conduct).

(2) Proceedings under that Chapter for a recovery order in respect of any recoverable property shall not be commenced after the expiration of the period of twelve years from the date on which the Scottish Ministers' right of action accrued.

(3) Proceedings under that Chapter are commenced when—

    (a) the proceedings are served, or

(b) an application is made for an interim administration order,
whichever is the earlier.

(4) The Scottish Ministers' right of action accrues in respect of any recoverable property—

(a) in the case of proceedings for a recovery order in respect of property obtained through unlawful conduct, when the property is so obtained,

(b) in the case of proceedings for a recovery order in respect of any other recoverable property, when the property obtained through unlawful conduct which it represents is so obtained.

(5) Expressions used in this section and Part 5 of that Act have the same meaning in this section as in that Part.'

(3) After Article 72 of the Limitation (Northern Ireland) Order 1989 (SI 1989/1339 (N.I. 11)) there is inserted—

'**72A. Actions for recovery of property obtained through unlawful conduct etc.**

(1) None of the time limits fixed by Parts II and III applies to any proceedings under Chapter 2 of Part 5 of the Proceeds of Crime Act 2002 (civil recovery of proceeds of unlawful conduct).

(2) Proceedings under that Chapter for a recovery order in respect of any recoverable property shall not be brought after the expiration of the period of twelve years from the date on which the Director's cause of action accrued.

(3) Proceedings under that Chapter are brought when—

(a) a claim form is issued, or

(b) an application is made for an interim receiving order,
whichever is the earlier.

(4) The Director's cause of action accrues in respect of any recoverable property—

(a) in the case of proceedings for a recovery order in respect of property obtained through unlawful conduct, when the property is so obtained,

(b) in the case of proceedings for a recovery order in respect of any other recoverable property, when the property obtained through unlawful conduct which it represents is so obtained.

(5) If—

(a) a person would (but for a time limit fixed by this Order) have a cause of action in respect of the conversion of a chattel, and

(b) proceedings are started under that Chapter for a recovery order in respect of the chattel,

Article 17(2) does not prevent his asserting on an application under section 281 of that Act that the property belongs to him, or the court making a declaration in his favour under that section.

(6) If the court makes such a declaration, his title to the chattel is to be treated as not having been extinguished by Article 17(2).

(7) Expressions used in this Article and Part 5 of that Act have the same meaning in this Article as in that Part.'

CHAPTER 3
RECOVERY OF CASH IN SUMMARY PROCEEDINGS

Searches

289. Searches

(1) If a customs officer or constable who is lawfully on any premises has reasonable grounds for suspecting that there is on the premises cash—
  (a) which is recoverable property or is intended by any person for use in unlawful conduct, and
  (b) the amount of which is not less than the minimum amount,
he may search for the cash there.

(2) If a customs officer or constable has reasonable grounds for suspecting that a person (the suspect) is carrying cash—
  (a) which is recoverable property or is intended by any person for use in unlawful conduct, and
  (b) the amount of which is not less than the minimum amount,
he may exercise the following powers.

(3) The officer or constable may, so far as he thinks it necessary or expedient, require the suspect—
  (a) to permit a search of any article he has with him,
  (b) to permit a search of his person.

(4) An officer or constable exercising powers by virtue of subsection (3)(b) may detain the suspect for so long as is necessary for their exercise.

(5) The powers conferred by this section—
  (a) are exercisable only so far as reasonably required for the purpose of finding cash,
  (b) are exercisable by a customs officer only if he has reasonable grounds for suspecting that the unlawful conduct in question relates to an assigned matter (within the meaning of the Customs and Excise Management Act 1979 (c. 2)).

(6) Cash means—
  (a) notes and coins in any currency,
  (b) postal orders,
  (c) cheques of any kind, including travellers' cheques,
  (d) bankers' drafts,
  (e) bearer bonds and bearer shares,
found at any place in the United Kingdom.

(7) Cash also includes any kind of monetary instrument which is found at any place in the United Kingdom, if the instrument is specified by the Secretary of State by an order made after consultation with the Scottish Ministers.

(8) This section does not require a person to submit to an intimate search or strip search (within the meaning of section 164 of the Customs and Excise Management Act 1979 (c. 2)).

290. Prior approval

(1) The powers conferred by section 289 may be exercised only with the appropriate approval unless, in the circumstances, it is not practicable to obtain that approval before exercising the power.

(2) The appropriate approval means the approval of a judicial officer or (if that is not practicable in any case) the approval of a senior officer.

(3) A judicial officer means—

    (a) in relation to England and Wales and Northern Ireland, a justice of the peace,

    (b) in relation to Scotland, the sheriff.

(4) A senior officer means—

    (a) in relation to the exercise of the power by a customs officer, a customs officer of a rank designated by the Commissioners of Customs and Excise as equivalent to that of a senior police officer,

    (b) in relation to the exercise of the power by a constable, a senior police officer.

(5) A senior police officer means a police officer of at least the rank of inspector.

(6) If the powers are exercised without the approval of a judicial officer in a case where—

    (a) no cash is seized by virtue of section 294, or

    (b) any cash so seized is not detained for more than 48 hours,

the customs officer or constable who exercised the powers must give a written report to the appointed person.

(7) The report must give particulars of the circumstances which led him to believe that—

    (a) the powers were exercisable, and

    (b) it was not practicable to obtain the approval of a judicial officer.

(8) In this section and section 291, the appointed person means—

    (a) in relation to England and Wales and Northern Ireland, a person appointed by the Secretary of State,

    (b) in relation to Scotland, a person appointed by the Scottish Ministers.

(9) The appointed person must not be a person employed under or for the purposes of a government department or of the Scottish Administration; and the terms and conditions of his appointment, including any remuneration or expenses to be paid to him, are to be determined by the person appointing him.

291. Report on exercise of powers

(1) As soon as possible after the end of each financial year, the appointed person must prepare a report for that year.

'Financial year' means—

    (a) the period beginning with the day on which this section comes into force and ending with the next 31 March (which is the first financial year), and

    (b) each subsequent period of twelve months beginning with 1 April.

(2) The report must give his opinion as to the circumstances and manner in which the powers conferred by section 289 are being exercised in cases where the customs officer or constable who exercised them is required to give a report under section 290(6).

(3) In the report, he may make any recommendations he considers appropriate.

(4) He must send a copy of his report to the Secretary of State or, as the case may be, the Scottish Ministers, who must arrange for it to be published.

(5) The Secretary of State must lay a copy of any report he receives under this section before Parliament; and the Scottish Ministers must lay a copy of any report they receive under this section before the Scottish Parliament.

292. Code of practice

(1) The Secretary of State must make a code of practice in connection with the exercise by customs officers and (in relation to England and Wales and Northern Ireland) constables of the powers conferred by virtue of section 289.

(2) Where he proposes to issue a code of practice he must—

    (a) publish a draft,

    (b) consider any representations made to him about the draft by the Scottish Ministers or any other person,

    (c) if he thinks it appropriate, modify the draft in the light of any such representations.

(3) He must lay a draft of the code before Parliament.

(4) When he has laid a draft of the code before Parliament he may bring it into operation by order.

(5) He may revise the whole or any part of the code issued by him and issue the code as revised; and subsections (2) to (4) apply to such a revised code as they apply to the original code.

(6) A failure by a customs officer or constable to comply with a provision of the code does not of itself make him liable to criminal or civil proceedings.

(7) The code is admissible in evidence in criminal or civil proceedings and is to be taken into account by a court or tribunal in any case in which it appears to the court or tribunal to be relevant.

293. Code of practice (Scotland)

(1) The Scottish Ministers must make a code of practice in connection with the exercise by constables in relation to Scotland of the powers conferred by virtue of section 289.

(2) Where they propose to issue a code of practice they must—

    (a) publish a draft,

    (b) consider any representations made to them about the draft,

    (c) if they think it appropriate, modify the draft in the light of any such representations.

(3) They must lay a draft of the code before the Scottish Parliament.

(4) When they have laid a draft of the code before the Scottish Parliament they may bring it into operation by order.

(5) They may revise the whole or any part of the code issued by them and issue the code as revised; and subsections (2) to (4) apply to such a revised code as they apply to the original code.

(6) A failure by a constable to comply with a provision of the code does not of itself make him liable to criminal or civil proceedings.

(7) The code is admissible in evidence in criminal or civil proceedings and is to be taken into account by a court or tribunal in any case in which it appears to the court or tribunal to be relevant.

Seizure and detention

294. Seizure of cash

(1) A customs officer or constable may seize any cash if he has reasonable grounds for suspecting that it is—

    (a) recoverable property, or

    (b) intended by any person for use in unlawful conduct.

(2) A customs officer or constable may also seize cash part of which he has reasonable grounds for suspecting to be—

    (a) recoverable property, or

    (b) intended by any person for use in unlawful conduct,

if it is not reasonably practicable to seize only that part.

(3) This section does not authorise the seizure of an amount of cash if it or, as the case may be, the part to which his suspicion relates, is less than the minimum amount.

295. Detention of seized cash

(1) While the customs officer or constable continues to have reasonable grounds for his suspicion, cash seized under section 294 may be detained initially for a period of 48 hours.

(2) The period for which the cash or any part of it may be detained may be extended by an order made by a magistrates' court or (in Scotland) the sheriff; but the order may not authorise the detention of any of the cash—

    (a) beyond the end of the period of three months beginning with the date of the order,

    (b) in the case of any further order under this section, beyond the end of the period of two years beginning with the date of the first order.

(3) A justice of the peace may also exercise the power of a magistrates' court to make the first order under subsection (2) extending the period.

(4) An application for an order under subsection (2)—

    (a) in relation to England and Wales and Northern Ireland, may be made by the Commissioners of Customs and Excise or a constable,

    (b) in relation to Scotland, may be made by the Scottish Ministers in connection with their functions under section 298 or by a procurator fiscal,

and the court, sheriff or justice may make the order if satisfied, in relation to any cash to be further detained, that either of the following conditions is met.

(5) The first condition is that there are reasonable grounds for suspecting that the cash is recoverable property and that either—

    (a) its continued detention is justified while its derivation is further investigated or consideration is given to bringing (in the United Kingdom or elsewhere) proceedings against any person for an offence with which the cash is connected, or

    (b) proceedings against any person for an offence with which the cash is connected have been started and have not been concluded.

(6) The second condition is that there are reasonable grounds for suspecting that the cash is intended to be used in unlawful conduct and that either—

    (a) its continued detention is justified while its intended use is further investigated or consideration is given to bringing (in the United Kingdom or elsewhere) proceedings against any person for an offence with which the cash is connected, or

    (b) proceedings against any person for an offence with which the cash is connected have been started and have not been concluded.

(7) An application for an order under subsection (2) may also be made in respect of any cash seized under section 294(2), and the court, sheriff or justice may make the order if satisfied that—

(a) the condition in subsection (5) or (6) is met in respect of part of the cash, and

(b) it is not reasonably practicable to detain only that part.

(8) An order under subsection (2) must provide for notice to be given to persons affected by it.

296. Interest

(1) If cash is detained under section 295 for more than 48 hours, it is at the first opportunity to be paid into an interest-bearing account and held there; and the interest accruing on it is to be added to it on its forfeiture or release.

(2) In the case of cash detained under section 295 which was seized under section 294(2), the customs officer or constable must, on paying it into the account, release the part of the cash to which the suspicion does not relate.

(3) Subsection (1) does not apply if the cash or, as the case may be, the part to which the suspicion relates is required as evidence of an offence or evidence in proceedings under this Chapter.

297. Release of detained cash

(1) This section applies while any cash is detained under section 295.

(2) A magistrates' court or (in Scotland) the sheriff may direct the release of the whole or any part of the cash if the following condition is met.

(3) The condition is that the court or sheriff is satisfied, on an application by the person from whom the cash was seized, that the conditions in section 295 for the detention of the cash are no longer met in relation to the cash to be released.

(4) A customs officer, constable or (in Scotland) procurator fiscal may, after notifying the magistrates' court, sheriff or justice under whose order cash is being detained, release the whole or any part of it if satisfied that the detention of the cash to be released is no longer justified.

Forfeiture

298. Forfeiture

(1) While cash is detained under section 295, an application for the forfeiture of the whole or any part of it may be made—

(a) to a magistrates' court by the Commissioners of Customs and Excise or a constable,

(b) (in Scotland) to the sheriff by the Scottish Ministers.

(2) The court or sheriff may order the forfeiture of the cash or any part of it if satisfied that the cash or part—

(a) is recoverable property, or

(b) is intended by any person for use in unlawful conduct.

(3) But in the case of recoverable property which belongs to joint tenants, one of whom is an excepted joint owner, the order may not apply to so much of it as the court thinks is attributable to the excepted joint owner's share.

(4) Where an application for the forfeiture of any cash is made under this section, the cash is to be detained (and may not be released under any power conferred by this Chapter) until any proceedings in pursuance of the application (including any proceedings on appeal) are concluded.

299. Appeal against forfeiture

(1) Any party to proceedings in which an order is made under section 298 for the forfeiture of cash who is aggrieved by the order may appeal—
   (a) in relation to England and Wales, to the Crown Court,
   (b) in relation to Scotland, to the Court of Session,
   (c) in relation to Northern Ireland, to a county court.

(2) An appeal under subsection (1) must be made within the period of 30 days beginning with the date on which the order is made.

(3) The appeal is to be by way of a rehearing.

(4) The court hearing the appeal may make any order it thinks appropriate.

(5) If the court upholds the appeal, it may order the release of the cash.

300. Application of forfeited cash

(1) Cash forfeited under this Chapter, and any accrued interest on it—
   (a) if forfeited by a magistrates' court in England and Wales or Northern Ireland, is to be paid into the Consolidated Fund,
   (b) if forfeited by the sheriff, is to be paid into the Scottish Consolidated Fund.

(2) But it is not to be paid in—
   (a) before the end of the period within which an appeal under section 299 may be made, or
   (b) if a person appeals under that section, before the appeal is determined or otherwise disposed of.

Supplementary

301. Victims and other owners

(1) A person who claims that any cash detained under this Chapter, or any part of it, belongs to him may apply to a magistrates' court or (in Scotland) the sheriff for the cash or part to be released to him.

(2) The application may be made in the course of proceedings under section 295 or 298 or at any other time.

(3) If it appears to the court or sheriff concerned that—
   (a) the applicant was deprived of the cash to which the application relates, or of property which it represents, by unlawful conduct,
   (b) the property he was deprived of was not, immediately before he was deprived of it, recoverable property, and
   (c) that cash belongs to him,
the court or sheriff may order the cash to which the application relates to be released to the applicant.

(4) If—
   (a) the applicant is not the person from whom the cash to which the application relates was seized,
   (b) it appears to the court or sheriff that that cash belongs to the applicant,
   (c) the court or sheriff is satisfied that the conditions in section 295 for the detention of that cash are no longer met or, if an application has been made under section 298, the court or sheriff decides not to make an order under that section in relation to that cash, and

(d) no objection to the making of an order under this subsection has been made by the person from whom that cash was seized,

the court or sheriff may order the cash to which the application relates to be released to the applicant or to the person from whom it was seized.

302. Compensation

(1) If no forfeiture order is made in respect of any cash detained under this Chapter, the person to whom the cash belongs or from whom it was seized may make an application to the magistrates' court or (in Scotland) the sheriff for compensation.

(2) If, for any period beginning with the first opportunity to place the cash in an interest-bearing account after the initial detention of the cash for 48 hours, the cash was not held in an interest-bearing account while detained, the court or sheriff may order an amount of compensation to be paid to the applicant.

(3) The amount of compensation to be paid under subsection (2) is the amount the court or sheriff thinks would have been earned in interest in the period in question if the cash had been held in an interest-bearing account.

(4) If the court or sheriff is satisfied that, taking account of any interest to be paid under section 296 or any amount to be paid under subsection (2), the applicant has suffered loss as a result of the detention of the cash and that the circumstances are exceptional, the court or sheriff may order compensation (or additional compensation) to be paid to him.

(5) The amount of compensation to be paid under subsection (4) is the amount the court or sheriff thinks reasonable, having regard to the loss suffered and any other relevant circumstances.

(6) If the cash was seized by a customs officer, the compensation is to be paid by the Commissioners of Customs and Excise.

(7) If the cash was seized by a constable, the compensation is to be paid as follows—

(a) in the case of a constable of a police force in England and Wales, it is to be paid out of the police fund from which the expenses of the police force are met,

(b) in the case of a constable of a police force in Scotland, it is to be paid by the police authority or joint police board for the police area for which that force is maintained,

(c) in the case of a police officer within the meaning of the Police (Northern Ireland) Act 2000 (c. 32), it is to be paid out of money provided by the Chief Constable.

(8) If a forfeiture order is made in respect only of a part of any cash detained under this Chapter, this section has effect in relation to the other part.

303. 'The minimum amount'

(1) In this Chapter, the minimum amount is the amount in sterling specified in an order made by the Secretary of State after consultation with the Scottish Ministers.

(2) For that purpose the amount of any cash held in a currency other than sterling must be taken to be its sterling equivalent, calculated in accordance with the prevailing rate of exchange.

CHAPTER 4
GENERAL

Recoverable property

304. Property obtained through unlawful conduct

(1) Property obtained through unlawful conduct is recoverable property.

(2) But if property obtained through unlawful conduct has been disposed of (since it was so obtained), it is recoverable property only if it is held by a person into whose hands it may be followed.

(3) Recoverable property obtained through unlawful conduct may be followed into the hands of a person obtaining it on a disposal by—

(a) the person who through the conduct obtained the property, or

(b) a person into whose hands it may (by virtue of this subsection) be followed.

305. Tracing property, etc.

(1) Where property obtained through unlawful conduct ('the original property') is or has been recoverable, property which represents the original property is also recoverable property.

(2) If a person enters into a transaction by which—

(a) he disposes of recoverable property, whether the original property or property which (by virtue of this Chapter) represents the original property, and

(b) he obtains other property in place of it,

the other property represents the original property.

(3) If a person disposes of recoverable property which represents the original property, the property may be followed into the hands of the person who obtains it (and it continues to represent the original property).

306. Mixing property

(1) Subsection (2) applies if a person's recoverable property is mixed with other property (whether his property or another's).

(2) The portion of the mixed property which is attributable to the recoverable property represents the property obtained through unlawful conduct.

(3) Recoverable property is mixed with other property if (for example) it is used—

(a) to increase funds held in a bank account,

(b) in part payment for the acquisition of an asset,

(c) for the restoration or improvement of land,

(d) by a person holding a leasehold interest in the property to acquire the freehold.

307. Recoverable property: accruing profits

(1) This section applies where a person who has recoverable property obtains further property consisting of profits accruing in respect of the recoverable property.

(2) The further property is to be treated as representing the property obtained through unlawful conduct.

308. General exceptions

(1) If—

(a) a person disposes of recoverable property, and

(b) the person who obtains it on the disposal does so in good faith, for value and without notice that it was recoverable property,

the property may not be followed into that person's hands and, accordingly, it ceases to be recoverable.

(2) If recoverable property is vested, forfeited or otherwise disposed of in pursuance of powers conferred by virtue of this Part, it ceases to be recoverable.

(3) If—

(a) in pursuance of a judgment in civil proceedings (whether in the United Kingdom or elsewhere), the defendant makes a payment to the claimant or the claimant otherwise obtains property from the defendant,

(b) the claimant's claim is based on the defendant's unlawful conduct, and

(c) apart from this subsection, the sum received, or the property obtained, by the claimant would be recoverable property,

the property ceases to be recoverable.

In relation to Scotland, 'claimant' and 'defendant' are to be read as 'pursuer' and 'defender'.

(4) If—

(a) a payment is made to a person in pursuance of a compensation order under Article 14 of the Criminal Justice (Northern Ireland) Order 1994 (S.I. 1994/2795 (N.I. 15)), section 249 of the Criminal Procedure (Scotland) Act 1995 (c. 46) or section 130 of the Powers of Criminal Courts (Sentencing) Act 2000 (c. 6), and

(b) apart from this subsection, the sum received would be recoverable property,

the property ceases to be recoverable.

(5) If—

(a) a payment is made to a person in pursuance of a restitution order under section 27 of the Theft Act (Northern Ireland) 1969 (c. 16 (N.I.)) or section 148(2) of the Powers of Criminal Courts (Sentencing) Act 2000 or a person otherwise obtains any property in pursuance of such an order, and

(b) apart from this subsection, the sum received, or the property obtained, would be recoverable property,

the property ceases to be recoverable.

(6) If—

(a) in pursuance of an order made by the court under section 382(3) or 383(5) of the Financial Services and Markets Act 2000 (c. 8) (restitution orders), an amount is paid to or distributed among any persons in accordance with the court's directions, and

(b) apart from this subsection, the sum received by them would be recoverable property,

the property ceases to be recoverable.

(7) If—

(a) in pursuance of a requirement of the Financial Services Authority under section 384(5) of the Financial Services and Markets Act 2000 (power of authority to require restitution), an amount is paid to or distributed among any persons, and

(b) apart from this subsection, the sum received by them would be recoverable property, the property ceases to be recoverable.

(8) Property is not recoverable while a restraint order applies to it, that is—
    (a) an order under section 41, 120 or 190, or
    (b) an order under any corresponding provision of an enactment mentioned in section 8(7)(a) to (g).

(9) Property is not recoverable if it has been taken into account in deciding the amount of a person's benefit from criminal conduct for the purpose of making a confiscation order, that is—
    (a) an order under section 6, 92 or 156, or
    (b) an order under a corresponding provision of an enactment mentioned in section 8(7)(a) to (g),

and, in relation to an order mentioned in paragraph (b), the reference to the amount of a person's benefit from criminal conduct is to be read as a reference to the corresponding amount under the enactment in question.

(10) Where—
    (a) a person enters into a transaction to which section 305(2) applies, and
    (b) the disposal is one to which subsection (1) or (2) applies,

this section does not affect the recoverability (by virtue of section 305(2)) of any property obtained on the transaction in place of the property disposed of.

309. Other exemptions

(1) An order may provide that property is not recoverable or (as the case may be) associated property if—
    (a) it is prescribed property, or
    (b) it is disposed of in pursuance of a prescribed enactment or an enactment of a prescribed description.

(2) An order may provide that if property is disposed of in pursuance of a prescribed enactment or an enactment of a prescribed description, it is to be treated for the purposes of section 278 as if it had been disposed of in pursuance of a recovery order.

(3) An order under this section may be made so as to apply to property, or a disposal of property, only in prescribed circumstances; and the circumstances may relate to the property or disposal itself or to a person who holds or has held the property or to any other matter.

(4) In this section, an order means an order made by the Secretary of State after consultation with the Scottish Ministers, and prescribed means prescribed by the order.

310. Granting interests

(1) If a person grants an interest in his recoverable property, the question whether the interest is also recoverable is to be determined in the same manner as it is on any other disposal of recoverable property.

(2) Accordingly, on his granting an interest in the property ('the property in question')—
    (a) where the property in question is property obtained through unlawful conduct, the interest is also to be treated as obtained through that conduct,
    (b) where the property in question represents in his hands property obtained through unlawful conduct, the interest is also to be treated as representing in his hands the property so obtained.

Insolvency

311. Insolvency

(1) Proceedings for a recovery order may not be taken or continued in respect of property to which subsection (3) applies unless the appropriate court gives leave and the proceedings are taken or (as the case may be) continued in accordance with any terms imposed by that court.

(2) An application for an order for the further detention of any cash to which subsection (3) applies may not be made under section 295 unless the appropriate court gives leave.

(3) This subsection applies to recoverable property, or property associated with it, if—

    (a) it is an asset of a company being wound up in pursuance of a resolution for voluntary winding up,

    (b) it is an asset of a company and a voluntary arrangement under Part 1 of the 1986 Act, or Part 2 of the 1989 Order, has effect in relation to the company,

    (c) an order under section 2 of the 1985 Act, section 286 of the 1986 Act or Article 259 of the 1989 Order (appointment of interim trustee or interim receiver) has effect in relation to the property,

    (d) it is an asset comprised in the estate of an individual who has been adjudged bankrupt or, in relation to Scotland, of a person whose estate has been sequestrated,

    (e) it is an asset of an individual and a voluntary arrangement under Part 8 of the 1986 Act, or Part 8 of the 1989 Order, has effect in relation to him, or

    (f) in relation to Scotland, it is property comprised in the estate of a person who has granted a trust deed within the meaning of the 1985 Act.

(4) An application under this section, or under any provision of the 1986 Act or the 1989 Order, for leave to take proceedings for a recovery order may be made without notice to any person.

(5) Subsection (4) does not affect any requirement for notice of an application to be given to any person acting as an insolvency practitioner or to the official receiver (whether or not acting as an insolvency practitioner).

(6) References to the provisions of the 1986 Act in sections 420 and 421 of that Act, or to the provisions of the 1989 Order in Articles 364 or 365 of that Order, (insolvent partnerships and estates of deceased persons) include subsections (1) to (3) above.

(7) In this section—

    (a) the 1985 Act means the Bankruptcy (Scotland) Act 1985 (c. 66),

    (b) the 1986 Act means the Insolvency Act 1986 (c. 45),

    (c) the 1989 Order means the Insolvency (Northern Ireland) Order 1989 (S.I. 1989/2405 (N.I. 19)),

and in subsection (8) 'the applicable enactment' means whichever enactment mentioned in paragraphs (a) to (c) is relevant to the resolution, arrangement, order or trust deed mentioned in subsection (3).

(8) In this section—

    (a) an asset means any property within the meaning of the applicable enactment or, where the 1985 Act is the applicable enactment, any property comprised in an estate to which the 1985 Act applies,

    (b) the appropriate court means the court which, in relation to the resolution, arrangement, order or trust deed mentioned in subsection (3), is the court for the purposes of the applicable enactment or, in relation to Northern Ireland, the High Court,

(c) acting as an insolvency practitioner has the same meaning as in section 433,

(d) other expressions used in this section and in the applicable enactment have the same meaning as in that enactment.

Delegation of enforcement functions

312. Performance of functions of Scottish Ministers by constables in Scotland

(1) In Scotland, a constable engaged in temporary service with the Scottish Ministers in connection with their functions under this Part may perform functions, other than those specified in subsection (2), on behalf of the Scottish Ministers.

(2) The specified functions are the functions conferred on the Scottish Ministers by—

(a) sections 244(1) and (2) and 256(1) and (7) (proceedings in the Court of Session),

(b) section 267(2) (trustee for civil recovery),

(c) sections 271(3) and (4) and 272(5) (agreements about associated and joint property),

(d) section 275(3) (pension schemes),

(e) section 282(1) (exemptions),

(f) section 283(5) and (8) (compensation),

(g) section 287(2) (financial threshold),

(h) section 293(1) (code of practice),

(i) section 298(1) (forfeiture),

(j) section 303(1) (minimum amount).

313. Restriction on performance of Director's functions by police

(1) In spite of section 1(6), nothing which the Director is authorised or required to do for the purposes of this Part may be done by—

(a) a member of a police force,

(b) a member of the Police Service of Northern Ireland,

(c) a person appointed as a police member of the National Criminal Intelligence Service under section 9(1)(b) of the Police Act 1997 (c. 50),

(d) a person appointed as a police member of the National Crime Squad under section 55(1)(b) of that Act.

(2) In this section—

(a) 'member of a police force' has the same meaning as in the Police Act 1996 (c. 16) and includes a person who would be a member of a police force but for section 97(3) of that Act (police officers engaged on service outside their force),

(b) 'member of the Police Service of Northern Ireland' includes a person who would be a member of the Police Service of Northern Ireland but for section 27(3) of the Police (Northern Ireland) Act 1998 (c. 32) (members of that service engaged on other police service).

Interpretation

314. Obtaining and disposing of property

(1) References to a person disposing of his property include a reference—

(a) to his disposing of a part of it, or

     (b) to his granting an interest in it,

(or to both); and references to the property disposed of are to any property obtained on the disposal.

  (2) A person who makes a payment to another is to be treated as making a disposal of his property to the other, whatever form the payment takes.

  (3) Where a person's property passes to another under a will or intestacy or by operation of law, it is to be treated as disposed of by him to the other.

  (4) A person is only to be treated as having obtained his property for value in a case where he gave unexecuted consideration if the consideration has become executed consideration.

315. Northern Ireland courts

In relation to the practice and procedure of courts in Northern Ireland, expressions used in this Part are to be read in accordance with rules of court.

316. General interpretation

  (1) In this Part—

'associated property' has the meaning given by section 245,

'cash' has the meaning given by section 289(6) or (7),

'constable', in relation to Northern Ireland, means a police officer within the meaning of the Police (Northern Ireland) Act 2000 (c. 32),

'country' includes territory,

'the court' (except in sections 253(2) and (3) and 262(2) and (3) and Chapter 3) means the High Court or (in relation to proceedings in Scotland) the Court of Session,

'dealing' with property includes disposing of it, taking possession of it or removing it from the United Kingdom,

'enforcement authority'—

     (a) in relation to England and Wales and Northern Ireland, means the Director,

     (b) in relation to Scotland, means the Scottish Ministers,

'excepted joint owner' has the meaning given by section 270(4),

'interest', in relation to land—

     (a) in the case of land in England and Wales or Northern Ireland, means any legal estate and any equitable interest or power,

     (b) in the case of land in Scotland, means any estate, interest, servitude or other heritable right in or over land, including a heritable security,

'interest', in relation to property other than land, includes any right (including a right to possession of the property),

'interim administration order' has the meaning given by section 256(2),

'interim receiving order' has the meaning given by section 246(2),

'the minimum amount' (in Chapter 3) has the meaning given by section 303,

'part', in relation to property, includes a portion,

'premises' has the same meaning as in the Police and Criminal Evidence Act 1984 (c. 60),

'property obtained through unlawful conduct' has the meaning given by section 242,

'recoverable property' is to be read in accordance with sections 304 to 310,

'recovery order' means an order made under section 266,

'respondent' means—

     (a) where proceedings are brought by the enforcement authority by virtue of Chapter 2, the person against whom the proceedings are brought,

(b) where no such proceedings have been brought but the enforcement authority has applied for an interim receiving order or interim administration order, the person against whom he intends to bring such proceedings,

'share', in relation to an excepted joint owner, has the meaning given by section 270(4),

'unlawful conduct' has the meaning given by section 241,

'value' means market value.

(2) The following provisions apply for the purposes of this Part.

(3) For the purpose of deciding whether or not property was recoverable at any time (including times before commencement), it is to be assumed that this Part was in force at that and any other relevant time.

(4) Property is all property wherever situated and includes—

(a) money,

(b) all forms of property, real or personal, heritable or moveable,

(c) things in action and other intangible or incorporeal property.

(5) Any reference to a person's property (whether expressed as a reference to the property he holds or otherwise) is to be read as follows.

(6) In relation to land, it is a reference to any interest which he holds in the land.

(7) In relation to property other than land, it is a reference—

(a) to the property (if it belongs to him), or

(b) to any other interest which he holds in the property.

(8) References to the satisfaction of the enforcement authority's right to recover property obtained through unlawful conduct are to be read in accordance with section 279.

(9) Proceedings against any person for an offence are concluded when—

(a) the person is convicted or acquitted,

(b) the prosecution is discontinued or, in Scotland, the trial diet is deserted simpliciter, or

(c) the jury is discharged without a finding.

PART 6

REVENUE FUNCTIONS

General functions

317. Director's general Revenue functions

(1) For the purposes of this section the qualifying condition is that the Director has reasonable grounds to suspect that—

(a) income arising or a gain accruing to a person in respect of a chargeable period is chargeable to income tax or is a chargeable gain (as the case may be) and arises or accrues as a result of the person's or another's criminal conduct (whether wholly or partly and whether directly or indirectly), or

(b) a company is chargeable to corporation tax on its profits arising in respect of a chargeable period and the profits arise as a result of the company's or another person's criminal conduct (whether wholly or partly and whether directly or indirectly).

(2) If the qualifying condition is satisfied the Director may serve on the Commissioners of Inland Revenue (the Board) a notice which—

(a) specifies the person or the company (as the case may be) and the period, and

(b) states that the Director intends to carry out, in relation to the person or the company (as the case may be) and in respect of the period, such of the general Revenue functions as are specified in the notice.

(3) Service of a notice under subsection (2) vests in the Director, in relation to the person or the company (as the case may be) and in respect of the period, such of the general Revenue functions as are specified in the notice; but this is subject to section 318.

(4) The Director—

(a) may at any time serve on the Board a notice of withdrawal of the notice under subsection (2);

(b) must serve such a notice of withdrawal on the Board if the qualifying condition ceases to be satisfied.

(5) A notice under subsection (2) and a notice of withdrawal under subsection (4) may be in respect of one or more periods.

(6) Service of a notice under subsection (4) divests the Director of the functions concerned in relation to the person or the company (as the case may be) and in respect of the period or periods specified in the notice.

(7) The vesting of a function in the Director under this section does not divest the Board or an officer of the Board of the function.

(8) If—

(a) apart from this section the Board's authorisation would be required for the exercise of a function, and

(b) the function is vested in the Director under this section,

the authorisation is not required in relation to the function as so vested.

(9) It is immaterial whether a chargeable period or any part of it falls before or after the passing of this Act.

318. Revenue functions regarding employment

(1) Subsection (2) applies if—

(a) the Director serves a notice or notices under section 317(2) in relation to a company and in respect of a period or periods, and

(b) the company is an employer.

(2) The general Revenue functions vested in the Director do not include functions relating to any requirement which—

(a) is imposed on the company in its capacity as employer, and

(b) relates to a year of assessment which does not fall wholly within the period or periods.

(3) Subsection (4) applies if—

(a) the Director serves a notice or notices under section 317(2) in relation to an individual and in respect of a year or years of assessment, and

(b) the individual is a self-employed earner.

(4) The general Revenue functions vested in the Director do not include functions relating to any liability to pay Class 2 contributions in respect of a period which does not fall wholly within the year or years of assessment.

(5) In this section in its application to Great Britain—

(a) 'self-employed earner' has the meaning given by section 2(1)(b) of the Social Security Contributions and Benefits Act 1992 (c. 4);

(b) 'Class 2 contributions' must be construed in accordance with section 1(2)(c) of that Act.

(6) In this section in its application to Northern Ireland—

(a) 'self-employed earner' has the meaning given by section 2(1)(b) of the Social Security Contributions and Benefits (Northern Ireland) Act 1992 (c. 7);

(b) 'Class 2 contributions' must be construed in accordance with section 1(2)(c) of that Act.

319. Source of income

(1) For the purpose of the exercise by the Director of any function vested in him by virtue of this Part it is immaterial that he cannot identify a source for any income.

(2) An assessment made by the Director under section 29 of the Taxes Management Act 1970 (c. 9) (assessment where loss of tax discovered) in respect of income charged to tax under Case 6 of Schedule D must not be reduced or quashed only because it does not specify (to any extent) the source of the income.

(3) If the Director serves on the Board a notice of withdrawal under section 317(4), any assessment made by him under section 29 of the Taxes Management Act 1970 is invalid to the extent that it does not specify a source for the income.

(4) Subsections (2) and (3) apply in respect of years of assessment whenever occurring.

320.   Appeals

(1) An appeal in respect of the exercise by the Director of general Revenue functions shall be to the Special Commissioners.

(2) The Presiding Special Commissioner may nominate one or more assessors to assist the Special Commissioners in any appeal to be heard by them in respect of the exercise by the Director of any of his Revenue functions.

(3) An assessor nominated under subsection (2)—

(a) must have special knowledge and experience of the matter to which the appeal relates, and

(b) must be selected from a panel of persons appointed for the purposes of this section by the Lord Chancellor after consultation with the Scottish Ministers.

(4) Regulations made under section 56B of the Taxes Management Act 1970 may include provision as to the manner in which an assessor nominated under subsection (2) is to assist the Special Commissioners.

(5) The remuneration of an assessor nominated under subsection (2) must be paid by the Lord Chancellor and must be at such rate as he decides.

Inheritance tax functions

321. Director's functions: transfers of value

(1) For the purposes of this section the qualifying condition is that the Director has reasonable grounds to suspect that—

(a) there has been a transfer of value within the meaning of the Inheritance Tax Act 1984 (c. 51), and

(b) the value transferred by it is attributable (in whole or part) to criminal property.

(2) If the qualifying condition is satisfied the Director may serve on the Board a notice which—

(a) specifies the transfer of value, and

(b) states that the Director intends to carry out the Revenue inheritance tax functions in relation to the transfer.

(3) Service of a notice under subsection (2) vests in the Director the Revenue inheritance tax functions in relation to the transfer.

(4) The Director—

(a) may at any time serve on the Board a notice of withdrawal of the notice under subsection (2);

(b) must serve such a notice of withdrawal on the Board if the qualifying condition ceases to be satisfied.

(5) Service of a notice under subsection (4) divests the Director of the Revenue inheritance tax functions in relation to the transfer.

(6) The vesting of a function in the Director under this section does not divest the Board or an officer of the Board of the function.

(7) It is immaterial whether a transfer of value is suspected to have occurred before or after the passing of this Act.

322. Director's functions: certain settlements

(1) For the purposes of this section the qualifying condition is that the Director has reasonable grounds to suspect that—

(a) all or part of the property comprised in a settlement is relevant property for the purposes of Chapter 3 of Part 3 of the Inheritance Tax Act 1984 (settlements without interest in possession), and

(b) the relevant property is (in whole or part) criminal property.

(2) If the qualifying condition is satisfied the Director may serve on the Board a notice which—

(a) specifies the settlement concerned,

(b) states that the Director intends to carry out the Revenue inheritance tax functions in relation to the settlement, and

(c) states the period for which he intends to carry them out.

(3) Service of a notice under subsection (2) vests in the Director the Revenue inheritance tax functions in relation to the settlement for the period.

(4) The Director—

(a) may at any time serve on the Board a notice of withdrawal of the notice under subsection (2);

(b) must serve such a notice of withdrawal on the Board if the qualifying condition ceases to be satisfied.

(5) Service of a notice under subsection (4) divests the Director of the Revenue inheritance tax functions in relation to the settlement for the period.

(6) The vesting of a function in the Director under this section does not divest the Board or an officer of the Board of the function.

(7) It is immaterial whether the settlement is commenced or a charge to tax arises or a period or any part of it falls before or after the passing of this Act.

General

323. Functions

(1) The general Revenue functions are such of the functions vested in the Board or in an officer of the Board as relate to any of the following matters—

(a) income tax;

(b) capital gains tax;

(c) corporation tax;

(d) national insurance contributions;

(e) statutory sick pay;

(f) statutory maternity pay;

(g) statutory paternity pay;

(h) statutory adoption pay;

(i) student loans.

(2) The Revenue inheritance tax functions are such functions vested in the Board or in an officer of the Board as relate to inheritance tax.

(3) But the general Revenue functions and the Revenue inheritance tax functions do not include any of the following functions—

(a) functions relating to the making of subordinate legislation (within the meaning given by section 21(1) of the Interpretation Act 1978 (c. 30));

(b) the function of the prosecution of offences;

(c) the function of authorising an officer for the purposes of section 20BA of the Taxes Management Act 1970 (c. 9) (orders for delivery of documents);

(d) the function of giving information under that section;

(e) the function of approving an officer's application for the purposes of section 20C of the Taxes Management Act 1970 (warrant to enter and search premises);

(f) the function of applying under that section.

(4) For the purposes of this section in its application to Great Britain—

(a) national insurance contributions are contributions payable under Part 1 of the Social Security Contributions and Benefits Act 1992 (c. 4);

(b) 'statutory sick pay' must be construed in accordance with section 151(1) of that Act;

(c) 'statutory maternity pay' must be construed in accordance with section 164(1) of that Act;

(d) 'statutory paternity pay' must be construed in accordance with section 171ZA of that Act;

(e) 'statutory adoption pay' must be construed in accordance with section 171ZL of that Act;

(f) 'student loans' must be construed in accordance with the Education (Student Loans) (Repayment) Regulations 2000 (S.I. 2000/944).

(5) For the purposes of this section in its application to Northern Ireland—

(a) national insurance contributions are contributions payable under Part 1 of the Social Security Contributions and Benefits (Northern Ireland) Act 1992 (c. 7);

(b) 'statutory sick pay' must be construed in accordance with section 147(1) of that Act;

(c) 'statutory maternity pay' must be construed in accordance with section 160(1) of that Act;

(d) 'statutory paternity pay' must be construed in accordance with any Northern

Ireland legislation which corresponds to Part 12ZA of the Social Security Contributions and Benefits Act 1992;

(e) 'statutory adoption pay' must be construed in accordance with any Northern Ireland legislation which corresponds to Part 12ZB of that Act;

(f) 'student loans' must be construed in accordance with the Education (Student Loans) (Repayment) Regulations (Northern Ireland) 2000 (S.R. 2000/121).

324. Exercise of Revenue functions

(1) This section applies in relation to the exercise by the Director of—
  (a) general Revenue functions;
  (b) Revenue inheritance tax functions.
(2) Paragraph (b) of section 1(6) does not apply.
(3) The Director must apply—
  (a) any interpretation of the law which has been published by the Board;
  (b) any concession which has been published by the Board and which is available generally to any person falling within its terms.
(4) The Director must also take account of any material published by the Board which does not fall within subsection (3).
(5) The Director must provide the Board with such documents and information as they consider appropriate.
(6) 'Concession' includes any practice, interpretation or other statement in the nature of a concession.

325. Declarations

(1) As soon as practicable after the appointment of a person as the Director he must make a declaration in the form set out in Schedule 8 before a member of the Board.
(2) Every member of the staff of the Agency who is authorised under section 1(6)(a) to carry out any of the functions of the Director under this Part must, as soon as practicable after being so authorised, make a declaration in the form set out in Schedule 8 before a person nominated by the Director for the purpose.

326. Interpretation

(1) Criminal conduct is conduct which—
  (a) constitutes an offence in any part of the United Kingdom, or
  (b) would constitute an offence in any part of the United Kingdom if it occurred there.
(2) But criminal conduct does not include conduct constituting an offence relating to a matter under the care and management of the Board.
(3) In applying subsection (1) it is immaterial whether conduct occurred before or after the passing of this Act.
(4) Property is criminal property if it constitutes a person's benefit from criminal conduct or it represents such a benefit (in whole or part and whether directly or indirectly); and it is immaterial—
  (a) who carried out the conduct;
  (b) who benefited from it.
(5) A person benefits from conduct if he obtains property as a result of or in connection with the conduct.

(6) If a person obtains a pecuniary advantage as a result of or in connection with conduct, he is to be taken to obtain as a result of or in connection with the conduct a sum of money equal to the value of the pecuniary advantage.

(7) References to property or a pecuniary advantage obtained in connection with conduct include references to property or a pecuniary advantage obtained in both that connection and some other.

(8) If a person benefits from conduct his benefit is the property obtained as a result of or in connection with the conduct.

(9) Property is all property wherever situated and includes—
    (a) money;
    (b) all forms of property, real or personal, heritable or moveable;
    (c) things in action and other intangible or incorporeal property.

(10) The following rules apply in relation to property—
    (a) property is obtained by a person if he obtains an interest in it;
    (b) references to an interest, in relation to land in England and Wales or Northern Ireland, are to any legal estate or equitable interest or power;
    (c) references to an interest, in relation to land in Scotland, are to any estate, interest, servitude or other heritable right in or over land, including a heritable security;
    (d) references to an interest, in relation to property other than land, include references to a right (including a right to possession).

(11) Any reference to an officer of the Board includes a reference to—
    (a) a collector of taxes;
    (b) an inspector of taxes.

(12) Expressions used in this Part and in the Taxes Acts have the same meaning as in the Taxes Acts (within the meaning given by section 118 of the Taxes Management Act 1970 (c. 9)).

(13) This section applies for the purposes of this Part.

PART 7
MONEY LAUNDERING

Offences

327. Concealing etc

(1) A person commits an offence if he—
    (a) conceals criminal property;
    (b) disguises criminal property;
    (c) converts criminal property;
    (d) transfers criminal property;
    (e) removes criminal property from England and Wales or from Scotland or from Northern Ireland.

(2) But a person does not commit such an offence if—
    (a) he makes an authorised disclosure under section 338 and (if the disclosure is made before he does the act mentioned in subsection (1)) he has the appropriate consent;

    (b) he intended to make such a disclosure but had a reasonable excuse for not doing so;

    (c) the act he does is done in carrying out a function he has relating to the enforcement of any provision of this Act or of any other enactment relating to criminal conduct or benefit from criminal conduct.

(3) Concealing or disguising criminal property includes concealing or disguising its nature, source, location, disposition, movement or ownership or any rights with respect to it.

328. Arrangements

(1) A person commits an offence if he enters into or becomes concerned in an arrangement which he knows or suspects facilitates (by whatever means) the acquisition, retention, use or control of criminal property by or on behalf of another person.

(2) But a person does not commit such an offence if—

    (a) he makes an authorised disclosure under section 338 and (if the disclosure is made before he does the act mentioned in subsection (1)) he has the appropriate consent;

    (b) he intended to make such a disclosure but had a reasonable excuse for not doing so;

    (c) the act he does is done in carrying out a function he has relating to the enforcement of any provision of this Act or of any other enactment relating to criminal conduct or benefit from criminal conduct.

329. Acquisition, use and possession

(1) A person commits an offence if he—

    (a) acquires criminal property;

    (b) uses criminal property;

    (c) has possession of criminal property.

(2) But a person does not commit such an offence if—

    (a) he makes an authorised disclosure under section 338 and (if the disclosure is made before he does the act mentioned in subsection (1)) he has the appropriate consent;

    (b) he intended to make such a disclosure but had a reasonable excuse for not doing so;

    (c) he acquired or used or had possession of the property for adequate consideration;

    (d) the act he does is done in carrying out a function he has relating to the enforcement of any provision of this Act or of any other enactment relating to criminal conduct or benefit from criminal conduct.

(3) For the purposes of this section—

    (a) a person acquires property for inadequate consideration if the value of the consideration is significantly less than the value of the property;

    (b) a person uses or has possession of property for inadequate consideration if the value of the consideration is significantly less than the value of the use or possession;

    (c) the provision by a person of goods or services which he knows or suspects may help another to carry out criminal conduct is not consideration.

330. Failure to disclose: regulated sector

(1) A person commits an offence if each of the following three conditions is satisfied.

(2) The first condition is that he—

    (a) knows or suspects, or

    (b) has reasonable grounds for knowing or suspecting,

that another person is engaged in money laundering.

(3) The second condition is that the information or other matter—

    (a) on which his knowledge or suspicion is based, or

    (b) which gives reasonable grounds for such knowledge or suspicion,

came to him in the course of a business in the regulated sector.

(4) The third condition is that he does not make the required disclosure as soon as is practicable after the information or other matter comes to him.

(5) The required disclosure is a disclosure of the information or other matter—

    (a) to a nominated officer or a person authorised for the purposes of this Part by the Director General of the National Criminal Intelligence Service;

    (b) in the form and manner (if any) prescribed for the purposes of this subsection by order under section 339.

(6) But a person does not commit an offence under this section if—

    (a) he has a reasonable excuse for not disclosing the information or other matter;

    (b) he is a professional legal adviser and the information or other matter came to him in privileged circumstances;

    (c) subsection (7) applies to him.

(7) This subsection applies to a person if—

    (a) he does not know or suspect that another person is engaged in money laundering, and

    (b) he has not been provided by his employer with such training as is specified by the Secretary of State by order for the purposes of this section.

(8) In deciding whether a person committed an offence under this section the court must consider whether he followed any relevant guidance which was at the time concerned—

    (a) issued by a supervisory authority or any other appropriate body,

    (b) approved by the Treasury, and

    (c) published in a manner it approved as appropriate in its opinion to bring the guidance to the attention of persons likely to be affected by it.

(9) A disclosure to a nominated officer is a disclosure which—

    (a) is made to a person nominated by the alleged offender's employer to receive disclosures under this section, and

    (b) is made in the course of the alleged offender's employment and in accordance with the procedure established by the employer for the purpose.

(10) Information or other matter comes to a professional legal adviser in privileged circumstances if it is communicated or given to him—

    (a) by (or by a representative of) a client of his in connection with the giving by the adviser of legal advice to the client,

    (b) by (or by a representative of) a person seeking legal advice from the adviser, or

    (c) by a person in connection with legal proceedings or contemplated legal proceedings.

(11) But subsection (10) does not apply to information or other matter which is communicated or given with the intention of furthering a criminal purpose.

(12) Schedule 9 has effect for the purpose of determining what is—
    (a) a business in the regulated sector;
    (b) a supervisory authority.

(13) An appropriate body is any body which regulates or is representative of any trade, profession, business or employment carried on by the alleged offender.

331. Failure to disclose: nominated officers in the regulated sector

(1) A person nominated to receive disclosures under section 330 commits an offence if the conditions in subsections (2) to (4) are satisfied.

(2) The first condition is that he—
    (a) knows or suspects, or
    (b) has reasonable grounds for knowing or suspecting,
that another person is engaged in money laundering.

(3) The second condition is that the information or other matter—
    (a) on which his knowledge or suspicion is based, or
    (b) which gives reasonable grounds for such knowledge or suspicion,
came to him in consequence of a disclosure made under section 330.

(4) The third condition is that he does not make the required disclosure as soon as is practicable after the information or other matter comes to him.

(5) The required disclosure is a disclosure of the information or other matter—
    (a) to a person authorised for the purposes of this Part by the Director General of the National Criminal Intelligence Service;
    (b) in the form and manner (if any) prescribed for the purposes of this subsection by order under section 339.

(6) But a person does not commit an offence under this section if he has a reasonable excuse for not disclosing the information or other matter.

(7) In deciding whether a person committed an offence under this section the court must consider whether he followed any relevant guidance which was at the time concerned—
    (a) issued by a supervisory authority or any other appropriate body,
    (b) approved by the Treasury, and
    (c) published in a manner it approved as appropriate in its opinion to bring the guidance to the attention of persons likely to be affected by it.

(8) Schedule 9 has effect for the purpose of determining what is a supervisory authority.

(9) An appropriate body is a body which regulates or is representative of a trade, profession, business or employment.

332. Failure to disclose: other nominated officers

(1) A person nominated to receive disclosures under section 337 or 338 commits an offence if the conditions in subsections (2) to (4) are satisfied.

(2) The first condition is that he knows or suspects that another person is engaged in money laundering.

(3) The second condition is that the information or other matter on which his knowledge or suspicion is based came to him in consequence of a disclosure made under section 337 or 338.

(4) The third condition is that he does not make the required disclosure as soon as is practicable after the information or other matter comes to him.

(5) The required disclosure is a disclosure of the information or other matter—
  (a) to a person authorised for the purposes of this Part by the Director General of the National Criminal Intelligence Service;
  (b) in the form and manner (if any) prescribed for the purposes of this subsection by order under section 339.

(6) But a person does not commit an offence under this section if he has a reasonable excuse for not disclosing the information or other matter.

333. Tipping off

(1) A person commits an offence if—
  (a) he knows or suspects that a disclosure falling within section 337 or 338 has been made, and
  (b) he makes a disclosure which is likely to prejudice any investigation which might be conducted following the disclosure referred to in paragraph (a).

(2) But a person does not commit an offence under subsection (1) if—
  (a) he did not know or suspect that the disclosure was likely to be prejudicial as mentioned in subsection (1);
  (b) the disclosure is made in carrying out a function he has relating to the enforcement of any provision of this Act or of any other enactment relating to criminal conduct or benefit from criminal conduct;
  (c) he is a professional legal adviser and the disclosure falls within subsection (3).

(3) A disclosure falls within this subsection if it is a disclosure—
  (a) to (or to a representative of) a client of the professional legal adviser in connection with the giving by the adviser of legal advice to the client, or
  (b) to any person in connection with legal proceedings or contemplated legal proceedings.

(4) But a disclosure does not fall within subsection (3) if it is made with the intention of furthering a criminal purpose.

334. Penalties

(1) A person guilty of an offence under section 327, 328 or 329 is liable—
  (a) on summary conviction, to imprisonment for a term not exceeding six months or to a fine not exceeding the statutory maximum or to both, or
  (b) on conviction on indictment, to imprisonment for a term not exceeding 14 years or to a fine or to both.

(2) A person guilty of an offence under section 330, 331, 332 or 333 is liable—
  (a) on summary conviction, to imprisonment for a term not exceeding six months or to a fine not exceeding the statutory maximum or to both, or
  (b) on conviction on indictment, to imprisonment for a term not exceeding five years or to a fine or to both.

Consent

335. Appropriate consent

(1) The appropriate consent is—
  (a) the consent of a nominated officer to do a prohibited act if an authorised disclosure is made to the nominated officer;

   (b) the consent of a constable to do a prohibited act if an authorised disclosure is made to a constable;

   (c) the consent of a customs officer to do a prohibited act if an authorised disclosure is made to a customs officer.

(2) A person must be treated as having the appropriate consent if—

   (a) he makes an authorised disclosure to a constable or a customs officer, and

   (b) the condition in subsection (3) or the condition in subsection (4) is satisfied.

(3) The condition is that before the end of the notice period he does not receive notice from a constable or customs officer that consent to the doing of the act is refused.

(4) The condition is that—

   (a) before the end of the notice period he receives notice from a constable or customs officer that consent to the doing of the act is refused, and

   (b) the moratorium period has expired.

(5) The notice period is the period of seven working days starting with the first working day after the person makes the disclosure.

(6) The moratorium period is the period of 31 days starting with the day on which the person receives notice that consent to the doing of the act is refused.

(7) A working day is a day other than a Saturday, a Sunday, Christmas Day, Good Friday or a day which is a bank holiday under the Banking and Financial Dealings Act 1971 (c. 80) in the part of the United Kingdom in which the person is when he makes the disclosure.

(8) References to a prohibited act are to an act mentioned in section 327(1), 328(1) or 329(1) (as the case may be).

(9) A nominated officer is a person nominated to receive disclosures under section 338.

(10) Subsections (1) to (4) apply for the purposes of this Part.

336. Nominated officer: consent

(1) A nominated officer must not give the appropriate consent to the doing of a prohibited act unless the condition in subsection (2), the condition in subsection (3) or the condition in subsection (4) is satisfied.

(2) The condition is that—

   (a) he makes a disclosure that property is criminal property to a person authorised for the purposes of this Part by the Director General of the National Criminal Intelligence Service, and

   (b) such a person gives consent to the doing of the act.

(3) The condition is that—

   (a) he makes a disclosure that property is criminal property to a person authorised for the purposes of this Part by the Director General of the National Criminal Intelligence Service, and

   (b) before the end of the notice period he does not receive notice from such a person that consent to the doing of the act is refused.

(4) The condition is that—

   (a) he makes a disclosure that property is criminal property to a person authorised for the purposes of this Part by the Director General of the National Criminal Intelligence Service,

   (b) before the end of the notice period he receives notice from such a person that consent to the doing of the act is refused, and

(c) the moratorium period has expired.

(5) A person who is a nominated officer commits an offence if—
    (a) he gives consent to a prohibited act in circumstances where none of the conditions in subsections (2), (3) and (4) is satisfied, and
    (b) he knows or suspects that the act is a prohibited act.

(6) A person guilty of such an offence is liable—
    (a) on summary conviction, to imprisonment for a term not exceeding six months or to a fine not exceeding the statutory maximum or to both, or
    (b) on conviction on indictment, to imprisonment for a term not exceeding five years or to a fine or to both.

(7) The notice period is the period of seven working days starting with the first working day after the nominated officer makes the disclosure.

(8) The moratorium period is the period of 31 days starting with the day on which the nominated officer is given notice that consent to the doing of the act is refused.

(9) A working day is a day other than a Saturday, a Sunday, Christmas Day, Good Friday or a day which is a bank holiday under the Banking and Financial Dealings Act 1971 (c. 80) in the part of the United Kingdom in which the nominated officer is when he gives the appropriate consent.

(10) References to a prohibited act are to an act mentioned in section 327(1), 328(1) or 329(1) (as the case may be).

(11) A nominated officer is a person nominated to receive disclosures under section 338.

Disclosures

337. Protected disclosures

(1) A disclosure which satisfies the following three conditions is not to be taken to breach any restriction on the disclosure of information (however imposed).

(2) The first condition is that the information or other matter disclosed came to the person making the disclosure (the discloser) in the course of his trade, profession, business or employment.

(3) The second condition is that the information or other matter—
    (a) causes the discloser to know or suspect, or
    (b) gives him reasonable grounds for knowing or suspecting,
that another person is engaged in money laundering.

(4) The third condition is that the disclosure is made to a constable, a customs officer or a nominated officer as soon as is practicable after the information or other matter comes to the discloser.

(5) A disclosure to a nominated officer is a disclosure which—
    (a) is made to a person nominated by the discloser's employer to receive disclosures under this section, and
    (b) is made in the course of the discloser's employment and in accordance with the procedure established by the employer for the purpose.

338. Authorised disclosures

(1) For the purposes of this Part a disclosure is authorised if—
    (a) it is a disclosure to a constable, a customs officer or a nominated officer by the alleged offender that property is criminal property,

(b) it is made in the form and manner (if any) prescribed for the purposes of this subsection by order under section 339, and

(c) the first or second condition set out below is satisfied.

(2) The first condition is that the disclosure is made before the alleged offender does the prohibited act.

(3) The second condition is that—

(a) the disclosure is made after the alleged offender does the prohibited act,

(b) there is a good reason for his failure to make the disclosure before he did the act, and

(c) the disclosure is made on his own initiative and as soon as it is practicable for him to make it.

(4) An authorised disclosure is not to be taken to breach any restriction on the disclosure of information (however imposed).

(5) A disclosure to a nominated officer is a disclosure which—

(a) is made to a person nominated by the alleged offender's employer to receive authorised disclosures, and

(b) is made in the course of the alleged offender's employment and in accordance with the procedure established by the employer for the purpose.

(6) References to the prohibited act are to an act mentioned in section 327(1), 328(1) or 329(1) (as the case may be).

339. Form and manner of disclosures

(1) The Secretary of State may by order prescribe the form and manner in which a disclosure under section 330, 331, 332 or 338 must be made.

(2) An order under this section may also provide that the form may include a request to the discloser to provide additional information specified in the form.

(3) The additional information must be information which is necessary to enable the person to whom the disclosure is made to decide whether to start a money laundering investigation.

(4) A disclosure made in pursuance of a request under subsection (2) is not to be taken to breach any restriction on the disclosure of information (however imposed).

(5) The discloser is the person making a disclosure mentioned in subsection (1).

(6) Money laundering investigation must be construed in accordance with section 341(4).

(7) Subsection (2) does not apply to a disclosure made to a nominated officer.

Interpretation

340. Interpretation

(1) This section applies for the purposes of this Part.

(2) Criminal conduct is conduct which—

(a) constitutes an offence in any part of the United Kingdom, or

(b) would constitute an offence in any part of the United Kingdom if it occurred there.

(3) Property is criminal property if—

(a) it constitutes a person's benefit from criminal conduct or it represents such a benefit (in whole or part and whether directly or indirectly), and

(b) the alleged offender knows or suspects that it constitutes or represents such a benefit.

(4) It is immaterial—
  (a) who carried out the conduct;
  (b) who benefited from it;
  (c) whether the conduct occurred before or after the passing of this Act.

(5) A person benefits from conduct if he obtains property as a result of or in connection with the conduct.

(6) If a person obtains a pecuniary advantage as a result of or in connection with conduct, he is to be taken to obtain as a result of or in connection with the conduct a sum of money equal to the value of the pecuniary advantage.

(7) References to property or a pecuniary advantage obtained in connection with conduct include references to property or a pecuniary advantage obtained in both that connection and some other.

(8) If a person benefits from conduct his benefit is the property obtained as a result of or in connection with the conduct.

(9) Property is all property wherever situated and includes—
  (a) money;
  (b) all forms of property, real or personal, heritable or moveable;
  (c) things in action and other intangible or incorporeal property.

(10) The following rules apply in relation to property—
  (a) property is obtained by a person if he obtains an interest in it;
  (b) references to an interest, in relation to land in England and Wales or Northern Ireland, are to any legal estate or equitable interest or power;
  (c) references to an interest, in relation to land in Scotland, are to any estate, interest, servitude or other heritable right in or over land, including a heritable security;
  (d) references to an interest, in relation to property other than land, include references to a right (including a right to possession).

(11) Money laundering is an act which—
  (a) constitutes an offence under section 327, 328 or 329,
  (b) constitutes an attempt, conspiracy or incitement to commit an offence specified in paragraph (a),
  (c) constitutes aiding, abetting, counselling or procuring the commission of an offence specified in paragraph (a), or
  (d) would constitute an offence specified in paragraph (a), (b) or (c) if done in the United Kingdom.

(12) For the purposes of a disclosure to a nominated officer—
  (a) references to a person's employer include any body, association or organisation (including a voluntary organisation) in connection with whose activities the person exercises a function (whether or not for gain or reward), and
  (b) references to employment must be construed accordingly.

(13) References to a constable include references to a person authorised for the purposes of this Part by the Director General of the National Criminal Intelligence Service.

PART 8
INVESTIGATIONS

CHAPTER 1
INTRODUCTION

341. Investigations

(1) For the purposes of this Part a confiscation investigation is an investigation into—
  (a) whether a person has benefited from his criminal conduct, or
  (b) the extent or whereabouts of his benefit from his criminal conduct.
(2) For the purposes of this Part a civil recovery investigation is an investigation into—
  (a) whether property is recoverable property or associated property,
  (b) who holds the property, or
  (c) its extent or whereabouts.
(3) But an investigation is not a civil recovery investigation if—
  (a) proceedings for a recovery order have been started in respect of the property in question,
  (b) an interim receiving order applies to the property in question,
  (c) an interim administration order applies to the property in question, or
  (d) the property in question is detained under section 295.
(4) For the purposes of this Part a money laundering investigation is an investigation into whether a person has committed a money laundering offence.

342. Offences of prejudicing investigation

(1) This section applies if a person knows or suspects that an appropriate officer or (in Scotland) a proper person is acting (or proposing to act) in connection with a confiscation investigation, a civil recovery investigation or a money laundering investigation which is being or is about to be conducted.
(2) The person commits an offence if—
  (a) he makes a disclosure which is likely to prejudice the investigation, or
  (b) he falsifies, conceals, destroys or otherwise disposes of, or causes or permits the falsification, concealment, destruction or disposal of, documents which are relevant to the investigation.
(3) A person does not commit an offence under subsection (2)(a) if—
  (a) he does not know or suspect that the disclosure is likely to prejudice the investigation,
  (b) the disclosure is made in the exercise of a function under this Act or any other enactment relating to criminal conduct or benefit from criminal conduct or in compliance with a requirement imposed under or by virtue of this Act, or
  (c) he is a professional legal adviser and the disclosure falls within subsection (4).
(4) A disclosure falls within this subsection if it is a disclosure—
  (a) to (or to a representative of) a client of the professional legal adviser in connection with the giving by the adviser of legal advice to the client, or
  (b) to any person in connection with legal proceedings or contemplated legal proceedings.
(5) But a disclosure does not fall within subsection (4) if it is made with the intention of furthering a criminal purpose.

(6) A person does not commit an offence under subsection (2)(b) if—
    (a) he does not know or suspect that the documents are relevant to the investigation, or
    (b) he does not intend to conceal any facts disclosed by the documents from any appropriate officer or (in Scotland) proper person carrying out the investigation.

(7) A person guilty of an offence under subsection (2) is liable—
    (a) on summary conviction, to imprisonment for a term not exceeding six months or to a fine not exceeding the statutory maximum or to both, or
    (b) on conviction on indictment, to imprisonment for a term not exceeding five years or to a fine or to both.

(8) For the purposes of this section—
    (a) 'appropriate officer' must be construed in accordance with section 378;
    (b) 'proper person' must be construed in accordance with section 412.

CHAPTER 2
ENGLAND AND WALES AND NORTHERN IRELAND

Judges and courts

343. Judges

(1) In this Chapter references to a judge in relation to an application must be construed in accordance with this section.

(2) In relation to an application for the purposes of a confiscation investigation or a money laundering investigation a judge is—
    (a) in England and Wales, a judge entitled to exercise the jurisdiction of the Crown Court;
    (b) in Northern Ireland, a Crown Court judge.

(3) In relation to an application for the purposes of a civil recovery investigation a judge is a judge of the High Court.

344. Courts

In this Chapter references to the court are to—
    (a) the Crown Court, in relation to an order for the purposes of a confiscation investigation or a money laundering investigation;
    (b) the High Court, in relation to an order for the purposes of a civil recovery investigation.

Production orders

345. Production orders

(1) A judge may, on an application made to him by an appropriate officer, make a production order if he is satisfied that each of the requirements for the making of the order is fulfilled.

(2) The application for a production order must state that—
    (a) a person specified in the application is subject to a confiscation investigation or a money laundering investigation, or

    (b) property specified in the application is subject to a civil recovery investigation.

(3) The application must also state that—

    (a) the order is sought for the purposes of the investigation;

    (b) the order is sought in relation to material, or material of a description, specified in the application;

    (c) a person specified in the application appears to be in possession or control of the material.

(4) A production order is an order either—

    (a) requiring the person the application for the order specifies as appearing to be in possession or control of material to produce it to an appropriate officer for him to take away, or

    (b) requiring that person to give an appropriate officer access to the material,

within the period stated in the order.

(5) The period stated in a production order must be a period of seven days beginning with the day on which the order is made, unless it appears to the judge by whom the order is made that a longer or shorter period would be appropriate in the particular circumstances.

346. Requirements for making of production order

(1) These are the requirements for the making of a production order.

(2) There must be reasonable grounds for suspecting that—

    (a) in the case of a confiscation investigation, the person the application for the order specifies as being subject to the investigation has benefited from his criminal conduct;

    (b) in the case of a civil recovery investigation, the property the application for the order specifies as being subject to the investigation is recoverable property or associated property;

    (c) in the case of a money laundering investigation, the person the application for the order specifies as being subject to the investigation has committed a money laundering offence.

(3) There must be reasonable grounds for believing that the person the application specifies as appearing to be in possession or control of the material so specified is in possession or control of it.

(4) There must be reasonable grounds for believing that the material is likely to be of substantial value (whether or not by itself) to the investigation for the purposes of which the order is sought.

(5) There must be reasonable grounds for believing that it is in the public interest for the material to be produced or for access to it to be given, having regard to—

    (a) the benefit likely to accrue to the investigation if the material is obtained;

    (b) the circumstances under which the person the application specifies as appearing to be in possession or control of the material holds it.

347. Order to grant entry

(1) This section applies if a judge makes a production order requiring a person to give an appropriate officer access to material on any premises.

(2) The judge may, on an application made to him by an appropriate officer and specifying the premises, make an order to grant entry in relation to the premises.

(3) An order to grant entry is an order requiring any person who appears to an appropriate officer to be entitled to grant entry to the premises to allow him to enter the premises to obtain access to the material.

348. Further provisions

(1) A production order does not require a person to produce, or give access to, privileged material.

(2) Privileged material is any material which the person would be entitled to refuse to produce on grounds of legal professional privilege in proceedings in the High Court.

(3) A production order does not require a person to produce, or give access to, excluded material.

(4) A production order has effect in spite of any restriction on the disclosure of information (however imposed).

(5) An appropriate officer may take copies of any material which is produced, or to which access is given, in compliance with a production order.

(6) Material produced in compliance with a production order may be retained for so long as it is necessary to retain it (as opposed to copies of it) in connection with the investigation for the purposes of which the order was made.

(7) But if an appropriate officer has reasonable grounds for believing that—

(a) the material may need to be produced for the purposes of any legal proceedings, and

(b) it might otherwise be unavailable for those purposes,

it may be retained until the proceedings are concluded.

349. Computer information

(1) This section applies if any of the material specified in an application for a production order consists of information contained in a computer.

(2) If the order is an order requiring a person to produce the material to an appropriate officer for him to take away, it has effect as an order to produce the material in a form in which it can be taken away by him and in which it is visible and legible.

(3) If the order is an order requiring a person to give an appropriate officer access to the material, it has effect as an order to give him access to the material in a form in which it is visible and legible.

350. Government departments

(1) A production order may be made in relation to material in the possession or control of an authorised government department.

(2) An order so made may require any officer of the department (whether named in the order or not) who may for the time being be in possession or control of the material to comply with it.

(3) An order containing such a requirement must be served as if the proceedings were civil proceedings against the department.

(4) If an order contains such a requirement—

(a) the person on whom it is served must take all reasonable steps to bring it to the attention of the officer concerned;

(b) any other officer of the department who is in receipt of the order must also take all reasonable steps to bring it to the attention of the officer concerned.

(5) If the order is not brought to the attention of the officer concerned within the period stated in the order (in pursuance of section 345(4)) the person on whom it is served must report the reasons for the failure to—

    (a) a judge entitled to exercise the jurisdiction of the Crown Court or (in Northern Ireland) a Crown Court judge, in the case of an order made for the purposes of a confiscation investigation or a money laundering investigation;

    (b) a High Court judge, in the case of an order made for the purposes of a civil recovery investigation.

(6) An authorised government department is a government department, or a Northern Ireland department, which is an authorised department for the purposes of the Crown Proceedings Act 1947 (c. 44).

351. Supplementary

(1) An application for a production order or an order to grant entry may be made ex parte to a judge in chambers.

(2) Rules of court may make provision as to the practice and procedure to be followed in connection with proceedings relating to production orders and orders to grant entry.

(3) An application to discharge or vary a production order or an order to grant entry may be made to the court by—

    (a) the person who applied for the order;

    (b) any person affected by the order.

(4) The court—

    (a) may discharge the order;

    (b) may vary the order.

(5) If an accredited financial investigator, a constable or a customs officer applies for a production order or an order to grant entry, an application to discharge or vary the order need not be by the same accredited financial investigator, constable or customs officer.

(6) References to a person who applied for a production order or an order to grant entry must be construed accordingly.

(7) Production orders and orders to grant entry have effect as if they were orders of the court.

(8) Subsections (2) to (7) do not apply to orders made in England and Wales for the purposes of a civil recovery investigation.

Search and seizure warrants

352. Search and seizure warrants

(1) A judge may, on an application made to him by an appropriate officer, issue a search and seizure warrant if he is satisfied that either of the requirements for the issuing of the warrant is fulfilled.

(2) The application for a search and seizure warrant must state that—

    (a) a person specified in the application is subject to a confiscation investigation or a money laundering investigation, or

    (b) property specified in the application is subject to a civil recovery investigation.

(3) The application must also state—

    (a) that the warrant is sought for the purposes of the investigation;

    (b) that the warrant is sought in relation to the premises specified in the application;

    (c) that the warrant is sought in relation to material specified in the application, or that there are reasonable grounds for believing that there is material falling within section 353(6), (7) or (8) on the premises.

(4) A search and seizure warrant is a warrant authorising an appropriate person—

    (a) to enter and search the premises specified in the application for the warrant, and

    (b) to seize and retain any material found there which is likely to be of substantial value (whether or not by itself) to the investigation for the purposes of which the application is made.

(5) An appropriate person is—

    (a) a constable or a customs officer, if the warrant is sought for the purposes of a confiscation investigation or a money laundering investigation;

    (b) a named member of the staff of the Agency, if the warrant is sought for the purposes of a civil recovery investigation.

(6) The requirements for the issue of a search and seizure warrant are—

    (a) that a production order made in relation to material has not been complied with and there are reasonable grounds for believing that the material is on the premises specified in the application for the warrant, or

    (b) that section 353 is satisfied in relation to the warrant.

353. Requirements where production order not available

(1) This section is satisfied in relation to a search and seizure warrant if—

    (a) subsection (2) applies, and

    (b) either the first or the second set of conditions is complied with.

(2) This subsection applies if there are reasonable grounds for suspecting that—

    (a) in the case of a confiscation investigation, the person specified in the application for the warrant has benefited from his criminal conduct;

    (b) in the case of a civil recovery investigation, the property specified in the application for the warrant is recoverable property or associated property;

    (c) in the case of a money laundering investigation, the person specified in the application for the warrant has committed a money laundering offence.

(3) The first set of conditions is that there are reasonable grounds for believing that—

    (a) any material on the premises specified in the application for the warrant is likely to be of substantial value (whether or not by itself) to the investigation for the purposes of which the warrant is sought,

    (b) it is in the public interest for the material to be obtained, having regard to the benefit likely to accrue to the investigation if the material is obtained, and

    (c) it would not be appropriate to make a production order for any one or more of the reasons in subsection (4).

(4) The reasons are—

    (a) that it is not practicable to communicate with any person against whom the production order could be made;

    (b) that it is not practicable to communicate with any person who would be required to comply with an order to grant entry to the premises;

    (c) that the investigation might be seriously prejudiced unless an appropriate person is able to secure immediate access to the material.

(5) The second set of conditions is that—
    (a) there are reasonable grounds for believing that there is material on the premises specified in the application for the warrant and that the material falls within subsection (6), (7) or (8),
    (b) there are reasonable grounds for believing that it is in the public interest for the material to be obtained, having regard to the benefit likely to accrue to the investigation if the material is obtained, and
    (c) any one or more of the requirements in subsection (9) is met.

(6) In the case of a confiscation investigation, material falls within this subsection if it cannot be identified at the time of the application but it—
    (a) relates to the person specified in the application, the question whether he has benefited from his criminal conduct or any question as to the extent or whereabouts of his benefit from his criminal conduct, and
    (b) is likely to be of substantial value (whether or not by itself) to the investigation for the purposes of which the warrant is sought.

(7) In the case of a civil recovery investigation, material falls within this subsection if it cannot be identified at the time of the application but it—
    (a) relates to the property specified in the application, the question whether it is recoverable property or associated property, the question as to who holds any such property, any question as to whether the person who appears to hold any such property holds other property which is recoverable property, or any question as to the extent or whereabouts of any property mentioned in this paragraph, and
    (b) is likely to be of substantial value (whether or not by itself) to the investigation for the purposes of which the warrant is sought.

(8) In the case of a money laundering investigation, material falls within this subsection if it cannot be identified at the time of the application but it—
    (a) relates to the person specified in the application or the question whether he has committed a money laundering offence, and
    (b) is likely to be of substantial value (whether or not by itself) to the investigation for the purposes of which the warrant is sought.

(9) The requirements are—
    (a) that it is not practicable to communicate with any person entitled to grant entry to the premises;
    (b) that entry to the premises will not be granted unless a warrant is produced;
    (c) that the investigation might be seriously prejudiced unless an appropriate person arriving at the premises is able to secure immediate entry to them.

(10) An appropriate person is—
    (a) a constable or a customs officer, if the warrant is sought for the purposes of a confiscation investigation or a money laundering investigation;
    (b) a member of the staff of the Agency, if the warrant is sought for the purposes of a civil recovery investigation.

354. Further provisions: general

(1) A search and seizure warrant does not confer the right to seize privileged material.
(2) Privileged material is any material which a person would be entitled to refuse to produce on grounds of legal professional privilege in proceedings in the High Court.
(3) A search and seizure warrant does not confer the right to seize excluded material.

355. Further provisions: confiscation and money laundering

(1) This section applies to—
    (a) search and seizure warrants sought for the purposes of a confiscation investigation or a money laundering investigation, and
    (b) powers of seizure under them.

(2) In relation to such warrants and powers, the Secretary of State may make an order which applies the provisions to which subsections (3) and (4) apply subject to any specified modifications.

(3) This subsection applies to the following provisions of the Police and Criminal Evidence Act 1984 (c. 60)—
    (a) section 15 (search warrants—safeguards);
    (b) section 16 (execution of warrants);
    (c) section 21 (access and copying);
    (d) section 22 (retention).

(4) This subsection applies to the following provisions of the Police and Criminal Evidence (Northern Ireland) Order 1989 (S.I. 1989/1341 (N.I. 12))—
    (a) Article 17 (search warrants—safeguards);
    (b) Article 18 (execution of warrants);
    (c) Article 23 (access and copying);
    (d) Article 24 (retention).

356. Further provisions: civil recovery

(1) This section applies to search and seizure warrants sought for the purposes of civil recovery investigations.

(2) An application for a warrant may be made ex parte to a judge in chambers.

(3) A warrant may be issued subject to conditions.

(4) A warrant continues in force until the end of the period of one month starting with the day on which it is issued.

(5) A warrant authorises the person it names to require any information which is held in a computer and is accessible from the premises specified in the application for the warrant, and which the named person believes relates to any matter relevant to the investigation, to be produced in a form—
    (a) in which it can be taken away, and
    (b) in which it is visible and legible.

(6) If—
    (a) the Director gives written authority for members of staff of the Agency to accompany the person a warrant names when executing it, and
    (b) a warrant is issued,
the authorised members have the same powers under it as the person it names.

(7) A warrant may include provision authorising a person who is exercising powers under it to do other things which—
    (a) are specified in the warrant, and
    (b) need to be done in order to give effect to it.

(8) Copies may be taken of any material seized under a warrant.

(9) Material seized under a warrant may be retained for so long as it is necessary to retain it (as opposed to copies of it) in connection with the investigation for the purposes of which the warrant was issued.

(10) But if the Director has reasonable grounds for believing that—
- (a) the material may need to be produced for the purposes of any legal proceedings, and
- (b) it might otherwise be unavailable for those purposes,

it may be retained until the proceedings are concluded.

Disclosure orders

357. Disclosure orders

(1) A judge may, on an application made to him by the Director, make a disclosure order if he is satisfied that each of the requirements for the making of the order is fulfilled.

(2) No application for a disclosure order may be made in relation to a money laundering investigation.

(3) The application for a disclosure order must state that—
- (a) a person specified in the application is subject to a confiscation investigation which is being carried out by the Director and the order is sought for the purposes of the investigation, or
- (b) property specified in the application is subject to a civil recovery investigation and the order is sought for the purposes of the investigation.

(4) A disclosure order is an order authorising the Director to give to any person the Director considers has relevant information notice in writing requiring him to do, with respect to any matter relevant to the investigation for the purposes of which the order is sought, any or all of the following—
- (a) answer questions, either at a time specified in the notice or at once, at a place so specified;
- (b) provide information specified in the notice, by a time and in a manner so specified;
- (c) produce documents, or documents of a description, specified in the notice, either at or by a time so specified or at once, and in a manner so specified.

(5) Relevant information is information (whether or not contained in a document) which the Director considers to be relevant to the investigation.

(6) A person is not bound to comply with a requirement imposed by a notice given under a disclosure order unless evidence of authority to give the notice is produced to him.

358. Requirements for making of disclosure order

(1) These are the requirements for the making of a disclosure order.

(2) There must be reasonable grounds for suspecting that—
- (a) in the case of a confiscation investigation, the person specified in the application for the order has benefited from his criminal conduct;
- (b) in the case of a civil recovery investigation, the property specified in the application for the order is recoverable property or associated property.

(3) There must be reasonable grounds for believing that information which may be provided in compliance with a requirement imposed under the order is likely to be of substantial value (whether or not by itself) to the investigation for the purposes of which the order is sought.

(4) There must be reasonable grounds for believing that it is in the public interest for the information to be provided, having regard to the benefit likely to accrue to the investigation if the information is obtained.

359. Offences

(1) A person commits an offence if without reasonable excuse he fails to comply with a requirement imposed on him under a disclosure order.

(2) A person guilty of an offence under subsection (1) is liable on summary conviction to—

    (a) imprisonment for a term not exceeding six months,

    (b) a fine not exceeding level 5 on the standard scale, or

    (c) both.

(3) A person commits an offence if, in purported compliance with a requirement imposed on him under a disclosure order, he—

    (a) makes a statement which he knows to be false or misleading in a material particular, or

    (b) recklessly makes a statement which is false or misleading in a material particular.

(4) A person guilty of an offence under subsection (3) is liable—

    (a) on summary conviction, to imprisonment for a term not exceeding six months or to a fine not exceeding the statutory maximum or to both, or

    (b) on conviction on indictment, to imprisonment for a term not exceeding two years or to a fine or to both.

360. Statements

(1) A statement made by a person in response to a requirement imposed on him under a disclosure order may not be used in evidence against him in criminal proceedings.

(2) But subsection (1) does not apply—

    (a) in the case of proceedings under Part 2 or 4,

    (b) on a prosecution for an offence under section 359(1) or (3),

    (c) on a prosecution for an offence under section 5 of the Perjury Act 1911 (c. 6) or Article 10 of the Perjury (Northern Ireland) Order 1979 (S.I. 1979/1714 (N.I. 19)) (false statements), or

    (d) on a prosecution for some other offence where, in giving evidence, the person makes a statement inconsistent with the statement mentioned in subsection (1).

(3) A statement may not be used by virtue of subsection (2)(d) against a person unless—

    (a) evidence relating to it is adduced, or

    (b) a question relating to it is asked,

by him or on his behalf in the proceedings arising out of the prosecution.

361. Further provisions

(1) A disclosure order does not confer the right to require a person to answer any privileged question, provide any privileged information or produce any privileged document, except that a lawyer may be required to provide the name and address of a client of his.

(2) A privileged question is a question which the person would be entitled to refuse to answer on grounds of legal professional privilege in proceedings in the High Court.

(3) Privileged information is any information which the person would be entitled to refuse to provide on grounds of legal professional privilege in proceedings in the High Court.

(4) Privileged material is any material which the person would be entitled to refuse to produce on grounds of legal professional privilege in proceedings in the High Court.

(5) A disclosure order does not confer the right to require a person to produce excluded material.

(6) A disclosure order has effect in spite of any restriction on the disclosure of information (however imposed).

(7) The Director may take copies of any documents produced in compliance with a requirement to produce them which is imposed under a disclosure order.

(8) Documents so produced may be retained for so long as it is necessary to retain them (as opposed to a copy of them) in connection with the investigation for the purposes of which the order was made.

(9) But if the Director has reasonable grounds for believing that—
  (a) the documents may need to be produced for the purposes of any legal proceedings, and
  (b) they might otherwise be unavailable for those purposes,
they may be retained until the proceedings are concluded.

362. Supplementary

(1) An application for a disclosure order may be made ex parte to a judge in chambers.

(2) Rules of court may make provision as to the practice and procedure to be followed in connection with proceedings relating to disclosure orders.

(3) An application to discharge or vary a disclosure order may be made to the court by—
  (a) the Director;
  (b) any person affected by the order.

(4) The court—
  (a) may discharge the order;
  (b) may vary the order.

(5) Subsections (2) to (4) do not apply to orders made in England and Wales for the purposes of a civil recovery investigation.

Customer information orders

363. Customer information orders

(1) A judge may, on an application made to him by an appropriate officer, make a customer information order if he is satisfied that each of the requirements for the making of the order is fulfilled.

(2) The application for a customer information order must state that—
  (a) a person specified in the application is subject to a confiscation investigation or a money laundering investigation, or
  (b) property specified in the application is subject to a civil recovery investigation and a person specified in the application appears to hold the property.

(3) The application must also state that—
  (a) the order is sought for the purposes of the investigation;

    (b) the order is sought against the financial institution or financial institutions specified in the application.

(4) An application for a customer information order may specify—

    (a) all financial institutions,

    (b) a particular description, or particular descriptions, of financial institutions, or

    (c) a particular financial institution or particular financial institutions.

(5) A customer information order is an order that a financial institution covered by the application for the order must, on being required to do so by notice in writing given by an appropriate officer, provide any such customer information as it has relating to the person specified in the application.

(6) A financial institution which is required to provide information under a customer information order must provide the information to an appropriate officer in such manner, and at or by such time, as an appropriate officer requires.

(7) If a financial institution on which a requirement is imposed by a notice given under a customer information order requires the production of evidence of authority to give the notice, it is not bound to comply with the requirement unless evidence of the authority has been produced to it.

364. Meaning of customer information

(1) 'Customer information', in relation to a person and a financial institution, is information whether the person holds, or has held, an account or accounts at the financial institution (whether solely or jointly with another) and (if so) information as to—

    (a) the matters specified in subsection (2) if the person is an individual;

    (b) the matters specified in subsection (3) if the person is a company or limited liability partnership or a similar body incorporated or otherwise established outside the United Kingdom.

(2) The matters referred to in subsection (1)(a) are—

    (a) the account number or numbers;

    (b) the person's full name;

    (c) his date of birth;

    (d) his most recent address and any previous addresses;

    (e) the date or dates on which he began to hold the account or accounts and, if he has ceased to hold the account or any of the accounts, the date or dates on which he did so;

    (f) such evidence of his identity as was obtained by the financial institution under or for the purposes of any legislation relating to money laundering;

    (g) the full name, date of birth and most recent address, and any previous addresses, of any person who holds, or has held, an account at the financial institution jointly with him;

    (h) the account number or numbers of any other account or accounts held at the financial institution to which he is a signatory and details of the person holding the other account or accounts.

(3) The matters referred to in subsection (1)(b) are—

    (a) the account number or numbers;

    (b) the person's full name;

    (c) a description of any business which the person carries on;

(d) the country or territory in which it is incorporated or otherwise established and any number allocated to it under the Companies Act 1985 (c. 6) or the Companies (Northern Ireland) Order 1986 (S.I. 1986/ 1032 (N.I. 6)) or corresponding legislation of any country or territory outside the United Kingdom;

(e) any number assigned to it for the purposes of value added tax in the United Kingdom;

(f) its registered office, and any previous registered offices, under the Companies Act 1985 or the Companies (Northern Ireland) Order 1986 (S.I. 1986/1032 (N.I. 6)) or anything similar under corresponding legislation of any country or territory outside the United Kingdom;

(g) its registered office, and any previous registered offices, under the Limited Liability Partnerships Act 2000 (c. 12) or anything similar under corresponding legislation of any country or territory outside Great Britain;

(h) the date or dates on which it began to hold the account or accounts and, if it has ceased to hold the account or any of the accounts, the date or dates on which it did so;

(i) such evidence of its identity as was obtained by the financial institution under or for the purposes of any legislation relating to money laundering;

(j) the full name, date of birth and most recent address and any previous addresses of any person who is a signatory to the account or any of the accounts.

(4) The Secretary of State may by order provide for information of a description specified in the order—
(a) to be customer information, or
(b) no longer to be customer information.

(5) Money laundering is an act which—
(a) constitutes an offence under section 327, 328 or 329 of this Act or section 18 of the Terrorism Act 2000 (c. 11), or
(b) would constitute an offence specified in paragraph (a) if done in the United Kingdom.

365. Requirements for making of customer information order

(1) These are the requirements for the making of a customer information order.

(2) In the case of a confiscation investigation, there must be reasonable grounds for suspecting that the person specified in the application for the order has benefited from his criminal conduct.

(3) In the case of a civil recovery investigation, there must be reasonable grounds for suspecting that—
(a) the property specified in the application for the order is recoverable property or associated property;
(b) the person specified in the application holds all or some of the property.

(4) In the case of a money laundering investigation, there must be reasonable grounds for suspecting that the person specified in the application for the order has committed a money laundering offence.

(5) In the case of any investigation, there must be reasonable grounds for believing that customer information which may be provided in compliance with the order is likely to be of substantial value (whether or not by itself) to the investigation for the purposes of which the order is sought.

(6) In the case of any investigation, there must be reasonable grounds for believing that it is in the public interest for the customer information to be provided, having regard to the benefit likely to accrue to the investigation if the information is obtained.

366. Offences

(1) A financial institution commits an offence if without reasonable excuse it fails to comply with a requirement imposed on it under a customer information order.

(2) A financial institution guilty of an offence under subsection (1) is liable on summary conviction to a fine not exceeding level 5 on the standard scale.

(3) A financial institution commits an offence if, in purported compliance with a customer information order, it—

    (a) makes a statement which it knows to be false or misleading in a material particular, or

    (b) recklessly makes a statement which is false or misleading in a material particular.

(4) A financial institution guilty of an offence under subsection (3) is liable—

    (a) on summary conviction, to a fine not exceeding the statutory maximum, or

    (b) on conviction on indictment, to a fine.

367. Statements

(1) A statement made by a financial institution in response to a customer information order may not be used in evidence against it in criminal proceedings.

(2) But subsection (1) does not apply—

    (a) in the case of proceedings under Part 2 or 4,

    (b) on a prosecution for an offence under section 366(1) or (3), or

    (c) on a prosecution for some other offence where, in giving evidence, the financial institution makes a statement inconsistent with the statement mentioned in subsection (1).

(3) A statement may not be used by virtue of subsection (2)(c) against a financial institution unless—

    (a) evidence relating to it is adduced, or

    (b) a question relating to it is asked,

by or on behalf of the financial institution in the proceedings arising out of the prosecution.

368. Disclosure of information

A customer information order has effect in spite of any restriction on the disclosure of information (however imposed).

369. Supplementary

(1) An application for a customer information order may be made ex parte to a judge in chambers.

(2) Rules of court may make provision as to the practice and procedure to be followed in connection with proceedings relating to customer information orders.

(3) An application to discharge or vary a customer information order may be made to the court by—

(a) the person who applied for the order;

(b) any person affected by the order.

(4) The court—

(a) may discharge the order;

(b) may vary the order.

(5) If an accredited financial investigator, a constable or a customs officer applies for a customer information order, an application to discharge or vary the order need not be by the same accredited financial investigator, constable or customs officer.

(6) References to a person who applied for a customer information order must be construed accordingly.

(7) An accredited financial investigator, a constable or a customs officer may not make an application for a customer information order or an application to vary such an order unless he is a senior appropriate officer or he is authorised to do so by a senior appropriate officer.

(8) Subsections (2) to (6) do not apply to orders made in England and Wales for the purposes of a civil recovery investigation.

Account monitoring orders

370. Account monitoring orders

(1) A judge may, on an application made to him by an appropriate officer, make an account monitoring order if he is satisfied that each of the requirements for the making of the order is fulfilled.

(2) The application for an account monitoring order must state that—

(a) a person specified in the application is subject to a confiscation investigation or a money laundering investigation, or

(b) property specified in the application is subject to a civil recovery investigation and a person specified in the application appears to hold the property.

(3) The application must also state that—

(a) the order is sought for the purposes of the investigation;

(b) the order is sought against the financial institution specified in the application in relation to account information of the description so specified.

(4) Account information is information relating to an account or accounts held at the financial institution specified in the application by the person so specified (whether solely or jointly with another).

(5) The application for an account monitoring order may specify information relating to—

(a) all accounts held by the person specified in the application for the order at the financial institution so specified,

(b) a particular description, or particular descriptions, of accounts so held, or

(c) a particular account, or particular accounts, so held.

(6) An account monitoring order is an order that the financial institution specified in the application for the order must, for the period stated in the order, provide account information of the description specified in the order to an appropriate officer in the manner, and at or by the time or times, stated in the order.

(7) The period stated in an account monitoring order must not exceed the period of 90 days beginning with the day on which the order is made.

371. Requirements for making of account monitoring order

(1) These are the requirements for the making of an account monitoring order.

(2) In the case of a confiscation investigation, there must be reasonable grounds for suspecting that the person specified in the application for the order has benefited from his criminal conduct.

(3) In the case of a civil recovery investigation, there must be reasonable grounds for suspecting that—

    (a) the property specified in the application for the order is recoverable property or associated property;

    (b) the person specified in the application holds all or some of the property.

(4) In the case of a money laundering investigation, there must be reasonable grounds for suspecting that the person specified in the application for the order has committed a money laundering offence.

(5) In the case of any investigation, there must be reasonable grounds for believing that account information which may be provided in compliance with the order is likely to be of substantial value (whether or not by itself) to the investigation for the purposes of which the order is sought.

(6) In the case of any investigation, there must be reasonable grounds for believing that it is in the public interest for the account information to be provided, having regard to the benefit likely to accrue to the investigation if the information is obtained.

372. Statements

(1) A statement made by a financial institution in response to an account monitoring order may not be used in evidence against it in criminal proceedings.

(2) But subsection (1) does not apply—

    (a) in the case of proceedings under Part 2 or 4,

    (b) in the case of proceedings for contempt of court, or

    (c) on a prosecution for an offence where, in giving evidence, the financial institution makes a statement inconsistent with the statement mentioned in subsection (1).

(3) A statement may not be used by virtue of subsection (2)(c) against a financial institution unless—

    (a) evidence relating to it is adduced, or

    (b) a question relating to it is asked,

by or on behalf of the financial institution in the proceedings arising out of the prosecution.

373. Applications

An application for an account monitoring order may be made ex parte to a judge in chambers.

374. Disclosure of information

An account monitoring order has effect in spite of any restriction on the disclosure of information (however imposed).

375. Supplementary

(1) Rules of court may make provision as to the practice and procedure to be followed in connection with proceedings relating to account monitoring orders.

(2) An application to discharge or vary an account monitoring order may be made to the court by—
    (a) the person who applied for the order;
    (b) any person affected by the order.
(3) The court—
    (a) may discharge the order;
    (b) may vary the order.
(4) If an accredited financial investigator, a constable or a customs officer applies for an account monitoring order, an application to discharge or vary the order need not be by the same accredited financial investigator, constable or customs officer.
(5) References to a person who applied for an account monitoring order must be construed accordingly.
(6) Account monitoring orders have effect as if they were orders of the court.
(7) This section does not apply to orders made in England and Wales for the purposes of a civil recovery investigation.

Evidence overseas

376. Evidence overseas

(1) This section applies if the Director is carrying out a confiscation investigation.
(2) A judge on the application of the Director or a person subject to the investigation may issue a letter of request if he thinks that there is evidence in a country or territory outside the United Kingdom—
    (a) that such a person has benefited from his criminal conduct, or
    (b) of the extent or whereabouts of that person's benefit from his criminal conduct.
(3) The Director may issue a letter of request if he thinks that there is evidence in a country or territory outside the United Kingdom—
    (a) that a person subject to the investigation has benefited from his criminal conduct, or
    (b) of the extent or whereabouts of that person's benefit from his criminal conduct.
(4) A letter of request is a letter requesting assistance in obtaining outside the United Kingdom such evidence as is specified in the letter for use in the investigation.
(5) The person issuing a letter of request must send it to the Secretary of State.
(6) If the Secretary of State believes it is appropriate to do so he may forward a letter received under subsection (5)—
    (a) to a court or tribunal which is specified in the letter and which exercises jurisdiction in the place where the evidence is to be obtained, or
    (b) to an authority recognised by the government of the country or territory concerned as the appropriate authority for receiving letters of request.
(7) But in a case of urgency the person issuing the letter of request may send it directly to the court or tribunal mentioned in subsection (6)(a).
(8) Evidence obtained in pursuance of a letter of request must not be used—
    (a) by any person other than the Director or a person subject to the investigation;
    (b) for any purpose other than that for which it is obtained.
(9) Subsection (8) does not apply if the authority mentioned in subsection (6)(b) consents to the use.
(10) Evidence includes documents and other articles.

(11) Rules of court may make provision as to the practice and procedure to be followed in connection with proceedings relating to the issue of letters of request by a judge under this section.

Code of practice

377. Code of practice

(1) The Secretary of State must prepare a code of practice as to the exercise by all of the following of functions they have under this Chapter—
  (a) the Director;
  (b) members of the staff of the Agency;
  (c) accredited financial investigators;
  (d) constables;
  (e) customs officers.
(2) After preparing a draft of the code the Secretary of State—
  (a) must publish the draft;
  (b) must consider any representations made to him about the draft;
  (c) may amend the draft accordingly.
(3) After the Secretary of State has proceeded under subsection (2) he must lay the code before Parliament.
(4) When he has done so the Secretary of State may bring the code into operation on such day as he may appoint by order.
(5) A person specified in subsection (1)(a) to (e) must comply with a code of practice which is in operation under this section in the exercise of any function he has under this Chapter.
(6) If such a person fails to comply with any provision of such a code of practice he is not by reason only of that failure liable in any criminal or civil proceedings.
(7) But the code of practice is admissible in evidence in such proceedings and a court may take account of any failure to comply with its provisions in determining any question in the proceedings.
(8) The Secretary of State may from time to time revise a code previously brought into operation under this section; and the preceding provisions of this section apply to a revised code as they apply to the code as first prepared.
(9) The following provisions do not apply to an appropriate officer in the exercise of any function he has under this Chapter—
  (a) section 67(9) of the Police and Criminal Evidence Act 1984 (c. 60) (application of codes of practice under that Act to persons other than police officers);
  (b) Article 66(8) of the Police and Criminal Evidence (Northern Ireland) Order 1989 (S.I. 1989/1341 (N.I. 12)) (which makes similar provision for Northern Ireland).

Interpretation

378. Officers

(1) In relation1 to a confiscation investigation these are appropriate officers—
  (a) the Director;
  (b) an accredited financial investigator;

   (c) a constable;

   (d) a customs officer.

(2) In relation to a confiscation investigation these are senior appropriate officers—

   (a) the Director;

   (b) a police officer who is not below the rank of superintendent;

   (c) a customs officer who is not below such grade as is designated by the Commissioners of Customs and Excise as equivalent to that rank;

   (d) an accredited financial investigator who falls within a description specified in an order made for the purposes of this paragraph by the Secretary of State under section 453.

(3) In relation to a civil recovery investigation the Director (and only the Director) is—

   (a) an appropriate officer;

   (b) a senior appropriate officer.

(4) In relation to a money laundering investigation these are appropriate officers—

   (a) an accredited financial investigator;

   (b) a constable;

   (c) a customs officer.

(5) For the purposes of section 342, in relation to a money laundering investigation a person authorised for the purposes of money laundering investigations by the Director General of the National Criminal Intelligence Service is also an appropriate officer.

(6) In relation to a money laundering investigation these are senior appropriate officers—

   (a) a police officer who is not below the rank of superintendent;

   (b) a customs officer who is not below such grade as is designated by the Commissioners of Customs and Excise as equivalent to that rank;

   (c) an accredited financial investigator who falls within a description specified in an order made for the purposes of this paragraph by the Secretary of State under section 453.

(7) But a person is not an appropriate officer or a senior appropriate officer in relation to a money laundering investigation if he is—

   (a) a member of the staff of the Agency, or

   (b) a person providing services under arrangements made by the Director.

379. Miscellaneous

'Document', 'excluded material' and 'premises' have the same meanings as in the Police and Criminal Evidence Act 1984 (c. 60) or (in relation to Northern Ireland) the Police and Criminal Evidence (Northern Ireland) Order 1989 (S.I. 1989/1341 (N.I. 12)).

CHAPTER 3
SCOTLAND

. . .

CHAPTER 4
INTERPRETATION

413. Criminal conduct

(1) Criminal conduct is conduct which—
    (a) constitutes an offence in any part of the United Kingdom, or
    (b) would constitute an offence in any part of the United Kingdom if it occurred there.

(2) A person benefits from conduct if he obtains property or a pecuniary advantage as a result of or in connection with the conduct.

(3) References to property or a pecuniary advantage obtained in connection with conduct include references to property or a pecuniary advantage obtained in both that connection and some other.

(4) If a person benefits from conduct his benefit is the property or pecuniary advantage obtained as a result of or in connection with the conduct.

(5) It is immaterial—
    (a) whether conduct occurred before or after the passing of this Act, and
    (b) whether property or a pecuniary advantage constituting a benefit from conduct was obtained before or after the passing of this Act.

414. Property

(1) Property is all property wherever situated and includes—
    (a) money;
    (b) all forms of property, real or personal, heritable or moveable;
    (c) things in action and other intangible or incorporeal property.

(2) 'Recoverable property' and 'associated property' have the same meanings as in Part 5.

(3) The following rules apply in relation to property—
    (a) property is obtained by a person if he obtains an interest in it;
    (b) references to an interest, in relation to land in England and Wales or Northern Ireland, are to any legal estate or equitable interest or power;
    (c) references to an interest, in relation to land in Scotland, are to any estate, interest, servitude or other heritable right in or over land, including a heritable security;
    (d) references to an interest, in relation to property other than land, include references to a right (including a right to possession).

415. Money laundering offences

(1) An offence under section 327, 328 or 329 is a money laundering offence.

(2) Each of the following is a money laundering offence—
    (a) an attempt, conspiracy or incitement to commit an offence specified in subsection (1);
    (b) aiding, abetting, counselling or procuring the commission of an offence specified in subsection (1).

416. Other interpretative provisions

(1) These expressions are to be construed in accordance with these provisions of this Part—

civil recovery investigation: section 341(2) and (3)

confiscation investigation: section 341(1)

money laundering investigation: section 341(4)

(2) In the application of this Part to England and Wales and Northern Ireland, these expressions are to be construed in accordance with these provisions of this Part—

account information: section 370(4)

account monitoring order: section 370(6)

appropriate officer: section 378

customer information: section 364

customer information order: section 363(5)

disclosure order: section 357(4)

document: section 379

order to grant entry: section 347(3)

production order: section 345(4)

search and seizure warrant: section 352(4)

senior appropriate officer: section 378.

(3) In the application of this Part to Scotland, these expressions are to be construed in accordance with these provisions of this Part—

account information: section 404(5)

account monitoring order: section 404(7)

customer information: section 398

customer information order: section 397(6)

disclosure order: section 391(4)

production order: section 380(5)

proper person: section 412

search warrant: section 387(4).

(4) 'Financial institution' means a person carrying on a business in the regulated sector.

(5) But a person who ceases to carry on a business in the regulated sector (whether by virtue of paragraph 5 of Schedule 9 or otherwise) is to continue to be treated as a financial institution for the purposes of any requirement under—

(a) a customer information order, or

(b) an account monitoring order,

to provide information which relates to a time when the person was a financial institution.

(6) References to a business in the regulated sector must be construed in accordance with Schedule 9.

(7) 'Recovery order', 'interim receiving order' and 'interim administration order' have the same meanings as in Part 5.

(8) References to notice in writing include references to notice given by electronic means.

(9) This section and sections 413 to 415 apply for the purposes of this Part.

PART 9

INSOLVENCY ETC.

Bankruptcy in England and Wales

417. Modifications of the 1986 Act

(1) This section applies if a person is adjudged bankrupt in England and Wales.

(2) the following property is excluded from his estate for the purposes of Part 9 of the 1986 Act—

    (a) property for the time being subject to a restraint order which was made under section 41, 120 or 190 before the order adjudging him bankrupt;

    (b) any property in respect of which an order under section 50 or 52 is in force;

    (c) any property in respect of which an order under section 128(3) is in force;

    (d) any property in respect of which an order under section 198 or 200 is in force.

(3) Subsection (2)(a) applies to heritable property in Scotland only if the restraint order is recorded in the General Register of Sasines or registered in the Land Register of Scotland before the order adjudging the person bankrupt.

(4) If in the case of a debtor an interim receiver stands at any time appointed under section 286 of the 1986 Act and any property of the debtor is then subject to a restraint order made under section 41, 120 or 190 the powers conferred on the receiver by virtue of that Act do not apply to property then subject to the restraint order.

418. Restriction of powers

(1) If a person is adjudged bankrupt in England and Wales the powers referred to in subsection (2) must not be exercised in relation to the property referred to in subsection (3).

(2) These are the powers—

    (a) the powers conferred on a court by sections 41 to 67 and the powers of a receiver appointed under section 48, 50 or 52;

    (b) the powers conferred on a court by sections 120 to 136 and Schedule 3 and the powers of an administrator appointed under section 125 or 128(3);

    (c) the powers conferred on a court by sections 190 to 215 and the powers of a receiver appointed under section 196, 198 or 200.

(3) This is the property—

    (a) property which is for the time being comprised in the bankrupt's estate for the purposes of Part 9 of the 1986 Act;

    (b) property in respect of which his trustee in bankruptcy may (without leave of the court) serve a notice under section 307, 308 or 308A of the 1986 Act (after-acquired property, tools, tenancies etc);

    (c) property which is to be applied for the benefit of creditors of the bankrupt by virtue of a condition imposed under section 280(2)(c) of the 1986 Act;

    (d) in a case where a confiscation order has been made under section 6 or 156 of this Act, any sums remaining in the hands of a receiver appointed under section 50, 52, 198 or 200 of this Act after the amount required to be paid under the confiscation order has been fully paid;

    (e) in a case where a confiscation order has been made under section 92 of this Act, any sums remaining in the hands of an administrator appointed under section

128 of this Act after the amount required to be paid under the confiscation order has been fully paid.

(4) But nothing in the 1986 Act must be taken to restrict (or enable the restriction of) the powers referred to in subsection (2).

(5) In a case where a petition in bankruptcy was presented or a receiving order or adjudication in bankruptcy was made before 29 December 1986 (when the 1986 Act came into force) this section has effect with these modifications—

   (a) for the reference in subsection (3)(a) to the bankrupt's estate for the purposes of Part 9 of that Act substitute a reference to the property of the bankrupt for the purposes of the 1914 Act;

   (b) omit subsection (3)(b);

   (c) for the reference in subsection (3)(c) to section 280(2)(c) of the 1986 Act substitute a reference to section 26(2) of the 1914 Act;

   (d) for the reference in subsection (4) to the 1986 Act substitute a reference to the 1914 Act.

419. Tainted gifts

(1) This section applies if a person who is adjudged bankrupt in England and Wales has made a tainted gift (whether directly or indirectly).

(2) No order may be made under section 339, 340 or 423 of the 1986 Act (avoidance of certain transactions) in respect of the making of the gift at any time when—

   (a) any property of the recipient of the tainted gift is subject to a restraint order under section 41, 120 or 190, or

   (b) there is in force in respect of such property an order under section 50, 52, 128(3), 198 or 200.

(3) Any order made under section 339, 340 or 423 of the 1986 Act after an order mentioned in subsection (2)(a) or (b) is discharged must take into account any realisation under Part 2, 3 or 4 of this Act of property held by the recipient of the tainted gift.

(4) A person makes a tainted gift for the purposes of this section if he makes a tainted gift within the meaning of Part 2, 3 or 4.

(5) In a case where a petition in bankruptcy was presented or a receiving order or adjudication in bankruptcy was made before 29 December 1986 (when the 1986 Act came into force) this section has effect with the substitution for a reference to section 339, 340 or 423 of the 1986 Act of a reference to section 27, 42 or 44 of the 1914 Act.

Sequestration in Scotland

420. Modifications of the 1985 Act

(1) This section applies if an award of sequestration is made in Scotland.

(2) The following property is excluded from the debtor's estate for the purposes of the 1985 Act—

   (a) property for the time being subject to a restraint order which was made under section 41, 120 or 190 before the award of sequestration;

   (b) any property in respect of which an order under section 50 or 52 is in force;

   (c) any property in respect of which an order under section 128(3) is in force;

(d) any property in respect of which an order under section 198 or 200 is in force.

(3) Subsection (2)(a) applies to heritable property in Scotland only if the restraint order is recorded in the General Register of Sasines or registered in the Land Register of Scotland before the award of sequestration.

(4) It shall not be competent to submit a claim in relation to a confiscation order to the permanent trustee in accordance with section 48 of the 1985 Act; and the reference here to a confiscation order is to any confiscation order that has been or may be made against the debtor under Part 2, 3 or 4 of this Act.

(5) If at any time in the period before the award of sequestration is made an interim trustee stands appointed under section 2(5) of the 1985 Act and any property in the debtor's estate is at that time subject to a restraint order made under section 41, 120 or 190, the powers conferred on the trustee by virtue of that Act do not apply to property then subject to the restraint order.

421. Restriction of powers

(1) If an award of sequestration is made in Scotland the powers referred to in subsection (2) must not be exercised in relation to the property referred to in subsection (3).

(2) These are the powers—
  (a) the powers conferred on a court by sections 41 to 67 and the powers of a receiver appointed under section 48, 50 or 52;
  (b) the powers conferred on a court by sections 120 to 136 and Schedule 3 and the powers of an administrator appointed under section 125 or 128(3);
  (c) the powers conferred on a court by sections 190 to 215 and the powers of a receiver appointed under section 196, 198 or 200.

(3) This is the property—
  (a) property which is for the time being comprised in the whole estate of the debtor within the meaning of section 31(8) of the 1985 Act;
  (b) any income of the debtor which has been ordered under section 32(2) of that Act to be paid to the permanent trustee;
  (c) any estate which under section 31(10) or 32(6) of that Act vests in the permanent trustee;
  (d) in a case where a confiscation order has been made under section 6 or 156 of this Act, any sums remaining in the hands of a receiver appointed under section 50, 52, 198 or 200 of this Act after the amount required to be paid under the confiscation order has been fully paid;
  (e) in a case where a confiscation order has been made under section 92 of this Act, any sums remaining in the hands of an administrator appointed under section 128 of this Act after the amount required to be paid under the confiscation order has been fully paid.

(4) But nothing in the 1985 Act must be taken to restrict (or enable the restriction of) the powers referred to in subsection (2).

(5) In a case where (despite the coming into force of the 1985 Act) the 1913 Act applies to a sequestration, subsection (3) above has effect as if for paragraphs (a) to (c) there were substituted—
  '(a) property which is for the time being comprised in the whole property of the debtor which vests in the trustee under section 97 of the 1913 Act;

(b) any income of the bankrupt which has been ordered under section 98(2) of that Act to be paid to the trustee;

(c) any estate which under section 98(1) of that Act vests in the trustee.'

(6) In a case where subsection (5) applies, subsection (4) has effect as if for the reference to the 1985 Act there were substituted a reference to the 1913 Act.

422. Tainted gifts

(1) This section applies if a person whose estate is sequestrated in Scotland has made a tainted gift (whether directly or indirectly).

(2) No decree may be granted under the Bankruptcy Act 1621 (c. 18) or section 34 or 36 of the 1985 Act (gratuitous alienations and unfair preferences), or otherwise, in respect of the making of the gift at any time when—

(a) any property of the recipient of the tainted gift is subject to a restraint order under section 41, 120 or 190, or

(b) there is in force in respect of such property an order under section 50, 52, 128(3), 198 or 200.

(3) Any decree made under the Bankruptcy Act 1621 (c. 18) or section 34 or 36 of the 1985 Act, or otherwise, after an order mentioned in subsection (2)(a) or (b) is discharged must take into account any realisation under Part 2, 3 or 4 of this Act of property held by the recipient of the tainted gift.

(4) A person makes a tainted gift for the purposes of this section if he makes a tainted gift within the meaning of Part 2, 3 or 4.

Bankruptcy in Northern Ireland

423. Modifications of the 1989 Order

(1) This section applies if a person is adjudged bankrupt in Northern Ireland.

(2) The following property is excluded from his estate for the purposes of Part 9 of the 1989 Order—

(a) property for the time being subject to a restraint order which was made under section 41, 120 or 190 before the order adjudging him bankrupt;

(b) any property in respect of which an order under section 50 or 52 is in force;

(c) any property in respect of which an order under section 128(3) is in force;

(d) any property in respect of which an order under section 198 or 200 is in force.

(3) Subsection (2)(a) applies to heritable property in Scotland only if the restraint order is recorded in the General Register of Sasines or registered in the Land Register of Scotland before the order adjudging the person bankrupt.

(4) If in the case of a debtor an interim receiver stands at any time appointed under Article 259 of the 1989 Order and any property of the debtor is then subject to a restraint order made under section 41, 120 or 190, the powers conferred on the receiver by virtue of that Order do not apply to property then subject to the restraint order.

424. Restriction of powers

(1) If a person is adjudged bankrupt in Northern Ireland the powers referred to in subsection (2) must not be exercised in relation to the property referred to in subsection (3).

(2) These are the powers—

    (a) the powers conferred on a court by sections 41 to 67 and the powers of a receiver appointed under section 48, 50 or 52;

    (b) the powers conferred on a court by sections 120 to 136 and Schedule 3 and the powers of an administrator appointed under section 125 or 128(3);

    (c) the powers conferred on a court by sections 190 to 215 and the powers of a receiver appointed under section 196, 198 or 200.

(3) This is the property—

    (a) property which is for the time being comprised in the bankrupt's estate for the purposes of Part 9 of the 1989 Order;

    (b) property in respect of which his trustee in bankruptcy may (without leave of the court) serve a notice under Article 280 or 281 of the 1989 Order (after-acquired property etc);

    (c) property which is to be applied for the benefit of creditors of the bankrupt by virtue of a condition imposed under Article 254(2)(c) of the 1989 Order;

    (d) in a case where a confiscation order has been made under section 6 or 156 of this Act, any sums remaining in the hands of a receiver appointed under section 50, 52, 198 or 200 of this Act after the amount required to be paid under the confiscation order has been fully paid;

    (e) in a case where a confiscation order has been made under section 92 of this Act, any sums remaining in the hands of an administrator appointed under section 128 of this Act after the amount required to be paid under the confiscation order has been fully paid.

(4) But nothing in the 1989 Order must be taken to restrict (or enable the restriction of) the powers mentioned in subsection (2).

(5) In a case where a petition in bankruptcy was presented or an adjudication in bankruptcy was made before 1 October 1991 (when the 1989 Order came into force) this section has effect with these modifications—

    (a) for the reference in subsection (3)(a) to the bankrupt's estate for the purposes of Part 9 of that Order substitute a reference to the property of the bankrupt for the purposes of the Bankruptcy Acts (Northern Ireland) 1857 to 1980;

    (b) omit subsection (3)(b);

    (c) for the reference in subsection (3)(c) to Article 254(2)(c) of the 1989 Order substitute a reference to Articles 28(4), (5)(c) and (11) and 30(6)(c) of the Bankruptcy Amendment (Northern Ireland) Order 1980 (S.I. 1980/561 (N.I. 4));

    (d) for the reference in subsection (4) to the 1989 Order substitute a reference to the Bankruptcy Acts (Northern Ireland) 1857 to 1980.

425. Tainted gifts

(1) This section applies if a person who is adjudged bankrupt in Northern Ireland has made a tainted gift (whether directly or indirectly).

(2) No order may be made under Article 312, 313 or 367 of the 1989 Order (avoidance of certain transactions) in respect of the making of the gift at any time when—

    (a) any property of the recipient of the tainted gift is subject to a restraint order under section 41, 120 or 190, or

    (b) there is in force in respect of such property an order under section 50, 52, 128(3), 198 or 200.

(3) Any order made under Article 312, 313 or 367 of the 1989 Order after an order mentioned in subsection (2)(a) or (b) is discharged must take into account any realisation under Part 2, 3 or 4 of this Act of property held by the recipient of the tainted gift.

(4) A person makes a tainted gift for the purposes of this section if he makes a tainted gift within the meaning of Part 2, 3 or 4.

(5) In a case where a petition in bankruptcy was presented or an adjudication in bankruptcy was made before 1 October 1991 (when the 1989 Order came into force) this section has effect with these modifications—

(a) for a reference to Article 312 of the 1989 Order substitute a reference to section 12 of the Bankruptcy Amendment Act (Northern Ireland) 1929 (c. 1 (N.I.));

(b) for a reference to Article 367 of the 1989 Order substitute a reference to section 10 of the Conveyancing Act (Ireland) 1634 (c. 3).

Winding up in England and Wales and Scotland

426. Winding up under the 1986 Act

(1) In this section 'company' means any company which may be wound up under the 1986 Act.

(2) If an order for the winding up of a company is made or it passes a resolution for its voluntary winding up, the functions of the liquidator (or any provisional liquidator) are not exercisable in relation to the following property—

(a) property for the time being subject to a restraint order which was made under section 41, 120 or 190 before the relevant time;

(b) any property in respect of which an order under section 50 or 52 is in force;

(c) any property in respect of which an order under section 128(3) is in force;

(d) any property in respect of which an order under section 198 or 200 is in force.

(3) Subsection (2)(a) applies to heritable property in Scotland only if the restraint order is recorded in the General Register of Sasines or registered in the Land Register of Scotland before the relevant time.

(4) If an order for the winding up of a company is made or it passes a resolution for its voluntary winding up the powers referred to in subsection (5) must not be exercised in the way mentioned in subsection (6) in relation to any property—

(a) which is held by the company, and

(b) in relation to which the functions of the liquidator are exercisable.

(5) These are the powers—

(a) the powers conferred on a court by sections 41 to 67 and the powers of a receiver appointed under section 48, 50 or 52;

(b) the powers conferred on a court by sections 120 to 136 and Schedule 3 and the powers of an administrator appointed under section 125 or 128(3);

(c) the powers conferred on a court by sections 190 to 215 and the powers of a receiver appointed under section 196, 198 or 200.

(6) The powers must not be exercised—

(a) so as to inhibit the liquidator from exercising his functions for the purpose of distributing property to the company's creditors;

(b) so as to prevent the payment out of any property of expenses (including the remuneration of the liquidator or any provisional liquidator) properly incurred in the winding up in respect of the property.

(7) But nothing in the 1986 Act must be taken to restrict (or enable the restriction of) the exercise of the powers referred to in subsection (5).

(8) For the purposes of the application of Parts 4 and 5 of the 1986 Act (winding up) to a company which the Court of Session has jurisdiction to wind up, a person is not a creditor in so far as any sum due to him by the company is due in respect of a confiscation order made under section 6, 92 or 156.

(9) The relevant time is—

    (a) if no order for the winding up of the company has been made, the time of the passing of the resolution for voluntary winding up;

    (b) if such an order has been made, but before the presentation of the petition for the winding up of the company by the court such a resolution has been passed by the company, the time of the passing of the resolution;

    (c) if such an order has been made, but paragraph (b) does not apply, the time of the making of the order.

(10) In a case where a winding up of a company commenced or is treated as having commenced before 29 December 1986, this section has effect with the following modifications—

    (a) in subsections (1) and (7) for 'the 1986 Act' substitute 'the Companies Act 1985';

    (b) in subsection (8) for 'Parts 4 and 5 of the 1986 Act' substitute 'Parts 20 and 21 of the Companies Act 1985'.

427. Tainted gifts

(1) In this section 'company' means any company which may be wound up under the 1986 Act.

(2) This section applies if—

    (a) an order for the winding up of a company is made or it passes a resolution for its voluntary winding up, and

    (b) it has made a tainted gift (whether directly or indirectly).

(3) No order may be made under section 238, 239 or 423 of the 1986 Act (avoidance of certain transactions) and no decree may be granted under section 242 or 243 of that Act (gratuitous alienations and unfair preferences), or otherwise, in respect of the making of the gift at any time when—

    (a) any property of the recipient of the tainted gift is subject to a restraint order under section 41, 120 or 190, or

    (b) there is in force in respect of such property an order under section 50, 52, 128(3), 198 or 200.

(4) Any order made under section 238, 239 or 423 of the 1986 Act or decree granted under section 242 or 243 of that Act, or otherwise, after an order mentioned in subsection (3)(a) or (b) is discharged must take into account any realisation under Part 2, 3 or 4 of this Act of property held by the recipient of the tainted gift.

(5) A person makes a tainted gift for the purposes of this section if he makes a tainted gift within the meaning of Part 2, 3 or 4.

(6) In a case where the winding up of a company commenced or is treated as having commenced before 29 December 1986 this section has effect with the substitution—

    (a) for references to section 239 of the 1986 Act of references to section 615 of the Companies Act 1985 (c. 6);

(b) for references to section 242 of the 1986 Act of references to section 615A of the Companies Act 1985;

(c) for references to section 243 of the 1986 Act of references to section 615B of the Companies Act 1985.

Winding up in Northern Ireland

428. Winding up under the 1989 Order

(1) In this section 'company' means any company which may be wound up under the 1989 Order.

(2) If an order for the winding up of a company is made or it passes a resolution for its voluntary winding up, the functions of the liquidator (or any provisional liquidator) are not exercisable in relation to the following property—

(a) property for the time being subject to a restraint order which was made under section 41, 120 or 190 before the relevant time;

(b) any property in respect of which an order under section 50 or 52 is in force;

(c) any property in respect of which an order under section 128(3) is in force;

(d) any property in respect of which an order under section 198 or 200 is in force.

(3) Subsection (2)(a) applies to heritable property in Scotland only if the restraint order is recorded in the General Register of Sasines or registered in the Land Register of Scotland before the relevant time.

(4) If an order for the winding up of a company is made or it passes a resolution for its voluntary winding up the powers referred to in subsection (5) must not be exercised in the way mentioned in subsection (6) in relation to any property—

(a) which is held by the company, and

(b) in relation to which the functions of the liquidator are exercisable.

(5) These are the powers—

(a) the powers conferred on a court by sections 41 to 67 and the powers of a receiver appointed under section 48, 50 or 52;

(b) the powers conferred on a court by sections 120 to 136 and Schedule 3 and the powers of an administrator appointed under section 125 or 128(3);

(c) the powers conferred on a court by sections 190 to 215 and the powers of a receiver appointed under section 196, 198 or 200.

(6) The powers must not be exercised—

(a) so as to inhibit the liquidator from exercising his functions for the purpose of distributing property to the company's creditors;

(b) so as to prevent the payment out of any property of expenses (including the remuneration of the liquidator or any provisional liquidator) properly incurred in the winding up in respect of the property.

(7) But nothing in the 1989 Order must be taken to restrict (or enable the restriction of) the exercise of the powers referred to in subsection (5).

(8) The relevant time is—

(a) if no order for the winding up of the company has been made, the time of the passing of the resolution for voluntary winding up;

(b) if such an order has been made, but before the presentation of the petition for the winding up of the company by the court such a resolution has been passed by the company, the time of the passing of the resolution;

    (c) if such an order has been made, but paragraph (b) does not apply, the time of the making of the order.

(9) In a case where a winding up of a company commenced or is treated as having commenced before 1 October 1991, this section has effect with the substitution for references to the 1989 Order of references to the Companies (Northern Ireland) Order 1986 (S.I. 1986/1032 (N.I. 6)).

429. Tainted gifts

(1) In this section 'company' means any company which may be wound up under the 1989 Order.

(2) This section applies if—

    (a) an order for the winding up of a company is made or it passes a resolution for its voluntary winding up, and

    (b) it has made a tainted gift (whether directly or indirectly).

(3) No order may be made under Article 202, 203 or 367 of the 1989 Order (avoidance of certain transactions) in respect of the making of the gift at any time when—

    (a) any property of the recipient of the tainted gift is subject to a restraint order under section 41, 120 or 190, or

    (b) there is in force in respect of such property an order under section 50, 52, 128(3), 198 or 200.

(4) Any order made under Article 202, 203 or 367 of the 1989 Order after an order mentioned in subsection (3)(a) or (b) is discharged must take into account any realisation under Part 2, 3 or 4 of this Act of property held by the recipient of the tainted gift.

(5) A person makes a tainted gift for the purposes of this section if he makes a tainted gift within the meaning of Part 2, 3 or 4.

Floating charges

430. Floating charges

(1) In this section 'company' means a company which may be wound up under—

    (a) the 1986 Act, or

    (b) the 1989 Order.

(2) If a company holds property which is subject to a floating charge, and a receiver has been appointed by or on the application of the holder of the charge, the functions of the receiver are not exercisable in relation to the following property—

    (a) property for the time being subject to a restraint order which was made under section 41, 120 or 190 before the appointment of the receiver;

    (b) any property in respect of which an order under section 50 or 52 is in force;

    (c) any property in respect of which an order under section 128(3) is in force;

    (d) any property in respect of which an order under section 198 or 200 is in force.

(3) Subsection (2)(a) applies to heritable property in Scotland only if the restraint order is recorded in the General Register of Sasines or registered in the Land Register of Scotland before the appointment of the receiver.

(4) If a company holds property which is subject to a floating charge, and a receiver has been appointed by or on the application of the holder of the charge, the powers

referred to in subsection (5) must not be exercised in the way mentioned in subsection (6) in relation to any property—

    (a) which is held by the company, and

    (b) in relation to which the functions of the receiver are exercisable.

(5) These are the powers—

    (a) the powers conferred on a court by sections 41 to 67 and the powers of a receiver appointed under section 48, 50 or 52;

    (b) the powers conferred on a court by sections 120 to 136 and Schedule 3 and the powers of an administrator appointed under section 125 or 128(3);

    (c) the powers conferred on a court by sections 190 to 215 and the powers of a receiver appointed under section 196, 198 or 200.

(6) The powers must not be exercised—

    (a) so as to inhibit the receiver from exercising his functions for the purpose of distributing property to the company's creditors;

    (b) so as to prevent the payment out of any property of expenses (including the remuneration of the receiver) properly incurred in the exercise of his functions in respect of the property.

(7) But nothing in the 1986 Act or the 1989 Order must be taken to restrict (or enable the restriction of) the exercise of the powers referred to in subsection (5).

(8) In this section 'floating charge' includes a floating charge within the meaning of section 462 of the Companies Act 1985 (c. 6).

Limited liability partnerships

431. Limited liability partnerships

(1) In sections 426, 427 and 430 'company' includes a limited liability partnership which may be wound up under the 1986 Act.

(2) A reference in those sections to a company passing a resolution for its voluntary winding up is to be construed in relation to a limited liability partnership as a reference to the partnership making a determination for its voluntary winding up.

Insolvency practitioners

432. Insolvency practitioners

(1) Subsections (2) and (3) apply if a person acting as an insolvency practitioner seizes or disposes of any property in relation to which his functions are not exercisable because—

    (a) it is for the time being subject to a restraint order made under section 41, 120 or 190, or

    (b) it is for the time being subject to an interim receiving order made under section 246 or an interim administration order made under section 256,

and at the time of the seizure or disposal he believes on reasonable grounds that he is entitled (whether in pursuance of an order of a court or otherwise) to seize or dispose of the property.

(2) He is not liable to any person in respect of any loss or damage resulting from the seizure or disposal, except so far as the loss or damage is caused by his negligence.

(3) He has a lien on the property or the proceeds of its sale—

    (a) for such of his expenses as were incurred in connection with the liquidation, bankruptcy, sequestration or other proceedings in relation to which he purported to make the seizure or disposal, and

    (b) for so much of his remuneration as may reasonably be assigned to his acting in connection with those proceedings.

(4) Subsection (2) does not prejudice the generality of any provision of the 1985 Act, the 1986 Act, the 1989 Order or any other Act or Order which confers protection from liability on him.

(5) Subsection (7) applies if—

    (a) property is subject to a restraint order made under section 41, 120 or 190,

    (b) a person acting as an insolvency practitioner incurs expenses in respect of property subject to the restraint order, and

    (c) he does not know (and has no reasonable grounds to believe) that the property is subject to the restraint order.

(6) Subsection (7) also applies if—

    (a) property is subject to a restraint order made under section 41, 120 or 190,

    (b) a person acting as an insolvency practitioner incurs expenses which are not ones in respect of property subject to the restraint order, and

    (c) the expenses are ones which (but for the effect of the restraint order) might have been met by taking possession of and realising property subject to it.

(7) Whether or not he has seized or disposed of any property, he is entitled to payment of the expenses under—

    (a) section 54(2), 55(3), 56(2) or 57(3) if the restraint order was made under section 41;

    (b) section 130(3) or 131(3) if the restraint order was made under section 120;

    (c) section 202(2), 203(3), 204(2) or 205(3) if the restraint order was made under section 190.

(8) Subsection (10) applies if—

    (a) property is subject to an interim receiving order made under section 246 or an interim administration order made under section 256,

    (b) a person acting as an insolvency practitioner incurs expenses in respect of property subject to the order, and

    (c) he does not know (and has no reasonable grounds to believe) that the property is subject to the order.

(9) Subsection (10) also applies if—

    (a) property is subject to an interim receiving order made under section 246 or an interim administration order made under section 256,

    (b) a person acting as an insolvency practitioner incurs expenses which are not ones in respect of property subject to the order, and

    (c) the expenses are ones which (but for the effect of the order) might have been met by taking possession of and realising property subject to it.

(10) Whether or not he has seized or disposed of any property, he is entitled to payment of the expenses under section 280.

433. Meaning of insolvency practitioner

(1) This section applies for the purposes of section 432.

(2) A person acts as an insolvency practitioner if he so acts within the meaning given by

section 388 of the 1986 Act or Article 3 of the 1989 Order; but this is subject to subsections (3) to (5).

(3) The expression 'person acting as an insolvency practitioner' includes the official receiver acting as receiver or manager of the property concerned.

(4) In applying section 388 of the 1986 Act under subsection (2) above—

    (a) the reference in section 388(2)(a) to a permanent or interim trustee in sequestration must be taken to include a reference to a trustee in sequestration;

    (b) section 388(5) (which includes provision that nothing in the section applies to anything done by the official receiver or the Accountant in Bankruptcy) must be ignored.

(5) In applying Article 3 of the 1989 Order under subsection (2) above, paragraph (5) (which includes provision that nothing in the Article applies to anything done by the official receiver) must be ignored.

Interpretation

434. Interpretation

(1) The following paragraphs apply to references to Acts or Orders—

    (a) the 1913 Act is the Bankruptcy (Scotland) Act 1913 (c. 20);

    (b) the 1914 Act is the Bankruptcy Act 1914 (c. 59);

    (c) the 1985 Act is the Bankruptcy (Scotland) Act 1985 (c. 66);

    (d) the 1986 Act is the Insolvency Act 1986 (c. 45);

    (e) the 1989 Order is the Insolvency (Northern Ireland) Order 1989 (S.I. 1989/2405 (N.I. 19)).

(2) An award of sequestration is made on the date of sequestration within the meaning of section 12(4) of the 1985 Act.

(3) This section applies for the purposes of this Part.

PART 10
INFORMATION

England and Wales and Northern Ireland

435. Use of information by Director

Information obtained by or on behalf of the Director in connection with the exercise of any of his functions may be used by him in connection with his exercise of any of his other functions.

436. Disclosure of information to Director

(1) Information which is held by or on behalf of a permitted person (whether it was obtained before or after the coming into force of this section) may be disclosed to the Director for the purpose of the exercise by the Director of his functions.

(2) A disclosure under this section is not to be taken to breach any restriction on the disclosure of information (however imposed).

(3) But nothing in this section authorises the making of a disclosure—

    (a) which contravenes the Data Protection Act 1998 (c. 29);

     (b) which is prohibited by Part 1 of the Regulation of Investigatory Powers Act 2000 (c. 23).

(4) This section does not affect a power to disclose which exists apart from this section.

(5) These are permitted persons—

     (a) a constable;

     (b) the Director General of the National Criminal Intelligence Service;

     (c) the Director General of the National Crime Squad;

     (d) the Director of the Serious Fraud Office;

     (e) the Commissioners of Inland Revenue;

     (f) the Commissioners of Customs and Excise;

     (g) the Director of Public Prosecutions;

     (h) the Director of Public Prosecutions for Northern Ireland.

(6) The Secretary of State may by order designate as permitted persons other persons who exercise functions which he believes are of a public nature.

(7) But an order under subsection (6) must specify the functions in respect of which the designation is made.

(8) Information must not be disclosed under this section on behalf of the Commissioners of Inland Revenue or on behalf of the Commissioners of Customs and Excise unless the Commissioners concerned authorise the disclosure.

(9) The power to authorise a disclosure under subsection (8) may be delegated (either generally or for a specified purpose)—

     (a) in the case of the Commissioners of Inland Revenue, to an officer of the Board of Inland Revenue;

     (b) in the case of the Commissioners of Customs and Excise, to a customs officer.

437. Further disclosure

(1) Subsection (2) applies to information obtained under section 436 from the Commissioners of Inland Revenue or from the Commissioners of Customs and Excise or from a person acting on behalf of either of them.

(2) Such information must not be further disclosed except—

     (a) for a purpose connected with the exercise of the Director's functions, and

     (b) with the consent of the Commissioners concerned.

(3) Consent under subsection (2) may be given—

     (a) in relation to a particular disclosure;

     (b) in relation to disclosures made in circumstances specified or described in the consent.

(4) The power to consent to further disclosure under subsection (2)(b) may be delegated (either generally or for a specified purpose)—

     (a) in the case of the Commissioners of Inland Revenue, to an officer of the Board of Inland Revenue;

     (b) in the case of the Commissioners of Customs and Excise, to a customs officer.

(5) Subsection (6) applies to information obtained under section 436 from a permitted person other than the Commissioners of Inland Revenue or the Commissioners of Customs and Excise or a person acting on behalf of either of them.

(6) A permitted person who discloses such information to the Director may make the disclosure subject to such conditions as to further disclosure by the Director as the

permitted person thinks appropriate; and the information must not be further disclosed in contravention of the conditions.

438. Disclosure of information by Director

(1) Information obtained by or on behalf of the Director in connection with the exercise of any of his functions may be disclosed by him if the disclosure is for the purposes of any of the following—

    (a) any criminal investigation which is being or may be carried out, whether in the United Kingdom or elsewhere;

    (b) any criminal proceedings which have been or may be started, whether in the United Kingdom or elsewhere;

    (c) the exercise of the Director's functions;

    (d) the exercise by the prosecutor of functions under Parts 2, 3 and 4;

    (e) the exercise by the Scottish Ministers of their functions under Part 5;

    (f) the exercise by a customs officer or a constable of his functions under Chapter 3 of Part 5;

    (g) safeguarding national security;

    (h) investigations or proceedings outside the United Kingdom which have led or may lead to the making of an external order within the meaning of section 447.

    (i) the exercise of a designated function.

(2) Subsection (1) does not apply to information obtained by the Director or on his behalf in connection with the exercise of his functions under Part 6.

(3) But such information may be disclosed by the Director—

    (a) to the Commissioners of Inland Revenue;

    (b) to the Lord Advocate for the purpose of the exercise by the Lord Advocate of his functions under Part 3.

(4) Information disclosed to the Lord Advocate under subsection (3)(b) may be further disclosed by him only to the Scottish Ministers for the purpose of the exercise by them of their functions under Part 5.

(5) If the Director makes a disclosure of information for a purpose specified in subsection (1) he may make any further disclosure of the information by the person to whom he discloses it subject to such conditions as he thinks fit.

(6) Such a person must not further disclose the information in contravention of the conditions.

(7) A disclosure under this section is not to be taken to breach any restriction on the disclosure of information (however imposed).

(8) But nothing in this section authorises the making of a disclosure—

    (a) which contravenes the Data Protection Act 1998 (c. 29);

    (b) which is prohibited by Part 1 of the Regulation of Investigatory Powers Act 2000 (c. 23).

(9) A designated function is a function which the Secretary of State thinks is a function of a public nature and which he designates by order.

Scotland

439. Disclosure of information to Lord Advocate and to Scottish Ministers

(1) Information which is held by or on behalf of a permitted person (whether it was obtained before or after the coming into force of this section) may be disclosed to

the Lord Advocate in connection with the exercise of any of his functions under Part 3 or to the Scottish Ministers in connection with the exercise of any of their functions under Part 5.

(2) A disclosure under this section is not to be taken to breach any restriction on the disclosure of information (however imposed).

(3) But nothing in this section authorises the making of a disclosure—
   (a) which contravenes the Data Protection Act 1998;
   (b) which is prohibited by Part 1 of the Regulation of Investigatory Powers Act 2000.

(4) This section does not affect a power to disclose which exists apart from this section.

(5) These are permitted persons—
   (a) a constable;
   (b) the Director General of the National Criminal Intelligence Service;
   (c) the Director General of the National Crime Squad;
   (d) the Director of the Serious Fraud Office;
   (e) the Commissioners of Inland Revenue;
   (f) the Commissioners of Customs and Excise;
   (g) the Director of Public Prosecutions;
   (h) the Director of Public Prosecutions for Northern Ireland.

(6) The Scottish Ministers may by order designate as permitted persons other persons who exercise functions which they believe are of a public nature.

(7) But an order under subsection (6) must specify the functions in respect of which the designation is made.

(8) Information must not be disclosed under this section on behalf of the Commissioners of Inland Revenue or on behalf of the Commissioners of Customs and Excise unless the Commissioners concerned authorise the disclosure.

(9) The power to authorise a disclosure under subsection (8) may be delegated (either generally or for a specified purpose)—
   (a) in the case of the Commissioners of Inland Revenue, to an officer of the Board of Inland Revenue;
   (b) in the case of the Commissioners of Customs and Excise, to a customs officer.

440. Further disclosure

(1) Subsection (2) applies to information obtained under section 439 from the Commissioners of Inland Revenue or from the Commissioners of Customs and Excise or from a person acting on behalf of either of them.

(2) Such information must not be further disclosed except—
   (a) for a purpose connected with the exercise of the functions of the Lord Advocate under Part 3 and of the Scottish Ministers under Part 5, and
   (b) with the consent of the Commissioners concerned.

(3) Consent under subsection (2) may be given—
   (a) in relation to a particular disclosure;
   (b) in relation to disclosures made in circumstances specified or described in the consent.

(4) The power to consent to further disclosure under subsection (2)(b) may be delegated (either generally or for a specified purpose)—
   (a) in the case of the Commissioners of Inland Revenue, to an officer of the Board of Inland Revenue;

(b) in the case of the Commissioners of Customs and Excise, to a customs officer.

(5) Subsection (6) applies to information obtained under section 439 from a permitted person other than the Commissioners of Inland Revenue or the Commissioners of Customs and Excise or a person acting on behalf of either of them.

(6) A permitted person who discloses such information to the Lord Advocate or to the Scottish Ministers may make the disclosure subject to such conditions as to further disclosure by the Lord Advocate or by the Scottish Ministers as the permitted person thinks appropriate; and the information must not be further disclosed in contravention of the conditions.

441. Disclosure of information by Lord Advocate and by Scottish Ministers

(1) Information obtained by or on behalf of the Lord Advocate in connection with the exercise of any of his functions under Chapter 3 of Part 5 may be disclosed to the Scottish Ministers in connection with the exercise of any of their functions under that Part.

(2) Information obtained by or on behalf of the Lord Advocate in connection with the exercise of any of his functions under Part 3 or by or on behalf of the Scottish Ministers in connection with the exercise of any of their functions under Part 5 may be disclosed by him or by them if the disclosure is for the purposes of any of the following—

(a) any criminal investigation which is being or may be carried out whether in the United Kingdom or elsewhere;

(b) any criminal proceedings which have been or may be started, whether in the United Kingdom or elsewhere;

(c) the exercise of the functions of the Lord Advocate under Part 3;

(d) the exercise of the functions of the Scottish Ministers under Part 5;

(e) the exercise by the prosecutor of functions under Parts 2, 3 and 4;

(f) the exercise of the Director's functions;

(g) the exercise by a customs officer or a constable of his functions under Chapter 3 of Part 5;

(h) safeguarding national security;

(i) investigations or proceedings outside the United Kingdom which have led or may lead to the making of an external order within the meaning of section 447;

(j) the exercise of a designated function.

(3) If the Lord Advocate makes a disclosure of information for a purpose specified in subsection (2) he may make any further disclosure of the information by the person to whom he discloses it subject to such conditions as he thinks fit.

(4) If the Scottish Ministers make a disclosure of information for a purpose specified in subsection (2) they may make any further disclosure of the information by the person to whom they disclose it subject to such conditions as they think fit.

(5) A person mentioned in subsection (3) or (4) must not further disclose the information in contravention of the conditions.

(6) A disclosure under this section is not to be taken to breach any restriction on the disclosure of information (however imposed).

(7) But nothing in this section authorises the making of a disclosure—

(a) which contravenes the Data Protection Act 1998 (c. 29);

(b) which is prohibited by Part 1 of the Regulation of Investigatory Powers Act 2000 (c. 23).

(8) This section does not affect a power to disclose which exists apart from this section.

(9) A designated function is a function which the Scottish Ministers think is a function of a public nature and which they designate by order.

Overseas purposes

442. Restriction on disclosure for overseas purposes

(1) Section 18 of the Anti-terrorism, Crime and Security Act 2001 (c. 24) (restrictions on disclosure of information for overseas purposes) applies to a disclosure of information authorised by section 438(1)(a) or (b) or 441(2)(a) or (b).

(2) In the application of section 18 of the Anti-terrorism, Crime and Security Act 2001 by virtue of subsection (1) section 20 of that Act must be ignored and the following subsection is substituted for subsection (2) of section 18 of that Act—

'(2) In subsection (1) the reference, in relation to a direction, to a relevant disclosure is a reference to a disclosure which—

(a) is made for a purpose authorised by section 438(1)(a) or (b) or 441(2)(a) or (b) of the Proceeds of Crime Act 2002, and

(b) is of any such information as is described in the direction.'.

PART 11
CO-OPERATION

443. Enforcement in different parts of the United Kingdom

(1) Her Majesty may by Order in Council make provision—

(a) for an order made by a court under Part 2 to be enforced in Scotland or Northern Ireland;

(b) for an order made by a court under Part 3 to be enforced in England and Wales or Northern Ireland;

(c) for an order made by a court under Part 4 to be enforced in England and Wales or Scotland;

(d) for an order made under Part 8 in one part of the United Kingdom to be enforced in another part;

(e) for a warrant issued under Part 8 in one part of the United Kingdom to be executed in another part.

(2) Her Majesty may by Order in Council make provision—

(a) for a function of a receiver appointed in pursuance of Part 2 to be exercisable in Scotland or Northern Ireland;

(b) for a function of an administrator appointed in pursuance of Part 3 to be exercisable in England and Wales or Northern Ireland;

(c) for a function of a receiver appointed in pursuance of Part 4 to be exercisable in England and Wales or Scotland.

(3) An Order under this section may include—

(a) provision conferring and imposing functions on the prosecutor and the Director;

(b) provision about the registration of orders and warrants;

(c) provision allowing directions to be given in one part of the United Kingdom about the enforcement there of an order made or warrant issued in another part;

(d) provision about the authentication in one part of the United Kingdom of an order made or warrant issued in another part.

(4) An Order under this section may—
   (a) amend an enactment;
   (b) apply an enactment (with or without modifications).

444. External requests and orders

(1) Her Majesty may by Order in Council—
   (a) make provision for a prohibition on dealing with property which is the subject of an external request;
   (b) make provision for the realisation of property for the purpose of giving effect to an external order.

(2) An Order under this section may include provision which (subject to any specified modifications) corresponds to any provision of Part 2, 3 or 4 or Part 5 except Chapter 3.

(3) An Order under this section may include—
   (a) provision about the functions of the Secretary of State, the Lord Advocate, the Scottish Ministers and the Director in relation to external requests and orders;
   (b) provision about the registration of external orders;
   (c) provision about the authentication of any judgment or order of an overseas court, and of any other document connected with such a judgment or order or any proceedings relating to it;
   (d) provision about evidence (including evidence required to establish whether proceedings have been started or are likely to be started in an overseas court);
   (e) provision to secure that any person affected by the implementation of an external request or the enforcement of an external order has an opportunity to make representations to a court in the part of the United Kingdom where the request is being implemented or the order is being enforced.

445. External investigations

(1) Her Majesty may by Order in Council make—
   (a) provision to enable orders equivalent to those under Part 8 to be made, and warrants equivalent to those under Part 8 to be issued, for the purposes of an external investigation;
   (b) provision creating offences in relation to external investigations which are equivalent to offences created by Part 8.

(2) An Order under this section may include—
   (a) provision corresponding to any provision of Part 8 (subject to any specified modifications);
   (b) provision about the functions of the Secretary of State, the Lord Advocate, the Scottish Ministers, the Director, the Director General of the National Criminal Intelligence Service, the Director of the Serious Fraud Office, constables and customs officers;
   (c) provision about evidence (including evidence required to establish whether an investigation is being carried out in a country or territory outside the United Kingdom).

321

(3) But an Order under this section must not provide for a disclosure order to be made for the purposes of an external investigation into whether a money laundering offence has been committed.

446. Rules of court

Rules of court may make such provision as is necessary or expedient to give effect to an Order in Council made under this Part (including provision about the exercise of functions of a judge conferred or imposed by the Order).

447. Interpretation

(1) An external request is a request by an overseas authority to prohibit dealing with relevant property which is identified in the request.

(2) An external order is an order which—
   (a) is made by an overseas court where property is found or believed to have been obtained as a result of or in connection with criminal conduct, and
   (b) is for the recovery of specified property or a specified sum of money.

(3) An external investigation is an investigation by an overseas authority into—
   (a) whether property has been obtained as a result of or in connection with criminal conduct, or
   (b) whether a money laundering offence has been committed.

(4) Property is all property wherever situated and includes—
   (a) money;
   (b) all forms of property, real or personal, heritable or moveable;
   (c) things in action and other intangible or incorporeal property.

(5) Property is obtained by a person if he obtains an interest in it.

(6) References to an interest, in relation to property other than land, include references to a right (including a right to possession).

(7) Property is relevant property if there are reasonable grounds to believe that it may be needed to satisfy an external order which has been or which may be made.

(8) Criminal conduct is conduct which—
   (a) constitutes an offence in any part of the United Kingdom, or
   (b) would constitute an offence in any part of the United Kingdom if it occurred there.

(9) A money laundering offence is conduct carried out in a country or territory outside the United Kingdom and which if carried out in the United Kingdom would constitute any of the following offences—
   (a) an offence under section 327, 328 or 329;
   (b) an attempt, conspiracy or incitement to commit an offence specified in paragraph (a);
   (c) aiding, abetting, counselling or procuring the commission of an offence specified in paragraph (a).

(10) An overseas court is a court of a country or territory outside the United Kingdom.

(11) An overseas authority is an authority which has responsibility in a country or territory outside the United Kingdom—
   (a) for making a request to an authority in another country or territory (including the United Kingdom) to prohibit dealing with relevant property,

(b) for carrying out an investigation into whether property has been obtained as a result of or in connection with criminal conduct, or

(c) for carrying out an investigation into whether a money laundering offence has been committed.

(12) This section applies for the purposes of this Part.

PART 12
MISCELLANEOUS AND GENERAL

Miscellaneous

448. Tax

Schedule 10 contains provisions about tax.

449. Agency staff: pseudonyms

(1) This section applies to a member of the staff of the Agency if—

(a) he is authorised (generally or specifically) by the Director to do anything for the purposes of this Act, and

(b) it is necessary or expedient for the purpose of doing the thing for the member of the staff of the Agency to identify himself by name.

(2) The Director may direct that such a member of the staff of the Agency may for that purpose identify himself by means of a pseudonym.

(3) For the purposes of any proceedings or application under this Act a certificate signed by the Director which sufficiently identifies the member of the staff of the Agency by reference to the pseudonym is conclusive evidence that that member of the staff of the Agency is authorised to use the pseudonym.

(4) In any proceedings or application under this Act a member of the staff of the Agency in respect of whom a direction under this section is in force must not be asked (and if asked is not required to answer) any question which is likely to reveal his true identity.

(5) Section 1(6) does not apply to anything done by the Director under this section.

450. Pseudonyms: Scotland

(1) This section applies to—

(a) any person named by the Scottish Ministers for the purpose of a civil recovery investigation under Part 8, or

(b) any person authorised by the Scottish Ministers for the purpose of such a civil recovery investigation to receive relevant information under section 391,

if it is necessary or expedient for the person to identify himself by name for that purpose.

(2) The Scottish Ministers may direct that such a person may for that purpose identify himself by means of a pseudonym.

(3) For the purposes of any proceedings or application under this Act, a certificate signed by the Scottish Ministers which sufficiently identifies the person by reference to the pseudonym is conclusive evidence that the person is authorised to use the pseudonym.

(4) In any proceedings or application under this Act a person in respect of whom a direction under this section is in force must not be asked (and if asked is not required to answer) any question which is likely to reveal his true identity.

451. Customs and Excise prosecutions

(1) Proceedings for a specified offence may be started by order of the Commissioners of Customs and Excise (the Commissioners).
(2) Such proceedings must be brought in the name of a customs officer.
(3) If the customs officer in whose name the proceedings are brought—
    (a) dies,
    (b) is removed or discharged, or
    (c) is absent,
the proceedings may be continued by a different customs officer.
(4) If the Commissioners investigate, or propose to investigate, any matter to help them to decide—
    (a) whether there are grounds for believing that a specified offence has been committed, or
    (b) whether a person is to be prosecuted for such an offence,
the matter must be treated as an assigned matter within the meaning of the Customs and Excise Management Act 1979 (c. 2).
(5) This section—
    (a) does not prevent any person (including a customs officer) who has power to arrest, detain or prosecute a person for a specified offence from doing so;
    (b) does not prevent a court from dealing with a person brought before it following his arrest by a customs officer for a specified offence, even if the proceedings were not started by an order under subsection (1).
(6) The following are specified offences—
    (a) an offence under Part 7;
    (b) an offence under section 342;
    (c) an attempt, conspiracy or incitement to commit an offence specified in paragraph (a) or (b);
    (d) aiding, abetting, counselling or procuring the commission of an offence specified in paragraph (a) or (b).
(7) This section does not apply to proceedings on indictment in Scotland.

452. Crown servants

(1) The Secretary of State may by regulations provide that any of the following provisions apply to persons in the public service of the Crown.
(2) The provisions are—
    (a) the provisions of Part 7;
    (b) section 342.

453. References to financial investigators

(1) The Secretary of State may by order provide that a specified reference in this Act to an accredited financial investigator is a reference to such an investigator who falls within a specified description.

(2) A description may be framed by reference to a grade designated by a specified person.

454. Customs officers

For the purposes of this Act a customs officer is a person commissioned by the Commissioners of Customs and Excise under section 6(3) of the Customs and Excise Management Act 1979 (c. 2).

455. Enactment

In this Act (except in section 460(1)) a reference to an enactment includes a reference to—
   (a) an Act of the Scottish Parliament;
   (b) Northern Ireland legislation.

General

456. Amendments

Schedule 11 contains miscellaneous and consequential amendments.

457. Repeals and revocations

Schedule 12 contains repeals and revocations.

458. Commencement

(1) The preceding provisions of this Act (except the provisions specified in subsection (3)) come into force in accordance with provision made by the Secretary of State by order.
(2) But no order may be made which includes provision for the commencement of Part 5, 8 or 10 unless the Secretary of State has consulted the Scottish Ministers.
(3) The following provisions come into force in accordance with provision made by the Scottish Ministers by order after consultation with the Secretary of State—
   (a) Part 3;
   (b) this Part, to the extent that it relates to Part 3.

459. Orders and regulations

(1) References in this section to subordinate legislation are to—
   (a) any Order in Council under this Act;
   (b) any order under this Act (other than one falling to be made by a court);
   (c) any regulations under this Act.
(2) Subordinate legislation—
   (a) may make different provision for different purposes;
   (b) may include supplementary, incidental, saving or transitional provisions.
(3) Any power to make subordinate legislation is exercisable by statutory instrument.
(4) A statutory instrument is subject to annulment in pursuance of a resolution of either House of Parliament if it contains subordinate legislation other than—
   (a) an order under section 75(7) or (8), 223(7) or (8), 282, 292(4), 309, 364(4), 377(4), 436(6), 438(9) or 458;

      (b) subordinate legislation made by the Scottish Ministers;

      (c) an Order in Council made under section 443 which makes provision only in relation to Scotland.

  (5) A statutory instrument is subject to annulment in pursuance of a resolution of the Scottish Parliament if it contains—

      (a) subordinate legislation made by the Scottish Ministers other than an order under section 142(6) or (7), 293(4), 398(4), 410(4), 439(6), 441(9) or 458;

      (b) an Order in Council made under section 443 which makes provision only in relation to Scotland.

  (6) No order may be made—

      (a) by the Secretary of State under section 75(7) or (8), 223(7) or (8), 282, 292(4), 309, 364(4), 377(4), 436(6) or 438(9) unless a draft of the order has been laid before Parliament and approved by a resolution of each House;

      (b) by the Scottish Ministers under section 142(6) or (7), 293(4), 398(4), 410(4), 439(6) or 441(9) unless a draft of the order has been laid before and approved by a resolution of the Scottish Parliament.

  (7) The Scottish Ministers must lay before the Scottish Parliament a copy of every statutory instrument containing an Order in Council made under section 444 or 445.

460. Finance

  (1) The following are to be paid out of money provided by Parliament—

      (a) any expenditure incurred by any Minister of the Crown under this Act;

      (b) any increase attributable to this Act in the sums payable out of money so provided under any other enactment.

  (2) Any sums received by the Secretary of State in consequence of this Act are to be paid into the Consolidated Fund.

461. Extent

  (1) Part 2 extends to England and Wales only.

  (2) In Part 8, Chapter 2 extends to England and Wales and Northern Ireland only.

  (3) These provisions extend to Scotland only—

      (a) Part 3;

      (b) in Part 8, Chapter 3.

  (4) Part 4 extends to Northern Ireland only.

  (5) The amendments in Schedule 11 have the same extent as the provisions amended.

  (6) The repeals and revocations in Schedule 12 have the same extent as the provisions repealed or revoked.

462. Short title

This Act may be cited as the Proceeds of Crime Act 2002.

SCHEDULES

SCHEDULE 1

ASSETS RECOVERY AGENCY

Director's terms of appointment

1.—(1) The Director holds office for the period determined by the Secretary of State on his appointment (or re-appointment) to the office.

(2) But—

(a) the Director may at any time resign by giving notice to the Secretary of State;

(b) the Secretary of State may at any time remove the Director from office if satisfied that he is unable or unfit to exercise his functions.

2. Subject to that, the Director holds office on the terms determined by the Secretary of State with the approval of the Minister for the Civil Service.

Staff

3.—(1) The members of staff of the Agency must include—

(a) a deputy to the Director who is to act as Director during any vacancy in that office or if the Director is absent, subject to suspension or unable to act, and

(b) an assistant to the Director with responsibilities in relation to the exercise of the Director's functions in Northern Ireland.

(2) But the Director must not appoint a person under sub-paragraph (1)(b) unless he first consults the Secretary of State.

4. The members of staff of the Agency hold office on the terms determined by the Director with the approval of the Minister for the Civil Service.

Finances

5.—(1) These amounts are to be paid out of money provided by Parliament—

(a) the remuneration of the Director and the staff of the Agency;

(b) any expenses incurred by the Director or any of the staff in the exercise of his or their functions.

(2) Subject to anything in this Act any sums received by the Director are to be paid into the Consolidated Fund.

Annual plan

6.—(1) The Director must, before the beginning of each financial year apart from the first, prepare a plan setting out how he intends to exercise his functions during the financial year (an annual plan).

(2) The annual plan must, in particular, set out how the Director intends to exercise his functions in Northern Ireland.

(3) The annual plan must also include a statement of—

(a) the Director's objectives for the financial year;

    (b) any performance targets which he has for the financial year (whether or not relating to his objectives);

    (c) his priorities for the financial year;

    (d) the financial resources expected to be available to him for the financial year;

    (e) his proposed allocation of those resources.

(4) Once the annual plan has been prepared the Director must send a copy to the Secretary of State for his approval.

(5) If the Secretary of State does not approve the annual plan—

    (a) he must give the Director his reasons for not approving it, and

    (b) he may require the Director to revise it in the manner specified by the Secretary of State.

(6) The Director must revise the annual plan, but if sub-paragraph (5)(b) applies he must do so in the manner specified by the Secretary of State.

(7) The Director must send a copy of the revised annual plan to the Secretary of State for his approval.

Annual report

7.—(1) The Director must, as soon as possible after the end of each financial year, prepare a report on how he has exercised his functions during the financial year.

(2) The report for any financial year apart from the first must include—

    (a) the Director's annual plan for the financial year, and

    (b) an assessment of the extent to which it has been carried out.

(3) The Director must send a copy of each report to the Secretary of State who must—

    (a) lay a copy of it before each House of Parliament, and

    (b) arrange for it to be published.

Meaning of 'financial year'

8. In this Schedule 'financial year' means—

    (a) the period beginning with the day on which section 1 comes into force and ending with the next 31 March (which is the first financial year), and

    (b) each subsequent period of twelve months beginning with 1 April.

Section 75

SCHEDULE 2

LIFESTYLE OFFENCES: ENGLAND AND WALES

Drug trafficking

1.—(1) An offence under any of the following provisions of the Misuse of Drugs Act 1971 (c. 38)—

    (a) section 4(2) or (3) (unlawful production or supply of controlled drugs);

    (b) section 5(3) (possession of controlled drug with intent to supply);

    (c) section 8 (permitting certain activities relating to controlled drugs);

    (d) section 20 (assisting in or inducing the commission outside the UK of an offence punishable under a corresponding law).

(2) An offence under any of the following provisions of the Customs and Excise Management Act 1979 (c. 2) if it is committed in connection with a prohibition or restriction on importation or exportation which has effect by virtue of section 3 of the Misuse of Drugs Act 1971—

(a) section 50(2) or (3) (improper importation of goods);
(b) section 68(2) (exploration of prohibited or restricted goods);
(c) section 170 (fraudulent evasion).

(3) An offence under either of the following provisions of the Criminal Justice (International Co-operation) Act 1990 (c. 5)—

(a) section 12 (manufacture or supply of a substance for the time being specified in Schedule 2 to that Act);
(b) section 19 (using a ship for illicit traffic in controlled drugs).

Money laundering

2. An offence under either of the following provisions of this Act—
(a) section 327 (concealing etc criminal property);
(b) section 328 (assisting another to retain criminal property).

Directing terrorism

3. An offence under section 56 of the Terrorism Act 2000 (c. 11) (directing the activities of a terrorist organisation).

People trafficking

4. An offence under section 25(1) of the Immigration Act 1971 (c. 77) (assisting illegal entry etc).

Arms trafficking

5.—(1) An offence under either of the following provisions of the Customs and Excise Management Act 1979 if it is committed in connection with a firearm or ammunition—
(a) section 68(2) (exportation of prohibited goods);
(b) section 170 (fraudulent evasion).

(2) An offence under section 3(1) of the Firearms Act 1968 (c. 27) (dealing in firearms or ammunition by way of trade or business).

(3) In this paragraph 'firearm' and 'ammunition' have the same meanings as in section 57 of the Firearms Act 1968 (c. 27).

Counterfeiting

6. An offence under any of the following provisions of the Forgery and Counterfeiting Act 1981 (c. 45)—
(a) section 14 (making counterfeit notes or coins);
(b) section 15 (passing etc counterfeit notes or coins);

(c) section 16 (having counterfeit notes or coins);

(d) section 17 (making or possessing materials or equipment for counterfeiting).

Intellectual property

7.—(1) An offence under any of the following provisions of the Copyright, Designs and Patents Act 1988 (c. 48)—

    (a) section 107(1) (making or dealing in an article which infringes copyright);

    (b) section 107(2) (making or possessing an article designed or adapted for making a copy of a copyright work);

    (c) section 198(1) (making or dealing in an illicit recording);

    (d) section 297A (making or dealing in unauthorised decoders).

  (2) An offence under section 92(1), (2) or (3) of the Trade Marks Act 1994 (c. 26) (unauthorised use etc of trade mark).

Pimps and brothels

8.—(1) An offence under any of the following provisions of the Sexual Offences Act 1956 (c. 69)—

    (a) section 2 (procuring a woman by threats);

    (b) section 3 (procuring a woman by false pretences);

    (c) section 9 (procuring a defective woman to have sexual intercourse);

    (d) section 22 (procuring a woman for prostitution);

    (e) section 24 (detaining a woman in a brothel);

    (f) section 28 (causing or encouraging prostitution etc of girl under 16);

    (g) section 29 (causing or encouraging prostitution of defective woman);

    (h) section 30 (man living on earnings of prostitution);

    (i) section 31 (woman exercising control over prostitute);

    (j) section 33 (keeping a brothel);

    (k) section 34 (letting premises for use as brothel).

  (2) An offence under section 5 of the Sexual Offences Act 1967 (c. 60) (living on the earnings of male prostitute).

Blackmail

9. An offence under section 21 of the Theft Act 1968 (c. 60) (blackmail).

Inchoate offences

10.—(1) An offence of attempting, conspiring or inciting the commission of an offence specified in this Schedule.

  (2) An offence of aiding, abetting, counselling or procuring the commission of such an offence.

SCHEDULE 3

. . .

SCHEDULE 4

. . .

SCHEDULE 5

. . .

Sections 247 and 257   SCHEDULE 6
POWERS OF INTERIM RECEIVER OR ADMINISTRATOR

Seizure

1. Power to seize property to which the order applies.

Information

2.—(1) Power to obtain information or to require a person to answer any question.

(2) A requirement imposed in the exercise of the power has effect in spite of any restriction on the disclosure of information (however imposed).

(3) An answer given by a person in pursuance of such a requirement may not be used in evidence against him in criminal proceedings.

(4) Sub-paragraph (3) does not apply—

(a) on a prosecution for an offence under section 5 of the Perjury Act 1911, section 44(2) of the Criminal Law (Consolidation) (Scotland) Act 1995 or Article 10 of the Perjury (Northern Ireland) Order 1979 (false statements), or

(b) on a prosecution for some other offence where, in giving evidence, he makes a statement inconsistent with it.

(5) But an answer may not be used by virtue of sub-paragraph (4)(b) against a person unless—

(a) evidence relating to it is adduced, or

(b) a question relating to it is asked,

by him or on his behalf in the proceedings arising out of the prosecution.

Entry, search, etc.

3.—(1) Power to—

(a) enter any premises in the United Kingdom to which the interim order applies, and

(b) take any of the following steps.

(2) Those steps are—

(a) to carry out a search for or inspection of anything described in the order,

(b) to make or obtain a copy, photograph or other record of anything so described,

(c) to remove anything which he is required to take possession of in pursuance of the order or which may be required as evidence in the proceedings under Chapter 2 of Part 5.

(3) The order may describe anything generally, whether by reference to a class or otherwise.

Supplementary

4.—(1) An order making any provision under paragraph 2 or 3 must make provision in respect of legal professional privilege (in Scotland, legal privilege within the meaning of Chapter 3 of Part 8).

(2) An order making any provision under paragraph 3 may require any person—

(a) to give the interim receiver or administrator access to any premises which he may enter in pursuance of paragraph 3,

(b) to give the interim receiver or administrator any assistance he may require for taking the steps mentioned in that paragraph.

Management

5.—(1) Power to manage any property to which the order applies.

(2) Managing property includes—

(a) selling or otherwise disposing of assets comprised in the property which are perishable or which ought to be disposed of before their value diminishes,

(b) where the property comprises assets of a trade or business, carrying on, or arranging for another to carry on, the trade or business,

(c) incurring capital expenditure in respect of the property.

Section 267   SCHEDULE 7
                  POWERS OF TRUSTEE FOR CIVIL RECOVERY

Sale

1. Power to sell the property or any part of it or interest in it.

Expenditure

2. Power to incur expenditure for the purpose of—

(a) acquiring any part of the property, or any interest in it, which is not vested in him,

(b) discharging any liabilities, or extinguishing any rights, to which the property is subject.

Management

3.—(1) Power to manage property.

(2) Managing property includes doing anything mentioned in paragraph 5(2) of Schedule 6.

Legal proceedings

4. Power to start, carry on or defend any legal proceedings in respect of the property.

Compromise

5. Power to make any compromise or other arrangement in connection with any claim relating to the property.

Supplementary

6.—(1) For the purposes of, or in connection with, the exercise of any of his powers—
  (a) power by his official name to do any of the things mentioned in sub-paragraph (2),
  (b) power to do any other act which is necessary or expedient.
(2) Those things are—
  (a) holding property,
  (b) entering into contracts,
  (c) suing and being sued,
  (d) employing agents,
  (e) executing a power of attorney, deed or other instrument.

Section 325   SCHEDULE 8
                         FORMS OF DECLARATIONS

The Director

'I, A.B., do solemnly declare that I will not disclose any information received by me in carrying out my functions under Part 6 of the Proceeds of Crime Act 2002 except for the purposes of those functions or for the purposes of any prosecution for an offence relating to inland revenue, or in such other cases as may be required or permitted by law.'

Members of the staff of the Agency

'I, A.B., do solemnly declare that I will not disclose any information received by me in carrying out the functions under Part 6 of the Proceeds of Crime Act 2002 which I may from time to time be authorised by the Director of the Assets Recovery Agency to carry out except for the purposes of those functions, or to the Director or in accordance with his instructions, or for the purposes of any prosecution for an offence relating to inland revenue, or in such other cases as may be required or permitted by law.'

SCHEDULE 9
REGULATED SECTOR AND SUPERVISORY AUTHORITIES

PART 1
REGULATED SECTOR

Business in the regulated sector

1.—(1) A business is in the regulated sector to the extent that it engages in any of the following activities—
  (a) accepting deposits by a person with permission under Part 4 of the Financial Services and Markets Act 2000 (c. 8) to accept deposits (including, in the case of a building society, the raising of money from members of the society by the issue of shares);
  (b) the business of the National Savings Bank;
  (c) business carried on by a credit union;
  (d) any home-regulated activity carried on by a European institution in respect of which the establishment conditions in paragraph 13 of Schedule 3 to the Financial Services and Markets Act 2000, or the service conditions in paragraph 14 of that Schedule, are satisfied;
  (e) any activity carried on for the purpose of raising money authorised to be raised under the National Loans Act 1968 (c. 13) under the auspices of the Director of Savings;
  (f) the activity of operating a bureau de change, transmitting money (or any representation of monetary value) by any means or cashing cheques which are made payable to customers;
  (g) any activity falling within sub-paragraph (2);
  (h) any of the activities in points 1 to 12 or 14 of Annex 1 to the Banking Consolidation Directive, ignoring an activity described in any of sub-paragraphs (a) to (g) above;
  (i) business which consists of effecting or carrying out contracts of long term insurance by a person who has received official authorisation pursuant to Article 6 or 27 of the First Life Directive.
  (2) An activity falls within this sub-paragraph if it constitutes any of the following kinds of regulated activity in the United Kingdom—
  (a) dealing in investments as principal or as agent;
  (b) arranging deals in investments;
  (c) managing investments;
  (d) safeguarding and administering investments;
  (e) sending dematerialised instructions;
  (f) establishing (and taking other steps in relation to) collective investment schemes;
  (g) advising on investments.
  (3) Paragraphs (a) and (i) of sub-paragraph (1) and sub-paragraph (2) must be read with section 22 of the Financial Services and Markets Act 2000, any relevant order under that section and Schedule 2 to that Act.
2.—(1) This paragraph has effect for the purposes of paragraph 1.

(2) 'Building society' has the meaning given by the Building Societies Act 1986 (c. 53).

(3) 'Credit union' has the meaning given by the Credit Unions Act 1979 (c. 34) or the Credit Unions (Northern Ireland) Order 1985 (S.I. 1985/1205 (N.I. 12)).

(4) 'European institution' means an EEA firm of the kind mentioned in paragraph 5(b) or (c) of Schedule 3 to the Financial Services and Markets Act 2000 (c. 8) which qualifies for authorisation for the purposes of that Act under paragraph 12 of that Schedule.

(5) 'Home-regulated activity' in relation to a European institution, means an activity—

(a) which is specified in Annex 1 to the Banking Consolidation Directive and in respect of which a supervisory authority in the home State of the institution has regulatory functions, and

(b) if the institution is an EEA firm of the kind mentioned in paragraph 5(c) of Schedule 3 to the Financial Services and Markets Act 2000, which the institution carries on in its home State.

(6) 'Home State', in relation to a person incorporated in or formed under the law of another member State, means that State.

(7) The Banking Consolidation Directive is the Directive of the European Parliament and Council relating to the taking up and pursuit of the business of credit institutions (No. 2000/12 EC).

(8) The First Life Directive is the First Council Directive on the co-ordination of laws, regulations and administrative provisions relating to the taking up and pursuit of the business of direct life assurance (No. 79/267/EEC).

Excluded activities

3. A business is not in the regulated sector to the extent that it engages in any of the following activities—

(a) the issue of withdrawable share capital within the limit set by section 6 of the Industrial and Provident Societies Act 1965 (c. 12) by a society registered under that Act;

(b) the acceptance of deposits from the public within the limit set by section 7(3) of that Act by such a society;

(c) the issue of withdrawable share capital within the limit set by section 6 of the Industrial and Provident Societies Act (Northern Ireland) 1969 by a society registered under that Act;

(d) the acceptance of deposits from the public within the limit set by section 7(3) of that Act by such a society;

(e) activities carried on by the Bank of England;

(f) any activity in respect of which an exemption order under section 38 of the Financial Services and Markets Act 2000 has effect if it is carried on by a person who is for the time being specified in the order or falls within a class of persons so specified.

PART 2
SUPERVISORY AUTHORITIES

4.—(1) Each of the following is a supervisory authority—

(a) the Bank of England;
(b) the Financial Services Authority;
(c) the Council of Lloyd's;
(d) the Director General of Fair Trading;
(e) a body which is a designated professional body for the purposes of Part 20 of the Financial Services and Markets Act 2000 (c. 8).

(2) The Secretary of State is also a supervisory authority in the exercise, in relation to a person carrying on a business in the regulated sector, of his functions under the enactments relating to companies or insolvency or under the Financial Services and Markets Act 2000.

(3) The Treasury are also a supervisory authority in the exercise, in relation to a person carrying on a business in the regulated sector, of their functions under the enactments relating to companies or insolvency or under the Financial Services and Markets Act 2000.

PART 3
POWER TO AMEND

5. The Treasury may by order amend Part 1 or 2 of this Schedule.

Section 448   SCHEDULE 10
                                        TAX

PART 1
GENERAL

1. Sections 75 and 77 of the Taxes Management Act 1970 (c. 9) (receivers: income tax and capital gains tax) shall not apply in relation to—
    (a) a receiver appointed under section 48, 50 or 52;
    (b) an administrator appointed under section 125 or 128;
    (c) a receiver appointed under section 196, 198 or 200;
    (d) an interim receiver appointed under section 246;
    (e) an interim administrator appointed under section 256.

PART 2
PROVISIONS RELATING TO PART 5
INTRODUCTORY

2.—(1) The vesting of property in the trustee for civil recovery or any other person by a recovery order or in pursuance of an order under section 276 is referred to as a Part 5 transfer.

(2) The person who holds the property immediately before the vesting is referred to as the transferor; and the person in whom the property is vested is referred to as the transferee.

(3) Any amount paid in respect of the transfer by the trustee for civil recovery, or another, to a person who holds the property immediately before the vesting is referred to (in relation to that person) as a compensating payment.

(4) If the recovery order provides or (as the case may be) the terms on which the order under section 276 is made provide for the creation of any interest in favour of a person who holds the property immediately before the vesting, he is to be treated instead as receiving (in addition to any payment referred to in sub-paragraph (3)) a compensating payment of an amount equal to the value of the interest.

(5) Where the property belongs to joint tenants immediately before the vesting and a compensating payment is made to one or more (but not both or all) of the joint tenants, this Part has effect separately in relation to each joint tenant.

(6) Expressions used in this paragraph have the same meaning as in Part 5 of this Act.

(7) 'The Taxes Act 1988' means the Income and Corporation Taxes Act 1988 (c. 1), and 'the Allowances Act 2001' means the Capital Allowances Act 2001 (c. 2).

(8) This paragraph applies for the purposes of this Part.

CAPITAL GAINS TAX

3.—(1) If a gain attributable to a Part 5 transfer accrues to the transferor, it is not a chargeable gain.

(2) But if a compensating payment is made to the transferor—
  (a) sub-paragraph (1) does not apply, and
  (b) the consideration for the transfer is the amount of the compensating payment.

(3) If a gain attributable to the forfeiture under section 298 of property consisting of—
  (a) notes or coins in any currency other than sterling,
  (b) anything mentioned in section 289(6)(b) to (d), if expressed in any currency other than sterling, or
  (c) bearer bonds or bearer shares,
accrues to the person who holds the property immediately before the forfeiture, it is not a chargeable gain.

(4) This paragraph has effect as if it were included in Chapter 1 of Part 2 of the Taxation of Chargeable Gains Act 1992 (c. 12).

INCOME TAX AND CORPORATION TAX

Accrued income scheme

4. If a Part 5 transfer is a transfer of securities within the meaning of sections 711 to 728 of the Taxes Act 1988 (transfers with or without accrued interest), sections 713(2) and (3) and 716 of that Act do not apply to the transfer.

Discounted securities

5. In the case of a Part 5 transfer of property consisting of a relevant discounted security (within the meaning of Schedule 13 to the Finance Act 1996 (c. 8)), it is not to be treated as a transfer for the purposes of that Schedule.

Rights to receive amounts stated in certificates of deposit etc.

6. In the case of a Part 5 transfer of property consisting of a right to which section 56(2) of the Taxes Act 1988 applies, or a right mentioned in section 56A(1) of that Act, (rights stated in certificates of deposit etc.) it is not to be treated as a disposal of the right for the purposes of section 56(2) of that Act.

Non-qualifying offshore funds

7. In the case of a Part 5 transfer of property consisting of an asset mentioned in section 757(1)(a) or (b) of the Taxes Act 1988 (interests in non-qualifying offshore funds etc.), it is not to be treated as a disposal for the purposes of that section.

Futures and options

8. In the case of a Part 5 transfer of property consisting of futures or options (within the meaning of paragraph 4 of Schedule 5AA to the Taxes Act 1988), it is not to be treated as a disposal of the futures or options for the purposes of that Schedule.

Loan relationships

9.—(1) Sub-paragraph (2) applies if, apart from this paragraph, a Part 5 transfer would be a related transaction for the purposes of section 84 of the Finance Act 1996 (c. 8) (debits and credits brought into account for the purpose of taxing loan relationships under Chapter 2 of Part 4 of that Act).

(2) The Part 5 transfer is to be disregarded for the purposes of that Chapter, except for the purpose of identifying any person in whose case any debit or credit not relating to the transaction is to be brought into account.

Exception from paragraphs 4 to 9

10. Paragraphs 4 to 9 do not apply if a compensating payment is made to the transferor.

Trading stock

11.—(1) Sub-paragraph (2) applies, in the case of a Part 5 transfer of property consisting of the trading stock of a trade, for the purpose of computing any profits of the trade for tax purposes.

(2) If, because of the transfer, the trading stock is to be treated for that purpose as if it had been sold in the course of the trade, the amount realised on the sale is to be treated for that purpose as equal to its acquisition cost.

(3) Sub-paragraph (2) has effect in spite of anything in section 100 of the Taxes Act 1988 (valuation of trading stock at discontinuance).

(4) In this paragraph, trading stock and trade have the same meaning as in that section.

CAPITAL ALLOWANCES

Plant and machinery

12.—(1) If there is a Part 5 transfer of plant or machinery, Part 2 of the Allowances Act 2001 is to have effect as if a transferor who has incurred qualifying expenditure were required to bring the disposal value of the plant or machinery into account in accordance with section 61 of that Act for the chargeable period in which the transfer occurs.

(2) But the Part 5 transfer is not to be treated as a disposal event for the purposes of Part 2 of that Act other than by virtue of sub-paragraph (1).

13.—(1) If a compensating payment is made to the transferor, the disposal value to be brought into account is the amount of the payment.

(2) Otherwise, the disposal value to be brought into account is the amount which would give rise neither to a balancing allowance nor to a balancing charge.

14.—(1) Paragraph 13(2) does not apply if the qualifying expenditure has been allocated to the main pool or a class pool.

(2) Instead, the disposal value to be brought into account is the notional written-down value of the qualifying expenditure incurred by the transferor on the provision of the plant or machinery.

(3) The notional written-down value is—

$$QE - A$$

where—

QE is the qualifying expenditure incurred by the transferor on the provision of the plant or machinery,

A is the total of all allowances which could have been made to the transferor in respect of the expenditure if—

(a) that expenditure had been the only expenditure that had ever been taken into account in determining his available qualifying expenditure, and

(b) all allowances had been made in full.

(4) But if—

(a) the Part 5 transfer of the plant or machinery occurs in the same chargeable period as that in which the qualifying expenditure is incurred, and

(b) a first-year allowance is made in respect of an amount of the expenditure,

the disposal value to be brought into account is that which is equal to the balance left after deducting the first year allowance.

15.—(1) Paragraph 13 does not apply if—

(a) a qualifying activity is carried on in partnership,

(b) the Part 5 transfer is a transfer of plant or machinery which is partnership property, and

(c) compensating payments are made to one or more, but not both or all, of the partners.

(2) Instead, the disposal value to be brought into account is the sum of—

(a) any compensating payments made to any of the partners, and

(b) in the case of each partner to whom a compensating payment has not been made, his share of the tax-neutral amount.

(3) A partner's share of the tax-neutral amount is to be determined according to the

339

profit-sharing arrangements for the twelve months ending immediately before the date of the Part 5 transfer.

16.—(1) Paragraph 13 does not apply if—
   (a) a qualifying activity is carried on in partnership,
   (b) the Part 5 transfer is a transfer of plant or machinery which is not partnership property but is owned by two or more of the partners ('the owners'),
   (c) the plant or machinery is used for the purposes of the qualifying activity, and
   (d) compensating payments are made to one or more, but not both or all, of the owners.

   (2) Instead, the disposal value to be brought into account is the sum of—
   (a) any compensating payments made to any of the owners, and
   (b) in the case of each owner to whom a compensating payment has not been made, his share of the tax-neutral amount.

   (3) An owner's share of the tax-neutral amount is to be determined in proportion to the value of his interest in the plant or machinery.

17.—(1) Paragraphs 12 to 16 have effect as if they were included in section 61 of the Allowances Act 2001.

   (2) In paragraphs 15 and 16, the tax-neutral amount is the amount that would be brought into account as the disposal value under paragraph 13(2) or (as the case may be) 14 if the provision in question were not disapplied.

Industrial buildings

18.—(1) If there is a Part 5 transfer of a relevant interest in an industrial building, Part 3 of the Allowances Act 2001 is to have effect as if the transfer were a balancing event within section 315(1) of that Act.

   (2) But the Part 5 transfer is not to be treated as a balancing event for the purposes of Part 3 of that Act other than by virtue of sub-paragraph (1).

19.—(1) If a compensating payment is made to the transferor, the proceeds from the balancing event are the amount of the payment.

   (2) Otherwise—
   (a) the proceeds from the balancing event are the amount which is equal to the residue of qualifying expenditure immediately before the transfer, and
   (b) no balancing adjustment is to be made as a result of the event under section 319 of the Allowances Act 2001.

20.—(1) Paragraph 19 does not apply to determine the proceeds from the balancing event if—
   (a) the relevant interest in the industrial building is partnership property, and
   (b) compensating payments are made to one or more, but not both or all, of the partners.

   (2) Instead, the proceeds from the balancing event are the sum of—
   (a) any compensating payments made to any of the partners, and
   (b) in the case of each partner to whom a compensating payment has not been made, his share of the amount which is equal to the residue of qualifying expenditure immediately before the Part 5 transfer.

   (3) A partner's share of that amount is to be determined according to the profit-sharing arrangements for the twelve months ending immediately before the date of the Part 5 transfer.

21. Paragraphs 18 to 20 have effect as if they were included in Part 3 of the Allowances Act 2001.

Flat conversion

22.—(1) If there is a Part 5 transfer of a relevant interest in a flat, Part 4A of the Allowances Act 2001 is to have effect as if the transfer were a balancing event within section 393N of that Act.

(2) But the Part 5 transfer is not to be treated as a balancing event for the purposes of Part 4A of that Act other than by virtue of sub-paragraph (1).

23.—(1) If a compensating payment is made to the transferor, the proceeds from the balancing event are the amount of the payment.

(2) Otherwise, the proceeds from the balancing event are the amount which is equal to the residue of qualifying expenditure immediately before the transfer.

24.—(1) Paragraph 23 does not apply to determine the proceeds from the balancing event if—

(a) the relevant interest in the flat is partnership property, and

(b) compensating payments are made to one or more, but not both or all, of the partners.

(2) Instead, the proceeds from the balancing event are the sum of—

(a) any compensating payments made to any of the partners, and

(b) in the case of each partner to whom a compensating payment has not been made, his share of the amount which is equal to the residue of qualifying expenditure immediately before the transfer.

(3) A partner's share of that amount is to be determined according to the profit-sharing arrangements for the twelve months ending immediately before the date of the transfer.

25. Paragraphs 22 to 24 have effect as if they were included in Part 4A of the Allowances Act 2001.

Research and development

26. If there is a Part 5 transfer of an asset representing qualifying expenditure incurred by a person, the disposal value he is required to bring into account under section 443(1) of the Allowances Act 2001 for any chargeable period is to be determined as follows (and not in accordance with subsection (4) of that section).

27.—(1) If a compensating payment is made to the transferor, the disposal value he is required to bring into account is the amount of the payment.

(2) Otherwise, the disposal value he is required to bring into account is nil.

28.—(1) Paragraph 27 does not apply to determine the disposal value to be brought into account if—

(a) the asset is partnership property, and

(b) compensating payments are made to one or more, but not both or all, of the partners.

(2) Instead, the disposal value to be brought into account is equal to the sum of any compensating payments.

29. Paragraphs 26 to 28 have effect as if they were included in Part 6 of the Allowances Act 2001.

EMPLOYEE ETC. SHARE SCHEMES

Share options

30. Section 135(6) of the Taxes Act 1988 (gains by directors and employees) does not make any person chargeable to tax in respect of any gain realised by the trustee for civil recovery.

Conditional acquisition of shares

31. Section 140A(4) of the Taxes Act 1988 (disposal etc. of shares) does not make the transferor chargeable to income tax in respect of a Part 5 transfer of shares or an interest in shares.

Shares acquired at an undervalue

32. Section 162(5) of the Taxes Act 1988 (employee shareholdings) does not make the transferor chargeable to income tax in respect of a Part 5 transfer of shares.

Shares in dependent subsidiaries

33. Section 79 of the Finance Act 1988 (c. 39) (charge on increase in value of shares) does not make the transferor chargeable to income tax in respect of a Part 5 transfer of shares or an interest in shares.

Section 456　　　　　　SCHEDULE 11
　　　　　　　　　　　AMENDMENTS

Introduction

1. The amendments specified in this Schedule shall have effect.

Parliamentary Commissioner Act 1967 (c. 13)

2.—(1) The Parliamentary Commissioner Act 1967 is amended as follows.
(2) In Schedule 2 (Departments etc. subject to investigation) at the appropriate place insert—
'Director of the Assets Recovery Agency.'
(3) In the Notes to that Schedule before paragraph 1 insert—
'A1 In the case of the Director of the Assets Recovery Agency an investigation under this Act may be conducted only in respect of the exercise of functions vested in him by virtue of a notice served on the Commissioners of Inland Revenue under section 317(2), 321(2) or 322(2) of the Proceeds of Crime Act 2002 (Inland Revenue functions).'

Police (Scotland) Act 1967 (c. 77)

3.—(1) The Police (Scotland) Act 1967 is amended as follows.
(2) In section 38(3B)(liability of Scottish Ministers for constables on central service)

after 'central service' insert 'or on temporary service as mentioned in section 38A(1)(aa) of this Act'.

(3) In section 38A(1) (meaning of 'relevant service') after paragraph (a) insert—

'(aa) temporary service with the Scottish Ministers in connection with their functions under Part 5 or 8 of the Proceeds of Crime Act 2002, on which a person is engaged with the consent of the appropriate authority;'.

Criminal Appeal Act 1968 (c. 19)

4.—(1) The Criminal Appeal Act 1968 is amended as follows.

(2) In section 33 (appeal to House of Lords) after subsection (1) insert—

'(1A) In subsection (1) above the reference to the prosecutor includes a reference to the Director of the Assets Recovery Agency in a case where (and to the extent that) he is a party to the appeal to the Court of Appeal.'

(3) In section 50(1) (meaning of sentence) after paragraph (c) insert—

'(ca) a confiscation order under Part 2 of the Proceeds of Crime Act 2002;

(cb) an order which varies a confiscation order made under Part 2 of the Proceeds of Crime Act 2002 if the varying order is made under section 21, 22 or 29 of that Act (but not otherwise);'.

Misuse of Drugs Act 1971 (c. 38)

5.—(1) Section 27 of the Misuse of Drugs Act 1971 (forfeiture) is amended as follows.

(2) In subsection (1) for 'a drug trafficking offence, as defined in section 1(3) of the Drug Trafficking Act 1994' substitute 'an offence falling within subsection (3) below'.

(3) After subsection (2) insert—

'(3) An offence falls within this subsection if it is an offence which is specified in—

(a) paragraph 1 of Schedule 2 to the Proceeds of Crime Act 2002 (drug trafficking offences), or

(b) so far as it relates to that paragraph, paragraph 10 of that Schedule.'

Immigration Act 1971 (c. 77)

6. In section 28L of the Immigration Act 1971, in paragraph (c) for the words '33 of the Criminal Law (Consolidation) (Scotland) Act 1995' substitute '412 of the Proceeds of Crime Act 2002'.

Rehabilitation of Offenders Act 1974 (c. 53)

7. In section 1 of the Rehabilitation of Offenders Act 1974 (rehabilitated persons and spent convictions) after subsection (2A) insert—

'(2B) In subsection (2)(a) above the reference to a fine or other sum adjudged to be paid by or imposed on a conviction does not include a reference to an amount payable under a confiscation order made under Part 2 or 3 of the Proceeds of Crime Act 2002.'

Rehabilitation of Offenders (Northern Ireland) Order 1978 (S.I. 1978/1908 (N.I. 27))

8. In Article 3 of the Rehabilitation of Offenders (Northern Ireland) Order 1978 (rehabilitated persons and spent convictions) after paragraph (2) insert—

'(2A) In paragraph (2)(a) the reference to a fine or other sum adjudged to be paid by or imposed on a conviction does not include a reference to an amount payable under a confiscation order made under Part 4 of the Proceeds of Crime Act 2002.'

Criminal Appeal (Northern Ireland) Act 1980 (c. 47)

9.—(1) The Criminal Appeal (Northern Ireland) Act 1980 is amended as follows.

(2) In section 30(3) (meaning of sentence) omit 'and' after paragraph (b) and after paragraph (c) insert—

'(d) a confiscation order under Part 4 of the Proceeds of Crime Act 2002;

(e) an order which varies a confiscation order made under Part 4 of the Proceeds of Crime Act 2002 if the varying order is made under section 171, 172 or 179 of that Act (but not otherwise).'

(3) In section 31 (appeal to House of Lords) after subsection (1) insert—

'(1A) In subsection (1) above the reference to the prosecutor includes a reference to the Director of the Assets Recovery Agency in a case where (and to the extent that) he is a party to the appeal to the Court of Appeal.'

Legal Aid, Advice and Assistance (Northern Ireland) Order 1981 (S.I. 1981/228 (N.I. 8))

10.—(1) Part I of Schedule 1 to the Legal Aid, Advice and Assistance (Northern Ireland) Order 1981 (proceedings for which legal aid may be given under Part II of the Order) is amended as follows.

(2) After paragraph 2 insert—

'2A.—(1) The following proceedings in the Crown Court under the Proceeds of Crime Act 2002—

(a) proceedings which relate to a direction under section 202(3) or 204(3) as to the distribution of funds in the hands of a receiver;

(b) applications under section 210 relating to action taken or proposed to be taken by a receiver;

(c) applications under section 211 to vary or discharge an order under any of sections 196 to 201 for the appointment of or conferring powers on a receiver;

(d) applications under section 220 or 221 for the payment of compensation;

(e) applications under sections 351(3), 362(3), 369(3) or 375(2) to vary or discharge certain orders made under Part 8.

(2) But sub-paragraph (1) does not apply in relation to a defendant (within the meaning of Part 4 of that Act) in the following proceedings—

(a) proceedings mentioned in head (b) of that sub-paragraph;

(b) an application under section 221 for the payment of compensation if the confiscation order was varied under section 179.'

(3) In paragraph 3 (courts of summary jurisdiction), after sub-paragraph (i) insert—

'(j) proceedings under sections 295, 297, 298, 301 and 302 of the Proceeds of Crime Act 2002'.

(4) The amendments made by this paragraph are without prejudice to the power to make regulations under Article 10(2) of the Legal Aid, Advice and Assistance

(Northern Ireland) Order 1981 amending or revoking the provisions inserted by this paragraph.

Civil Jurisdiction and Judgments Act 1982 (c. 27)

11. In section 18 of the Civil Jurisdiction and Judgments Act 1982 (enforcement of United Kingdom judgments in other parts of the United Kingdom) in subsection (3) (exceptions) insert after paragraph (c)—

'(d) an order made under Part 2, 3 or 4 of the Proceeds of Crime Act 2002 (confiscation).'

Civic Government (Scotland) Act 1982 (c. 45)

12.—(1) The Civic Government (Scotland) Act 1982 is amended as follows.
(2) In section 86A(3) (application of Part VIIA) for 'sections 21(2) and 28(1) of the Proceeds of Crime (Scotland) Act 1995' substitute 'section 21(2) of the Proceeds of Crime (Scotland) Act 1995 and Part 3 of the Proceeds of Crime Act 2002'.
(3) In paragraph 8 of Schedule 2A (interpretation) for the definition of 'restraint order' substitute—
' "restraint order" means a restraint order made under Part 3 of the Proceeds of Crime Act 2002'.

Criminal Justice Act 1982 (c. 48)

13. In Part 2 of Schedule 1 to the Criminal Justice Act 1982 (offences excluded from early release provisions) after the entry relating to the Drug Trafficking Act 1994 insert—

'PROCEEDS OF CRIME ACT 2002

Section 327 (concealing criminal property etc).
Section 328 (arrangements relating to criminal property).
Section 329 (acquisition, use and possession of criminal property).'

Police and Criminal Evidence Act 1984 (c. 60)

14.—(1) The Police and Criminal Evidence Act 1984 is amended as follows.
(2) In section 56 (right to have someone informed when arrested) for subsection (5A) substitute—
'(5A) An officer may also authorise delay where he has reasonable grounds for believing that—
(a) the person detained for the serious arrestable offence has benefited from his criminal conduct, and
(b) the recovery of the value of the property constituting the benefit will be hindered by telling the named person of the arrest.
(5B) For the purposes of subsection (5A) above the question whether a person has benefited from his criminal conduct is to be decided in accordance with Part 2 of the Proceeds of Crime Act 2002.'

(3) In section 58 (access to legal advice) for subsection (8A) substitute—

'(8A) An officer may also authorise delay where he has reasonable grounds for believing that—

(a) the person detained for the serious arrestable offence has benefited from his criminal conduct, and

(b) the recovery of the value of the property constituting the benefit will be hindered by the exercise of the right conferred by subsection (1) above.

(8B) For the purposes of subsection (8A) above the question whether a person has benefited from his criminal conduct is to be decided in accordance with Part 2 of the Proceeds of Crime Act 2002.'

(4) In section 116 (meaning of serious arrestable offence) in subsection (2) for paragraph (c) and the word 'and' immediately preceding it substitute—

'(c) any offence which is specified in paragraph 1 of Schedule 2 to the Proceeds of Crime Act 2002 (drug trafficking offences),

(d) any offence under section 327, 328 or 329 of that Act (certain money laundering offences).'

Bankruptcy (Scotland) Act 1985 (c. 66)

15.—(1) The Bankruptcy (Scotland) Act 1985 is amended as follows.

(2) In section 5(4) (meaning of 'qualified creditor') for the words from 'has the meaning' to '1995' substitute 'means a confiscation order under Part 2, 3 or 4 of the Proceeds of Crime Act 2002'.

(3) In section 7(1) (meaning of 'apparent insolvency') for the words from 'has the meaning assigned' where second occurring to 'said Act of 1994' where second occurring substitute '"confiscation order" and "restraint order" mean a confiscation order or a restraint order made under Part 2, 3 or 4 of the Proceeds of Crime Act 2002'.

(4) After section 31 (vesting of estate at date of sequestration) insert—

'31A. Property subject to restraint order

(1) This section applies where—

(a) property is excluded from the debtor's estate by virtue of section 420(2)(a) of the Proceeds of Crime Act 2002 (property subject to a restraint order),

(b) an order under section 50, 52, 128, 198 or 200 of that Act has not been made in respect of the property, and

(c) the restraint order is discharged.

(2) On the discharge of the restraint order the property vests in the permanent trustee as part of the debtor's estate.

(3) But subsection (2) does not apply to the proceeds of property realised by a management receiver under section 49(2)(d) or 197(2)(d) of that Act (realisation of property to meet receiver's remuneration and expenses).

31B. Property in respect of which receivership or administration order is made

(1) This section applies where—

(a) property is excluded from the debtor's estate by virtue of section 420(2)(b), (c) or (d) of the Proceeds of Crime Act 2002 (property in respect of which an order for the appointment of a receiver or administrator under certain provisions of that Act is in force), and

(b) a confiscation order is made under section 6, 92 or 156 of that Act,

(c) the amount payable under the confiscation order is fully paid, and

(d) any of the property remains in the hands of the receiver or administrator (as the case may be).

(2) The property vests in the permanent trustee as part of the debtor's estate.

31C. Property subject to certain orders where confiscation order discharged or quashed

(1) This section applies where—

(a) property is excluded from the debtor's estate by virtue of section 420(2)(a), (b), (c) or (d) of the Proceeds of Crime Act 2002 (property in respect of which a restraint order or an order for the appointment of a receiver or administrator under that Act is in force),

(b) a confiscation order is made under section 6, 92 or 156 of that Act, and

(c) the confiscation order is discharged under section 30, 114 or 180 of that Act (as the case may be) or quashed under that Act or in pursuance of any enactment relating to appeals against conviction or sentence.

(2) Any property in the hands of a receiver appointed under Part 2 or 4 of that Act or an administrator appointed under Part 3 of that Act vests in the permanent trustee as part of the debtor's estate.

(3) But subsection (2) does not apply to the proceeds of property realised by a management receiver under section 49(2)(d) or 197(2)(d) of that Act (realisation of property to meet receiver's remuneration and expenses).'

(5) In section 55 (effect of discharge) after subsection (2) insert—

'(3) In subsection (2)(a) above the reference to a fine or other penalty due to the Crown includes a reference to a confiscation order made under Part 2, 3 or 4 of the Proceeds of Crime Act 2002.'.

Insolvency Act 1986 (c. 45)

16.—(1) The Insolvency Act 1986 is amended as follows.

(2) In section 281 (effect of discharge) after subsection (4) insert—

'(4A) In subsection (4) the reference to a fine includes a reference to a confiscation order under Part 2, 3 or 4 of the Proceeds of Crime Act 2002.'

(3) After section 306 insert—

'306A. Property subject to restraint order

(1) This section applies where—

(a) property is excluded from the bankrupt's estate by virtue of section 417(2)(a) of the Proceeds of Crime Act 2002 (property subject to a restraint order),

(b) an order under section 50, 52, 128, 198 or 200 of that Act has not been made in respect of the property, and

(c) the restraint order is discharged.

(2) On the discharge of the restraint order the property vests in the trustee as part of the bankrupt's estate.

(3) But subsection (2) does not apply to the proceeds of property realised by a management receiver under section 49(2)(d) or 197(2)(d) of that Act (realisation of property to meet receiver's remuneration and expenses).

306B. **Property in respect of which receivership or administration order made**

(1) This section applies where—
    (a) property is excluded from the bankrupt's estate by virtue of section 417(2)(b), (c) or (d) of the Proceeds of Crime Act 2002 (property in respect of which an order for the appointment of a receiver or administrator under certain provisions of that Act is in force),
    (b) a confiscation order is made under section 6, 92 or 156 of that Act,
    (c) the amount payable under the confiscation order is fully paid, and
    (d) any of the property remains in the hands of the receiver or administrator (as the case may be).
(2) The property vests in the trustee as part of the bankrupt's estate.

306C. **Property subject to certain orders where confiscation order discharged or quashed**

(1) This section applies where—
    (a) property is excluded from the bankrupt's estate by virtue of section 417(2)(a), (b), (c) or (d) of the Proceeds of Crime Act 2002 (property in respect of which a restraint order or an order for the appointment of a receiver or administrator under that Act is in force),
    (b) a confiscation order is made under section 6, 92 or 156 of that Act, and
    (c) the confiscation order is discharged under section 30, 114 or 180 of that Act (as the case may be) or quashed under that Act or in pursuance of any enactment relating to appeals against conviction or sentence.
(2) Any such property in the hands of a receiver appointed under Part 2 or 4 of that Act or an administrator appointed under Part 3 of that Act vests in the trustee as part of the bankrupt's estate.
(3) But subsection (2) does not apply to the proceeds of property realised by a management receiver under section 49(2)(d) or 197(2)(d) of that Act (realisation of property to meet receiver's remuneration and expenses).'

Criminal Justice Act 1988 (c. 33)

17.—(1) The Criminal Justice Act 1988 is amended as follows.
(2) The following provisions shall cease to have effect—
    (a) sections 71 to 102;
    (b) Schedule 4.
(3) In section 151(4) (Customs and Excise power of arrest) omit 'and' after paragraph (a), and after paragraph (b) insert—
    '(c) a money laundering offence;'
(4) In section 151(5) for the words after 'means' substitute 'any offence which is specified in—
    (a) paragraph 1 of Schedule 2 to the Proceeds of Crime Act 2002 (drug trafficking offences), or
    (b) so far as it relates to that paragraph, paragraph 10 of that Schedule.'

(5) In section 151 after subsection (5) insert—

'(6) In this section "money laundering offence" means any offence which by virtue of section 415 of the Proceeds of Crime Act 2002 is a money laundering offence for the purposes of Part 8 of that Act.'

(6) In section 152(4) (remands of suspected drugs offenders to customs detention) for the words after 'means' substitute 'any offence which is specified in—

(a) paragraph 1 of Schedule 5 to the Proceeds of Crime Act 2002 (drug trafficking offences), or

(b) so far as it relates to that paragraph, paragraph 10 of that Schedule.'

Extradition Act 1989 (c. 33)

18.—(1) The Extradition Act 1989 is amended as follows.

(2) In section 22 (extension of purposes of extradition for offences under Acts giving effect to international conventions) in subsection (4)(h)—

(a) for sub-paragraph (i) substitute—

'(i) any offence which is specified in—

(a) paragraph 1 of Schedule 2 to the Proceeds of Crime Act 2002 (drug trafficking offences), or

(b) so far as it relates to that paragraph, paragraph 10 of that Schedule;

(ia) any offence which by virtue of section 415 of the Proceeds of Crime Act 2002 is a money laundering offence for the purposes of Part 8 of that Act;';

(b) for sub-paragraph (ii) substitute—

'(ii) any offence which is specified in—

(a) paragraph 2 of Schedule 4 to the Proceeds of Crime Act 2002, or

(b) so far as it relates to that paragraph, paragraph 10 of that Schedule;

(iia) any offence which by virtue of section 415 of the Proceeds of Crime Act 2002 is a money laundering offence for the purposes of Part 8 of that Act;';

(c) omit 'and' after sub-paragraph (ii) and for sub-paragraph (iii) substitute—

'(iii) any offence which is specified in—

(a) paragraph 1 of Schedule 5 to the Proceeds of Crime Act 2002 (drug trafficking offences), or

(b) so far as it relates to that paragraph, paragraph 10 of that Schedule; and

(iv) any offence which by virtue of section 415 of the Proceeds of Crime Act 2002 is a money laundering offence for the purposes of Part 8 of that Act;'.

(3) In paragraph 15 of Schedule 1 (deemed extension of jurisdiction of foreign states)—

(a) for paragraph (j) substitute—

'(j) any offence which is specified in—

(i) paragraph 1 of Schedule 2 to the Proceeds of Crime Act 2002 (drug trafficking offences), or

(ii) so far as it relates to that paragraph, paragraph 10 of that Schedule;

(ja) any offence which by virtue of section 415 of the Proceeds of Crime Act 2002 is a money laundering offence for the purposes of Part 8 of that Act;';

(b) for paragraph (k) substitute—

'(k) any offence which is specified in—

(i) paragraph 2 of Schedule 4 to the Proceeds of Crime Act 2002, or

(ii) so far as it relates to that paragraph, paragraph 10 of that Schedule;

(ka) any offence which by virtue of section 415 of the Proceeds of Crime Act 2002 is a money laundering offence for the purposes of Part 8 of that Act;';

(c) for paragraph (m) substitute—

'(m) any offence which is specified in—

    (i) paragraph 1 of Schedule 5 to the Proceeds of Crime Act 2002 (drug trafficking offences), or

    (ii) so far as it relates to that paragraph, paragraph 10 of that Schedule;

(ma) any offence which by virtue of section 415 of the Proceeds of Crime Act 2002 is a money laundering offence for the purposes of Part 8 of that Act;'.

Police and Criminal Evidence (Northern Ireland) Order 1989
(S.I. 1989/1341 (N.I. 12))

19.—(1) The Police and Criminal Evidence (Northern Ireland) Order 1989 is amended as follows.

(2) In Article 57 (right to have someone informed when arrested) for paragraph (5A) substitute—

'(5A) An officer may also authorise delay where he has reasonable grounds for believing that—

(a) the person detained for the serious arrestable offence has benefited from his criminal conduct, and

(b) the recovery of the value of the property constituting the benefit will be hindered by telling the named person of the arrest.

(5B) For the purposes of paragraph (5A) the question whether a person has benefited from his criminal conduct is to be decided in accordance with Part 4 of the Proceeds of Crime Act 2002.'

(3) In Article 59 (access to legal advice) for paragraph (8A) substitute—

'(8A) An officer may also authorise delay where he has reasonable grounds for believing that—

(a) the person detained for the serious arrestable offence has benefited from his criminal conduct, and

(b) the recovery of the value of the property constituting the benefit will be hindered by the exercise of the right conferred by paragraph (1).

(8B) For the purposes of paragraph (8A) the question whether a person has benefited from his criminal conduct is to be decided in accordance with Part 4 of the Proceeds of Crime Act 2002.'

(4) In Article 87 (meaning of serious arrestable offence) in paragraph (2) for subparagraph (aa) substitute—

'(aa) any offence which is specified in paragraph 1 of Schedule 5 to the Proceeds of Crime Act 2002 (drug trafficking offences);

(ab) any offence under section 327, 328 or 329 of that Act (certain money laundering offences);'.

Insolvency (Northern Ireland) Order 1989
(S.I. 1989/2405 (N.I. 19))

20.—(1) The Insolvency (Northern Ireland) Order 1989 is amended as follows.

(2) In Article 255 (effect of discharge) after paragraph (4) insert—

'(4A) In paragraph (4) the reference to a fine includes a reference to a confiscation order under Part 2, 3 or 4 of the Proceeds of Crime Act 2002.'

(3) After Article 279 insert—

'279A. Property subject to restraint order

(1) This Article applies where—
- (a) property is excluded from the bankrupt's estate by virtue of section 423(2)(a) of the Proceeds of Crime Act 2002 (property subject to a restraint order),
- (b) an order under section 50, 52, 128, 198 or 200 of that Act has not been made in respect of the property, and
- (c) the restraint order is discharged.

(2) On the discharge of the restraint order the property vests in the trustee as part of the bankrupt's estate.

(3) But paragraph (2) does not apply to the proceeds of property realised by a management receiver under section 49(2)(d) or 197(2)(d) of that Act (realisation of property to meet receiver's remuneration and expenses).

279B. Property in respect of which receivership or administration order made

(1) This Article applies where—
- (a) property is excluded from the bankrupt's estate by virtue of section 423(2)(b),
- (c) or (d) of the Proceeds of Crime Act 2002 (property in respect of which an order for the appointment of a receiver or administrator under certain provisions of that Act is in force),
- (b) a confiscation order is made under section 6, 92 or 156 of that Act,
- (c) the amount payable under the confiscation order is fully paid, and
- (d) any of the property remains in the hands of the receiver or administrator (as the case may be).

(2) The property vests in the trustee as part of the bankrupt's estate.

279C. Property subject to certain orders where confiscation order discharged or quashed

(1) This Article applies where—
- (a) property is excluded from the bankrupt's estate by virtue of section 423(2)(a), (b), (c) or (d) of the Proceeds of Crime Act 2002 (property in respect of which a restraint order or an order for the appointment of a receiver or administrator under that Act is in force),
- (b) a confiscation order is made under section 6, 92 or 156 of that Act, and
- (c) the confiscation order is discharged under section 30, 114 or 180 of that Act (as the case may be) or quashed under that Act or in pursuance of any enactment relating to appeals against conviction or sentence.

(2) Any such property in the hands of a receiver appointed under Part 2 or 4 of that Act or an administrator appointed under Part 3 of that Act vests in the trustee as part of the bankrupt's estate.

(3) But paragraph (2) does not apply to the proceeds of property realised by a management receiver under section 49(2)(d) or 197(2)(d) of that Act (realisation of property to meet receiver's remuneration and expenses).'

Criminal Justice (International Co-operation) Act 1990 (c. 5)

21. In section 13(6) of the Criminal Justice (International Co-operation) Act 1990 (information not to be disclosed except for certain purposes)—

    (a) omit 'the Drug Trafficking Act 1994 or the Criminal Justice (Scotland) Act 1987';

    (b) at the end insert 'or of proceedings under Part 2, 3 or 4 of the Proceeds of Crime Act 2002'.

Pension Schemes Act 1993 (c. 48)

22.—(1) The Pension Schemes Act 1993 is amended as follows.

    (2) In section 10 (protected rights and money purchase benefits), after subsection (5) insert—

'(6) Where, in the case of a scheme which makes such provision as is mentioned in subsection (2) or (3), any liability of the scheme in respect of a member's protected rights ceases by virtue of a civil recovery order, his protected rights are extinguished or reduced accordingly.'

    (3) In section 14 (earner's guaranteed minimum), after subsection (2) insert—

'(2A) Where any liability of a scheme in respect of an earner's guaranteed minimum pension ceases by virtue of a civil recovery order, his guaranteed minimum in relation to the scheme is extinguished or reduced accordingly.'

    (4) In section 47 (further provisions relating to guaranteed minimum pensions), in subsection (6), after 'but for' insert 'section 14(2A) and'.

    (5) In section 68B (safeguarded rights), at the end insert 'including provision for such rights to be extinguished or reduced in consequence of a civil recovery order made in respect of such rights'.

    (6) In section 181(1) (general interpretation), after the definition of 'Category A retirement pension' insert—

'"civil recovery order" means an order under section 266 of the Proceeds of Crime Act 2002 or an order under section 276 imposing the requirement mentioned in section 277(3).'

Pension Schemes (Northern Ireland) Act 1993 (c. 49)

23.—(1) The Pension Schemes (Northern Ireland) Act 1993 is amended as follows.

    (2) In section 6 (protected rights and money purchase benefits), after subsection (5) insert—

'(6) Where, in the case of a scheme which makes such provision as is mentioned in subsection (2) or (3), any liability of the scheme in respect of a member's protected rights ceases by virtue of a civil recovery order, his protected rights are extinguished or reduced accordingly.'

    (3) In section 10 (earner's guaranteed minimum), after subsection (2) insert—

'(2A) Where any liability of a scheme in respect of an earner's guaranteed minimum pension ceases by virtue of a civil recovery order, his guaranteed minimum in relation to the scheme is extinguished or reduced accordingly.'

    (4) In section 43 (further provisions relating to guaranteed minimum pensions), in subsection (6), after 'but for' insert 'section 10(2A) and'.

(5) In section 64B (safeguarded rights), at the end insert 'including provision for such rights to be extinguished or reduced in consequence of a civil recovery order made in respect of such rights'.

(6) In section 176(1) (general interpretation), after the definition of 'Category A retirement pension' insert—

' "civil recovery order" means an order under section 266 of the Proceeds of Crime Act 2002 or an order under section 276 imposing the requirement mentioned in section 277(3).'

Criminal Justice and Public Order Act 1994 (c. 31)

24. In section 139(12) of the Criminal Justice and Public Order Act 1994 (search powers) in paragraph (b) of the definition of 'items subject to legal privilege' for 'section 40 of the Criminal Justice (Scotland) Act 1987' substitute 'section 412 of the Proceeds of Crime Act 2002'.

Drug Trafficking Act 1994 (c. 37)

25.—(1) The Drug Trafficking Act 1994 is amended as follows.

(2) The following provisions shall cease to have effect—

    (a) sections 1 to 54;

    (b) in sections 55(4)(a) (orders to make material available) and 56(3)(a) and (4)(a) (authority for search) the words 'or has benefited from';

    (c) in section 59 (disclosure of information held by government departments), subsections (1) to (10) and in subsection (11) the words 'An order under subsection (1) above, and,';

    (d) in section 60(6) (Customs and Excise prosecution powers), in the definition of 'specified offence', in paragraph (a) the words 'Part III or' and paragraph (c) and the word 'or' immediately preceding it;

    (e) in section 60(6) the words from 'and references to the institution of proceedings' to the end;

    (f) in section 60, subsections (7) and (8);

    (g) in section 61 (extension of certain offences to the Crown), subsections (2) to (4);

    (h) sections 62, 63(1), (2) and (3)(a) and 64 (interpretation);

    (i) in section 68(2) (extent—Scotland), paragraphs (a) to (c) and in paragraph (g) the words '1, 41, 62' and '64';

    (j) in section 68(3) (extent—Northern Ireland), paragraph (a) and in paragraph (d) the word '64'.

(3) In section 59(12)(b) for the words 'referred to in subsection (1) above' substitute 'specified in an order under section 55(2)'.

(4) After section 59 insert the following section—

'59A. Construction of sections 55 to 59

(1) This section has effect for the purposes of sections 55 to 59.

(2) A reference to a constable includes a reference to a customs officer.

(3) A customs officer is a person commissioned by the Commissioners of Customs and Excise under section 6(3) of the Customs and Excise Management Act 1979 (c. 2).

(4) Drug trafficking means doing or being concerned in any of the following (whether in England and Wales or elsewhere)—

    (a) producing or supplying a controlled drug where the production or supply contravenes section 4(1) of the Misuse of Drugs Act 1971 or a corresponding law;

    (b) transporting or storing a controlled drug where possession of the drug contravenes section 5(1) of that Act or a corresponding law;

    (c) importing or exporting a controlled drug where the importation or exportation is prohibited by section 3(1) of that Act or a corresponding law;

    (d) manufacturing or supplying a scheduled substance within the meaning of section 12 of the Criminal Justice (International Co-operation) Act 1990 where the manufacture or supply is an offence under that section or would be such an offence if it took place in England and Wales;

    (e) using any ship for illicit traffic in controlled drugs in circumstances which amount to the commission of an offence under section 19 of that Act.

(5) In this section 'corresponding law' has the same meaning as in the Misuse of Drugs Act 1971.'

(5) In section 60 after subsection (6) insert—

'(6A) Proceedings for an offence are instituted—

    (a) when a justice of the peace issues a summons or warrant under section 1 of the Magistrates' Courts Act 1980 (issue of summons to, or warrant for arrest of, accused) in respect of the offence;

    (b) when a person is charged with the offence after being taken into custody without a warrant;

    (c) when a bill of indictment is preferred under section 2 of the Administration of Justice (Miscellaneous Provisions) Act 1933 in a case falling within paragraph (b) of subsection (2) of that section (preferment by direction of the criminal division of the Court of Appeal or by direction, or with the consent, of a High Court judge).

(6B) Where the application of subsection (6A) would result in there being more than one time for the institution of proceedings they must be taken to have been instituted at the earliest of those times.'

(6) In section 61(1) for 'sections 49(2), 50 to 53 and 58' substitute 'section 58'.

(7) In section 68(2)(d), for '59(10)' substitute '59(11)'.

Criminal Justice (Northern Ireland) Order 1994 (S.I. 1994/2795 (N.I. 15))

26. In Article 16 of the Criminal Justice (Northern Ireland) Order 1994 in paragraph (a) after 'Proceeds of Crime (Northern Ireland) Order 1996' insert 'or Part 4 of the Proceeds of Crime Act 2002'.

Proceeds of Crime Act 1995 (c. 11)

27. Section 15(2) and (3) of the Proceeds of Crime Act 1995 (investigation into benefit to be treated as the investigation of an offence for the purposes of sections 21 and 22 of the Police and Criminal Evidence Act 1984) shall cease to have effect.

Proceeds of Crime (Scotland) Act 1995 (c. 43)

28.—(1) The Proceeds of Crime (Scotland) Act 1995 is amended as follows.

(2) The following provisions in the Act shall cease to have effect—
  (a) Part I, except section 2(7);
  (b) in section 28, subsections (1)(a) and (2) and in subsection (5) the words '(including a restraint order made under and within the meaning of the 1994 Act)';
  (c) section 29;
  (d) in section 31, subsection (2) and in subsection (4) the words 'or (2)';
  (e) sections 35 to 39;
  (f) in section 40, subsections (1)(a), (2) and (4);
  (g) in section 42, subsections (1)(a) and (b);
  (h) in section 43, in subsection (1) the words ', confiscation order' and subsection (2);
  (i) in section 45, subsection (1)(a);
  (j) section 47;
  (k) in section 49, in subsection (1) the definitions of 'the 1988 Act', 'the 1994 Act' and 'confiscation order' and subsection (4).
(3) The following provisions in Schedule 1 to the Act shall cease to have effect—
  (a) in paragraph 1(1)(b) the words 'or a confiscation order', in paragraph 1(2)(a) the words 'subject to paragraph (b) below', paragraph 1(2)(b) and in paragraph 1(3)(a)(i) the words 'or confiscation order';
  (b) in paragraph 2(1)(a) the words ', and if appointed (or empowered) under paragraph 1(1)(b) above where a confiscation order has been made';
  (c) paragraph 4;
  (d) in paragraph 5(1) the words 'Part I of';
  (e) in paragraph 8(2) the words ', unless in a case where a confiscation order has been made there are sums available to be applied in payment of it under paragraph 4(4)(b) above,';
  (f) in paragraph 10(1) the words 'or the recipient of a gift caught by Part I of this Act or an implicative gift' and paragraphs 10(2) and 10(3);
  (g) in paragraph 12(1)(a) the words 'paragraph (a) or (b) of section 4(1) or'.
(4) The following provisions in Schedule 2 to the Act shall cease to have effect—
  (a) in paragraph 1(2) the words 'and 35 to 38';
  (b) in paragraph 2, in sub-paragraph (1) the words 'realisable or', in sub-paragraph (2) the words 'and 35 to 38', sub-paragraph (5).
  (c) in paragraph 3(2) the words 'and 35 to 38' and paragraphs 3(4) and (5);
  (d) in paragraph 4(2) the words 'and 35 to 38';
  (e) paragraph 6(2)(a).
(5) In section 28(9) (restraint orders) for 'Subsections (2)(a) and' substitute 'Subsection'.
(6) In section 42 (enforcement) in subsections (2)(a), (c) and (d) for 'Part I,' substitute 'Part'.

Criminal Procedure (Scotland) Act 1995 (c. 46)

29.—(1) The Criminal Procedure (Scotland) Act 1995 is amended as follows.
(2) In section 109(1) (intimation of appeal) for 'section 10 of the Proceeds of Crime (Scotland) Act 1995 (postponed confiscation orders)' substitute 'section 99 of the Proceeds of Crime Act 2002 (postponement)'.
(3) In section 205B(5) (minimum sentence for third drug trafficking offence) for the definition of 'drug trafficking offence' substitute—

'"drug trafficking offence" means an offence specified in paragraph 2 or (so far as it relates to that paragraph) paragraph 10 of Schedule 4 to the Proceeds of Crime Act 2002;'.

(4) In section 219(8)(b) (fines: imprisonment for non-payment) for '14(2) of the Proceeds of Crime (Scotland) Act 1995' substitute '118(2) of the Proceeds of Crime Act 2002'.

Police Act 1996 (c. 16)

30.—(1) Section 97 of the Police Act 1996 (police officers engaged on service outside their force) is amended as follows.

(2) In subsection (1) after paragraph (cc) insert—

'(cd) temporary service with the Assets Recovery Agency on which a person is engaged with the consent of the appropriate authority;'.

(3) In subsection (6)(a) after '(cc)' insert '(cd)'.

(4) In subsection (8) after '(cc)' insert '(cd)'.

Proceeds of Crime (Northern Ireland) Order 1996 (S.I. 1996/1299 (N.I. 9)

31.—(1) The Proceeds of Crime (Northern Ireland) Order 1996 is amended as follows.

(2) Parts II and III shall cease to have effect.

(3) The following provisions shall also cease to have effect—

(a) in Article 2 (interpretation) in paragraph (2) from the definition of 'charging order' to the definition of 'external confiscation order' and from the definition of 'modifications' to the definition of 'restraint order' and paragraphs (3) to (10) and (12);

(b) Article 3 (definition of 'property' etc.);

(c) in Article 49 (additional investigation powers), in paragraph (1) sub-paragraph (c) and the word 'and' immediately preceding it, in paragraph (1A) sub-paragraph (c) and the word 'and' immediately preceding it, paragraph (4) and in paragraph (5) the definitions of 'customs officer' and 'relevant property';

(d) in Article 52 (supplementary provisions) in paragraph (2) sub-paragraph (b) and the word 'and' immediately preceding it, and paragraph (3);

(e) in Article 54 (disclosure of information held by government departments) paragraphs (1) to (10) and (13) and in paragraph (11) the words 'An order under paragraph (1) and,';

(f) in Article 55 (Customs and Excise prosecution powers), in paragraph (6) in the definition of 'specified offence' in paragraph (a) the words 'Part III or' and paragraph (c) and the word 'or' immediately preceding it, and paragraph (7);

(g) Article 56(2) to (4) (extension of certain offences to the Crown);

(h) in Schedule 2 paragraph 3.

(4) In Article 49(1) (additional investigation powers)—

(a) for 'county court' substitute 'Crown Court';

(b) in sub-paragraph (a) for the words from 'an investigation' to the end of head (ii) substitute 'a confiscation investigation';

(c) in sub-paragraph (b) after 'and who is' insert 'an accredited financial investigator'.

(5) In Article 49(1A)—
   (a) after 'application made by' insert 'the Director of the Assets Recovery Agency or';
   (b) for 'county court' substitute 'Crown Court';
   (c) in sub-paragraph (a) for the words from 'an investigation' to the end of head (ii) substitute 'a confiscation investigation';
   (d) in sub-paragraph (b) after 'if' insert 'the Director or';
   (e) after 'authorise' insert 'the Director or';
   (f) for 'paragraphs 3 and 3A' where it twice occurs substitute 'paragraph 3A'.

(6) In Article 49(5) insert at the appropriate place in alphabetical order—
'"accredited financial investigator" has the meaning given by section 3(5) of the Proceeds of Crime Act 2002;
"confiscation investigation" has the same meaning as it has for the purposes of Part 8 of that Act by virtue of section 341(1);'.

(7) In Article 50(1) (order to make material available)—
   (a) for sub-paragraphs (a) and (b) substitute 'drug trafficking';
   (b) for 'county court' substitute 'Crown Court'.

(8) In Article 50(4)(a), for heads (i) to (iii) substitute 'has carried on drug trafficking'.

(9) In Article 50(8) for 'county court' substitute 'Crown Court'.

(10) In Article 51(1) (authority for search)—
   (a) for sub-paragraphs (a) and (b) substitute 'drug trafficking';
   (b) for 'county court' substitute 'Crown Court'.

(11) In Article 51(3)(a) for heads (i) to (iii) substitute 'has carried on drug trafficking'.

(12) In Article 51(4)—
   (a) in sub-paragraph (a) for heads (i) to (iii) substitute 'has carried on drug trafficking';
   (b) in sub-paragraph (b)(i) for the words from 'the question' to the end substitute 'drug trafficking'.

(13) In Article 52(1)(a) (supplementary provisions), for heads (i) to (ii) substitute 'drug trafficking'.

(14) In Article 54 (disclosure of information held by government departments) in paragraph (12)(b) for 'referred to in paragraph (1)' substitute 'specified in an order under Article 50(2)'.

(15) After Article 54 insert the following Article—

'54A. Construction of Articles 49 to 54

(1) This Article has effect for the purposes of Articles 49 to 54.

(2) A reference to a constable includes a reference to a customs officer.

(3) A customs officer is a person commissioned by the Commissioners of Customs and Excise under section 6(3) of the Customs and Excise Management Act 1979.

(4) Drug trafficking means doing or being concerned in any of the following (whether in Northern Ireland or elsewhere)—
   (a) producing or supplying a controlled drug where the production or supply contravenes section 4(1) of the Misuse of Drugs Act 1971 or a corresponding law;
   (b) transporting or storing a controlled drug where possession of the drug contravenes section 5(1) of that Act or a corresponding law;

    (c) importing or exporting a controlled drug where the importation or exportation is prohibited by section 3(1) of that Act or a corresponding law;

    (d) manufacturing or supplying a scheduled substance within the meaning of section 12 of the Criminal Justice (International Co-operation) Act 1990 where the manufacture or supply is an offence under that section or would be such an offence if it took place in Northern Ireland;

    (e) using any ship for illicit traffic in controlled drugs in circumstances which amount to the commission of an offence under section 19 of that Act.

  (5) In this Article 'corresponding law' has the same meaning as in the Misuse of Drugs Act 1971.'

(16) In Article 55 after paragraph (6) insert—

  '(6A) Proceedings for an offence are instituted—

    (a) when a summons or warrant is issued under Article 20 of the Magistrates' Courts (Northern Ireland) Order 1981 in respect of the offence;

    (b) when a person is charged with the offence after being taken into custody without a warrant;

    (c) when an indictment is preferred under section 2(2)(c), (e) or (f) of the Grand Jury (Abolition) Act (Northern Ireland) 1969.

(6B) Where the application of paragraph (6A) would result in there being more than one time for the institution of proceedings they must be taken to have been instituted at the earliest of those times.'

(17) In Article 56(1) (extension of certain offences to the Crown), for 'Articles 44, 45, 46, 47(2), 48 and' substitute 'Article'.

(18) In Schedule 2 (financial investigations) in paragraph 3A—

    (a) in sub-paragraph (1) for 'any conduct to which Article 49 applies' substitute 'his criminal conduct';

    (b) after that paragraph insert—

'(1A) For the purposes of sub-paragraph (1) the question whether a person has benefited from his criminal conduct is to be decided in accordance with Part 4 of the Proceeds of Crime Act 2002.'

Crime (Sentences) Act 1997 (c. 43)

32.—(1) The Crime (Sentences) Act 1997 is amended as follows.

  (2) In section 35 (fine defaulters) in subsection (1)(a) after 'Drug Trafficking Act 1994' insert 'or section 6 of the Proceeds of Crime Act 2002'.

  (3) In section 40 (fine defaulters) in subsection (1)(a) after 'Drug Trafficking Act 1994' insert 'or section 6 of the Proceeds of Crime Act 2002'.

Crime and Punishment (Scotland) Act 1997 (c. 48)

33. The following provisions of the Crime and Punishment (Scotland) Act 1997 shall cease to have effect—

  (a) section 15(3),

  (b) in Schedule 1, paragraph 20.

Police (Northern Ireland) Act 1998 (c. 32)

34.—(1) Section 27 of the Police (Northern Ireland) Act 1998 (members of the Police Service engaged on other police service) is amended as follows.

(2) In subsection (1) after paragraph (c) insert—

'(ca) temporary service with the Assets Recovery Agency on which a member of the Police Service of Northern Ireland is engaged with the consent of the Chief Constable;'.

(3) In subsection (5)(b) after '(c)' insert '(ca)'.

(4) In subsection (7) for 'or (c)' there is substituted '(c) or (ca)'.

Crime and Disorder Act 1998 (c. 37)

35. In Schedule 8 to the Crime and Disorder Act 1998 paragraphs 115 and 116 shall cease to have effect.

Access to Justice Act 1999 (c. 22)

36.—(1) Schedule 2 to the Access to Justice Act 1999 (services excluded from the Community Legal Service) is amended as follows.

(2) In paragraph 2(2), after paragraph (d) insert 'or

(e) under the Proceeds of Crime Act 2002 to the extent specified in paragraph 3,'

and omit the 'or' at the end of paragraph (c).

(3) In paragraph 2(3) (magistrates courts), after '2001' insert—

'(l) for an order or direction under section 295, 297, 298, 301 or 302 of the Proceeds of Crime Act 2002,'

and omit the 'or' at the end of paragraph (j).

(4) After paragraph 2 insert—

'3(1) These are the proceedings under the Proceeds of Crime Act 2002—

(a) an application under section 42(3) to vary or discharge a restraint order or an order under section 41(7);

(b) proceedings which relate to a direction under section 54(3) or 56(3) as to the distribution of funds in the hands of a receiver;

(c) an application under section 62 relating to action taken or proposed to be taken by a receiver;

(d) an application under section 63 to vary or discharge an order under any of sections 48 to 53 for the appointment of or conferring powers on a receiver;

(e) an application under section 72 or 73 for the payment of compensation;

(f) proceedings which relate to an order under section 298 for the forfeiture of cash;

(g) an application under section 351(3), 362(3), 369(3) or 375(2) to vary or discharge certain orders made under Part 8.

(2) But sub-paragraph (1) does not authorise the funding of the provision of services to a defendant (within the meaning of Part 1 of that Act) in relation to—

(a) proceedings mentioned in paragraph (b);

(b) an application under section 73 for the payment of compensation if the confiscation order was varied under section 29.'

359

Powers of Criminal Courts (Sentencing) Act 2000 (c. 6)

37.—(1) The Powers of Criminal Courts (Sentencing) Act 2000 is amended as follows.

(2) In section 110(5) (minimum sentence for third drug trafficking offence) for the definition of 'drug trafficking offence' there is substituted—

'"drug trafficking offence" means an offence which is specified in—

  (a) paragraph 1 of Schedule 2 to the Proceeds of Crime Act 2002 (drug trafficking offences), or

  (b) so far as it relates to that paragraph, paragraph 10 of that Schedule.'

(3) In section 133 (review of compensation orders) in subsection (3)(c) after 'Criminal Justice Act 1988' insert ', or Part 2 of the Proceeds of Crime Act 2002,'.

Financial Services and Markets Act 2000 (c. 8)

38. In Schedule 1 to the Financial Services and Markets Act 2000 (provisions relating to the Financial Services Authority) after paragraph 19 insert—

  '19A. For the purposes of this Act anything done by an accredited financial investigator within the meaning of the Proceeds of Crime Act 2002 who is—

  (a) a member of the staff of the Authority, or

  (b) a person appointed by the Authority under section 97, 167 or 168 to conduct an investigation,

must be treated as done in the exercise or discharge of a function of the Authority.'

Terrorism Act 2000 (c. 11)

39.—(1) Schedule 8 to the Terrorism Act 2000 (detention) is amended as follows.

(2) In paragraph 8 (authorisation of delay in exercise of detained person's rights) for sub-paragraph (5) substitute—

  '(5) An officer may also give an authorisation under sub-paragraph (1) if he has reasonable grounds for believing that—

  (a) the detained person has benefited from his criminal conduct, and

  (b) the recovery of the value of the property constituting the benefit will be hindered by—

    (i) informing the named person of the detained person's detention (in the case of an authorisation under sub-paragraph (1)(a)), or

    (ii) the exercise of the right under paragraph 7 (in the case of an authorisation under sub-paragraph (1)(b)).

(5A) For the purposes of sub-paragraph (5) the question whether a person has benefited from his criminal conduct is to be decided in accordance with Part 2 of the Proceeds of Crime Act 2002.'

(3) In paragraph 17(3) (grounds for authorising delay or requiring presence of senior officer), in paragraph (d) for 'Part VI of the Criminal Justice Act 1988, Part I of the Proceeds of Crime (Scotland) Act 1995' substitute 'Part 2 or 3 of the Proceeds of Crime Act 2002'.

(4) For paragraph 17(4) (further grounds for authorising delay in exercise of detained person's rights) substitute—

  '(4) This sub-paragraph applies where an officer mentioned in paragraph 16(4) or (7) has reasonable grounds for believing that—

    (a) the detained person has benefited from his criminal conduct, and

    (b) the recovery of the value of the property constituting the benefit will be hindered by—

        (i) informing the named person of the detained person's detention (in the case of an authorisation under paragraph 16(4)), or

        (ii) the exercise of the entitlement under paragraph 16(6) (in the case of an authorisation under paragraph 16(7)).

(4A) For the purposes of sub-paragraph (4) the question whether a person has benefited from his criminal conduct is to be decided in accordance with Part 3 of the Proceeds of Crime Act 2002.'

(5) In paragraph 34 (authorisation for withholding information from detained person) for sub-paragraph (3) substitute—

'(3) A judicial authority may also make an order under sub-paragraph (1) in relation to specified information if satisfied that there are reasonable grounds for believing that—

    (a) the detained person has benefited from his criminal conduct, and

    (b) the recovery of the value of the property constituting the benefit would be hindered if the information were disclosed.

(3A) For the purposes of sub-paragraph (3) the question whether a person has benefited from his criminal conduct is to be decided in accordance with Part 2 or 3 of the Proceeds of Crime Act 2002.'

Criminal Justice and Police Act 2001 (c. 16)

40.—(1) The Criminal Justice and Police Act 2001 is amended as follows.

    (2) In section 55 (obligation to return excluded and special procedure material) in subsection (5) (powers in relation to which section does not apply as regards special procedure material) omit 'and' after paragraph (b), and after paragraph (c) insert—
'and

    (d) section 352(4) of the Proceeds of Crime Act 2002,'.

    (3) In section 60 (cases where duty to secure seized property arises) in subsection (4) (powers in relation to which duty does not arise as regards special procedure material) omit 'or' after paragraph (b), and after paragraph (c) insert—
'or

    (d) section 352(4) of the Proceeds of Crime Act 2002,'.

    (4) In section 64 (meaning of appropriate judicial authority) in subsection (3) after paragraph (a) omit 'and' and insert—
'(aa) the power of seizure conferred by section 352(4) of the Proceeds of Crime Act 2002, if the power is exercisable for the purposes of a civil recovery investigation (within the meaning of Part 8 of that Act);'.

    (5) In section 65 (meaning of 'legal privilege')—

    (a) in subsection (1)(b) for the words '33 of the Criminal Law (Consolidation) (Scotland) Act 1995 (c. 39)' substitute '412 of the Proceeds of Crime Act 2002';

    (b) after subsection (3) insert—

'(3A) In relation to property which has been seized in exercise, or purported exercise, of—

    (a) the power of seizure conferred by section 352(4) of the Proceeds of Crime Act 2002, or

Sch 12, Proceeds of Crime Act 2002

(b) so much of any power of seizure conferred by section 50 as is exercisable by reference to that power,

references in this Part to an item subject to legal privilege shall be read as references to privileged material within the meaning of section 354(2) of that Act.'

(6) In Part 1 of Schedule 1 (powers of seizure to which section 50 applies) at the end add—

'73A. Proceeds of Crime Act 2002 (c. 00)

The power of seizure conferred by section 352(4) of the Proceeds of Crime Act 2002 (seizure of material likely to be of substantial value to certain investigations).'

(7) In Part 3 of Schedule 1 (powers of seizure to which section 55 applies) at the end add—

'110. Proceeds of Crime Act 2002 (c. 00)

The power of seizure conferred by section 352(4) of the Proceeds of Crime Act 2002 (seizure of material likely to be of substantial value to certain investigations).'

Section 457

SCHEDULE 12
REPEALS AND REVOCATIONS

Short title and chapter	Extent of repeal or revocation
Misuse of Drugs Act 1971 (c. 38)	In section 21 the words 'or section 49 of the Drug Trafficking Act 1994'. In section 23(3A) the words 'or section 49 of the Drug Trafficking Act 1994'.
Criminal Appeal (Northern Ireland) Act 1980 (c. 47)	In section 30(3) the word 'and' after paragraph (b).
Police and Criminal Evidence Act 1984 (c. 60)	In section 65— (a) the definitions of 'drug trafficking' and 'drug trafficking offence'; (b) the words from 'references in this Part' to 'in accordance with the Drug Trafficking Act 1994'.
Criminal Justice Act 1988 (c. 33)	Sections 71 to 102. In section 151(4) the word 'and' after paragraph (a). In section 172— (a) in subsection (2) the words from 'section 76(3)' to 'extending to Scotland'; (b) in subsection (4) the words from 'sections 90' to 'section 93E'. Schedule 4.
Housing Act 1988 (c. 50)	In Schedule 17, paragraphs 83 and 84.
Extradition Act 1989 (c. 33)	In section 22(4)(h) the word 'and' after sub-paragraph (ii).

not marked as table

362

Short title and chapter	Extent of repeal or revocation
Police and Criminal Evidence (Northern Ireland) Order 1989 (S.I. 1989/1341 (N.I. 12))	In Article 53— (a) the definitions of 'drug trafficking' and 'drug trafficking offence'; (b) the words from 'References in this Part' to 'Order 1996'.
Criminal Justice (International Co-operation) Act 1990 (c. 5)	In section 13(6) the words 'the Drug Trafficking Act 1994 or'. Section 14. In Schedule 4, paragraph 1.
Criminal Justice (Confiscation) (Northern Ireland) Order 1990 (S.I. 1990/2588 (N.I. 17))	In Article 37— (a) paragraph (2); (b) in paragraphs (3) and (4) sub-paragraph (b) and the word 'and' before it; (c) paragraph (5).
Criminal Justice Act 1993 (c. 36)	Section 21(3)(e) to (g). Sections 27 to 35. In Schedule 4, paragraph 3. In Schedule 5, paragraph 14.
Criminal Justice and Public Order Act 1994 (c. 33)	In Schedule 9, paragraph 36.
Drug Trafficking Act 1994 (c. 37)	Sections 1 to 54. In sections 55(4)(a) and 56(3)(a) and (4)(a) the words 'or has benefited from'. In section 59, subsections (1) to (10) and in subsection (11) the words 'An order under subsection (1) above, and'. In section 60(6), in the definition of 'specified offence', in paragraph (a) the words 'Part III or' and paragraph (c) and the word 'or' immediately preceding it. In section 60(6), the words from 'and references to the institution of proceedings' to the end. Section 60(7) and (8). Section 61(2) to (4). Sections 62, 63(1), (2) and (3)(a) and 64. In section 68(2), paragraphs (a) to (c) and in paragraph (g) the words '1, 41, 62' and '64'. In section 68(3), paragraph (a) and in paragraph (d) the word '64'. In Schedule 1, paragraphs 3, 4(a), 8, 21 and 26.
Proceeds of Crime Act 1995 (c. 11)	Sections 1 to 13. Section 15(1) to (3).

Short title and chapter	Extent of repeal or revocation
Proceeds of Crime Act 1995 (c. 11)	Section 16(2), (5) and (6). Schedule 1.
Criminal Law (Consolidation) (Scotland) Act 1995 (c. 39)	Part V.
Criminal Procedure (Consequential Provisions) (scotland) Act 1995 (c. 40)	In Schedule 3, paragraph 4(2). In Schedule 4, paragraphs 69 and 94.
Private International Law (Miscellaneous Provisions) Act 1995 (c. 42)	Section 4(3).
Proceeds of Crime (Scotland) Act 1995 (c. 43)	Part I, except section 2(7). In section 28, subsections (1)(a) and (2) and in subsection (5) the words '(including a restraint order made under and within the meaning of the 1994 Act)' Section 29. In section 31, subsection (2), in subsection (4) the words 'or (2)'. Sections 35 to 39. In section 40, subsections (1)(a), (2) and (4). In section 42, subsections (1)(a) and (b). In section 43, in subsection (1) the words 'confiscation order', subsection (2). Section 45(1)(a). Section 47. In section 49, in subsection (1) the definitions of 'the 1988 Act', 'the 1994 Act' and 'confiscation order' and subsection (4). In Schedule 1, in paragraph 1, in sub-paragraph (1)(b) the words 'or a confiscation order', in sub-paragraph (2)(a) the words 'subject to paragraph (b) below', sub-paragraph (2)(b), in sub-paragraph (3)(a)(i) the words 'or confiscation order' In Schedule 1, in paragraph 2, in sub-paragraph (1)(a) the words ', and if appointed (or empowered) under paragraph 1(1)(b) above where a confiscation order has been made', paragraph 4, in paragraph 5(1) the words 'Part I of', in paragraph 8(2) the words from ', unless in a case where a confiscation order has been' to '4(4)(b) above,' In Schedule 1, in paragraph 10(1) the words 'or the recipient of a gift caught by Part I of this Act or

Short title and chapter	Extent of repeal or revocation
Proceeds of Crime (Scotland) Act 1995 (c. 43) (*cont.*)	an implicative gift', paragraphs 10(2) and (3), in paragraph 12(1)(a) the words 'paragraph (a) or (b) of section 4(1) or'. In Schedule 2, in paragraph 1(2) the words 'and 35 to 38', in paragraph 2(1) the words 'realisable or', in paragraph 2(2) the words 'and 35 to 38', paragraph 2(5), in paragraph 3(2) the words 'and 35 to 38', paragraphs 3(4) and (5), in paragraph 4(2) the words 'and 35 to 38', paragraph 6(2)(a).
Proceeds of Crime (Northern Ireland) Order 1996 (S.I. 1996/1299 (N.I. 9))	Parts II and III. In Article 2 in paragraph (2) from the definition of 'charging order' to the definition of 'external confiscation order' and from the definition of 'modifications' to the definition of 'restraint order' and paragraphs (3) to (10) and (12). Article 3. In Article 49, in paragraph (1) sub-paragraph (c) and the word 'and' immediately preceding it, in paragraph (1A) sub-paragraph (c) and the word 'and' immediately preceding it, paragraph (4) and in paragraph (5) the definitions of 'customs officer' and 'relevant property'. In Article 52 in paragraph (2) sub-paragraph (b) and the word 'and' immediately preceding it, and paragraph (3). In Article 54 paragraphs (1) to (10) and (13) and in paragraph (11) the words 'An order under paragraph (1) and,'. In Article 55, in paragraph (6) in the definition of 'specified offence' in paragraph (a) the words 'Part III or' and paragraph (c) and the word 'or' immediately preceding it, and paragraph (7). Article 56(2) to (4). In Schedule 2— (a) in paragraph 1(3) '3 or'; (b) paragraph 3; (c) in paragraphs 4(2), 5(1) and 6(1) '3'. In Schedule 3, paragraphs 1 to 3 and 18.
Justices of the Peace Act 1997 (c. 25)	In Schedule 5, paragraphs 23 and 36.
Crime and Punishment (Scotland) Act 1997 (c. 48)	Section 15(3). In Schedule 1, paragraph 20.
Crime and Disorder Act 1998 (c. 37)	Section 83. In Schedule 1, paragraphs 115 and 116.

Short title and chapter	Extent of repeal or revocation
Crime and Disorder Act 1998 (c. 37) (*cont.*)	In Schedule 8, paragraph 114. In Schedule 9, paragraph 8.
Access to Justice Act 1999 (c. 22)	In Schedule 2— (a) in paragraph 2(2) the word 'or' at the end of paragraph (c); (b) in paragraph 2(3) the word 'or' at the end of paragraph (j). In Schedule 13, paragraphs 139 and 172.
Powers of Criminal Courts (Sentencing) Act 2000 (c. 6)	In Schedule 9, paragraphs 105 to 113 and 163 to 173.
Terrorism Act 2000 (c. 11)	In Schedule 15, paragraphs 6, 10 and 11(2).
Criminal Justice and Police Act 2001 (c. 16)	In section 55(5) paragraph (a) and the word 'and' after paragraph (b). In section 60(4) paragraph (a) and the word 'or' after paragraph (b). In section 64(3) the word 'and' after paragraph (a). In Schedule 1, paragraphs 47 and 105.
Financial Investigations (Northern Ireland) Order 2001 (S.I. 2001/1866 (N.I. 1))	Articles 3(2)(b) and 4(1)(a) and (c), (2), (3) and (5).
Land Registration Act 2002 (c. 9)	In Schedule 11, paragraphs 22 and 32.
This Act	Section 248(2)(a) and (4).

The Magistrates' Courts (Detention and Forfeiture of Cash) Rules 2002 (SI 2002/2998)

Made	*2nd December 2002*
Laid before Parliament	*9th December 2002*
Came into force	*30th December 2002*

The Lord Chancellor, in exercise of the powers conferred on him by section 144 and 145(1)(a) of the Magistrates' Courts Act 1980,[1] after consultation with the Rule Committee appointed under the said section 144, hereby makes the following Rules:

Citation and commencement

1. These Rules may be cited as the Magistrates' Courts (Detention and Forfeiture of Cash) Rules 2002 and shall come into force on 30th December 2002.

Interpretation

2. In these Rules—
  (a) "the Act" means the Proceeds of Crime Act 2002;[2]
  (b) "justices' clerk" means the justices' clerk for the justices who are to hear or have heard an application;
  (c) words and expressions used have the same meaning as in Chapter 3 of Part 5 of the Act;
  (d) a reference to a form is a reference to a form set out in the Schedule to these Rules or a form with the same effect.

Prior approval of searches for cash

3.—(1) An application to a justice of the peace under section 290(1) of the Act for prior approval of a search for cash under section 289 of the Act may be made without notice.
  (2) A justice of the peace may grant such an application without a hearing and may conduct any hearing in private.

First application for the continued detention of seized cash

4.—(1) The first application under section 295(4) of the Act for an order under section 295(2) of the Act for the continued detention of cash seized under section 294 of the Act shall be made in form A and shall be sent to the justices' chief executive for the petty sessions area of the court before which the applicant wishes to make the application.

---

[1] 1980, c. 43.   [2] 2002, c 29.

(2) But where the reasonable grounds for suspicion which led to the seizure of cash to which an application under section 295(4) of the Act relates are connected to the reasonable grounds for suspicion which led to the seizure of other cash to which a previous order made under section 295(2) of the Act relates, then the application may be sent to the justices' chief executive for the petty sessions area of the court which made the previous order.

(3) Except where paragraph (4) or paragraph (7) applies, a copy of the written application and notification of the hearing of the application shall be given by the applicant to the person from whom the cash was seized.

(4) Where seized cash is found in a means of unattended dispatch, such as an unattended letter, parcel or container, copies of the written application and notification of the hearing of the application shall be sent by the applicant to the sender and intended recipient of the means of unattended dispatch.

(5) But where paragraph (4) applies the applicant is not required to send copies of the written application and notification of the hearing to a sender or intended recipient who cannot be identified.

(6) Where paragraph (4) applies, the court shall not decline to hear an application solely on the ground that it has not been proved that the sender and intended recipient have been given a copy of the written application and notification of the hearing.

(7) Where unattended cash is seized (other than where the cash is found in a means of unattended dispatch) the applicant need not give a copy of the written application and notification of the hearing to any person.

(8) An order for the continued detention of seized cash shall be in Form B.

(9) The justices' chief executive shall give—

    (a) notice of the order in Form C, and

    (b) a copy of the order,

to the person from whom the cash was seized and to any other person known to be affected by the order.

Further applications for the continued detention of seized cash

5.—(1) An application under section 295(4) of the Act for a further order under section 295(2) of the Act for the continued detention of cash shall be made in Form A and shall be sent to the justices' chief executive to whom the first application under section 295(4) of the Act was sent.

(2) The applicant shall send a copy of the application to every person to whom notice of previous related orders made under section 295(2) of the Act has been given.

(3) The justices' clerk shall fix a date for the hearing of the application, which, unless he directs otherwise, shall not be earlier than seven days from the date on which it is fixed, and the justices' chief executive shall notify that date to the applicant and every person to whom notice of the previous orders has been given.

(4) A further order for the continued detention of seized cash shall be in Form B.

(5) The justices' chief executive shall give a copy of the order to every person to whom notice of the previous related orders has been given.

(6) The justices' chief executive shall also give—

    (a) notice of the order in Form C, and

    (b) a copy of the order,

to any person other than one referred to in paragraph (5) known to be affected by the order.

Applications for the release of detained cash

6.—(1) An application under section 297(3) or 301(1) of the Act for the release of detained cash shall be made in writing and sent to the justices' chief executive for the petty sessions area of the court before which the applicant wishes to make the application.

(2) But if the applicant has been given notice of an order under section 295(2) of the Act in respect of the detained cash, then the application shall be sent to the justices' chief executive who sent him that notice.

(3) The justices' chief executive shall send a copy of the application to—

(a) the Commissioners of Customs and Excise, if the cash which is the subject of the application was seized by a customs officer;

(b) the chief officer of the police force to which the constable belongs (or in the case of a constable who is a member of the National Crime Squad, the Director General of that Squad), if the cash which is the subject of the application was seized by a constable; and

(c) every person to whom notice of the order made under section 295(2) of the Act has been given.

(4) The justices' clerk shall fix a date for the hearing of the application, which, unless he directs otherwise, shall not be earlier than seven days from the date on which it is fixed, and the justices' chief executive shall notify that date to the applicant and to every person to whom a copy of the application is required to be sent under paragraph (3).

(5) At the hearing of an application under section 301(1) of the Act, the court may, if it thinks fit, order that the applicant shall be joined as a party to all the proceedings in relation to the detained cash.

(6) A direction under section 297(2) of the Act shall be in Form D, an order under section 301(3) of the Act shall be in Form E and an order under section 301(4) of the Act shall be in Form F.

(7) A direction under section 297(2) of the Act and an order under section 301(3) or (4) of the Act shall provide for the release of the cash within seven days of the date of the making of the order or direction, or such longer period as, with the agreement of the applicant, may be specified, except that cash shall not be released whilst section 298(4) of the Act applies.

Application for forfeiture of detained cash

7.—(1) An application under section 298(1) of the Act for the forfeiture of detained cash shall be in Form G and shall be sent to the justices' chief executive to whom applications for the continued detention of the cash under section 295(4) of the Act have been sent.

(2) Where no applications in respect of the cash have been made under section 295(4) of the Act, the application shall be sent to—

(a) the justices' chief executive for the petty sessions area of the court before which the applicant wishes to make the application; or

(b) where the reasonable grounds for suspicion which led to the seizure of cash to which the application for forfeiture relates are connected to the reasonable grounds for suspicion which led to the seizure of cash to which an order made under section 295(2) of the Act relates, to the justices' chief executive for the petty sessions area of the court which made the order under section 295(2).

(3) The applicant shall send a copy of the application to every person to whom notice of an order made under section 295(2) of the Act in respect of the detained cash has been given and to any other person identified by the court as being affected by the application.

(4) The justices' clerk shall set a date for a directions hearing, which, unless he directs otherwise, shall not be earlier than seven days from the date on which it is fixed, and the justices' chief executive shall notify that date to the applicant and to every person to whom a copy of the application is required to be sent under paragraph (3).

(5) At the directions hearing, the court may give directions relating to the management of the proceedings, including directions as to the date for the hearing of the application.

(6) If neither the person from whom the cash was seized, nor any other person who is affected by the detention of the cash, seeks to contest the application, the court may decide the application at the directions hearing.

(7) An order for the forfeiture of detained cash under section 298(2) of the Act shall be in Form H and a copy of the order shall be given by the justices' chief executive to every person to whom notice of an order made under section 295(2) of the Act in respect of the detained cash has been given and to any other person known to be affected by the order.

Application for compensation

8.—(1) An application under section 302(1) for compensation shall be made in writing and sent to the justices' chief executive for the petty sessions area of the court before which the applicant wishes to make the application.

(2) But if the applicant has been given notice of an order under section 295(2) of the Act in respect of the cash which is the subject of the application, then the application shall be sent to the justices' chief executive who sent him that notice.

(3) The justices' chief executive shall send a copy of the application to—
  (a) the Commissioners of Customs and Excise, if the cash which is the subject of the application was seized by a customs officer;
  (b) the chief officer of the police force to which the constable belongs (or in the case of a constable who is a member of the National Crime Squad, the Director General of that Squad), if the cash which is the subject of the application was seized by a constable.

The justices' clerk shall fix a date for the hearing of the application, which, unless he directs otherwise, shall not be earlier than seven days from the date on which it is fixed, and the justices' chief executive shall notify the applicant and the person referred to in paragraph (3) of that date.

Notice

9. Any notification or document required to be given or sent to any person under these Rules may be given by post or by facsimile to his last known address, or to any other address given by that person for the purpose of service of documents under these Rules.

Transfer of proceedings

10.—(1) Any person who is a party to, or affected by, proceedings under Chapter 3 of Part 5 of the Act may, at any time, make an application to the court dealing with the matter for the proceedings to be transferred to a different petty sessions area.

(2) Any such application shall be made in writing and sent to the justices' chief executive for the petty sessions area in which the proceedings are being dealt with and shall specify the grounds on which it is made.

(3) The justices' chief executive shall send a copy of the application to the parties to the proceedings and any other person affected by the proceedings.

(4) The justices' clerk shall fix a date for the hearing of the application, which, unless he directs otherwise, shall not be earlier than seven days from the date on which it is fixed, and the justices' chief executive shall notify the date to the applicant and every person to whom a copy of the application is required to be sent under paragraph (3).

(5) The court may grant the application if it is satisfied that it would be more convenient or fairer for proceedings to be transferred to a different petty sessions area.

(6) If the application is granted—

  (a) the justices' chief executive shall give a copy of the order to the parties to the proceedings and any other person affected by the proceedings;

  (b) the justices' chief executive shall send all relevant papers to the justices' chief executive for the petty sessions area to which proceedings are transferred;

  (c) any further proceedings under Chapter 3 of Part 5 of the Act in respect of the cash to which the proceedings relate shall be dealt with in the petty sessions area to which proceedings are transferred;

  (d) any requirement under these Rules to make an application to a justices' chief executive shall be read as a requirement to make an application to the justices' chief executive for the petty sessions area to which proceedings are transferred.

Procedure at hearings

11.—(1) At the hearing of an application under Chapter 3 of Part 5 of the Act, any person to whom notice of the application has been given may attend and be heard on the question of whether the application should be granted, but the fact that any such person does not attend shall not prevent the court from hearing the application.

(2) Subject to the foregoing provisions of these Rules, proceedings on such an application shall be regulated in the same manner as proceedings on a complaint, and accordingly for the purposes of these Rules, the application shall be deemed to be a complaint, the applicant a complainant, the respondents to be defendants and any notice given by the justices' chief executive under rules 5(3), 6(4), 7(4), 8(4) or 10(4) to be a summons: but nothing in this rule shall be construed as enabling a warrant of arrest to be issued for failure to appear in answer to any such notice.

(3) At the hearing of an application under Chapter 3 of Part 5 of the Act, the court shall require the matters contained in the application to be sworn by the applicant under oath, may require the applicant to answer any questions under oath and may require any response from the respondent to the application to be made under oath.

(4) The court shall record or cause to be recorded the substance of any statements made under oath which are not already recorded in the written application.

Irvine of Lairg,
C.
2nd December 2002

SCHEDULE

Rules 4(1) and 5(1) and Rule 2

FORM A

First/Further** application for continued detention of seized cash
(Section 295(4) Proceeds of Crime Act 2002; MC (Detention and Forfeiture of Cash) Rules
2002 rr 4(1), 5(1)

Magistrates' Court

(Code)

Date

Name of person from whom cash seized

Address*

Names and addresses of any other persons likely to be affected by an order for detention of
the cash (if known)

Amount seized/Estimated amount seized (only in the case of a first application for continued detention) **

Amount to which reasonable grounds of suspicion apply/Estimated amount to which reasonable grounds for suspicion apply (only in the case of a first application for continued
detention) ** where it is not reasonably practicable to detain only that part

Date of seizure

Time of seizure

Place of seizure

Date of latest order for continued detention of seized cash (if any)

Amount detained under latest order for continued detention (if any)

Amounts released since the latest order for continued detention (if any)

I,

of

(official address and position of applicant)

Constable/Customs Officer **, apply for an order under section 295(2) of the Proceeds of
Crime Act 2002 authorising the continued detention of cash in the sum of and will state
upon oath that one of the two grounds below is satisfied in relation to all of the cash/ the
sum of but it is not reasonably practicable to detain only that part of the cash **;

1. There are reasonable grounds for suspecting that the cash is recoverable property and
that either—

(a) its continued detention is justified while its derivation is further investigated or consideration is given to bringing (in the United Kingdom or elsewhere) proceedings against any person for an offence with which the cash is connected, or

(b) proceedings against any person for an offence with which the cash is connected have been started and have not been concluded.

2. There are reasonable grounds for suspecting that the cash is intended to be used in unlawful conduct and that either—

(a) its continued detention is justified while its intended use is further investigated or consideration is given to bringing (in the United Kingdom or elsewhere) proceedings against any person for an offence with which the cash is connected, or

(b) proceedings against any person for an offence with which the cash is connected have been started and have not been concluded.

(state grounds)

Signed

To: The Justices' Chief Executive

Magistrates' Court

Notes to the Applicant—

First Application—You must give a copy of this application and notification of the hearing of it to the person from whom the cash was seized * * *.

Further Application—This application must wherever possible be submitted to the justices' chief executive at least seven days before the expiry of the last period of detention that was ordered by the court. You must give a copy of this application to the person from whom the cash was seized and any other person specified in any order made under section 295(2) of the Proceeds of Crime Act 2002 ***.

*In the case of a means of unattended dispatch such as a letter, parcel or container, insert names and addresses, if known, of sender and intended recipient. In the case of any other unattended cash, state that you believe the cash was unattended and explain your grounds for believing that the cash was unattended.

**Delete as appropriate

*** In the case of a means of unattended dispatch such as a letter, parcel or container, the copy application and, if applicable, notification of hearing should be given to the sender and intended recipient (if known), rather than the person from whom the cash was seized. In the case of any other unattended cash, there is no requirement to give the copy application and, if applicable, notification of hearing to the person from whom the cash was seized.

Rules 4(8) and 5(4)

FORM B

First/Further** order for continued detention of seized cash

(Section 295(2) Proceeds of Crime Act 2002; MC (Detention and Forfeiture of Cash) Rules 2002 rr 4(8), 5(4))

Magistrates' Court

(Code)

Date

Name of person from whom cash was seized*

Address*

Names and addresses of any other persons identified by the court as being affected by this order

Amount seized/Estimated amount seized (only in the case of a first order for continued detention)**

Amount to which reasonable grounds of suspicion apply/Estimated amount to which reasonable grounds for suspicion apply (only in the case of a first order for continued detention)** where it is not reasonably practicable to detain only that part

Date of seizure

Time of seizure

Place of seizure

Date of latest order for continued detention of seized cash (if any)

Amount detained under latest order for continued detention (if any)

Amounts released since the latest order for continued detention (if any)

On the application of

after hearing oral evidence from

and representations from

It is ordered that the sum of

be further detained for a period of

(state a period up to a maximum of three months from the date of this order, and not beyond the end of a period of two years from the date of the first order) or until its release may be otherwise ordered, whichever is the earlier.

Notice of this order shall be given without delay to the person from whom the cash was seized and to any other person affected by it. Such notice shall be in Form C and shall be accompanied by a copy of this order.

Justice of the Peace

[or by Order of the Court, Clerk of the Court]

*In the case of a means of unattended dispatch such as a letter, parcel or container, insert names and addresses, if known, of sender and intended recipient. In the case of any other unattended cash, state that the cash was unattended and state the grounds given by the applicant for believing that the cash was unattended.

**Delete as appropriate

Rules 4(9) and 5(6)

FORM C

Notice to persons affected by an order for continued detention of seized cash

(Section 295(8) of the Proceeds of Crime Act 2002; MC (Detention and Forfeiture of Cash) Rules 2002 rr 4(9), 5(6))

Magistrates' Court

(Code)

Date

Name of person from whom cash was seized*

Amount seized/Estimated amount seized (only in the case of a first order for continued detention)**

Amount to which reasonable grounds of suspicion apply/Estimated amount to which reasonable grounds for suspicion apply (only in the case of a first order for continued detention) ** where it is not reasonably practicable to detain only that part

Date of seizure

Time of seizure

Place of seizure

On (date) an order was made under section 295(2) the Proceeds of Crime Act 2002 authorising the continued detention of cash in the sum of for a period of

A copy of the order accompanies this notice.

The person from whom the cash was seized may apply for the release of the detained cash or any part of it under section 297 of that Act. If the cash was in a letter, parcel, container or other means of unattended dispatch, the sender or the intended recipient may make the application.

A person who claims that any cash detained or any part of it belongs to him, may apply for the release of the detained cash or part of it under section 301 of that Act if either—

1. he was deprived of it or of property which it represents by criminal conduct and the property he was deprived of was not, immediately before he was deprived of it, recoverable property; or

2. the conditions for detaining the cash are no longer met or the court decides not to make a forfeiture order in respect of the cash and no objection has been made by the person from whom the cash was seized.

An application under section 297 or 301 of the Proceeds of Crime Act 2002 should be made in writing to the justices' chief executive at the magistrates' court which made the order for continued detention of seized cash.

The application should state the grounds relied on and identify as clearly as possible the cash referred to.

At the end of the above-mentioned period of detention an application may be made for the further detention of the cash. An application may also be made to forfeit the cash.

You will be notified if an application is made, or if any other person makes an application to the court for the release of the detained cash.

If you intend to consult a solicitor about these proceedings you should do so at once and hand this notice and the copy of the order to him.

Signed

(Justices' Chief Executive)

*In the case of a means of unattended dispatch such as a letter, parcel or container, insert names, if known, of sender and intended recipient. In the case of any other unattended cash, state that the cash was unattended and state the grounds given by the applicant for believing that the cash was unattended.

**Delete as appropriate

Rule 6(6)

FORM D

Direction for the release of detained cash under section 297(2) of the Proceeds of Crime Act 2002(MC (Detention and Forfeiture of Cash) Rules 2002 r 6(6))

Magistrates' Court(Code)Date

On the application of (name of applicant)of (address)

after hearing oral evidence fromand representations from

It is directed that the sum of which represents the whole/part* of the sum seized, together with any interest accruing thereon in accordance with section 296(1) of the Proceeds of Crime Act 2002, be released to orto the order of (name)

on or before(specify a date, not more than seven days from the date of this direction unless a later date is agreed by the applicant)

Cash is not to be released under this direction where section 298(4) of the Proceeds of Crime Act 2002 (which provides that detained cash may not be released whilst forfeiture proceedings are ongoing) applies. Justice of the Peace[or by Order of the Court, Clerk of the Court]

*Delete as appropriate

Rule 6(6)

FORM E

Order for the release of detained cash under section 301(3) of the Proceeds of Crime Act 2002(MC (Detention and Forfeiture of Cash) Rules 2002 r 6(6))

Magistrates' Court(Code)Date

On the application of (name of applicant)of (address)

after hearing oral evidence fromand representations from

It appears to the court that
1. the sum below belongs to the applicant,
2. the applicant was deprived of it or of property which it represents by criminal conduct, and
3. the property the applicant was deprived of was not, immediately before he was deprived of it, recoverable property.

It is ordered that the sum of which represents the whole/part* of the sum seized, together with any interest accruing thereon in accordance with section 296(1) of the Proceeds of Crime Act 2002, be released to or to the order of (name)

on or before(specify a date, not more than seven days from the date of this order unless a later date is agreed by the applicant)

Cash is not to be released under this direction where section 298(4) of the Proceeds of Crime Act 2002 (which provides that detained cash may not be released whilst forfeiture proceedings are ongoing) applies.

Justice of the Peace[or by Order of the Court, Clerk of the Court]

*Delete as appropriate

Rule 6(6)

FORM F

Order for the release of detained cash under section 301(4) of the Proceeds of Crime Act 2002 (MC (Detention and Forfeiture of Cash) Rules 2002 r 6(6))

Magistrates' Court

(Code)

Date

On the application of (name of applicant)

of (address)

after hearing oral evidence from

and representations from

It appears to the court that
1. the sum below was not seized from the applicant,
2. the sum below belongs to the applicant,
3. the conditions in section 295 of the Proceeds of Crime Act 2002 for detaining the sum below are no longer met or the court has decided not to order forfeiture of the sum below under section 298(2) of the Proceeds of Crime Act 2002, and
4. no objection to the making of this order has been made by the person from whom the sum below was seized/the cash was unattended*.

It is ordered that the sum of which represents the whole/part* of the sum seized, together with any interest accruing thereon in accordance with section 296(1) of the Proceeds of Crime Act 2002, be released to or to the order of (name)

on or before

(specify a date, not more than seven days from the date of this order unless a later date is agreed by the applicant)

Cash is not to be released under this direction where section 298(4) of the Proceeds of Crime Act 2002 (which provides that detained cash may not be released whilst forfeiture proceedings are ongoing) applies.

Justice of the Peace

[or by Order of the Court, Clerk of the Court]

*Delete as appropriate

Rule 7(1)

FORM G

Application for forfeiture of detained cash

(Section 298(1) of the Proceeds of Crime Act 2002; MC (Detention and Forfeiture of Cash) Rules 2002 r 7(1))

Magistrates' Court

(Code)

Date

Name of person from whom cash seized*

Address*

Names and addresses of any other persons identified by the court as being affected by this application

Amount seized

Date of seizure

Time of seizure

Place of seizure

Date of latest order for continued detention of seized cash (if any)

Amount detained under latest order for continued detention (if any)

Amounts released since the latest order for continued detention (if any)

I

of

(official address and position of applicant)

Constable/Customs Officer**, apply for an order under 298(2) of the Proceeds of Crime Act 2002 for the forfeiture of cash in the sum of together with any interest accruing thereon pursuant to section 296(1) of that Act, on the grounds that the cash is recoverable property or is intended by any person for use in unlawful conduct.

(state grounds)

To: The Justices' Chief Executive

Magistrates' Court

Note to the Applicant—You must send a copy of this application to the person from whom the cash was seized and any other person specified in any order made under section 295(2) of the Proceeds of Crime Act 2002***.

Note to copy recipients—If you are not the person from whom the cash was seized but the cash belongs to you and the court decides not to make a forfeiture order, you may apply to the court under section 301(4) of the Proceeds of Crime Act 2002 for the cash to be released to you. You can make an application before the court makes its decision on forfeiture. However, the court will not be able to release the cash to you until the forfeiture proceedings are finished.

*In the case of a means of unattended dispatch such as a letter, parcel or container, insert names and addresses, if known, of sender and intended recipient. In the case of any other unattended cash, state that you believe the cash was unattended and explain your grounds for believing that the cash was unattended.

**Delete as appropriate

*** In the case of a means of unattended dispatch such as a letter, parcel or container, the copy application and, if applicable, notification of hearing should be given to the sender and intended recipient (if known), rather than the person from whom the cash was seized. In the case of any other unattended cash, there is no requirement to give the copy application and, if applicable, notification of hearing to the person from whom the cash was seized.

Rule 7(7)

FORM H

Order for forfeiture of detained cash (section 298(2) of the Proceeds of Crime Act 2002; MC (Detention and Forfeiture of Cash) Rules 2002 r 7(7))

Magistrates' Court

(Code)

Date

Name of person from whom cash was seized*

Address*

Names and addresses of any other persons whom the court has identified as being affected by the above-mentioned order

Amount seized

Date of seizure

Time of seizure

Place of seizure

Date of latest order for continued detention of seized cash (if any)

Amount detained under latest order for continued detention (if any)

Amounts released since the latest order for continued detention (if any)

On the application of

after hearing oral evidence

and representations from

It is ordered that the whole/part** of the above-mentioned cash be forfeited.

Sum forfeited

Justice of the Peace

[or by Order of the Court, Clerk of the Court]

Note to the parties to these proceedings—Any party to the proceedings in which this forfeiture order is made may appeal against the order to the Crown Court under section 299 of the Proceeds of Crime Act 2002. The appeal must be brought before the end of the period of 30 days beginning with the date on which this order was made.

*In the case of a means of unattended dispatch such as a letter, parcel or container, insert names, if known, of sender and intended recipient. In the case of any other unattended cash, state that the cash was unattended and state the grounds given by the applicant for believing that the cash was unattended.

**Delete as appropriate

EXPLANATORY NOTE

(This note is not part of the Rules)

These Rules prescribe the procedure to be followed for applications to a magistrates' court for the detention, further detention, forfeiture or release of cash seized under Chapter 3 of Part 5 of the Proceeds of Crime Act 2002. Cash may be seized by a constable or customs officer on reasonable suspicion that the cash represents the benefit from unlawful conduct or is intended for use in unlawful conduct. The Rules also prescribe the procedure to be followed for applications to a magistrates' court for compensation where no forfeiture order is made. In addition, the Rules prescribe the forms to be used in connection with the applications and hearings.

Code of Practice Issued Under Section 377 of the Proceeds of Crime Act 2002

INTRODUCTION

1. This code of practice governs the exercise of the investigation powers in Chapter 2 of Part 8 of the Proceeds of Crime Act 2002 ("the Act"). It is issued by the Home Secretary under section 377 of the Act. The code provides guidance as to how such powers in respect of confiscation, civil recovery and money laundering investigations are to be used in England, Wales and Northern Ireland. There is a separate code of practice in respect of the Scottish powers in Chapter 3 issued by Scottish Ministers under section 410. These powers of investigation are not available where cash has been detained under Chapter 3 of Part 5, where an interim receiving order or an administration order has been made or where civil recovery proceedings have started. They are also not available for Revenue investigations (Part 6).

2. Where a person fails to comply with any provision of the code, he is not by reason only of that failure liable to any criminal or civil proceedings, but the code is admissible as evidence in such proceedings and a court may take account of any failure to comply with its provisions in determining any questions in the proceedings.

3. A summary of the powers and access to them is provided in the table attached to this code. Also annexed to the code are models of the warrants and orders, and information in support of applications. These act as models for appropriate officers, but are not prescribed forms. They have been designed for the purposes of confiscation and money laundering investigations, civil recovery investigation applications may require significant amendments.

PERSONS COVERED BY THE CODE

4. The code places obligations on all those who either apply for or execute the five powers of investigation in England, Wales and Northern Ireland. Chapter 2 has a basic framework by which appropriate officers apply for and execute the investigation powers. A definition of appropriate officer is found at section 378. These are variously the Director of the Assets Recovery Agency ("the Agency"[1]), an accredited financial investigator[2], a constable and a

---

[1] Throughout this code references to the Agency mean the Assets Recovery Agency, unless some other meaning is obviously implied.

[2] An accredited financial investigator is a civilian investigator accredited by the Director of the Agency to have access to some or all of the powers of investigation. The accredited financial

customs officer. The identity of the appropriate officer in each case depends on the type of investigation and the specific power.

5. A search and seizure warrant (sections 352(5) and 353(10)) must be executed by an appropriate *person*. An appropriate person is a constable or customs officer in respect of warrants issued in respect of a confiscation or money laundering investigation, and a member of the staff of the Agency in respect of a civil recovery investigation. These persons' actions will also be covered by this code of practice.

6. The disclosure order (section 357(1)) is only available to the Director. Under section 1(6) of the Act, the Director may authorise a member of the staff of the Agency or a person providing services under arrangements made and authorised by him to perform his functions. The code therefore also applies to persons to whom the Director has delegated investigation powers. They should look for references to 'the Director' in determining their obligations. When the Director delegates this responsibility, he or she will provide written authority, which the person must produce when acting as the Director under the Act and this code.

7. The code should be readily available at all police stations for consultation by police and members of the public. It should also form part of the published instructions or guidance for customs officers. The Agency will also make arrangements for the code to be available to any interested party (whether in a hard form or electronically). Government Departments and other bodies who have accredited financial investigators operating the powers of investigation should also make arrangements for the code to be available to both their staff and members of the public on request.

8. The code only applies to functions carried out under Chapter 2 of Part 8. Those carrying out functions under Part 8 do not have to have regard to other codes of practice, e.g. those issued under the Police and Criminal Evidence Act 1984 ("PACE") or section 292 of the Act. However, if an officer is also performing an additional and separate function, e.g. a search for cash under section 289 of the Act, they must have regard to any connected code.

9. The production order and search warrant provisions under the Drug Trafficking Act 1994 have not been repealed and will continue to be available in respect of investigations into the **offences** of drug trafficking. This code does not relate to those provisions. However, appropriate officers and financial investigators should be aware that the powers of investigation into the **benefit** of drug trafficking under the Drug Trafficking Act are now repealed and have been replaced by the provisions of the Act, and therefore are covered by this code.

GENERAL PROVISIONS RELATING TO ALL THE ORDERS AND WARRANTS

Action to be taken before an application is made

10. The powers of investigation may involve significant interference with privacy of those whose premises are searched; on whom personal information is obtained; or whose personal information, material or documents are seen and/or seized by an appropriate officer

---

investigator will also have to fall within a category given in an order issued by the Home Secretary under section 453 of the Act.

or appropriate person. This places an obligation upon those operating the powers of investigation to ensure that the application for the order or warrant is fully and clearly justified. In particular, appropriate officers should consider at every stage whether the necessary objectives can be achieved by less intrusive means.

11. Officers should be aware that the operation of the Act is subject to the Human Rights Act 1998 and consider their use of the powers of investigation accordingly. The use of the powers which impact upon individuals' rights under the ECHR (European Convention on Human Rights) must be proportionate to the outcome being sought.

12. An appropriate officer will have to satisfy a judge that any infringement of, for example, a person's right to privacy under Article 8 of the ECHR is proportionate to the benefit to be gained from making an order or warrant. The appropriate officer must satisfy himself or herself of these issues, as with the other requirements for the making of orders/warrants, before an application is made. This becomes a greater consideration in respect of orders and warrants made against people who are not themselves under investigation.

13. Before a judge can grant any of the Part 8 orders or warrants, he will have to be satisfied that the statutory requirements are met. For each order or warrant to be granted, there is a statutory requirement that there must be reasonable grounds for suspecting that a person has benefited from his criminal conduct, has committed a money laundering offence (except in the case of the disclosure order which is not available for investigation of money laundering offences) or that the property specified in the application can be recovered under Part 5 of the Act.

14. Reasonable grounds for suspicion depend on the circumstances in each case. There must be an objective basis for that suspicion based on facts and/or information. Reasonable suspicion can never be supported on the basis of personal factors alone without reliable supporting information. Where information is received which appears to justify an application the appropriate officer concerned must take reasonable steps to check that the information is accurate, recent and has not been provided maliciously or irresponsibly. An application must not be made on the basis of information from an anonymous source unless there is corroboration.

15. In respect of each order or warrant to be granted, there is a statutory requirement that there must be reasonable grounds for believing that the material or information is likely to be of substantial value (whether or not by itself) to the investigation. The appropriate officer must be satisfied that the material or information will progress the investigation.

16. There is also a statutory requirement that there must be reasonable grounds for believing that it is in the public interest that the material or information is obtained or accessed by the appropriate officer. The appropriate officer must make sure that the public interest in obtaining the order outweighs the disadvantages to the person against whom the order is being made. For example, an application for an account monitoring order against a bank should not normally be made unless the appropriate officer considers that this may lead to the identification of monies greater than the anticipated cost to the bank in complying with the order[3], or that the appropriate officer suspects that the information will be of substantial benefit with regards to the serious nature of the investigation.

17. The appropriate officer must satisfy himself or herself that all of these statutory requirements are satisfied before making the application.

---

[3] The appropriate officer is under no obligation to divulge the anticipated cost he or she has decided.

18. The Act only requires appropriate officers to obtain authorisation for their applications in respect of customer information orders. However, appropriate officers should, where practicable, obtain internal authorisation in respect of applications for the other orders and warrants. The appropriate officer should therefore obtain the authorisation of a senior officer (at least inspector rank in the police or the equivalent rank of seniority within the department or agency for which the appropriate officer works). This does not apply to disclosure orders which are only available to the Director.

Action to be taken in making an application

19. All the applications for the powers of investigation may be made ex parte to a judge in chambers[4]. In deciding whether the application should be ex parte, the appropriate officer should consider the benefit of not holding the proceedings inter partes[5]. An obvious and probably most common reason would be so as not to alert the persons connected to an investigation that such is ongoing. Inter partes proceedings might enable the person to move material and thereby frustrate the investigation. However, where a production order is directed at a financial institution (who would be the respondent), the institution should normally be notified of the intention of making an application for an investigation order— the application hearing could then be held inter partes.

20. An application in respect of a civil recovery investigation must be made to a High Court judge in accordance with the relevant civil procedure rules and Practice Direction.

21. The following must be included in an application for an order or warrant:–

• the name of the person who is under investigation or who holds property which is under investigation and confirmation that the information sought is for the purposes of the investigation. If the application is for an order against a different person to the one under investigation, he or she must also be named on the application and there must be an explanation of the person's connection to the investigation;

• the grounds on which the application is made; and

• confirmation that none of the material or information sought is or consists of items subject to legal privilege or excluded material (with the exception of information relating to a client's name and address which is subject to legal privilege requested under a disclosure order). This does not apply to customer information orders and account monitoring orders as the type of information requested will not be that which could be subject to legal privilege.

22. The identity of an informant need not be disclosed when making an application, but the appropriate officer should be prepared to deal with any questions the judge may have about the accuracy of information provided by that source or any other related matters.

23. The person applying must be ready to satisfy the judge that he or she is an appropriate officer (see section 378) who may apply for the order or warrant[6].

---

[4] This means that an appropriate officer can apply for an order or warrant without notifying the respondent that the application is being contemplated or made.

[5] Inter partes applications are those notified to the respondent of the contemplated order or warrant. They are therefore aware of the application and can be represented at the hearing.

[6] This could be a police or customs officer's warrant card. This could also be documentation confirming the status of accredited financial investigators, the Director and persons authorised by the Director to perform his functions.

Action to be taken in serving an order or warrant

24. In all cases, the investigatory powers should be exercised courteously and with respect for the persons and property of those concerned.

25. In deciding the method of service of the order, the appropriate officer should take into account all the circumstances of the investigation, including the possible need to prove that service was effected, and the person or body on whom the order is served. Search and seizure warrants are executed by an 'appropriate person' who must also have regard to these actions in service of the warrant.

26. When serving the order, warrant or (in the case of a disclosure order and customer information order) notice under the order, a covering letter must be provided which includes the following information (unless it is already included in order or the notice):

- the name of the subject of the order or the name by which he or she is known;
- a warning in plain language that failure without reasonable excuse to comply with the requirement is an offence and could result in prosecution;
- a warning that disclosure of information about the investigation may contravene section 342 ('offences of prejudicing investigation'), and that if anyone contacts the respondent about the investigation they should report this to the appropriate officer or appropriate person;
- that the warning given does not constitute a criminal caution, nor has the consequences of one;
- a general description of the investigation in connection with which the requirement is made; [it is not necessary to specify the name of the person or property subject to the investigation on the order, although this must be imparted to the judge at the application stage];
- that the subject of the order should seek legal advice or ask the appropriate officer about any doubts or concerns they may have, or for guidance on complying with the order;
- the duty not to falsify, conceal, destroy or otherwise dispose of, or cause or permit the falsification, concealment, destruction or disposal of relevant documents which are relevant to any confiscation, civil recovery or money laundering investigation which the subject of the order knows or suspects is being or is about to be conducted ; and a warning that to do so is an offence punishable by up to five years imprisonment and an unlimited fine;
- the duty not to disclose to any other person information or any other matter which is likely to prejudice any confiscation, civil recovery or money laundering investigation which the subject of the order knows or suspects is being or is about to be conducted and a warning to do so is an offence punishable by up to five years imprisonment and an unlimited fine, and
- the right to apply for a variation or discharge of the order (not applicable in search and seizure warrants).

27. When serving a notice under a disclosure order or a customer information order, the appropriate officer must inform the respondent of his right to refuse to comply with any requirement imposed on him or her unless the appropriate officer has, if required to do so, produced evidence of his authority to issue that notice.

28. Where it appears to the appropriate officer or person that the recipient of an order or warrant has genuine difficulty in reading or understanding English he or she should

attempt to serve a copy of the order on a person known to the recipient who, in the opinion of the appropriate officer or person, is able to explain or translate what is happening. If this is not practicable the appropriate officer or person should attempt to engage an interpreter or translator to effect service of the order or warrant.

29. Sections 359(1) and 366(1) provide that an offence is committed if, without reasonable excuse, a person or financial institution fails to comply with a requirement imposed by a disclosure or customer information order. The other orders are treated as orders of the court and therefore attract contempt proceedings if they are not complied with. The recipient of the order should be warned in plain language that failure without reasonable excuse to comply with the requirement of an order is an offence that could result in prosecution, imprisonment and/or a fine.

30. What in law amounts to a reasonable excuse may depend on the facts of each particular case and will be a matter for decision by a court. But the fact that a person has already been questioned in connection with the same or a connected investigation, that the question relates to activities outside the jurisdiction or that a truthful answer to a question would tend to incriminate the interviewee or some other person is unlikely, in itself, to amount to a reasonable excuse.

31. Section 449 of the Act empowers the Director to direct that a member of staff of the Agency may identify himself or herself by means of a pseudonym when authorised to carry out functions under the Act. An application may be made or service of an order or warrant may be carried out using a pseudonym. A certificate signed by the Director is sufficient to identify a member of staff of the Agency and the member of staff may not be asked any question which is likely to reveal his or her true identity. The pseudonym provision does not extend to appropriate officers working outside the Agency, for example police officers or accredited financial investigators, working for a government department.

32. No document may be removed or accessed and no information sought which is subject to legal privilege (with the one limited exception in respect of the disclosure order as explained in that part of the code). A respondent has the right to withhold material and information sought which is subject to legal privilege The Act relies upon the evolving definition of legal privilege as in caselaw which is relied upon in High Court proceedings. The current caselaw broadly defines the concept as communications between a lawyer and his client regarding contemplated or actual legal proceedings. However such communications made in the furtherance of a criminal purpose are not privileged.

33. None of the powers of investigation allow access to excluded material. Excluded material is defined at section 11 of PACE and includes journalistic material and medical records.

34. Where an appropriate person is executing a search and seizure warrant, he may by virtue of Part 2 of the Criminal Justice and Police Act 2001, seize privileged or excluded material if it is not reasonably practicable for him to determine on the premises whether the material he is seizing includes privilege or excluded material

35. Aside from the legal privilege provision, requirements for information made under the powers of investigation take precedence in spite of any restriction on the disclosure of information, however imposed. They therefore take precedence over any contractual duties of confidentiality and the common law duty of confidence.

Action to be taken in receiving an application for an extension of a time limit

36. It is for the appropriate officer to set the time limit for replies to requirements made under disclosure orders and customer information orders. Where the subject of one of

these orders asks for more time to comply with a requirement made under one of these orders, the appropriate officer must consider the request. When he has made his decision, the appropriate officer must set out his decision and the reasons for it in a letter to the subject of the order. The circumstances in which it would be suitable for appropriate officers to consider an extension might be obtaining legal advice, difficulty in obtaining requested information and/or documents and an interviewee's unavailability. The letter conveying the appropriate officer's decision must be served in the same way as the original notice under the order was served.

37. Where a solicitor acting on behalf of the subject of the order makes the application for an extension of time, the letter may be served on the solicitor.

38. Time limits for compliance with a production order and an account monitoring order are set out on the face of the order—(see sections 345(5) and 370(6)). Therefore they cannot be extended unless the subject of the order applies to the court for a variation of the order. If the appropriate officer receives a request for an extension of the time limit to comply with a production order or an account monitoring order, he or she should direct the subject of the order to the court[7].

Record of Proceedings

39. The appropriate officer must keep or cause to be kept a record of the exercise of the powers conferred by the provisions of Chapter 2 of Part 8.

40. The record must, in relation to each requirement, include:

- a copy of the order or warrant and copies of notices given under an order;
- a copy of the application for the order or warrant;
- the date on which the order, warrant or notice was served;
- the date of receipt of and reason for any request for an extension of the time allowed to comply with the order;
- the decision in respect of any such request and the date on which it was notified to the subject of the order;
- the date and place that the information or documents were received in response to the order; and,
- receipts provided in accordance with the provisions of this code.

Retention of documents and information

41. If documents or information are provided which were not required to be provided under the terms of the order, no account of that document or information must be taken of it in the investigation and it must be returned to the provider of the material.

42. Appropriate officers should follow established local procedures on the retention and return of documents, material and information. Intelligence that arises during the appropriate officer's investigation may be passed to the National Criminal Intelligence Service,

---

[7] This underlines the importance of an appropriate officer requesting a reasonable time limit at the time of his application for a production order or an account monitoring order. The appropriate officer should liase where possible with the subject of the order. Realistic time limits in orders will reduce later applications to the court for extensions of time.

police, customs, the Assets Recovery Agency and/or other departments and agencies (provided there is a legal basis in place either in statute or common law for the passing of information between those bodies for that purpose).

VARIATION AND DISCHARGE APPLICATIONS

43. Where an appropriate officer applies to the court to vary or discharge an order or warrant made under Chapter 2 of Part 8 of the Act, he should, as far as is practicable, follow the same procedure as for the original application. There is no requirement for the same appropriate officer to make the variation or discharge application but if it is a different officer, that officer should be in a position to explain the genuine change of circumstances. These applications are inter partes[8].

PRODUCTION ORDERS

44. Persons to whom this part of the code applies must familiarise themselves with the introduction section which sets out general instructions relating to all the orders and warrants.

Definition

45. A production order is an order which can be served on any person or institution, for example a financial institution, requiring the production of material; this might include documents such as bank statements (section 345(4)).

Statutory requirements

46. The application must specify a person who is subject to a confiscation investigation or a money laundering investigation or property which is subject to a civil recovery investigation. The application must also state that the order is sought for the purposes of a civil recovery, confiscation or money laundering investigation. It must identify the specific material sought or describe the type of material sought and it must specify a person who appears to possess or be in control of the material. It must also state whether production of the material or access to the material is required.

47. The person named in the order must either produce the material, or provide access to it, as directed by the order. This is within a period decided at the judge's discretion, but section 345(5) provides seven days as the normal period.

Persons who may apply for a production order

48. As with the other orders, an application may be made by an appropriate officer; the definition depends on the type of investigation (section 378).

---

[8] Unlike an application for an investigation order, both the applicant and respondent are notified of an application for a variation or discharge of the order. They therefore both have the opportunity to be represented before the judge.

Particular action to be taken before an application for a production order

49. The appropriate officer must ascertain, as specifically as is possible in the circumstances, the nature of the material concerned and, where relevant, its location.

50. The appropriate officer must also make enquiries to establish what, if anything, is known about the likely occupier of the premises where the material is believed to be located and the nature of the premises themselves; and to obtain any other information relevant to the application.

51. The appropriate officer must consider whether he or she requires production of the material or access to it. In most circumstances he or she would want production, so as to retain it. There are occasions however where, for example, he or she may simply want sight of information contained in larger material, e.g. an entry in a register.

52. The 7 day time limit for the production of material will apply unless it appears to the judge that a shorter or longer period would be appropriate. Reasons which the appropriate officer might put to the judge for changing the 7 day period are that the investigation may be prejudiced unless there is a shorter time limit, or that it would not be reasonably practicable for the subject of the production order to comply with the seven day time limit due to the nature or amount of documentation required. There will be cases when the best practice is to contact the subject of the production order (e.g. a financial institution) before the application is made to discuss a reasonable time limit.

Particular action to be taken executing a production order

53. When a production order is served on a person, business or institution under section 345(4)(a) of the Act, the order or the covering letter must, in addition to the matters specified in paragraph 26 of the general section , state:

- that the order was made under section 345(4)(a) of the Act;
- the material or class of material required to be furnished;
- the period of time within which such documents must be furnished.

54. Where an order is made under section 345(4)(b) of the Act (for access to material), the order or covering letter must, in addition, state:

- that the order was made under section 345(4)(b) of the Act;
- the material or class of material required to satisfy the production order;
- the appropriate officer's right of access to such material;

55. Section 350 deals with service of a production order on a government department. Where a production order is served on a government department, it must be served in the way that civil proceedings would be served on the department. This means that officers should look at the list of government departments published by the Cabinet Office under section 17 of the Crown Proceedings Act 1947 in order to find the correct address for service. A list is available on the Treasury Solicitor's website (www.treasury-solicitor.gov.uk/). In many cases, the correct procedure will be to serve the order on the Treasury Solicitor. A production order served on a government department can contain a requirement for the person on whom the order is served and anyone else who receives to bring it to the attention of the official who holds the material even if they are unknown at that stage.

Particular provisions relating to the handling and retention of documents produced or accessed in response to a production order

56. When executing a production order, an appropriate officer should ask for the material specified in the production order to be produced. This request may, if considered necessary, include a request to see the index of files held on the premises if there is one. The appropriate officer may inspect any files which, according to the index, appear to contain any of the material specified in the order or material falling within the class of material specified in the order.

57. When asking for material to be produced in accordance with an order the appropriate officer should direct the request to a person in authority and with responsibility for the material.

58. An appropriate officer may remove any material covered by the production order, except where the production order is made under section 345(4)(b) and only allows access to, rather than removal of, the material.

59. An appropriate officer may photograph or copy or have photographed or copied any material which he or she has power to remove. If a copy of the material is sufficient, it should be copied on site and the original returned. If this is not practicable, the material should be copied and the original returned as soon as possible after it has been removed.

60. Where an appropriate officer requires material to be produced from a computer in a form which may be taken away or to which access can be given in a legible form (for example a computer printout or a removable computer disk), in accordance with section 349, care should be taken to ensure that, the person producing the material in this form does not delete evidence from the computer, either deliberately or accidentally.

61. The appropriate officer should complete, unless it is impracticable to do so, a list of the articles or documents removed and give a copy of it and receipt to the occupier and the subject of the order, if present, before leaving the premises. In any event, the appropriate officer must make or have made a record of the articles removed and or accessed in compliance with a production order. A copy of any such record shall be given to the subject of the order within 7 days of the removal or access of the material.

Order to grant entry

62. An appropriate officer should consider at the application stage if he or she considers the right to enter premises is necessary in order to satisfy the production order. It might be used, for example, to enable an appropriate officer to be granted entry to a building in circumstances where a production order had been made in respect of material in a particular company's office in that building.

63. An order to grant entry differs from a search and seizure warrant in that the order to grant entry is to overcome any physical obstacle in serving the production order. It does not include the power to search the premises.

SEARCH AND SEIZURE WARRANTS

64. Persons to whom this part of the code applies must familiarise themselves with the introduction section which sets out general instructions relating to all the orders and warrants.

Definition

65. A search and seizure warrant (defined at section 352(4)) can be issued in the three circumstances set out below, and enables the appropriate person to enter and search the premises specified in the warrant, and to retain material which is likely to be of substantial value to the investigation. The search and seizure warrant does not include a power to stop a person, make an arrest or to search a person. The legislation and the code only apply to searches of premises. For the purpose of this code and the legislation "premises" is defined in section 23 of Police and Criminal Evidence Act 1984. The definition provides that premises includes any place and, in particular, includes any vehicle, vessel, aircraft or hovercraft, any offshore installation, any tent or moveable structure.

66. This code does not apply to searches conducted under other legislation or section 289 of the Act, and does not apply to searches conducted with consent without a search and seizure warrant.

Persons who can apply for and/or execute search and seizure warrants

67. As with the other powers of investigation, the code deals with appropriate *officers'* power to make an application for a search and seizure warrant and their right to retain material. This part of the code also deals with appropriate *persons'* powers to execute the warrants, namely to search the premises and seize and retain relevant material found on premises.

68. As detailed in the general section it is an appropriate officer who must make an application for a search and seizure warrant. This is defined at section 378 as the Director of the Assets Recovery Agency, an accredited financial investigator, a constable or a customs officer, depending on the type of investigation in respect of which the warrants is being requested. The person who is carrying out the investigation will normally make the application. The search warrant must be executed by an appropriate person. As detailed in the introduction, section 352(5) of the Act provides that an appropriate person is a constable or customs officer for search and seizure warrants in respect of confiscation and money laundering investigations, and a member of the staff of the Assets Recovery Agency for warrants in respect of civil recovery investigations.

Statutory requirements

69. A search and seizure warrant may only be issued if one of three statutory requirements are met.

70. The first requirement is met if a production order has not been complied with and there are reasonable grounds for believing that the material specified in the production order is on the premises specified in the search and seizure warrant.

71. The second requirement is met if the material which is sought can be identified, but it is not practicable to communicate with the person against whom a production order might be made or with any person against whom an order to grant entry to premises might be made. This might be satisfied, for example, where the person who owns the material or who controls access to the premises on which the material is held is abroad and therefore it is not possible to communicate with that person. In such circumstances, it is clear that a production order in respect of that person would have no effect. In order for this requirement to be met, the judge must also be satisfied that the investigation might be seriously prejudiced unless immediate access to the premises is secured.

72. The third requirement is met if there are reasonable grounds for believing that there is material on the premises which cannot be identified precisely enough for the purposes of a production order and that the material relates to property or a person specified in the application (appropriate officers should have regard to section 353 of the Act for full details). This might be satisfied where it is impossible to describe the material in precise detail, but it is known that suspect material belonging to a person is on the premises. In order for this requirement to be met, the judge must also be satisfied that it is not practicable to communicate with anyone who might grant entry to the premises or that entry to the premises will not be granted unless a warrant is produced or that the investigation might be seriously prejudiced unless immediate access to the premises is secured.

Particular action to be taken before an application for a search and seizure warrant

73. The appropriate officer must note that a search and seizure warrant is the most invasive of the powers of investigation.

74. The appropriate officer should consider why he needs a search and seizure warrant rather than a production order with an order to grant entry.

75. The appropriate officer must ascertain as specifically as is possible in the circumstances the nature of the material to be specified in the application and its location.

76. The appropriate officer must also make reasonable enquiries to establish what, if anything, is known about the likely occupier of the premises and the nature of the premises themselves; whether they have been previously searched and if so how recently; and obtain any other information relevant to the application.

Particular action in making an application for a search and seizure warrant

77. An application for a search and seizure warrant must include:

- the name of the person who is subject to a confiscation investigation or a money laundering investigation or the property which is subject to a civil recovery investigation;
- that the warrant is sought for the purposes of that investigation;
- which of the conditions under section 352(6)(a), 353(3) or (5) of the Act apply to the application—and why a production order is not appropriate;
- the name (if any) and address of the premises to be searched and the object of the search;
- the material which is sought or that there are reasonable grounds for believing that there is relevant material on the premises which cannot be identified;

78. If an application for a search and seizure warrant is refused, no further application may be made for a warrant to search those premises unless supported by additional grounds which subsequently come to light.

Particular action to be taken executing a search and seizure warrant

79. If the appropriate officer who made the application is different from the appropriate person authorised to execute the warrant, the appropriate officer should explain the background and decision to apply for the warrant to the appropriate person. The appropriate person will thereby have the relevant information which will help him to execute the warrant.

Time of searches

80. Searches made under a warrant must be made within one calendar month from the date of issue of the warrant.

81. Where the extent or complexity of a search means that it is likely to take a long time to complete, the appropriate person may wish to consider whether the seize and sift powers may appropriately be used (see paragraph 34).

Entry other than with consent

82. Before entering the premises, the appropriate person must first attempt to communicate with the occupier, or any other person entitled to grant access to the premises, by explaining the authority under which entry is sought to the premises, showing the warrant and asking the occupier to allow entry, unless:

- the premises to be searched are known to be unoccupied;
- the occupier and any other person entitled to grant access are known to be absent; or
- there are reasonable grounds for believing that to alert the occupier or any other person entitled to grant access by attempting to communicate with them would frustrate the object of the search or endanger the person concerned or other people.

83. Before a search begins, the appropriate person must identify him or herself (subject to the provisions relating to pseudonyms of Agency staff) and show an official form of identification, state the purpose of the search and the grounds for undertaking it. The appropriate person does not need to comply with this provision if the circumstances detailed at paragraph 82 apply.

Notice of powers and rights

84. The appropriate person must, unless it is impractical to do so, provide the occupier of the premises with a copy of the warrant and in addition to the matters specified in paragraph 26 of the general section, a notice in a standard format[9]:

- summarising the extent of the powers of search and seizure conferred in the Act;
- explaining the rights of the occupier of the premises and of the owner of the material seized under this code and as set out in the section 355 Order in connection with warrants issued in respect of a confiscation investigation or a money laundering investigation, or the Practice Direction applying safeguards to civil warrants in respect of a civil recovery investigation;
- stating that a copy of this code is available to be consulted and giving an address at which it can be obtained.

85. If the occupier is present, copies of the notice mentioned above, and of the warrant must, if practicable, be given to the occupier before the search begins, unless the appropriate person reasonably believes that to do so would frustrate the object of the search or endanger the officers concerned or other people. If the occupier is not present, copies of the

---

[9] If this information is on the warrant then there is no need for it to be also detailed and served on a separate notice.

notice and of the warrant should be left in a prominent place on the premises or appropriate part of the premises and endorsed with the name of the appropriate person (or, if authorised, the pseudonym used by a member of staff of the Agency) and the date and time of the search. The warrant itself must be endorsed to show that this has been done.

Conduct of searches

86. Premises may be searched only to the extent necessary to achieve the object of the search, having regard to the size and nature of whatever is sought. No search may continue once the appropriate person is satisfied that whatever is being sought is not on the premises. This does not prevent a further search of the same premises if additional grounds come to light which support a further application for a search warrant. Examples would be when as a result of new information it is believed that articles previously not found or additional articles are on the premises.

87. Searches must be conducted with due consideration for the property and privacy of the occupier of the premises searched, and with no more disturbance than necessary. They should be conducted at a reasonable time of day unless there are reasonable grounds to suspect that this would frustrate the search. Officers might want to consider the possibility of using reasonable force as a last resort if this appears to be the only way in which to give effect to their power of search.

88. The occupier must be asked whether he or she wishes a friend, neighbour or other person to witness the search. That person must be allowed to do so unless the appropriate person has reasonable grounds for believing that the presence of the person asked for would seriously hinder the investigation or endanger persons present. A search need not be unreasonably delayed for this purpose. A record of the action taken under this paragraph, including the grounds for refusing a request from the occupier, must be made on the premises search record (see below). This requirement also relates to business and commercial properties if practicable, as well as private addresses.

89. A person is not required to be cautioned prior to being asked questions that are solely necessary for the purpose of furthering the proper and effective conduct of a search. Examples would include questions to discover who is the occupier of specified premises, to find a key to open a locked drawer or cupboard or to otherwise seek co-operation during the search or to determine whether a particular item is liable to be seized.

Leaving premises

90. If premises have been entered by force the appropriate person must, before leaving them, be satisfied that they are secure either by arranging for the occupier or the occupier's agent to be present or by any other appropriate means.

Seizure of material

91. An appropriate person may seize:

- anything covered by the warrant;
- anything covered by the powers in Part 2 of the Criminal Justice and Police Act 2001 ("the 2001 Act") which allow an appropriate person to seize property from premises where it is not reasonably practicable to determine on the premises whether he

is entitled to seize it and retain it for sifting or examination in secure conditions elsewhere; and

- anything that the appropriate person has the power to seize not covered by the warrant which is discovered during the course of the search (e.g. cash under section 294 of the Act). However, this is incidental to the search powers and a warrant must not be applied for to search for other material other than that specified in the application. A search must not continue after it appears that there is no more material covered by the warrant on the premises, even if the appropriate person suspects that there are other items which he or she may want to seize.

92. Appropriate persons must be aware of section 59 of the Criminal Justice and Police Act 2001 which allows persons with a relevant interest in material which has been seized to make an application to a judicial authority for the return of the material. Appropriate persons must also be aware of the subsequent duty to secure in section 60.

93. An appropriate person may photograph, image or copy, or have photographed, copied or imaged, any material which he has power to seize. An appropriate person must have regard to his or her statutory obligation not to retain any original material when a photograph or copy would be sufficient.

94. Where an appropriate person considers that information which is held in a computer and is accessible from the premises specified in the warrant is relevant to the investigation, the officer may require the information to be produced from the computer in a form which can be taken away (for example a computer printout or a removable computer disk). Care should be taken to ensure that the person producing the material in this form does not delete evidence from the computer, either deliberately or accidentally.

Particular record of proceedings in executing a search and seizure warrant

95. Where premises have been searched under a warrant issued under Chapter 2 of Part 8 of the Act, the appropriate person must make or have made a record of the search. The record shall include:

- the address of the premises searched;
- the date, time and duration of the search;
- the warrant under which the search was made (a copy of the warrant shall be appended to the record or kept in a place identified in the record);
- subject to the provisions relating to pseudonyms of Agency staff, the name of the appropriate person and the names of all other persons involved in the search;
- the names of any people on the premises if they are known;
- any grounds for refusing the occupier's request to have someone present during the search as set out in paragraph 88;
- either a list of any material seized or a note of where such a list is kept and, if not covered by a warrant, the grounds for their seizure;
- whether force was used, and, if so, the reason why it was used; and
- details of any damage caused during the search, and the circumstances in which it was caused; and,
- confirmation that premises were left secured and by what means.

96. The warrant must be endorsed by the appropriate person to show:

- whether any material was seized;
- the date and time at which it was executed;
- subject to the provisions relating to pseudonyms of Agency staff, the name of the appropriate person who executed it; and
- whether a copy of the warrant, together with a copy of the Notice of Powers and Rights, was handed to the occupier; or whether it was endorsed and left on the premises together with the copy notice and, if so, where.

Search register

97. A search register must be maintained at each sub-divisional or equivalent police station, each Customs office and at the Assets Recovery Agency. All search records which are required to be made shall be made, copied, or referred to in the register. However, police stations are not required to set up a separate register in addition to the one maintained for searches covered by the PACE Codes of Practice.

Specific procedures for seize and sift powers

98. Part 2 of the Criminal Justice and Police Act 2001 provides persons who are lawfully on any premises and exercising powers of search and seizure with limited powers to seize material from premises so that they can sift through it or otherwise examine it elsewhere. These powers may be exercised where it is not reasonably practicable to determine on the premises whether or not the person is entitled to seize it. All appropriate persons conducting searches under the Act are permitted to use these powers. Appropriate persons must be careful that they only exercise these powers where it is essential to do so and that they do not remove any more material than is absolutely necessary. The removal of large volumes of material, much of which may not ultimately be retainable, may have serious implications for the owners, particularly where they are involved in business. Appropriate persons must always give careful consideration to whether removing copies or images of relevant material or data would be a satisfactory alternative to removing the originals. Where originals are taken, appropriate persons must always be prepared to facilitate the provision of copies or images for the owners where that is reasonably practicable.

99. Property seized under section 50 of the 2001 Act must be kept securely and separately from any other material seized under other powers. Section 51 is not relevant as the search and seizure powers under the Act do not extend to seizing material from the person. An examination under section 53 to determine what material may be retained in accordance with the Act must be carried out at soon as practicable, allowing the person from whom the material was seized, or a person with an interest in the material, an opportunity of being present or represented. The appropriate person must ensure that he or she has the facilities for the sift to be conducted in suitable surroundings and that persons from whom the material was seized or who have an interest in the material or their representative can be present.

100. It is the responsibility of the appropriate person to ensure that, where appropriate, property is returned in accordance with sections 53 to 55 of the 2001 Act. Material which is not retainable (i.e. because it is legally privileged material, excluded material or falls outside the terms of the warrant) must be separated from the rest of the seized property and

returned as soon as reasonably practicable after the examination of all the seized property has been completed. Delay is only warranted if very clear and compelling reasons exist. For example, the unavailability of the person to whom the material is to be returned or the need to agree a convenient time to return a very large volume of material. Legally privileged or excluded material which cannot be retained must be returned as soon as reasonably practicable and without waiting for the whole examination to be completed. As set out in section 58 of the 2001 Act, material must be returned to the person from whom it was seized, except where it is clear that some other person has a better right to it. Unlike most other legislation, the Proceeds of Crime Act allows for the seizure and retention of special procedure material. Special procedure material is defined at section 14 of the Police and Criminal Evidence Act 1984 and refers to journalistic and other confidential material acquired or created in the course of a trade, business, profession or unpaid office.

101. Where an officer involved in the investigation has reasonable grounds to believe that a person with a relevant interest in property seized under section 50 of the 2001 Act intends to make an application under section 59 for the return of any legally privileged or excluded material, the officer in charge of the investigation must be informed and the material seized must be kept secure in accordance with section 61.

102. The responsibility for ensuring property is properly secured rests ultimately with the appropriate person and the appropriate officer, even if there is a separate person delegated with this specific task. Securing involves making sure that the property is not examined, copied or put to any other use except with the consent of the applicant or in accordance with the directions of the appropriate judicial authority. Any such consent or directions must be recorded in writing and signed by both the applicant or judicial authority and the appropriate person.

103. Where an appropriate person exercises a power of seizure conferred by section 50 of the 2001 Act that appropriate person must at the earliest opportunity and unless it is impracticable to do so, provide the occupier of the premises or the person from whom the property was seized with a written notice:

- specifying what has been seized in reliance on the powers conferred by that section;
- specifying the grounds on which those powers have been exercised;
- setting out the effect of sections 59 to 61 of the 2001 Act which cover the grounds on which a person with a relevant interest in seized property may apply to a judicial authority for its return and the duty of officers to secure property in certain circumstances where such an application is made;
- specifying the name and address of the person to whom notice of an application to the appropriate judicial authority in respect of any of the seized property must be given; and
- specifying the name and address of the person to whom an application may be made to be allowed to attend the initial examination of the property (i.e. police station, customs office, office of the accredited financial investigator or an Agency building).

104. If the occupier is not present but there is some other person there who is in charge of the premises, the notice must be given to that person. If there is no one on the premises to whom the notice may appropriately be given, it should either be left in a prominent place on the premises or attached to the exterior of the premises so that it will easily be found.

Retention

105. Anything which has been seized may be retained only for as long as is necessary in connection with the investigation for the purposes of which the warrant was issued or (in the case of confiscation or money laundering investigations) in order to establish its lawful owner, where there are reasonable grounds for believing that it has been obtained in consequence of the commission of an offence.

106. Property must not be retained if a photograph or copy would suffice for the purposes of evidence in the prospective court proceedings following the investigation.

Rights of owners etc.

107. If property is retained, the occupier of the premises on which it was seized or the person who had custody or control of it immediately prior to its seizure must on request be provided with a list or description of the property within a reasonable time.

108. That person or their representative must be allowed supervised access to the property to examine it or have it photographed or copied, or must be provided with a photograph or copy, in either case within a reasonable time of any request and at their own expense, unless the appropriate officer has reasonable grounds for believing that this would prejudice the investigation or any proceedings. A record of the grounds must be made in any case where access is denied.

CUSTOMER INFORMATION ORDERS

109. Persons to whom this part of the code applies must familiarise themselves with the introduction section which sets out general instructions relating to all the orders and warrants.

Definition

110. A customer information order compels a financial institution covered by the application to provide any 'customer information' it has relating to the person specified in the application. 'Customer information' is defined at section 364 of the Act. A 'financial institution' means a person carrying on a business in the regulated sector. Regulated sector is defined at Schedule 9 to the Act.

Persons who can apply for a customer information order

111. An appropriate officer must have the authorisation of a senior appropriate officer to make an application for a customer information order. A senior appropriate officer for a confiscation investigation is the Director or a police officer who is not below the rank of superintendent, a customs officer at Pay Band 9 or above or a financial investigator accredited for the function of authorising such applications. For money laundering investigations, a senior appropriate officer is a police officer who is not below the rank of superintendent, a customs officer at Pay Band 9 or above or a financial investigator accredited for the function of authorising such applications. For civil recovery investigations, the senior appropriate officer is the Director. If an investigator is accredited to both apply for

and authorise the making of an application for a customer information order, he or she can make such an application without an additional separate authorisation. A police officer who is not below the rank of superintendent, an customs officer at Pay Band 9 or above or the Director can also make such an application without an additional separate authorisation

Statutory requirements

112. The application must specify a person who is subject to a confiscation investigation or money laundering investigation or a person who holds property subject to a civil recovery investigation. It must state that the order is sought for the purposes of that investigation. It must specify the financial institutions from which the appropriate officer wishes to obtain customer information, whether this is done by a list or a description of financial institution. A description of financial institutions may include all financial institutions within a specific geographical area or who specialise in a particular form of account.

Particular action to be taken before an application for a customer information order is made

113. The appropriate officer must carefully consider his existing evidence and information so as to limit the number or scope of financial institutions. This would include researching his own force or agency's intelligence systems, the Police National Computer and the National Criminal Intelligence Service. He or she should consider what benefit the customer information he or she may obtain may have, either in itself or as the lead to other avenues of investigation. He or she should also consider whether the information he or she wishes to gain could not be acquired as effectively and efficiently from material which could be obtained by way of a production order. The appropriate officer should consider the cost both to himself or herself and the financial institutions.

114. On receiving a request for authorisation for an application for a customer information order, the senior appropriate officer must consider similar issues. He or she should particularly consider the proportionality of requesting the customer information, against the believed benefit to the investigation. The senior appropriate officer should also consider the broader issues of law enforcement such as the benefit to the community of removing the suspected proceeds from circulation.

Particular action to be taken executing a customer information order

115. Section 363(5) of the Act requires a financial institution to provide any customer information which it has relating to the person specified in the application if it is given notice in writing by an appropriate officer. Section 363(6) gives the appropriate office power to request the manner and the time by which the financial institution provides the information. The appropriate officer is expected to impose a reasonable time limit depending on the nature of the institution and the information which is requested. There will be cases when the best practice is to contact the financial institution before the notice is served to discuss a reasonable time limit.

116. A notice given under a customer information order should include the following:

• the name of the financial institution;
• the name of the person about whom customer information is sought;

- the financial institution's right to refuse to comply with any requirement made of them unless the appropriate officer has, if asked to do so, produced evidence of his authority;
- the period of time within which the customer information must be furnished;
- the manner in which such information must be furnished;
- the place at which the information is to be furnished;
- where the appropriate officer thinks that the customer information includes information in relation to accounts held in any other name which it appears to the appropriate officer that the specified person may have used, that other name;
- where the appropriate officer thinks that the customer information includes information in relation to accounts held in the name of any company or limited liability partnership, which the specified person is or in which it appears to the appropriate officer that the specified person has or had an interest, the name and all known addresses of that company or limited liability partnership;
- all addresses known by the appropriate officer to have been used by the specified person possibly relating to accounts that may have been or are held by the financial institution;
- the date of birth or approximate age of that person if an individual, or any known identification information in respect of a company or limited liability partnership ;
- such other information as the appropriate officer considers would assist the respondent in complying with the requirement; and
- the financial institution's right not to have information furnished used in evidence against it in criminal proceedings other than in the circumstances specified in section 367(2).

Particular record of proceedings under a customer information order

117. The appropriate officer should keep a copy of the customer information order and all the notices issued to financial institutions under a customer information order. He or she should also keep a record of all the information supplied in response to the notices.

118. The appropriate officer should consider the customer information he or she has obtained and consider whether a production order or account monitoring order would be the next step to obtain further information and material to support the investigation.

ACCOUNT MONITORING ORDERS

119. Persons to whom this part of the code applies must familiarise themselves with the introduction section which sets out general instructions relating to all the orders and warrants.

Definition

120. An account monitoring order is an order that requires a specified financial institution to provide account information on a specified account for a specified period, up to 90 days in the manner and at or by the times specified in the order. 'Account information' is information relating to an account held at a financial institution—this would most commonly be transaction details. There is no bar on an appropriate officer making a repeat application for an account monitoring order immediately after an account monitoring order has expired.

Persons who can apply for an account monitoring order

121. As with the other orders, an application may be made by an appropriate officer; the definition depends on the type of investigation (see section 378 of the Act).

Statutory requirements

122. The application must specify a person who is subject to a confiscation investigation or money laundering investigation or a person who holds property subject to a civil recovery investigation. It must state that the order is sought for the purposes of that investigation. It must specify the financial institution from which the appropriate officer wishes to obtain the account information. The application must state that the order is sought in relation to account information about the specified person. It must specify the account information which is sought, whether by reference to specific accounts or accounts of a general description.

123. The order also sets the manner and deadline by which the financial institution must produce account information and the period for which the order should last.

Particular action to be taken before an application for an account monitoring order

124. The appropriate officer has to consider to his investigation the benefit of obtaining information from an account, and whether this information could be as easily obtained by using a production order. He should consider whether in relation to a confiscation investigation he should consider making (or where he is not an accredited financial investigator, asking someone else to make) an application for a restraint order on the account (under section 42 or 191).

125. The appropriate officer should also consider what account information he or she should request. If, for example, the appropriate officer requires information on certain transactions, he or she should consider whether he or she could meaningfully limit the information he or she requires to amounts over a certain threshold or identity of the source of the deposit or destination of a withdrawal.

126. The period to be specified for compliance with any requirement shall be set by the judge on the order. A reasonable time limit to suggest to the judge might be that the information should be provided within 24 hours on all transactions unless it appears that it would not be reasonably practicable for the subject of the account monitoring order to comply with this time limit. There will be cases when the best practice is to contact the subject of the account monitoring order (i.e. the relevant financial institution) before the application is made to discuss types of transaction and the reporting process.

127. Appropriate officers should consider the time period they wish the account monitoring order to cover. The appropriate officer should not treat the 90 day maximum as the standard time limit. They must carefully consider and justify to the judge the requirement for the time period requested.

Particular action to be taken executing an account monitoring order

128. When an account monitoring order is served on a financial institution, the covering letter, in addition to the matters specified in paragraph 26 of the general section, should include the following (unless it is already included in the order):

- the name of the financial institution;
- the identity of the person(s) who hold the account to be monitored, including as much identity information as is known by the appropriate officer;
- the accounts in relation to which the information is required, whether this is a specific account or a general description of accounts;
- the account information required (in as specific detail as possible, for example a general description of the nature of the transactions);
- the period for which the account monitoring order will have effect;
- the period of time within which such information must be furnished to the appropriate officer (e.g. within 24 hours of a particular transaction taking place);
- the manner in which such information must be furnished;
- such other information as the appropriate officer considers would assist the respondent in complying with the requirements of the account monitoring order;
- the financial institution's right not to have information furnished used in evidence against it in criminal proceedings other than in the circumstances specified in section 367(2).

Particular record of proceedings under an account monitoring order

129. The appropriate officer should keep a record of all the account information supplied in response to the order.

DISCLOSURE ORDERS

130. The Director must familiarise himself or herself with the introduction section which sets out general instructions relating to all the orders and warrants.

Definition

131. A disclosure order is an order authorising the Director to give notice in writing to any person requiring him or her to answer questions, to provide information or to produce documents with respect to any matter relevant to the investigation in relation to which the order is sought.

132. Once a disclosure order has been made, the Director may use the extensive powers set out in section 357(4) of the Act throughout his investigation. Thus, unlike the other orders which have to be applied for separately on each occasion, a disclosure order gives the Director continuing powers for the purposes of the investigation. The Director must serve a notice on any person he wishes to question or to ask to provide information or documents. The disclosure order is only available for confiscation and civil recovery investigations. The disclosure order is not available for money laundering investigations. In keeping with the other powers the disclosure order is not available for revenue investigations under Part 6 of the Act.

133. Under section 357(6), where a person is given a notice under a disclosure order, he can require that evidence of the authority to give the notice be provided. Where this happens, a copy of the disclosure order should be given to the person.

Persons who can apply for a disclosure order

134. Only the Director of the Assets Recovery Agency can apply for a disclosure order, and only in respect of his own investigations. He or she cannot apply for and execute a disclosure order on behalf of another agency (i.e. police, customs or other body with the power to conduct a confiscation investigation).

Statutory requirements

135. The Director has to satisfy the judge that a civil recovery or confiscation investigation is going on and the order is sought for the purposes of that investigation.

Particular action to be taken in making an application

136. An application for a disclosure order must state:

- the name of the person who is subject to a confiscation investigation or the property which is subject to a civil recovery investigation;
- that the order is sought for the purposes of that investigation;
- if it is a confiscation investigation, that the investigation is being undertaken by the Director or by one of his staff;
- whether the Director is likely to require answers to questions and/or information and/or documents;
- if practicable, the name of the person or persons against whom the power may be used; and
- the grounds on which the application is made (including details of the investigation);
- why a disclosure order is required in preference to the other powers of investigation.

Particular action to be taken in executing a disclosure order

Providing of information and production of documents

137. Production of documents or information in response to a disclosure order should follow similar processes to those set out for production orders. The Director must give notice in writing to anyone whom he wishes to provide information or documents. In addition to the general requirements at paragraph 26, this notice should include, where applicable;

- whether the Director wants the respondent to provide information under section 357(4)(b) or produce documents under section 357(4)(c) of the Act;
- if the Director requires information, a description of the information required;
- if the Director requires documents, the documents or class of documents required;

Interview

138. The disclosure order also contains a power to ask questions. The preferred course of asking questions is to conduct a formalised interview in accordance with the procedure set out below.

Invitation to interview

139. The Director must send the interviewee a notice served under the disclosure order which must contain:

- the right of the Director to interview the interviewee under section 357(4)(a) of the Act;
- the purpose of the interview, which may be as detailed as the Director thinks necessary;
- the interviewee's right not to have statements made by him used in evidence in criminal proceedings against him or her other than in the circumstances specified in section 360(2);
- his or her right to be accompanied at any interview by a solicitor and/or a qualified accountant;
- his or her right, if he or she is a juvenile[10], is mentally disordered or mentally handicapped, to be accompanied at any interview by an appropriate adult;
- details of the place at which the interview is to take place, and
- where attendance is not required at once, the time and date of the interview.

Legal and Financial advice

140. In this code, a 'solicitor' means a solicitor who holds a current practising certificate, a trainee solicitor, a duty solicitor representative or an accredited representative included on the register of representatives maintained by the Legal Services Commission. A 'qualified accountant' means a person who is a member or fellow of the Institute of Chartered Accountants in England and Wales, or the Institute of Chartered Accountants of Scotland, or the Institute of Chartered Accountants in Ireland, or the Association of Chartered Certified Accountants or who would, for the purposes of the audit of company accounts be regarded by virtue of section 33 of the Companies Act 1989, as holding an approved overseas qualification.

141. In urgent cases a person who is not suspected of any unlawful conduct may be prepared to answer questions without the presence of a solicitor and/or qualified accountant. If a person to be interviewed requests access to legal or financial advice before complying with a requirement to be interviewed in a notice served under a disclosure order, the Director should normally consent and set a reasonable time limit for obtaining such advice. In the exceptional cases set out below the Director can refuse such a request depending on the circumstances of the case and the information or material which is being requested.

142. A person who requests legal and/or financial advice may not be interviewed or continue to be interviewed until they have received such advice unless:

(a) the person conducting the interview has reasonable grounds for believing that:

    (i) the consequent delay would be likely to lead to interference with or harm to evidence connected with the investigation; or

    (ii) the delay would alert another person whom the person conducting the interview thinks might have information relevant to the investigation and alerting that person would prejudice the investigation;

---

[10] if anyone appears to be under the age of 17 then he or she shall be treated as a juvenile for the purposes of this code in the absence of clear evidence to show that he or she is older

(b) a solicitor and/or qualified accountant has been contacted and has agreed to attend but the Director considers that awaiting their arrival would cause unreasonable delay to the process of investigation This decision must be made by the Director him or herself and cannot be taken by a person delegated to perform his or her functions under section 1(6) of the Act;

(c) the solicitor and/or qualified accountant whom the person has nominated:

   (i)   cannot be contacted; or
   (ii) has previously indicated that they do not wish to be contacted; or
   (iii) having been contacted, has declined to attend and the person being interviewed declines to consult another solicitor and/or qualified accountant; or,

(d) the person who wanted legal and/or financial advice changes his or her mind.

143. In a case falling within paragraph (a), once sufficient information has been obtained to avert the risk of interference or harm to evidence or of alerting another person so as to prejudice the investigation, questioning must cease until the interviewee has received legal or financial advice.

144. In a case falling within paragraph (d), the interview may be started or continued without further delay provided that the person has given his or her agreement in writing to being interviewed without receiving legal or financial advice and that the person conducting the interview has inquired into the person's reasons for the change of mind and has given authority for the interview to proceed. Confirmation of the person's agreement, his or her change of mind and his or her reasons (where given) must be recorded in the written interview record at the beginning or re-commencement of interview.

145. If a solicitor wishes to send a non-accredited or probationary representative to provide advice on his behalf, then that person is also recognised as a 'legal adviser' and must be admitted to the interview unless the Director considers that this will hinder the investigation.

146. In exercising his discretion as to whether to admit a legal adviser who is not a solicitor, the person conducting the interview should take into account in particular whether the identity and status of the non-accredited or probationary representative have been satisfactorily established; whether he or she is of suitable character to provide legal advice (a person with a criminal record is unlikely to be suitable unless the conviction was for a minor offence and is not recent); and any other matters in any written letter of authorisation provided by the solicitor on whose behalf the person is attending.

147. If the person conducting the interview refuses access to a non-accredited or probationary representative or a decision is taken that such a person should not be permitted to remain at an interview, he or she must forthwith notify a solicitor on whose behalf the non-accredited or probationary representative was to have acted or was acting, and give him or her an opportunity to make alternative arrangements. The interviewee must also be informed.

Persons who may be present at interviews

148. Interviews must be conducted in private by the person conducting the interview. Another member of the Agency must be present at all times. Only persons whose presence is sanctioned by this code should be present. It is up to the interviewee to arrange the presence of any solicitor and/or qualified accountant. When doing so he or she should ensure that the person he or she selects is available to attend. Where the provisions of this code

require the presence of an appropriate adult or an interpreter and no such person attends with the interviewee the person conducting the interview must, before commencing or restarting any interview, secure the attendance of such a person.

149. The person conducting the interview may be accompanied by a person to assist in handling documents and carrying out such other support tasks as will assist the person conducting the interview to perform his duties. Such a person has no power to require the interviewee to do anything and need not disclose his name or address provided a record of these is made by the person conducting the interview.

150. If the person conducting the interview has any suspicion, or is told in good faith, that a person is or appears to be (without clear evidence to the contrary)

- under seventeen years of age;
- mentally disordered;
- mentally handicapped; or
- mentally incapable of understanding the significance of questions put to him or her or his or her replies.[11]

he or she shall not be interviewed unless an appropriate adult is present.

The 'appropriate adult'

151. In this code 'the appropriate adult' means:

(a) in the case of a juvenile:

(i) his or her parent or guardian (or, if the juvenile is in care a member of staff of the care authority/agency or voluntary organisation. The term 'in care' is used in this code to cover all cases in which a juvenile is 'looked after' by a local authority under the terms of the Children Act 1989);

(ii) a social worker;

(iii) failing either of the above, another responsible adult aged 18 or over who is not a member of staff of the Agency or any law enforcement or prosecuting body.

(b) in the case of a person who is mentally disordered or mentally handicapped:

(i) a relative, guardian or other person responsible for his or her care and custody;

(ii) someone who has experience of working with mentally disordered or mentally handicapped people but who is not a member of staff of the Agency or any law enforcement or prosecuting body (such as an approved social worker as defined by the Mental Health Act 1983, a specialist social worker or a community psychiatric nurse); or

(iii) failing either of the above, some other responsible adult aged 18 or over who is not a member of staff of the Agency or any law enforcement or prosecuting body.

---

[11] 'Mental disorder' is defined in section 1(2) of the Mental Health Act 1983 as 'mental illness, arrested or incomplete development of mind, psychopathic disorder and any other disorder or disability of the mind'. Where the person conducting the interview has any doubt about the mental state or capacity of an interviewee, that person should be treated as mentally vulnerable and an appropriate adult should be called.

152. A person, including a parent or guardian, should not be an appropriate adult if he or she is suspected of involvement in the unlawful conduct to which the civil recovery investigation relates or the criminal conduct to which the confiscation investigation relates is involved in the investigation or has received admissions from the juvenile prior to attending to act as the appropriate adult. If the parent of a juvenile is estranged from the juvenile, he or she should not be asked to act as the appropriate adult if the juvenile expressly and specifically objects to his presence.

153. A person should always be given an opportunity, when an appropriate adult is called to the interview, to consult privately with a solicitor and/or a qualified accountant in the absence of the appropriate adult if they wish to do so.

Role of persons who may be present at interviews

Solicitor and Qualified Accountant

154. The main role of any solicitor or qualified accountant is to see that it is conducted in a fair and proper manner. He or she may not answer questions on behalf of the interviewee but he or she may intervene:

- to seek clarification of questions put during the interview;
- to challenge a question put by the Director which he or she considers improper;
- to challenge the manner in which a question is put;
- if the client may have a reasonable excuse for failure to comply with the disclosure order, to advise him or her whether or not to reply to a question; or
- give the interviewee advice.

155. Any request for legal or financial advice and the action taken on it shall be recorded on the record and/or taped. If a person has asked for legal or financial advice and an interview is begun in the absence of a solicitor or qualified accountant (or the solicitor or qualified accountant has been required to leave an interview), a note shall be made in the interview record.

156. The solicitor or qualified accountant may read any documents shown to, or produced by, the interviewee at the interview.

Appropriate Adult

157. Where the appropriate adult is present at an interview, he or she shall be informed that he or she is not expected to act simply as an observer, and that the purposes of their presence are, first, to advise the person being questioned and to observe whether or not the interview is being conducted properly and fairly, and secondly, to facilitate communication with the person being interviewed.

Physical Disability

158. A person who is blind or seriously visually impaired may be accompanied by his guide dog. The person conducting the interview shall ensure that the person who is blind or seriously visually impaired has his or her solicitor, relative, the appropriate adult or some other person likely to take an interest in him or her (and not involved in the investigation) available to help in the checking of any documentation. Where this code requires written consent then the person who is assisting may be asked to sign instead if the interviewee so wishes.

159. An interviewee who is seriously physically impaired may be accompanied by an able-bodied adult aged 18 or over to provide such physical assistance, as the interviewee requires. Such a person may take no part in the interview and has none of the rights of an appropriate adult.

Interpreters

160. A person must not be interviewed in the absence of a person capable of acting as interpreter if:

- he or she has difficulty in understanding English and the person conducting the interview cannot speak the person's own language; or
- he or she is deaf or has difficulty with hearing or speaking,

unless the interviewee agrees in writing that the interview may proceed without an interpreter.

161. An interpreter shall also be called if a juvenile is interviewed and the appropriate adult appears to be deaf or there is doubt about his or her hearing or speaking ability, unless he or she agrees in writing that the interview should proceeds without one.

162. The interpreter must be provided at the Director's expense. The person conducting the interview must ascertain, as far as is practicable, that the interpreter and interviewee understand each other, and this must be noted on the interview record. An appropriate adult may not act as the interpreter.

163. The interviewing officer must ensure that the interpreter makes a note of the interview at the time in the language of the person being interviewed for use in the event of his or her being called to give evidence, and certifies its accuracy. The person conducting the interview shall allow sufficient time for the interpreter to make a note of each question and answer after each question and answer has been put or given and interpreted. The interviewee shall be given the opportunity to read it or, in the case of an interviewee who is not deaf or has difficulty in hearing, have it read to him and sign it as correct or to indicate the respects in which he considers it inaccurate[12].

164. Action taken to call an interpreter under this section and any agreement to be interviewed in the absence of an interpreter must be recorded in writing and or taped.

Excluding Persons from the Interview

165. The person conducting the interview may exclude from the interview a person whose presence is authorised[13] by the provisions of this code if it appears to the person conducting the interview that the person is mentally disordered (see footnote 11).

166. Subject to paragraph 166, the person conducting the interview may exclude from the interview a person whose presence is authorised[14] only if he or she has reason to believe that the person is personally involved in the matter under investigation or that the person has, by improper conduct, hindered the proper conduct of the interview. Before excluding any person the person conducting the interview shall state his or her reason and note this on the interview record. What amounts to improper conduct will depend on the

---

[12] The interpreter must make a note of the interview even if it is also being tape-recorded.

[13] Persons whose presence is authorised are a solicitor, a qualified accountant, an appropriate adult, a person providing assistance and an interpreter.

[14] Ibid.

circumstances of each case. It would almost always be improper conduct for a person to prompt the interviewee, to provide the interviewee with written answers to the questions, to answer questions on behalf of the interviewee or to interrupt the interview for any reason other than to make a proper representation. Exclusion of any person from an interview is a serious matter which may be subject to comment in court. The person conducting the interview should therefore be prepared to justify his decision.

167. If the person conducting the interview has excluded a person from the interview room under paragraph 166 or 167, he or she should adjourn the interview. The interviewee must then be informed that he has the right to seek another person to act in the same role as the person who was excluded. If the interviewee wished the interview to continue, then the interviewer should record this decision and continue with the interview.

168. If the person conducting the interview considers that a solicitor or qualified accountant is acting in such a way, he or she must cease questioning the interviewee, and whilst the tape recorder is still operating, speak to the solicitor or qualified accountant. After speaking to the solicitor or qualified accountant, the person conducting the interview must decide whether or not the interview should continue in the presence of that solicitor or qualified accountant. If he or she decides that it should not, the interviewee must be given the opportunity to consult another solicitor or qualified accountant before the interview continues and that solicitor must be given an opportunity to be present at the interview.

169. The removal of a solicitor from an interview is a serious step and, if it occurs, the person conducting the interview must consider whether the incident should be reported to the Law Society.

Conduct of interviews

170. As far as practicable interviews should take place in interview rooms which must be adequately heated, lit and ventilated.

171. People being questioned or making statements must not be required to stand.

172. Breaks from interviewing must be made at recognised meal times. Short breaks for refreshment must also be provided at intervals of approximately two hours, subject to the interviewer's discretion to delay a break if there are reasonable grounds for believing that it would prejudice the outcome of the investigation.

173. Where an interview, is adjourned for any reason and is to be resumed at the same place later the same day it shall be sufficient for the person conducting the interview to inform the interviewee of the time or resumption and no notice in writing requiring attendance at that time shall be necessary. The details of the adjournment should be noted in the interview record.

174. Where an interview, is adjourned for any reason and is to be resumed either at a different place or on a different day the person conducting the interview must serve another notice under the disclosure order on the interviewee requiring him to attend at that place or on that day.

The interviewer's obligations at the interview

175. The person conducting the interview must then caution the interviewee as follows:

'You are required by law to answer all the questions I put to you unless you have a reasonable excuse for not doing so. If you fail, without reasonable excuse, to answer a question or if you knowingly or recklessly make a statement which is false you will be committing an offence for which you may be prosecuted. Do you understand?'

The person conducting the interview should also inform the interviewee that this is not a criminal caution and any responses will not be used to incriminate the interviewee.

176. The person conducting the interview must, if asked to do so, produce evidence of his authority to require the interviewee to answer questions under the disclosure order.

177. The person conducting the interview may ask such further questions as appear to him or her to be necessary to ascertain the entitlement of any person to be present.

178. The person conducting the interview must ask the interviewee whether he or she suffers from any condition which may impair his ability to understand what is taking place or if he or she is due to take any medication before the time at which the Director estimates that the interview will end. The interviewee must be free to take medication during a routine break in the interview. When a break is to be taken during the interview, the fact that a break is to be taken, the reason for it and the time shall be recorded.

179. The person conducting the interview must offer the interviewee the opportunity to ask any questions to clarify the purpose, structure and conduct of the interview.

180. Before concluding the interview the person conducting the interview must ask the interviewee if he or she has any complaint to make about anything which has taken place at the interview.

181. If a question and answer record has been taken of the interview because it was not tape-recorded, the person conducting the interview must afford the interviewee the opportunity to read the record. If the interviewee is for any reason unable to read the note or if the interviewee declines to do so the person conducting the interview must read, or cause it to be read, aloud. The person conducting the interview must invite the interviewee to comment on the note and will add to it any comments made. The interviewee must be invited to sign the note. The person conducting the interview must then record the time in the presence of the interviewee. If the interviewee is unable for any reason to sign the note he or she may authorise any person, present at the interview to sign it on his behalf. Where the interviewee refuses to sign the note, or to have it signed on his behalf; the person conducting the interview must record that fact and any reason given for the refusal on the note.

182. Whenever this code requires a person to be given certain information he or she does not have to be given it if he or she is incapable at the time of understanding what is said to him or her, or is violent or likely to become violent or is in urgent need of medical attention, but he or she must be given it as soon as practicable.

Tape Recording

183. Interviews should be tape-recorded. A record of certain matters arising from the interview should also be made contemporaneously. The matters to be recorded in the note are listed at the end of this section.

Recording and the sealing of master tapes

184. Tape recording of interviews must be carried out openly to instil confidence in its reliability as an impartial and accurate record of the interview.

185. One tape that shall be the master tape must be sealed before it leaves the presence of the interviewee. A second tape will be used as a working copy. The master tape is either one of the two tapes used in a twin deck machine or the only tape used in a single deck machine.

The working copy is either the second tape used in a twin deck machine or a copy of the master tape made by a single deck machine.

Interviews to be taped recorded

186. The person conducting the interview may authorise that the interview not be taped where it is not reasonably practicable to do so. This could be due to failure of the equipment or lack of a suitable interview room or recorder if the person conducting the interview has reasonable grounds for considering that the interview should not be delayed until the failure has been rectified or a suitable room or recorder becomes available.

187. In such cases the interview must be recorded in writing. In all cases the person conducting the interview shall make a note in specific terms of the reasons for not tape recording

Commencement of interviews

188. When the interviewee is brought into the interview room the person conducting the interview must without delay, but in the sight of the interviewee, load the tape recorder with clean tapes and set it to record. The tapes must be unwrapped or otherwise opened in the presence of the interviewee.

189. The person conducting the interview must:

- inform the interviewee that he or she is the Director or has delegated authority (see section 1(6) of the Act);
- give his or her name and that of any other persons present (subject to the provision on pseudonyms of Agency staff);
- inform the interviewee of the purpose for which any person accompanying the person conducting the interview is present;
- ask the interviewee to state his full name and address and date of birth;
- ask any person present with the interviewee to state their name, business address[15] and capacity in which he or she is present;
- state the date, time of commencement and place of the interview;
- state that the interviewee has the opportunity to request legal and/or financial advice;
- state and obtain the confirmation of the reasons under paragraph 141 et seq for there being no legal representation if this be the case;
- inform the interviewee of his or her right:

  (a) to consult in private at any time with any solicitor, qualified accountant or appropriate adult present with him or her at any interview;
  (b) to be questioned fairly;
  (c) to be given an opportunity at the end of the interview to clarify anything he or she has said or to say anything further if he or she wishes;
  (d) to be allowed a break in any interview which last for more than two hours.

- inform the interviewee that the interview is being tape-recorded;

---

[15] If persons present do not have a business address (e.g. a parent), they should provide a home address.

- state that the interviewee will be given a notice about what will happen to the tapes. and
- attempt to estimate the likely length of the interview and inform the interviewee.

Objections and complaints by the suspect

190. If the interviewee raises objections to the interview being tape-recorded either at the outset or during the interview or during a break in the interview, the person conducting the interview must explain the fact that the interview is being tape-recorded and that the provisions of this code require that the interviewee's objections shall be recorded on tape. When any objections have been recorded on tape or the interviewee has refused to have their objections recorded, the person conducting the interview may turn off the recorder. In this eventuality the person conducting the interview must say that he or she is turning off the recorder, give his or her reasons for doing so and then turn it off. The person conducting the interview must then make a written record of the interview. If, however, the person conducting the interview reasonably considers that he or she may proceed to put questions to the interviewee with the tape recorder still on, the person conducting the interview may do so.

Changing tapes

191. When the recorder indicates that the tapes have only a short time left to run, the person conducting the interview must tell the interviewee that the tapes are coming to an end and round off that part of the interview. If the person conducting the interview wishes to continue the interview but does not already have a second set of tapes, he or she must obtain a set. The interviewee must not be left unattended in the interview room. The person conducting the interview must remove the tapes from the tape recorder and insert the new tapes, which must be unwrapped or otherwise opened in the interviewee's presence. The tape recorder must then be set to record on the new tapes. Care must be taken, particularly when a number of sets of tapes have been used, to ensure that there is no confusion between the tapes. This may be done by marking the tapes with an identification number immediately they are removed from the tape recorder.

Taking a break during interview

192. When a break is to be taken during the course of an interview and the interview room is to be vacated by the interviewee, the fact that a break is to be taken, the reason for it and the time must be recorded on tape. The tapes must then be removed from the tape recorder and the procedures for the conclusion of an interview set out in paragraphs 199 to 202 below followed.

193. When a break is to be a short one and both the interviewee and the person conducting the interview are to remain in the interview room the fact that a break is to be taken, the reasons for it and the time must be recorded on tape. The tape recorder may be turned off. There is, however, no need to remove the tapes and when the interview is recommenced the tape recording shall be continued on the same tapes. The time at which the interview recommences must be recorded on tape.

Failure of recording equipment

194. If there is a failure of equipment, which can be rectified quickly, for example by inserting new tapes, the appropriate procedures set out in paragraph 191 shall be followed. When the recording is resumed the person conducting the interview must explain what has happened and record the time the interview recommences. If, however, it will not be possible to

continue recording on that particular tape recorder and no replacement recorder or recorder in another interview room is readily available, the interview may continue without being tape-recorded.

Removing tapes from the recorder

195. Where tapes are removed from the recorder in the course of an interview, they must be retained and the procedures set out in paragraphs 199 to 202 below followed.

Conclusion of interview

196. The person conducting the interview must inform the interviewee that he or she has no further questions and offer the interviewee an opportunity to clarify anything he or she has said and to say anything further he or she wishes. Any solicitor, qualified accountant or appropriate adult present at the interview along with the interviewee, must be given the opportunity to ask the interviewee any question the purpose of which is to clarify any ambiguity in an answer given by the interviewee or to give the interviewee an opportunity to answer any question which he or she has refused previously to answer.

197. At the conclusion of the interview, including the taking and reading back of any written statement, the time must be recorded and the tape recorder switched off. The master tape must be sealed with a master tape label. The Director must sign the label and ask the interviewee and any appropriate adult and other third party present during the interview to sign it also. If the interviewee or the appropriate adult refuses to sign the label, the person conducting the interview must sign it

198. The interviewee must be handed a notice, which explains the use, which will be made of the tape recording and the arrangements for access to it. A copy of the tape must be supplied as soon as practicable to the interviewee, if court proceedings are connected to interview are commenced (i.e. a confiscation or civil recovery proceedings).

After the interview

199. Where the interview is not subsequently used in confiscation or civil recovery proceedings the tapes must nevertheless be kept securely in accordance with the provisions below.

Tape security

200. The person conducting the interview must make arrangements for master tapes to be kept securely and their movements accounted for.

201. The person conducting the interview has no authority to break the seal on a master tape, which may be required for civil recovery or confiscation proceedings. If it is necessary to gain access to the master tape, the person conducting the interview must arrange for its seal to be broken in the presence of another member of the Agency. The interviewee or his legal adviser must be informed of the intention to break the seal on the master tape and given a reasonable opportunity to be present. If the interviewee or his legal representative is present he or she must be invited to reseal and sign the master tape. If either refuses or neither is present another member of the Agency shall do this.

202. Where no court proceedings result, it is the responsibility of the Director to establish arrangements for the breaking of the seal on the master tape, where this becomes necessary.

Particular record of action taken under a disclosure order

203. In addition to the general provisions on taking records, the Director shall also keep copies of notices in writing issued under a disclosure order (see section 357(4)) together with full details of their issue and response.

204. The record of an interview should contain the following, as appropriate

- a copy of the invitation to interview letter;
- the date and place and time of the interview;
- the time the interview began and ended, the time of any breaks in the interview and, subject to the provisions relating to pseudonyms of Agency staff, the names of all those present;
- any request made for financial or legal advice, and action taken on that request;
- that the person conducting the interview told the interviewee everything he was required to tell him or her under this code;
- the name of person(s) excluded from the interview room, and the reason for that decision; and,
- the presence of an interpreter, and the reason for this.

205. In respect of interviews conducted under the authority of section 357(4)(a), the record of the interview should be held with a transcript of the interview. Documents produced at the interview should also be listed on a note of the action taken under disclosure order. Receipts should be given to the interviewee and this should also be recorded.

206. In respect of requests for information under section 357(4)(b) or documents under section 357(4)(c) he or she should keep a copy of the disclosure order together with all the notices requesting information and/or documents under the disclosure order. The Director should also keep a record of all the documents and information submitted in response to the notices. Receipts should be sent to the supplier of the material if requested.

Summary of the Powers of Investigation under the Proceeds of Crime Act 2002

Purpose of power	Who can apply for it—confiscation investigation?	Who can apply for it —money laundering investigation?	Who can apply for it—civil recovery investigation?
Production order Obtain material already in existence relating to a known person e.g. bank statements and correspondence	(1) Director of the Agency (2) Any constable (3) Any customs officer (4) AFI with relevant accreditation[16]	(1) Any constable (2) Any customs officer (3) AFI with relevant accreditation	Director of the Agency
Search and seizure warrant (1) Search premises where production order not complied with; or (2) Search premises where production order likely to be ineffective and seize material	(1) Director of the Agency (2) Any constable (3) Any customs officer (4) AFI with relevant accreditation and authorisation	(1) Any constable (2) Any customs officer (3) AFI with relevant accreditation	Director of the Agency
Disclosure order Require any person to produce documents, provide information or answer questions relating to investigation	Director of the Agency	Not available in a money laundering investigation	Director of the Agency
Customer information order Trawl financial institutions for accounts in the name of a particular person or organisation	(1) Director of the Agency (2) Any constable with superintendent authorisation (3) Any customs officer with officer at Pay Band 9 authorisation (4) AFI with relevant accreditation and authorisation	(1) Any constable with superintendent authorisation (2) Any customs officer with officer at Pay Band 9 authorisation (3) AFI with relevant accreditation and authorisation	Director of the Agency
Account monitoring order Monitor future transactions through a known account for up to 90 days	(1) Director of the Agency (2) Any constable (3) Any customs officer (4) AFI with relevant accreditation and authorisation	(1) Any constable (2) Any customs officer (3) AFI with relevant accreditation	Director of the Agency

[16] Accredited financial investigator (a civilian investigator accredited by the Director of the Agency to have access to some or all of the powers of investigation) who falls within a description given in an order issued by the Home Secretary.

APPLICATION FOR PRODUCTION ORDER

(SECTION 345 PROCEEDS OF CRIME ACT 2002)

The application of **{appropriate officer}** an appropriate officer as defined by section 378 Proceeds of Crime Act 2002 of the **{name of force/agency}** who upon **{oath/affirmation}** states:

{name of person} is subject to a **{confiscation investigation / money laundering investigation}** and

(i)   There are reasonable grounds for suspecting that **{name of person}** has **{benefited from criminal conduct} {committed a money laundering offence}**;

(ii) There are reasonable grounds for believing that material which may be provided in compliance with the order is likely to be of substantial value (whether or not by itself) to the investigation for the purposes of which the order is sought; and

(iii) There are reasonable grounds for believing it is in the public interest for the material to be provided or for access to be given to it having regard to the benefit likely to accrue to the investigation if the information is obtained and the circumstances in which the material is held.

An order is sought against **{specify the person who appears to be in possession or control of material}** who appears to be in possession or control of material, specifically **{specify the material sought, including where applicable account numbers and the period required}** which does not include material or information that is or consists of items subject to legal privilege or excluded material to **{produce it to {name of appropriate officer} or another appropriate officer} {give {name of appropriate officer} or another appropriate officer access to it}** within **{seven days/other as appropriate}**

The order is sought for the purposes of the investigation on the grounds outlined in the **{written} {oral}** information.

Signature   Date

417

PRODUCTION ORDER

(SECTION 345 PROCEEDS OF CRIME ACT 2002)

IN THE CROWN COURT AT...   DATE...

Penal Notice
A failure to comply with the terms of this order may constitute a contempt of court for which you may be imprisoned or fined.

To: **{person/organisation}**

An application having been made in pursuance of Section 345 **{(4)(a)} {(4)(b)}** Proceeds of Crime Act 2002

By: **{appropriate officer}**   Of the **{name force/agency}**

I am satisfied, having heard the application, that the requirements for making a production order under section 346 Proceeds of Crime Act 2002 are fulfilled.

You are ordered to **{produce to {name of appropriate officer} or another appropriate officer} {give {name of appropriate officer} or another appropriate officer access to}** material, specifically **{insert details of material to be provided or given access to}** which does not consist of items subject to legal privilege for a period **{state dates between}** within **{7 days / other period as appropriate)** from the date of this order.

Where the material consists of information contained on a computer, it must be **{produced/access given to it}** in a form which is visible and legible **{and can be taken away}**.

1. It is an offence to prejudice a confiscation or money laundering investigation or prospective investigation by making a disclosure about it or by tampering with documents relevant to the investigation. You should not therefore falsify, conceal, destroy or otherwise dispose of, or cause or permit the falsification, destruction or disposal of, relevant documents, nor disclose to any other person information or any other matter which is likely to prejudice any investigation into confiscation or money laundering investigation. The penalty for this offence on summary conviction is imprisonment for six months or a fine or both and on conviction on indictment of 5 years imprisonment or a fine or both.

2. Anyone served with, notified or affected by this order may apply to the court at any time to vary or discharge this order (or so much of it as affects that person), but they must first inform the applicant **{giving 2 clear days notice}**.

3. If you have any doubts or concerns about this order you should seek legal advice and / or contact **{address and contact details of appropriate officer}**

Court Stamp   Signature of Judge

                                             Date

APPLICATION FOR
SEARCH AND SEIZURE WARRANT

(SECTION 352 PROCEEDS OF CRIME ACT 2002)

The application of **{appropriate officer}** an appropriate officer as defined by section 378 Proceeds of Crime Act 2002 of the **{name of force/agency}** who upon **{oath/affirmation}** states:

{name of person} is subject to a **{confiscation investigation / money laundering investigation}** and a search warrant is sought in relation to material which does not consist of or include privileged or excluded material held on premises situated at **{specify premises}** and:

{On **{date}** a production order under section 345 Proceeds of Crime Act 2002 was made at **{name of Court}** Crown Court by **{His/Her}** Honour **{name of Judge}** which has not been complied with and there are reasonable grounds for believing that the material is on the premises.}

Alternatively

There are reasonable grounds for suspecting that **{name of person}** has **{benefited from criminal conduct}** **{committed a money laundering offence}**, and the **{first/ second}** set of conditions are satisfied; that

[first]

(i) {There are reasonable grounds for believing that material on the specified premises is likely to be of substantial value (whether or not by itself) to the investigation for the purposes of which the warrant is sought ,

(ii) There are reasonable grounds for believing it is in the public interest for the material to be obtained, having regard to the benefit likely to accrue to the investigation if the information is obtained, and

(iii) It would not be appropriate to make a production order for the following {reason/s};}

[second]

(i) {there are reasonable grounds for believing that there is material on the premises specified in the application for the warrant and that the material;

{In relation to a confiscation investigation cannot be identified at the time of the application but it—

a) relates to the person specified in the application, the question whether he has benefited from his criminal conduct or any question as to the extent or whereabouts of his benefit from his criminal conduct, and

b) is likely to be of substantial value (whether or not by itself) to the investigation for the purposes of which the warrant is sought.}

{In relation to a money laundering investigation it cannot be identified at the time of the application but it—

a) relates to the person specified in the application or the question whether he has committed a money laundering offence, and

419

b) is likely to be of substantial value (whether or not by itself) to the investigation for the purposes of which the warrant is sought.}

(ii) It is in the public interest for the material to be obtained, having regard to the benefit likely to accrue to the investigation if the material is to be obtained, and}

[applies to first and second]

i. {that it is not practicable to communicate with any person against whom the production order could be made;}
ii. {that it is not practicable to communicate with any person who would be required to comply with an order to grant entry to the premises;}
iii. {that the investigation might be seriously prejudiced unless an appropriate person is able to secure immediate access to the material.}

The warrant is sought for the purposes of the investigation on the grounds outlined in the written information.

Signature

Applicant Name

Date

SEARCH AND SEIZURE WARRANT

(SECTION 352 PROCEEDS OF CRIME ACT 2002)

IN THE CROWN COURT AT...   DATE...

Penal Notice
A failure to comply with the terms of this order may constitute a contempt of court for which you may be imprisoned or fined.

To: **{person/organisation}**

An application having been made in pursuance of Section 352 Proceeds of Crime Act 2002

By: **{appropriate officer}**   Of the **{name force/agency}**

I am satisfied, having heard the application, that the requirements for issuing a search and seizure warrant under section 352 Proceeds of Crime Act 2002 are fulfilled.

I hereby authorise **{name and address of appropriate person}** to enter and search premises situated at **{specify premises}** and seize and retain material which does not consist of items subject to legal privilege or excluded material.

Court Stamp   Signature of Judge

                    Date

APPLICATION FOR
CUSTOMER INFORMATION ORDER

(SECTION 363 PROCEEDS OF CRIME ACT 2002)

The application of **{appropriate officer}** an appropriate officer as defined by section 378 Proceeds of Crime Act 2002 of the **{name of force/agency}** who upon **{oath/affirmation}** states:

{name of person} is subject to a **{confiscation investigation / money laundering investigation}** and

(1) There are reasonable grounds for suspecting that **{name of person}** has **{benefited from criminal conduct} {committed a money laundering offence}**;

(2) There are reasonable grounds for believing that customer information which may be provided in compliance with the order is likely to be of substantial value (whether or not by itself) to the investigation for the purposes of which the order is sought; and,

(3) There are reasonable grounds for believing it is in the public interest for the customer information to be provided or for access to be given to it having regard to the benefit likely to accrue to the investigation if the information is obtained

An order is sought against **{specify all financial institutions, particular description/s of institutions or a particular institution/s}** in relation to customer information as defined by section 364 Proceeds of Crime Act to provide the information to **{name of appropriate officer}** or another appropriate officer in such manner, and at or by such time or times specified in the written notice.

The order is sought for the purposes of the investigation on the grounds outlined in the **{written} {oral}** information.

Signature   Date

Authorised by **{name of Senior Authorising Officer)**
            {rank / position}

CUSTOMER INFORMATION ORDER

(SECTION 363 PROCEEDS OF CRIME ACT 2002)

IN THE CROWN COURT AT...   DATE...

Penal Notice
A failure to comply with the terms of this order may constitute a contempt of court for which you may be imprisoned or fined.

To: **{specify all financial institutions, particular description/s of institutions or a particular institution/s**

An application having been made in pursuance of section 363 Proceeds of Crime Act 2002

By: **{appropriate officer}**   of the **{name force/agency}**

I am satisfied, having heard the application, that the requirements for making a customer information order under section 365 Proceeds of Crime Act 2002 are fulfilled.

You are ordered, on receipt of written notice from an appropriate officer, to provide any customer information, as defined by section 364 Proceeds of Crime Act 2002, held by you in relation to **{name of person and any other information that could assist in identification}** to **{name and address of appropriate officer}** or another appropriate officer in such a manner, and at such a time, as an appropriate officer requires.

Court Stamp   Signature of Judge

                                  Date

CUSTOMER INFORMATION ORDER

NOTICE IN WRITING

To **{details of institution}**

This is a notice in writing in pursuance of the terms of a customer information order granted on {date of order} **at** {details of Crown Court} **by** {His/Her} **Honour** {name of judge}

Penal Notice

By virtue of section 366 of the Proceeds of Crime Act 2002, you are required, on receipt of this written notice, to provide any customer information, as defined by section 364 Proceeds of Crime Act 2002, held by you in relation to **{name of person and any other information that could assist in identification}** to **{name of appropriate officer}** or another appropriate officer by **{insert details of the manner in which the information is to be provided} {at or by} {insert the time or times at or by the information is to be provided}**

"Customer information" is information whether a person holds, or has held, an account or accounts (whether solely or jointly with another) and where that person is an individual

a. the account number or numbers;
b. the person's full name;
c. date of birth;
d. most recent and any previous address;
e. date or dates on which he or she began to hold the account or accounts, and if he or she has ceased to hold the account or any accounts, the date or dates on which he or she did so;
f. such evidence of his or her identity obtained by you under or for the purposes of any legislation relating to money ;
g. the full name, date of birth and most recent address, and any previous addresses, of any person who holds, or has held, an account at your institution jointly with him or her;
h. the account number or numbers of any other account or accounts held at your institution to which he or she is a signatory and details of the person holding the other account or accounts;

and where the specified person is a company, limited liability partnership or similar body incorporated or established outside the UK,

i. the account number or numbers;
j. the person's full name;
k. a description of any business which the person carries on;
l. the country or territory in which it is incorporated or otherwise established and any number allocated to it under the Companies Act 1985 (c.6) or the Companies (Northern Ireland) Order 1986 (S.I.1986/1032 (N.I. 6)) or corresponding legislation of any country or territory outside the United Kingdom;
m. any number assigned to it for the purposes of value added tax in the United Kingdom;
n. its registered office, and previous registered offices, under the Companies Act 1985

424

(c.6) or the Companies (Northern Ireland) Order 1986 (S.I.1986/1032 (N.I. 6)) or anything similar under corresponding legislation of any country or territory outside the United Kingdom under the Companies Act 1985 or corresponding legislation of any country or territory outside the United Kingdom;

o. its registered office, and previous registered offices, under the Limited Liability Partnerships Act 2000 (c.12) or corresponding legislation of any country or territory outside Great Britain;

p. the date or dates on which it began to hold the account or accounts and, if it has ceased to hold the account or any of the accounts, the date on which it did so;

q. such evidence of its identity as was obtained by you for the purposes of any legislation relating to money laundering;

r. the full name, date of birth and most recent address and any previous addresses of any person who is signatory to the account or any of the accounts.

A financial institution has a right to refuse to comply with any requirement under the terms of a customer information order unless the appropriate officer has, if required to do so, produced evidence of authority to issue notice.

A financial institution commits an offence if, without reasonable excuse, it fails to comply with a requirement imposed on it under a customer information order and is liable on summary conviction to a fine.

A financial institution commits an offence if, in purported compliance with a customer information order, it makes a statement it knows to be false or misleading in a material particular, or recklessly makes a statement which is false or misleading in a material particular and is liable on summary conviction or on conviction on indictment to a fine.

A statement made by a financial institution in response to a customer information order may not be used in evidence against it in criminal proceedings except on a prosecution for an offence outlined above, on a prosecution for another offence where, in giving evidence, the financial institution makes a statement inconsistent with the statement made in response, or in confiscation proceedings in England and Wales or Northern Ireland

It is an offence to prejudice a confiscation or money laundering investigation or prospective investigation by making a disclosure about it or by tampering with documents relevant to the investigation. You should not therefore falsify, conceal, destroy or otherwise dispose of, or cause or permit the falsification, destruction or disposal of, relevant documents, nor disclose to any other person information or any other matter which is likely to prejudice any investigation into confiscation or money laundering investigation. The penalty for this offence on summary conviction is imprisonment for six months or a fine or both and on conviction on indictment of 5 years imprisonment or a fine or both.

Anyone served with, notified or affected by this order may apply to the court at any time to vary or discharge this order (or so much of it as affects that person), but they must first inform the applicant {giving 2 clear days notice}. If any evidence is to be relied upon in support of the application, the substance of it must be communicated in writing to the applicant in advance.

If you have any doubts or concerns about this order you should seek legal advice and / or contact {**contact details of appropriate officer**}.

Signature

Name

Date

APPLICATION FOR
ACCOUNT MONITORING ORDER

(SECTION 370 PROCEEDS OF CRIME ACT 2002)

The application of **{appropriate officer}** an appropriate officer as defined by section 378 Proceeds of Crime Act 2002 of the **{name of force/agency}** who upon **{oath/affirmation}** states:
{name of person} is subject to a **{confiscation investigation / money laundering investigation}** and

(1) There are reasonable grounds for suspecting that **{name of person}** has **{benefited from criminal conduct}** **{committed a money laundering offence}**;
(2) There are reasonable grounds for believing that account information which may be provided in compliance with the order is likely to be of substantial value (whether or not by itself) to the investigation for the purposes of which the order is sought; and,
(3) There are reasonable grounds for believing it is in the public interest for the material to be provided or for access to be given to it having regard to the benefit likely to accrue to the investigation if the information is obtained

An order is sought against **{name/details of financial institution}** in relation to account information, specifically **{description of account information}** to provide the information to **{name of appropriate officer}** or another appropriate officer in such manner, and at or by such time or times specified in the order.

The order is sought for the purposes of the investigation on the grounds outlined in the **{written}** **{oral}** information.

Signature   Date

426

ACCOUNT MONITORING ORDER
(SECTION 370 PROCEEDS OF CRIME ACT 2002)

IN THE CROWN COURT AT... DATE...

Penal Notice

A failure to comply with the terms of this order may constitute a contempt of court for which you may be imprisoned or fined.

To: **{person/organisation}**

An application having been made in pursuance of Section 370 Proceeds of Crime Act 2002

By: **{appropriate officer}**   Of the **{name force/agency}**

I am satisfied, having heard the application, that the requirements for making an account monitoring order under section 371 Proceeds of Crime Act 2002 are fulfilled.

You are ordered to provide account information, specifically **{insert details of information to be provided including the description of the material}** for a period **{enter amount of days}** not exceeding 90 days from the date of this order, to **{name of appropriate officer}** or another appropriate officer by **{insert details of the manner in which the information is to be provided} {at or by} {insert the time or times at or by the information is to be provided}**

1. It is an offence to prejudice a confiscation or money laundering investigation or prospective investigation by making a disclosure about it or by tampering with documents relevant to the investigation. You should not therefore falsify, conceal, destroy or otherwise dispose of, or cause or pe.rmit the falsification, destruction or disposal of, relevant documents, nor disclose to any other person information or any other matter which is likely to prejudice any investigation into confiscation or money laundering investigation. The penalty for this offence on summary conviction is imprisonment for six months or a fine or both and on conviction on indictment of 5 years imprisonment or a fine or both.

2. Anyone served with, notified or affected by this order may apply to the court at any time to vary or discharge this order (or so much of it as affects that person), but they must first inform the applicant **{giving 2 clear days notice}**.

3. If you have any doubts or concerns about this order you should seek legal advice and / or contact **{address and contact details of appropriate officer}**.

Court Stamp   Signature of Judge

                                                 Date

The Proceeds of Crime Act 2002 (Failure to Disclose Money Laundering: Specified Training) Order 2003 (SI 2003/171)

Made	*29th January 2003*
Laid before Parliament	*3rd February 2003*
Came into force	*24th February 2003*

The Secretary of State, in exercise of the powers conferred upon him by section 330(7)(b) of the Proceeds of Crime Act 2002,[1] hereby makes the following Order:

1. This Order may be cited as the Proceeds of Crime Act 2002 (Failure to Disclose Money Laundering: Specified Training) Order 2003 and shall come into force on 24th February 2003.

2. The training specified for the purposes of section 330 of the Proceeds of Crime Act 2002 is the training required to be provided under regulation 5(1)(c) of the Money Laundering Regulations 1993.[2]

EXPLANATORY NOTE

(This note is not part of the Order)

This Order specifies training for the purposes of section 330 of the Proceeds of Crime Act 2002. If a person has not been provided by his employer with the specified training, he may have a defence to the offence in section 330 of failure to disclose money laundering by a person in the regulated sector. The defence only applies where the employee does not actually know or suspect that another person is engaged in money laundering, but would still commit the offence by virtue of having reasonable grounds for knowing or suspecting that another person is engaged in money laundering.

The training specified is the training required to be provided under regulation 5(1)(c) of the Money Laundering Regulations 1993. Regulation 5(1)(c) requires that a person carrying

---

[1] 2002, c. 29.

[2] S.I. 1993/1933; relevant amending instruments are regulation 11 of the Banking Consolidation Directive (Consequential Amendments) Regulations 2000 (S.I. 2000/2952), regulation 3 of the Money Laundering Regulations 2001 (S.I. 2001/3641) and articles 438 and 439 of the Financial Services and Markets Act 2000 (Consequential Amendments and Repeals) Order 2001 (S.I. 2001/3649).back

out relevant financial business must provide employees whose duties include the handling of relevant financial business with training from time to time in the recognition and handling of transactions carried out by, or on behalf of, any person who is, or appears to be, engaged in money laundering. Relevant financial business is defined in regulation 4 of the Money Laundering Regulations 1993.

The Proceeds of Crime Act 2002 (References to Financial Investigators) Order 2003 (SI 2003/172)

Made	*29th January 2003*
Laid before Parliament	*3rd February 2003*
Came into force	*24th February 2003*

The Secretary of State, in exercise of the powers conferred on him by sections 453 and 459(2) of the Proceeds of Crime Act 2002,[1] hereby makes the following Order:

1. This Order may be cited as the Proceeds of Crime Act 2002 (References to Financial Investigators) Order 2003 and shall come into force on 24th February 2003.

2. A reference to an accredited financial investigator in the Proceeds of Crime Act 2002 which is specified in column 1 of the Schedule to this Order is a reference to an accredited financial investigator who falls within the description specified in relation to that reference in column 2 of the Schedule to this Order.

Bob Ainsworth
Parliamentary Under-Secretary of State

Home Office
29th January 2003

THE SCHEDULE

Article 2

Column 1	Column 2
Section 42(2)(c) (application for restraint order under Part 2)	An accredited financial investigator who is— (a) a constable of a police force in England and Wales;[2] (b) a member of staff of a police force in England and Wales; (c) a customs officer; (d) a member of staff of the Financial Services Authority;

---

[1] 2002 c. 29.

[2] Police force has the meaning given to it in section 101 of the Police Act 1996 (c. 16) by virtue of Schedule 1 to the Interpretation Act 1978 (c. 30), as amended by Schedule 7 to the Police Act 1996.

Column 1	Column 2
	(e) a member of staff of the Inland Revenue; (f) a member of staff of the Medicines and Healthcare Products Regulatory Agency;[3] (g) a member of staff of the Department for Work and Pensions; (h) a member of staff of the Investigation Branch of the Department for Environment, Food and Rural Affairs; (i) a member of staff of the Rural Payments Agency;[4] or (j) a member of staff of the Department of Trade and Industry.
Section 68(3)(c) (authorisation for application for restraint order under Part 2)	An accredited financial investigator who is a member of staff of— (a) the Financial Services Authority and is not below the grade designated by the Financial Services Authority as Head of Department; (b) the Inland Revenue and is not below the grade designated by the Commissioners of Inland Revenue as grade 6;[5] (c) the Medicines and Healthcare Products Regulatory Agency and is not below the grade designated by the Secretary of State for Health as integrated pay band 3 (upper);[6] (d) the Department for Work and Pensions and is not below the grade designated by the Secretary of State for Work and Pensions as Senior Executive Officer;[7] (e) the Investigation Branch of the Department for Environment, Food and Rural Affairs and is not below the grade designated by the Secretary of State for Environment, Food and Rural Affairs as Senior Investigation Officer;[8] (f) the Rural Payments Agency and is not below the grade designated by the Chief Executive of the Agency as Senior Investigation Officer;[9] or (g) the Department of Trade and Industry and is a Deputy Chief Investigation Officer or Chief Investigation Officer not below the grade designated by the Secretary of State for Trade and Industry as range 9.[10]

[3] The Medicines and Healthcare Products Regulatory Agency is part of the Department of Health.

[4] The Rural Payments Agency is part of the Department for Environment, Food and Rural Affairs.

[5] The grading of posts in relation to the Inland Revenue has been delegated to the Commissioners of Inland Revenue by the Minister for the Civil Service under the Civil Service (Management Functions) Act 1992 (c. 61).

[6] The grading of posts in relation to the Department of Health has been delegated to the Secretary of State for Health by the Minister for the Civil Service under the Civil Service (Management Functions) Act 1992 (c. 61). The Secretary of State has retained responsibility for the grading of posts in relation to the Agency.

[7] The grading of posts in relation to the Department for Work and Pensions has been delegated to the Secretary of State for Work and Pensions by the Minister for the Civil Service under the Civil Service (Management Functions) Act 1992 (c. 61).

[8] The grading of posts in relation to the Department for Environment, Food and Rural Affairs has been delegated to the Secretary of State for Environment, Food and Rural Affairs by the Minister for the Civil Service under the Civil Service (Management Functions) Act 1992 (c. 61).

[9] The grading of posts in relation to the Agency has been delegated to the Chief Executive of the Agency by the Secretary of State for Environment, Food and Rural Affairs.

[10] The grading of posts in relation to the Department of Trade and Industry has been delegated to the Secretary of State for Trade and Industry by the Minister for the Civil Service under the Civil Service (Management Functions) Act 1992 (c. 61).

Column 1	Column 2
Section 191(2)(c) (application for restraint order under Part 4)	An accredited financial investigator who is— (a) a constable of the Police Service of Northern Ireland;[11] (b) a member of staff of the Police Service of Northern Ireland; (c) a customs officer; (d) a member of staff of the Financial Services Authority; (e) a member of staff of the Inland Revenue; (f) a member of staff of the Medicines and Healthcare Products Regulatory Agency; (g) a member of staff of the Department for Social Development in Northern Ireland; or (h) a member of staff of the Department of Health, Social Services and Public Safety in Northern Ireland.
Section 216(3)(c) (authorisation for application for restraint order under Part 4)	An accredited financial investigator who is a member of staff of— (a) the Financial Services Authority and is not below the grade designated by the Financial Services Authority as Head of Department; (b) the Inland Revenue and is not below the grade designated by the Commissioners of Inland Revenue as grade 6; (c) the Medicines and Healthcare Products Regulatory Agency and is not below the grade designated by the Secretary of State for Health as integrated pay band 3 (upper); or (d) the Department for Social Development in Northern Ireland and is not below the grade designated by the Department of Finance and Personnel in Northern Ireland[12] as Deputy Principal.
Section 378(1)(b) (appropriate officers for the purposes of confiscation investigations)	In relation to England and Wales, an accredited financial investigator who is a member of staff of— (a) a police force in England and Wales; (b) the Serious Fraud Office;[13] (c) the Financial Services Authority; (d) the Inland Revenue; (e) the Medicines and Healthcare Products Regulatory Agency; (f) the Department for Work and Pensions; (g) the Investigations Branch of the Department for Environment, Food and Rural Affairs; (h) the Rural Payments Agency; or (i) the Department of Trade and Industry. In relation to Northern Ireland, an accredited financial investigator who is a member of staff of— (a) the Police Service of Northern Ireland; (b) the Serious Fraud Office; (c) the Financial Services Authority; (d) the Inland Revenue; (e) the Medicines and Healthcare Products Regulatory Agency;

---

[11] Police Service of Northern Ireland has the meaning given to it in the Police (Northern Ireland) Act 2000 (c. 32), by virtue of Schedule 1 to the Interpretation Act 1978 (c. 30), as amended by Section 78 of and Schedule 6 to the Police (Northern Ireland) Act 2000.

[12] The function of grading of posts in relation to Northern Ireland Departments is exercisable by the Department of Finance and Personnel by virtue of a prerogative order made under section 23(3) of the Northern Ireland Act 1998 (c. 47).

[13] The Serious Fraud Office is constituted under the Criminal Justice Act 1987 (c. 38).

Column 1	Column 2
	(f) the Department for Social Development in Northern Ireland; or
	(g) the Department of Health, Social Services and Public Safety in Northern Ireland.
Section 378(2)(d) (senior appropriate officers for the purposes of confiscation investigations)	In relation to England and Wales, an accredited financial investigator who is a member of staff of—
	(a) the Serious Fraud Office and is not below the grade designated by the Director of the Serious Fraud Office as grade 6;[14]
	(b) the Financial Services Authority and is not below the grade designated by the Financial Services Authority as Head of Department;
	(c) the Inland Revenue and is not below the grade designated by the Commissioners of Inland Revenue as grade 6;
	(d) the Medicines and Healthcare Products Regulatory Agency and is not below the grade designated by the Secretary of State for Health as integrated pay band 3 (upper);
	(e) the Department for Work and Pensions and is not below the grade designated by the Secretary of State for Work and Pensions as Senior Executive Officer;
	(f) the Investigation Branch of the Department for Environment, Food and Rural Affairs and is not below the grade designated by the Secretary of State for Environment, Food and Rural Affairs as Senior Investigation Officer;
	(g) the Rural Payments Agency and is not below the grade designated by the Chief Executive of the Agency as Senior Investigation Officer; or
	(h) the Department of Trade and Industry and is a Deputy Chief Investigation Officer or Chief Investigation Officer not below the grade designated by the Secretary of State for Trade and Industry as range 9.
	In relation to Northern Ireland, an accredited financial investigator who is a member of staff of—
	(a) the Serious Fraud Office and is not below the grade designated by the Director of the Serious Fraud Office as grade 6;
	(b) the Financial Services Authority and is not below the grade designated by the Financial Services Authority as Head of Department;
	(c) the Inland Revenue and is not below the grade designated by the Commissioners of Inland Revenue as grade 6;
	(d) the Medicines and Healthcare Products Regulatory Agency and is not below the grade designated by the Secretary of State for Health as integrated pay band 3 (upper); or
	(e) the Department for Social Development in Northern Ireland and is not below the grade designated by the Department of Finance and Personnel in Northern Ireland as Deputy Principal.
Section 378(4)(a) (appropriate officers for the purposes of money laundering investigations)	In relation to England and Wales, an accredited financial investigator who is a member of staff of—
	(a) a police force in England and Wales;
	(b) the Serious Fraud Office;
	(c) the Medicines and Healthcare Products Regulatory Agency;

---

[14] The grading of posts in relation to the Serious Fraud Office has been delegated to the Director of the Serious Fraud Office by the Minister for the Civil Service under the Civil Service (Management Functions) Act 1992 (c. 61).back

Column 1	Column 2
	(d) the Department for Work and Pensions; or
	(e) the Department of Trade and Industry.
	In relation to Northern Ireland, an accredited financial investigator who is a member of staff of—
	(a) the Police Service of Northern Ireland;
	(b) the Serious Fraud Office;
	(c) the Medicines and Healthcare Products Regulatory Agency; or
	(d) the Department for Social Development in Northern Ireland.
Section 378(6)(c) (senior appropriate officers for the purposes of money laundering investigations)	In relation to England and Wales, an accredited financial investigator who is a member of staff of— (a) the Serious Fraud Office and is not below the grade designated by the Director of the Serious Fraud Office as grade 6; (b) the Medicines and Healthcare Products Regulatory Agency and is not below the grade designated by the Secretary of State for Health as integrated pay band 3 (upper); (c) the Department for Work and Pensions and is not below the grade designated by the Secretary of State for Work and Pensions as Senior Executive Officer; or (d) the Department of Trade and Industry and is a Deputy Chief Investigation Officer or Chief Investigation Officer not below the grade designated by the Secretary of State for Trade and Industry as range 9.
	In relation to Northern Ireland, an accredited financial investigator who is a member of staff of— (a) the Serious Fraud Office and is not below the grade designated by the Director of the Serious Fraud Office as grade 6; (b) the Medicines and Healthcare Products Regulatory Agency and is not below the grade designated by the Secretary of State for Health as integrated pay band 3 (upper); or (c) the Department for Social Development in Northern Ireland who is not below the grade designated by the Department of Finance and Personnel in Northern Ireland as Deputy Principal.

EXPLANATORY NOTE

(This note is not part of the Order)

This Order provides that references to accredited financial investigators in the Proceeds of Crime Act 2002 ("the Act") are to be read as references to accredited financial investigators within the description specified in this Order. Accredited financial investigators may apply for restraint orders under Parts 2 and 4 of the Act and may apply for orders and warrants in relation to confiscation investigations and money laundering investigations under Part 8 of the Act.

The Proceeds of Crime Act 2002 (Recovery from Pension Schemes) Regulations 2003 (SI 2003/291)

Made	*12th February 2003*
Laid before Parliament	*17th February 2003*
Came into force	*17th March 2003*

The Secretary of State, in exercise of the powers conferred on him by sections 273(2)(a), 275(1) to (3) and 459(2) of the Proceeds of Crime Act 2002,[1] and after consultation with the Scottish Ministers, hereby makes the following Regulations:

Citation, commencement and interpretation

1.—(1) These Regulations may be cited as the Proceeds of Crime Act 2002 (Recovery from Pension Schemes) Regulations 2003 and shall come into force on 17th March 2003.

(2) In these Regulations—

"the Act" means the Proceeds of Crime Act 2002;

"destination arrangement" means a pension arrangement under which some or all of the rights are derived, directly or indirectly, from a pension sharing transaction;

"pension recovery order" means a recovery order made by virtue of section 273(2) of the Act;

"pension sharing transaction" means an order or provision falling within section 28(1) of the Welfare Reform and Pensions Act 1999[2] (activation of pension sharing) or article 25(1) of the Welfare Reform and Pensions (Northern Ireland) Order 1999[3] (activation of pension sharing);

"relevant person" means the person whose rights under a pension scheme are the subject of a pension recovery order; and

"valuation date" means a date within the period prescribed by regulation 5 in respect of which the trustees or managers of the pension scheme decide to value the relevant person's pension rights in accordance with regulation 2 or 3.

Calculation and verification of the value of rights under pension schemes

2.—(1) This regulation applies where the High Court or the Court of Session makes a pension recovery order, other than in respect of rights derived from a pension sharing transaction under a destination arrangement in a pension scheme.

---

[1] 2002 c. 29. (Section 275(3) is cited because of the meaning ascribed to the words "regulations" and "prescribed".

[2] 1999 c. 30.

[3] S.I. 1999/3147 (N.I. 11).

(2) The trustees or managers of the pension scheme in respect of which the pension recovery order has been made must calculate and verify the cash equivalent of the value at the valuation date of the rights which are the subject of the pension recovery order and must pay to the trustee for civil recovery a sum equal to that cash equivalent.

(3) In relation to the calculation and verification by the trustees or managers of the cash equivalent referred to in paragraph (2)—

(a) in the case of a pension scheme wholly or mainly administered in England and Wales, regulation 3 of the Pensions on Divorce etc. (Provision of Information) Regulations 2000[4] (information about pensions and divorce: valuation of pension benefits), except paragraph (2) thereof, shall have effect as it has effect for the valuation of benefits in connection with the supply of information in connection with domestic and overseas divorce etc. in England and Wales, with the modification that, for "the date on which the request for the valuation was received" in each case where it appears in that regulation, there shall be substituted "the valuation date for the purposes of the Proceeds of Crime Act 2002 (Recovery from Pension Schemes) Regulations 2003";

(b) in the case of a pension scheme wholly or mainly administered in Scotland, regulation 3 of the Divorce etc. (Pensions) (Scotland) Regulations 2000[5] (valuation), except paragraph (11) thereof, shall have effect as it has effect for the valuation of benefits in connection with the supply of information in connection with divorce in Scotland, with the modification that, for "the relevant date" in each case where it appears in that regulation, there shall be substituted "the valuation date for the purposes of the Proceeds of Crime Act 2002 (Recovery from Pension Schemes) Regulations 2003"; and

(c) in the case of a pension scheme wholly or mainly administered in Northern Ireland, regulation 3 of the Pensions on Divorce etc. (Provision of Information) Regulations (Northern Ireland) 2000[6] (information about pensions on divorce: valuation of pension benefits), except paragraph (2) thereof, shall have effect as it has effect for the valuation of benefits in connection with the supply of information in connection with domestic and overseas divorce etc. in Northern Ireland, with the modification that, for "the date on which the request for the valuation was received" in each case where it appears in that regulation, there shall be substituted "the valuation date for the purposes of the Proceeds of Crime Act 2002 (Recovery from Pension Schemes) Regulations 2003".

Calculation and verification of the value of rights under destination arrangements

3.—(1) This regulation applies where the High Court or the Court of Session makes a pension recovery order in respect of rights derived from a pension sharing transaction under a destination arrangement in a pension scheme.

(2) The trustees or managers of the pension scheme in respect of which the pension recovery order has been made must calculate and verify the cash equivalent of the value at the valuation date of the rights which are the subject of the pension recovery order and must pay to the trustee for civil recovery a sum equal to that cash equivalent.

---

[4] S.I. 2000/1048.
[5] S.S.I. 2000/112; to which there are amendments not relevant to these Regulations.
[6] S.R. 2000/142 to which there are amendments not relevant to these Regulations.

(3) In relation to the calculation and verification by the trustees or managers of the cash equivalent referred to in paragraph (2)—

    (a) in the case of a pension arrangement in a scheme that is wholly or mainly administered in either England and Wales or Scotland, regulation 24 of the Pension Sharing (Pension Credit Benefit) Regulations 2000[7] (manner of calculation and verification of cash equivalents) shall have effect as it has effect for the calculation and verification of pension credit for the purposes of those regulations; and

    (b) in the case of a pension arrangement in a scheme that is wholly or mainly administered in Northern Ireland, regulation 24 of the Pension Sharing (Pension Credit Benefit) Regulations (Northern Ireland) 2000[8] (manner of calculation and verification of cash equivalents) shall have effect as it has effect for the calculation and verification of pension credit for the purposes of those regulations.

Approval of manner of calculation and verification of the value of rights

4.—(1) This regulation applies where the relevant person is also a trustee or manager of the pension scheme in respect of which the pension recovery order has been made.

(2) When the trustees or managers of the pension scheme have, under regulation 2 or 3, calculated and verified the value of the rights which are the subject of a pension recovery order, the manner in which the trustees or managers have calculated and verified the value of the rights must be approved by—

    (a) a Fellow of the Institute of Actuaries;[9] or

    (b) a Fellow of the Faculty of Actuaries.[10]

(3) Where the person referred to in paragraph (2) is not able to approve the manner in which the trustees or managers have calculated and verified the value of the rights which are the subject of a pension recovery order, he must give notice in writing of that fact to the trustee for civil recovery and the trustees or managers of the scheme.

(4) Where the trustees or managers of the scheme have been given notice under paragraph (3), they must re-calculate and re-verify the value of the rights which are the subject of a pension recovery order for the purposes of regulation 2 or 3.

Time for compliance with a pension recovery order

5.—(1) In this regulation, "the prescribed period" means the period prescribed for the purposes of section 273(2)(a) of the Act.

(2) Subject to paragraphs (3) and (4), the prescribed period is the period of 60 days beginning on the day on which the pension recovery order is made.

(3) Where an application for permission to appeal the pension recovery order is made within the period referred to in paragraph (2), the prescribed period is the period of 60 days beginning on—

    (a) the day on which permission to appeal is finally refused;

    (b) the day on which the appeal is withdrawn; or

    (c) the day on which the appeal is dismissed,

as the case may be.

---

[7] S.I. 2000/1054.   [8] S.R. 2000/146 as amended by S.R. 2000/335.

[9] The Institute of Actuaries is at Staple Inn Hall, High Holborn, London WC1V 7QJ.

[10] The Faculty of Actuaries is at Maclaurin House, 18 Dublin Street, Edinburgh EH1 3PP.

(4) Where the person referred to in regulation 4(2) gives notice, in accordance with regulation 4(3) and within the period referred to in paragraph (2), to the trustee for civil recovery and trustees or managers of the scheme that he is unable to approve the manner in which the trustees or managers have calculated the value of the rights which are the subject of the pension recovery order, the prescribed period is the period of 60 days beginning on the day on which such notice is given.

EXPLANATORY NOTE

(This note is not part of the Regulations)

These Regulations make provision as to the exercise by trustees or managers of pension schemes of their powers when a civil recovery order made under section 273(2) of the Proceeds of Crime Act 2002 (c. 29) ("the Act") requires them to make a payment to the trustee for civil recovery in respect of the rights of a member of that scheme.

Regulation 1 provides for citation, commencement and interpretation.

Regulation 2 provides for the calculation and verification of the cash equivalent of the value of pension rights which are recoverable property under a recovery order made under the Act. This is by reference to the method applying for the purposes of the provision of information in respect of pensions on divorce, separation and nullity under the Pensions on Divorce etc. (Provision of Information) Regulations 2000 (S.I. 2000/1048) and the equivalent regulations applying in Scotland and Northern Ireland.

Regulation 3 makes similar provision to regulation 2 where the pension rights are derived directly or indirectly from a pension sharing transaction.

Regulation 4 makes provision for the circumstances where the person with the pension rights which are recoverable property is a trustee or manager of the scheme in question. In these circumstances, an actuary must approve the method of calculation and verification of the cash equivalent value. The actuary must be a member of the Faculty or Institute of Actuaries.

Regulation 5 prescribes the period for paying the amount of those pension rights to the trustee for civil recovery.

These Regulations have only a negligible cost for business: a regulatory impact assessment is therefore not necessary.

The Crown Court (Confiscation, Restraint and Receivership) Rules 2003 (SI 2003/421)

Made	*20th February 2003*
Laid before Parliament	*27th February 2003*
Came into force	*24th March 2003*

We, the Crown Court Rule Committee, in exercise of the powers conferred upon us by sections 52, 84(1), (5A) and (6), and 86 of the Supreme Court Act 1981[1] and sections 91 and 446 of the Proceeds of Crime Act 2002,[2] hereby make the following Rules:

PART I

Introduction

Citation and commencement

1. These Rules may be cited as the Crown Court (Confiscation, Restraint and Receivership) Rules 2003 and shall come into force on 24th March 2003.

Interpretation

2. In these Rules—

    (a) "the Act" means the Proceeds of Crime Act 2002;

    (b) "business day" means any day other than—

        (i) a Saturday, Sunday, Christmas Day or Good Friday; or

        (ii) a bank holiday under the Banking and Financial Dealings Act 1971,[3] in England and Wales;

    (c) "court officer" means a member of the Crown Court staff;

    (d) "document" means anything in which information of any description is recorded;

    (e) "hearsay evidence" means evidence consisting of hearsay within the meaning of section 1(2) of the Civil Evidence Act 1995;[4]

    (f) "restraint proceedings" means proceedings under sections 42 and 58(2) and (3) of the Act;

    (g) "receivership proceedings" means proceedings under sections 48, 49, 50, 51, 52, 53, 54(4), 56(4), 59(2) and (3), 60(2) and (3), 62 and 63 of the Act;

---

[1] 1981 c. 54; sub-sections 84(5A) and (6) were substituted by the Civil Procedure Act 1997 (c. 12).

[2] 2002 c. 29.   [3] 1971 c. 80.   [4] 1995 c. 38.

(h) "witness statement" means a written statement signed by a person which contains the evidence, and only that evidence, which that person would be allowed to give orally;

(i) words and expressions used have the same meaning as in Part 2 of the Act.

3.—(1) This rule shows how to calculate any period of time for doing any act which is specified by these Rules for the purposes of any proceedings under Part 2 of the Act or by an order of the Crown Court in restraint proceedings or receivership proceedings.

(2) A period of time expressed as a number of days shall be computed as clear days.

(3) In this rule "clear days" means that in computing the number of days—

(a) the day on which the period begins; and

(b) if the end of the period is defined by reference to an event, the day on which that event occurs are not included.

(4) Where the specified period is 5 days or less and includes a day which is not a business day that day does not count.

4. When the period specified by these Rules or by an order of the Crown Court under Part 2 of the Act for doing any act at the court office falls on a day on which the office is closed, that act shall be in time if done on the next day on which the court office is open.

PART II

Confiscation Proceedings

Statements in connection with confiscation orders

5.—(1) When the prosecutor or the Director is required, under section 16 of the Act, to give a statement to the Crown Court, the prosecutor or the Director, as the case may be, must also, as soon as practicable, serve a copy of the statement on the defendant.

(2) Any statement given to the Crown Court by the prosecutor or the Director under section 16 of the Act must, in addition to the information required by the Act, include the following information—

(a) the name of the defendant;

(b) the name of the person by whom the statement is made and the date on which it is made;

(c) where the statement is not given to the Crown Court immediately after the defendant has been convicted, the date on which and the place where the relevant conviction occurred.

(3) Where, under section 17 of the Act, the Crown Court orders the defendant to indicate the extent to which he accepts each allegation in a statement given by the prosecutor or the Director, the defendant must indicate this in writing to the prosecutor or the Director (as the case may be) and must give a copy to the Crown Court.

(4) Where the Crown Court orders the defendant to give to it any information under section 18 of the Act, the defendant must provide the information in writing and must, as soon as practicable, serve a copy of it on—

(a) the prosecutor, if the prosecutor asked the court to proceed under section 6 of the Act; or

(b) the Director, if the Director asked the court to proceed under section 6 of the Act.

Postponement of confiscation proceedings

6. The Crown Court may grant a postponement under section 14(1)(b) of the Act without a hearing.

Application for reconsideration of decision to make confiscation order or benefit assessed for purposes of confiscation order

7.—(1) This rule applies where the prosecutor or Director makes an application under section 19, 20 or 21 of the Act.

(2) The application must be in writing and give details of—

(a) the name of the defendant;

(b) the date on which and the place where any relevant conviction occurred;

(c) the date on which and the place where any relevant confiscation order was made or varied;

(d) the grounds for the application; and

(e) an indication of the evidence available to support the application.

(3) The application must be lodged with the Crown Court.

(4) The application must be served on the defendant at least 7 days before the date fixed by the court for hearing the application, unless the Crown Court specifies a shorter period.

Application for reconsideration of available amount

8.—(1) This rule applies where the prosecutor, the Director or a receiver makes an application under section 22 of the Act for a new calculation of the available amount.

(2) The application must be in writing and may be supported by a witness statement.

(3) The application and any witness statement must be lodged with the Crown Court.

(4) The application and any witness statement must be served on—

(a) the defendant;

(b) the receiver, if the prosecutor or the Director is making the application and a receiver has been appointed under section 50 or 52 of the Act; and

(c) if the receiver is making the application—

(i) the prosecutor; or

(ii) if the Director is appointed as the enforcement authority under section 34 of the Act, the Director,

at least 7 days before the date fixed by the court for hearing the application, unless the Crown Court specifies a shorter period.

Variation of confiscation order due to inadequacy of available amount

9.—(1) This rule applies where the defendant or a receiver makes an application under section 23 of the Act for the variation of a confiscation order.

(2) The application must be in writing and may be supported by a witness statement.

(3) The application and any witness statement must be lodged with the Crown Court.

(4) The application and any witness statement must be served on—

(a) the prosecutor, or if the Director is appointed as the enforcement authority under section 34, the Director;

(b) the defendant, if the receiver is making the application; and

(c) the receiver, if the defendant is making the application and a receiver has been appointed under section 50 or 52 of the Act, at least 7 days before the date fixed by the court for hearing the application, unless the Crown Court specifies a shorter period.

Application by justices' chief executive to discharge confiscation order

10.—(1) This rule applies where a justices' chief executive makes an application under section 24 or 25 of the Act for the discharge of a confiscation order.

(2) The application must be in writing and give details of—
- (a) the confiscation order;
- (b) the amount outstanding under the order; and
- (c) the grounds for the application.

(3) The application must be served on—
- (a) the defendant;
- (b) the prosecutor; and
- (c) any receiver appointed under section 50 of the Act.

(4) The Crown Court may determine the application without a hearing unless a person listed in paragraph (3) indicates, within 7 days after the application was served on him, that he would like to make representations.

(5) If the Crown Court makes an order discharging the confiscation order, the court must, at once, send a copy of the order to—
- (a) the justices' chief executive who applied for the order;
- (b) the defendant;
- (c) the prosecutor; and
- (d) any receiver appointed under section 50 of the Act.

Application for variation of confiscation order made against an absconder

11.—(1) This rule applies where the defendant makes an application under section 29 of the Act for the variation of a confiscation order made against an absconder.

(2) The application must be in writing and supported by a witness statement which must give details of—
- (a) the confiscation order made against an absconder under section 6 of the Act as applied by section 28 of the Act;
- (b) the circumstances in which the defendant ceased to be an absconder;
- (c) the defendant's conviction of the offence or offences concerned; and
- (d) the reason why he believes the amount required to be paid under the confiscation order was too large.

(3) The application and witness statement must be lodged with the Crown Court.

(4) The application and witness statement must be served on the prosecutor or, if the Director is appointed as the enforcement authority under section 34 of the Act, the Director at least 7 days before the date fixed by the court for hearing the application, unless the Crown Court specifies a shorter period.

Application for discharge of confiscation order made against an absconder

12.—(1) This rule applies if the defendant makes an application under section 30 of the Act for the discharge of a confiscation order.

(2) The application must be in writing and supported by a witness statement which must give details of—
- (a) the confiscation order made under section 28 of the Act;

   (b) the date on which the defendant ceased to be an absconder;

   (c) the acquittal of the defendant if he has been acquitted of the offence concerned; and

   (d) if the defendant has not been acquitted of the offence concerned—

      (i)   the date on which the defendant ceased to be an absconder;

     (ii) the date on which the proceedings taken against the defendant were instituted and a summary of steps taken in the proceedings since then; and

    (iii) any indication given by the prosecutor that he does not intend to proceed against the defendant.

(3) The application and witness statement must be lodged with the Crown Court.

(4) The application and witness statement must be served on the prosecutor or, if the Director is appointed as the enforcement authority under section 34 of the Act, the Director at least 7 days before the date fixed by the court for hearing the application, unless the Crown Court specifies a shorter period.

(5) If the Crown Court orders the discharge of the confiscation order, the court must serve notice on the magistrates' court responsible for enforcing the order if the Director has not been appointed as the enforcement authority under section 34 of the Act.

Application for increase in term of imprisonment in default

13.—(1) This rule applies where the prosecutor or the Director makes an application under section 39(5) of the Act to increase the term of imprisonment in default of payment of a confiscation order.

(2) The application must be made in writing and give details of—

   (a) the name and address of the defendant;

   (b) the confiscation order;

   (c) the grounds for the application; and

   (d) the enforcement measures taken, if any.

(3) On receipt of the application, the court must—

   (a) at once, send to the defendant and, if the Director has not been appointed as the enforcement authority under section 34 of the Act, the magistrates' court responsible for enforcing the order, a copy of the application; and

   (b) fix a time, date and place for the hearing and notify the applicant and the defendant of that time, date and place.

(4) If the Crown Court makes an order increasing the term of imprisonment in default, the court must, at once, send a copy of the order to—

   (a) the applicant;

   (b) the defendant;

   (c) where the defendant is in custody at the time of the making of the order, the person having custody of the defendant; and

   (d) if the Director has not been appointed as the enforcement authority under section 34 of the Act, the magistrates' court responsible for enforcing the order.

Compensation—general

14.—(1) This rule applies to an application for compensation under section 72 of the Act.

(2) The application must be in writing and may be supported by a witness statement.

(3) The application and any witness statement must be lodged with the Crown Court.

(4) The application and any witness statement must be served on—

(a) the person alleged to be in default; and

(b) the person by whom the compensation would be payable under section 72(9) of the Act (or if the compensation is payable out of a police fund under section 72(9)(a), the chief officer of the police force concerned),

at least 7 days before the date fixed by the court for hearing the application, unless the Crown Court directs otherwise.

Compensation—confiscation order made against absconder

15.—(1) This rule applies to an application for compensation under section 73 of the Act.

(2) The application must be in writing and supported by a witness statement which must give details of—

(a) the confiscation order made under section 28 of the Act;

(b) the variation or discharge of the confiscation order under section 29 or 30 of the Act;

(c) the realisable property to which the application relates; and

(d) the loss suffered by the applicant as result of the confiscation order.

(3) The application and witness statement must be lodged with the Crown Court.

(4) The application and witness statement must be served on the prosecutor or, if the Director is appointed as the enforcement authority under section 34, the Director at least 7 days before the date fixed by the court for hearing the application, unless the Crown Court specifies a shorter period.

PART III

Restraint Proceedings

Application for restraint order

16.—(1) This rule applies where the prosecutor, the Director or an accredited financial investigator makes an application for a restraint order under section 42 of the Act.

(2) The application may be made without notice.

(3) The application must be in writing and supported by a witness statement which must—

(a) give the grounds for the application;

(b) to the best of the witness's ability, give full details of the realisable property in respect of which the applicant is seeking the order and specify the person holding that realisable property;

(c) give the grounds for, and full details of, any application for an ancillary order under section 41(7) of the Act for the purposes of ensuring that the restraint order is effective; and

(d) where the application is made by an accredited financial investigator, include a statement that he has been authorised to make the application under section 68 of the Act.

Restraint orders

17.—(1) The Crown Court may make a restraint order subject to exceptions, including, but not limited to, exceptions for reasonable living expenses and reasonable legal expenses, and for the purpose of enabling any person to carry on any trade, business or occupation.

(2) But the Crown Court must not make an exception for legal expenses where this is prohibited by section 41(4) of the Act.

(3) An exception to a restraint order may be made subject to conditions.

(4) The Crown Court must not require the applicant for a restraint order to give any undertaking relating to damages sustained as a result of the restraint order by a person who is prohibited from dealing with realisable property by the restraint order.

(5) The Crown Court may require the applicant for a restraint order to give an undertaking to pay the reasonable expenses of any person, other than a person who is prohibited from dealing with realisable property by the restraint order, which are incurred in complying with the restraint order.

(6) A restraint order must include a statement that disobedience of the order, either by a person to whom the order is addressed, or by another person, may be contempt of court and the order must include details of the possible consequences of being held in contempt of court.

(7) Unless the Crown Court directs otherwise, a restraint order made without notice has effect until the court makes an order varying or discharging the restraint order.

(8) The applicant for a restraint order must—

(a) serve copies of the restraint order and of the witness statement made in support of the application on the defendant and any person who is prohibited from dealing with realisable property by the restraint order; and

(b) notify any person whom the applicant knows to be affected by the restraint order of the terms of the restraint order.

Application for discharge or variation of restraint order by person affected by order

18.—(1) This rule applies where a person affected by a restraint order makes an application to the Crown Court under section 42(3) of the Act to discharge or vary the restraint order or any ancillary order made under section 41(7) of the Act.

(2) The application must be in writing and may be supported by a witness statement.

(3) The application and any witness statement must be lodged with the Crown Court.

(4) The application and any witness statement must be served on the person who applied for the restraint order and any person who is prohibited from dealing with realisable property by the restraint order (if he is not the person making the application) at least 2 days before the date fixed by the court for hearing the application, unless the Crown Court specifies a shorter period.

Application for variation of restraint order by the person who applied for the order

19.—(1) This rule applies where the applicant for a restraint order makes an application under section 42(3) of the Act to the Crown Court to vary the restraint order or any ancillary order made under section 41(7) of the Act (including where the court has already made a restraint order and the applicant is seeking to vary the order in order to restrain further realisable property).

(2) The application may be made without notice if the application is urgent or if there are reasonable grounds for believing that giving notice would cause the dissipation of realisable property which is the subject of the application.

(3) The application must be in writing and must be supported by a witness statement which must—

(a) give the grounds for the application;

    (b) where the application is for the inclusion of further realisable property in the order give full details, to the best of the witness's ability, of the realisable property in respect of which the applicant is seeking the order and specify the person holding that realisable property; and

    (c) where the application is made by an accredited financial investigator, include a statement that he has been authorised to make the application under section 68 of the Act.

(4) The application and witness statement must be lodged with the Crown Court.

(5) Except where, under paragraph (2), notice of the application is not required to be served, the application and witness statement must be served on any person who is prohibited from dealing with realisable property by the restraint order at least 2 days before the date fixed by the court for hearing the application, unless the Crown Court specifies a shorter period.

(6) If the court makes an order for the variation of a restraint order, the applicant must serve copies of the order and of the witness statement made in support of the application on—

    (a) the defendant;

    (b) any person who is prohibited from dealing with realisable property by the restraint order (whether before or after the variation); and

    (c) any other person whom the applicant knows to be affected by the order.

Application for discharge of a restraint order by the person who applied for the order

20.—(1) This rule applies where the applicant for a restraint order makes an application under section 42(3) of the Act to discharge the order or any ancillary order made under section 41(7) of the Act.

(2) The application may be made without notice.

(3) The application must be in writing and must state the grounds for the application.

(4) If the court makes an order for the discharge of a restraint order, the applicant must serve copies of the order on—

    (a) the defendant;

    (b) any person who is prohibited from dealing with realisable property by the restraint order (whether before or after the discharge); and

    (c) any other person whom the applicant knows to be affected by the order.

PART IV

Receivership Proceedings

Application for appointment of a management or enforcement receiver

21.—(1) This rule applies to an application for the appointment of a management receiver under section 48(1) of the Act and an application for the appointment of an enforcement receiver under section 50(1) of the Act.

(2) The application may be made without notice if—

    (a) the application is joined with an application for a restraint order under rule 16;

    (b) the application is urgent; or

    (c) there are reasonable grounds for believing that giving notice would cause the dissipation of realisable property which is the subject of the application.

(3) The application must be in writing and must be supported by a witness statement which must—

(a) give the grounds for the application;

(b) give full details of the proposed receiver;

(c) to the best of the witness's ability, give full details of the realisable property in respect of which the applicant is seeking the order and specify the person holding that realisable property;

(d) where the application is made by an accredited financial investigator, include a statement that he has been authorised to make the application under section 68 of the Act; and

(e) if the proposed receiver is not a member of staff of the Assets Recovery Agency, the Crown Prosecution Service or the Commissioners of Customs and Excise and the applicant is asking the court to allow the receiver to act—

(i) without giving security; or

(ii) before he has given security or satisfied the court that he has security in place, explain the reasons why that is necessary.

(4) Where the application is for the appointment of an enforcement receiver, the applicant must provide the Crown Court with a copy of the confiscation order made against the defendant.

(5) The application and witness statement must be lodged with the Crown Court.

(6) Except where, under paragraph (2), notice of the application is not required to be served, the application and witness statement must be lodged with the Crown Court and served on—

(a) the defendant;

(b) any person who holds realisable property to which the application relates; and

(c) any other person whom the applicant knows to be affected by the application,

at least 7 days before the date fixed by the court for hearing the application, unless the Crown Court specifies a shorter period.

(7) If the court makes an order for the appointment of a receiver, the applicant must serve copies of the order and of the witness statement made in support of the application on—

(a) the defendant;

(b) any person who holds realisable property to which the order applies; and

(c) any other person whom the applicant knows to be affected by the order.

Application for conferral of powers on management receiver, enforcement receiver or Director's receiver

22.—(1) This rule applies to an application for the conferral of powers on a management receiver under section 49(1) of the Act, an enforcement receiver under section 51(1) of the Act or a Director's receiver under section 53(1) of the Act.

(2) The application may be made without notice if the application is to give the receiver power to take possession of property and—

(a) the application is joined with an application for a restraint order under rule 16;

(b) the application is urgent; or

(c) there are reasonable grounds for believing that giving notice would cause the dissipation of the property which is the subject of the application.

(3) The application must be made in writing and supported by a witness statement which must—

    (a) give the grounds for the application;

    (b) give full details of the realisable property in respect of which the applicant is seeking the order and specify the person holding that realisable property; and

    (c) where the application is made by an accredited financial investigator, include a statement that he has been authorised to make the application under section 68 of the Act.

(4) Where the application is for the conferral of powers on an enforcement receiver or Director's receiver, the applicant must provide the Crown Court with a copy of the confiscation order made against the defendant.

(5) The application and witness statement must be lodged with the Crown Court.

(6) Except where, under paragraph (2), notice of the application is not required to be served, the application and witness statement must be served on—

    (a) the defendant;

    (b) any person who holds realisable property in respect of which a receiver has been appointed or in respect of which an application for a receiver has been made;

    (c) any other person whom the applicant knows to be affected by the application; and

    (d) the receiver (if one has already been appointed),

at least 7 days before the date fixed by the court for hearing the application, unless the Crown Court specifies a shorter period.

(7) If the court makes an order for the conferral of powers on a receiver, the applicant must serve copies of the order on—

    (a) the defendant;

    (b) any person who holds realisable property in respect of which the receiver has been appointed; and

    (c) any other person whom the applicant knows to be affected by the order.

Applications for discharge or variation of receivership orders and applications for other orders

23.—(1) This rule applies to applications under section 62(3) of the Act for orders (by persons affected by the action of receivers) and applications under section 63(1) of the Act for the discharge or variation of orders relating to receivers.

(2) The application must be made in writing and lodged with the Crown Court.

(3) The application must be served on the following persons (except where they are the person making the application)—

    (a) the person who applied for appointment of the receiver;

    (b) the defendant;

    (c) any person who holds realisable property in respect of which the receiver has been appointed;

    (d) the receiver; and

    (e) any other person whom the applicant knows to be affected by the application,

at least 7 days before the date fixed by the court for hearing the application, unless the Crown Court specifies a shorter period.

(4) If the court makes an order for the discharge or variation of an order relating to a receiver under section 63(2), the applicant must serve copies of the order on any persons whom he knows to be affected by the order.

Sums in the hands of receivers

24.—(1) This rule applies where the amount payable under a confiscation order has been fully paid and any sums remain in the hands of an enforcement receiver or Director's receiver.

(2) The receiver must make an application to the Crown Court for directions as to the distribution of the sums in his hands.

(3) The application and any evidence which the receiver intends to rely on in support of the application must be served on—

(a) the defendant; and

(b) any other person who held (or holds) interests in any property realised by the receiver,

at least 7 days before the date fixed by the court for hearing the application, unless the Crown Court specifies a shorter period.

(4) If any of the provisions listed in paragraph (5) (provisions as to the vesting of funds in a trustee in bankruptcy) apply, then the Crown Court must make a declaration to that effect.

(5) These are the provisions—

(a) section 31B of the Bankruptcy (Scotland) Act 1985;[5]

(b) section 306B of the Insolvency Act 1986;[6] and

(c) article 279B of the Insolvency (Northern Ireland) Order 1989.[7]

Security

25.—(1) This rule applies where the Crown Court appoints a receiver under section 48, 50 or 52 of the Act and the receiver is not a member of staff of the Assets Recovery Agency, the Crown Prosecution Service or of the Commissioners of Customs and Excise (and it is immaterial whether the receiver is a permanent or temporary member or he is on secondment from elsewhere).

(2) The Crown Court may direct that before the receiver begins to act, or within a specified time, he must either—

(a) give such security as the Crown Court may determine; or

(b) file with the Crown Court and serve on all parties to any receivership proceedings evidence that he already has in force sufficient security,

to cover his liability for his acts and omissions as a receiver.

(3) The Crown Court may terminate the appointment of a receiver if he fails to—

(a) give the security; or

(b) satisfy the court as to the security he has in force,

by the date specified.

Remuneration

26.—(1) This rule applies where the Crown Court appoints a receiver under section 48, 50 or 52 of the Act and the receiver is not a member of staff of the Assets Recovery Agency, the Crown Prosecution Service or of the Commissioners of Customs and Excise (and it is immaterial whether the receiver is a permanent or temporary member or he is on secondment from elsewhere).

---

[5] 1985 c. 66.   [6] 1986 c. 45.   [7] S.I. 1989/2405 (N.I. 19).

449

(2) The receiver may only charge for his services if the Crown Court—
   (a) so directs; and
   (b) specifies the basis on which the receiver is to be remunerated.
(3) Unless the Crown Court orders otherwise, in determining the remuneration of the receiver, the Crown Court shall award such sum as is reasonable and proportionate in all the circumstances and which takes into account—
   (a) the time properly given by him and his staff to the receivership;
   (b) the complexity of the receivership;
   (c) any responsibility of an exceptional kind or degree which falls on the receiver in consequence of the receivership;
   (d) the effectiveness with which the receiver appears to be carrying out, or to have carried out, his duties; and
   (e) the value and nature of the subject matter of the receivership.
(4) The Crown Court may refer the determination of a receiver's remuneration to be ascertained by the taxing authority of the Crown Court and rules 15 to 18 of the Crown Court Rules 1982[8] shall have effect as if the taxing authority was ascertaining costs.
(5) A receiver appointed under section 48 of the Act is to receive his remuneration by realising property in respect of which he is appointed, in accordance with section 49(2)(d) of the Act.
(6) A receiver appointed under section 50 of the Act is to receive his remuneration by applying to the justices' chief executive for payment under section 55(4)(b) of the Act.
(7) A receiver appointed under section 52 of the Act is to receive his remuneration by applying to the Director for payment under section 57(4)(b) of the Act.

Accounts

27.—(1) The Crown Court may order a receiver appointed under section 48, 50 or 52 of the Act to prepare and serve accounts.
(2) A party to receivership proceedings served with such accounts may apply for an order permitting him to inspect any document in the possession of the receiver relevant to those accounts.
(3) Any party to receivership proceedings may, within 14 days of being served with the accounts, serve notice on the receiver—
   (a) specifying any item in the accounts to which he objects;
   (b) giving the reason for such objection; and
   (c) requiring the receiver within 14 days of receipt of the notice, either—
      (i) to notify all the parties who were served with the accounts that he accepts the objection; or
      (ii) if he does not accept the objection, to apply for an examination of the accounts in relation to the contested item.
(4) When the receiver applies for the examination of the accounts he must at the same time lodge with the Crown Court—
   (a) the accounts; and
   (b) a copy of the notice served on him under this rule.

---

[8] S.I. 1982/1109, to which there are amendments not relevant in this context.

(5) If the receiver fails to comply with paragraph (3)(c) of this rule, any party to receivership proceedings may apply to the Crown Court for an examination of the accounts in relation to the contested item.

(6) At the conclusion of its examination of the accounts the court will certify the result.

Non-compliance by receiver

28.—(1) If a receiver appointed under section 48, 50 or 52 of the Act fails to comply with any rule, practice direction or direction of the Crown Court, the Crown Court may order him to attend a hearing to explain his non-compliance.

(2) At the hearing, the Crown Court may make any order it considers appropriate, including—

(a) terminating the appointment of the receiver;

(b) reducing the receiver's remuneration or disallowing it altogether; and

(c) ordering the receiver to pay the costs of any party.

PART V

Other Applications

Distress and forfeiture

29.—(1) This rule applies to applications under sections 58(2) and (3), 59(2) and (3) and 60(2) and (3) of the Act for leave of the Crown Court to levy distress against property or exercise a right of forfeiture by peaceable re-entry in relation to a tenancy, in circumstances where the property or tenancy is the subject of a restraint order or a receiver has been appointed in respect of the property or tenancy.

(2) The application must be made in writing to the Crown Court.

(3) The application must be served on—

(a) the person who applied for the restraint order or the order appointing the receiver; and

(b) any receiver appointed in respect of the property or tenancy,

at least 7 days before the date fixed by the court for hearing the application, unless the Crown Court specifies a shorter period.

Application for registration of Scottish or Northern Ireland Order

30.—(1) This rule applies to an application for registration of an order under article 6 of the Proceeds of Crime Act 2002 (Enforcement in different parts of the United Kingdom) Order 2002.[9]

(2) The application may be made without notice.

(3) The application must be in writing and may be supported by a witness statement which must—

(a) exhibit the order or a certified copy of the order; and

(b) to the best of the witness's ability, give full details of the realisable property located in England and Wales in respect of which the order was made and specify the person holding that realisable property.

---

[9] S.I. 2002/3133.

(4) If the court registers the order, the applicant must serve notice of the registration on—
  (a) any person who holds realisable property to which the order applies; and
  (b) any other person whom the applicant knows to be affected by the order.
(5) The permission of the Crown Court under rule 60 is not required to serve the notice outside England and Wales.

Application to vary or set aside registration

31.—(1) An application to vary or set aside registration of an order under article 6 of the Proceeds of Crime Act 2002 (Enforcement in different parts of the United Kingdom) Order 2002 may be made to the Crown Court by—
  (a) any person who holds realisable property to which the order applies; and
  (b) any other person affected by the order.
(2) The application must be in writing and may be supported by a witness statement.
(3) The application and any witness statement must be lodged with the Crown Court.
(4) The application must be served on the person who applied for registration at least 7 days before the date fixed by the court for hearing the application, unless the Crown Court specifies a shorter period.
(5) No property in England and Wales may be realised in pursuance of the order before the Crown Court has decided the application.

Register of orders

32.—(1) The Crown Court must keep, under the direction of the Lord Chancellor, a register of the orders registered under article 6 of the Proceeds of Crime Act 2002 (Enforcement in different parts of the United Kingdom) Order 2002.
(2) The register must include details of any variation or setting aside of a registration under rule 31 and of any execution issued on a registered order.
(3) If the person who applied for registration of an order which is subsequently registered notifies the Crown Court that the court which made the order has varied or discharged the order, details of the variation or discharge, as the case may be, must be entered in the register.

PART VI

Provisions Applicable only to Restraint and Receivership Proceedings

Joining of applications

33. An application for the appointment of a management receiver or enforcement receiver under rule 21 may be joined with—
  (a) an application for a restraint order under rule 16; and
  (b) an application for the conferral of powers on the receiver under rule 22.

Applications to be dealt with in writing

34. Applications in restraint proceedings and receivership proceedings are to be dealt with without a hearing, unless the Crown Court orders otherwise.

Business in chambers

35. Restraint proceedings and receivership proceedings may be heard in chambers.

Power of court to control evidence

36.—(1) When hearing restraint proceedings and receivership proceedings, the Crown Court may control the evidence by giving directions as to—

(a) the issues on which it requires evidence;

(b) the nature of the evidence which it requires to decide those issues;

(c) the way in which the evidence is to be placed before the court.

(2) The court may use its power under this rule to exclude evidence that would otherwise be admissible.

(3) The court may limit cross-examination in restraint proceedings and receivership proceedings.

Evidence of witnesses

37.—(1) The general rule is that, unless the Crown Court orders otherwise, any fact which needs to be proved in restraint proceedings or receivership proceedings by the evidence of a witness is to be proved by their evidence in writing.

(2) Where evidence is to be given in writing under this rule, any party may apply to the Crown Court for permission to cross-examine the person giving the evidence.

(3) If the Crown Court gives permission under paragraph (2) but the person in question does not attend as required by the order, his evidence may not be used unless the court gives permission.

Witness summons

38.—(1) Any party to restraint proceedings or receivership proceedings may apply to the Crown Court to issue a witness summons requiring a witness to—

(a) attend court to give evidence; or

(b) produce documents to the court.

(2) Rule 23 of the Crown Court Rules 1982[10] applies to an application under this rule as it applies to an application under section 2 of the Criminal Procedure (Attendance of Witnesses) Act 1965.[11]

Hearsay evidence

39. Section 2(1) of the Civil Evidence Act 1995[12] (duty to give notice of intention to rely on hearsay evidence) does not apply to evidence in restraint proceedings and receivership proceedings.

---

[10] Rule 23 was substituted by rule 2 of the Crown Court (Miscellaneous Amendments) Rules 1999 (S.I. 1999/598).

[11] 1965 c. 69.

[12] 1995 c. 38. Sections 2 to 4 of the Civil Evidence Act 1995 apply to restraint proceedings by virtue of section 46 of the Proceeds of Crime Act 2002 (c. 29).

Disclosure and inspection of documents

40.—(1) This rule applies where, in the course of restraint proceedings or receivership proceedings, an issue arises as to whether property is realisable property.

(2) The Crown Court may make an order for disclosure of documents.

(3) Part 31 of the Civil Procedure Rules 1998[13] as amended from time to time shall have effect as if the proceedings were proceedings in the High Court.

Court documents

41.—(1) Any order which the Crown Court issues in restraint proceedings or receivership proceedings must—

    (a) state the name and judicial title of the person who made it;

    (b) bear the date on which it is made; and

    (c) be sealed by the Crown Court.

(2) The Crown Court may place the seal on the order—

    (a) by hand; or

    (b) by printing a facsimile of the seal on the order whether electronically or otherwise.

(3) A document purporting to bear the court's seal shall be admissible in evidence without further proof.

Consent orders

42.—(1) This rule applies where all the parties to restraint proceedings or receivership proceedings agree the terms in which an order should be made.

(2) Any party may apply for a judgment or order in the terms agreed.

(3) The Crown Court may deal with an application under paragraph (2) without a hearing.

(4) Where this rule applies—

    (a) the order which is agreed by the parties must be drawn up in the terms agreed;

    (b) it must be expressed as being "By Consent";

    (c) it must be signed by the legal representative acting for each of the parties to whom the order relates or by the party if he is a litigant in person.

(5) Where an application is made under this rule, then the requirements of any other rule as to the procedure for making an application do not apply.

Slips and omissions

43.—(1) The Crown Court may at any time correct an accidental slip or omission in an order made in restraint proceedings or receivership proceedings.

(2) A party may apply for a correction without notice.

Supply of documents from court records

44.—(1) No document relating to restraint proceedings or receivership proceedings may be supplied from the records of the Crown Court for any person to inspect or copy unless the Crown Court grants permission.

(2) An application for permission under paragraph (1) must be made on notice to the parties to the proceedings.

---

[13] S.I. 1998/3132 (L. 17), to which there are amendments not relevant to these Rules.

Disclosure of documents in criminal proceedings

45.—(1) This rule applies where—
    (a) proceedings for an offence have been started in the Crown Court and the defendant has not been either convicted or acquitted on all counts; and
    (b) an application for a restraint order under section 42(1) of the Act has been made.
(2) The judge presiding at the proceedings for the offence may be supplied from the records of the Crown Court with documents relating to restraint proceedings and any receivership proceedings.
(3) Such documents must not otherwise be disclosed in the proceedings for the offence.

Preparation of documents

46.—(1) Every order in restraint proceedings or receivership proceedings will be drawn up by the Crown Court unless—
    (a) the Crown Court orders a party to draw it up;
    (b) a party, with the permission of the Crown Court, agrees to draw it up; or
    (c) the order is made by consent under rule 42.
(2) The Crown Court may direct that—
    (a) an order drawn up by a party must be checked by the Crown Court before it is sealed; or
    (b) before an order is drawn up by the Crown Court, the parties must lodge an agreed statement of its terms.
(3) Where an order is to be drawn up by a party—
    (a) he must lodge it with the Crown Court no later than 7 days after the date on which the court ordered or permitted him to draw it up so that it can be sealed by the Crown Court; and
    (b) if he fails to lodge it within that period, any other party may draw it up and lodge it.
(4) Nothing in this rule shall require the Crown Court to accept a document which is illegible, has not been duly authorised, or is unsatisfactory for some other similar reason.

Change of solicitor

47.—(1) This rule applies where—
    (a) a party for whom a solicitor is acting in restraint proceedings or receivership proceedings wants to change his solicitor;
    (b) a party, after having represented himself in such proceedings, appoints a solicitor to act on his behalf (except where the solicitor is appointed only to act as an advocate for a hearing); or
    (c) a party, after having been represented by a solicitor in such proceedings, intends to act in person.
(2) Where this rule applies, the party or his solicitor (where one is acting) must—
    (a) lodge notice of the change at the Crown Court; and
    (b) serve notice of the change on every other party and, where paragraph (1)(a) or (c) applies, on the former solicitor.
(3) The notice lodged at the Crown Court must state that notice has been served as required by paragraph (2)(b).
(4) Subject to paragraph (5), where a party has changed his solicitor or intends to act in person, the former solicitor will be considered to be the party's solicitor unless and until—

    (a) notice is served in accordance with paragraph (2); or

    (b) the Crown Court makes an order under rule 48 and the order is served as required by paragraph (3) of that rule.

(5) Where the certificate of a LSC funded client is revoked or discharged—

    (a) the solicitor who acted for that person will cease to be the solicitor acting in the proceedings as soon as his retainer is determined under regulation 4 of the Community Legal Service (Costs) Regulations 2000;[14] and

    (b) if that person wishes to continue, where he appoints a solicitor to act on his behalf paragraph (2) will apply as if he had previously represented himself in the proceedings.

(6) "Certificate" in paragraph (5) means a certificate issued under the Funding Code (approved under section 9 of the Access to Justice Act 1999[15]) and "LSC funded client" means an individual who receives services funded by the Legal Services Commission as part of the Community Legal Service within the meaning of Part I of the Access to Justice Act 1999.

Application by solicitor for declaration that solicitor has ceased to act

48.—(1) A solicitor may apply to the Crown Court for an order declaring that he has ceased to be the solicitor acting for a party to restraint proceedings or receivership proceedings.

(2) Where an application is made under this rule—

    (a) notice of the application must be given to the party for whom the solicitor is acting, unless the Crown Court directs otherwise; and

    (b) the application must be supported by evidence.

(3) Where the Crown Court makes an order that a solicitor has ceased to act, the solicitor must serve a copy of the order on every party to the proceedings.

Application by other party for declaration that solicitor has ceased to act

49.—(1) Where—

    (a) a solicitor who has acted for a party to restraint proceedings or receivership proceedings—

        (i)   has died;

        (ii) has become bankrupt;

        (iii) has ceased to practise; or

        (iv) cannot be found; and

    (b) the party has not given notice of a change of solicitor or notice of intention to act in person as required by rule 47,

any other party may apply to the Crown Court for an order declaring that the solicitor has ceased to be the solicitor acting for the other party in the proceedings.

(2) Where an application is made under this rule, notice of the application must be given to the party to whose solicitor the application relates unless the Crown Court directs otherwise.

(3) Where the Crown Court makes an order under this rule, the applicant must serve a copy of the order on every other party to the proceedings.

---

[14] S.I. 2000/441, amended by S.I. 2001/882.   [15] 1999 c. 22.

Order for costs

50.—(1) This rule applies where the Crown Court is deciding whether to make an order for costs under rule 12 of the Crown Court Rules 1982 in restraint proceedings or receivership proceedings.

(2) The court has discretion as to—
  (a) whether costs are payable by one party to another;
  (b) the amount of those costs; and
  (c) when they are to be paid.

(3) If the court decides to make an order about costs—
  (a) the general rule is that the unsuccessful party will be ordered to pay the costs of the successful party; but
  (b) the court may make a different order.

(4) In deciding what order (if any) to make about costs, the court must have regard to all of the circumstances, including—
  (a) the conduct of all the parties; and
  (b) whether a party has succeeded on part of an application, even if he has not been wholly successful.

(5) The orders which the court may make under rule 12 of the Crown Court Rules 1982 include an order that a party must pay—
  (a) a proportion of another party's costs;
  (b) a stated amount in respect of another party's costs;
  (c) costs from or until a certain date only;
  (d) costs incurred before proceedings have begun;
  (e) costs relating to particular steps taken in the proceedings;
  (f) costs relating only to a distinct part of the proceedings; and
  (g) interest on costs from or until a certain date, including a date before the making of an order.

(6) Where the court would otherwise consider making an order under paragraph (5)(f), it must instead, if practicable, make an order under paragraph (5)(a) or (c).

(7) Where the court has ordered a party to pay costs, it may order an amount to be paid on account before the costs are assessed.

Assessment of costs

51.—(1) Where the Crown Court has made an order for costs in restraint proceedings or receivership proceedings it may either—
  (a) make an assessment of the costs itself; or
  (b) order assessment of the costs under rule 14 of the Crown Court Rules 1982.

(2) In either case, the Crown Court or the taxing authority, as the case may be, must—
  (a) only allow costs which are proportionate to the matters in issue; and
  (b) resolve any doubt which it may have as to whether the costs were reasonably incurred or reasonable and proportionate in favour of the paying party.

(3) The Crown Court or the taxing authority, as the case may be, is to have regard to all the circumstances in deciding whether costs were proportionately or reasonably incurred or proportionate and reasonable in amount.

(4) In particular, the Crown Court or the taxing authority must give effect to any orders which have already been made.

(5) The Crown Court or the taxing authority must also have regard to—

    (a) the conduct of all the parties, including in particular, conduct before, as well as during, the proceedings;

    (b) the amount or value of the property involved;

    (c) the importance of the matter to all the parties;

    (d) the particular complexity of the matter or the difficulty or novelty of the questions raised;

    (e) the skill, effort, specialised knowledge and responsibility involved;

    (f) the time spent on the application; and

    (g) the place where and the circumstances in which work or any part of it was done.

Time for complying with an order for costs

52. A party to restraint proceedings or receivership proceedings must comply with an order for the payment of costs within 14 days of—

    (a) the date of the order if it states the amount of those costs;

    (b) if the amount of those costs is decided later under rule 14 of the Crown Court Rules 1982, the date of the taxing authority's decision; or

    (c) in either case, such later date as the Crown Court may specify.

Application of costs rules

53. These Rules do not apply to the assessment of costs in proceedings to the extent that section 11 of the Access to Justice Act 1999 applies and provisions made under that Act make different provision.

PART VII

General Provisions

Statements of truth

54.—(1) Any witness statement required to be served by these Rules must be verified by a statement of truth contained in the witness statement.

(2) A statement of truth is a declaration by the person making the witness statement to the effect that the witness statement is true to the best of his knowledge and belief and that he made the statement knowing that, if it were tendered in evidence, he would be liable to prosecution if he wilfully stated in it anything which he knew to be false or did not believe to be true.

(3) The statement of truth must be signed by the person making the witness statement.

(4) If the person making the witness statement fails to verify the witness statement by a statement of truth, the Crown Court may direct that it shall not be admissible as evidence.

Use of witness statements for other purposes

55.—(1) Except as provided by this rule, a witness statement served in proceedings under Part 2 of the Act may be used only for the purpose of the proceedings in which it is served.

(2) Paragraph (1) does not apply if and to the extent that—

    (a) the witness gives consent in writing to some other use of it;

(b) the Crown Court gives permission for some other use; or

(c) the witness statement has been put in evidence at a hearing held in public.

Expert evidence

56.—(1) A party to proceedings under Part 2 of the Act who wishes to adduce expert evidence (whether of fact or opinion) in the proceedings must, as soon as practicable—

(a) serve on the other parties a statement in writing of any finding or opinion which he proposes to adduce by way of such evidence; and

(b) serve on any party who requests it in writing, a copy of (or if it appears to the party proposing to adduce the evidence to be more practicable, a reasonable opportunity to examine)—

(i) the record of any observation, test, calculation or other procedure on which the finding or opinion is based; and

(ii) any document or other thing or substance in respect of which the observation, test, calculation or other procedure mentioned in sub-paragraph (i) has been carried out.

(2) A party may serve notice in writing waiving his right to be served with any of the matters mentioned in paragraph (1) above and, in particular, may agree that the statement mentioned in sub-paragraph (a) may be given to him orally and not served in writing.

(3) If a party who wishes to adduce expert evidence in proceedings under Part 2 of this Act fails to comply with this rule he may not adduce that evidence in those proceedings without the leave of the court, except where rule 57 applies.

Exceptions to procedure for expert evidence

57.—(1) If a party has reasonable grounds for believing that the disclosure of any evidence in compliance with rule 56 might lead to the intimidation, or attempted intimidation, of any person on whose evidence he intends to rely in the proceedings, or otherwise to the course of justice being interfered with, he shall not be obliged to comply with those requirements in relation to that evidence, unless the Crown Court orders otherwise.

(2) Where, in accordance with paragraph (1), a party considers that he is not obliged to comply with the requirements imposed by rule 56 with regard to any evidence in relation to any other party, he must serve notice in writing on that party stating—

(a) that the evidence is being withheld; and

(b) the reasons for withholding the evidence.

Service of documents

58.—(1) Rules 28 and 30 of the Crown Court Rules 1982[16] shall not apply in restraint proceedings and receivership proceedings.

(2) Where these Rules require service of a document, then, unless the Crown Court directs otherwise, the document may be served by any of the following methods—

(a) in all cases, by delivering the document personally to the party to be served;

(b) if no solicitor is acting for the party to be served by delivering the document at, or by sending it by first-class post to, his residence or his last-known residence;

---

[16] S.I. 1982/1109. Rule 30 was inserted by the Crown Court (Amendment) Rules 1991 (S.I. 1991/1288).

    (c) if a solicitor is acting for the party to be served—
        (i) by delivering the document at, or sending it by first-class post to, the solicitor's business address; or
       (ii) where the solicitor's business address includes a numbered box at a document exchange, by leaving the document at that document exchange or at a document exchange which transmits documents on every business day to that document exchange; or
      (iii) if the solicitor has indicated that he is willing to accept service by facsimile transmission, by sending a legible copy of the document by facsimile transmission to the solicitor's office.

(3) A document shall, unless the contrary is proved, be deemed to have been served—
    (a) in the case of service by first-class post, on the second business day after posting;
    (b) in the case of service in accordance with paragraph (2)(c)(ii), on the second business day after the day on which it is left at the document exchange; and
    (c) in the case of service in accordance with paragraph (2)(c)(iii), where it is transmitted on a business day before 4 p.m., on that day and in any other case, on the next business day.

(4) An order made in restraint proceedings or receivership proceedings may be enforced against the defendant or any other person affected by it notwithstanding that service of a copy of the order has not been effected in accordance with this rule if the Crown Court is satisfied that the person had notice of the order by being present when the order was made.

Service by an alternative method

59.—(1) Where it appears to the Crown Court that there is a good reason to authorise service by a method not otherwise permitted by these Rules, the court may make an order permitting service by an alternative method.

(2) An application for an order permitting service by an alternative method—
    (a) must be supported by evidence;
    (b) may be made without notice.

(3) An order permitting service by an alternative method must specify—
    (a) the method of service; and
    (b) the date when the document will be deemed to be served.

Service outside the jurisdiction

60.—(1) Where these Rules require a document to be served on someone who is outside England and Wales, it may be served outside England and Wales with the permission of the Crown Court.

(2) Where a document is to be served outside England and Wales it may be served by any method permitted by the law of the country in which it is to be served.

(3) Nothing in this rule or in any court order shall authorise or require any person to do anything in the country where the document is to be served which is against the law of that country.

(4) Where these Rules require a document to be served a certain period of time before the date of a hearing and the recipient does not appear at the hearing, the hearing must not take place unless the Crown Court is satisfied that the document has been duly served.

Certificates of service

61.—(1) Where these Rules require that the applicant for an order in restraint proceedings or receivership proceedings serve a document on another person, the applicant must lodge a certificate of service with the Crown Court within 7 days of service of the document.

(2) The certificate must state—

    (a) the method of service;

    (b) the date of service; and

    (c) if the document is served under rule 59, such other information as the court may require when making the order permitting service by an alternative method.

(3) Where a document is to be served by the Crown Court in restraint proceedings and receivership proceedings and the court is unable to serve it, the court must send a notice of non-service stating the method attempted to the party who requested service.

EXPLANATORY NOTE

(This note is not part of the Rules)

These Rules make provision for the procedure to be followed in proceedings in the Crown Court under Part 2 of the Proceeds of Crime Act 2002, which makes provision about confiscation orders and ancillary orders such as the making of restraint orders and the appointment of receivers.

Part I of the Rules makes introductory provision. Part II deals with confiscation proceedings. Part III deals with restraint proceedings. Part IV deals with receivership proceedings. Part V deals with other applications, including applications for registration of orders made in Scotland or Northern Ireland. Part VI makes general provision applicable only to restraint proceedings and receivership proceedings, whereas Part VII contains general provision which applies to all proceedings.

Prior to the passing of the Proceeds of Crime Act 2002, all restraint proceedings and receivership proceedings were dealt with in the High Court. Therefore, many of the rules applicable to restraint proceedings and receivership proceedings make provision corresponding to Civil Procedure Rules, as permitted by section 91 of the Proceeds of Crime Act 2002.

The Crown Court (Amendment) Rules 2003 (SI 2003/422)

Made	*20th February 2003*
Laid before Parliament	*27th February 2003*
Came into force	*24th March 2003*

We, the Crown Court Rule Committee, in exercise of the powers conferred upon us by sections 84(1) and 86 of the Supreme Court Act 1981[1] and sections 351(2), 362(2), 369(2) and 375(1) of the Proceeds of Crime Act 2002,[2] hereby make the following Rules:

1. These Rules may be cited as the Crown Court (Amendment) Rules 2003 and shall come into force on 24th March 2003.

2. The Crown Court Rules 1982[3] are amended as follows.

3. In rule 25B[4]—

    (a) in paragraph (1), for "section 27 of the Drug Trafficking Offences Act 1986 or section 93H of the Criminal Justice Act 1988", there is substituted "section 93H of the Criminal Justice Act 1988[5], section 55 of the Drug Trafficking Act 1994,[6] or section 345 of the Proceeds of Crime Act 2002[7]";

    (b) in paragraph (1), for "the person required to comply with it", there is substituted "any person affected by it";

    (c) in paragraph (1), after "a Circuit judge" there is inserted "or, in the case of an order under the Proceeds of Crime Act 2002, a judge entitled to exercise the jurisdiction of the Crown Court";

    (d) in paragraph (2), for "to a constable at the police station from which the application for the order was made, together with a notice indicating", there is substituted—

    "—

        (a) to a constable at the police station specified in the order; or

        (b) where the application for the order was made under the Proceeds of Crime Act 2002 and was not made by a constable, to the office of the appropriate officer

---

[1] 1981 c. 54.

[2] 2002 c. 29.

[3] S.I. 1982/1109; relevant amending instruments are S.I. 1986/2151, S.I. 1995/2618 and S.I. 2001/4012.

[4] Rule 25B was inserted by S.I. 1986/2151 and amended by S.I. 1995/2618.

[5] 1988 c. 33; section 93H was inserted by section 11 of the Proceeds of Crime Act 1995 (c. 11).

[6] 1994 c. 37.

[7] 2002 c. 29.

who made the application, as specified in the order,
in either case together with a notice indicating";

(e) in paragraph (3), after "a Circuit judge" there is inserted "or, in the case of an order under the Proceeds of Crime Act 2002, a judge entitled to exercise the jurisdiction of the Crown Court";

(f) in paragraph (4), before the definition of "constable", there is inserted " "appropriate officer" has the meaning given to it by section 378 of the Proceeds of Crime Act 2002;".

4. In rule 25C[8]—

(a) for the heading, there is substituted "Account monitoring orders under the Terrorism Act 2000 and the Proceeds of Crime Act 2002";

(b) in paragraph (2), for "other than a police officer", there is substituted "other than the person who applied for the account monitoring order";

(c) in paragraph (2), after "the Terrorism Act 2000", there is inserted "or section 375(2) of the Proceeds of Crime Act 2002";

(d) in paragraph (2), for "to a police officer at the police station specified in the order, together with a notice indicating", there is substituted—

"—

(a) to a police officer at the police station specified in the account monitoring order; or

(b) where the application for the account monitoring order was made under the Proceeds of Crime Act 2002 and was not made by a constable, to the office of the appropriate officer who made the application, as specified in the account monitoring order,

in either case together with a notice indicating";

(e) after paragraph (2), there is inserted—

" (3) In this rule—

"appropriate officer" has the meaning given to it by section 378 of the Proceeds of Crime Act 2002;

references to the person who applied for an account monitoring order must be construed in accordance with section 375(4) and (5) of the Proceeds of Crime Act 2002."

5. After Rule 25C, there is inserted—

" **Customer information orders under the Proceeds of Crime Act 2002**

25D.—(1) Where any person other than the person who applied for the customer information order proposes to make an application under section 369(3) of the Proceeds of Crime Act 2002 for the discharge or variation of a customer information order, he shall, not later than 48 hours before the application is to be made, give a copy of the proposed application—

(a) to a police officer at the police station specified in the customer information order; or

(b) where the application for the customer information order was not made by a constable, to the office of the appropriate officer who made the application, as specified in the customer information order,

in either case together with a notice indicating the time and place at which the application for a discharge or variation is to be made.

(2) In this rule—

---

[8] Rule 25C was inserted by S.I. 2001/4012.

"appropriate officer" has the meaning given to it by section 378 of the Proceeds of Crime Act 2002;

references to the person who applied for the customer information order must be construed in accordance with section 369(5) and (6) of the Proceeds of Crime Act 2002.

Proof of identity and accreditation

25E.—(1) This rule applies where—

(a) an appropriate officer makes an application under section 345 (production orders), section 363 (customer information orders) or section 370 (account monitoring orders) of the Proceeds of Crime Act 2002 for the purposes of a confiscation investigation or a money laundering investigation; or

(b) the Director of the Assets Recovery Agency makes an application under section 357 of the Proceeds of Crime Act 2002 (disclosure orders) for the purposes of a confiscation investigation.

(2) Subject to section 449 of the Proceeds of Crime Act 2002 (which makes provision for members of staff of the Assets Recovery Agency to use pseudonyms), the appropriate officer or the Director of the Assets Recovery Agency, as the case may be, must provide the judge with proof of his identity and, if he is an accredited financial investigator, his accreditation under section 3 of the Proceeds of Crime Act 2002.

(3) In this rule—

"appropriate officer" has the meaning given to it by 378 of the Proceeds of Crime Act 2002;

"confiscation investigation" and "money laundering investigation" have the meanings given to them by section 341 of the Proceeds of Crime Act 2002.".

EXPLANATORY NOTE

(This note is not part of the Rules)

These Rules amend the Crown Court Rules 1982 in consequence of the enactment of the Proceeds of Crime Act 2002 ("the Act"). Part 8 of the Act deals with investigations into the proceeds of crime and makes provision for applications to be made to Crown Court judges for various orders and warrants.

Rule 3 amends the existing provision in rule 25B of the Crown Court Rules 1982 about production orders so that it also covers production orders made under Part 8 of the Act. Rule 4 amends the existing provision in rule 25C of the Crown Court Rules 1982 about account monitoring orders so that it also covers account monitoring orders made under Part 8 of the Act. However, no amendment is made to rule 25C(1) as the court is not to serve account monitoring orders made under the Act. Rule 5 inserts a new rule 25D making provision about the discharge and variation of customer information orders under the Act and a new rule 25E which provides for applicants under Part 8 of the Act to prove their identity.

The Criminal Appeal (Confiscation, Restraint and Receivership) Rules 2003 (SI 2003/428)

Made	*20th February 2003*
Laid before Parliament	*28th February 2003*
Came into force	*24th March 2003*

We, the Crown Court Rule Committee, in exercise of the powers conferred upon us by sections 84(1), 86 and 87(4) of the Supreme Court Act 1981,[1] and with the concurrence of the Treasury under section 84(7) of the Supreme Court Act 1981, hereby make the following Rules:

PART I

Introduction

Citation and commencement

1. These Rules may be cited as the Criminal Appeal (Confiscation, Restraint and Receivership) Rules 2003 and shall come into force on 24th March 2003.

Interpretation

2. In these Rules—
  "the 1968 Act" means the Criminal Appeal Act 1968;[2]
  "the 2002 Act" means the Proceeds of Crime Act 2002;[3]
  "appellant" means a person who brings or seeks to bring an appeal;
  "defendant" has the meaning given to it in Part 2 of the 2002 Act;
  "the Director of the Assets Recovery Agency" is the Director appointed under section 1 of the 2002 Act;
  "the Order" means the Proceeds of Crime Act 2002 (Appeals under Part 2) Order 2003;[4]
  "the principal rules" means the Criminal Appeal Rules 1968;[5]
  "respondent" means—
  (i)   a person other than the appellant who was a party to the proceedings in the Crown Court and who is affected by an appeal; and
  (ii) a person who is permitted by the Court of Appeal to be a party to the appeal;

---

[1] 1981 c. 54.   [2] 1968 c. 19.   [3] 2002 c. 29.   [4] S.I. 2003/82.
[5] S.I. 1968/1262, to which there are amendments not relevant in this context.

"the registrar" means the registrar of criminal appeals of the Court of Appeal;

references to the Court of Appeal are to the criminal division of the Court of Appeal;

a reference to a form is a reference to a form set out in the Schedule to these Rules or a form with the same effect;

references to a single judge are to any judge of the Court of Appeal or of the High Court.

PART II

Provisions Applicable only to Appeals under Section 31 of the 2002 Act

Notice of appeal

3.—(1) Where an appellant wishes to apply to the Court of Appeal for leave to appeal under section 31 of the 2002 Act, he must serve a notice of appeal in Form 1 on—

(a) the appropriate officer of the Crown Court; and

(b) the defendant.

(2) When the notice of the appeal is served on the defendant, it must be accompanied by a respondent's notice in Form 2 for the defendant to complete and a notice which—

(a) informs the defendant that the result of an appeal could be that the Court of Appeal would increase a confiscation order already imposed on him, make a confiscation order itself or direct the Crown Court to hold another confiscation hearing;

(b) informs the defendant of any right he has under article 6 of the Order to be present at the hearing of the appeal, although he may be in custody:

(c) invites the defendant to serve notice on the registrar if he wishes—

  (i) to apply to the Court of Appeal for leave to be present at proceedings for which leave is required under article 6 of the Order; or

  (ii) to present any argument to the Court of Appeal on the hearing of the application or, if leave is given, the appeal, and whether he wishes to present it in person or by means of a legal representative;

(d) draws to the defendant's attention the effect of rule 16 (supply of documentary and other exhibits); and

(e) advises the defendant to consult a solicitor as soon as possible.

(3) The appellant must provide the appropriate officer of the Crown Court with a certificate of service stating that he has served the notice of appeal on the defendant in accordance with paragraph (2) or explaining why he has been unable to effect service.

Respondent's notice

4.—(1) This rule applies where a defendant is served with a notice of appeal under rule 3.

(2) If the defendant wishes to oppose the application for leave to appeal, he must, not later than 14 days after the date on which he received the notice of appeal, serve on the registrar and on the appellant a notice in Form 2—

(a) stating the date on which he received the notice of appeal;

(b) summarising his response to the arguments of the appellant; and

(c) specifying the authorities which he intends to cite.

(3) The time for giving notice under this rule may be extended by the registrar, a single judge or by the Court of Appeal.

(4) Where the registrar refuses an application under paragraph (3) for the extension of time, the defendant shall be entitled to have his application determined by a single judge.

(5) Where a single judge refuses an application under paragraph (3) or (4) for the extension of time, the defendant shall be entitled to have his application determined by the Court of Appeal.

Amendment and abandonment of appeal

5.—(1) The appellant may amend a notice of appeal served under rule 3 or abandon an appeal under section 31 of the 2002 Act—

(a) without the permission of the Court at any time before the Court of Appeal have begun hearing the appeal; and

(b) with the permission of the Court after the Court of Appeal have begun hearing the appeal,

by serving notice in writing on the registrar.

(2) Where the appellant serves a notice abandoning an appeal under paragraph (1), he must send a copy of it to—

(a) the defendant;

(b) the proper officer of the court of trial; and

(c) the magistrates' court responsible for enforcing any confiscation order which the Crown Court has made.

(3) Where the appellant serves a notice amending a notice of appeal under paragraph (1), he must send a copy of it to the defendant.

(4) Where an appeal is abandoned under paragraph (1), the application for leave to appeal or appeal shall be treated, for the purposes of section 85 of the 2002 Act, as having been refused or dismissed by the Court of Appeal.

PART III

Provisions Applicable only to Appeals under Section 43 or 65 of the 2002 Act

Leave to appeal

6.—(1) Leave to appeal to the Court of Appeal under section 43 or section 65 of the 2002 Act will only be given where—

(a) the Court of Appeal considers that the appeal would have a real prospect of success; or

(b) there is some other compelling reason why the appeal should be heard.

(2) An order giving leave may limit the issues to be heard and be made subject to conditions.

Notice of appeal

7.—(1) Where an appellant wishes to apply to the Court of Appeal for leave to appeal under section 43 or 65 of the 2002 Act, he must serve a notice of appeal in Form 3 on the appropriate officer of the Crown Court.

(2) Unless the registrar, a single judge or the Court of Appeal directs otherwise, the appellant must serve the notice of appeal, accompanied by a respondent's notice in Form 4 for the respondent to complete, on—

    (a) each respondent;

    (b) any person who holds realisable property to which the appeal relates; and

    (c) any other person affected by the appeal,

    as soon as practicable and in any event not later than 7 days after the notice of appeal is served on the appropriate officer of the Crown Court.

(3) The appellant must serve the following documents with his notice of appeal—

    (a) four additional copies of the notice of appeal for the Court of Appeal;

    (b) four copies of any skeleton argument;

    (c) one sealed copy and four unsealed copies of any order being appealed;

    (d) four copies of any witness statement or affidavit in support of the application for leave to appeal;

    (e) four copies of a suitable record of the reasons for judgment of the Crown Court;

    (f) four copies of the bundle of documents used in the Crown Court proceedings from which the appeal lies.

(4) Where it is not possible to serve all of the documents referred to in paragraph (3), the appellant must indicate which documents have not yet been served and the reasons why they are not currently available.

(5) The appellant must provide the appropriate officer of the Crown Court with a certificate of service stating that he has served the notice of appeal on each respondent in accordance with paragraph (2) and including full details of each respondent or explaining why he has been unable to effect service.

Respondent's notice

8.—(1) This rule applies to an appeal under section 43 or 65 of the 2002 Act.

(2) A respondent may serve a respondent's notice on the registrar.

(3) A respondent who—

    (a) is seeking leave to appeal from the Court of Appeal; or

    (b) wishes to ask the Court of Appeal to uphold the decision of the Crown Court for reasons different from or additional to those given by the Crown Court,

    must serve a respondent's notice on the registrar.

(4) A respondent's notice must be in Form 4 and where the respondent seeks leave to appeal to the Court of Appeal it must be requested in the respondent's notice.

(5) A respondent's notice must be served on the registrar not later than 14 days after—

    (a) the date the respondent is served with notification that the Court of Appeal has given the appellant leave to appeal; or

    (b) the date the respondent is served with notification that the application for leave to appeal and the appeal itself are to be heard together.

(6) Unless the registrar, a single judge or the Court of Appeal directs otherwise, the respondent serving a respondent's notice must serve the notice on the appellant and any other respondent—

    (a) as soon as practicable; and

    (b) in any event not later than 7 days,

    after it is served on the registrar.

Amendment and abandonment of appeal

9.—(1) The appellant may amend a notice of appeal served under rule 7 or abandon an appeal under section 43 or 65 of the 2002 Act—

(a) without the permission of the Court at any time before the Court of Appeal have begun hearing the appeal; and

(b) with the permission of the Court after the Court of Appeal have begun hearing the appeal,

by serving notice in writing on the registrar.

(2) Where the appellant serves a notice under paragraph (1), he must send a copy of it to each respondent.

Stay

10. Unless the Court of Appeal or the Crown Court orders otherwise, an appeal under section 43 or 65 of the 2002 Act shall not operate as a stay of any order or decision of the Crown Court.

Striking out appeal notices and setting aside or imposing conditions on leave to appeal

11.—(1) The Court of Appeal may—

(a) strike out the whole or part of a notice of appeal served under rule 7; or

(b) impose or vary conditions upon which an appeal under section 43 or 65 of the 2002 Act may be brought.

(2) The Court of Appeal will only exercise its powers under paragraph (1) where there is a compelling reason for doing so.

(3) Where a party is present at the hearing at which leave to appeal was given, he may not subsequently apply for an order that the Court of Appeal exercise its powers under sub-paragraph (1)(b).

Hearing of appeals

12.—(1) This rule applies to appeals under section 43 or 65 of the 2002 Act.

(2) Every appeal will be limited to a review of the decision of the Crown Court unless the Court of Appeal considers that in the circumstances of an individual appeal it would be in the interests of justice to hold a re-hearing.

(3) The Court of Appeal will allow an appeal where the decision of the Crown Court was—

(a) wrong; or

(b) unjust because of a serious procedural or other irregularity in the proceedings in the Crown Court.

(4) The Court of Appeal may draw any inference of fact which it considers justified on the evidence.

(5) At the hearing of the appeal a party may not rely on a matter not contained in his notice of appeal unless the Court of Appeal gives permission.

PART IV

General provisions

Extension of time

13.—(1) An application to extend the time limit for giving notice of application for leave to appeal under Part 2 of the 2002 Act must—

    (a) be included in the notice of appeal; and

    (b) state the grounds for the application.

(2) The parties may not agree to extend any date or time limit set by these Rules or by the Order.

Other applications

14. Rule 3 of the principal rules (application relating to bail, leave to be present or reception of evidence)[6] shall apply in relation to an application—

    (a) by the defendant to be given leave by the court to be present at proceedings for which leave is required under article 6 of the Order;

    (b) by a party to an appeal under Part 2 of the 2002 Act that, under article 7 of the Order, a witness be ordered to attend or that the evidence of a witness be received by the Court of Appeal,

as it applies in relation to applications under Part I of the 1968 Act and the forms in which rule 3 of the principal rules require notice to be given may be modified as necessary.

Examination of witness by court

15.—(1) Rule 9 of the principal rules (examination of witness by court) shall apply in relation to an order of the court under article 7 of the Order to require a person to attend for examination as it applies in relation to such an order of the court under Part I of the 1968 Act.

(2) The form in which rule 9 of the principal rules requires the order of the court to be made may be modified as necessary.

Supply of documentary and other exhibits

16. Rule 8 of the principal rules (supply of documentary and other exhibits) shall apply in relation to an appellant or respondent under Part 2 of the 2002 Act as it applies in relation to an appellant and respondent under Part I of the 1968 Act.

Registrar's power to require information from court of trial

17. The registrar may require the Crown Court to provide the Court of Appeal with any assistance or information which they may require for the purposes of exercising their jurisdiction under Part 2 of the 2002 Act, the Order or these Rules.

Hearing by single judge

18. Rule 11 of the principal rules (hearing by single judge) shall apply in relation to a judge exercising any of the powers referred to in article 8 of the Order or the powers in rules 4(3) and (4), 7(2), 8(6) and 23(1), (2) and (4), as it applies in relation to a judge exercising the powers referred to in section 31(2) of the 1968 Act or rule 5 of the principal rules.

Determination by full court

19.—(1) Rule 12 of the principal rules (determination by full court) shall apply where a single judge has refused an application by a party to exercise in his favour any of the

---

[6] Rule 3 was amended by S.I. 1978/1118 and S.I. 1987/1977.back

powers listed in article 8 of the Order or the power in rule 4(3) or (4) as it applies where the judge has refused to exercise the powers referred to in section 31(2) of the 1968 Act.

(2) The form in which rule 12 of the principal rules requires notice to be given may be modified as necessary.

Notice of determination

20.—(1) This rule applies where a single judge or the Court of Appeal has determined an application or appeal under the Order or under Part 2 of the 2002 Act.

(2) The registrar must, as soon as practicable, serve notice of the determination on all of the parties to the proceedings.

(3) Where a single judge or the Court of Appeal has disposed of an application for leave to appeal or an appeal under section 31 of the 2002 Act, the registrar must also, as soon as practicable, serve the order on the proper officer of the court of trial and any magistrates' court responsible for enforcing any confiscation order which the Crown Court has made.

Record of proceedings and transcripts

21.—(1) Rules 18, 19 and 20 of the principal rules shall apply in relation to proceedings in respect of which an appeal lies to the Court of Appeal under Part 2 of the 2002 Act as they apply in relation to proceedings in respect of which an appeal lies to the Court of Appeal under Part I of the 1968 Act.

(2) The Director of the Assets Recovery Agency shall be treated as an interested party for the purposes of rule 19 of the principal rules as it applies by virtue of this rule.

Appeal to House of Lords

22.—(1) An application to the Court of Appeal for leave to appeal to the House of Lords under Part 2 of the 2002 Act must be made—

(a) orally after the decision of the Court of Appeal from which an appeal lies to the House of Lords; or

(b) in Form 5, in accordance with article 12 of the Order and served on the registrar.

(2) The application may be abandoned at any time before it is heard by the Court of Appeal by serving notice in writing on the registrar.

(3) Rule 11 of the principal rules (hearing by single judge) applies in relation to a judge exercising any of the powers referred to in article 15 of the Order, as it applies in relation to a judge exercising the powers referred to in section 31(2) of the 1968 Act or rule 5 of the principal rules.

(4) Rule 12 of the principal rules (determination by full court) applies where a single judge has refused an application by a party to exercise in his favour any of the powers listed in article 15 of the Order as it applies where the judge has refused to exercise the powers referred to in section 31(2) of the 1968 Act.

(5) The form in which rule 12 of the principal rules requires notice to be given may be modified as necessary.

Service of documents

23.—(1) Where these Rules require service of a document on the registrar then, unless the registrar, a single judge or the Court of Appeal directs otherwise, the document may be served by any of the following methods—

   (a) in the case of a defendant who is in custody, by delivering it to the person who has custody of him;

   (b) by addressing it to the registrar and delivering it at, or sending it by first-class post to, his office in the Royal Courts of Justice, London WC2.

(2) Where these Rules require service of a document on the appropriate officer of the Crown Court then, unless the registrar, a single judge or the Court of Appeal directs otherwise, the document may be served by any of the following methods—

   (a) in the case of a defendant who is in custody, by delivering it to the person who has custody of him;

   (b) by delivering it to, or sending it by first-class post to, the appropriate officer at the Crown Court centre at which the decision being appealed against was made.

(3) A person who has custody of a defendant and to whom the defendant delivers a document under paragraph (1)(a) or (2)(a) must endorse on it the date of delivery and forward it to the registrar or the appropriate officer of the Crown Court, as the case may be.

(4) Where these Rules require the service of a document on any other person then, unless the registrar, a single judge or the Court of Appeal directs otherwise, the document may be served by any of the following methods—

   (a) in all cases, by delivering the document personally to the party to be served;

   (b) if no solicitor is acting for the party to be served by delivering the document at, or by sending it by first-class post to, his residence or his last-known residence;

   (c) if a solicitor is acting for the party to be served—

     (i) by delivering the document at, or sending it by first-class post to, the solicitor's address for service; or

     (ii) where the solicitor's address for service includes a numbered box at a document exchange, by leaving the document at that document exchange or at a document exchange which transmits documents on every business day to that document exchange; or

     (iii) if the solicitor has indicated that he is willing to accept service by facsimile transmission, by sending a legible copy of the document by facsimile transmission to the solicitor's office.

SCHEDULE

Rule 2

FORM 1

Rule 3

The Court of Appeal Criminal Division

NOTICE and GROUNDS of application for leave to appeal and appeal by the prosecutor or the Director of the Assets Recovery Agency

Section 31 Proceeds of Crime Act 2002

CAO No. / /

The Appellant

(Prosecutor or Director of Assets Recovery Agency)

Name:

Address:

Post Code:

Confiscation Hearing at Crown Court

Name of Judge:

Dates of Hearing:

Indictment Number:

Ruling in respect of which application for leave to appeal is made:

Grounds of Appeal

1. Specify the question of fact or law in respect of which the appeal is brought (and where appropriate, such facts of the case as are necessary for the proper consideration of the question of law).

2. Summarise the arguments that you intend to put to the Court of Appeal (specifying any authorities to be cited).

Signature

Signature of appellant:

Date: **For Criminal Appeal Office Use**

Received (date):

Acknowledged (date):

FORM 2

Rules 3 and 4

The Court of Appeal Criminal Division

The Criminal Appeal (Confiscation, Restraint and Receivership) Rules 2003

NOTICE and GROUNDS of opposition to application for leave to appeal and appeal by Prosecutor or Director of Assets Recovery Agency

Section 31 Proceeds of Crime Act 2002

  CAO No. / /

The Respondent

(Give full name. If in custody give Prison and address where detained)

Surname:

Forenames:

Address:

Post Code:

Date of Birth:

Prison Index No (where approximate)

Confiscation Hearing at Crown Court

Name of Judge:

Dates of Hearing:

Indictment Number:

Date on which appellant's notice of appeal was received:

The Respondent is applying:

(Please tick as appropriate)

for an extension of time in which to give notice of opposition to appeal

(give reasons below)

to be given leave to be present on the hearing of the appeal or any proceedings preliminary or incidental to it (if respondent is in custody)

(give reasons below)

to oppose the application for leave to appeal

If you require an extention of time in which to give notice of opposition to appeal or wish to be present at the hearing of the appeal state reasons:

Grounds

Summarise the arguments you intend to put to the Court of Appeal, specifying any authorities to be cited.

Signature

Signature of respondent:	Details of any person signing on behalf of the respondent:	
	Name:	
	Solicitor/Counsel*	*Delete as appropriate
	Address:	
Date:	Post Code:	
	Solicitor's Ref:	

For Prison Use		**For Criminal Appeal Office Use**
This notice was handed to me by the respondent today.	Received (date):	
Signed: (Prison Officer)		
Date:	Acknowledged (date):	
Respondent's Index No:		

FORM 3

Rule 7

The Court of Appeal Criminal Division

NOTICE and GROUNDS of application for leave to appeal and appeal against restraint or receivership decision

Sections 43 and 65 Proceeds of Crime Act 2002

CAO No. / /

Details of the case

Crown Court centre:

Case number:

Name of defendant:

(sections 88(3) and 40(9) Proceeds of Crime Act 2002)

Are you (please tick as appropriate):

the person who applied for the order

the defendant

a person affected by the order or decision

Your (appellant's) name and address

(Give full name. If in custody give Prison and address where detained)

Your full name:

Address:

Post Code:

Date of Birth:

Prison Index No (where appropriate):

Details of the order(s), part(s) of order(s) or decision(s) you want to appeal

Name of Judge:

Date of order(s) or decision(s):

Description of order(s) or decision(s)

If only part of an order is appealed, write out that part (or those parts):

Grounds for appeal

Specify the question(s) in respect of which the appeal is brought.

Arguments in support of grounds

Summarise the arguments you intend to put to the Court of Appeal, specifying any authorities to be cited.

What decision are you asking the Court of Appeal to make?

I am asking that (please tick as appropriate):

the order(s), parts of order(s) or decision(s) I am appealing against be set aside

the order(s), parts of order(s) or decision(s) I am appealing against be varied and the following order(s) or decision(s) substituted

a re-hearing by the Crown Court be ordered

the Court of Appeal makes the following additional orders

Other applications

(section 43(3)(b) and section 65(6)(b) Proceeds of Crime Act 2002)

I wish the Court of Appeal to make the following additional orders.

Part A

I apply for an order (a draft of which is attached) that:

because:

Part B

I wish to rely on (please tick as appropriate):

evidence in Part C

witness statement (affidavit)

Part C

I wish to rely on the following evidence in support of this application:

Supporting documents

If you do not yet have a document that you intend to use to support your appeal, identify it, give the date when you expect it to be available and give the reasons why it is not currently available in the box below.

Please tick the papers you are filing with this notice and any you will be filing later.

Four additional copies of this notice

Four copies of your skeleton argument *(if separate)*

One sealed copy and four unsealed copies of any order being appealed

Four copies of any witness statements or affidavits in support of any application included in this notice

Four copies of a suitable record of the reasons for the judgment of the Crown Court

Four copies of the bundle of documents used in the Crown Court proceedings

Signature

Signature of appellant:	Details of any person signing on behalf of the appellant:	
	Name:	
	Solicitor/Counsel*	*Delete as appropriate
	Address:	
Date:	Post Code:	
	Solicitor's Ref:	

For Prison Use	**For Criminal Appeal Office Use**
This notice was handed to me by the appellant today.	Received (date):
Signed: (Prison Officer)	
Date:	Acknowledged (date):
Appellant's Index No:	

FORM 4

Rules 7 and 8

The Court of Appeal Criminal Division

NOTICE and GROUNDS of opposition to application for leave to appeal and appeal against restraint or receivership decision

Sections 43 and 65 Proceeds of Crime Act 2002

CAO No. / /

Details of the case

Crown Court centre:

Case number:

Name of defendant:

(sections 88(3) and 40(9) Proceeds of Crime Act 2002)

Are you (please tick as appropriate):

the person who applied for the order

the defendant

a person affected by the order or decision

478

Your (respondent's) name and address

Your full name:

Address:

Post Code:

Date of Birth:

Prison Index No. (where appropriate):

Details of the order(s), part(s) of order(s) or decision(s) you want to appeal

Name of Judge:

Date of order(s) or decision(s):

Description of order(s) or decision(s):

If only part of an order is appealed, write out that part (or those parts):

Grounds for appeal or for upholding the order

I (please tick as appropriate):

appeal the order(s) or decision(s) of the Crown Court

wish the Court of Appeal to uphold the order(s) or decision(s) of the Crown Court on different or additional grounds

because:

Arguments in support of grounds

Summarise the arguments you intend to put to the Court of Appeal, specifying any authorities to be cited.

What decision are you asking the appeal court to make?

I am asking that (please tick as appropriate):

the order(s), parts of order(s) or decision(s) I am appealing against be set aside

the order(s), parts of order(s) or decision(s) I am appealing against be varied and the following order(s) or decision(s) substituted

a re-hearing by the Crown Court be ordered

the Court of Appeal makes the following additional orders

the Court of Appeal upholds the order(s), parts of order(s) or decision(s) but for the following different or additional reasons

Other applications

(section 43(3)(b) and section 65(6)(b) Proceeds of Crime Act 2002)

I wish the Court of Appeal to make the following additional orders.

Part A

I apply for an order (a draft of which is attached) that:

because:

Part B

I wish to rely on (please tick as appropriate):

evidence in Part C

witness statement (affidavit)

Part C

I wish to rely on the following evidence in support of this application:

Supporting documents

If you do not yet have a document that you intend to use to support your appeal, identify it, give the date when you expect it to be available and give the reasons why it is not currently available in the box below.

Please tick the papers you are filing with this notice and any you will be filing later.

Four additional copies of this notice

Four copies of your skeleton argument *(if separate)*

Four copies of any witness statements or affidavits in support of any application included in this notice

Reasons why you have not supplied a document and date when you expect it to be available.

Signature

Signature of respondent:	Details of any person signing on behalf of the respondent:	
	Name:	
	Solicitor/Counsel*	*Delete as appropriate
	Address:	
Date:	Post Code:	
	Solicitor's Ref:	

For Prison Use	**For Criminal Appeal Office Use**
This notice was handed to me by the respondent today.	Received (date):
Signed: (Prison Officer)	
Date:	Acknowledged (date):
Respondent's Index No:	

FORM 5

Rule 22

The Court of Appeal Criminal Division

NOTICE of application for leave to appeal to the House of Lords

Sections 33, 44 and 66 Proceeds of Crime Act 2002

CAO No. / /

Details of the Defendant

(sections 88(3) and 40(9) Proceeds of Crime Act 2002)

(Give full name. If in custody give Prison and address where detained.)

Surname:

Forenames:

Address:

Post Code:

Date of Birth:

Prison Index No. (where appropriate):

Date the Court of Appeal gave reasons for its decision

The Defendant/Prosecutor/Other party to proceedings before the Court of Appeal will apply to the Court of Appeal:

(Delete as appropriate)

to certify that a point of law of general public importance is involved in the decision of the Court of Appeal

and if the Court so certifies:

for leave to appeal to the House of Lords against the decision of the Court of Appeal

to extend the time within which an application to the Court or the House of Lords for leave to appeal to the House of Lords may be made to be given leave to be present on the hearing of the appeal or any proceedings preliminary or incidental to it (if appellant is in custody)

Grounds of Application

Signature

Signature of appellant:	Details of any person signing on behalf of the appellant:	
	Name:	
	Solicitor/Counsel*	*Delete as appropriate
	Address:	
Date:	Post Code:	
	Solicitor's Ref:	
For Prison Use		**For Criminal Appeal Office Use**
This notice was handed to me by the appellant today.		Received (date):
Signed:	(Prison Officer)	
Date:		Acknowledged (date):
Appellant's Index No:		

EXPLANATORY NOTE

(This note is not part of the Rules)

These Rules make provision as to procedure in the criminal division of the Court of Appeal for the purposes of three new appeals introduced by the Proceeds of Crime Act 2002 ("the 2002 Act").

The first is an appeal under section 31 of the 2002 Act to the Court of Appeal (and from there to the House of Lords under section 33 of the 2002 Act) by the prosecutor or Director of the Assets Recovery Agency against a confiscation order or a failure of the Crown Court to make a confiscation order. The second is an appeal under section 43 of the 2002 Act to the Court of Appeal (and from there to the House of Lords under section 44 of the 2002 Act) in respect of decisions of the Crown Court about restraint orders. The third is an appeal under section 65 of the 2002 Act to the Court of Appeal (and from there to the House of Lords under section 66 of the 2002 Act) in respect of decisions of the Crown Court about receivers.

All three appeals are to be heard in the criminal division of the Court of Appeal by virtue of section 89(2) of the 2002 Act.

Part I of these Rules makes introductory provision. Part II deals with appeals under section 31 of the 2002 Act. Part III deals with appeals under sections 43 and 65 of the 2002 Act. Part IV makes general provision.

APPENDIX 10

The Money Laundering Regulations 2003 (SI 2003/3075)

Made   *28th November 2003*
Laid before Parliament   *28th November 2003*
Coming into force in accordance with regulation 1(2)

ARRANGEMENT OF REGULATIONS
PART I: GENERAL

PART II: OBLIGATIONS ON PERSONS WHO CARRY ON RELEVANT BUSINESS

PART III: MONEY SERVICE OPERATORS AND HIGH VALUE DEALERS

PART IV: MISCELLANEOUS

SCHEDULES

Whereas the Treasury are a government department designated[1] for the purposes of section 2(2) of the European Communities Act 1972[2] in relation to measures relating to preventing the use of the financial system for the purpose of money laundering;

Now therefore the Treasury, in exercise of the powers conferred on them by—

    (i) section 2(2) of the European Communities Act 1972, and

---

[1] S.I. 1992/1711.

[2] 1972 c. 68. By virtue of the amendment of section 1(2) made by section 1 of the European Economic Area Act 1993 (c. 51) regulations may be made under section 2(2) to implement obligations of the United Kingdom created by or arising under the Agreement on the European Economic Area signed at Oporto on 2nd May 1992 (Cm 2073) and the Protocol adjusting that Agreement signed at Brussels on 17th March 1993 (Cm 2183).

(ii) sections 168(4)(b), 402(1)(b), 417(1)[3] and 428(3) of the Financial Services and Markets Act 2000,[4]

hereby make the following Regulations:

PART I: GENERAL

Citation, commencement etc.

1.—(1) These Regulations may be cited as the Money Laundering Regulations 2003.

(2) These Regulations come into force—

  (a) for the purposes of regulation 10 in so far as it relates to a person who acts as a high value dealer, on 1st April 2004;

  (b) for the purposes of regulation 2(3)(h), on 31st October 2004;

  (c) for the purposes of regulation 2(3)(i), on 14th January 2005;

  (d) for all other purposes, on 1st March 2004.

(3) These Regulations are prescribed for the purposes of sections 168(4)(b) and 402(1)(b) of the 2000 Act.

(4) The following Regulations are revoked—

  (a) the Money Laundering Regulations 1993;[5]

  (b) the Financial Services and Markets Act 2000 (Regulations Relating to Money Laundering) Regulations 2001;[6]

  (c) the Money Laundering Regulations 2001.[7]

Interpretation

2.—(1) In these Regulations—

"the 2000 Act" means the Financial Services and Markets Act 2000;

"applicant for business" means a person seeking to form a business relationship, or carry out a one-off transaction, with another person acting in the course of relevant business carried on by that other person in the United Kingdom;

"applicant for registration" means an applicant for registration as a money service operator, or as a high value dealer;

"the appropriate judicial authority" means—

  (a) in England and Wales, a magistrates' court,

  (b) in Scotland, the sheriff,

  (c) in Northern Ireland, a court of summary jurisdiction;

"authorised person" has the meaning given by section 31(2) of the 2000 Act;

"the Authority" means the Financial Services Authority;

"the Banking Consolidation Directive" means Directive 2000/12/EC of the European Parliament and of the Council of 20th March 2000 relating to the taking up and pursuit of the business of credit institutions as last amended by Directive 2002/87/EC of the European Parliament and of the Council of 16th December 2002;[8]

---

[3] See the definition of "prescribed".   [4] 2000 c. 8.

[5] S.I. 1993/1933, amended by S.I. 1994/1696, S.I. 1998/1129, S.I. 2000/2952, S.I. 2001/3641 and 3649.

[6] S.I. 2001/1819.   [7] S.I. 2001/3641.

[8] OJ L 126, 26.5.2000, p.1; OJ L 35, 11.2.2003, p.1.

"business relationship" means any arrangement the purpose of which is to facilitate the carrying out of transactions on a frequent, habitual or regular basis where the total amount of any payments to be made by any person to any other in the course of the arrangement is not known or capable of being ascertained at the outset;

"cash" means notes, coins or travellers' cheques in any currency;

"the Commissioners" means the Commissioners of Customs and Excise;

"constable" includes a person commissioned by the Commissioners and a person authorised for the purposes of these Regulations by the Director General of the National Criminal Intelligence Service;

"EEA State" means a State which is a contracting party to the agreement on the European Economic Area signed at Oporto on 2nd May 1992 as it has effect for the time being;

"estate agency work" has the meaning given by section 1 of the Estate Agents Act 1979[9] save for the omission of the words "(including a business in which he is employed)" in subsection (1) and includes a case where, in relation to a disposal or acquisition, the person acts as principal;

"high value dealer" means a person who carries on the activity mentioned in paragraph (2)(n);

"the Life Assurance Consolidation Directive" means Directive 2002/83/EC of the European Parliament and of the Council of 5th November 2002 concerning life assurance;[10]

"justice" means a justice of the peace or, in relation to Scotland, a justice within the meaning of section 307 of the Criminal Procedure (Scotland) Act 1995;[11]

"money laundering" means an act which falls within section 340(11) of the Proceeds of Crime Act 2002[12] or an offence under section 18 of the Terrorism Act 2000;[13]

"the Money Laundering Directive" means Council Directive 91/308/EEC of 10th June 1991 on prevention of the use of the financial system for the purpose of money laundering as amended by Directive 2001/97/EC of the European Parliament and of the Council of 4th December 2001;[14]

"money service business" means any of the activities mentioned in paragraph (2)(d) (so far as not excluded by paragraph (3)) when carried on by way of business;

"money service operator" means a person who carries on money service business other than a person who carries on relevant business falling within any of sub-paragraphs (a) to (c) of paragraph (2);

"nominated officer" has the meaning given by regulation 7;

"officer" (except in regulations 7, 10 and 27) has the meaning given by section 1(1) of the Customs and Excise Management Act 1979;[15]

"officer in overall charge of the investigation" means the person whose name and address are endorsed on the order concerned as being the officer so in charge;

---

[9] 1979 c. 38. Section 1 was amended by the Law Reform (Miscellaneous Provisions) (Scotland) Act 1985 (c. 73), Schedule 1, Pt I, para. 40, the Planning (Consequential Provisions) Act 1990 (c. 11), Schedule 2, para. 42, the Planning (Consequential Provisions) (Scotland) Act 1997 (c. 11), Schedule 2, para. 28 and by S.I. 2001/1283.

[10] OJ L 345, 19.12.2002, p.1.   [11] 1995 c. 46.   [12] 2002 c. 29.

[13] 2000 c. 11.   [14] OJ L 166, 28.6.1991, p.77; OJ L 344, 28.12.2001, p.76.

[15] 1979 c. 2.

487

"one-off transaction" means any transaction other than one carried out in the course of an existing business relationship;

"operator" means a money service operator;

"recorded information" includes information recorded in any form and any document of any nature whatsoever;

"registered number" has the meaning given by regulation 9(2);

"relevant business" has the meaning given by paragraph (2);

"the review procedure" means the procedure under regulation 21;

"satisfactory evidence of identity" has the meaning given by paragraphs (5) and (6);

"supervisory authority" has the meaning given by paragraphs (7) and (8);

"tribunal" means a VAT and duties tribunal.

(2) For the purposes of these Regulations, "relevant business" means—

    (a) the regulated activity of—

        (i)   accepting deposits;

        (ii)   effecting or carrying out contracts of long-term insurance when carried on by a person who has received official authorisation pursuant to Article 4 or 51 of the Life Assurance Consolidation Directive;

        (iii) dealing in investments as principal or as agent;

        (iv) arranging deals in investments;

        (v)   managing investments;

        (vi) safeguarding and administering investments;

        (vii) sending dematerialised instructions;

        (viii) establishing (and taking other steps in relation to) collective investment schemes;

        (ix) advising on investments; or

        (x)   issuing electronic money;

    (b) the activities of the National Savings Bank;

    (c) any activity carried on for the purpose of raising money authorised to be raised under the National Loans Act 1968[16] under the auspices of the Director of Savings;

    (d) the business of operating a bureau de change, transmitting money (or any representation of monetary value) by any means or cashing cheques which are made payable to customers;

    (e) any of the activities in points 1 to 12 or 14 of Annex 1 to the Banking Consolidation Directive (which activities are, for convenience, set out in Schedule 1 to these Regulations) when carried on by way of business, ignoring an activity falling within any of sub-paragraphs (a) to (d);

    (f) estate agency work;

    (g) operating a casino by way of business;

    (h) the activities of a person appointed to act as an insolvency practitioner within the meaning of section 388 of the Insolvency Act 1986[17] or Article 3 of the Insolvency (Northern Ireland) Order 1989;[18]

    (i) the provision by way of business of advice about the tax affairs of another person by a body corporate or unincorporate or, in the case of a sole practitioner, by an individual;

---

[16] 1968 c. 13.   [17] 1986 c. 45.   [18] S.I. 1989/2405 (N.I. 19).

(j) the provision by way of business of accountancy services by a body corporate or unincorporate or, in the case of a sole practitioner, by an individual;

(k) the provision by way of business of audit services by a person who is eligible for appointment as a company auditor under section 25 of the Companies Act 1989[19] or Article 28 of the Companies (Northern Ireland) Order 1990;[20]

(l) the provision by way of business of legal services by a body corporate or unincorporate or, in the case of a sole practitioner, by an individual and which involves participation in a financial or real property transaction (whether by assisting in the planning or execution of any such transaction or otherwise by acting for, or on behalf of, a client in any such transaction);

(m) the provision by way of business of services in relation to the formation, operation or management of a company or a trust; or

(n) the activity of dealing in goods of any description by way of business (including dealing as an auctioneer) whenever a transaction involves accepting a total cash payment of 15,000 euro or more.

(3) Paragraph (2) does not apply to—

(a) the issue of withdrawable share capital within the limit set by section 6 of the Industrial and Provident Societies Act 1965[21] by a society registered under that Act;

(b) the acceptance of deposits from the public within the limit set by section 7(3) of that Act by such a society;

(c) the issue of withdrawable share capital within the limit set by section 6 of the Industrial and Provident Societies Act (Northern Ireland) 1969[22] by a society registered under that Act;

(d) the acceptance of deposits from the public within the limit set by section 7(3) of that Act by such a society;

(e) activities carried on by the Bank of England;

(f) any activity in respect of which an exemption order under section 38 of the 2000 Act has effect if it is carried on by a person who is for the time being specified in the order or falls within a class of persons so specified;

(g) any activity (other than one falling within sub-paragraph (f)) in respect of which a person was an exempted person for the purposes of section 45 of the Financial Services Act 1986[23] immediately before its repeal;

(h) the regulated activities of arranging deals in investments or advising on investments, in so far as the investment consists of rights under a regulated mortgage contract;

(i) the regulated activities of dealing in investments as agent, arranging deals in investments, managing investments or advising on investments, in so far as the investment consists of rights under, or any right to or interest in, a contract of insurance which is not a qualifying contract of insurance; or

(j) the Official Solicitor to the Supreme Court when acting as trustee in his official capacity.

(4) The following must be read with section 22 of the 2000 Act, any relevant order under that section and Schedule 2 to that Act—

---

[19] 1989 c. 40.   [20] S.I. 1990/593 (N.I. 5).   [21] 1965 c. 12.   [22] 1969 c. 24 (N.I.).
[23] 1986 c. 60. This Act was repealed as from 1st December 2001 by S.I. 2001/3649, art. 3(1)(c).

   (a) paragraphs (2)(a) and (3)(h) and (i);
   (b) regulation 25 (authorised persons operating a bureau de change);
   (c) references in these Regulations to a contract of long-term insurance.
(5) For the purposes of these Regulations, and subject to paragraph (6), "satisfactory evidence of identity" is evidence which is reasonably capable of establishing (and does in fact establish to the satisfaction of the person who obtains it) that the applicant for business is the person he claims to be.
(6) Where the person who obtains the evidence mentioned in paragraph (5) knows or has reasonable grounds for believing that the applicant for business is a money service operator, satisfactory evidence of identity must also include the applicant's registered number (if any).
(7) For the purposes of these Regulations, each of the following is a supervisory authority—
(a) the Bank of England;
   (b) the Authority;
   (c) the Council of Lloyd's;
   (d) the Office of Fair Trading;
   (e) the Occupational Pensions Regulatory Authority;
   (f) a body which is a designated professional body for the purposes of Part 20 of the 2000 Act;
   (g) the Gaming Board for Great Britain.
(8) The Secretary of State and the Treasury are each a supervisory authority in the exercise, in relation to a person carrying on relevant business, of their respective functions under the enactments relating to companies or insolvency or under the 2000 Act.
(9) In these Regulations, references to amounts in euro include references to equivalent amounts in another currency.
(10) For the purpose of the application of these Regulations to Scotland, "real property" means "heritable property".

PART II: OBLIGATIONS ON PERSONS WHO CARRY ON RELEVANT BUSINESS

Systems and training etc. to prevent money laundering

3.—(1) Every person must in the course of relevant business carried on by him in the United Kingdom—
   (a) comply with the requirements of regulations 4 (identification procedures), 6 (record-keeping procedures) and 7 (internal reporting procedures);
   (b) establish such other procedures of internal control and communication as may be appropriate for the purposes of forestalling and preventing money laundering; and
   (c) take appropriate measures so that relevant employees are—
      (i) made aware of the provisions of these Regulations, Part 7 of the Proceeds of Crime Act 2002 (money laundering) and sections 18 and 21A of the Terrorism Act 2000;[24] and

---

[24] Section 21A was inserted by the Anti-terrorism, Crime and Security Act 2001 (c. 24), Schedule 2, Part 3, para. 5.

      (ii) given training in how to recognise and deal with transactions which may be related to money laundering.

(2) A person who contravenes this regulation is guilty of an offence and liable—

    (a) on conviction on indictment, to imprisonment for a term not exceeding 2 years, to a fine or to both;

    (b) on summary conviction, to a fine not exceeding the statutory maximum.

(3) In deciding whether a person has committed an offence under this regulation, the court must consider whether he followed any relevant guidance which was at the time concerned—

    (a) issued by a supervisory authority or any other appropriate body;

    (b) approved by the Treasury; and

    (c) published in a manner approved by the Treasury as appropriate in their opinion to bring the guidance to the attention of persons likely to be affected by it.

(4) An appropriate body is any body which regulates or is representative of any trade, profession, business or employment carried on by the alleged offender.

(5) In proceedings against any person for an offence under this regulation, it is a defence for that person to show that he took all reasonable steps and exercised all due diligence to avoid committing the offence.

(6) Where a person is convicted of an offence under this regulation, he shall not also be liable to a penalty under regulation 20 (power to impose penalties).

Identification procedures

4.—(1) In this regulation and in regulations 5 to 7—

    (a) "A" means a person who carries on relevant business in the United Kingdom; and

    (b) "B" means an applicant for business.

(2) This regulation applies if—

    (a) A and B form, or agree to form, a business relationship;

    (b) in respect of any one-off transaction—

        (i) A knows or suspects that the transaction involves money laundering; or

        (ii) payment of 15,000 euro or more is to be made by or to B; or

    (c) in respect of two or more one-off transactions, it appears to A (whether at the outset or subsequently) that the transactions are linked and involve, in total, the payment of 15,000 euro or more by or to B.

(3) A must maintain identification procedures which—

    (a) require that as soon as is reasonably practicable after contact is first made between A and B—

        (i) B must produce satisfactory evidence of his identity; or

        (ii) such measures specified in the procedures must be taken in order to produce satisfactory evidence of B's identity;

    (b) take into account the greater potential for money laundering which arises when B is not physically present when being identified;

    (c) require that where satisfactory evidence of identity is not obtained, the business relationship or one-off transaction must not proceed any further; and

    (d) require that where B acts or appears to act for another person, reasonable measures must be taken for the purpose of establishing the identity of that person.

Exceptions

5.—(1) Except in circumstances falling within regulation 4(2)(b)(i), identification procedures under regulation 4 do not require A to take steps to obtain evidence of any person's identity in any of the following circumstances.

(2) Where A has reasonable grounds for believing that B—

    (a) carries on in the United Kingdom relevant business falling within any of sub-paragraphs (a) to (e) of regulation 2(2), is not a money service operator and, if carrying on an activity falling within regulation 2(2)(a), is an authorised person with permission under the 2000 Act to carry on that activity;

    (b) does not carry on relevant business in the United Kingdom but does carry on comparable activities to those falling within sub-paragraph (a) and is covered by the Money Laundering Directive; or

    (c) is regulated by an overseas regulatory authority (within the meaning given by section 82 of the Companies Act 1989) and is based or incorporated in a country (other than an EEA State) whose law contains comparable provisions to those contained in the Money Laundering Directive.

(3) Where—

    (a) A carries out a one-off transaction with or for a third party pursuant to an introduction effected by a person who has provided a written assurance that evidence of the identity of all third parties introduced by him will have been obtained and recorded under procedures maintained by him;

    (b) that person identifies the third party; and

    (c) A has reasonable grounds for believing that that person falls within any of sub-paragraphs (a) to (c) of paragraph (2).

(4) In relation to a contract of long-term insurance—

    (a) in connection with a pension scheme taken out by virtue of a person's contract of employment or occupation where the contract of long-term insurance—

        (i) contains no surrender clause; and

        (ii) may not be used as collateral for a loan; or

    (b) in respect of which a premium is payable—

        (i) in one instalment of an amount not exceeding 2,500 euro; or

        (ii) periodically and where the total payable in respect of any calendar year does not exceed 1,000 euro.

(5) Where the proceeds of a one-off transaction are payable to B but are instead directly reinvested on his behalf in another transaction—

    (a) of which a record is kept; and

    (b) which can result only in another reinvestment made on B's behalf or in a payment made directly to B.

Record-keeping procedures

6.—(1) A must maintain procedures which require the retention of the records prescribed in paragraph (2) for the period prescribed in paragraph (3).

(2) The records are—

    (a) where evidence of identity has been obtained under the procedures stipulated by regulation 4 (identification procedures) or pursuant to regulation 8 (casinos)—

        (i) a copy of that evidence;

        (ii) information as to where a copy of that evidence may be obtained; or

      (iii) information enabling the evidence of identity to be re-obtained, but only where it is not reasonably practicable for A to comply with paragraph (i) or (ii); and

    (b) a record containing details relating to all transactions carried out by A in the course of relevant business.

(3) In relation to the records mentioned in paragraph (2)(a), the period is—

    (a) where A and B have formed a business relationship, at least five years commencing with the date on which the relationship ends; or

    (b) in the case of a one-off transaction (or a series of such transactions), at least five years commencing with the date of the completion of all activities taking place in the course of that transaction (or, as the case may be, the last of the transactions).

(4) In relation to the records mentioned in paragraph (2)(b), the period is at least five years commencing with the date on which all activities taking place in the course of the transaction in question were completed.

(5) Where A is an appointed representative, his principal must ensure that A complies with this regulation in respect of any relevant business carried out by A for which the principal has accepted responsibility pursuant to section 39(1) of the 2000 Act.

(6) Where the principal fails to do so, he is to be treated as having contravened regulation 3 and he, as well as A, is guilty of an offence.

(7) "Appointed representative" has the meaning given by section 39(2) of the 2000 Act and "principal" has the meaning given by section 39(1) of that Act.

Internal reporting procedures

7.—(1) A must maintain internal reporting procedures which require that—

    (a) a person in A's organisation is nominated to receive disclosures under this regulation ("the nominated officer");

    (b) anyone in A's organisation to whom information or other matter comes in the course of relevant business as a result of which he knows or suspects or has reasonable grounds for knowing or suspecting that a person is engaged in money laundering must, as soon as is practicable after the information or other matter comes to him, disclose it to the nominated officer or a person authorised for the purposes of these Regulations by the Director General of the National Criminal Intelligence Service;

    (c) where a disclosure is made to the nominated officer, he must consider it in the light of any relevant information which is available to A and determine whether it gives rise to such knowledge or suspicion or such reasonable grounds for knowledge or suspicion; and

    (d) where the nominated officer does so determine, the information or other matter must be disclosed to a person authorised for the purposes of these Regulations by the Director General of the National Criminal Intelligence Service.

(2) Paragraph (1) does not apply where A is an individual who neither employs nor acts in association with any other person.

(3) Paragraph (1)(b) does not apply in relation to a professional legal adviser where the information or other matter comes to him in privileged circumstances.

(4) Information or other matter comes to a professional legal adviser in privileged circumstances if it is communicated or given to him—

    (a) by (or by a representative of) a client of his in connection with the giving by the adviser of legal advice to the client;

(b) by (or by a representative of) a person seeking legal advice from the adviser; or

(c) by a person in connection with legal proceedings or contemplated legal proceedings.

(5) But paragraph (4) does not apply to information or other matter which is communicated or given with the intention of furthering a criminal purpose.

(6) "Professional legal adviser" includes any person in whose hands information or other matter may come in privileged circumstances.

Casinos

8.—(1) A person who operates a casino by way of business in the United Kingdom must obtain satisfactory evidence of identity of any person before allowing that person to use the casino's gaming facilities.

(2) A person who fails to do so is to be treated as having contravened regulation 3.

PART III: MONEY SERVICE OPERATORS AND HIGH VALUE DEALERS

Registration

Registers of money service operators and high value dealers

9.—(1) The Commissioners must maintain a register of operators.

(2) The Commissioners must allocate to every registered operator a number, which is to be known as his registered number.

(3) The Commissioners must maintain a register of high value dealers.

(4) The Commissioners may keep the registers in any form they think fit.

Requirement to be registered

10.—(1) A person who acts as an operator or as a high value dealer must first be registered by the Commissioners.

(2) An applicant for registration must—

(a) make an application to be registered in such manner as the Commissioners may direct; and

(b) furnish the following information to the Commissioners—

    (i)   his name and (if different) the name of the business;

    (ii) his VAT registration number or, if he is not registered for VAT, any other reference number issued to him by the Commissioners;

    (iii) the nature of the business;

    (iv) the address of each of the premises at which he proposes to carry on the business;

    (v) any agency or franchise agreement relating to the business, and the names and addresses of all relevant principals, agents, franchisors or franchisees;

    (vi) the name of the nominated officer (if any); and

    (vii) whether any person concerned (or proposed to be concerned) in the management, control or operation of the business has been convicted of money laundering or an offence under these Regulations.

(3) At any time after receiving an application for registration and before determining it, the Commissioners may require the applicant for registration to furnish them, within 21

days beginning with the date of being requested to do so, with such further information as they reasonably consider necessary to enable them to determine the application.

(4) Any information to be furnished to the Commissioners under this regulation must be in such form or verified in such manner as they may specify.

(5) In this regulation, "the business" means money service business (or, in the case of a high value dealer, the business of dealing in goods) which the applicant for registration carries on or proposes to carry on.

(6) In paragraph (2)(b)(vii), the reference to "money laundering or an offence under these Regulations" includes an offence referred to in regulation 2(3) of the Money Laundering Regulations 1993 or an offence under regulation 5 of those Regulations.

Supplementary information

11.—(1) If at any time after a person has furnished the Commissioners with any information under regulation 10—

(a) there is a change affecting any matter contained in that information; or

(b) it becomes apparent to that person that the information contains an inaccuracy;

he must supply the Commissioners with details of the change or, as the case may be, a correction of the inaccuracy (hereafter "supplementary information") within 30 days beginning with the date of the occurrence of the change (or the discovery of the inaccuracy) or within such later time as may be agreed with the Commissioners.

(2) The supplementary information must be supplied in such manner as the Commissioners may direct.

(3) The obligation in paragraph (1) applies also to changes affecting any matter contained in any supplementary information supplied pursuant to this regulation.

Determination of application to register

12.—(1) The Commissioners may refuse to register an applicant for registration if, and only if—

(a) any requirement of—

(i) paragraphs (2) to (4) of regulation 10 (requirement to be registered);

(ii) regulation 11 (supplementary information); or

(iii) regulation 14 (fees);

has not been complied with; or

(b) it appears to them that any information furnished pursuant to regulation 10 or 11 is false or misleading in a material particular.

(2) The Commissioners must, by the end of the period of 45 days beginning with the date on which they receive the application or, where applicable, the date on which they receive any further information required under regulation 10(3), give notice in writing to the applicant for registration of—

(a) their decision to register him and, in the case of an applicant for registration as an operator, his registered number; or

(b) the following matters—

(i) their decision not to register him;

(ii) the reasons for their decision;

(iii) the review procedure; and

(iv) the right to appeal to a tribunal.

Cancellation of registration

13.—(1) The Commissioners may cancel the registration of an operator or high value dealer if, at any time after registration, it appears to them that they would have had grounds to refuse registration under paragraph (1) of regulation 12 (determination of application to register).

(2) Where the Commissioners decide to cancel the registration of an operator or high value dealer, they must forthwith inform him, in writing, of—

(a) their decision and the date from which the cancellation takes effect;

(b) the reasons for their decision;

(c) the review procedure; and

(d) the right to appeal to a tribunal.

Fees

14.—(1) The Commissioners may charge a fee—

(a) to an applicant for registration; and

(b) to an operator or high value dealer annually on the anniversary of his registration by them under these Regulations.

(2) The Commissioners may charge under paragraph (1) such fees as they consider will enable them to meet any expenses incurred by them in carrying out any of their functions under these Regulations or for any incidental purpose.

(3) Without prejudice to the generality of paragraph (2), a fee may be charged in respect of each of the premises at which the operator, high value dealer or applicant for registration carries on (or proposes to carry on) money service business or relevant business falling within regulation 2(2)(n).

Powers of the Commissioners

Entry, inspection etc.

15.—(1) Where an officer has reasonable cause to believe that any premises are used in connection with money service business or relevant business falling within regulation 2(2)(n), he may at any reasonable time enter and inspect the premises and inspect any recorded information or currency found on the premises.

(2) An operator or high value dealer must—

(a) furnish to an officer, within such time and in such form as the officer may reasonably require, such information relating to the business as the officer may reasonably specify; and

(b) upon demand made by the officer, produce or cause to be produced for inspection by the officer at such place, and at such time, as the officer may reasonably require, any recorded information relating to the business.

(3) An officer may take copies of, or make extracts from, any recorded information produced under paragraph (2).

Order for access to recorded information

16.—(1) Where, on an application by an officer, a justice is satisfied that there are reasonable grounds for believing—

(a) that an offence under these Regulations is being, has been or is about to be committed by an operator or high value dealer; and

    (b) that any recorded information which may be required as evidence for the purpose of any proceedings in respect of such an offence is in the possession of any person;

he may make an order under this regulation.

(2) An order under this regulation is an order that the person who appears to the justice to be in possession of the recorded information to which the application relates must—

    (a) give an officer access to it;

    (b) permit an officer to take copies of, or make extracts from, any information produced; or

    (c) permit an officer to remove and take away any of it which he reasonably considers necessary;

not later than the end of the period of 7 days beginning with the date of the order or the end of such longer period as the order may specify.

(3) Where the recorded information consists of information stored in any electronic form, an order under this regulation has effect as an order to produce the information in a form in which it is visible and legible, or from which it can readily be produced in a visible and legible form, and, if the officer wishes to remove it, in a form in which it can be removed.

Procedure where recorded information is removed

17.—(1) An officer who removes any recorded information in the exercise of a power conferred by regulation 16 must, if so requested by a person showing himself—

    (a) to be the occupier of premises from which the information was removed; or

    (b) to have had custody or control of the information immediately before the removal;

provide that person with a record of what he has removed.

(2) The officer must provide the record within a reasonable time from the making of the request for it.

(3) Subject to paragraph (7), if a request for permission to be granted access to anything which—

    (a) has been removed by an officer; and

    (b) is retained by the Commissioners for the purposes of investigating an offence;

is made to the officer in overall charge of the investigation by a person who had custody or control of the thing immediately before it was so removed or by someone acting on behalf of such a person, that officer must allow the person who made the request access to it under the supervision of an officer.

(4) Subject to paragraph (7), if a request for a photograph or copy of any such thing is made to the officer in overall charge of the investigation by a person who had custody or control of the thing immediately before it was so removed, or by someone acting on behalf of such a person, that officer must—

    (a) allow the person who made the request access to it under the supervision of an officer for the purpose of photographing it or copying it; or

    (b) photograph or copy it, or cause it to be photographed or copied.

(5) Where anything is photographed or copied under paragraph (4)(b), the photograph or copy must be supplied to the person who made the request.

(6) The photograph or copy must be supplied within a reasonable time from the making of the request.

(7) There is no duty under this regulation to grant access to, or supply a photograph or a copy of, anything if the officer in overall charge of the investigation for the purposes of

which it was removed has reasonable grounds for believing that to do so would prejudice—

(a) that investigation;

(b) the investigation of an offence other than the offence for the purposes of the investigation of which the recorded information was removed; or

(c) any criminal proceedings which may be brought as a result of—

    (i) the investigation of which he is in charge; or

    (ii) any such investigation as is mentioned in sub-paragraph (b).

Failure to comply with requirements under regulation 17

18.—(1) Where, on an application made as mentioned in paragraph (2), the appropriate
judicial authority is satisfied that a person has failed to comply with a requirement
imposed by regulation 17, the authority may order that person to comply with the
requirement within such time and in such manner as may be specified in the order.

(2) An application under paragraph (1) may only be made—

(a) in the case of a failure to comply with any of the requirements imposed by regulation 17(1) and (2), by the occupier of the premises from which the thing in question
was removed or by the person who had custody or control of it immediately before
it was so removed;

(b) in any other case, by the person who had such custody or control.

(3) In England and Wales and Northern Ireland, an application for an order under this
regulation is to be made by complaint; and sections 21 and 42(2) of the Interpretation
Act (Northern Ireland) 1954[25] apply as if any reference in those provisions to any
enactment included a reference to this regulation.

Entry, search etc.

19.—(1) Where a justice is satisfied on information on oath that there is reasonable ground
for suspecting that an offence under these Regulations is being, has been or is about to
be committed by an operator or high value dealer on any premises or that evidence of
the commission of such an offence is to be found there, he may issue a warrant in writing authorising any officer to enter those premises, if necessary by force, at any time
within one month from the time of the issue of the warrant and search them.

(2) A person who enters the premises under the authority of the warrant may—

(a) take with him such other persons as appear to him to be necessary;

(b) seize and remove any documents or other things whatsoever found on the premises
which he has reasonable cause to believe may be required as evidence for the purpose of proceedings in respect of an offence under these Regulations; and

(c) search or cause to be searched any person found on the premises whom he has reasonable cause to believe to be in possession of any such documents or other things;
but no woman or girl may be searched except by a woman.

(3) The powers conferred by a warrant under this regulation may not be exercised—

(a) outside such times of day as may be specified in the warrant; or

(b) if the warrant so provides, otherwise than in the presence of a constable in uniform.

---

[25] 1954 c. 33 (N.I.).

(4) An officer seeking to exercise the powers conferred by a warrant under this regulation or, if there is more than one such officer, that one of them who is in charge of the search must provide a copy of the warrant endorsed with his name as follows—

  (a) if the occupier of the premises concerned is present at the time the search is to begin, the copy must be supplied to the occupier;

  (b) if at that time the occupier is not present but a person who appears to the officer to be in charge of the premises is present, the copy must be supplied to that person;

  (c) if neither sub-paragraph (a) nor (b) applies, the copy must be left in a prominent place on the premises.

Penalties, review and appeals

Power to impose penalties

20.—(1) The Commissioners may impose a penalty of such amount as they consider appropriate, not exceeding £5,000, on a person to whom regulation 10 (requirement to be registered) applies, where that person fails to comply with any requirement in regulation 3 (systems and training etc. to prevent money laundering), 10, 11 (supplementary information), 14 (fees) or 15 (entry, inspection etc.).

(2) The Commissioners must not impose a penalty on a person where there are reasonable grounds for them to be satisfied that the person took all reasonable steps for securing that the requirement would be complied with.

(3) Where the Commissioners decide to impose a penalty under this regulation, they must forthwith inform the person, in writing, of—

  (a) their decision to impose the penalty and its amount;

  (b) their reasons for imposing the penalty;

  (c) the review procedure; and

  (d) the right to appeal to a tribunal.

(4) Where a person is liable to a penalty under this regulation, the Commissioners may reduce the penalty to such amount (including nil) as they think proper.

Review procedure

21.—(1) This regulation applies to the following decisions of the Commissioners—

  (a) a decision under regulation 12 to refuse to register an applicant;

  (b) a decision under regulation 13 to cancel the registration of an operator or high value dealer;

  (c) a decision under regulation 20 to impose a penalty.

(2) Any person who is the subject of a decision as mentioned in paragraph (1) may by notice in writing to the Commissioners require them to review that decision.

(3) The Commissioners need not review any decision unless the notice requiring the review is given before the end of the period of 45 days beginning with the date on which written notification of the decision was first given to the person requiring the review.

(4) A person may give a notice under this regulation to require a decision to be reviewed for a second or subsequent time only if—

  (a) the grounds on which he requires the further review are that the Commissioners did not, on any previous review, have the opportunity to consider certain facts or other matters; and

(b) he does not, on the further review, require the Commissioners to consider any facts or matters which were considered on a previous review except in so far as they are relevant to any issue to which the facts or matters not previously considered relate.

(5) Where the Commissioners are required under this regulation to review any decision they must either—

(a) confirm the decision; or

(b) withdraw or vary the decision and take such further steps (if any) in consequence of the withdrawal or variation as they consider appropriate.

(6) Where the Commissioners do not, within 45 days beginning with the date on which the review was required by a person, give notice to that person of their determination of the review, they are to be assumed for the purposes of these Regulations to have confirmed the decision.

Appeals to a VAT and duties tribunal

22. On an appeal from any decision by the Commissioners on a review under regulation 21, the tribunal have the power to—

(a) quash or vary any decision of the Commissioners, including the power to reduce any penalty to such amount (including nil) as they think proper; and

(b) substitute their own decision for any decision quashed on appeal.

Miscellaneous

Prosecution of offences by the Commissioners

23.—(1) Proceedings for an offence under these Regulations may be instituted by order of the Commissioners.

(2) Such proceedings may be instituted only against an operator or high value dealer or, where such a person is a body corporate, a partnership or an unincorporated association, against any person who is liable to be proceeded against under regulation 27 (offences by bodies corporate etc.).

(3) Any such proceedings which are so instituted must be commenced in the name of an officer.

(4) In the case of the death, removal, discharge or absence of the officer in whose name any such proceedings were commenced, those proceedings may be continued by another officer.

(5) Where the Commissioners investigate, or propose to investigate, any matter with a view to determining—

(a) whether there are grounds for believing that an offence under these Regulations has been committed by any person mentioned in paragraph (2); or

(b) whether such a person should be prosecuted for such an offence;

that matter is to be treated as an assigned matter within the meaning of the Customs and Excise Management Act 1979.

(6) In exercising their power to institute proceedings for an offence under these Regulations, the Commissioners must comply with any conditions or restrictions imposed in writing by the Treasury.

(7) Conditions or restrictions may be imposed under paragraph (6) in relation to—

(a) proceedings generally; or

(b) such proceedings, or categories of proceedings, as the Treasury may direct.

Recovery of fees and penalties through the court

24. Where any fee is charged, or any penalty is imposed, by virtue of these Regulations—

    (a) if the person from whom it is recoverable resides in England and Wales or Northern Ireland, it is recoverable as a civil debt; and

    (b) if that person resides in Scotland, it may be enforced in the same manner as an extract registered decree arbitral bearing a warrant for execution issued by the sheriff court of any sheriffdom in Scotland.

Authorised persons operating a bureau de change

25.—(1) No authorised person may, as from 1st April 2004, carry on the business of operating a bureau de change unless he has first informed the Authority that he proposes to do so.

(2) Where an authorised person ceases to carry on that business, he must inform the Authority forthwith.

(3) Any information to be supplied to the Authority under this regulation must be in such form or verified in such manner as the Authority may specify.

(4) Any requirement imposed by this regulation is to be treated as if it were a requirement imposed by or under the 2000 Act.

(5) Any function of the Authority under this regulation is to be treated as if it were a function of the Authority under the 2000 Act.

PART IV: MISCELLANEOUS

Supervisory authorities etc. to report evidence of money laundering

26.—(1) Where a supervisory authority, in the light of any information obtained by it, knows or suspects, or has reasonable grounds for knowing or suspecting, that someone has or may have been engaged in money laundering, the supervisory authority must disclose the information to a constable as soon as is reasonably practicable.

(2) Where a supervisory authority passes the information to any other person who has such knowledge or suspicion or such reasonable grounds for knowledge or suspicion as is mentioned in paragraph (1), he may disclose the information to a constable.

(3) Where any person within paragraph (6), in the light of any information obtained by him, knows or suspects or has reasonable grounds for knowing or suspecting that someone has or may have been engaged in money laundering, he must, as soon as is reasonably practicable, disclose that information either to a constable or to the supervisory authority by whom he was appointed or authorised.

(4) Where information has been disclosed to a constable under this regulation, he (or any person obtaining the information from him) may disclose it in connection with the investigation of any criminal offence or for the purpose of any criminal proceedings, but not otherwise.

(5) A disclosure made under this regulation is not to be taken to breach any restriction on the disclosure of information (however imposed).

(6) Persons within this paragraph are—

    (a) a person or inspector appointed under section 65 or 66 of the Friendly Societies Act 1992;[26]

---

[26] 1992 c. 40.

(b) an inspector appointed under section 49 of the Industrial and Provident Societies Act 1965 or section 18 of the Credit Unions Act 1979;[27]

(c) an inspector appointed under section 431, 432, 442 or 446 of the Companies Act 1985[28] or under Article 424, 425, 435 or 439 of the Companies (Northern Ireland) Order 1986;[29]

(d) a person or inspector appointed under section 55 or 56 of the Building Societies Act 1986;[30]

(e) a person appointed under section 167, 168(3) or (5), 169(1)(b) or 284 of the 2000 Act, or under regulations made as a result of section 262(2)(k) of that Act, to conduct an investigation; and

(f) a person authorised to require the production of documents under section 447 of the Companies Act 1985, Article 440 of the Companies (Northern Ireland) Order 1986 or section 84 of the Companies Act 1989.

Offences by bodies corporate etc.

27.—(1) If an offence under regulation 3 committed by a body corporate is shown—

(a) to have been committed with the consent or the connivance of an officer; or

(b) to be attributable to any neglect on his part;

the officer as well as the body corporate is guilty of an offence and liable to be proceeded against and punished accordingly.

(2) If an offence under regulation 3 committed by a partnership is shown—

(a) to have been committed with the consent or the connivance of a partner; or

(b) to be attributable to any neglect on his part;

the partner as well as the partnership is guilty of an offence and liable to be proceeded against and punished accordingly.

(3) If an offence under regulation 3 committed by an unincorporated association (other than a partnership) is shown—

(a) to have been committed with the consent or the connivance of an officer of the association or a member of its governing body; or

(b) to be attributable to any neglect on the part of such an officer or member;

that officer or member as well as the association is guilty of an offence and liable to be proceeded against and punished accordingly.

(4) If the affairs of a body corporate are managed by its members, paragraph (1) applies in relation to the acts and defaults of a member in connection with his functions of management as if he were a director of the body.

(5) In this regulation—

(a) "partner" includes a person purporting to act as a partner; and

(b) "officer", in relation to a body corporate, means a director, manager, secretary, chief executive, member of the committee of management, or a person purporting to act in such a capacity.

Prohibitions in relation to certain countries

28.—(1) The Treasury may direct any person who carries on relevant business—

(a) not to enter a business relationship;

(b) not to carry out any one-off transaction; or

---

[27] 1979 c. 34.   [28] 1985 c. 6.   [29] S.I. 1986/1032 (N.I. 6).   [30] 1986 c. 53.

(c) not to proceed any further with a business relationship or one-off transaction;
in relation to a person who is based or incorporated in a country (other than an EEA State) to which the Financial Action Task Force has decided to apply counter-measures.

(2) A person who fails to comply with a Treasury direction is to be treated as having contravened regulation 3.

Minor and consequential amendments

29. The provisions mentioned in Schedule 2 to these Regulations have effect subject to the amendments there specified, being minor amendments and amendments consequential on the provisions of these Regulations.

Transitional provisions

30.—(1) Nothing in these Regulations obliges any person who carries on relevant business falling within any of sub-paragraphs (a) to (e) of regulation 2(2) to maintain identification procedures which require evidence to be obtained in respect of any business relationship formed by him before 1st April 1994.

(2) Nothing in these Regulations obliges any person who carries on relevant business falling within any of sub-paragraphs (f) to (n) of regulation 2(2)—

(a) to maintain identification procedures which require evidence to be obtained in respect of any business relationship formed by him before 1st March 2004; or

(b) to maintain internal reporting procedures which require any action to be taken in respect of any knowledge, suspicion or reasonable grounds for knowledge or suspicion which came to that person before 1st March 2004.

SCHEDULE 1

Regulation 2(2)(e)

ACTIVITIES LISTED IN ANNEX 1 TO
THE BANKING CONSOLIDATION DIRECTIVE

1. Acceptance of deposits and other repayable funds.
2. Lending.
3. Financial leasing.
4. Money transmission services.
5. Issuing and administering means of payment (eg credit cards, travellers' cheques and bankers' drafts).
6. Guarantees and commitments.
7. Trading for own account or for account of customers in—
   (a) money market instruments (cheques, bills, certificates of deposit, etc.);
   (b) foreign exchange;
   (c) financial futures and options;
   (d) exchange and interest-rate instruments;
   (e) transferable securities.

8. Participation in securities issues and the provision of services related to such issues.
9. Advice to undertakings on capital structure, industrial strategy and related questions and advice as well as services relating to mergers and the purchase of undertakings.
10. Money broking.
11. Portfolio management and advice.
12. Safekeeping and administration of securities.
13. Credit reference services.
14. Safe custody services.

SCHEDULE 2

Regulation 29

MINOR AND CONSEQUENTIAL AMENDMENTS
PART I: PRIMARY LEGISLATION

Value Added Tax Act 1994 (c. 23)

1.—(1) Section 83 of the Value Added Tax Act 1994 is amended as follows.
(2) In paragraph (zz), for "regulation 16 of the Money Laundering Regulations 2001", substitute "regulation 21 of the Money Laundering Regulations 2003".

Northern Ireland Act 1998 (c. 47)

2.—(1) Paragraph 25 of Schedule 3 (reserved matters) to the Northern Ireland Act 1998 is amended as follows.
(2) For "1993" substitute "2003".

PART II: SECONDARY LEGISLATION

The Cross-Border Credit Transfers Regulations 1999 (S.I. 1999/1876)

3.—(1) Regulation 12 of the Cross-Border Credit Transfers Regulations 1999 is amended as follows.
(2) For paragraph (2) substitute—

" (2) In this regulation "enactments relating to money laundering" means section 18 of the Terrorism Act 2000, section 340(11) of the Proceeds of Crime Act 2002 and the Money Laundering Regulations 2003.".

The Terrorism Act 2000 (Crown Servants and Regulators) Regulations 2001 (S.I. 2001/192)

4.—(1) The Terrorism Act 2000 (Crown Servants and Regulators) Regulations 2001 are amended as follows.
(2) In regulation 2, for the definition of "relevant financial business" substitute—

" "relevant business" has the meaning given by regulation 2(2) of the Money Laundering Regulations 2003.".

(3) In regulation 3, for "relevant financial business" substitute "relevant business".

The Representation of the People (England and Wales) Regulations 2001 (S.I. 2001/341)

5.—(1) The Representation of the People (England and Wales) Regulations 2001 are amended as follows.
(2) In regulation 114(3)(b)[31]—
    (i)   for "1993" substitute "2003"; and
    (ii) omit ", the Money Laundering Regulations 2001".

The Representation of the People (Northern Ireland) Regulations 2001 (S.I. 2001/400)

6.—(1) The Representation of the People (Northern Ireland) Regulations 2001 are amended as follows.
(2) In regulation 107(3)(b)[32]—
    (i)   in paragraph (i), for "1993" substitute "2003";
    (ii) omit paragraph (ii); and
    (iii) in paragraph (iii), omit the words "either of" and "sets of".

The Representation of the People (Scotland) Regulations 2001 (S.I. 2001/497)

7.—(1) The Representation of the People (Scotland) Regulations 2001 are amended as follows.
(2) In regulation 113(3)(b)[33]—
    (i)   for "1993" substitute "2003"; and
    (ii) omit ", the Money Laundering Regulations 2001".

The Proceeds of Crime Act 2002 (Failure to Disclose Money Laundering:
Specified Training) Order 2003 (S.I. 2003/171)

8.—(1) The Proceeds of Crime Act 2002 (Failure to Disclose Money Laundering: Specified Training) Order 2003 is amended as follows.
(2) In article 2, for "regulation 5(1)(c) of the Money Laundering Regulations 1993" substitute "regulation 3(1)(c)(ii) of the Money Laundering Regulations 2003".

---

[31] Inserted by regulation 15 of the Representation of the People (England and Wales) (Amendment) Regulations 2002 (S.I. 2002/1871).
[32] Inserted by regulation 21 of the Representation of the People (Northern Ireland) (Amendment) Regulations 2002 (S.I. 2002/1873).
[33] Inserted by regulation 14 of the Representation of the People (Scotland) (Amendment) Regulations 2002 (S.I. 2002/1872).

EXPLANATORY NOTE

(This note is not part of the Regulations)

These Regulations replace the Money Laundering Regulations 1993 and 2001 with updated provisions which reflect Directive 2001/97/EC of the European Parliament and of the Council amending Council Directive 91/308/EEC on prevention of the use of the financial system for the purpose of money laundering. A Transposition Note setting out how the main elements of Directive 2001/97/EC will be transposed into UK law is available from the Financial Systems and International Standards Team, HM Treasury, 1 Horse Guards Road, London SW1A 2HQ. The Transposition Note is also on HM Treasury's website (http://www.hm-treasury.gov.uk/). A regulatory impact assessment has been prepared and placed in the library of each House of Parliament. A copy is likewise available from the Treasury and can be found on the Treasury's website.

Where business relationships are formed, or one-off transactions are carried out, in the course of relevant business (defined in regulation 2), the persons carrying out such relevant business are required to maintain certain identification procedures (regulation 4), record-keeping procedures (regulation 6) and internal reporting procedures (regulation 7) and to establish other appropriate procedures for the purpose of forestalling or preventing money laundering (regulation 3(1)(b)). They are also required to train their employees in those procedures and, more generally, in the recognition of money laundering transactions and the law relating to money laundering (regulation 3(1)(c)). A person who fails to maintain the procedures or carry out the training is guilty of a criminal offence (regulation 3(2)). Casino operators must obtain satisfactory evidence of the identity of all people using their gaming facilities (regulation 8).

Regulation 9 requires the Commissioners of Customs and Excise to keep a register of money service operators and a register of high value dealers and regulations 10-11 state the registration requirements placed on such persons. Regulation 12 lists the grounds on which registration may be refused by the Commissioners, including where information which has been supplied is incomplete, false or misleading. Regulation 13 lists the circumstances in which registration may be cancelled by the Commissioners. Regulation 14 allows the Commissioners to charge fees.

Regulations 15 to 19 state the powers of the Commissioners in relation to money service operators and high value dealers, including a power to enter and inspect premises. Where there are reasonable grounds for believing that an offence under the Regulations is being, has been or is about to be committed by a money service operator or high value dealer, the Commissioners may seek a court order requiring any person in possession of certain information to allow them access to it. Regulation 19 allows the Commissioners to enter premises with a warrant, to search persons and to take away documents. Regulation 20 allows the Commissioners to impose a civil penalty in certain circumstances. Regulation 21 provides a mechanism for a formal review by the Commissioners of their decisions. Regulation 22 provides for appeals against the Commissioners' decisions to be heard by a VAT tribunal. Regulation 23 allows the Commissioners to prosecute offences under the Regulations. Regulation 24 allows fees and penalties to be recovered as a civil debt. Regulation 25 requires people who are authorised by the Financial Services Authority ("the FSA") to inform the FSA before they operate bureaux de change.

Regulation 26 requires supervisory authorities (defined in regulation 20) and various other people who obtain information indicative of money laundering to inform a constable. Regulation 28 allows the Treasury to require people who carry on relevant business to refrain from doing business with people in certain non-EEA States.

APPENDIX 11

Practice Direction—Proceeds of Crime Act 2002 Parts 5 and 8: Civil Recovery

CONTENTS OF THIS PRACTICE DIRECTION

ANNEX
SCOPE AND INTERPRETATION

1.1 Section I of this practice direction contains general provisions about proceedings in the High Court under Parts 5 and 8 of the Proceeds of Crime Act 2002.

1.2 Section II contains provisions about applications to the High Court under Part 5 of the Act for—
   (a) a recovery order; and
   (b) an interim receiving order.

1.3 Section III contains provisions about applications to the High Court under Part 8 of the Act for any of the following types of order or warrant in connection with a civil recovery investigation—
   (a) a production order;
   (b) a search and seizure warrant;
   (c) a disclosure order;
   (d) a customer information order; and
   (e) an account monitoring order.

1.4 Section IV of this practice direction contains further provisions about applications for each of the specific types of order and warrant listed in paragraph 1.3 above.

1.5 In this practice direction—
   (1) 'the Act' means the Proceeds of Crime Act 2002;
   (2) 'the Director' means the Director of the Assets Recovery Agency, or any person authorised by him to act on his behalf in accordance with section 1(6) of the Act; and
   (3) other expressions used have the same meaning as in the Act.

SECTION I—GENERAL PROVISIONS

Venue

2.1 A claim or application to the High Court under Part 5 or Part 8 of the 2002 Act must be issued in the Administrative Court.

2.2 The Administrative Court will thereupon consider whether to transfer the claim or application to another Division or Court of the High Court.

Use of pseudonyms by Agency staff

3.1 If a member of staff of the Assets Recovery Agency gives written or oral evidence in any proceedings using a pseudonym in accordance with section 449 of the Act—

(1) the court must be informed that the witness is using a pseudonym; and

(2) a certificate under section 449(3) of the Act must be filed or produced.

SECTION II—PROCEEDINGS UNDER PART 5 OF THE ACT

Claim for a recovery order

4.1 A claim by the Director for a recovery order must be made using the CPR Part 8 procedure.

4.2 The claim form must—

(1) identify the property in relation to which a recovery order is sought;

(2) state, in relation to each item or description of property –

(a) whether the property is alleged to be recoverable property or associated property; and

(b) either—

(i) who is alleged to hold the property; or

(ii) where the Director is unable to identify who holds the property, the steps that have been taken to try to establish their identity;

(3) set out the matters relied upon in support of the claim; and

(4) give details of the person nominated by the Director to act as trustee for civil recovery in accordance with section 267 of the Act.

4.3 The evidence in support of the claim must include the signed, written consent of the person nominated by the Director to act as trustee for civil recovery if appointed by the court.

Application for an interim receiving order

5.1 An application for an interim receiving order must be made –

(1) to a High Court judge; and

(2) in accordance with Part 23.

5.2 The application may be made without notice in the circumstances set out in section 246(3) of the Act.

5.3 Part 69 (court's power to appoint a receiver) and its practice direction apply to an application for an interim receiving order with the following modifications –

(1) paragraph 2.1 of the practice direction supplementing Part 69 does not apply;

(2) the Director's written evidence must, in addition to the matters required by paragraph 4.1 of that practice direction, also state in relation to each item or description of property in respect of which the order is sought –

(a) whether the property is alleged to be –

(i) recoverable property; or

(ii) associated property,

and the facts relied upon in support of that allegation; and
    (b) in the case of any associated property –
        (i) who is believed to hold the property; or
        (ii) if the Director is unable to establish who holds the property, the steps that have been taken to establish their identity; and
  (3) the Director's written evidence must always identify a nominee and include the information in paragraph 4.2 of that practice direction.

5.4 There must be filed with the application notice a draft of the order sought. This should if possible also be supplied to the court on disk in a form compatible with the word processing software used by the court.

Application for directions

6.1 An application for directions as to the exercise of the interim receiver's functions may, under section 251 of the Act, be made at any time by—
  (1) the interim receiver;
  (2) any party to the proceedings; and
  (3) any person affected by any action taken by the interim receiver, or who may be affected by any action proposed to be taken by him.

6.2 The application must always be made by application notice, which must be served on—
  (1) the interim receiver (unless he is the applicant);
  (2) every party to the proceedings; and
  (3) any other person who may be interested in the application.

Application to vary or discharge an interim receiving order

7.1 An application to vary or discharge an interim receiving order may be made at any time by—
  (1) the Director; or
  (2) any person affected by the order.

7.2 A copy of the application notice must be served on—
  (1) every party to the proceedings;
  (2) the interim receiver; and
  (3) any other person who may be affected by the court's decision.

SECTION III—APPLICATIONS UNDER PART 8 OF THE ACT

How to apply for an order or warrant

8.1 An application by the Director for an order or warrant under Part 8 of the Act in connection with a civil recovery investigation must be made—
  (1) to a High Court judge;
  (2) by filing an application notice.

8.2 The application may be made without notice.

Confidentiality of court documents

9.1 CPR rule 5.4 does not apply to an application under Part 8 of the Act, and paragraphs 9.2 and 9.3 below have effect in its place.

9.2 When an application is issued, the court file will be marked 'Not for disclosure' and, unless a High Court judge grants permission, the court records relating to the application (including the application notice, documents filed in support, and any order or warrant that is made) will not be made available by the court for any person to inspect or copy, either before or after the hearing of the application.

9.3 An application for permission under paragraph 9.2 must be made on notice to the Director in accordance with Part 23.

(Rule 23.7(1) requires a copy of the application notice to be served as soon as practicable after it is filed, and in any event at least 3 days before the court is to deal with the application.)

Application notice and evidence

10.1 The application must be supported by written evidence, which must be filed with the application notice.

10.2 The evidence must set out all the matters on which the Director relies in support of the application, including any matters required to be stated by the relevant sections of the Act, and all material facts of which the court should be made aware.

10.3 There must also be filed with the application notice a draft of the order sought. This should if possible also be supplied to the court on disk in a form compatible with the word processing software used by the court.

Hearing of the application

11.1 The application will be heard and determined in private, unless the judge hearing it directs otherwise.

Variation or discharge of order or warrant

12.1 An application to vary or discharge an order or warrant may be made by—
(1) the Director; or
(2) any person affected by the order or warrant.

12.2 An application under paragraph 12.1 to stop an order or warrant from being executed must be made immediately upon it being served.

12.3 A person applying to vary or discharge a warrant must first inform the Director that he is making the application.

12.4 The application should be made to the judge who made the order or issued the warrant or, if he is not available, to another High Court judge.

SECTION IV—FURTHER PROVISIONS ABOUT SPECIFIC APPLICATIONS UNDER PART 8 OF THE ACT

Production order

13.1 The application notice must name as a respondent the person believed to be in possession or control of the material in relation to which a production order is sought.

13.2 The application notice must specify—
   (1) whether the application is for an order under paragraph (a) or (b) of section 345(4) of the Act;
   (2) the material, or description of material, in relation to which the order is sought; and
   (3) the person who is believed to be in possession or control of the material.

13.3 An application under section 347 of the Act for an order to grant entry may be made either—
   (1) together with an application for a production order; or
   (2) by separate application, after a production order has been made.

13.4 An application notice for an order to grant entry must—
   (1) specify the premises in relation to which the order is sought; and
   (2) be supported by written evidence explaining why the order is needed.

13.5 A production order, or an order to grant entry, must contain a statement of the right of any person affected by the order to apply to vary or discharge the order.

Search and seizure warrant

14.1 The application notice should name as respondent the occupier of the premises to be subject to the warrant, if known.

14.2 The evidence in support of the application must state—
   (1) the matters relied on by the Director to show that one of the requirements in section 352(6) of the Act for the issue of a warrant is satisfied;
   (2) details of the premises to be subject to the warrant, and of the possible occupier or occupiers of those premises;
   (3) the name and position of the member of the staff of the Agency who it is intended will execute the warrant.

14.3 There must be filed with the application notice drafts of—
  (1) he warrant; and
  (2) a written undertaking by the person who is to execute the warrant to comply with paragraph 13.8 of this practice direction.

14.4 A search and seizure warrant must—
  (1) specify the statutory power under which it is issued and, unless the court orders otherwise, give an indication of the nature of the investigation in respect of which it is issued;
  (2) state the address or other identification of the premises to be subject to the warrant;
  (3) state the name of the member of staff of the Agency who is authorised to execute the warrant;
  (4) set out the action which the warrant authorises the person executing it to take under the relevant sections of the Act;
  (5) give the date on which the warrant is issued;
  (6) include a statement that the warrant continues in force until the end of the period of one month beginning with the day on which it is issued;
  (7) contain a statement of the right of any person affected by the order to apply to discharge or vary the order.

14.5 An example of a search and seizure warrant is annexed to this practice direction. This example may be modified as appropriate in any particular case.

14.6 Rule 40.2 applies to a search and seizure warrant.

  (Rule 40.2 requires every judgment or order to state the name and judicial title of the person making it, to bear the date on which it is given or made, and to be sealed by the court.)

14.7 Upon the issue of a warrant the court will provide to the Director—
  (1) the sealed warrant; and
  (2) a copy of it for service on the occupier or person in charge of the premises subject to the warrant.

14.8 A person attending premises to execute a warrant must, if the premises are occupied produce the warrant on arrival at the premises, and as soon as possible thereafter personally serve a copy of the warrant and an explanatory notice on the occupier or the person appearing to him to be in charge of the premises.

14.9 The person executing the warrant must also comply with any order which the court may make for service of any other documents relating to the application.

Disclosure order

15.1 The application notice should normally name as respondents the persons on whom the Director intends to serve notices under the disclosure order sought.

15.2 A disclosure order must—
  (1) give an indication of the nature of the investigation for the purposes of which the order is made;
  (2) set out the action which the order authorises the Director to take in accordance with section 357(4) of the Act;
  (3) contain a statement of—
    (a) the offences relating to disclosure orders under section 359 of the Act; and
    (b) the right of any person affected by the order to apply to discharge or vary the order.

15.3 Where, pursuant to a disclosure order, the Director gives to any person a notice under section 357(4) of the Act, he must also at the same time serve on that person a copy of the disclosure order.

Customer information order

16.1 The application notice should normally (unless it is impracticable to do so because they are too numerous) name as respondents the financial institution or institutions to which it is proposed that an order should apply.

16.2 A customer information order must—
  (1) specify the financial institution, or description of financial institutions, to which it applies;
  (2) state the name of the person in relation to whom customer information is to be given, and any other details to identify that person;
  (3) contain a statement of—
    (a) the offences relating to disclosure orders under section 366 of the Act; and
    (b) the right of any person affected by the order to apply to discharge or vary the order.

16.3 Where, pursuant to a customer information order, the Director gives to a financial institution a notice to provide customer information, he must also at the same time serve a copy of the order on that institution.

Account monitoring order

17.1 The application notice must name as a respondent the financial institution against which an account monitoring order is sought.

17.2 The application notice must—
  (1) state the matters required by section 370(2) and (3) of the Act; and
  (2) give details of—
    (a) the person whose account or accounts the application relates to;
    (b) each account or description of accounts in relation to which the order is sought, including if known the number of each account and the branch at which it is held;

(c) the information sought about the account or accounts;

(d) the period for which the order is sought;

(e) the manner in which, and the frequency with which, it is proposed that the financial institution should provide account information during that period.

17.3 An account monitoring order must contain a statement of the right of any person affected by the order to apply to vary or discharge the order.

ANNEX

IN THE HIGH COURT OF JUSTICE DIVISION CLAIM NO.   OF 20

CLAIMANT:

DIRECTOR OF THE ASSETS RECOVERY AGENCY

[insert address]

PREMISES TO WHICH THIS WARRANT RELATES:

[insert address]

WARRANT TO ENTER PREMISES AND EXERCISE POWERS UNDER SECTIONS 352–354 AND 356 OF THE PROCEEDS OF CRIME ACT 2002

To [insert name of person/organisation], who is believed to be the occupier of the premises described above ("the premises") and to any person in charge of, or operating at or from, the premises:

You should read the terms of this warrant and the accompanying notice very carefully. You are advised to consult a solicitor as soon as possible. If you intentionally obstruct or fail to comply with any requirement of a member of staff of the Assets Recovery Agency exercising his or her powers under the warrant, you may be committing a contempt of court for which you may be imprisoned or fined.

An application was made on *[insert date]* by Counsel for the Director of the Assets Recovery Agency ("the Director") to The Honourable Mr Justice *[insert date]* ("the Judge") for a warrant under section 352 of the Proceeds of Crime Act 2002 ("the Act").

The Judge read the evidence in support of the application and was satisfied that the requirement for the issue of a warrant in section 352(6)[(a)][(b)] of the Act has been met.

As a result of the application, this warrant in relation to the premises was issued by the Judge on *[insert date]*.

1. This warrant is issued in respect of a civil recovery investigation by the Assets Recovery Agency in relation to *[indicate the property subject to the investigation]* ("the investigation").

2. This warrant continues in force until the end of the period of one month starting with the day on which it is issued and may be executed on any one or more days within that period.

3. By this warrant *[insert name]*, a member of staff of the Assets Recovery Agency, is authorised to produce the warrant [at any time] *[insert any restriction on times or days of the week]* and on producing the warrant:):
   (a) to enter and search the premises;
   (b) to seize any material found there which in their opinion is likely to be of substantial value (whether or not by itself) to the investigation;
   (c) to require any information which is held in a computer and is accessible from the premises, and which they believe relates to any matter relevant to the investigation, to be produced in a form—
       (i) in which it can be taken away; and
       (ii) in which it is visible and legible;
   (d) to take copies of any material seized;
   (e) to retain material seized under the warrant for so long as it is necessary to retain it in connection with the investigation.

4. In this warrant, the term "premises" includes any place and, in particular includes—
   (a) any vehicle, vessel, aircraft or hovercraft;
   (b) any offshore installation; and
   (c) any tent or movable structure.

You are entitled to apply to the court to vary or discharge this warrant. If you intend to make such an application, you must first inform the [Assets Recovery Agency] [person named in paragraph 3]. An application to stop the warrant from being executed must be made immediately upon it being served

DATED this [   ] day of [   ] 20
THE HONOURABLE

Guidance to Solicitors and Applicants Seeking Community Legal Service Funding for Proceedings under the Proceeds of Crime Act 2002 Involving the Assets Recovery Agency © 2004 Legal Services Commission

Note: this guidance note is primarily intended to provide greater information to solicitors acting for defendants in proceedings brought by the Assets Recovery Agency. If you are a defendant in these proceedings, please contact a solicitor at the earliest opportunity and take a copy of this note with you. If you need assistance locating a suitable solicitor, you can contact CLS Directory Line (tel: 0845 608 1122).

INTRODUCTION

The Proceeds of Crime Act 2002 established the Assets Recovery Agency (ARA), an agency dedicated to investigating and recovering proceeds of crime. Among the functions of the ARA is a role in the new civil recovery scheme, created by the Act, to recover the proceeds of alleged unlawful conduct in cases where a criminal conviction has not been obtained and is unlikely to be obtained.

The purpose of this paper is to provide general guidance to defendants in proceedings brought by the ARA and their solicitors regarding the availability of Community Legal Service (CLS) funding for these proceedings and the procedures used to consider applications for funding in these cases.

AVAILABILITY OF LEGAL AID IN CIVIL RECOVERY PROCEEDINGS

Proceedings for which CLS funding is available

All High Court proceedings under Part 5 of the Proceeds of Crime Act 2002 and all proceedings under Parts 2, 5 or 8 of the Act that are listed in paragraph 3 of Schedule 2 of the Access to Justice Act 1999 are civil proceedings for which CLS funding is available, subject to meeting the required means and merits tests (these are discussed in greater detail below).

Civil Recovery by the Assets Recovery Agency

Proceedings for civil recovery in the High Court under Chapter 2 of Part 5 of the Proceeds of Crime Act can only be brought by the Assets Recovery Agency. CLS funding is available for these proceedings. This can apply to both a respondent against whom the agency is proceeding or a third party who claims to be an innocent owner of property.

Investigations by the Assets Recovery Agency

Under Chapter 2 of Part 8 the High Court can make a range of orders to support investigations into whether a person has benefited from criminal conduct, holds recoverable property or has committed a money laundering offence. CLS funding is available for the following proceedings under Part 8:

(a) Application under section 351(3) to discharge or vary a production order or an order to grant entry;
(b) Application under section 362(3) to discharge or vary a disclosure order;
(c) Application under section 369(3) to discharge or vary a customer information order;
(d) Application under section 375(2) to discharge or vary an account monitoring order.

Exclusions

In some cases, despite the fact that the type of proceedings is within the scope of CLS funding, they may nevertheless be excluded from funding under paragraph 1 of Schedule 2. This paragraph lists particular types of proceedings that cannot be funded under CLS. In reality none of the proceedings listed in this paragraph are likely to arise in the proceedings brought by the ARA.

The exclusion in this paragraph that would have arisen most often, which excludes all matters arising out of the carrying on of a business, has been avoided by way of a Direction made by the Secretary of State on 24 May 2004. This direction states that the Commission is authorised to fund services on behalf of a defendant in Proceeds of Crime Act 2002 proceedings that are in scope of the scheme, despite the fact that the provision of those services may be excluded by reason of paragraph 1(h) (matters arising out of the carrying on of a business) of that Schedule.

Funding Criteria

Where CLS funding is available for proceedings under the Proceeds of Crime Act 2002 as specified above, applications for Legal Representation will be subject to the normal CLS criteria for scope, means and merits. The Commission has, however, ensured that account is taken of the special nature of these proceedings when considering applications in these cases.

Merits

The proceedings for which CLS funding is available are defined as civil proceedings under the Proceeds of Crime Act 2002. However, as these proceedings are new, and are likely to raise a number of important issues in the period during which an amount of precedent develops in this area, the Commission has set a more flexible merits test for these proceedings, than for other civil proceedings within the scope of CLS funding.

Therefore, the Commission applies an "interests of justice" test to determine whether an application should be funded on merits. This test is essentially whether it is in the interests of justice to provide funding to the client. In deciding whether it is in the interests of justice to fund any particular applicant, we will take into account:

(a) The importance of the issues to the applicant; that is, how seriously the client will be affected by the court making or not making the order in question.
(b) Whether there are complex legal and factual issues that could not fairly be determined without legal representation for the applicant.
(c) Whether the applicant suffers from any lack of understanding of the issues, including any language problem or disability.
(d) Whether the case requires extensive legal preparation, for example in the tracing of witnesses, or advocacy skills.

Means

CLS funding for these proceedings will only be available to applicants who are financially eligible for such funding in accordance with the Commission's standard financial eligibility limits, as set out in the Community Legal Service (Financial) Regulations 2000 as amended. In order to determine whether or not an applicant qualifies financially the Commission will require them to complete a Means Assessment Form setting out their full financial circumstances.

In assessing disposable income and capital the Commission will not take into account any assets that have already been frozen under the Proceeds of Crime Act. However all the applicant's (and their partner's, if they have one) other disposable income and capital will be taken into account. The regulations provide that if an applicant has a partner (whether married or not) their means are aggregated, unless the partner is established to have a contrary interest in the proceedings.

The Commission's experience to date has shown that defendants in proceedings brought by the ARA generally have complex financial circumstances. The Commission therefore refers all applications for funding in these cases to our Special Investigations Unit (SIU) in order to determine the financial eligibility of the applicant. The Commission is authorised, by the applicant's and their partner's Declaration and Authorisation on the application form, to seek information on the applicant's, or their partner's financial circumstances from third parties. That includes the ARA.

If funding is provided, and proceedings are successfully defended, the statutory charge will apply. The statutory charge means that any property that is recovered or maintained for a funded client must be used to repay the cost of the case to the CLS fund. Where seized assets have not been taken into account on the basis that they are the subject matter of the dispute, success in the proceedings resulting in the release of assets to the client will be treated as a recovery or preservation. Any assets so recovered must therefore be paid to the solicitor and on to the Commission—see Regulations 18 and 20 of the CLS (Costs) Regulations 2000.

PROCEDURES

CLS funding for Legal Representation in these proceedings is Licensed Work. Both suppliers with a civil franchise in any category, and those with a criminal franchise are licensed to undertake work in relation to these proceedings. Application must therefore be made to the Commission for certificates to authorise such work. All applications must be submitted to the Commission's Special Cases Unit (SCU) at 29–37 Red Lion Street, London WC1R 4PP, DX 170 London/Chancery Lane. Normal CLS means and merits forms must be supplied (CLS APP1 for merits and the appropriate means forms).

Processes within SCU

Once an application is received by SCU, it will make an in principle merits decision in respect of the application as soon as possible. The target time for this decision is 5 days from receipt of the application. However, should any additional information be required before a decision can be reached, this will be delayed. We aim to ensure such information will be sought within 5 days.

Once notified of the merits decision, solicitors will be asked to submit a costed case plan. Upon receipt of this plan, SCU will agree the level of funding and an appropriate work package through the case plan, or raise further queries, again with a target time of within 5 days.

Should a dispute arise over work plans or merits refusals, this will be referred to the Commission's Funding Review Committee (FRC).

Processes within SIU

As stated above, the Commission refers all applications for funding in these cases to SIU in order to determine the financial eligibility of the applicant. It is expected that SCU will refer cases to SIU as soon as possible after receipt in order that both units are able to consider the application at the same time.

Once SIU has received an application, SIU will review the client's deciareda income and determine whether the application is out of scope on that basis. The application may be refused at this stage.

If the client indicates that they or their partner are in receipt of a passported benefit (Income Support or Income based Job Seekers Allowance) SIU will confirm this with the Department for Work and Pensions. If confirmation is received the application will usually be approved on means at that time.

In all other cases, SIU will write to relevant sources of information, including the ARA, to seek financial information from them in relation to the applicant. Upon receipt of all information initially sought, SIU will determine whether the client is likely to have a partner or assets available from other sources. If such assets appear unlikely then a decision may be made at that time to discontinue the investigation and to approve the means on the basis of the client's income/assets alone. Otherwise all parties will be notified that a full SIU investigation will commence. During any investigation SIU has a target time to deal with all correspondence of within 10 days of receipt.

Emergency Funding

In some cases it will be necessary to provide services to an applicant while the investigation of the applicant's means are on going. Emergency Funding may be available for this work.

Under the existing rules, suppliers who hold a contract (whether civil or criminal) with the Commission are able to self-grant emergency Legal Representation under the usual emergency criteria (see section 12 of the Funding Code Guidance). However, due to the complex nature of these cases, the Commission would prefer that individual applications for emergency funding be made directly to SCU, on the appropriate CLS App 6 form. The Commission has undertaken that in relation to proceedings brought by the ARA, any application for emergency funding will be viewed in as favourable light as possible pending a decision on means.

Solicitors must bear in mind that an emergency application must satisfy the standard Criteria for Legal Representation together with the Criteria for Full Representation contained in the General Funding Code. In addition, where an application for emergency representation is made the solicitor must advise the client about the nature and consequences of emergency representation. In particular, they must be told:

(a) an emergency certificate will only help a client about urgent matters and will not be a substitute for full Legal Representation;

(b) the client's means will still have to be assessed by the Commission, so:

　(i) if the client does not co-operate, this may result not only in no grant of full Legal Representation but also in withdrawal of the emergency certificate.

　(ii) if the client turns out to be outside the eligibility limits or fails to accept an offer of Legal Representation and pay any assessed contribution, the emergency representation will be withdrawn and in either case this may mean the client having to pay all the legal costs personally and having no costs protection in relation to the opponent's costs;

(c) the emergency certificate will only cover urgent legal work and will be strictly limited as to scope and duration.

Providing information to the ARA

The ARA is able, as a party to these proceedings, to seek updates from the Commission on the progress of a legal aid application. Where such a request is made, the Commission will provide the ARA with confirmation that a grant has been made, or not, and also any chronological information regarding the progress of the application. The Commission will not, however, disclose any information that has been received by the Commission in connection with any individual application for funding to the ARA.

WORKING WITH THE COMMISSION

It should be noted that any failure to co-operate with the Commission's investigations, or a failure to disclose any relevant fact, may lead to a refusal or withdrawal of funding at any time. In addition, whether during assessment or after funding is granted, Regulation 13 of the Community Legal Service (Financial) Regulations 2000 provides that the Commission must be informed of any change in the applicant's (or their partner's) financial circumstances, which might affect the terms on which the applicant is assessed as eligible for funding.

FURTHER INFORMATION

• The leaflet *A Practical Guide to Community Legal Service* funding explains how the Commission (LSC) funds civil legal services, how to apply and the tests which you need to be able to meet to qualify. Section 5 of the leaflet deals with legal representation in the High Court, where cases under these Parts of the Act are heard.

• The Commission's Funding Code, which sets out the decision-making guidance of the Commission, is available on the Commission's website: www.legalservices.gov.uk.

- The Commission also has an on-line financial eligibility calculator, to assist applicants in determining whether they may be financially eligible for funding. The results of the calculator are indicative only, and it can be found on the Just Ask website: http://www. justask.org.uk/legalhelp/calculator.

Index